COMPUTERS

ABOUT THE AUTHORS

Dr. Nancy Long and **Dr. Larry Long**, partners at Long and Associates, work as a team. Nancy has a decade of teaching and administrative experience at all levels of education: elementary, secondary, college, and continuing education. Her wealth of knowledge in the areas of pedagogy and reading education is evident throughout the text.

Larry is a lecturer, author, columnist, consultant, and educator in the field of information services. His many books cover a broad spectrum of computer and information services topics, from BASIC to MIS strategic planning. He has also written numerous articles on management, computers, and information services. Larry's "Turnaround Time" column appears in *Computerworld* and in several sister affiliates throughout the world. He is the editor of *INTRO,* a newsletter for introductory computer education. Larry presents a variety of MIS seminars in the United States and abroad and is a frequent speaker at professional conferences. His consulting practice enables him to interact with all levels of management in virtually every industry type. Larry has over a decade of classroom experience at Lehigh University and the University of Oklahoma, and continues to be an active lecturer at Lehigh.

The authors met and married while students at the University of Oklahoma, where they received their degrees. Nancy received a Ph.D. in Reading Education and Educational Psychology, an M.S. in Personnel Services, and a B.S. in Elementary Education. Larry received Ph.D., M.S., and B.S. degrees in Industrial Engineering and holds certification as a C.D.P. and a Professional Engineer.

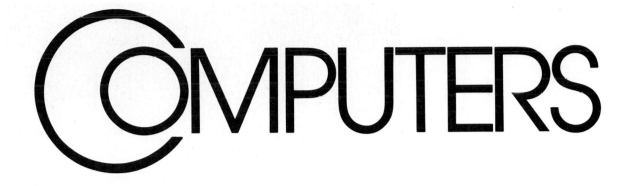

COMPUTERS

Larry Long

Nancy Long

PRENTICE-HALL, INC., Englewood Cliffs, New Jersey 07632

Library of Congress Cataloging in Publication Data

Long, Nancy (date)
    Computers

    Includes index.
      1. Computers.   2. Electronic data processing.
I. Long, Larry E. II. Title.
QA76.L576 1986   004 85–12404
ISBN 0–13–163619–7

© 1986 by Prentice-Hall, Inc., Englewood Cliffs, New Jersey 07632

Printed in the United States of America

10 9 8 7 6 5 4 3 2 1

Editorial/production supervision: Nancy Milnamow
Interior design: Janet Schmid
Art supervision: Janet Schmid
Cover design: Janet Schmid
Cover art: Symbolics, Inc.
Interior illustrations: Fine Line
Page layout supervision: Gail Cocker
Manufacturing buyer: Ed O'Dougherty
Acquisitions editor: Marcia Horton

ISBN 0-13-163619-7   01

Prentice-Hall International, (UK) Limited, *London*
Prentice-Hall of Australia Pty. Limited, *Sydney*
Prentice-Hall Canada Inc., *Toronto*
Prentice-Hall Hispanoamericana, S.A., *Mexico*
Prentice-Hall of India Private Limited, *New Delhi*
Prentice-Hall of Japan, Inc., *Tokyo*
Prentice-Hall of Southeast Asia Pte. Ltd., *Singapore*
Editora Prentice-Hall do Brasil, Ltda., *Rio de Janeiro*
Whitehall Books Limited, *Wellington, New Zealand*

CHAPTER OPENING PHOTOGRAPHS

Chapters 1, 3, 8, 12, 16–Genigraphics Corporation

Chapters 2, 5, 7, 11, 13, 14, Integrated Software, BASIC–Melvin L. Prueitt, Los Alamos National Laboratory

Chapter 4–Aydin Controls

Chapter 6–AVL

Chapter 9–Intergraph Corporation

Chapter 10–Courtesy of International Business Machines Corporation

Chapter 15–Program of Computer Graphics, Cornell University

Chapter 17–TRW Inc.

OVERVIEW

PART IV

PART V

INTEGRATED MICROCOMPUTER SOFTWARE   S.1

BASIC PROGRAMMING   B.1

CONTENTS

PART II

HARDWARE AND DATA COMMUNICATIONS TECHNOLOGY

PART III

SOFTWARE AND DATA MANAGEMENT

PART IV

INFORMATION SYSTEMS

PART V

OPPORTUNITY
RESPONSIBILITY,
AND CHALLENGE

INTEGRATED MICROCOMPUTER SOFTWARE

BASIC PROGRAMMING

LEARNING MODULE I: BASIC Basics   B.4

LEARNING MODULE II: Getting Started in BASIC   B.13

LEARNING MODULE III: Adding to Your Foundation   B.35

LEARNING MODULE IV: Generating Reports   B.47

LEARNING MODULE V: Writing Interactive Inquiry Programs   B.67

PREFACE TO THE STUDENT

The computer revolution is upon us and computers are fast becoming a way of life. The material in this text offers an overview of this exciting and challenging field. Once you have read and understood its content, you will be poised to play an active role in this revolution.

Getting the Most from This Text

Every sentence, every piece of art, and every photo was selected with you in mind. The layout and organization of the text and its content are designed to be interesting; to present concepts in a logical and informative manner; and to provide a reference for the reinforcement of classroom lectures.

Reading a Chapter. A good way to approach each chapter is to:

1. Look over the Student Learning Objectives.
2. Turn to the back of the chapter and read the Summary and Important Terms.
3. Read over major headings and subheadings and think how they are related.
4. Read the chapter and note the important terms that are in **boldface** type and in *italic* type.
5. Relate photos and photo captions to the textual material (a picture is worth a thousand words).
6. Go over the Summary Outline and Important Terms again, paying particular attention to the boldface terms.
7. Take the Self Test.
8. Reread those sections that you do not fully understand.
9. Answer the questions in the Review Exercises.

The Rainbow. Color is used throughout the book to add another dimension to the learning process. There are many instances where concepts can be reinforced and made easier to understand with a spectrum of colors. We call this the *functional use of color*. For example, the spectrum of discussion items often runs:

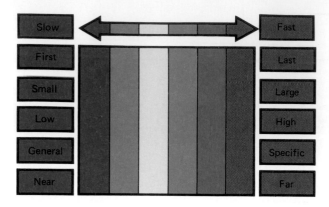

These spectrums are visually represented in the book by the spectrum of prismatic colors in the *rainbow*. Red, the first color in the rainbow, would represent such concepts as the first step, the smallest portion, or the general concept. Each increment in a conceptual spectrum is represented by the subsequent colors of the rainbow: orange, yellow, green, blue, and violet. In an illustration that has three steps, for example, the last step would always be represented with yellow (the third color). This functional use of color is designed to help you relate the textual material to the illustrations.

The text is supported by an optional *Study Guide,* a *Software Supplement,* and *Video Tapes.* Ask your instructor about the availability of these learning supplements.

You, Computers, and the Future

Whether you are pursuing a career as a writer, social worker, computer specialist, dancer, attorney, physician, shop supervisor, politician, or are involved in virtually any other career, the knowledge you gain from this course will ultimately prove beneficial. Keep your course notes and this book because they will provide valuable reference material in other courses and in your career. The chapter material addresses a broad range of computer concepts which pop up frequently in other classes, at work, and even at home. The skills sections on *Integrated Microcomputer Software* and *BASIC Programming* will prove valuable if you anticipate working with electronic spreadsheets, doing word processing, or writing programs.

The career opportunities are there for those with an understanding and a working knowledge of computers. Less than 5% of the population is computer literate, yet employers of virtually every discipline are seeking to hire people who can take advantage of the computer revolution.

The use of computers for information processing is in its infancy. By taking this course, you are getting in on the ground floor. Each class you attend and each page you turn will present a learning experience that will let you advance one step closer to an understanding of how computers are making the world a better place in which to live and work. Most importantly, you will be gaining the knowledge necessary to become an active participant in what is the most exciting decade of technological innovation and change in recorded history.

PREFACE TO THE INSTRUCTOR

Instructors of every discipline are keenly aware of the tremendous impact that computers have had on their fields of study and on society in general. In most colleges and universities, this faculty awareness has led to recommendations that a course on "computers" be made a general education requirement. For some, such a course is a reality; for others, students flock in mass to take the "intro computer course" as an elective. Whether required or an elective, the introductory computer course is consistently one of the most popular courses and is taken by students from every curriculum. This text and its comprehensive support package are designed especially to meet the teaching and learning needs of such a course.

We have been fortunate in that we have talked with hundreds of your colleagues in academe. Your feedback was loud and clear: write a book that can be used in a class of students who have a variety of skill levels, interests, and career orientations. In this book, we accommodate a breadth of students by addressing a broad range of computer concepts, applications, issues, and concerns. And we have attempted to write in a style that can be understood by average learners, yet challenges the more advanced students.

Learning about computers can be an exciting journey. This theme is evident throughout the book. When we wrote this book we wanted students to turn the page because they want to, not because they had to.

Concepts, Awareness, and Skills

The textual material is designed to strike a balance between concepts, awareness, and skills. Most will agree that the computer literate must have a grasp of certain computer concepts. But it is also important that the students have a heightened sensitivity to the impact of computers on society, both now and in the future. Learning a computer skill is also important because it helps the students to gain confidence in computers and in their ability to effectively use them.

Chapters 1–17.   The focus of Chapters 1–17 is on *concepts* and developing the students' computer *awareness,* but always within the context of *application.* Introductory computer concepts are discussed and illustrated throughout the text by using applications from a wide variety of working environments and disciplines. Controversial issues, problems, and trends are presented with candor to heighten the students' awareness of the social implications of the implementation of more and more computer technology.

Integrated Microcomputer Software. The special sections at the back of the book on *Integrated Microcomputer Software* and *BASIC Programming* have a skills orientation. The section on micro software provides generic, yet detailed coverage of data management, electronic spreadsheets, graphics, word processing, and communications software. Once the student has read and understood the principles, the student can easily relate what has been learned to the specifics of your hardware/software environment. With a little practice, the student has a computer skill.

When used in conjunction with hands-on exposure to specific operational software packages, there is sufficient material and exercises in the *Integrated Microcomputer Software* section, Chapter 4 (Computer Systems—Micros), Chapter 6 (Inside the Computer), Chapter 7 (Data Storage Devices and Media), Chapter 8 (Input/Output Devices), and the *Software Supplement* to support a complete course in the use and application of common microcomputer software packages.

BASIC Programming. BASIC is presented in a special section to permit you the flexibility to introduce BASIC at any point in the course. The *BASIC Programming* section is divided into nine learning modules so that the student can systematically progress through increasingly sophisticated levels of understanding. If you only wish to expose the student to BASIC and assign a few simple programs, then Modules I, II, and III will suffice. Modules IV, V, and VI take the student up to an intermediate skill level. Modules VII and VIII introduce advanced features and techniques, and Module IX presents an overview and examples of the 1985 ANS BASIC.

The material and exercises in the *BASIC Programming* section, Chapter 15 (Programming Concepts), and the *Software Supplement* are sufficient to support a complete course in BASIC.

Software Supplement. The *Software Supplement* (see "Support Material" section of this preface) enables the student to gain skills in the use and operation of a computer.

Approach

Functional Use of Color. The design of this book is integral to its pedagogy. Rather than simply use color for splash, we decided to take advantage of the four-color design and add another dimension to the presentation of the material. We call it the *functional use of color.* Throughout the book a "spectrum" of ideas is related to a spectrum of prismatic colors so that the student can more easily relate the ideas to one another and to illustrations and textual material. The functional use of color is explained and illustrated in more detail in the "Preface to the Student."

Level of Detail. Content material is presented at a *consistent level of detail.* That is, we carefully avoided going off the deep end on some topics. Considerable thought was given by us and by your colleagues as to whether a topic should be covered and at what level it should be covered. Also, the reading level was carefully monitored to avoid the problems associated with inappropriate levels of presentation.

Ahead of Date. Advances in computer technology continue to come in rapid succession. Because a book is often used in the classroom for several years, being "up-to-date" isn't good enough—you have to be *ahead-of-date*. That is exactly what we have attempted to do. To be in a position to do this, we have maintained a close association with people who are working on the perimeters of computer technology. They have provided us with a solid perspective on what we might anticipate in the near future and during the last half of the 1980s. These perspectives are reflected in the text: today's computers are "generationless"; "workstation" is preferred to "terminal"; the new ANS BASIC is introduced; programming languages are placed in six generations; the QWERTY/Dvorak keyboard changeover is addressed; proto-typing is part of systems development; and the list goes on. We avoided clinging to tradition for tradition's sake. Things are moving too fast.

Photos.   The *photographs* are an integral part of the text and the learning experience. Computers and the people who use them are more than words and diagrams—they are dynamic and alive. We wanted to project this energy to the student and one way to do this is through photos and their captions. We carefully selected over 400 photos that enhance understanding of the core material and create a visually stimulating text. Photo placement is key to the design of the book. When we talk about an application, a situation, a computing device, or perhaps a person, there is usually a support photo and descriptive caption on the same page.

Flexibility in Assignment of Material

We recognize that no two colleges (or even instructors) will emphasize the same mix of concepts, awareness, and skills in an introductory computer course. To provide you and your colleagues with as much flexibility as possible, we have included more than enough material for a single course. This gives you plenty of latitude to "pick and choose" those parts of the chapters or the special sections on integrated micro software and BASIC that are most appropriate to your teaching environment. Chapters often assigned out of sequence (e.g., Chapter 15, Programming Concepts) were written to be rela-tively independent of other chapters. Sections within chapters are numbered for ease of selective assignment.

Organization

The concepts and awareness portion of the text is divided into five parts.

Part I—Computers: Today and Yesterday   presents background information to help clarify the student's perspective on computers. Trends, fundamental concepts of a computer system, myths, categories of computer usage, an overview of computer appplications, controversial issues, and the history of computers are discussed.

Part II—Hardware and Data Communications Technology   presents an over-view of a variety of computer systems (micros, minis, mainframes), an opera-tional description of computers and computer peripheral devices, and an introduction to data communications.

Part III—Software and Data Management   presents a survey of programming languages, software concepts, and approaches to data manipulation and infor-mation retrieval.

Part IV—Information Systems expands on computer-based information systems and applications of the computer by examining how computers are used in business and industry, and in government, health, and education. This part also includes a discussion of a systematic procedure by which information systems are conceived, designed, developed, implemented, and evaluated. The concepts and activity of programming are introduced in some detail.

Part V—Opportunity, Responsibility, and Challenge presents the student with the breadth of career opportunities awaiting those with an interest in pursuing a computer-related career and for those with a computer knowledge who pursue other careers. A perspective is given on how computers will be used and how they will impact society in the future.

The *Integrated Microcomputer Software* and *BASIC Programming* sections are positioned at the end of the text so that these skill topics can be introduced at any point in the course.

Chapter organization is consistent throughout the text. The *chapter body* is prefaced by *Student Learning Objectives.* In the body of the chapter, all major headings are numbered (i.e., 1–1, 1–2, and so on) to facilitate selective assignment and to provide an easy crossreference to all related material in the supplements. Important terms and phrases are highlighted in **boldface** print. Informative photos, interesting box items, "Memory Bits" (outlines of key points), and cartoons are interspersed throughout each chapter. Words and phrases to be emphasized appear in *italics.* Each chapter concludes with a *Summary Outline and Important Terms, Review Exercises* (concepts and discussion), and a *Self Test.*

Support Material

The *Instructor's Resource Manual* contains (for each chapter): Student Learning Objectives, Teaching Hints, Lecture Notes, Supplementary Material, Answers to End-Of-Chapter Review Exercises, and Exercises and Project Assignments. The lecture notes are in an outline format. Any detailed explanation is supplementary to the text and is included as a teaching tool. Boldface terms, discussion questions, and references to appropriate transparencies are embedded in the outline. The format is similar for the special sections on micro software and BASIC.

The *Instructor's Resource Manual* also includes the *test bank.* The test bank is organized by numbered section heads within each chapter to facilitate question selection and uniform coverage of the material. A computerized version of the *test bank* is available on *diskettes* for popular microcomputers. Instructors can select specific questions or request that the exams be generated randomly. When printed, the exam is ready for duplication. An answer sheet is also produced.

The two-color student *Study Guide* is organized to support the chapter objectives. Each chapter contains: Student Learning Objectives, Chapter Overview, Reinforcement Activities (list of important terms, and completion, true/false, and multiple choice questions), Application Questions, Stimulation Activities (discussion questions and projects), and Software Exercises to accompany the *Software Supplement.* It also has comprehensive sections on Integrated Microcomputer Software and BASIC Programming. A "Guide to the Videotape Series" is included in the *Study Guide.*

The comprehensive *Software Supplement,* called "SuperSoftware," is designed to instruct, intrigue, and motivate. The design philosophy of this supplement is to actively involve students through interactive communication with the computer. Graphic images and icons enhance the software's "user friendliness." SuperSoftware has two main menus: one is organized by chapter and the other by topic.

Interesting programs such as "Introduction to the PC" and "Internal Operation of the Computer" provide instruction on the hardware. A number of programs are designed to encourage students to become familiar with the computer. For example, the student can draw with "Compu-Sketch," compose and play music, or journey through computer history on a time machine. There are also plenty of application simulations, such as airline reservation systems and home banking.

The concepts underlying microcomputer software are demonstrated through imaginative simulations of data management software, electronic spreadsheets, word processing, graphics, communications, and an idea processor. Some of these programs are partially functional. The BASIC programming software is organized by learning module. For each learning module, the software demonstrates the BASIC concepts introduced in that module, has syntax and logic debugging exercises, and contains the example programs in the book.

SuperSoftware even has a full-blown tutorial on keyboarding. And there is much, much more. The software supplement contains enough material for a full term's worth of laboratory activities.

All of the above software is available for the IBM PC (and IBM PC compatibles). A substantial subset is available for the Apple II. Any institution adopting this book for educational use will be awarded a site license to use "SuperSoftware." For others, the software is available on an annual rental agreement.

Eight *Video Tapes* set the material in the text in motion. Each video addresses a particular facet of the use and application of computers.

Color Transparency Acetates (70) and black-line *Transparency Masters* (150), which support material in the text and the *Instructor's Resource Manual,* are provided to facilitate in-class explanation.

PC-Write (word processing), *PC-Calc* (electronic spreadsheet), and *PC-File* (database management) freeware (for IBM PC) will be made available to adopters of *Computers* at a substantially reduced rate.

INTRO, the newsletter for introductory computer education, is distributed periodically to adopters of this text. *INTRO* is intended to help instructors keep abreast of teaching innovations for introductory computer courses and of a rapidly changing technology. Surveys of what others are teaching and how they are teaching it are taken and reported in the newsletter. The newsletter also provides a forum for the exchange of ideas.

Acknowledgements

We are very proud of *Computers* and its comprehensive support package. And so are hundreds of others that have made significant contributions: editors, artists, programmers, set designers, professors, cartoonists, production schedulers, dummiers, proofreaders, and many more. We thank them, one and all, for their untiring effort and commitment to excellence.

A publishing tradition is to place only the names of the authors on the cover of the book—but if this ever changes, we think a few other names should be included, for *Computers* is their book too. Marcia Horton, our editor, spearheaded this project with the perfect blend of passion, compassion, and sense of purpose. Three very wise men, Executive Editors Jim Fegen and Chuck Iossi, and President of Technical Publishing, Hank Kennedy, were always happy to share their editorial and fiscal wisdom when we needed it. Production Editor Nancy Milnamow, Buyer Ed O'Dougherty, and Manufacturing Manager David Hetherington used their magic to transform a manuscript into a book. Janet Schmid's imaginative art direction is apparent on every page. Gail Cocker and Bob Lentz added their special touch to the text. Joe Heider, Niels Nielsen and the marketing team assembled a very imaginative marketing package. Rick Smith produced and directed a set of video tapes that perfectly complement the book. Super Martin Chamberlain did the programming for SuperSoftware. Editorial Assistant Karen Grant performed some logistical wizardry. Andy Kreutzer co-authored the *Study Guide* and gave us a lot of good ideas during the development of the manuscript.

Over 400 companies have in some way participated in this project. They have provided information, photos, software, examples, and, most of all, their precious time. We wish to thank them for their valuable contribution.

Computers is a product of collective thinking—and a lot of thinking went into this book. In that regard, we are truly grateful for the committed efforts of our colleagues: Sally Anthony, San Diego State University; Harvey R. Blessing, Essex Community College; Wayne Bowen, Black Hawk Community College; Michael Brown, DeVry Institute of Technology, Chicago; J. Patrick Fenton, West Valley College; Ken Griffin, University of Central Arkansas; Nancy Harrington, Trident Technical College; Grace C. Hertlein, California State University; Shirley Hill, California State University; Cynthia Kachik, Santa Fe Community College; Sandra Lehmann, Morraine Park Technical Institute; Michael Lichtenstein, DeVry Institute of Technology, Chicago; Dennis R. Martin, Kennebec Valley Vocational Technical Institute; William McDaniel, Jr., Northern Virginia Community College at Alexandria; Edward L. Nock, DeVry Institute of Technology, Columbus; Louis Noe, Ivy Technical Institute; Frank O'Brien, Milwaukee Area Technical College; Alvin Ollenburger, University of Minnesota; Beverly Oswalt, University of Central Arkansas; James Phillips, Lexington Community College; Nancy Roberts, Lesley College; Richard Siebert, Morton College; Bob Spear, Prince George's Community College; and Thomas Voight, Franklin University.

Dedication

We dedicate this book to our wonderful and loving parents—Carl and Barbara Rothlisberger, and Pete and Marie Long.

Nancy Long, Ph.D.   Larry Long, Ph.D.

COMPUTERS

PART

COMPUTERS: TODAY AND YESTERDAY

- To grasp the scope of computer literacy.
- To distinguish computer myth from computer reality.
- To distinguish between data and information.
- To understand the relationship between the levels of the hierarchy of data organization.
- To describe the fundamental components of a computer system.
- To identify and describe uses of the computer.

CHAPTER

1

The World of Computers

1-1 COMPUTER LITERACY DEFINED

Companies promote *it* for their employees. Parents demand *it* for their children. Those who have *it* believe they have a competitive edge. Those who don't have *it* seek *it* out. "*It*" is **computer literacy**. We are rapidly becoming a computer-literate society.

Until recently, **computers** were found only in environmentally controlled rooms behind locked doors. Only computer professionals dared enter these secured premises. In contrast, today, computers are found in millions of homes and just about *every* office. In fact, there is a computer for one in *every* eight people. In a couple of years, the ratio will be one in four. Eventually, all of us will have at least one computer and use it *every* day in our work and leisure.

What Is Computer Literacy?   A decade ago, the term "computer literacy" had little meaning. Either you were a computer professional who had dedicated years of study to computers, or you were not. Only computer professionals were computer literate. Well, things have changed. Computers are for everyone!

In a few months, you will achieve computer literacy. So, what does this mean to you? You will:

1.   Feel comfortable in the use and operation of a computer system.
2.   Be able to make the computer work for you through judicious development *or* use of **software**. (Software refers collectively to a set of machine-readable instructions, called **programs**, that cause the computer to perform desired functions.)
3.   Be able to interact with the computer—that is, generate input to the computer and interpret output from the computer.
4.   Understand how computers are impacting society, now and in the future.
5.   Be an intelligent consumer of computer-related products and services.

Computers have become as much a part of the office as the telephone. This company conducts opinion surveys on everything from product recognition to political preference. These pollsters rely on computers to help collect, store, and analyze the data. (Provided by Datapoint ® Corporation. All rights reserved.)

2

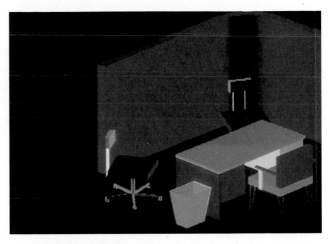

With a personal computer, you are the boss! Computing capabilities similar to those of much larger computers are within an arm's reach. This woman is updating her guest list and creating an imaginative invitation for an upcoming party. (Courtesy of Apple Computer, Inc.)

Interior designers use computer graphics to test possible office arrangements. It's a lot easier to move an "electronic" desk than a real one. (Calma Company)

The precise, untiring movement of computer-controlled industrial robots helps assure quality in the assembly of electrical components. (AT&T Technologies)

Computer literacy is achieved through study, practice, and interest in the topic. There is no "quick fix" that will result in your becoming a computer-literate person. A magazine article, a few television shows, or a computer demonstration may serve to heighten your interest, but these are *side trips* on the way to computer literacy. You are about to embark on an emotional and intellectual *journey* that will stimulate your imagination, challenge your every resource from physical dexterity to intellect, and, perhaps, alter your sense of perspective. Computer literacy is more than learning—it's an adventure. Enjoy your journey into the world of computers!

1-2 WHY COMPUTER LITERACY?

There are four main reasons to become computer literate:

1. To realize that the computer revolution is upon us and computers are impacting the way we live, work, and play.
2. To overcome any fear of computers.
3. To learn the lingo, called computerese.
4. To attain a level of computer education that will enable you to take full advantage of the opportunities afforded by the computer revolution.

The Computer Revolution.   In a little more than three decades, computer technology has come a very long way. The first commercial computer was large enough to fill a gymnasium and was considered too expensive for all but the largest companies. Today, the small **personal computers** that we use for all kinds of domestic and business applications are thousands of times faster and more powerful than the first commercial computers. If the automobile industry had experienced similar progress, a new car would now cost less than a gallon of gas!

The *computer revolution* is upon us. This unprecedented technical revolution has made computers a *part of life*. With the rapid growth in the number and variety of computer applications, they are rapidly becoming a *way of life*.

In our private lives, computers may speed the checkout process at supermarkets, enable 24-hour banking, provide up-to-the-minute weather information, and, of course, entertain us with video games. And if that is not enough, computers are the culprits behind our "conversations" with elevators, automobiles, and vending machines.

In our professional lives, the computer is an integral tool in the performance of many jobs. In the theater, set directors create and view sets on the computer before constructing them. Sociologists use the computer to analyze demographic patterns. Writers use word processing systems to check spelling, grammar, and style. Geologists rely on an "expert" computer system for guidance in the quest for minerals. Financial analysts examine up-to-the-minute securities information on their workstations. Computer artists have millions (yes, millions!) of colors from which to choose.

On the down side, the computer revolution has raised serious social issues. Personal information is more accessible, and therefore more vulnerable to abuse. The take in an average "electronic" heist is a hundred times that of the more traditional bank robbery. One computer-controlled robot can replace four or more workers. These and other automation issues are discussed in Chapter 2, "Computers in Society—Today," and throughout the book.

Computers, and technology in general, have potential for both good and bad. Numerous surveys have attempted to evaluate public opinion on computers and automation. The findings show that the overwhelming majority believe that computers enhance the quality of life. The people of the world have become committed to a better way of life through computers, and it is unlikely that the momentum toward this goal will change. It is our responsibility to ensure that this inevitable evolution of computer technology is directed to the benefit of society.

While watching a college football game, this sports writer composed a story for the morning paper on his portable personal computer. After the game he edited the copy, then transmitted the story electronically over a telephone line to the newspaper's computer system.
(Photo supplied courtesy of Epson America)

DO YOU HAVE CYBERPHOBIA?

Cyberphobia (si′ ber fō′ bē ə): The irrational fear of and aversion to computers.

- Do you think robots will inherit the earth?
- Do you avoid automatic teller machines?
- When you hear programmers talk about RAM, do you envision a collision?
- Are you afraid that the computer will break if you press the wrong key?
- Are you suspicious of others who use a computer, thinking they know more than you do?

- Do you believe that "The computer did it"?
- Do you fold, spindle, or mutilate computer cards without remorse?

If you answer "yes" to any four of these questions, then you probably have cyberphobia! People who wrap the computer in a shroud of mystique will continue to be cyberphobics. Those who pursue computer knowledge will become computer literate and benefit from the computer's endless capabilities.

Fear of the Unknown. Computers are synonymous with change, and any type of change is usually met with some resistance. We can attribute much of this resistance to a lack of knowledge about computers and, perhaps, to a fear of the unknown. It is human nature to fear that which we don't understand, be it the Extra Terrestrial or computers.

Fear of the computer is so widespread that psychologists have created a name for it: **cyberphobia**. Cyberphobia is the irrational fear of, and aversion to, computers. In truth, computers are merely machines and don't merit being the focus of such fear. If you are a cyberphobic, you will soon see that your fears are unfounded.

Computerese. A by-product of the computer revolution is a new language called **computerese**. Computerese is a mixture of English and computer jargon, which could just as well be ancient hieroglyphics to the novice. With the expanded use and acceptance of computers both at home and at work, it is becoming more and more important to be fluent in computerese. You may be happy to know that you are already well along your way to fluency in computerese. You are probably familiar with about half of the computerese vocabulary. For example, you know:

window	write	block	record
read	job	bug	flag
run	word	page	trace
bit	memory	host	loop
menu	field	gateway	load

Your familiarity with these terms is the good news. Now for the bad news: they all mean something different in computerese. In computerese, you don't "walk through a *gateway*," "apply for a *job*," "wave a *flag*," or "*load* a truck." As you will learn, a parallel often exists between the computerese usage and the common definition of familiar words. But, before you become fluent in computerese, you will need to learn many new vocabulary words, such as *byte* and *ROM*.

As oil companies automate the distribution of gasoline and the handling of credit transactions, service station attendants are learning to use computers. (Chevron Corporation)

Opportunity. Computers provide many opportunities for us to improve the quality of both our private and professional lives. The challenge is to take advantage of these opportunities. People, like you, who are willing to put forth the effort and accept the challenge will be the ones who benefit the most.

For some, this course will be a stepping stone to more advanced topics and, perhaps, a career in information systems or computer science. For others, this course will provide a solid foundation that will prove helpful in the pursuit of virtually any career. In either case, you will be prepared to play an active role in the age of information.

1–3 COMPUTERS ARE FOR EVERYONE

From Dirt to Data. Two centuries ago, 90 of every 100 people worked to produce food. As people became more efficient in the production of food, an *agrarian society* gave way to the growth of an *industrial society*. Today, two people produce enough food for the other 98, and the industrial society is making way for an emerging *information society*.

The trend in today's factories is paralleling that of the farm 200 years earlier. If history repeats itself—and most experts believe it will—automation will continue to reduce the number of workers needed to produce manufactured goods. And sometime in the near future, our industrial society will mature into an information society.

In the information society, workers will concentrate their energy on providing a myriad of information services. Today, it is a bit difficult to imagine a society that may become desperately dependent on certain information services. Let's put it into perspective. How would our nineteenth-century forefathers react to our need for television and hair dryers? Who among us would give up our hair dryer!

Two centuries ago, our agrarian society began to evolve into an industrial society. Today, we are rapidly transitioning to an information society where "knowledge" workers depend on computer-generated information to accomplish their jobs.
(Harris Corporation, Computer Systems Division)

"Computers are for everyone. . . ."
(By permission of Bob Glueckstein)

And so it will be with the inevitable information services. Grocery shopping will be done from the comfort of our own homes. When diagnosing a patient, physicians will routinely ask for a second opinion—from the computer, of course. National elections will be completed in minutes. Some factories will have no windows or light—robots don't need to see.

User-Friendly Computers.   Members of the information society will in some way support information-related services. Just as the emergence of the industrial revolution can be attributed to the steam engine, the central focus of the information society will be the computer. Fortunately, today's computers are for everyone. And that's good, because virtually everybody will be using them!

Computers and software are being designed to be **user friendly**. Being user friendly means that someone with only a computer-literacy-level exposure to computers can make effective use of the computer and its software. Ten years ago, such was not the case. If you didn't have a computer science degree and the mental agility of a wizard, you were out of luck.

Users, Professionals, and Hackers.   The majority of white collar workers and a growing number of blue collar workers use the computer in some way every day. These people are referred to as **end users** or, simply, **users**. Traditionally, users have relied on the technical expertise of professional programmers and systems analysts when it comes to writing programs and selecting computers. But more and more users have taken a keen interest in computers and have educated themselves to the point that they can write their own programs, are comfortable with very sophisticated user-friendly software, and are intelligent consumers of computers and software.

Many of these sophisticated users are **hackers**, a name given to computer enthusiasts who use the computer as a source of enjoyment. Hackers all over the country have formed clubs and associations to share interesting computer discoveries. Hackers are old and young, manager and laborer, ecolo-

These programmers and systems analysts work in an information systems department for a medical instruments manufacturer. Their current project is a human resources information system that will help managers more effectively use the skills of their workers. The system will match the tasks with the skills of the individual workers.
(Honeywell, Inc.)

I DON'T REALLY USE A COMPUTER EVERY DAY, DO I?

You might think that using a computer means sitting down at a computer workstation and doing a little programming. Think again!

1. A *computer-controlled environmental system* adjusts the room temperature to be just right when you awake in the morning. It even heats up the water in time for your shower.

2. You preprogrammed the computer in your *microwave oven* (time and temperature settings) for scrambled eggs and sausage.

3. "And the weather will be. . . ." Both radio and TV weather forecasters use computer-enhanced signals from satellites to predict the *weather forecasts*.

4. You're off. Your car has several computer systems. A *computerized warning system* checks systems and "tells" you which ones are not ready: "Fasten your seat belt." "A door is open." A *computerized fuel control system* feeds the exact mixture of fuel and air to the engine.

5. Traffic seems to be running smoothly this morning. Must be that *automated traffic control system* that optimizes the flow of traffic.

6. When you get to work, you check your *electronic mailbox* for messages. Hmmm, the boss wants some order-status information. Guess you should make an inquiry to the *on-line order entry system*. And, how does your *electronic calendar* look today? Any important meetings?

7. Lunch time already, and only 47 cents in cash! No problem. Just stop at an *automatic teller machine* on your way to lunch.

8. Ah, home after a hard day. Tap into an *information network service* to pay a few bills, do a little "home" shopping, or, perhaps, review the entertainment options for the evening.

gist and geologist, all sharing a common bond: to explore the seemingly infinite capabilities of their computers. On occasion, hackers have carried their enthusiasm for computers beyond the limits of the law. It is perfectly legal for willing hackers to share files and ideas, but it is not legal for hackers to use their computers to tap into sensitive business and government data bases. Unauthorized access to data bases will be discussed in more detail in Chapter 13, "Information Systems in Government, Health, and Education."

The Information Services Department.   Most companies have a computer center and the personnel to support their **information systems**. An information system is a computer-based system that provides data processing capability and information for making decisions. This combination of computing equipment (called **hardware**), the software that instructs the computers what to do, and the people who run the computers and develop the software is often referred to as the information services department or the data processing (DP) department.

The information services department handles the organization's information needs in the same way that the finance department handles the organization's money needs. The department provides data processing and information-related services to virtually every business area. For example, programmers and systems analysts might work with a plant manager and engineers to develop a computer-based production and inventory-control system. Employment opportunities in an information services department and elsewhere are discussed in Chapter 16, "Jobs and Career Opportunities."

1-4   COMPUTER MYTHOLOGY

Computers are inanimate; they have only the logic capability that is programmed by human intelligence—no more, no less. As you will see in your venture toward computer literacy, the mystique surrounding computers is unwarranted. Nevertheless, certain myths have evolved about computers. Let's take time to dispel these myths.

Myth No. 1: "Computers stifle creativity."   A recent poll revealed that two-thirds of the population believe they will eventually end up working for computers and not using their brains for creativity. Music composers, architects, accountants, nurses, and people in a hundred other professions who have *used* computers could easily dispel this widely held myth.

With computers handling more and more routine tasks, we have more time to be creative. For this industrial engineer, time-consuming calculations are handled by the computer, thereby giving him more time to create the most efficient layout for a kitchen appliances plant.
(Courtesy of Apple Computer, Inc.)

When using a computer in composing music, a musician need not break concentration to manually draw each note on a staff. As a note is played, it is immediately displayed in music notation on a video display screen. With the laborious task of documenting the creation being handled by the computer, the composer's efforts can be devoted to the creative aspects of the composition. This is just one of many examples of how computers *enhance* creativity.

Myth No. 2: "The computer did it."   Major newspapers and magazines routinely carry headlines reinforcing the myth that "the computer did it"—headlines such as "Payroll Foulup Attributed to Computer Error" or "Erroneous Tax Assessment Blamed on Computer." The computer has no feelings and is the perfect scapegoat.

Computers do fail. But, with the proper safeguards, failures are noted before they do any harm; the only thing lost is a little time. Most of the time errors can be traced to a breakdown in procedures or a human error (oops!).

Myth No. 3: "Computers cause loss of jobs."   A recent study by the U.S. Department of Labor revealed that computer-related job displacement has been more than offset by the jobs created. The implementation of a computer system may cause the elimination of jobs devoted to certain routine tasks, but the people holding these jobs are usually retrained and moved to positions with greater opportunities. In general, the computer industry is experiencing enormous growth. The net effect is the creation, not the loss, of jobs.

Society is in transition from an industrial to an information society. During this transition, the complexion of jobs will dramatically change.

Myth No. 4: "Computers can do anything."   The Heuristic Algorithmic computer (HAL) of Arthur Clarke's *2001: A Space Odyssey* is a classic invention of this imaginative science fiction writer. HAL and other similarly conceived computers are far removed from the reality of modern computers. A timely example is George Orwell's fictionalized, but very vivid, portrayal of Big Brother in the novel *1984*. The year 1984 has come and gone and we still do not have an electronic dictator, nor will we ever. Big Brother is not technologically feasible or sociologically possible.

HAL could see, learn, and reason. In reality, the state-of-the-art of computer technology in these areas is still in the embryonic stages of research. This is not to say that we will never see robots such as C-3PO of the *Star Wars* films. Perhaps we will, but not for a long while.

Myth No. 5: "You have to be good at mathematics to be good at computers." Not only engineers and mathematicians, but sociologists, teachers, and people from almost every area of interest have had success in using computers. Computers are for everyone.

Myth No. 6: "Computers are synonymous with programming."   The novice tends to associate all computer-related activities with programming. Relatively few users actually write their own programs. Most will rely on user-friendly software to obtain the information they need. Programming is an integral part of the development of information systems, but at least a dozen other computer-related careers do not involve programming. A knowledge of programming, however, is always an asset to those who work with computers.

1-5   FROM DATA TO INFORMATION _____

Up to now we have talked quite a bit about information, but little about the origin of information—data. **Data** (the plural of *datum*) are the raw material from which information is derived. **Information** is comprised of data that have been collected and processed into a meaningful form.

We routinely deal with the concepts of data and information in our everyday experiences. We use data to produce information that will help us make decisions. For example, when we wake up in the morning we collect two pieces of data. We look at the time, then recall from our memory the time when our first class begins, or when we are to be at work. Then we subtract the current time from the starting time of the class (or work). This mental computation provides information on how much time we have to get ready and go. Based on this information, we make a decision to hurry up or to relax and take it easy. We produce information from data to help us make decisions for thousands of situations each day. In many ways, the contents of this book are just an extension of concepts with which you are already familiar.

1-6   THE HIERARCHY OF DATA ORGANIZATION: A PREVIEW _____

So that you can better appreciate discussions of hardware, you will need a fundamental understanding of how data are organized in a computer system. This section contains a *brief overview* of the *hierarchy of data organization* (see Figure 1–1). An in-depth treatment of the topic is provided in Chapter 11, "Data Organization and File Processing." Although you may not be familiar with this terminology, you are probably familiar with the concept of the hierarchy of data organization.

In Chapter 6, "Inside the Computer," we will introduce how computers store data as 1s and 0s, or binary digits, called **bits**. But for now, it is enough to say that the bit is the lowest level of the hierarchy of data organization. A series of *bits* can be configured to represent a *character*. For example, the bit configurations of 01000001 and 01000010 represent the characters A and B inside a computer (see Figure 1–1).

At the next level of the hierarchy, characters are combined to represent the value of a **data element**. The data element, sometimes called a **field**, is the smallest logical unit of data. Some examples are name, employee number, and price. Related data elements are then grouped to form **logical records**, or simply **records**. In Figure 1–1, for example, the data elements of name, on-campus residence hall, and room number are grouped to form the student name-and-address record.

At the fourth level of the hierarchy, records with the same data elements are combined to form a **file**. In Figure 1–1, the file contains the names and on-campus addresses of all students. This permanent source of student data is called a **master file**. A **transaction file** might contain the data elements of name and a *new* address. Compare the student master file to a transaction file that is used to periodically update the data on a master file.

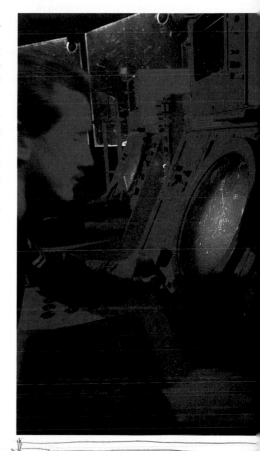

Radar provides the source of data for this air traffic control system. As the radar scans the sky, data on aircraft altitude, direction of flight, and speed are entered into the computer system. The system produces visual information that enables this controller to direct aircraft to a safe landing.
(Courtesy Burroughs Corporation)

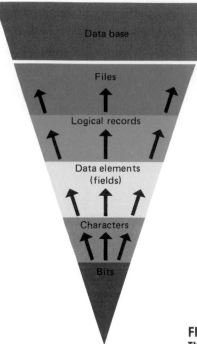

Student name and address master; registration master; financial aids master

Bob Buck, etc.; Nancy Wells, etc.; Jane Jenkins, etc; . . .

Bob Buck, Gower Hall, Rm 311

Bob Buck

B

0100 0010

FIGURE 1–1
The Hierarchy of Data Organization

A **data base**, the next level in the hierarchy, contains several different record types and defines their relationships. We will wait until Chapter 11 to discuss more about data base concepts. At that time you will have a better understanding of hardware, software, and uses of data. For now, just keep in mind that a data base is an organization's data resource for all computer-based information.

Supervisors at this plant rely on computers to help them schedule the maintenance and repair of diesel engines. The system lets supervisors make inquiries to a data base about the status of any diesel engine at the plant.
(Santa Fe Industries)

1-7 UNCOVERING THE "MYSTERY" OF COMPUTERS _____

The Four Components.   Computers may be technically complex, but they are conceptually simple. A computer system has only four fundamental components—**input**, *processing*, **output**, and *storage*. Note that a *computer system* (not a *computer*) has four components. The actual computer is the processing component and is combined with the other three to form a **computer system** (see Figures 1–2 and 1–3).

The relationship of data to a computer system is best explained by an analogy to gasoline and an automobile. Data are to a computer system as gas is to a car. Data provide the fuel for a computer system. A computer system without data is like a car with an empty gas tank: no gas, no go; no data, no information.

How a Computer System Works.   A computer system can be likened to the biological system of the human body. Your brain is the processing component. Your eyes and ears are input components that send signals to the

FIGURE 1–2
The Four Fundamental Components of a Microcomputer System
In a microcomputer system, the storage and processing components are often contained in the same physical unit. In the illustration, the diskette storage medium is inserted into the unit that contains the processor.

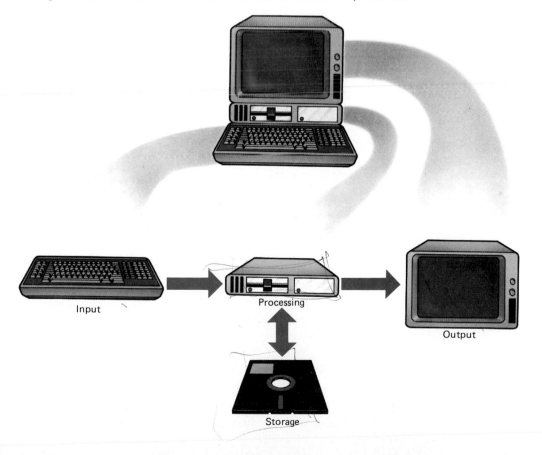

Input

Processing

Output

Storage

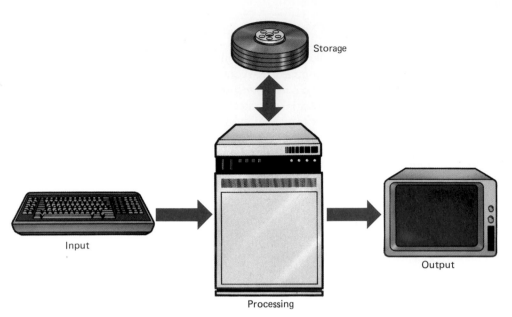

Storage

Input

Processing

Output

FIGURE 1-3
The Four Fundamental Components of a Computer System
In larger computer systems, each of the four components is contained in a
separate physical unit.

brain. If you see someone approaching, your brain matches the visual image
of this person with others in your memory (storage component). If the visual
image is matched in memory with that of a friend, your brain sends signals
to your vocal chords and right arm (output components) to greet your friend
with a "Hello" and a handshake. Computer system components interact in
a similar way.

The grade-reporting system in Figure 1–4 illustrates how data are entered
and how the four computer system components interact to produce information. The grades that instructors give students are the *input* to the system
and are *stored* on the student master file. Remember, the storage component
of a computer system stores data, not information!

The grade report is produced when the *processing* component, or the
computer, executes a program. In this example, the student record is recalled
from storage, and the term and the cumulative grade-point averages are calculated. The *output* is the printed grade reports. Other programs extract data
from the student master file to produce a dean's list and other reports.

In Figure 1–4, the student name, course number, and letter grade are
data. Letter-grade data are associated with course and student data to produce
information (in this case, the grade report). The letter grades are then used
to compute the average grade for the term. Therefore, letter-grade *data* serve
as input to the computation of average-grade *information*.

The Hardware.   In the grade example, data are entered (input) on a **video
display terminal (VDT)**. A video display terminal is a device with a typewriterlike keyboard for input and a televisionlike (video) screen for output. The

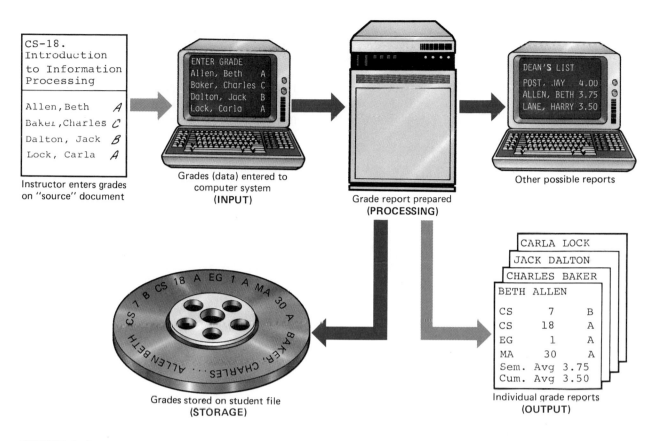

FIGURE 1-4
Grade Reporting System
This grade reporting system illustrates input, storage, processing, and output.

This advertising executive's personal computer has a keyboard for input and both a video display terminal and a printer for output.
(Dataproducts Corporation)

The components of a mainframe computer system are not as apparent as those of a microcomputer. The processing component is the box in the middle. The printer (output) is on the left. Input is on the operator console in the foreground. The other boxes are for permanent and temporary storage of data and programs.
(Courtesy of International Business Machines Corporation)

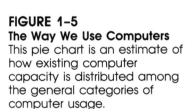

grade reports are then output on a device called a **printer**. There is a wide variety of input and output devices. The variety of hardware devices that make up a computer system are discussed in detail in Part II, "Hardware and Data Communications Technology."

The principles discussed above apply equally to personal computers, also called **microcomputers**, and **mainframe computers**. Each has the four components and uses data to produce information in a similar manner. The difference is that personal computers are more limited in their capabilities and are designed primarily for use by one person at a time. Mainframe computers can service many users at the same time, perhaps the entire college faculty at once. Chapters 4 and 5 on computer systems discuss microcomputers and mainframe computers in detail.

1-8   HOW DO WE USE COMPUTERS?

For the purpose of this discussion, we will classify the uses of computers into six general categories: *information systems/data processing*, *personal computing*, *science and research*, *process control*, *education*, and *artificial intelligence*. Figure 1–5 shows how the sum total of existing computer capacity

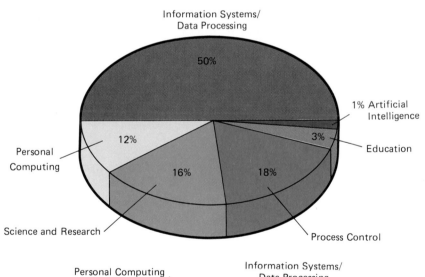

FIGURE 1-5
The Way We Use Computers
This pie chart is an estimate of how existing computer capacity is distributed among the general categories of computer usage.

FIGURE 1-6
The Way We Will Use Computers in the Future
This pie chart is an estimate of how computer capacity in the year 2000 might be distributed among the general categories of computer usage.

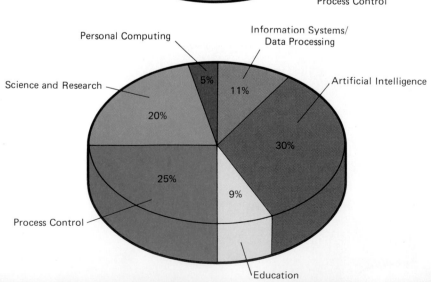

While meeting with a customer, this pharmaceutical sales representative uses a workstation that is linked to the company's central computer center to request up-to-the-minute pricing information and to enter orders. The customer is even given a copy of the order before the representative leaves.
(Copyright 1984 GTE Telenet Communications Corporation)

is apportioned to each of these general categories. In the years ahead, look for personal computing, process control, education, and artificial intelligence to grow rapidly and become larger shares of the computer "pie." Figure 1-6 illustrates how computing capabilities might be used in the year 2000.

Information Systems/Data Processing

The bulk of existing computer power is dedicated to *information systems* and *data processing*. This category includes all uses of computers for business purposes. Example applications include payroll systems, airline reservation systems, student registration systems, hospital patient billing systems, office automation systems, and countless others.

To get a feeling for the widespread influence of computers, let's take a look at how the computer services a typical manufacturing organization's data processing and information needs. Consider the organization of ZIMCO Enterprises, as illustrated in Figure 1-7.

FIGURE 1-7
User Group Interaction with Information Services
Every division at ZIMCO Enterprises (a fictitious name) is in some way supported by the Information Services Organization. The solid lines show organizational authority and the dotted lines show information flow.

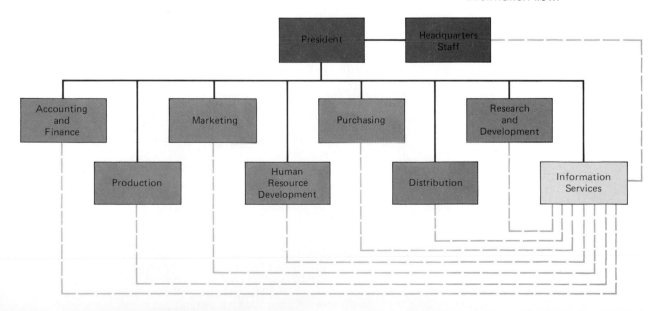

- In the *accounting* division, all financial/accounting systems are computerized.
- ZIMCO's *production* division uses information systems for such applications as inventory control and production scheduling.
- As competition becomes keener, the *marketing* division has turned to the information services division for assistance in fine tuning the marketing effort.
- The *human resources development* division has automated the basic personnel functions of employment history and career planning.
- The *purchasing* division has replaced cumbersome manual systems with computer-based systems that extend their buying power through selective, time-phased purchasing.
- The *research and development* division relies on the information services division to support a variety of technical programs that include simulation and computer-aided design.
- ZIMCO's *headquarters staff* and top management routinely make "what if" inquiries, such as "What *if* the advertising budget were increased by 20%, how might sales be affected?"

The influence of computer information systems is just as pervasive in hospitals, government agencies, or colleges. A wide variety of information systems for virtually every industry are described and discussed throughout the remainder of the book.

Personal Computing

Individuals and companies are purchasing small, inexpensive personal computers for a variety of business and domestic applications. An entire personal computer system, also called a microcomputer, easily sits on a desktop and can be controlled by one person. The growth of this general area, called **personal computing**, has surpassed even the most adventurous forecasts

Microcomputers have become part of the scenery in every academic discipline. This student is using a computer to analyze the results of a chemical experiment.
(Courtesy of Apple Computer, Inc.)

of the mid-1970s. By 1990, personal computers will be as commonplace as color television sets are now. Even now, personal computers actually outnumber mainframe computers. But, of course, a single mainframe computer may have the processing capacity of 1,000 personal computers.

Typical domestic applications for personal computing include: home budgeting, personal mailing lists, video games, computer-assisted instruction, word processing, and use of commercially available information services. To take advantage of available information services, personal computers are linked to mainframe computers that provide information, such as air travel schedules, restaurant menus, stock reports, and a host of other services.

During the mid-1970s, personal computers were used primarily by hackers in the home. But today, just about every office, be it a psychiatrist's office, a government agency, or a plant manager's office, has at least one personal computer. These powerful personal computers are used in many of the traditional ways in which computers have supported business: payroll, accounting, inventory management, and so on. But, for the most part, personal computers are used by individuals for *personal* computing and information needs.

A very popular use of personal computers is a series of commercially available programs that can interact with one another. These programs, collectively known as *integrated software*, permit the user the flexibility to move data between various applications. These applications include *data management*, *electronic spreadsheets*, *graphics*, *word processing*, and *communications*. The *function* of each of these applications is described in Chapter 4, "Computer Systems—Micros." The *concepts* and *use* of these applications are described in considerable detail in a special *Integrated Microcomputer Software* section following Chapter 17.

Science and Research

Engineers and scientists routinely use the computer as a tool in experimentation and design. Mechanical engineers use computers to simulate the effects of a wind tunnel to analyze the aerodynamics of an automobile prototype. Political scientists collect and analyze demographic data, such as median income and housing starts, to predict voting trends. Chemists use computer graphics to create three-dimensional views of an experimental molecule. There are at least as many science and research applications for the computer as there are scientists and engineers.

Process Control

Computers used for **process control** accept data in a continuous *feedback loop*. In a feedback loop, the process generates data that become input to the computer. As the data are received and interpreted by the computer, the computer initiates action to control the ongoing process. For example, process-control computers monitor and control the environment within skyscrapers (see Figure 1–8).

An aircraft inertial navigation system is another good example of a computer being used for process control. The aircraft's on-board computer uses star-tracking and radar inputs to keep on course. These directional inputs

The computer's ability to analyze large volumes of data is enabling research and development scientists to investigate the perimeters of knowledge.
(Phillips Petroleum Company)

A central computer system monitors and controls the drilling and pumping systems in this exploratory off-shore oil rig in the Norwegian North Sea. (Phillips Petroleum Company)

are continuously analyzed by the computer. If, for example, a wind change is detected, the computer activates the automatic pilot to compensate for the wind's new direction.

Tiny "computers on a chip" are being embedded in artificial hearts and other organs. Once the organs are implanted in the body, the computer monitors critical inputs, such as blood pressure and flow, then takes corrective action to ensure stability of operation.

FIGURE 1–8
Process-Control Feedback Loop
Computer-based environmental control systems monitor and control the temperature and humidity in thousands of buildings.

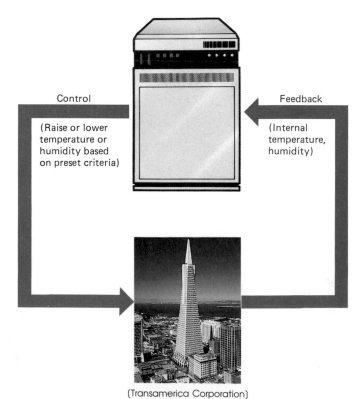

Control

(Raise or lower temperature or humidity based on preset criteria)

Feedback

(Internal temperature, humidity)

(Transamerica Corporation)

Education

Computers can interact with students to enhance the learning process. Relatively inexpensive hardware that is capable of multidimensional communication (sound, print, graphics, and color) has resulted in a phenomenal growth of the computer as an educational tool in both the home and the classroom. Computer based education will not replace teachers and books, but educators are in agreement that *computer-assisted instruction*, or CAI for short, is having a profound impact on traditional modes of education.

Computers have been used for drill and practice for over a decade. Only recently has sophisticated CAI been economically feasible. Now, powerful personal computers have added a dimension that is not possible with books and the traditional classroom lecture. The student controls the pace of learning and can interact directly with the computer system. Through interactive computer graphics, a CAI system can demonstrate certain concepts more effectively than books or even teachers. The teacher-book-CAI approach has spawned a new era in education. The software supplement to this text provides many examples of sophisticated CAI.

Artificial Intelligence

Humans Are Born, Not Manufactured. Today's computers can simulate many human capabilities, such as reaching, grasping, calculating, speaking, remembering, comparing numbers, and drawing. Researchers are working to expand these capabilities and, therefore, the power of computers to include the ability to reason, to learn or "accumulate knowledge," to strive for self-improvement, and to simulate human sensory capabilities. This general area of research is known as **artificial intelligence (AI)**.

"Artificial intelligence?" To some, the mere mention of artificial intelligence creates visions of electromechanical automatons replacing human beings. The misconceptions by novices are probably rooted in the unfortunate phrasing of the term artificial intelligence. In computerese, **intelligence** refers to computer processing capability. "Artificial" seemed a logical adjective. But, as anyone involved in the area of artificial intelligence will tell you, there is, and will always be, a distinct difference between humans and machines. Computers will never be capable of simulating the distinctly human qualities of creativity, humor, and emotions!

Humans will always be the masters of computers. Any "intelligence" given a computer is our gift to technology.

Computer Simulation of Human Capabilities. Computer systems with artificial intelligence can see, smell, feel, write, speak, and interpret spoken words. To varying degrees, these artificial intelligence capabilities are possible with current technology.

The simulation of human sensory capabilities is extremely complex. For example, a computer does not actually *see* and interpret an image the way a human does. The image is first detected by a camera and is **digitized**—that is, translated to a form that computers can interpret. The digitized image is then compared to other digitized images stored in the computer's data base. Through a matching process, the computer interprets the image.

This tiny silicon chip, sometimes called a "computer on a chip," contains one million electronic circuits. The human brain has 10 trillion circuit elements, about 10 million times as many as this state-of-the-art silicon chip. (TRW Inc.)

Voice inflections, grammatical exceptions, and words that have several meanings have combined to make speech interpretation and voice synthesis difficult, but not impossible. "I'm OK!" differs from "I'm OK?" and, out of context, "I read often" can be interpreted in the present or the past tense. For humans, distinguishing these subtle differences is second nature. For machines, these subtleties must be programmed and made part of the permanent data base.

Expert Systems.   **Expert systems** provide "expert" advice and guidance in a wide range of activities, from locomotive maintenance to surgery. An expert system is an interactive system that responds to questions, asks for clarification, makes recommendations, and generally aids in the decision-making process. At the heart of an expert system is a **knowledge base**.

A knowledge base is *not* a data base. The traditional data base environment, as illustrated in the example of Section 1–5, deals with data that have a static relationship between the elements. That is, a student record has a fixed relationship between a course record and a faculty record. A knowledge base is created by *knowledge engineers*, who translate the knowledge of real, live human experts into rules and strategies. A knowledge base is heuristic; that is, it provides the expert system with the capability to recommend directions for user inquiry. It also encourages further investigation into areas that

Locomotive mechanics get troubleshooting help with this computer-based expert system. The mechanic simply keys in responses to questions asked by the "expert" about the malfunction. Through interactive questioning, the expert system eventually identifies the cause of the malfunction and demonstrates repair procedures on the video monitor (screen at left).
(General Electric Company)

may be important to a certain line of questioning, but not apparent to the user. Moreover, a knowledge base grows because it "learns" from user feedback. An expert system learns by "remembering"; that is, it stores occurrences of the past in its knowledge base. For example, a recommendation that sends a user on a "wild goose chase" is thereafter deleted as a viable strategy for similar future inquiries.

In effect, expert systems simulate the human thought process. To varying degrees, they can reason, draw inferences, and make judgments. Here is how an expert system works. Let's use a medical diagnosis system as an example. Upon examination of a patient, a physician might interact with an expert diagnosis system to get help in diagnosing the patient's illness or, perhaps, to get a second opinion. First, the doctor would relate the symptoms to the expert system: male of age 10, temperature of 103 degrees, and swollen glands about the neck. Needing more information, the expert system might ask the doctor to examine the parotid gland for swelling. Receiving an affirmative answer, the system might ask a few more questions and perhaps even for lab reports before giving a diagnosis. A final question put to the physician might be whether or not the patient had been previously afflicted with or immunized for parotitis. If not, the expert system diagnoses the illness as parotitis, otherwise known as the mumps.

Computer-based expert systems have fared well against real expert physicians in effectiveness of diagnosis of illnesses. Other expert systems help crews repair telephone lines and computer vendors configure computer systems to customer specifications. Still others help geologists explore for minerals by interpreting data on rock formations, ages, and types.

Some computer industry observers believe that expert systems are the wave of the future and that each of us will have "expert" help and guidance in our respective professions. Others say "no way." Time will tell!

MEMORY BITS
CATEGORIES OF COMPUTER USAGE
■ Information systems/data processing
■ Personal computing
■ Science and research
■ Process control
■ Education
■ Artificial intelligence

1-9 COMPUTER LITERACY AND OPPORTUNITY _____

Computer literacy is the door to opportunity in many professions. Many organizations have already set computer literacy as a prerequisite for employment, and the number is growing. Others require it for promotion. Once you complete this course, the door is open. Your marketability for employment is improved. You have an advantage over those of your peers who are computer illiterate. If you are or will become a self-employed professional, such as an attorney, an engineer, or a physician, computer-literacy education will provide you with the prerequisite knowledge that you will need to maintain a competitive edge.

Once you attain computer literacy, the rate at which you can learn more about computers is accelerated. Your base of knowledge will grow so that you will be better equipped to keep pace with a rapidly changing technology.

If you decide to pursue a career in computers and information systems, you will find that the opportunities have never been better. These jobs have no geographic or industry restrictions. You can work in a hospital in New York, in a bank in Colorado, or on a ranch in Texas. It is inevitable that the ever-widening vistas for computer applications will create more and greater

YOU'RE NEVER TOO OLD (OR YOUNG) FOR CAMP

"Going off to camp" can take on a new meaning for those who head for a growing number and variety of "computer camps." These can range from the traditional outdoor camps that may feature hands-on computer experience as a special choice of activities, to cruise ships, to vacation resorts, to an eight-hour classroom setting.

Each camp is different: teaching style, the computer-to-camper ratio, the instructor-to-camper ratio, the approach to instruction, the price, and the balance of activities.

In addition to generally familiarizing campers with computers, common curriculum offerings include: computer literacy, programming in such languages as LOGO and BASIC, using robotics, creating with computer graphics, applying word processing, problem solving, and, of course, having fun.

Club Med and other vacation getaways, on land and sea, now include "learning computers" as one of their recreational activities.
(Club Med Sales, Inc.)

career opportunities. Today, there are at least a dozen well-defined information systems jobs (i.e., programmer, systems analyst, data base administrator, operator, information systems consultant, information systems auditor, and so on). Next year, there will be more. The variety of possible computer/information systems career paths is discussed in detail in Chapter 16, "Jobs and Career Opportunities."

SUMMARY OUTLINE AND IMPORTANT TERMS

1-1   COMPUTER LITERACY DEFINED.   **Computer literacy** is achieved through study, practice, and interest in the topic. Computer-literate people know how to purchase, use, and operate a computer system and to make it work for them. The computer-literate person is also aware of the computer's impact on society.

1-2   WHY COMPUTER LITERACY?   People study computers: because the computer is impacting the way we live, work, and play; to overcome **cyberphobia**; to learn **computerese**; and to be in a better position to take advantage of opportunities afforded by the computer revolution. Each year computers, both in general and at a more personal level (**personal computers**), are having a greater influence on our lives.

1-3 COMPUTERS ARE FOR EVERYONE. After existing for millenia as an agrarian society, the people of the world progressed to an industrial society. Today, what is emerging is an information society. In an information society, computers are for everyone: **users** in all environments, computer professionals, and **hackers**. Companies, like individuals, depend on **information systems** and the capabilities of computing **hardware** for their information needs.

1-4 COMPUTER MYTHOLOGY. The computer mystique has caused our society to build certain myths around computers. These myths revolve around a "thinking" machine that is threatening to society's general well-being. But, in reality, computers are inanimate and are capable of only that logic programmed by human intelligence.

1-5 FROM DATA TO INFORMATION. **Data** are the raw material from which information is derived. **Information** is comprised of data that have been collected and processed into a meaningful form.

1-6 THE HIERARCHY OF DATA ORGANIZATION: A PREVIEW. A string of **bits** is combined to form a character. Characters are combined to represent the values of **data elements**, also called **fields**. Related data elements are grouped to form **records**. Records with the same data elements combine to become a **file**. A **data base** contains several different record types and defines their relationships.

1-7 UNCOVERING THE "MYSTERY" OF COMPUTERS. A **computer system** is not as complex as we are sometimes led to believe. Personal computers, also called **microcomputers**, and **mainframe computers** are all computer systems, and each has only four fundamental components: **input** (e.g., a **VDT** keyboard), processing (executing a program), **output** (e.g., a **printer**), and storage.

1-8 HOW DO WE USE COMPUTERS?. The uses of computers can be classified into six general categories:

- **Information systems/data processing**—the computer is used to process data and produce business information.
- **Personal computing**—the computer is used for a variety of business and domestic "personal" applications.
- **Science and research**—the computer is used as a tool in experimentation and design.
- **Process control**—the computer is used to control a process by accepting and evaluating data in a continuous feedback loop.
- **Education**—the computer is used to communicate with a student for the purpose of enhancing the learning process.
- **Artificial intelligence**—the computer is used in applications that simulate such human capabilities as reaching, speaking, drawing, smelling, and the abilities to reason, learn, and strive for self-improvement.

1-9 COMPUTER LITERACY AND OPPORTUNITY. Computer literacy is the door to opportunity in many professions.

REVIEW EXERCISES

Concepts

1. What are the four fundamental components of a computer system?
2. Which component of a computer system executes the program?
3. Name and give an example for each level of the hierarchy of data organization.
4. Associate the following with the appropriate category of computer usage: continuous feedback loop, experimentation, home use, CAI, speech, and business systems.
5. What are the primary functions of an organization's information services department?
6. What is the basic difference between an expert system's knowledge base and a data base?
7. Suppose you are the president of a college. Give examples of "what if" questions that you would like to submit to the college's student information system. One example might be, "What if enrollment increased 20%, how would class size be affected in the Psychology Department?"
8. Describe the relationship between data and information.
9. What are the five components of integrated software?

Discussion

10. If programming is only 15% to 30% of the total effort, what other activities are involved in developing computer-based information systems?
11. The computer has had far-reaching effects on our lives. How has the computer impacted your life?
12. What is your concept of computer literacy? In what ways do you think achieving computer literacy will impact your domestic life? Business life?
13. At what age should computer literacy education begin?
14. Discuss how the complexion of jobs will change as we evolve from an industrial society to an information society. Give several examples.
15. The use of computers tends to stifle creativity. Argue for or against this statement.
16. Research in artificial intelligence is accelerating much faster than anyone would have imagined in 1980. Perhaps this increase in research can be attributed to AI's potential for increasing productivity in the plant and improving decision making. Is this the case, or will it mean fewer paychecks? Discuss.

SELF-TEST (by section) _____

1-1. To be computer literate, you must be able to write computer pro-
      grams. (T/F)

1-2. The irrational fear of, or aversion to, computers is called_____ .

1-3. A computer enthusiast is: (a) user friendly, (b) a hacker, or (c) a
      computerist.

1-4. A solid knowledge of upper-division mathematics is a prerequisite
      to becoming computer literate. (T/F)

1-5. _____ are the raw material from which_____ is derived.

1-6. Related data elements are grouped to form_____ .

1-7. A printer is an example of which of the four computer system compo
      nents?

1-8. The greatest amount of available computing capacity is dedicated
      to the information systems/data processing category of computer
      usage. (T/F)

1-9. There are fewer than six well-defined computer-related jobs. (T/F)

Self-Test answers.   1–1, F; 1–2, cyberphobia; 1–3, b; 1–4, F; 1–5, data, information;
1–6, records; 1–7, output; 1–8, T; 1–9, F.

STUDENT LEARNING OBJECTIVES

- To put society's dependence on computers in perspective.
- To identify and discuss controversial computer-related issues.
- To discuss growth patterns, trends, and problems related to computers and information processing.
- To know when to use a computer.
- To appreciate the scope and influence of computers in society.
- To learn ways in which the computer can enhance our lives.

CHAPTER 2

Computers in Society— Today

2

Reaching the Point of No Return. Albert Einstein said that "Concern for man himself and his fate must always form the chief interest of all technical endeavors." There are those who believe that a rapidly advancing computer technology exhibits little regard for "man himself and his fate." They contend that computers are overused, misused, and generally detrimental to society. This group argues that the computer is dehumanizing and is slowly forcing society into a pattern of mass conformity. To be sure, the "computer revolution" is presenting society with difficult and complex problems, but they can be overcome.

Whether it is good or bad, society has reached the point of no return with regard to its dependence on computers. Stiff business competition means a continued and growing use of computers. On the more personal level, we are reluctant to forfeit the everyday conveniences made possible by computers. More and more of us find that our personal computers are an integral part of our daily activities.

Society's dependence on computers is not always apparent. For example, today's automobile assembly line is almost as computer dependent as it is people dependent: an inventory-management system makes sure that parts are delivered to the right assembly point at the right time; a computer-controlled robot does the welding; and the movement of the assembly line is controlled by a process-control computer.

Give Up My Computer? Never! Ask a secretary to trade a word processing system for a typewriter. Ask a physician for an alternative to a computer-controlled intensive care unit. Ask airline executives how long they could continue to operate without their on-line reservation system. Ask yourself if you would give up the convenience of remote banking at automatic teller machines.

A manager of a dry cleaning shop examines monthly revenues for each of the various articles of clothing (e.g., shirts, pants, coats). Obtaining this valuable information is a breeze with a computer. Six months earlier, before the computer was installed, the same report would have taken a week to compile.
(Texas Instruments, Inc.)

Our dependence on food has evolved into the joy of gourmet eating, and so it is, or can be, with computers. Dependence is not necessarily bad as long as we keep it in perspective. We can't passively assume that computers will continue to enhance the quality of our lives. It's our obligation to learn to understand computers so that we can better direct their application to society's benefit. Only through understanding can we control the misuse or abuse of computer technology.

2-2 CONTROVERSY: ANOTHER WORD FOR COMPUTER

A by-product of the computer revolution is intense controversy. The emotions of both the general public and the computer community run high on computer-related issues. Some of the more heated issues are discussed below.

Privacy of Personal Information

Sources of Personal Data. The issue of greatest concern to the general public is the privacy of personal information. Some people fear that computer-based record keeping offers too much of an opportunity for abuse of an individual's privacy. There is indeed reason for concern. For example, credit card users unknowingly leave a "trail" of activities and interests that, when examined and evaluated, can provide a rather comprehensive personal profile.

The date and location are recorded for all credit card transactions. In effect, when you make a charge for a lunch, gasoline, or clothing, you are creating a chronological record of where you have been and your spending habits. From this information, a good analyst could compile a very accurate picture of your life style. For example, the analyst could predict how you

The accumulation of personal data has become a matter of concern to our information society. Whether you realize it, you are continuously contributing data about yourself to some computer systems. For example, when you request a long-distance telephone number from an operator, your number and the requested number are recorded in a computer system. In this and most instances, personal data are collected as a matter of record and not for the purpose of abuse.
(Computer Consoles Inc.)

dress by knowing the type of clothing stores you patronize. On a more personal level, records are kept that detail the duration, time, and numbers of all your telephone calls. With computers, these numbers can easily be matched with people. So each time you make a phone call, you also leave a record of who you call. Enormous amounts of personal data are maintained on everyone: the IRS, your college, your employer, your creditors, and on and on.

We would hope that information about us is up to date and accurate. Laws permit us to examine our records, but first we must find them. You cannot just write to the federal government and request to see your files. To be completely sure that you examine all your federal records for completeness and accuracy, you would have to write, and probably visit, each of the approximately 5,800 agencies that maintain computer-based files on individuals. The same is true of computer-based personal data maintained in the private sector.

Abuses of Personal Information. Most will agree that the potential exists for abuse, but are these data being abused? Some say yes. Consider the states that sell lists containing the addresses and data on their licensed drivers. At the request of a manager of several petite women's clothing stores, a state provided the manager with a list of all licensed drivers in the state who were women, between the ages of 21 and 40, less than 5 feet 3 inches tall, and under 120 pounds. You be the judge. Is the sale of such a list an abuse of personal information?

Personal information has become the product of a growing industry. Companies have been formed that do nothing but sell information about people. Not only are the people involved not asked for permission to use

"According to this, your total is $47.32, your last name is Robertson, and you won't have a nice day until 1988."
(By permission of Brian Hansen)

their data, they are seldom even told that their personal information is being sold! A great deal of personal data can be extracted from public records. For example, one company sends people to county courthouses all over the United States to gather publicly-accessible data on those people who have recently filed papers to purchase a home. Mailing lists are then sold to insurance companies, landscape companies, congresspersons seeking new votes, lawyers seeking new clients, and so on. Those placed on the mailing list eventually become targets of commerce and special interest.

The use of personal information for profit and other purposes is growing at such a rapid rate that, for all practical purposes, the abuse of this information has slipped from beneath the legislative umbrella. Antiquated laws, combined with judicial unfamiliarity with computers, make policing and prosecuting abuses of personal information difficult and, in many cases, impossible.

Computer Matching.   Computer matching is a procedure whereby separate data bases are examined and individuals common to both are identified. Computer matching has been referred to as Orwellian by some. Auditors think it is a great help in their jobs.

The focus of most computer matching applications is to identify those persons engaged in wrongdoing. Federal employees are being matched against those with delinquent student loans. Wages are then garnished to repay the loan. In another computer matching case, a $30 million fraud was uncovered when questionable financial transactions were traced to common participants.

The Potential for Security.   Computer experts feel that the integrity of personal data can be more secure in computer data bases than in file cabinets. They contend that we can continue to be the masters and not the victims if we implement proper safeguards for the maintenance and release of this information, and enact effective legislation to cope with the abuse of personal information.

Computer Crime

It is estimated that each year the total loss from computer crime is greater than the sum total of all robberies. In fact, no one really knows the extent of computer crime because much of it is either undetected or unreported (most often the latter). In those cases involving banks, officers may elect to write off the loss rather than announce the crime and risk the loss of good will from their customers. Computer crime is on the rise. There are many types of computer crimes, ranging from the use of an unauthorized password by a student to a billion-dollar insurance fraud.

Computer crime requires the cooperation of an experienced computer specialist. A common street thug does not have the knowledge or the opportunity to pull off a computer crime. The sophistication of the crime, however, makes it no less criminal.

Computer crime is a relatively recent phenomenon. Legislation, the criminal justice system, and industry are not yet adequately prepared to cope with it. Only a few police and FBI agents in the entire country have been trained to handle cases involving computer crime. And when a case comes to court, few judges have the background necessary to understand the testimony.

This is one of ten aisles in a large magnetic tape library. The entire library is secured in a vault to protect the privacy of millions of individuals whose personal data are stored on these tapes.
(TRW Inc.)

Recognizing the potential severity of computer crime, the legal system and industry are trying to speed up precautionary measures. Some say that we are still moving too slowly and that a Three Mile Island-level catastrophe is the only thing that will make industry and government believe how severe computer crime can be.

The Culprits.   There is a growing concern that the media is glorifying the illegal entry and use of computer systems by overzealous hackers. These "electronic vandals" have tapped into everything from local credit agencies to top-secret defense systems. The evidence of unlawful entry, perhaps a revised record or access during nonoperating hours, is called a *footprint*.

A few hackers and computer professionals have chosen computer crime as a profession. But the threat of computer crime may be even greater from managers and consultants, because they are in the best position to pull off a computer crime. They know how the systems operate, and they know the passwords needed to gain access to the systems.

Software Piracy.   Software is protected by the Copyright Law of 1974, just as books are protected by copyright laws. This makes the duplication of copyright software illegal. This unlawful thievery of someone else's programs is sometimes called *software piracy*. The term *pilferage* is used to describe the situation where a company purchases a software product without a site-usage license agreement, then copies and distributes it throughout the company.

It may cost more to reproduce a book than to buy it, but a $750 commercial software product can be reproduced for $2.50 (price of storage medium) in less than a minute. Many software pirates have found the temptation too great to resist. Vendors of software for personal computers estimate that for every software product sold, two more are illegally copied. Software piracy is a serious problem, and software vendors are acting vigorously to prosecute people and companies who violate their copyrights.

Software is subject to copyright laws because it, like books, can be reproduced. Unlawful duplication of copyright software is called software piracy. Microcomputer software that is distributed on diskettes is the most vulnerable to software pirates.
(Photograph provided by Tandem Computers Incorporated)

Legislators at both the state and Federal levels are working to draft effective legislation to better cope with the privacy of personal information and computer crime.
(General Instrument Corporation)

Computer Legislation

The abuse of personal information and computer crime are critical issues confronting lawmakers. Laws that have been enacted are quite inadequate to deal with these issues. Fortunately, legislation is being drafted at the federal level and by most states to define computer crime, its punishment, and what constitutes proper handling of personal data. At the federal level, several pieces of legislation have been introduced, but to date no comprehensive legislation has become law. About 60% of the states have enacted some kind of legislation. In some states it is now a felony to steal or abuse data.

Once we have definitive legislation, prosecution of computer crimes becomes another issue. Even when a computer crime is brought to the attention of the authorities, prosecutors lack sufficient technical knowledge to prepare a case. A judge and jury understand the concept of armed robbery and have a relative feel for the appropriate punishment, but what about computer crimes? Sophisticated computer crimes can be extremely complex and well beyond the understanding of most prosecutors, judges, and jurors. Legislation must be enacted and prosecution issues resolved before the criminal justice system can begin to cope with computer crime.

Electronic Funds Transfer

The "Cashless Society."   The growing number of *automatic teller machines* (*ATM*) have made *electronic funds transfer* (*EFT*) very visible to the public. In EFT, money is transferred "electronically" from bank to bank, and from account to account, via computers. Each weekday, the financial institutions of the world use EFT to transfer over 1 trillion dollars. Applications of EFT

This grocery store has the capability to operate without cash transfers. The customer swipes her bank card (containing account number and authorization data) through a badge reader and enters a personal identification number on the keyboard, both of which are connected to a network of banking computers. The customer then enters the amount of the purchase. This amount is deducted from her bank account and credited to that of the grocery store.
(Diebold, Incorporated)

are being implemented all around us. A few automatic teller machines and automatic payroll transfer systems have been operational for a decade. Now, the number of installed ATMs is doubling each year. Some banks offer *home banking* services that permit customers to pay bills and perform banking transactions from their personal computers without leaving home.

The debate rages on as we move closer to a "cashless society." Is this a reasonable and prudent manner in which to handle money? It is well within the state of the art to just about eliminate money transactions and make the transition to a cashless society.

EFT: Pro and Con.   Sometime in the future, the scope of EFT may be expanded because the buyer will be able to use a universal "smart" card (smart, because of the tiny embedded computer), and perhaps a password, to purchase everything from candy bars to automobiles. Upon purchasing an item, a buyer would give the card to the seller. The seller would use the purchaser's card to log the sale on a *point-of-sale (POS)* terminal that is linked to a network of banking computers. The amount of the sale would then be transferred from the buyer's account to the seller's account.

The advantages of an expanded use of EFT are noteworthy. EFT would eliminate the cumbersome administrative work associated with handling of money and checks. It would also eliminate the need to carry money, eliminate rubber checks and counterfeit money, and minimize the possibility of error. It would provide a detailed record of all transactions. And, EFT would also eliminate the cost of making money. The cost of manufacturing a penny now exceeds the value of the coin!

The disadvantages are equally noteworthy. The critical issue is EFT's potential for the abuse of personal information. EFT generates a chronological record of all purchases (see the discussion in the earlier section on "Privacy of Personal Information"). In effect, this type of system permits everything from a person's life style to location to be monitored. Opponents of EFT are also concerned about EFT's vulnerability to crime.

With untold amounts of money being electronically transferred among the banks of the world, the banking industry is a prime target for computer crime. Bank robbers have graduated from guns and dynamite to computers and software. A technology called **cryptography** is available to ensure the integrity of funds transfer. Incredibly, only a few banks use it. This crime-prevention technology involves the *encryption* and *decryption* of data. Since the data sent over communications channels (e.g., telephone lines) are the most vulnerable, these devices "scramble" the data into messages that are almost impossible to decode.

It will not be long after the first billion-dollar computer "heist" that all banks will install cryptography hardware. Cryptography may become a way of life for all transmission of data to and from remote locations if hackers continue to violate data security. Cryptography is discussed in Chapter 9, "Data Communications."

Even though there is a trend toward more electronic funds transfer, some experts feel that EFT is about to reach its peak of acceptance. Others feel that total EFT is inevitable within the next ten years.

Automation

Concern over the effects of automation began two hundred years ago with the industrial revolution, and the public is still concerned. To many people, computers mean automation, and automation means loss of jobs. Just as the industrial revolution created hundreds of new job opportunities, so will the information revolution (see Section 1–2, "Why Computer Literacy?").

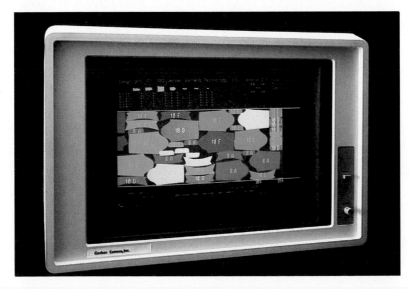

Foot apparel patterns are first laid out using computer-aided design (CAD). The pattern specifications are then input to a computer-controlled cutter that uses an "intelligent" knife to cut the material.
(Gerber Scientific Inc.)

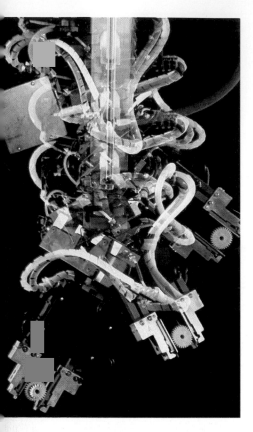

The robot shown here (in multiple exposures) mounts a gear to a computer printer assembly. Before robots, workers in this assembly plant were primarily involved with manual tasks; now they are concerned with tasks that tap their cognitive resources. These tasks include production scheduling, quality control, and the design and programming of robots.
(Courtesy of International Business Machines Corporation)

There is no doubt that the emergence of computer technology has resulted in the elimination of jobs involving routine, monotonous, and sometimes hazardous tasks. However, the elimination of these jobs has been offset by the creation of more challenging jobs. For the most part, people whose jobs have been eliminated have been displaced to jobs carrying greater responsibilities and offering more opportunities. It is common for bookkeepers to become systems analysts, for draftpersons to advance to computer-aided design, and for secretaries to become specialists in a myriad of computer applications from word processing to data management. This pattern is repeated thousands of times each month.

Automation will continue to eliminate and create jobs. Historically, advancement in technology has increased overall productivity in certain areas, thereby cutting the number of workers needed. In addition, a new wave of jobs is created in the wake of cutbacks in traditional areas. With the cost of labor increasing and the cost of computers decreasing, the trend to automation of routine activities will probably continue. However, to realize a smooth transition to an automated environment, industry and government must recognize that they have a social responsibility to retrain those who will be displaced to other jobs.

National Data Base

Like EFT, the technology is available to establish a national data base. Many have proposed a national data base as a central respository for all personal data. An individual would be assigned a unique identification number at birth. This ID number would replace the social security number, motor vehicle operator's license number, student identification number, and dozens of other identification numbers.

A national data base would consolidate the personal data now stored on tens of thousands of manual and computer-based files. The national data base could contain an individual's name, past and present addresses, dependent data, work history, medical history, marital history, tax data, criminal records, military history, credit rating and history, and so on. Proponents of the national data base recognize that the above data are currently maintained, but they are redundant and often inaccurate or out of date. Their contention is that at least the national data base would be accurate and up to date.

Those who are for a national data base list certain advantages. For instance, a national data base could provide the capability to monitor the activities of criminal suspects; to virtually eliminate welfare fraud; to quickly identify illegal aliens; to make an individual's medical history available at any hospital in the country; to take the 10-year census almost automatically; and to generate valuable information. Medical researchers could isolate geographic areas that have inordinately high incidences of certain illnesses. The Bureau of Labor Statistics could monitor real, as opposed to reported, employment levels on a daily basis. The information possibilities are endless.

Those who oppose the national data base call it impersonal and an invasion of privacy. Their feelings are that any advantages are more than offset by the potential for abuse of such a data base.

The creation of a national data base is an extremely complex undertaking, the social implications notwithstanding. It is unlikely that we will see such a data base within this decade. However, with the growing concern about welfare fraud, tax evasion, crime, and the influx of illegal aliens, the national data base may be an increasingly appealing alternative.

2-3 WHEN TO USE A COMPUTER

Computer System Capabilities

Before we discuss when to use a computer, let's find out what it can do. In a nutshell, computers are fast, accurate, and reliable; they don't forget anything; and they don't complain. Now for the details:

Speed.   The smallest unit of time in the human experience is, realistically, the second. With the second as the only means of comparison, it is difficult for us to comprehend the time scale of computers. Even the operations (the execution of an instruction) for personal computers are measured in thousandths of a second, or **milliseconds**. Operations for larger processors are measured in **microseconds**, **nanoseconds**, and **picoseconds** (one millionth, one billionth, and one trillionth of a second, respectively). To give you a feel for the speed of processors, a beam of light travels down the length of this page in about one nanosecond!

For the most part, hospitals, clinics, and doctor's offices maintain patient medical records in manila folders. The medical community would like to see critical patient data made a part of a national data base. In this way, if you are in an auto accident 1,000 miles from home, the emergency room doctor can immediately find out such information as your blood type and the drugs that might cause an allergic reaction.
(Texas Instruments, Inc.)

A computer's speed is measured in millions of instructions per second, or MIPS. An instruction may be to add two numbers or to compare two numbers. The computer in this public works consulting firm can execute more instructions in one second than an average person will take steps in a lifetime.
(Control Data Corporation)

COMPUTERS TAKE A HIKE

Computers go just about anywhere anymore, even up Mt. Everest. One recent three-month expedition retraced the 1924 steps of George Leigh-Mallory and Andrew Irvine's unsuccessful attempt to reach the summit of Mt. Everest.

On this expedition, however, the climbers used the computer as a tool to: monitor the expedition members' health; monitor the food consumption for both the humans and the yaks; determine the weather's influence on the day's plans; and decide on the best route to the summit.

A portable computer and printer shared a tent with 16 Tibetan porters at the 21,000-foot base camp (the peak is at 29,028 feet). The hardware worked perfectly, even at 40°F below zero.

The Santa Fe Railroad's Network Management System at Topeka, Kansas monitors the location and movement of every train in the system. System reliability is critical in this computer-dependent system.
(Santa Fe Industries)

Accuracy. You may work for years before experiencing a system error, such as an updating of the wrong record or an incorrect addition. Errors do occur in computer-based information systems, but precious few can be directly attributed to the computer system. The vast majority of these errors can be traced to a program logic error, a procedural error, or erroneous data. These are *human errors*. Hardware errors are usually detected and corrected by the computer system itself.

Reliability. Computer systems are particularly adept at repetitive tasks. They don't take sick days and coffee breaks, and they seldom complain. Anything below 99.9% *uptime* is usually unacceptable. Unfortunately, *downtime* sometimes occurs at the most inconvenient times. For some companies, any downtime is unacceptable. For example, automobile manufacturers must have their computers operational at all times. If the computers fail in an automobile assembly plant, the line is shut down and thousands of people become idle. These companies provide *backup* computers that take over if the main computers fail.

Memory Capability. Computer systems have total and instant recall of data and an almost unlimited capacity to store these data. A typical mainframe computer system will have billions of characters, and perhaps thousands of graphic images, stored and available for instant recall. Ten times that amount might be stored off-line (that is, the data must be loaded to the computer system) on interchangeable magnetic tapes and disks. A million characters of magnetic tape storage costs about a nickel. To give you a benchmark for comparison, this book contains approximately 1,500,000 characters.

Computers or People?

Some tasks are better suited for *computers* than for *people*, and vice versa. Programmers and systems analysts routinely compare the capabilities of computers and people when they must decide whether to automate a particular task or to let it remain a human task. To provide you with a guide for comparison, tasks are lumped into the following four categories:

The Computer Is Not Appropriate. The number and variety of tasks that can be done by a computer system are amazing, but many tasks are still done best and at less expense by people. For example, a computer-based supplies inventory system in a small law firm is probably more trouble than it is worth. Since the inventory in a law firm is composed primarily of office supplies, it is surely easier for the office manager to visually check the level of supplies than to update an inventory system each time a note pad or a pencil is removed from the supply cabinet.

The Computer Will Help People to Do Their Job Better.   The computer assists supermarket checkers to accurately tally a customer's bill and, at the same time, update the inventory. Computers provide a cross-check for nurses in intensive care units. Both nurses and a computer monitor the vital signs of critically ill patients.

The Computer Will Eliminate the Need for Human Involvement.   Before computers, banking transactions involving withdrawals, deposits, and checks were sorted and posted manually. This time-consuming and somewhat boring task is now done by computers. As another example, computerized industrial robots handle materials in areas with intense heat and hazardous chemicals that were formerly worked by humans.

The Computer Is the Only Alternative.   Some tasks would be impossible without the computer. For example, space shuttle astronauts pilot their space-craft to an Earth landing; however, during most of the mission the spacecraft is maneuvered through space by hundreds of complex systems, all monitored and controlled by computers. The requirement for split-second timing and the simultaneous control of hundreds of systems placed the piloting of these spacecraft beyond human capabilities.

During the diving competition at the XXI Olympiad in Los Angeles, computer technology was used to help judges record and report the scores for each dive. This is a case of the computer helping people to do a better job.
(AT&T Technologies)

2-4   APPLICATIONS OF THE COMPUTER: LIMITED ONLY BY OUR IMAGINATION

Twenty years ago, *space* and *distance* were formidable obstacles to what we could and could not do with the computer. But today, *microminiaturization* and *data communications* have removed these obstacles. Microminiaturization of electronic circuitry has made it possible to put computers in wristwatches. Computers with capabilities similar to those of the mainframe computers of the early 1960s are about the size of a fingernail. Data communications satellites make it possible for computers in the United States to communicate with computers in Japan, France, or in any other country (see Chapter 9 on communications).

The door is now open for applications of the computer that were only dreams or fantasies two decades ago. The number and the type of computer applications are limited only by our imaginations. This section contains a brief overview of a variety of familiar computer applications. You have proba-bly had occasion to use each of these information systems at one time or another. Other applications in other fields of endeavor will be presented throughout the book in the textual material, in photo captions, and in the special-interest boxes.

Microminiaturization of computers and satellite data communications have opened up new vistas for computer applications. This communications satellite is being released from the space shuttle over the Gulf of Mexico (the state of Florida is visible just below the horizon). This small silicon chip holds 256 thousand pieces of data.
(NASA)
(AT&T Technologies)

Health Care

A drug-interaction system helps physicians and pharmacists prepare and administer the proper drug to a patient. Literally thousands of drugs can be prescribed by an attending physician, and a mistake in selecting drug pairs could cause an adverse chemical reaction that might be serious, even fatal.

Over the years, physicians and pharmacists have compiled a drug-interaction data base that identifies those drug pairs that should not be prescribed together. With new drugs being introduced almost daily, pharmacists cannot rely on their memory to keep abreast of possible adverse interactions. It would take an army of pharmacists to manually check the thousands of possible interactions for each prescription.

In a drug-interaction system, the pharmacist enters the name of the drug or drugs prescribed and the patient's name (see Figure 2–1). The computer accesses the patient's record and checks other drugs that the patient is presently taking. The possible drug interactions are checked against the drug-interaction data base and potentially hazardous interactions are identified. This system minimizes the possibility of an adverse drug interaction and a potentially fatal accident.

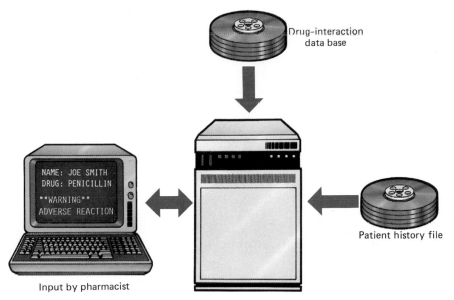

FIGURE 2-1
Drug-interaction System
Drugs currently being administered to Joe Smith are matched against penicillin and the drug-interaction data base to check for a possible adverse reaction.

Airlines

An airline reservation system is a classic example of an information system that reflects an up-to-the-minute status. An airline reservations agent communicates with a centralized computer via a remote terminal to update the data base the moment a seat on any flight is filled or becomes available.

An airline reservation system does much more than keep track of flight reservations. Departure and arrival times are closely monitored so that ground crew activities can be coordinated. The system offers many kinds of management information needs: the number of passenger miles flown, profit per passenger on a particular flight, percent of arrivals on time, average number of empty seats on each flight for each day of the week, and so on.

It is interesting that airlines overbook almost every flight; that is, they book seats they do not have. The number of extra seats sold is based on historical no-show statistics that are compiled from the reservation system data base. Although these statistics provide good guidelines, occasionally everyone does show up!

Before each flight, the pilot and copilot get a weather briefing and pick up a "computer" flight plan. Just as cars travel on highways, airplanes travel on airways. Based on wind speed and direction, the computer selects the best airway route and projects a flying time for each leg. The flight plan also suggests flying altitudes that minimize fuel consumption. (AT&T Technologies)

This farm scene was created by a computer artist. Just as a writer can edit a manuscript using word processing, an artist can easily make changes to computer art pieces. The artist can change this scene from bright sun to dusk, or from summer colors to fall colors.
(Mindset Corporation)

Art

The computer is an *image processor* as well as an *information processor*. Computer art is now a well-accepted art form in the artistic community. Computer art is gaining great visibility on television and as a regular feature on the covers of magazines.

The computer gives the artist enormous flexibility in creating a piece of art. The basic reds, greens, and blues can be mixed to create up to 16.8 million colors! The artist can do just about anything with an image. For example, a square box can be elongated, stood on end, enlarged or reduced, moved, multiplied, rotated in three dimensions, distorted, and so on. Computer art can be dynamic as well as static. That is, the image can be created to take on different forms as it is viewed.

Let's say the artist would like a barn to be a slightly paler shade of red to better blend with the landscape. The artist pushes a few keys and the barn is "painted" a different color.

Banking

The use of the ever-present **automatic teller machine (ATM)** is an application of **electronic funds transfer (EFT)**. ATMs are strategically placed throughout the city and linked to a central computer. ATMs enable bank customers to deposit, withdraw, and transfer funds from or to their various accounts. As each money transaction is completed, the customer's record is updated and the customer is provided with a printed receipt (see Figure 2–2). The widespread acceptance of the convenience afforded by ATMs has prompted the banking industry to expand the scope of this service. Recognizing that our society is becoming increasingly mobile, participating banks are linking their computers so that customers can complete banking transactions on ATMs anywhere in the country.

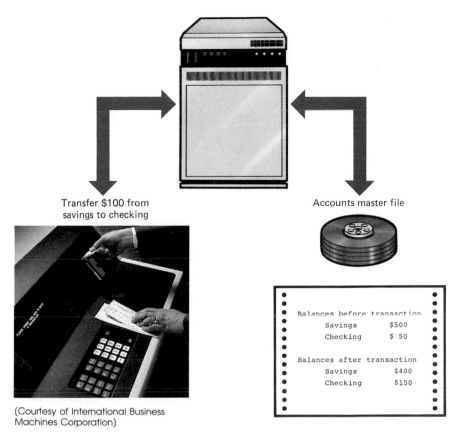

Transfer $100 from
savings to checking

Accounts master file

```
Balances before transaction
      Savings        $500
      Checking       $ 50

Balances after transaction
      Savings        $400
      Checking       $150
```

(Courtesy of International Business
Machines Corporation)

FIGURE 2–2
Banking Transactions at an
Automatic Teller Machine
The electronic funds transfer
(EFT) of $100 from savings to
checking causes the accounts
master file to be updated.

The city of Chicago's
automated traffic control
system is one example of how
a municipal government uses
computers for process control
applications. Other process
control uses include control of
the water distribution system
and temperature control of city
buildings. Many of these office
buildings have process control
computers that monitor fire
alarm and security systems.
(Commonwealth Edison)

Municipal Government

Have you ever driven an automobile through a city with an automated traffic-control system? If so, you would soon notice how the traffic signals are coordinated to minimize delays and optimize traffic flow. Traffic sensors are strategically placed throughout the city to feed data continuously to the computer on the volume and direction of traffic flow.

The computer system that activates the traffic signals is programmed to "plan ahead." That is, if the sensors locate a group of cars traveling together, then traffic signals are timed accordingly. An automated traffic-control system is a good example of the continuous feedback loop in a computerized process-control system.

Retail Sales

In the retail sales industry (see Figure 2–3), transactions are recorded on cash-register-like computer terminals at the **point of sale (POS)**. Each point-of-sale terminal is linked to a central computer and a shelf-item master file. To record a sale, the sales clerk enters only the item number. The current price and item description are retrieved from the item master file. A sales ticket and customer receipt are printed automatically. The item master file is always up to date because the file is updated each time an item is sold.

FIGURE 2–3
Point-of-Sale (POS) System
POS systems permit retailers to check a customer's line of credit, update inventory, and record each sale on the customer master file.

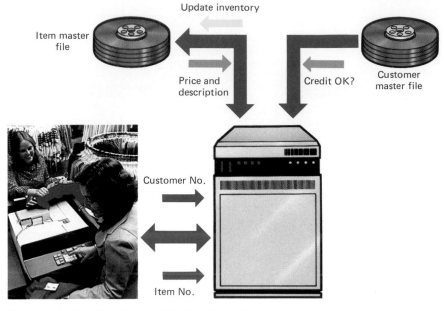

(Courtesy of International Business Machines Corporation)

Without taking a physical inventory, managers know which items are moving, which are not, and when to order and restock an item.

Some point-of-sale systems go one step further than this; they also handle credit transactions. When a customer purchases an item on credit, the sales clerk enters the customer number. The point-of-sale system automatically checks the amount of the purchase against the customer's credit limit. An "OK" light on the terminal is a signal to the sales clerk that the transaction can be completed.

YES, THAT COKE MACHINE SAID "THANK YOU!"

No, it's not an alien from another planet boxed in a red and white spaceship, nor is it Santa dressed in a square suit. That creature with a voice and musical background is, instead, a talking vendor for Coca-Cola. And it's bringing lots of smiles to consumers who aren't expecting a vocal vendor!

The vendor introduces itself with a polite, "Hello, I'm a talking Coca-Cola vending machine." If the money deposited is insufficient, a voice advises the consumer, "You need to put in more money," and follows with, "Make your selection, please." After dispensing the package, the vendor says, "Thanks for using the talking vendor. Please come again!" A friendly reminder, "Don't forget your change," concludes the conversation if change is given.

The voice of the talking vendor is not a recording, and no tapes or motors produce the speech. A small computer stores a digital voice pattern in its memory. When coins are deposited, the changer senses a signal and recalls a particular voice pattern from memory. The programmed sentences travel in electronic form to a speaker located above the vendor's selection buttons. The result is heard as words . . . in English, Spanish, Japanese, German, and Italian.

The computer-based vending machine is not just talk! It gives the buyer several purchase options. Buy a Coke and play a video game. Buy two and get a discount or maybe a cents-off coupon. It offers several sizes of containers and products from cans to two-liter bottles, *and* it can even make change for paper money.

Source: Courtesy of The Coca-Cola Company.

2-5 OVERSIGHTS AND FORESIGHT

Oversights

For whatever reasons, business, industry, and government have elected not to implement computer applications that are well within the state of the art of computer technology. Many cost-effective systems are working in the laboratory but have not been implemented in practice. The implementation of these potentially beneficial systems has lagged behind the state of the art of computer technology by five to ten years. Some "oversights" are presented below.

Several experimental homes have implemented computer-controlled lighting, temperature, and security systems. Such systems would start the coffee maker so that we could awaken to the aroma of freshly brewed coffee. They would even help with the paying of the bills. This technology is available today and is relatively inexpensive if properly designed and installed during construction. In any case, such a system would pay for itself in a couple of years through energy savings alone.

Although some sophisticated computer-controlled medical equipment is now available, physicians rarely use the computer for assistance in diagnosing patients' illnesses. This is, however, a natural application for a computer.

A "cashless society" is technologically and economically possible. In a cashless society, the amount of a purchase would be transferred automatically from the purchaser's bank account to the vendor's bank account. The billing, payment, and collection problems would be eliminated, along with the need to write checks and remember to mail them.

There are many reasons why these cost-effective and potentially beneficial computer applications have not been implemented. Among those are historical momentum, resistance to change, limited education, and lack of available resources. In the case of domestic-control systems, it is probably a matter of education, both of the builder and the homeowner. In the case of computer diagnosis of illness, some physicians are reluctant to admit that the computer is a valuable aid in diagnosis. In the case of the cashless society, the question of invasion of privacy is yet to be resolved.

These and hundreds of other "oversights" will be on the shelf until enough people with enough knowledge and know-how are available to appreciate their potential. This is where you come in!

Foresight

Some computer applications are probably inevitable but beyond the current state of the art of the technology. For example, it is only a matter of time before the computer will be able to interpret a wide range of vocal commands. When this technology becomes reality and is combined with existing synthesized-speech technology, we should be able to have a meaningful verbal dialogue with a computer. Instead of keying in a computer program on a keyboard, you would simply enter each line verbally. In word processing, for example, a manager would dictate directly to the computer system, thereby eliminating the need for a secretary to transcribe the dictation.

Computers are now partners to millions of workers. This labor negotiator carries his portable computer to all negotiating sessions so that pertinent facts and figures can be retrieved immediately. Those on the other side of the negotiating table will be at a disadvantage unless they also invited their "electronic" partners.
(Photo courtesy of Hewlett-Packard Company)

The cashless society may someday become a reality, but not soon. Most banks are still doing everything they can to break "the wall," the point at which more than 33% of their customers use ATMs. An ATM transaction costs the bank less than half that of a teller transaction. Some banks pay customers as much as $5 just to give an ATM a try; other banks have begun to charge customers for teller transactions.
(Courtesy Burroughs Corporation)

A quadraplegic demonstrates an experimental computer-based hand-control system. The system is intended to help quadraplegics grip objects more firmly, aiding in such everyday tasks as combing hair and brushing teeth.
(Wright State University, Dayton, Ohio)

We are still a few steps away, but life-saving computer implants are only around the corner. These tiny computers will control mechanical devices that can replace organs that have ceased to function. Other medical research has given paraplegics renewed hope that they may someday walk again with the assistance of a computerized nervous system. Encouraging research leads us to believe that the computer will play a vital role in tomorrow's medical "miracles."

Within a few years, pocket computers will be as common as the pocket comb. From virtually anywhere, we will be able to use our pocket computers to read 50 different newspapers, turn on the heat at home, call a cab, order groceries, buy shares of stock, make hotel reservations, or study the Chinese language. Our pocket computers will also serve as counterfeitproof "credit cards."

As we evolve to an information society, the computer will continue to have a profound impact. For example, the rapid growth of personal computers in the home, as well as the services offered for these computers, is expected to alter the demographics of cities. Personal computers in the home are also a link to the office. With the information and tools (computers and software) available in the home, trips to the office will be less frequent. This will, of course, encourage an even greater urban spread, therefore changing existing cities and creating new cities.

These are just a few of the many inevitable uses of computer technology that will emerge with the information society. More applications of the future are discussed in Chapter 17, "Computers in Society—Tomorrow."

2-6 OUR COMMITMENT TO COMPUTERS _____

Computers and information systems have enhanced our life styles to the point that most of us take the computer for granted. There is nothing wrong with this attitude, but we must recognize that society has made a very real commitment to computers. We have passed the point of no return. The dependence of government and industry on computers cannot be overlooked. Turn off the computer system for a day in almost any organization and observe the consequences. Most organizations would cease to function.

IS COMPUTERESE CHANGING THE WAY WE TALK?

"Yesterday, I **exited** the **port** at the **back end** of my **main**house and **walked through** the **gateway** to the **micro**shed **workstation** where I **retrieved** a few **productivity tools** for **maintenance**. My wife saw me **displayed** in the **window** and **transmitted** concern about the **density** of the grass.

I **interpreted** her **transmission** as a **command**, **booted** my **machine**, and **initialized** the **project** according to a **standardized methodology** that is based on a **top-down looping algorithm**. At termination, I **compiled** and **dumped** the grass on a **spreadsheet** at the **front end** of the **main**house. From there, a **common carrier uploads** the grass **overflow**, then **downloads** it to an **off-site location** for **permanent storage**."

In other words . . .

"Yesterday, I was in the backyard. My wife saw me and asked me to cut the grass. I mowed the yard and put the clippings near the street for the trash collector."

Of course, the above scenario is an exaggeration, but each year a few more computerese terms are creeping into our everyday conversations. Managers talk in terms of "output"; profit is stated in terms of "K"; people are "brought on-line"; an error is a "bug"; and workflow is "I/O."

This dependence is not necessarily bad. Why give up a good thing? Computers are here, they are reliable, and they will continue to improve the quality of life. We are the masters of our fate, not technology. Even so, we must be ever mindful of society's commitment to computers and strive to give proper direction to the evolution of the information society. In so doing, we have a responsibility to weigh the benefits, burdens, and consequences of each successive level of automation.

SUMMARY OUTLINE AND IMPORTANT TERMS _____

2–1 COMPUTERS: DO WE REALLY NEED THEM?   Society has reached a point of no return with regard to dependence on computers. Business competition demands the use of computers. We are also reluctant to give up those personal conveniences made possible by the computer. Only through understanding can we control the misuse or abuse of computer technology.

2–2 CONTROVERSY: ANOTHER WORD FOR COMPUTER.   The emotions of both the general public and the computer community run high on computer-related issues. Privacy of personal information is perhaps the issue of greatest concern. Other issues include computer crime, computer legislation, electronic funds transfer, automation, and a national data base.

2–3 WHEN TO USE THE COMPUTER.   The computer is fast, accurate, reliable, and has an enormous memory capacity. But, having no innate intelligence, the computer is relatively inflexible. The computer is, therefore, best for repetitive tasks that involve frequent interaction with stored data.

2-4   APPLICATIONS OF THE COMPUTER: LIMITED ONLY BY OUR IMAGI-
      NATION.   Recent innovations in microminiaturization of circuitry
      and data communications have opened the door for computer appli-
      cations that were only dreams or fantasies two decades ago. Com-
      puter-based information systems can be found in diverse business
      and government environments, including health care, transportation,
      art, banking (e.g., **ATM** and **EFT**), municipal government, and retail
      sales (e.g., **POS**).

2-5   OVERSIGHTS AND FORESIGHT.   Although society has been the
      beneficiary of a wide variety of computer applications, much more
      can be done with existing technology. Historical momentum, resis-
      tance to change, limited education, and lack of resources have slowed
      the development of computer applications that are technologically
      feasible.

          It is only a matter of time before current research provides the
      technological capability for even more sophisticated computer appli-
      cations. Some say it is inevitable that within the 1980s people will
      be able to have a meaningful dialogue with a computer.

2-6   OUR COMMITMENT TO COMPUTERS.   Our society has made a
      commitment to computers and the way of life made possible by
      computers. Government and industry have become dependent on
      computers for routine operations. The marriage of computers and
      organizations has been a happy one, but a commitment must accom-
      pany this interdependence. Therefore, we must all become aware
      of the benefits, burdens, and consequences of each successive level
      of automation.

REVIEW EXERCISES

Concepts

1. How have the system design constraints of space and distance been overcome?
2. Why is EFT a controversial issue?
3. Why would a judge sentence one person to ten years for an unarmed robbery of $25 from a convenience store and another to 18 months for computer fraud of millions of dollars?
4. What is the objective of computer matching?
5. What is the technology called that involves the encryption and decryption of data?
6. Compare the information processing capabilities of humans to that of computers with respect to speed, accuracy, reliability, and memory.
7. Describe what is meant by software pilferage.
8. Light travels at 186,000 miles per second. How many milliseconds does it take for a beam of light to travel across the United States, a distance of about 3,000 miles?

Discussion

9. Some companies are experimenting with placing small computer chips in charge cards as a means to thwart theft and fraud. Describe how you feel the computer would be used during the processing of a charge transaction. Speculate on the data that are input to, output from, permanently stored, and processed by the charge card computer.

10. Comment on how computers are changing our traditional patterns of personal communication.

11. Comment on how computers are changing our traditional patterns of recreation.

12. List and discuss applications, other than those mentioned in the text, for a national data base.

13. Do you feel society's dependence on computers is good or bad? What would you suggest be done to improve the situation?

14. Describe what yesterday would have been like if you did not use the capabilities of computers. Keep in mind that businesses with which you deal rely on computers and that many of your appliances are computer-based.

15. Why would a bank officer elect not to report a computer crime?

16. Argue for or against a "cashless society."

17. Discuss areas in which losses of jobs can be directly attributed to computerization. Identify jobs that may have been created as a result of this computerization.

18. Discuss an information processing task for which the computer is not appropriate, and discuss another for which the computer is the only alternative.

SELF-TEST (by section)

2-1. It would take at least a month to retool a typical automobile assembly line so that it could function without computers. (T/F)

2-2. The evidence of unlawful entry to a computer system is called a _____ .

2-3. A microsecond is 1,000 times longer than a nanosecond. (T/F)

2-4. It is unlikely that computer art will ever be accepted by the artistic community. (T/F)

2-5. A "cashless society" is technologically and economically possible. (T/F)

2-6. If the number of computer applications continues to grow at the present rate, our computer-independent society will be dependent on computers by the year 2000. (T/F)

Self-Test answers.   2–1, F; 2–2, footprint; 2–3, T; 2–4, F; 2–5, T; 2–6, F.

STUDENT LEARNING OBJECTIVES

- To put the technological development of hardware and software into historical perspective.
- To identify and describe the feats of computer pioneers.
- To acquire a frame of reference for the computer innovations of the future.

CHAPTER

3

Historical Perspective

3

3-1 THE LIVING HISTORY

The history of computers is of special significance to us, for many of its most important events have occurred within our own lifetimes. The last two decades have been the most exciting part of the short, but event-filled, history of the electronic computer. In terms of the way people live and work, John V. Atanasoff's invention of the computer (1942) can be considered one of the most significant events in history.

The history of computers, as presented in this chapter, will provide you with a historical perspective and a feel for the "roots" of the modern computer. An appreciation of the trials and successes of the past encourages us to be positive about the future.

3-2 EARLY HISTORY: WE'VE COME A LONG WAY

The history of modern electronic computers may have begun in 1942, but several earlier events helped to set the stage.

The Abacus.   The abacus was probably the original mechanical counting device. It has been traced back at least 5,000 years, and its effectiveness has withstood the test of time. It is still used both to illustrate the principles of counting to school children and for modern business applications. When a Chinese restaurant owner was asked why he used an abacus for computing the bill rather than a hand calculator, he simply stated that for him the abacus was faster.

The Pascaline.   Inventor and painter Leonardo da Vinci (1452–1519) sketched ideas for a mechanical adding machine. A century and a half later, the French philosopher and mathematician Blaise Pascal (1623–1662) finally invented and built the first mechanical adding machine. It was called the Pascaline and used gear-driven counting wheels to do addition. Although Pascal was praised throughout Europe for his accomplishments, the Pascaline was a dismal financial failure. Since Pascal was the only person who could repair it, businessmen considered it impractical. Besides, at that time, human labor for arithmetic calculations was less expensive than the Pascaline.

Pascal's counting-wheel design was, however, used by all mechanical calculators until the mid-1960s. Mechanical calculators were then made obsolete by the electronic calculator.

The abacus has been used for counting and computation for millennia.
(The Computer Museum, Boston, MA)

Blaise Pascal's early work on mechanical calculators is recognized today in the popular computer programming language that bears his name.
(Courtesy of International Business Machines Corporation)

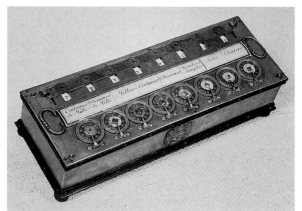

Pascal built the Pascaline to help his father, a tax collector, calculate tax revenues. The numbers for each digit position were arranged on wheels so that a single revolution of one wheel resulted in one-tenth of a revolution of the wheel to its immediate left.
(Courtesy of International Business Machines Corporation)

Babbage's Folly.   Charles Babbage (1793–1871), an English visionary and Cambridge professor, might have hastened the development of computers had he and his inventive mind been born 100 years later. He advanced the state of computational hardware by inventing a "difference engine," capable of computing mathematical tables. In 1834, while working on advances to the difference engine, Babbage conceived the idea of an "analytical engine." In essence, this was a general-purpose computer. As designed, his analytical engine would add, subtract, multiply, and divide in automatic sequence at a rate of 60 additions per minute. The design called for thousands of gears and drives that would cover the area of a football field and be powered by a locomotive engine. Skeptics nicknamed his machine "Babbage's Folly." Babbage worked on his analytical engine until his death.

Babbage's detailed drawings described the characteristics embodied in the modern electronic computer. Had Babbage lived in the era of electronic technology and precision parts, he might have advanced the birth of the electronic computer by several decades. Ironically, his work was forgotten to the extent that some pioneers in the development of the electronic computer were completely unaware of his ideas on memory, printers, punched cards, and sequential program control.

Concepts used in today's general-purpose computer were introduced over 100 years ago by Charles Babbage.
(Courtesy of International Business Machines Corporation)

3-3 TWO CENTURIES OF PUNCHING HOLES IN CARDS

The First Punched Card.   The Jacquard weaving loom, invented in 1801 by the Frenchman Joseph-Marie Jacquard (1753-1834) and still in use today, is controlled by **punched cards**. In the operation of Jacquard's loom, holes are strategically punched in cards and the cards are sequenced to indicate a particular weaving design.

Babbage's Difference Engine was the first practical mechanical calculator.
(New York Public Library Picture Collection)

Jacquard's weaving loom used punched-card technology in the early nineteenth century. The loom is considered the first significant use of binary automation.
(Courtesy of International Business Machines Corporation)

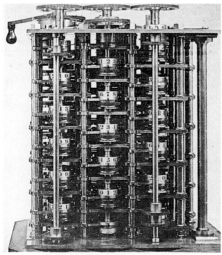

Herman Hollerith was awarded an honorary doctrate from Columbia University for his invention of the punched-card tabulating machine. Workers at the Bureau of the Census were not as excited about his invention. Fearing that it would replace them, they turned it off whenever the supervisor was not looking.
(Courtesy of International Business Machines Corporation)

Dr. Hollerith's punched-card tabulating machine had three parts. Clerks at the Bureau of the Census entered data into the cards with a hand punch. Cards were read and sorted by a 24-bin sorter box. The tabulator, which was electrically connected to the sorter box, summarized the totals on its numbered dials.
(Courtesy of International Business Machines Corporation)

The development of Jacquard's loom is steeped in social irony. Jacquard was a practicing weaver who spent what little spare time he had improving loom technology so that he and other textile workers could improve their plight in life. They were working 16 hours a day, with no days off! Fearing unemployment, textile workers, the very people whom he tried to help, called him a traitor. Sound familiar?

Charles Babbage wanted to use the punched-card concept of the Jacquard loom for his analytical engine. In 1843, Lady Ada Augusta Lovelace suggested that cards could be prepared that would instruct Babbage's engine to repeat certain operations. Because of her suggestion, some people call Lady Lovelace the first programmer. Since we do not know the extent to which her idea was implemented, the identification of the first programmer is still a matter of debate.

The Emergence of Automated Data Processing.   The U.S. Bureau of the Census did not complete the 1880 census until almost 1888. Bureau management concluded that before long the ten-year census would take more than ten years to complete! The Census Bureau commissioned Herman Hollerith, a statistician, to apply his expertise in the use of punched cards to take the 1890 census. With punched-card processing and Hollerith's punched-card tabulating machine, the census was completed in just $2\frac{1}{2}$ years and saved the bureau over $5,000,000. Thus began the emergence of automated data processing. Dr. Hollerith's work proved once again that "necessity is the mother of invention."

Hollerith's idea for the punched card came, not from Jacquard or Babbage, but from "punch photography." Railroads of the day issued tickets with physical descriptions of the passengers. Conductors punched holes in tickets that noted a passenger's hair and eye color and the nose shape. Hollerith's daughter later said that "This gave him the idea for making a punch photograph of every person to be tabulated."

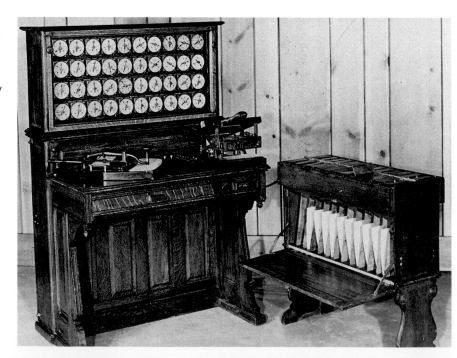

Hollerith founded the Tabulating Machine Company and marketed his products all over the world. The demand for his machines spread even to Russia. Russia's first census, taken in 1897, was recorded with Hollerith's tabulating machine. In 1911, the Tabulating Machine Company merged with several other companies to form the Computing-Tabulating-Recording Company.

Electromechanical Accounting Machines.   Tabulating-machine results had to be posted by hand until 1919, when the Computing-Tabulating-Recording Company announced the printer/lister. The printer/lister revolutionized the way companies did business. To better reflect the scope of their business interests, in 1924 the company was renamed the International Business Machines Corporation (IBM).

For decades, through the mid-1950s, punched-card technology improved with the addition of more punched-card devices and more sophisticated capabilities. Since each card usually contained a record (e.g., an employee's name and address), punched-card processing also became known as **unit-record processing** (one card = one record). Although interactive programming and on-line data entry (both discussed later) have made punched-card devices economically obsolete, we can still find isolated occurrences of them in today's computer centers.

The **electromechanical accounting machine (EAM)** family of punched-card devices includes the *card punch*, *verifier*, *reproducer*, *summary punch*, *interpreter*, *sorter*, *collator*, *calculator*, and the *accounting machine*.

Most of these devices were "programmed" to perform a particular operation by the insertion of a prewired control panel. A different panel was "wired" for each type of operation to be performed.

Ten years after joining the Computer-Tabulating-Recording Corporation in 1914, Thomas J. Watson, Sr. became General Manager, changed the name of the company to International Business Machines Corporation, and moved into this building. Watson ran IBM until a few months before his death at age 82 in 1956. His son, Thomas J. Watson, Jr., lead IBM into the age of computers.
(Courtesy of International Business Machines Corporation)

The 80-column card was the standard for punched-card data processing for over 50 years. The smaller 96-column card was introduced by IBM in the late 1960s for use with their small business computers.
(Courtesy of International Business Machines Corporation)

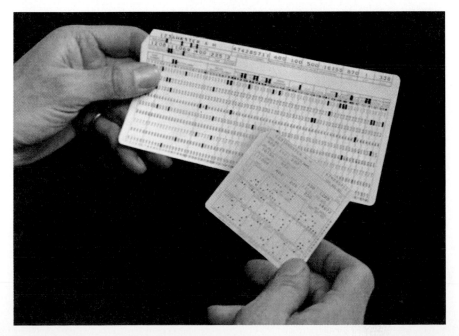

Electromechanical accounting machine (EAM) installations handled data processing activities during the 1940s and 1950s.
(Courtesy of International Business Machines Corporation)

Punched-Card Processing.   A machine-room operator in a punched-card installation had a physically demanding job. Some machine rooms resembled a factory. Punched cards and printed output were moved from one device to the next on hand trucks. The noise was no less intense than that in an automobile assembly plant. Today's machine-room operators use their brains rather than their backs.

To prepare punched-card files for processing, the cards had to be **sorted** (sequenced by employee last name, part number, and so on) and **collated** (two or more files combined for processing—e.g., name and address file with payroll file). Because punched-card devices operate independently, several steps, called **machine runs**, are required to produce a given output. In a run, each file is "read" one card at a time. In most modern information systems, only that portion of the data base that is needed is processed, usually in one run.

3–4 COMPUTER PIONEERS

Atanasoff and Berry.   An early patent on a device that most people thought to be the first electronic digital computer was invalidated in 1973 by a federal court ruling, and Dr. John V. Atanasoff was officially credited with the invention of the electronic digital computer. Dr. Atanasoff, a professor at Iowa State University, developed the first electronic digital computer during the years 1937 to 1942. He called his invention the Atanasoff-Berry Computer or, simply, the *ABC*. A graduate student, Clifford Berry, was instrumental in helping Dr. Atanasoff build the ABC computer.

THE FIRST ELECTRONIC DIGITAL COMPUTER

"The world's first automatic electronic digital computer was constructed in this building in 1939 by John Vincent Atanasoff, a mathematician and physicist on the Iowa State faculty, who conceived the idea, and by Clifford Edward Berry, a physics graduate student."

These words appear on a metal plaque attached to the lobby wall of the old physics building on the Iowa State University campus.

For years, computer historians stated that the ENIAC, built at the University of Pennsylvania by J. Presper Eckert and John W. Mauchly, was the first electronic digital computer. But history was changed by a court decision on October 19, 1973, when Judge Earl R. Larsen ruled that "Eckert and Mauchly did not themselves first invent the automatic electronic digital computer, but instead derived that subject matter from one Dr. John Vincent Atanasoff."

During the years 1935–1938, Dr. John V. Atanasoff had begun to think about a machine that could reduce the time it took for him and his physics students to make long, complicated mathematical calculations. The decisions he made on such aspects as an electronic medium with vacuum tubes, the base-2 numbering system, memory, and logic circuits set the direction for the development of the modern computer.

In 1939, Professor Atanasoff and his graduate student, Clifford E. Berry, assembled a prototype of the ABC computer (Atanasoff Berry Computer), which by 1942 was a workable model. However, neither Iowa State, the business world, nor the scientific community showed much interest in the ABC. For example, the Iowa State University alumnus magazine ran a short article in 1942 about two "devices" developed on the campus by the Science Division, "which, following the war, will meet important needs." The article described "an improved swivel mounting for microscopes . . ." and "a machine that can solve linear algebraic equations involving 30 unknowns many times faster than any present device." Iowa State University patented the microscope, but not the ABC computer.

When Dr. Atanasoff contacted IBM about what he called his "computing machine proper," the company responded that "IBM never will be interested in an electronic computing machine."

In 1984 Iowa State University presented Atanasoff with the university's highest award for an alumnus—the Distinguished Achievement Citation.

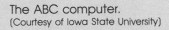

The ABC computer.
(Courtesy of Iowa State University)

Dr. John V. Atanasoff, inventor of the electronic digital computer, is seen at a banquet given in his honor by Iowa State University. A binary memory drum, the only major piece of the ABC that remains, can be seen in the foreground.
(Courtesy of Iowa State University)

The ABC was born of frustration. Dr. Atanasoff later explained that one night in the winter of 1937, "nothing was happening" with respect to creating an electronic device that could help solve physics problems. His "despair grew," so he got in his car and drove for several hours across the state of Iowa and the Mississippi River. Finally, he stopped at an Illinois roadhouse for a drink. It was in this roadhouse that Dr. Atanasoff overcame his creative block and conceived ideas that would lay the foundation for the evolution of the modern computer.

Mauchly and Eckert.   After talking with Dr. Atanasoff, reading notes describing the principles of the ABC, and seeing the ABC, Dr. John W. Mauchly collaborated with J. Presper Eckert to develop a machine that would compute trajectory tables for the U.S. Army. The end product, a large-scale fully operational electronic computer, was completed in 1946 and called the *ENIAC* (*E*lectronic *N*umerical *I*ntegrator *A*nd *C*omputer). The ENIAC, built for World War II applications, was completed in 30 months by a team of scientists working around the clock.

A thousand times faster than its electromechanical predecessors, the ENIAC was a major breakthrough in computer technology. It could do 5,000 additions per minute and 500 multiplications per minute. It weighed 30 tons and occupied 1,500 square feet of floor space. Unlike computers of today that operate in binary (0, 1), the ENIAC operated in decimal (0, 1, 2, . . . 9) and required ten vacuum tubes to represent one decimal digit. With over 18,000 vacuum tubes, the ENIAC needed a great amount of electricity. Legend has it that the ENIAC, built at the University of Pennsylvania, dimmed the lights of Philadelphia whenever it was activated.

The imposing scale and general applicability of the ENIAC signaled the beginning of the first generation of computers.

The ENIAC, recognized as the first all-electronic general-purpose digital computer, signaled the beginning of the first generation of computers. The ENIAC could perform calculations 1,000 times faster than its electromechanical predecessors. The two men in the foreground are its inventors, J. Presper Eckert and Dr. John W. Mauchly.
(United Press International Photo)

3-5 COMPUTER GENERATIONS

The First Generation of Computers (1946 through 1959)

The UNIVAC I.   The **first generation of computers** was characterized by the most prominent feature of the ENIAC—*vacuum tubes*. Through 1950, several other notable computers were built, each contributing significant advancements. These advancements included binary arithmetic, random access, and the concept of stored programs. These computer concepts, which are common in today's computers, are discussed later in the book.

They say history repeats itself, and so it did with the installation of the first commercial computer in the U.S. Bureau of the Census in 1951. The computer, called the Universal Automatic Computer (*UNIVAC I* for short), was developed by Mauchly and Eckert for the Remington-Rand Corporation. This put the Sperry UNIVAC Division of what became the Sperry Corporation years ahead of the competition. The federal government got their money's worth out of the UNIVAC I: the Census Bureau used it for 12 years!

Today we take for granted that computers can be used to predict winners in national elections. Predictions are often made on the national returns before the polls close in the West Coast states. In late 1951, CBS News became a believer when the UNIVAC I correctly predicted Dwight Eisenhower's victory over Adlai Stevenson in the presidential election with only 5% of the votes counted. Today, sophisticated information systems are essential tools for comprehensive television election coverage.

By 1951, other manufacturers, primarily in the punched-card and electronics industries, were beginning to enter the commercial computer market. This group included Burroughs, Honeywell, International Business Machines (IBM), and Radio Corporation of America (RCA).

IBM Enters the Computer Market.   The first electromechanical computer, called the *Mark I*, was the result of IBM-sponsored research. Howard Aiken, a Harvard University professor, completed the Mark I in 1944. The Mark I was essentially a serial collection of electronic calculators and had many simi-

The first generation of computers was characterized by its use of vacuum tube technology.
(AT&T Technologies)

The MARK I Automatic Sequence Controlled Calculator, a cooperative effort between IBM and Dr. Howard Aiken of Harvard, was begun in 1939 and completed in 1944. The slower electromechanical MARK I was no match for the all-electronic ENIAC.
(Courtesy of International Business Machines Corporation)

"GIANT BRAIN" PREDICTS IKE THE WINNER IN 1952 ELECTION

Written Before the Election

The radio and TV networks hope to end the suspense as quickly as possible on election night. In order to detect instantly any significant trends in the voting, CBS has arranged to use Univac, an all-electronic automatic computer, known familiarly as the "Giant Brain." Because it is too big (25,000 lbs.) to be moved to Manhattan, CBS will train a TV camera on the machine at Remington Rand's offices in Philadelphia.

This week, and for the rest of the month, a staff of researchers is feeding 1944 and 1948 election results of each state into the Giant Brain. With all this material digested and memorized, the machine will be able on election night to respond every hour with a comparative analysis of the total population and electoral votes for each candidate.

NBC has its own smaller electronic brain. Called Monrobot, it will also recall the past and help predict the outcome of the current election at the earliest possible hour. Says ABC's News Director John Madigan, professing a disdain for such electronic gimmicks: "We'll report our results through Elmer Davis, John Daly, Walter Winchell, Drew Pearson—and about 20 other human brains."

Written After the Election

The New York Times reported on "the first use on Election Night of the super-duper electronic brains, which can think in terms of a couple

Dr. Eckert instructs newsman Walter Cronkite in the use of the UNIVAC I computer prior to the 1952 presidential election.
(Sperry Corporation)

of quintillion mathematical problems at one time. Both gadgets were more of a nuisance than a help."

"The CBS pride was called 'Univac,' which at the critical moment refused to work with anything like the efficiency of a human being. The mishap caused the CBS stars, Walter Cronkite, Ed Murrow, and Eric Sevareid, to give 'Univac' a rough ride for the rest of the evening in a most amusing sidelight to the CBS coverage."

It was a rough start, but, today, computers are as much a part of election night as political rhetoric and flag waving.

larities to Babbage's analytical engine. Three years after completing the Mark I, Aiken became aware of Babbage's work and remarked, "If Babbage would have lived 75 years later, I would have been out of a job."

The Mark I was a significant improvement in the state of the art, and several years later the ENIAC was offered to IBM, but IBM's management still felt that computers would not replace punched-card equipment. At the time, IBM held a virtual monopoly on punched-card data processing equipment and was doing quite well with meat slicers and scales for delicatessens, time clocks, and other products. Not until the success of the UNIVAC I did IBM make the decision and the commitment to develop and market computers.

This first-generation computer replaced a large installation of electromechanical accounting machines and was leased for slightly more than $30,000 per month. That is a lot of money today, but think how much it was in the 1950s!
(Courtesy of International Business Machines Corporation)

IBM's first entry into the commercial computer market was the *IBM 701* in 1953. IBM introduced the IBM 701 with a bang—literally. It blew up during the demonstration for the press! After a slow, but exciting, beginning, the IBM 701 became a commercially viable product. However, the *IBM 650*, introduced in 1954, is probably the reason that IBM enjoys such a healthy share of today's computer market. Unlike some of its competitors, the IBM 650 was designed as a logical upgrade to existing punched-card machines. That is, it processed data in a manner that resembled the traditional punched-card data processing. Companies were much more willing to accept the IBM 650—with its familiar approach to data processing—than the competitive alternatives.

If not for the IBM 650, the punched card that is affectionately known as the "IBM card" would probably have been called the "UNIVAC card." IBM management went out on a limb and estimated sales of 50. This figure was greater than the number of installed computers in the United States at that time. Computers were seldom sold outright during the first and second generation, but IBM actually leased more than 1,000. The rest is history.

IBM, with over 70% of the mainframe market and an established position as a leader in the personal computer market, has been the dominant force in the worldwide computer market for over three decades.

The Computer Industry Comes of Age.   By the late 1950s a number of other manufacturers, including Control Data Corporation (CDC), General Electric (GE), and National Cash Register (NCR), had decided to commit their resources to computers and test the water. Each new entrant to the computer business made significant contributions to the state of the art of computer technology.

Scores of other companies marketed punched cards, printout forms, machine-room accessories, and other items needed to support the computer/information processing industry. By 1960, the computer industry was established and was beginning to influence the direction of industry in general. IBM remained the dominant computer vendor, even though other vendors manufactured comparable computer systems. Competition among vendors was, and remains today, fiercely competitive.

The Second Generation of Computers (1959 through 1964)

To most people, the invention of the *transistor* meant small portable radios. To those in the data processing business, it signaled the start of the **second generation of computers**. The transistor meant more powerful, more reliable, and less expensive computers that would occupy less space and give off less heat than vacuum-tube powered computers.

The expense item should be emphasized. The cost of a computer during the first, second, and part of the third generation represented a significant portion of a company's budget. Computers were expensive. Cost per instruction executed can be used to compare the cost of computers over the last three decades. Significant innovations, spurred by intense competition, have resulted in enormous increases in computer performance and substantial reductions in price. This trend, established with the introduction of second-generation computers, continues today. If the automobile industry had realized the price/performance improvements of the computer industry (see Figure 3–1), we would all have a Rolls Royce as a second car.

FIGURE 3–1
The Cost of Computers
Advancing computer technology makes it possible for more instructions to be executed at less cost each year.

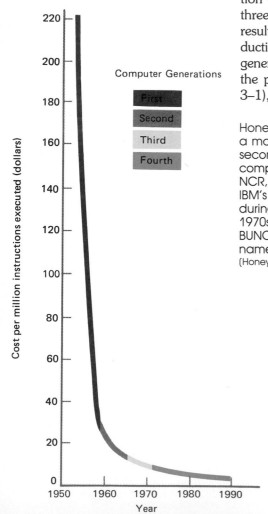

Honeywell established itself as a major competitor during the second generation of computers. Burroughs, Univac, NCR, CDC, and Honeywell, IBM's biggest competitors during the 1960s and early 1970s, became known as the BUNCH (the first initial of each name).
(Honeywell, Inc.)

The dominant characteristics of the second generation were:

1. The transistor.

2. Limited **compatibility** within a manufacturer's line of computers. Programs written for one computer usually required modification before they could be run on a different computer. This meant that if a company upgraded to a larger computer system, they might be required to reprogram some or all of their existing programs.

3. No compatibility between manufacturers.

4. Continued orientation to tape sequential processing. Sequential processing is good for processing transactions and for printing reports, but not for making inquiries.

5. Low-level, symbolic programming languages (discussed in Chapter 10, "Programming Languages and Software Concepts").

The Third Generation of Computers (1964–1971)

Characteristics. What some computer historians consider to be the single most important event in the history of computers occurred when IBM announced their *System 360* line of computers on April 7, 1964. The System 360 ushered in the **third generation of computers**. *Integrated circuits* did for the third generation what transistors did for the second generation. The System 360s and the third-generation computers of Honeywell, NCR, CDC, UNIVAC, Burroughs, GE, and other manufacturers made all previously installed computers obsolete.

The compatibility problems of second-generation computers were almost eliminated in third-generation computers. However, third-generation computers differed radically from second-generation computers. The change was revolutionary, not evolutionary, and caused conversion nightmares for thousands of computer users. In time, the conversion of information systems from second-generation to third-generation hardware was written off as the price of progress.

By the mid-1960s, it became apparent that almost every computer installation could expect rapid growth. An important characteristic of third-generation computers was **upward compatibility**, which meant that a company could buy a computer from a particular vendor and then upgrade to a more powerful computer without having to redesign and reprogram existing information systems.

Third-generation computers work so quickly that they provide the capability to run more than one program concurrently **(multiprogramming)**. For example, at any given time the computer might be printing payroll checks, accepting orders, and testing programs. Although third-generation computers continued to provide tape-processing capabilities, the computer systems were developed to encourage the use of random processing and rotating magnetic disks. Random processing and magnetic disks enabled computers to process only that portion of the file that was needed. Multiprogramming and disk processing set the stage around 1967 for the introduction of data communications and "on-line" systems. These devices and concepts are discussed in detail in Part II, "Hardware and Data Communications Technology."

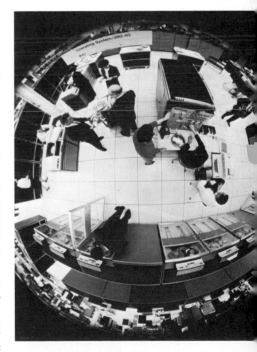

Business Week reported IBM's announcement of their System 360 line of computers saying that, "In the annals of major product changes, it is like Ford's switch from the Model T to the Model A." This fish eye view of the System 360 captures the essence of its "360°" name.
(Courtesy of International Business Machines Corporation)

The third generation of computers was characterized by its use of integrated circuits. Each vacuum tube in the first-generation computer represented a single piece of binary datum, on or off. In contrast, this integrated circuit is only $\frac{1}{4}$ inch square and can represent thousands of binary digits.
(Courtesy of AT&T Bell Laboratories)

The Race Was On.   Most third-generation computers were conceived and designed to be responsive to the needs of both the business and scientific communities. In fact, the name for the IBM System 360 computers was derived from the "all-encompassing" 360 degrees of a circle. It soon became apparent to computer vendors that market demands were not being met by their lines of computers—and the race was on!

There were "holes," or product demands, in the computer market when the third generation of computer systems was introduced in 1964, and there are still holes in the market today. Vendors are continually developing new and better computers to meet ever-changing demands. Even though hundreds of different computers are available, vendors are still identifying requirements that are not adequately met by existing computers.

The Minicomputer.   The demand for small computers in business and for scientific applications was so great that several companies manufactured only small computers. These became known as **minicomputers**. Digital Equipment Corporation (DEC) and Data General Corporation took an early lead in the sale and manufacturer of "minis."

Having difficulty conceiving a name for this third-generation minicomputer, IBM's board of directors noted that it was 11:30 AM and time for lunch. The IBM 1130, as it was eventually named, was aimed at meeting the demand for small business and scientific computers.
(Courtesy of International Business Machines Corporation)

The Fourth Generation of Computers

Most computer vendors classify their computers as being in the **fourth generation of computers**, and a few call theirs the "fifth generation." The first three generations were characterized by significant technological breakthroughs in electronics—the use of vacuum tubes, then transistors, and then integrated circuits. Some people prefer to pinpoint the start of the fourth generation as 1971, with the introduction of *large-scale integration* (more circuits per unit space) of electronic circuitry. However, other computer designers argue that if we accept this premise, then there have probably been a fifth, a sixth, and maybe a seventh generation since 1971.

The base technology of today's computers is still the integrated circuit. This is not to say that two decades have passed without any significant innovations. In truth, the computer industry has experienced a mind-boggling succession of advances in the further miniaturization of circuitry, data communications, the design of computer hardware and software, and input/output devices.

The 1970s.   During the 1970s, the most prolific line of computers was the IBM *System 370*. Each System 370 computer could deliver two to five times the power of its System 360 counterpart at only a slight increase in cost. The same price/performance ratio was evident in subsequent third-generation upgrades by other vendors (such as CDC's Cyber series). Getting "more bang for the buck" has become a tradition in the computer industry; today it is not only anticipated, it is expected.

The Microprocessor.   One of the most significant contributions to the emergence of the fourth generation of computers is the **microprocessor**. The microprocessor, which can be contained on a single silicon chip, is a product of the microminiaturization of electronic circuitry. It is sometimes called a "computer on a chip." The first fully operational microprocessor was invented in 1971. Today, there are more microprocessors on Earth than there are people. This device can be purchased for as little as a few dollars and can be found in everything from elevators to satellites.

The Microcomputer.   The microprocessor is the processing component of the small, relatively inexpensive, but powerful *microcomputer*. The microcomputer, also called a *personal computer*, has made it possible for small businesses and individuals to own computers. The microcomputer and personal computer are discussed in detail in Chapter 4, "Computer Systems—Micros."

The microcomputer was a product of the fourth generation of computers. In 1983, the total number of all microcomputers sold surpassed the total of all other computers. (Photo courtesy of Hewlett-Packard Company)

Generationless Computers

We may have defined our last generation of computers and begun the era of **generationless computers**. Even though computer manufacturers talk of "fifth"- and "sixth"-generation computers, this talk is more a marketing ploy than a reflection of reality. Advocates of the concept of generationless computers say that even though technological innovations are coming in rapid succession, no single innovation is, or will be, significant enough to characterize another generation of computers.

3-6   AND SOFTWARE HAS A HISTORY, TOO _____

Hardware and software are as inseparable as bread and butter, football and fall, or politicians and promises. A historical perspective on one should be accompanied by a historical perspective on the other.

Programming

The Stored-Program Concept.   The quantum leap in technology brought about by the ENIAC was offset by the cumbersome method of programming the machine. Switches had to be set and wires inserted into a series of panels resembling those used by telephone operators of the period. Each time a different program was to be run, the switches had to be reset and the wires repositioned. This task usually took several hours. Not only did early programmers spend countless hours setting switches and wiring boards, but then they had to cross their fingers and hope that the computer would run long enough to complete the program without breaking down!

Mauchly and Eckert, ENIAC's designers, realized that a better method of programming was necessary to make the computer a truly general-purpose machine. In 1949, they worked with a mathematician named John Von Neumann (1903–1957) to develop a computer that would store a program the way it stored data. The introduction of the "stored-program" concept enabled computers to execute one program, then electronically load and ready another program for execution within a matter of minutes.

Von Neumann reconceived one of Lady Augusta Lovelace's concepts 90 years after her death. Lady Lovelace had suggested that the conditional transfer instruction be used in Babbage's analytical engine. This type of instruction would permit the sequence in which the instructions were executed to be altered based on certain criteria. For example, in payroll processing a set of instructions is executed for salaried personnel and a different set is executed for hourly personnel. The conditional transfer instruction and the introduction of the stored-program concept made the general-purpose computer a reality.

Programming Languages.   Today, computer operations are directed by a *program* that is written by a *programmer* in a particular *programming language*. In the *first generation* of languages (not to be confused with generations of computers), programs were written in **machine language** and consisted entirely of 1s and 0s. Imagine the difficulty in keeping track of the sequence of program instructions made up entirely of 1s and 0s, not to mention the eyestrain! The *second-generation* language, called **assembler**

Itojo

"Ladies and Gentleman . . .
THE FIFTH GENERATION!"
(By permission of Brian Hansen)

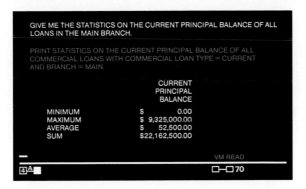

GIVE ME THE STATISTICS ON THE CURRENT PRINCIPAL BALANCE OF ALL
LOANS IN THE MAIN BRANCH.

PRINT STATISTICS ON THE CURRENT PRINCIPAL BALANCE OF ALL
COMMERCIAL LOANS WITH COMMERCIAL LOAN TYPE = CURRENT
AND BRANCH = MAIN.

	CURRENT PRINCIPAL BALANCE
MINIMUM	$ 0.00
MAXIMUM	$ 9,325,000.00
AVERAGE	$ 52,500.00
SUM	$22,162,500.00

VM READ

□—□70

When programming in fourth-generation languages, programmers enter instructions that look very much like plain English.
(© Artifical Intelligence Corporation)

language, used symbols. For example, an "A" might represent a series of 1s and 0s that told the computer to add two numbers. Both machine and assembler languages required the programmer to write a program instruction for each operation to be performed.

In the *third generation*, **procedure-oriented languages** allowed the programmer to write instructions that combined a number of computer operations. One instruction could direct the computer to perform several operations. Most applications for early computers were scientific, and so the first procedure-oriented language, **FORTRAN**, developed in 1955, had the aim of making it easier for scientists and engineers to write programs. A few years later, in 1959, **COBOL** was introduced for business applications.

In the *fourth-generation* languages, first introduced in the late 1970s, the programmer tells the computer "what to do" and not necessarily "how to do it." As you can see, the trend in program-language development is to make each new language easier to use while reducing the number of programming instructions required for each programming task.

The hierarchy of programming languages is discussed in detail in Chapter 10, "Programming Languages and Software Concepts."

Unbundling.   In 1969, IBM announced the **unbundling** of their products. Simply stated, unbundling meant that previously "free" software, education, and services would be billed separately from the hardware. Prior to unbundling, IBM and other manufacturers provided software as part of the hardware lease or purchase agreement—therefore, companies had little incentive to produce and market software. IBM's unbundling was the incentive the software industry needed. Overnight, the software industry was born. Today, over 2,000 software vendors market more than 25,000 products.

3-7   UPDATE: WHERE ARE WE NOW? _____

Someone being exposed today to computer systems and information processing for the first time might look back on the short but interesting history of computers (see the chronological perspective, Figure 3–2) and wish he or she had been in on the ground floor. In the history of computers, however, *now* is the ground floor.

The computer today is where the airplane was a year after the Wright brother's history-making flight. With respect to the development and application of computer technology, we have only just begun!

FIGURE 3-2
Chronology of Computer History

Year	Historic Event	Processing	Input	Output	Storage (secondary)	Software	Systems Concepts	Information Systems Organization	Information Systems Personnel
1940	World War II begins	Electro-mechanical accounting machines ABC computer	Punched card Paper tape Mark sense	Punched card Paper tape Printer	Punched card Paper tape	Wired panels Switches	Data processing (DP)	Centralized punched card departments	
	And ends	1st generation (vacuum tubes) ENIAC				Machine language Stored program			Programmer
1950		UNIVAC I (1st commercial)				Assembler language			
	Ike elected President	IBM 650							Operator Data entry Systems analyst
	Sputnik launched	2nd generation (transistors)	Magnetic ink character recognition (MICR)	Plotters MICR	Magnetic tape Magnetic disk	Compilers FORTRAN COBOL LISP		Trend to large centralized information systems departments	Librarian Programmer (systems and applications)
1960	JF Kennedy assassinated	Minicomputer 3rd generation (integrated circuits) IBM 360 family	Optical character recognition (OCR)	OCR	Mass storage devices	Multiprogramming RPG PL/I BASIC APL LOGO	Management information systems (MIS)		Control clerk
		Computer networks	Keyboard (on-line) Light pen	Voice (recorded) Soft copy (VDT)					
	Apollo II lands on moon			Computer output microfilm (COM) Graphics (VDT)	IK RAM chip Floppy disk	Pascal Word processing			Data base administrator
1970		4th generation (large-scale integration) Microprocessors Microcomputers	Mouse			Query languages		Trend to decentralization and distributed processing	Project leader
	Watergate burglary			Color graphics					Education coordinator Documentalist Office automation specialist
		Personal computers	Hand print	High-speed laser printers		UNIX operating system Application generators	Information resource management (IRM) Decision support systems (DDS)		
	USA's 200th birthday	Word processors	Voice	Voice (synthesized)		Electronic spreadsheet Ada			MIS long-range planner
		Distributed processing	Vision input systems		Video disk			Information centers	User-analyst Information center specialist
1980	Mt. St. Helens erupts				Optical laser disk	Integrated micro software			
	E.T. lands	Pocket computers multiuser micros							User liaison
	Reagan begins second term						Expert systems		Microcomputer specialist
	XXII Olympiad				1 megabit RAM chip				
1990									

This chart includes events that are discussed in this chapter and throughout the book.

A MILESTONE IN HISTORY

The year 1982 was filled with notable events, people, and situations. However, when *Time* magazine made their annual selection for Man of the Year, they chose a machine: the computer.

The Man of the Year is someone or something that has had the greatest influence, be it good or evil, during the year. *Time* editors chose the computer because they felt it would change the way people live.

The managing editor said that the personal computer "will salvage the American economy rather than hurt it" and "a decade from now, looking back at 1982, we would say that this was the moment the computer revolution was recognized by the population as a whole."

Source: Excerpts reprinted by permission of *The Wall Street Journal*, © Dow Jones and Company, Inc. (1982). All rights reserved. (Photo courtesy of Hewlett-Packard Company)

SUMMARY OUTLINE AND IMPORTANT TERMS _____

3–1 THE LIVING HISTORY.   The most exciting part of the short but glorious history of the modern computer has transpired during our own lifetimes. An appreciation of this history provides a frame of reference for future events.

3–2 EARLY HISTORY: WE'VE COME A LONG WAY.   Early mechanical computers include the abacus, the Pascaline, and Charles Babbage's difference engine. Babbage later invented an analytical machine with design characteristics similar to those of the modern electronic computer.

3–3 TWO CENTURIES OF PUNCHING HOLES IN CARDS.   Some computer historians feel Lady Ada Lovelace became the first programmer when she suggested that punched cards, fashioned after those used on the Jacquard loom, to represent repetitive operations on Babbage's analytical machine.

Herman Hollerith and the U.S. Bureau of the Census collaborated and used **punched-card** technology to introduce automated data processing to the business world. Punched-card technology and **electromechanical accounting machines (EAM)** were used for routine data processing tasks for half a century. Punched-card processing, or **unit-record processing**, required cards to be **sorted** and **collated** before **machine runs**.

3–4 COMPUTER PIONEERS.   Dr. John V. Atanasoff and Clifford Berry developed the first electronic computer between 1937 and 1942. They called it the ABC. Dr. John W. Mauchly and J. Presper Eckert, Jr., expanded on Dr. Atanasoff's basic design concepts to produce the first full-scale computer. It was called the ENIAC.

3-5   COMPUTER GENERATIONS.   Vacuum-tube technology character-
       ized the **first-generation of computers**. IBM started late, but
       passed the early front-runner, UNIVAC, to secure the dominant posi-
       tion in the computer industry. Early first-generation computers were
       punch-card oriented, with later versions relying more on magnetic tape.
            Second-generation computers used transistor technology,
       which made computers less expensive and, therefore, more available
       to more organizations. These tape-oriented computers had limited
       compatibility and used low-level programming languages.
            Integrated circuits replaced transistors in **third-generation
       computers**. Computer manufacturers provided disk-oriented sys-
       tems with **upward compatibility** and **multiprogramming** cap-
       ability. Data communications and on-line systems are also products
       of the third generation.
            Fourth-generation computers are associated with the large-
       scale integration of electronic circuitry. A product of this technology
       is the **microprocessor**. This "computer on a chip" made it economi-
       cally feasible for individuals to own personal computers.
            Computer technology is advancing at such a rapid pace that
       we may have begun the era of the **generationless computer**.

3-6   AND SOFTWARE HAS A HISTORY, TOO.   The ENIAC and other
       early computers required the operators to manipulate switches and
       reset wires to get the computer to perform a particular set of opera-
       tions. This cumbersome method of "programming" prompted re-
       search that resulted in the stored-program concept and a hierarchy
       of programming languages, which, like hardware, has evolved in
       generations. **Machine languages** comprise the first generation of
       programming languages; **assembler languages** the second; and
       procedure-oriented languages (e.g., **FORTRAN** and **COBOL**)
       the third. In the fourth and subsequent generations, the programmer
       tells the computer "what to do" and not necessarily "how to do it."
            In 1969, IBM **unbundled** their software from their hardware.
       This event signaled the birth of the software industry.

3-7   UPDATE: WHERE ARE WE NOW?   The computer industry is in its
       infancy, and perhaps the most significant events in computer history
       will result from the efforts and innovation of your generation.

REVIEW EXERCISES

Concepts

1. Group the following items by generation of programming languages:
    assembler language, COBOL, "what to do" not "how to do it," and
    machine language.

2. What is considered the original mechanical accounting device?

3. A computer can be placed on a single silicon chip no larger than a
    fingernail. What is this computer called?

4. What is the equipment called that was used for data processing prior
    to computers? What medium did these devices use for data storage?

5. What electrical components are usually associated with each of the first three generations of computers?

6. Briefly describe the major achievements of the following pioneers in computers and automation: Babbage, Mauchly and Eckert, Lovelace, Hollerith, Atanasoff, and Pascal.

7. Group the following items by generation of computers: multiprogramming, UNIVAC I, transistor, minicomputer, microprocessor, integrated circuits, and ENIAC.

Discussion

8. Of those computer-manufacturing companies mentioned in this chapter, which ones still manufacture computers? Can you name five more manufacturers of computers?

9. Compare the history of computers with the history of aviation. Use the history of aviation to draw conclusions about the future of computers.

10. Discuss the social irony surrounding Jacquard's invention of a punched-card weaving loom. Relate this irony to current events.

11. According to the author, we may have entered the era of generationless computers. Support or discredit the author's premise.

12. What is unbundling, and what effect did it have on the software industry?

13. What do you think the computer historians of the year 2000 will say about computer advances during the 1980s?

14. The first computer predictions for a presidential election occurred in 1951. Since then, accurate predictions are often made before the polls close. Discuss the advantages and disadvantages of such predictions.

SELF-TEST (by section)

3-1. John V. Atanasoff's invention of the computer in 1933 is considered one of the significant events in history. (T/F)

3-2. _____ 's detailed drawings of his analytical engine described the characteristics embodied in the modern electronic computer.

3-3. Lady Augusta Lovelace is universally acclaimed to be the first programmer. (T/F)

3-4. The ENIAC was developed to compute trajectory tables for the U.S. Army. (T/F)

3-5. Multiprogramming and upward _____ were characteristics of the third generation of computers.

3-6. FORTRAN was the first programming language to take advantage of Von Neumann's stored-program concept. (T/F)

3-7. In the history of computers, we have only just begun. (T/F)

Self-Test answers. 3–1, F; 3–2, Babbage; 3–3, F; 3–4, T; 3–5, compatibility; 3–6, F; 3–7, T.

PART II

HARDWARE AND DATA COMMUNICATIONS TECHNOLOGY

STUDENT LEARNING OBJECTIVES

- To describe a computer and its operational capabilities.
- To identify the types of microcomputers.
- To demonstrate an awareness of the broad range of uses for microcomputers.
- To know what to look for when buying a microcomputer.

CHAPTER 4

Computer Systems– Micros

4-1 WHAT IS A COMPUTER? _____

Technically speaking, the computer is any counting device. But in the context of modern technology, we'll define the **computer** as *an electronic device capable of interpreting and executing programmed commands for input, output, computation, and logic operations*. The computer, also called a **processor**, is the "intelligence" of a *computer system*. Remember from Chapter 1 that *input/output* and *data storage* hardware components are "configured" with the *processing* component (the computer) to make up a computer system (see Figures 1–2 and 1–3).

Let's discuss the operational capabilities of a computer system just a bit further.

Input/Output Operations

The computer *reads* from input and storage devices. The computer *writes* to output and storage devices. Before data can be processed, they must be "read" from an input device or data storage device. Input data are usually entered by an operator on a video display terminal (VDT) or retrieved from a data storage device, such as a magnetic disk drive. Once data have been processed, they are "written" to an output device, such as a printer, or to a data storage device. Input/output (I/O) operations are illustrated in Figure 4–1.

Processing Operations

The computer is totally objective. That is, any two computers instructed to perform the same operation will arrive at the same result. This is because the computer can perform only *computation* and *logic operations*.

FIGURE 4–1
Input/Output Operation
Grades are read, the student master file is updated (grades "written"), and a program causes the processing necessary to produce the grade report.

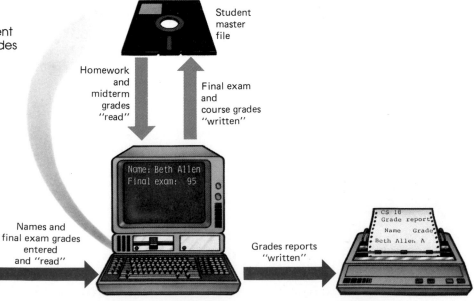

Student master file

Homework and midterm grades "read"

Final exam and course grades "written"

Name: Beth Allen
Final exam: 95

CS 18
Grade report
Name   Grade
Beth Allen   A

Names and final exam grades entered and "read"

Grades reports "written"

The computational capabilities of the computer include adding, subtracting, multiplying, and dividing. Logic capability permits the computer to make comparisons between numbers and between words. In the grade-reporting system example of Chapter 1 (Figure 1–4), the computer calculates the grade average in a computation operation (e.g., $(32+24)/16 \rightarrow 3.5$). In a logic operation, the computer compares the student's grade to 3.0 to determine whether a student qualifies for the Dean's List. If the grade average is greater than or equal to 3.0 (i.e., grade $>= 3.0$), then the student is placed on the Dean's List.

4-2 COMPUTER SYSTEMS: A ROSE IS A ROSE IS A ROSE . . .

The most distinguishing characteristic of any computer system is its "size" or computing capacity. Computers have been classified as *microcomputers*, *minicomputers*, *superminicomputers*, *midicomputers*, *maxicomputers*, and *supercomputers*. From this list you might think that these terms were coined by fashion designers. Such is not the case. The minicomputer preceded the miniskirt!

Now, and even in the past, these computer classifications have defied definition. Even though it is doubtful that any two computer specialists would describe a minicomputer or a supercomputer in the same way, these terms are still frequently used. Rapid advances in computer technology have caused what used to be distinguishing characteristics (e.g., physical size, cost, memory capacity, and so on) to become blurred.

All computers, no matter how small or large, have the same fundamental capabilities. Just as "a rose, is a rose, is a rose . . ." (Gertrude Stein), "a computer, is a computer, is a computer. . . ." Keep this in mind as we discuss *microcomputer systems* in this chapter and *mainframe computer systems* in Chapter 5. It should be emphasized that these are relative categories, and what people call a mainframe computer system today may be called a microcomputer system at some time in the future.

In all probability you have been exposed to a microcomputer or a minicomputer system. Most high schools have several small computer systems and offer courses in BASIC programming. An increasing number of students have personal computers in their homes. Others use them at work. If you were not exposed to computers in high school or at work, and you don't own one, don't feel left out. The vast array of video games that challenge our physical dexterity and mental quickness are also computers.

4-3 MICROS AND PERSONAL COMPUTERS: SMALL BUT POWERFUL

The Evolution of the Microcomputer

Microprocessors. Here is a tough one. What is smaller than a dime and found in wristwatches, sewing machines, and jukeboxes? The answer: a **micro-**

This micro is configured with a keyboard for input, a video monitor and a printer for output, and two disk drives for storage of data and programs. This micro is unique in that the printer and monitor are contained in the same physical unit.
(TRW, Inc.)

THE MAC FAC

Apple's Macintosh factory in Fremont, California, is packed with factory-of-the-future technology. It is designed to build at least one Mac computer every 27 seconds. That's over 1,000 every day!

The Mac was designed to be easily mass produced. Much of the actual assembly process is automated. Each of its printed circuit boards is passed through diagnostic tests before it is mounted in the unit. The boards are tested by—you guessed it—a Macintosh.

Once assembled, the completed unit is run through its paces. First, a program is run to ask Mac a few "questions." If Mac responds correctly, it then travels, via conveyer, to the "burn-in" racks for further testing. While on the racks, the computer reads and writes to the same disk for 24 hours—one hour on and one hour off.

The Macintosh Factory.
(Courtesy of Apple Computer, Inc.)

In the spirit of keeping it in the family, a single Macintosh controls each of the factory's burn-in racks.

Many automobile engine functions are monitored and controlled by this microprocessor-based engine control kit.
(RCA)

processor. Microprocessors play a very important role in our lives. You probably have a dozen or more of them at home and may not know it. They are in telephones, ovens, televisions, greeting cards, cars, and, of course, personal computers.

The microprocessor is a product of the microminiaturization of electronic circuitry; it is literally a "computer on a chip." The first fully operational microprocessor was demonstrated in March 1971. Since that time the microprocessor, which can be purchased for as little as a few dollars, has been integrated into thousands of mechanical and electronic devices. For example, microprocessors, which are now smaller than a dime, are used in elevators and ski boot bindings.

Microprocessors make it possible for elevators to converse with us. The microprocessor activates a *voice synthesizer* that reminds us which floor we are on and when the elevator is too full. The microprocessor is connected to sensors that monitor the weight of the elevator. If the elevator is overloaded, passengers are "asked" (via electronically generated speech) to lighten the load. Have you ever entered an elevator and noticed that all of the floors are lit up? This can't happen in modern microprocessor-based elevators. The microprocessor compares the approximate number of people (input from weight sensors) against the number of floor selections. If they don't match, the microprocessor cancels all selections and "requests" that floors be reentered. In these elevators, a mischievous child (or an adolescent adult) will get no satisfaction.

There may be a future for microprocessors in ski equipment. Malfunctioning ski boot bindings are the major cause of ski-related injuries. In theory, the bindings are supposed to release the boot from the ski during a fall.

Recently, a major breakthrough in ski boot binding technology promises to reduce the number of injuries attributed to bindings. Microprocessors in ski boot bindings retain in memory a mathematical model of a skier's leg movements. These microprocessors are linked to a dynamometer that measures critical pressure points on the ski. The microprocessor-based bindings can monitor subtle movements not detected by mechanical bindings. Movements not consistent with the mathematical model activate the release mechanism.

In a few years, virtually everything that is mechanical or electronic will incorporate microprocessor technology into the design.

Microcomputers. The microprocessor is sometimes confused with its famous offspring, the **microcomputer**. A keyboard, video monitor, and memory were attached to the microprocessor and—the microcomputer was born! Suddenly, owning a computer became an economic reality for individuals and small businesses.

In a microcomputer, the microprocessor, electronic circuitry for handling input/output signals from the peripheral devices, and "memory chips" are mounted on a single circuit board, called a **motherboard**. Before being attached to the circuit board, the microprocessor and other chips are mounted to a *carrier*. Carriers have standard-sized pin connectors that permit the chips to be attached to the motherboard.

The motherboard is the "guts" of a microcomputer. The motherboard is what distinguishes one microcomputer from another. The motherboard is simply "plugged" into one of several slots designed for circuit boards. Most micros have several empty slots so that you can purchase optional capabilities in the form of *add-in* boards. For example, you can purchase more memory, a board that permits graphics output, or a modem (a device that permits data communications between computers). These capabilities are discussed in more detail in later chapters.

Microcomputer Defined. But what is a microcomputer? During the last decade, people have described microcomputers in terms of cost, physical dimensions, size of primary storage, and amount of data processed at a time, but all definitions proved confusing. A **micro** is just a small computer. Perhaps the best definition of a micro is *any computer that you can pick up and carry*. But don't be misled by the "micro" prefix. You can pick up and carry some very powerful computers!

A microcomputer is also called a **personal computer** or **PC**. The label "personal computer" was associated with microcomputers because it was designed for use by one person at a time. For the most part, this one-to-one relationship still holds true. However, some micros or PCs can handle several users simultaneously. Multiuser micros are discussed later.

Pocket, Lap, and Desktop PCs. Personal computers come in three different physical sizes: *pocket PCs*, *lap PCs*, and *desktop PCs*. The pocket and lap PCs are light (a few ounces to 8 pounds), compact, and do not require an external power source—so they earn the "portable" label as well. There are also a number of "transportable" desktop PCs on the market, but they are more cumbersome to move. They fold up to about the size of a small suitcase, weigh about 25 pounds, and usually require an external power source. Most

The processing capabilities of a microcomputer are contained on a circuit board called the motherboard. The motherboard is inserted into a "card cage" to complete the connection to the other components.
(Cromemco, Inc.)

A 6½ by 2¾ inch pocket PC, ⅜ inches thick, is attached to a battery recharger and a printer. When detached from the recharger unit, this small portable computer can easily fit into a purse or a coat pocket.
(Courtesy of Radio Shack, A Division of Tandy Corporation)

An architect packs his blueprints and a lap PC. The computer comes in handy when a client asks for on-the-spot cost estimates for proposed changes.
(Courtesy of Apple Computer, Inc.)

desktop PCs are not designed for frequent movement and are, therefore, not considered portable.

The power of a PC is not necessarily in proportion to its size. A few lap PCs can run circles around some of the desktops. Some user conveniences, however, must be sacrificed to achieve portability. For instance, the miniature keyboards on pocket PCs make data entry and interaction with the computer difficult and slow. On lap PCs, the display screen is small and does not hold as much text as a display on a desktop PC.

Home and Business PCs. Some people make a distinction between *home* and *business* microcomputers. Actually, the differences are primarily cosmetic. For example, home computers may use a television for a monitor and the keyboard may be less durable, but internally these computers are very similar. For instance, they may have the same motherboard. The "home" and "business" labels are more for marketing than for technical differentiation.

Most "home" PCs cost less and have slightly less processing capacity than "business" PCs, but the home computer is often found in the office, and vice versa. The bottom line is that any computer in a home is a home computer. For this reason, future discussions of micros and PCs will not distinguish between the home and business varieties. Ironically, the number one use of computers in the home is for business work done at home!

The microcomputer is used in small businesses operated by druggists, veterinarians, attorneys, plumbers, and hundreds of other professions. To the engineer and scientist, the microcomputer has become almost as commonplace as the hand calculator of the 1970s and the slide rule before that. The minimal cost and almost unlimited applications for the microcomputer have made it the darling of the computer industry. A little more than a

This project manager carries his transportable PC home on weekends to review the schedule of project activities for the coming week. To prepare the computer for movement, the keyboard is detached and fastened in position to cover the monitor. A handle is attached to the back of the micro.
(Sperry Corporation)

Parts inventory and customer records are maintained on this micro at an automobile service center.
(Courtesy of Apple Computer, Inc.)

decade ago, no one had heard of a microcomputer. Now, the dollar amount of microcomputer sales is about equal to that of mainframes that cost ten to 2,000 times as much. The number of microcomputers sold in one month today exceeds the total number of operational computers in existence in the United States ten years ago.

Why Are Micros and Personal Computers So Popular?

When you use a micro or personal computer, the capabilities of a complete computer system are at the tip of your fingers. Some are more powerful than computers that once handled the data processing requirements of large banks. PCs and their support software are designed to be user friendly; therefore, they are easy to use and understand. The wide variety of software available for microcomputers offers something for almost everyone, from video games to word processing to education to home finances to inventory control.

These reasons for the micro's popularity pale when we talk of the *real* reason for its unparalleled success—it is just plain fun to use, whether for personal, business, or scientific computing.

Configuring a Microcomputer

The microcomputer is the smallest computer system. Even so, it has the same components as mainframe computer systems: input, output, storage, and processing. As you might expect, the input/output components are much slower, and the storage component has a smaller capacity than have the larger systems.

The computer and its peripheral devices are called the computer system **configuration**. The configuration of a microcomputer can vary. The most typical micro configuration consists of

During a tennis match, a tennis-knowledgeable scorer uses a micro with a special keyboard to enter data on each point played. After or during the match, the data can be summarized and printed for coaches or television commentators. The statistics highlight a player's strengths, weaknesses, and patterns of play.
(CompuTennis™, Sports Software, Inc.)

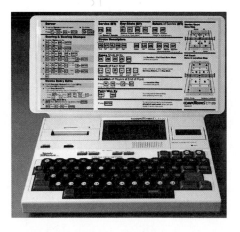

A portable micro is configured here with all the trimmings: a printer, a power supply (in front of the carrying case), the keyboard and processor unit (which also contains one disk drive), a mouse (for input), another disk drive, a modem (under telephone) for making connections to other computers, and a joy stick (far right). These add-ons are discussed in Chapters 7, 8, and 9. The processor unit is the central focus of the system. Cables from each device are connected to the input/output ports at the rear of the processor unit.
(Courtesy of Apple Computer, Inc.)

1. A computer.
2. A keyboard for input.
3. A televisionlike display called a **monitor** for **soft copy** (temporary) output.
4. A printer for **hard copy** (printed) output.
5. One or two disk drives for permanent storage of data and programs.

In some microcomputer systems these components are purchased as separate physical units, then linked together. In others, two, three, and even all of the components can be contained in a single unit. With a few rare exceptions, the printer is a separate unit.

The storage medium of most microcomputers is normally a **diskette** or a **microdisk**. The diskette can be compared to a phonograph record, but it is thinner, more flexible, and permanently enclosed within a $5\frac{1}{4}$-inch square jacket. Because the diskette is flexible, like a page in this book, it is also called a **flexible disk** or a **floppy disk**. Some microcomputers use rigid microdisks ($3\frac{1}{4}$ or $3\frac{1}{2}$ inches in diameter) for storage. The more powerful microcomputers use hard disks. These and other storage media are discussed in detail in Chapter 7, "Data Storage Devices and Media."

Just about any input or output device that can be linked to a mainframe computer can also be linked to a microcomputer. The wide variety of input/output devices, from the *mouse* (a device that moves the blinking cursor on a display screen) to the *voice synthesizer* (a device that produces electronic speech), are discussed in Chapter 8, "Input/Output Devices."

In keeping with conversational computerese, we will drop the "system" from "microcomputer system." Therefore, all future references to a personal computer or a microcomputer imply a microcomputer *system*.

Multiuser Micros

In the early 1960s, mainframe computer systems were able to service only one user at a time. By the mid-1960s, technological improvements made it possible for computers to service several users simultaneously. A quarter of a century later, some mainframes service thousands of users. We can draw a parallel between what happened to the mainframe in the 1960s and what is happening to microcomputers today. Until recently, micros were "personal" computers—for individual use only. But technological improvements have been so rapid that it has become difficult for a single user to tap the full potential of state-of-the-art micros. To tap this unused potential, hardware and software vendors are marketing products that permit several users on the system at once.

These multiuser micros are configured with up to 12 keyboard/monitor pairs, called **workstations**. These workstations, usually located in the same office, share the microcomputer's resources and its peripheral devices. With a multiuser micro, a secretary can be transcribing dictation at one workstation, a manager can be doing financial analysis at another workstation, and a clerk can be entering data to a data base at another workstation. All of this is taking place at the same time on the same multiuser micro.

Micros as Workstations

A workstation is the hardware that allows you to interact with a computer system, be it a mainframe or a multiuser micro. A video display terminal (VDT) is a workstation. A microcomputer can also be a workstation. With the installation of an optional data communications adapter, a micro has the flexibility to serve as a *stand-alone* computer system or as an "intelligent" workstation to a mainframe computer.

The term "intelligent" is applied to workstations that can also operate as stand alone computer systems, independent of the mainframe. For example, you can dial-up any one of a number of information services on travel, securities, and consumer goods, link your micro to the telephone line and remote computer, then use your micro as a workstation to obtain information. Both the micro and the VDT can transmit and receive data from a remote computer, but only the micro workstation can process and store the data independently. We will talk more about micros as workstations in Chapters 8 and 9.

Several other workstations can be connected to this microcomputer to make it a multiuser system.
(Courtesy of International Business Machines Corporation)

4-4   HOW ARE MICROS USED?

Microcomputers are used in all six of the categories of computer use discussed in Chapter 1: information systems; science and research; process control; education; personal computing; and artificial intelligence.

Information Systems/Data Processing

PCs in Small Organizations.   The microcomputer has opened up a new world for information systems/data processing. Prior to the microcomputer, even the smallest minicomputer could not be economically justified in very small businesses. Now, with powerful microcomputer systems costing less than $5,000, it is common to find a microcomputer in an office with one or two professional people. Attorneys, psychiatrists, and public accountants have many cost-effective applications that can be handled easily by a microcomputer.

Attorneys use their micros to keep track of their case loads and to generate

The reaction of this doctor and nurse reconfirms what millions of people have come to learn: micros are not only a source of valuable information, they also can be fun.
(Photo supplied courtesy of Epson America)

standard legal documents, such as wills and real estate transactions. Psychiatrists use their micros to schedule patients, monitor accounts, and ensure the availability of supplies. Certified Public Accountants rely on their micros to perform routine accounting functions for their clients. All these professionals use their systems for word processing. Off-the-shelf software packages can be purchased for each of these applications.

The opportunities for lawyers, doctors, and accountants to use the computer are apparent. The need for computers may not be so obvious in some professions, but the need is just as great. For example, a portable computer was carried by mountain climbers on an ascent of Mount Everest. During the three-month trip, 16 mountaineers used the computer to monitor their health, food consumption, and energy consumption and to measure snowfall and temperature. The computer system analyzed a variety of inputs and alerted the mountaineers of potentially dangerous situations.

PCs in Large Organizations. The micro is equally applicable for information systems in larger companies. Even though a larger company may already have one or several mainframe computers, these computers are shared by all departments. A micro, however, is readily available and can be used to support small information systems that are unique to a particular department or individual.

Within most organizations there are scores of applications for which a micro is more appropriate than a mainframe. For example, the photography department of a major computer vendor, such as CDC or Honeywell, has thousands of product photos. Rather than rely on the company's information services department, the photographers keep track of the photos on a microcomputer. A particular photograph is categorized by product and situation (e.g., with or without people). When someone requests a photo, the photographer has only to enter the specifications of the request and the information system replies with currency, status, and inventory information for all photos meeting the prescribed specifications.

Integrated Microcomputer Software. Software vendors now market *integrated software* that makes it easy for even a computer novice to create a "personal" information system. Integrated software gives users the flexibility to move data between several applications: data management, electronic spreadsheets, graphics, word processing, and communications. The function of each of the applications, which can also be purchased as independent units, is briefly described below. Their concepts and uses are described in considerable detail in the special section, "Integrated Microcomputer Software," that follows Chapter 17.

With integrated software, you can move easily between entering data with data management software and manipulating the data with electronic spreadsheet software. Data can be passed freely between the various pieces of software. For example, a spreadsheet can be created from a data base. The data can be analyzed by the spreadsheet software and displayed as a bar chart with the graphics software. A paragraph of explanation can be added using word processing. Then, both the chart and the explanation can be transmitted with the communications software to a mainframe computer for distribution to other departments. This type of transmission (micro-to-another-computer) is called **uploading**. The reverse is called *downloading*.

Data Management. Data management software permits the user to create and maintain a data base, and also to extract information from the data base. The user first identifies the format of the data, then designs a display screen format that will permit interactive entry and revision of the data. Once it is part of the data base, a record can be deleted or changed. The user can also retrieve and summarize data, based on certain criteria (e.g., list all salespersons over quota for July). Also, data can be sorted for display in a variety of formats (e.g., listing salespersons by total sales, or listing them alphabetically).

Electronic Spreadsheet. A popular microcomputer application is the **electronic spreadsheet**. The spreadsheet contains a tabular structure of rows and columns. The user, instead of manually writing the entries in the rows and columns of a worksheet, has them stored in an "electronic" data base, which can contain thousands of entries. Obviously, all entries in a large matrix cannot be displayed at the same time, so the data are displayed in **windows**, or parts of the total matrix. The user can display one or several windows on the screen at one time.

The applications of electronic spreadsheets are endless. Think of anything that has rows and columns. For example, spreadsheet software is often used to work with profit and loss statements, sales forecasts, and budget summaries and to maintain and calculate student grades.

The intersection of a row and column is called a *cell* and is referenced by its position within the matrix. In a profit and loss statement, for example, the entry in cell A4 (the first or A column, row 4) might be "Cost of Goods Sold," and the entry in cell B4 might be "$30,780." Columns are lettered and rows numbered. Cell entries can be either words or numbers.

Once the data are entered for a profit and loss statement, an electronic spreadsheet permits the user to manipulate and analyze the data. For example, the user can "electronically" increase sales by 20% per year and the cost of goods sold by 10% per year, then see how these changes affect profit over the next three years.

Graphics. Graphics software enables you to create a variety of presentation graphics based on data in a data base or a spreadsheet. These graphics take the form of bar charts, pie charts, and line charts.

A director of personnel in a consumer goods company uses data management and electronic spreadsheet software to ask "what if" questions regarding a proposal for a new benefits package for the company's 1,200 union workers.
(Quotron Systems, Inc.)

Spice up a presentation with colorful graphics by using a microcomputer. Graphics software permits you to prepare a screen that can be produced instantly on a print for previewing or as a 35mm slide for use in a presentation.
(Digital Research Inc.)

A pie chart is easily produced from a spreadsheet containing regional sales data. Each slice of the "pie" might depict the sales for each region as a percentage of total sales. The slices are in proportion. For example, if sales in the northeast region are $10 million and sales in the southwest region $5 million, then the northeast region slice is shown twice the size of that of the southwest region.

Word Processing. **Word processing** is using the computer to enter text, to store it on magnetic storage media, to manipulate it in preparation for output, and to produce a hard copy. Numerous applications involve written communications: letters, reports, memos, and so on. As well as being a component in integrated microcomputer software, word processing is also part of a set of applications collectively referred to as *office automation*. Office automation applications are discussed in detail in Chapter 12, "Information Systems in Business and Industry."

If you use word processing to prepare your reports, you will only have to key in the initial draft. Revisions and corrections can be made on the disk before the report is printed in final form. If you forgot a word or need to add a paragraph, you do not have to retype a page or, in the worst case, the whole report. For example, the original text for this book was keyed in only once on a microcomputer. Editorial changes (all 345,128 of them) were then entered by the authors on keyboards before the final manuscript was submitted to the publisher.

Communications. *Communications* software is available for micros that, in essence, makes the micro a terminal. But a micro can do more than a terminal can. It not only can transmit and receive data from a remote computer, it can process and store data as well. The software automatically "dials-up" the desired remote computer, then it "logs-on" (establishes a communications link with the remote computer). Once on-line, you can communicate with the remote computer or download data and work with the data using the micro as a stand-alone computer.

Science and Research

The computer, in general, and the microcomputer, in particular, have revolutionized the scientist's approach to research and the engineer's capabilities in design. The micro is a *stand-alone* (independent) computer for most routine tasks, and it serves as a terminal when connected to more powerful computers for tasks that require greater computing capacity.

A microcomputer was the basis for well-publicized research at Wright State University that may someday enable paraplegics to walk with the assistance of a computer.

Micros permit scientists to do sophisticated statistical analysis, then use "graphics" software to summarize the data in the form of graphs and charts.

Process Control

The microcomputer has enough computational power to handle most computer-controlled processes. In the home, micros can control the interior climate by activating temperature- and humidity-control devices; serve as the nerve center for security/fire systems that automatically notify police or fire officials in emergency; activate lights throughout the premises; activate the sprinkler system if there is too little rainfall; and wake you up in the morning with a radio alarm and the smell of fresh-perked coffee.

In the commercial environment, micros can be used for the same applications as in the home, for traffic-signal control, control of oil flow through pipelines, and hundreds more.

Education

Personal computers are becoming as much a part of the educational process as teachers (well, almost). They are commonly found in elementary schools and are part of the learning process in high schools, universities, and businesses. Education is one of the primary reasons people buy personal computers for their homes.

The interactive capability of the micro, coupled with its multidimensional output capability (sound, color graphics, and other visual stimuli), makes the micro a natural learning tool that encourages logical and creative thinking. Micros enable us to test our knowledge of subject matter, and they teach us new information in subject areas where our understanding is not clear. Numerous educational software courses are available to help elementary students learn such topics as arithmetic and reading and to help adults learn such topics as French and computer programming.

About 50 colleges have made owning a PC a prerequisite for admission. These colleges are encouraging their professors to view the computer as an effective pedagogical tool and to plan their courses accordingly. By the end of the decade, the number of colleges adopting the PC entrance requirement may be in the hundreds. Someday, courses may require computers as well as texts!

Personal Computing

Domestic and Business Applications.   Education, entertainment, and a variety of domestic and business applications form the foundation of personal computing. Domestic applications include some of the following: maintaining an up-to-date asset inventory of household items; storing names and addresses for a personal mailing list; maintaining records for and preparing income tax returns; creating and monitoring a household budget; keeping an appointment and social calendar; handling household finances (e.g., checkbook balancing, paying of bills, coupon refunding); and writing letters. You can purchase software for all of these applications, and you can probably obtain software for your special interest, whether it be astrology, charting biorhythms, composing music, or dieting. Virtually any business application (e.g., payroll, grade reporting) discussed in this book can be supported on a personal computer.

Video Games.   A popular pastime with those who own or have access to a personal computer is playing the almost endless variety of video games. Personal computers have revolutionized home entertainment. Card games

Until the mid-1970s, the drilling of deep off-shore wells was a difficult undertaking. It was almost impossible for a human to hold the ship steady for the time required to drill the well. Now that task is handled by a microcomputer. It does this by locking on to a satellite fix and activating propulsion systems to counter movements of the ship caused by the ocean current and the wind.
(Combustion Engineering, Inc.)

COMPUTERS GO TO COLLEGE

As the job market tightens, colleges are looking to give their students a competitive edge. With computer knowledge becoming a job prerequisite for many positions, some colleges have made the purchase of a personal computer a prerequisite for admission. Personal computers are versatile in that they can be used as stand-alone computers or they can be linked to the college's central mainframe computer or other personal computers.

Wouldn't it be great to: Run a bibliographic search from your dorm room or home? Make changes to a report without retyping it? Run a case search for a law class? Use the computer for math homework calculations?

Besides requiring students to have their own personal computers, college officials have placed computers in lounges, libraries, and other common areas.

Playing Cupid may not have been what administrators had in mind, but true love has bloomed as a result of messages exchanged via electronic mail. It's not uncommon to log on and find messages from students who are lonely and who just want to "talk." Talk evolves into amorous notes, and amorous notes evolve into a meeting, and. . . .

At some colleges, owning a computer has been made a prerequisite for admission.
(Courtesy of Apple Computer, Inc.)

Instead of making hard copies of class assignments, instructors key in their assignments, which are then "delivered" to each student's electronic mailbox. Students can correspond with their instructors through their computer to get help with assignments. They can even "talk" to other students at connected colleges. The computer is drawing students from all disciplines closer together and has opened up a whole world of new relationships.

The same personal computer that is used to monitor the family budget can just as easily take you to a king's castle with knights and fair maidens.
(Courtesy of International Business Machines Corporation)

and checkers have taken a back seat to video games, such as Pac Man, Space Invaders, Asteroids, Donkey Kong (all are now classics), and literally hundreds of others. These video games provide us with an opportunity to compete, have fun, *and* improve mental acuity and manual dexterity. Many of us, at one time or another, have been hypnotized by the heat of competition while attempting to eat little dots or destroy invading starships.

The innovators who create these video games have large followings and are treated like rock stars. These arcade heroes, called designers, are programmers, and they even have fan clubs. Only six years ago no one in the computer community would have dreamed that programmers would become national personalities and receive hundreds of letters each week. Some designers even receive six-figure bonuses, just like professional athletes.

Information Services.   Personal computers are normally used as stand-alone computer systems, but they can also double as remote terminals. This dual-function capability provides you with the flexibility to work with the PC as a stand-alone system or to link with a larger computer and take advantage of its increased capacity. Your PC is your link to a wide variety of information services. The personal computer can be used in conjunction with the telephone system to transmit data to and receive data from an *information network*.

A growing trend among personal computer enthusiasts is to subscribe to the services of an information network. These information networks have one or several large computer systems that offer such services as hotel and airline reservations, real estate listings, home banking, a variety of educational programs, horoscopes, news, electronic mail (where one person with a PC can send a message to another), stock prices, shopping services, electronic bulletin boards, and even video games. This list is only a sample of what is available now, and what is to come. Eventually, we will probably use our PCs to register our votes while linked to a government information network.

This general category of computer applications is called **videotext**. A videotext system provides certain services to an end user through a communications link. The link is between a mainframe computer, with one or several data bases, and a terminal or a personal computer. The two-way videotext systems provide the end user with text and graphic information on a variety of topics (see above) and permit the end user to enter data (e.g., to make reservations for airlines, or to transfer money from a savings to a checking account).

Retailers of consumer goods and services are already making plans to provide extended services to those who have personal computers. Instead of spending time searching for items in a supermarket, all you will have to do is "page" through menus on your PC display screen and select the items you want. The selections will be transmitted to the grocer's computer, then automatically retrieved and packaged for you to pick up. Eventually, competition will demand that goods be delivered. Look for shop-at-home systems to be available in the near future.

Home banking services permit you to complete banking transactions on your personal computer while on-line with the bank's computer. Existing home banking services also permit you to pay bills and make inquiries about the status of your accounts. Home banking services are often packaged with other information services.

These and many other time-saving applications should eventually make personal computers a "must-have" item in every home and business. Some PCs are already priced lower than a good pair of sneakers!

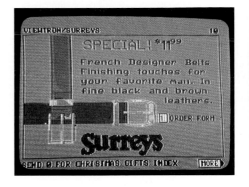

A PC user can take advantage of many information services by establishing a communications link with a large computer system. For example, with two-way videotext, you can browse through a "catalog" of items and place your order while sitting in front of your PC. Forecasters estimate that by 1990 up to 20% of all retail sales will be transacted on personal computers via videotext systems.
(Mindset Corporation)

Artificial Intelligence

The last wave of technological innovations have resulted in microcomputers with enough capacity to handle artificial intelligence (AI) applications. In the past, AI applications were limited to large mainframe computers. For the most part this is still the case, but micros can support small expert systems and simulate many human tasks, such as speaking, reading, and, to a limited extent, vision.

4-5 BUYING A MICRO

Retail Sales

Where to Buy.   Microcomputers and personal computers can be purchased at thousands of convenient locations. The TRS-80 series is sold at Radio Shack stores. Retail chains, such as ComputerLand, ENTRÉ Computer Center, 20/20, and MicroAge, market and service a variety of small computer systems. Micros are also sold in most department stores. The demand for micros has encouraged major computer system manufacturers, such as IBM, to·open retail stores (IBM Product Centers).

You don't always have to buy a computer at a retail store. If you know what you want, you can call any of several mail order services, give them a credit card number, and your PC will be delivered to your doorstep. A couple of prominent vendors will not sell their micros to mail order houses, but the mail order houses get them anyway through the PC "black market." It seems as if a black market always surfaces for high-demand products.

Prior to 1975, computer vendors sold their products through their own field marketing representatives. The first retail outlet was opened in 1975, and today more than 20,000 retail stores specialize in computer sales. Several times that many that sell microcomputers as part of their product line. And this is only the beginning.

The Perks of Employment.   You might be able to acquire a micro through your employer. Many companies offer their employees a "computer perk." In cooperation with vendors, companies make volume purchases of PCs at discount rates, then offer them to employees at substantial savings. This plan benefits everybody. The manufacturers sell their computers and the employees get an inexpensive PC. But the real reason behind the plan is to encourage "computer literacy." Employees inevitably begin to use and understand computers, and in the long run their computer savvy is translated into improved productivity in their jobs.

Computer stores the world over routinely hold seminars and product briefings for their customers. This IBM product center is in the Tokyo business district.
(Courtesy of International Business Machines Corporation)

Micro Manufacturers

Visions of tremendous profit opportunities have lured scores of companies into developing products to meet the growing demand for microcomputers and personal computers. Dollar signs blurred the vision of some executives as they put micros on the market before they were fully tested. This strategy backfired on several companies and resulted in embarrassing failures. Other firms built and marketed good products that made their founders millionaires almost overnight.

The number of personal computer manufacturers may have peaked in 1983, with over 150 companies manufacturing about 700 PCs. Recent failures of both small and large companies have caused potential entrepreneurs to think twice before going head-to-head with dozens of established, well-financed companies. Industry analysts are predicting that at least half of the existing micro vendors will not survive the decade.

Tandy Corporation, with an existing national network of Radio Shack electronics stores, was a natural to enter the microcomputer market—and indeed it did. Its TRS-80 microcomputer series, introduced in 1977, has established records for computer sales.

One of the biggest business success stories was written by Apple Computer, Inc. In 1977, a couple of microcomputer enthusiasts, Steven Jobs and Stephen Wozniak, set up business in a garage. The rest is history. The success of the Apple computer series is proof of the almost insatiable demand for the personal computer.

An inexpensive way to own your own personal computer is to make it—from a kit, of course. And, yes, there are Heath kits for personal computers. You do not have to be an electronics wizard to assemble one of these kits. People with relatively little background in computers and electronics have successfully assembled personal computers.

Commodore Business Machines, Apple, Tandy, Compaq, Epson, Zenith, and Kaypro are just a few of many manufacturers of microcomputers. Computer giants such as IBM, DEC, and Xerox did not enter the microcomputer market until 1981. The giants may have had a late start, but they are making up for lost time by taking bigger and bigger shares of the micro market. Almost immediately after it was announced, the IBM PC became an industry phenomenon. During the first half of the 1980s it was the industry standard. At one time, over 30 companies manufactured IBM PC-compatible micros. These supposedly would run the same software and accomplish the same functions as the IBM PC. A few IBM PC-compatible micros are indeed completely compatible, but others are only partially compatible.

Choosing a Microcomputer

Buying a microcomputer can be a harrowing experience, or it can be a thrilling and fulfilling one. If you approach the purchase of a micro haphazardly, expect the former. If you go about the acquisition methodically and with purpose, expect the latter. This section contains some hints for the evaluation and selection of a microcomputer.

Steven P. Jobs (in photo), formerly chairman of the board of Apple Computer, Inc., and Stephen Wozniak started Apple Computer in 1977. In five years, Apple Computer moved from Job's garage to a spot on the Fortune 500, a list of the 500 largest corporations in the United States.
(Courtesy of Apple Computer, Inc.)

Salespersons at computer retail stores are usually happy to show you what options are available for a particular microcomputer. Available in most retail stores are "demo disks" that, when loaded to a PC, demonstrate the features of a software package.
(Courtesy of International Business Machines Corporation)

Steps to Buying a Micro

1. *Achieve computer literacy*. You don't buy an automobile before you learn how to drive, and you shouldn't buy a microcomputer without a good understanding of its capabilities and limitations. By the time you finish this course, you will have the knowledge to make informed decisions when buying a micro.

2. *Determine your information and computer usage needs*. There is an old adage, "If you don't know where you are going, any road will get you there." The statement is certainly true of choosing a PC. "Knowing where you are going" can be translated to mean "How do you plan to use the PC?"

   Do you wish to develop your own software or purchase commercially available software packages? Or perhaps do both? If you want to write your own programs, then you must select the programming language best suited to your application needs (see Chapter 10, "Programming Languages and Software Concepts"). All microcomputers support the BASIC programming language (see the special section, "BASIC Programming"). If you plan on purchasing the software, determine which general application areas you wish to have supported on the proposed PC (e.g., spreadsheet, accounting, word processing, home banking).

3. *Assess availability of software and information services*. Determine what software and information services are available to meet your prescribed needs. Good sources of this type of information include a wide variety of periodicals (e.g., *PC*, *Byte*, *Creative Computing*, *Computerworld*, and *Personal Computing*, to name a few); salespersons at computer stores; and acquaintances who have knowledge in the area.

MEMORY BITS

STEPS TO BUYING A MICROCOMPUTER
1. Achieve computer literacy
2. Determine your information and computer usage needs
3. Assess availability of software and information services
4. Investigate hardware options
5. Determine features desired
6. "Test drive" several alternatives
7. Select and buy

4. *Investigate hardware options*. If you select a specific software product and/or an information service in Step 3, your selection may dictate the general computer system configuration requirements and, in some cases, a specific microcomputer system. In all likelihood, you will have several, if not a dozen, hardware alternatives available to you. Become familiar with the features, and options, of each alternative system.

5. *Determine features desired*. You can go with a "minimum" configuration, or you can add a few "bells and whistles." Expect to pay for each feature in convenience, quality, and speed that you add to the minimum configuration. For example, people are usually willing to pay a little extra for the added convenience of a two-disk system, even though one disk will suffice. On the other hand, a color monitor may be an unnecessary luxury for some applications. The peripherals that you select depend very much on your specific needs and volume of usage. For example, the type of printer that you choose would depend on the volume of hard copy output that you anticipate, whether or not you need graphics output, whether or not you need letter-quality print, and so on.

6. *"Test drive" several alternatives*. Once you have selected several software and hardware alternatives, spend enough time to gain some familiarity with them. Do you prefer one keyboard over another? Does a word processing system fully use the features of the hardware? Is one system easier to understand and use than another? Use these sessions to answer any questions that you might have about the hardware or software. Salespersons at most retail stores are happy to give you a test drive; just ask.

7. *Select and buy*. Apply your criteria, select, then buy your hardware and software.

Factors to Consider

1. *Future computing needs*. What will your computer and information processing needs be in the future? Most micros provide room for growth; that is, you can add more memory and other peripheral devices as you need them. Make sure the system you select can grow with your needs.

2. *Who will use the system?* Plan not only for yourself but for others in your home or office who will also use the system. Get their input and consider their needs along with yours.

(By permission of Bob Glueckstein)

3. *Availability of software*. Software is developed for one or several micro-computers, but not for all microcomputers. As you might expect, a more extensive array of software is available for the more popular micros. However, don't overlook some of the less visible vendors if their products, in your mind, are superior to the other alternatives.

4. *Service*. Computing hardware is very reliable. Even so, the possibility exists that one or several of the components will eventually malfunction and have to be repaired. Before purchasing a micro, identify a reliable source of hardware maintenance. Most retailers service what they sell. If a retailer says that the hardware must be returned to the manufacturer for repair, choose another retailer or another system.

   Most retailers or vendors will offer a variety of maintenance contracts. Maintenance contract options range from on-site repair that covers all parts and service to carry-in service that does not include parts. Most domestic users elect to treat their micros like their TVs and autos: when the warranty runs out, they pay for repairs as they are needed. Under normal circumstances, this strategy will prove the least expensive. Some businesses will purchase a maintenance contract for the convenience that it offers.

   Service extends beyond hardware maintenance. Service is also an organization's willingness to respond to your inquiries, before *and* after the sale. Some retailers and vendors offer classes in programming and in the use of the hardware and software that they sell.

5. *Obsolescence*. "I'm going to buy one as soon as the price goes down a little more." If you adopt this strategy, you may never purchase a computer. If you wait another six months, you will probably be able to get a more powerful micro for less money. But what about the lost opportunity?

   There is, however, a danger in purchasing a micro that is near or at the end of its life cycle. Focus your search on micros with state-of-the-art technology. Even though you may get a substantial discount on the older micro, you will normally get more for your money with the newer micro.

6. *Other costs*. The cost of the actual microcomputer system is the major expense, but there are numerous incidental expenses that can mount up and may influence your selection of a micro. If you have a spending limit, consider these costs when purchasing the hardware (the cost ranges listed are for a first-time user): software ($100–$1,500), maintenance (0–$500/year), diskettes ($50–$200), furniture (0–$350), insurance (0–$20), and printer ribbons, paper, and other supplies ($40–$150).

SUMMARY OUTLINE AND IMPORTANT TERMS _____

4-1   WHAT IS A COMPUTER?   The **computer**, or **processor**, is an electronic device capable of interpreting and executing programmed commands for input, output, computation, and logic operations. Computer system capabilities are defined as either input/output or processing. Processing capabilities are subdivided into computation and logic operations.

4-2 COMPUTER SYSTEMS: A ROSE IS A ROSE IS A ROSE. . . . The most distinguishing characteristic of any computer system is its "size" or computing capacity. All computers, no matter how large or small, have the same fundamental capabilities.

4-3 MICROCOMPUTERS AND PERSONAL COMPUTERS: SMALL BUT POWERFUL. **Microprocessors** not only set the stage for **microcomputers**, but they are found in dozens of devices about the home. The **motherboard** in a microcomputer contains the electronic circuitry for processing and I/O operations, and some memory. The **micro**, also called a **personal computer** or **PC**, comes in pocket, lap, and desktop sizes.

The most common **configuration** for a micro is a keyboard for input, a **monitor** for **soft copy** output, a printer for **hard copy** output, and disk drives for permanent storage of data on **diskettes** or **microdisks**. A diskette is also called a **flexible disk** or **floppy disk**. Multiuser micros are configured with several **workstations**. Micros can be used as stand-alone computer systems or they can serve as "intelligent" workstations to mainframe computers.

4-4 HOW ARE MICROS USED? Microcomputers are used in all six categories of computer usage. In information systems/data processing, micros handle virtually all information processing tasks in small organizations, and they handle specific departmental information needs in larger organizations. The most popular use of micros in the business environment is integrated software: data management, **electronic spreadsheet**, graphics, **word processing**, and communications.

Micros have revolutionized approaches to research. They can handle most computer-controlled processes and have become an integral part of the educational process.

Education, entertainment, and a variety of domestic and business applications form the foundation of personal computing. Personal computers can be used to transmit and receive data from information networks. You can even "go shopping" via **videotext**.

Micro technology has become powerful enough to perform certain artificial intelligence applications.

4-5 BUYING A MICRO. Micros and PCs can be purchased at computer and traditional retail stores everywhere. A number of computer vendors, such as Apple and Tandy Corporation, specialize in microcomputers, but in recent years the vendors of mainframe computers, such as DEC and IBM, have made micros a major segment of their product lines.

Buying a microcomputer, whether for home or business, should be approached methodically and with purpose. Factors to consider when buying a micro include: future computing needs; who will use the system; availability of software; service; obsolescence; and other costs.

REVIEW EXERCISES

Concepts

1. Which of the five components of integrated software would be most helpful in writing a term paper?
2. What do you look for when you "test drive" a microcomputer before purchasing it?
3. What is a motherboard?
4. Describe a multiuser micro.
5. What is the relationship between a microprocessor and a microcomputer?
6. What is the software capability that enables viewing of electronic spreadsheet data and a bar graph at the same time?
7. List at least six information network services.
8. In terms of physical size, how are PCs categorized?
9. What is the name given to printed output? Output on a monitor?
10. In computerese, what is meant by "read" and "write"?
11. How are microcomputers used in process control?
12. Briefly describe the function of each of the five applications in integrated software.

Discussion

13. Home banking services are available only to those who have home computers with communications capabilities. To encourage customer participation, some banks offer this service at a price that is below their cost. Excess cost is then passed on to all customers. Is this fair? Explain.
14. The number one use of computers in the home is for business work done at home. Is there a contradiction when one speaks of "business" microcomputers and "home" microcomputers? Explain.
15. Is the use of such terms as microcomputer, minicomputer, midicomputer, supercomputer, and so on a help or a hindrance to distinguishing between the computing capacities of computer systems? Explain.
16. List at least ten products that are smaller than a breadbox and use microprocessors. Select one of the ten and describe the function of its microprocessor.
17. What options would you like to have on your own personal micro that are not included in a minimum configuration? Why?
18. Discuss at least five domestic applications for personal computers.
19. How might a microcomputer help in the day-to-day administration of an academic department at a college (e.g., Psychology Department, Nursing Department)?

SELF-TEST (by section)

4-1. The two types of processing operations performed by computers are _____ and _____ .

4-2. The most distinguishing characteristic of any computer system is its computing capacity. (T/F)

4-3. A microcomputer cannot serve as a workstation linked to a mainframe computer. (T/F)

4-4. The transmission of data from a micro to a mainframe is called uploading. (T/F)

4-5. The most important consideration in buying a microcomputer is whether or not a long-term service contract is available. (T/F)

Self-Test answers.   4–1, computation, logic; 4–2, T; 4–3, F; 4–4, T; 4–5, F.

STUDENT LEARNING OBJECTIVES

- To distinguish between micros and mainframes.
- To contrast the concepts of on-line and off-line.
- To demonstrate awareness of the relative size, scope, characteristics, and variety of available computer systems.
- To describe the functions and relationships of the various processors in a computer system.
- To discuss the concept of distributed processing.
- To describe applications of special-purpose computer systems.

CHAPTER

5

Computer Systems— Mainframes

5-1 COMPUTER SYSTEM CONCEPTS

Micros versus Mainframes. *Micros* are computer systems. *Mainframes* are computer systems. Each offers a variety of input and output alternatives, and each is supported by a wide variety of packaged software. There are, of course, obvious differences in size and capabilities. Everything associated with a mainframe is larger in scope: execution of programs is faster; on-line disk storage has more capacity; printer speeds are much faster; mainframes service many workstations; and they cost more.

Besides size and capability, the single most distinguishing characteristic of a mainframe computer is the manner in which it is used. Mainframe computers, with their expanded processing capabilities, provide a computing resource that can be shared by an entire organization, not just a single user. For example, it is common in a company for the finance, personnel, and accounting departments to share the resources of a mainframe, possibly all at the same time. We discussed the microcomputer environment in Chapter 4. This chapter focuses on the mainframe environment and also covers special-purpose computers, which can be either micros or mainframes.

The clean lines of this large mainframe computer system hide the thousands of integrated circuits, miles of wire, and even gold, that make up the inner workings of a computer system. This data center provides information processing support for hundreds of end users.
(Courtesy Burroughs Corporation)

All airline reservation systems are on-line systems. The workstations at ticketing counters in airports are on-line to a centralized computer facility. Each time an agent writes a ticket and assigns a passenger a seat, the master record for that flight is immediately updated to reflect the addition of one more passenger.
(Texas Instruments, Inc.)

On-line versus Off-line.   In a computer system, the input, output, and data storage components receive data from, and transmit data to, the processor over electrical cables or "lines." These hardware components are said to be **on-line** to the processor. Hardware devices that are not accessible to, or under the control of, a processor are said to be **off-line**. The concepts of on-line and off-line apply also to data. Data are said to be *on-line* if they can be accessed and manipulated by the processor. All other data are *off-line*.

Consider the payroll example in Figure 5–1. In an *off-line* operation, all supervisors complete the weekly time sheets. The time sheets are then collected and *batched* for input to the computer system. When transactions are grouped together for processing, it is called **batch processing**.

Before the data can be entered and the payroll checks printed, the payroll master file must be placed on-line. To do this, the master file is retrieved manually from a library of disk files and "loaded" to a storage component called a disk drive. Once loaded, the payroll master file is on-line. The process is analogous to selecting the phonograph record that you wish to play and mounting it on the turntable.

An operator at a VDT enters the data contained on the time sheets directly into the computer system in an *on-line* operation. Employee data, such as name, social security number, pay rate, and deductions, are retrieved from the payroll master file and combined with the number of hours worked to produce the payroll checks. The payroll checks are produced on a printer, which is an output device.

Since the payroll checks are printed on continuous preprinted forms, they must be separated before they can be distributed to the employees. In an *off-line* operation, a machine called a burster separates and stacks the payroll checks.

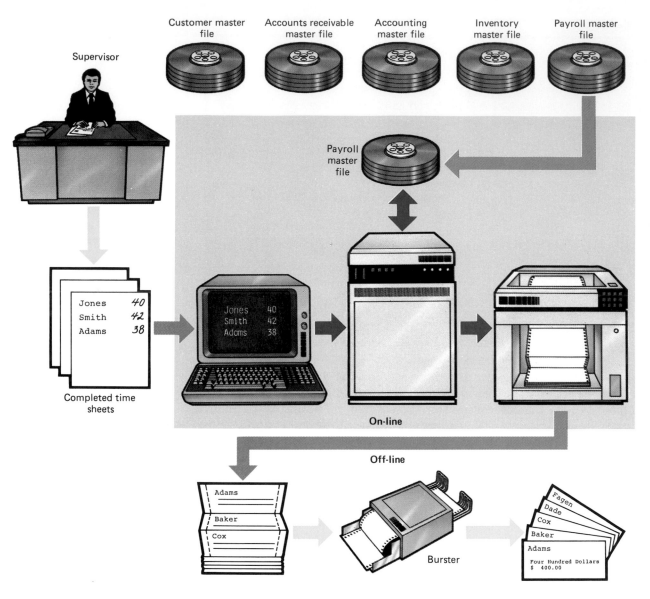

FIGURE 5–1
On-Line and Off-Line Operations
Those processing activities, hardware, and files that are not controlled by, or accessible to, the computer are referred to as off-line.

5–2   MINICOMPUTERS

Until the late 1960s, all computers were mainframe computers, and they were expensive—too expensive for all but the largest companies. About that time vendors introduced smaller, but slightly "watered down," computers that were more affordable to smaller companies. The industry dubbed these small computers **minicomputers**, or simply **minis**. The name has stuck, even though some of today's so-called minis are many times as powerful as the largest mainframes of the early 1970s (see Figure 5–2).

FIGURE 5–2
Micro, Mini, and Mainframe Computing Capacities
The computing capacity of a micro, mini, or mainframe increases with advancing technology.

There is no clear-cut or generally accepted definition for a minicomputer. The passing of time and a rapidly changing technology have blurred the distinction between categories of computers. The more powerful multiuser micros look very much like small minis, but minis are now accomplishing processing tasks that have traditionally been associated with mainframes. Minis bridge the gap between micros and mainframes, but the manner in which they are used makes them more characteristic of mainframes than of micros. Creating a rigorous definition of a minicomputer is like trying to grab a speeding bullet. Since technology has created a moving target, we will describe the minicomputer simply as the line of computers just larger than the microcomputer. You can pick up and carry a micro, but not a mini. Minicomputers are simply small mainframe computers.

Minicomputers usually serve as stand-alone computer systems for small businesses (ten to 400 employees) and as remote computer systems linked to a large centralized computer (see Section 5–4). Minis are also common in research groups, engineering firms, and colleges.

Minis have most of the operational capabilities of mainframe computers that are a thousand times faster. They just perform their tasks more slowly. Minicomputer input, output, and storage devices are similar in appearance and function to those used on much larger systems. However, the printers are not quite as fast, the storage capacity is smaller, and fewer workstations can be serviced. Figure 5–3 illustrates a midsize minicomputer system configuration that provides information systems support for a mail order sporting goods retailer with $40 million in sales. The components illustrated in Figure 5–3 are described on the following page.

Minicomputers are being designed to operate in a normal office environment. Most minicomputers, such as the one in this management consulting firm, do not require special accommodations for temperature and humidity control.
(AT&T Information Systems)

Computing capacity

- Micros
- Minis
- Mainframes

1975 1980 1985 1990

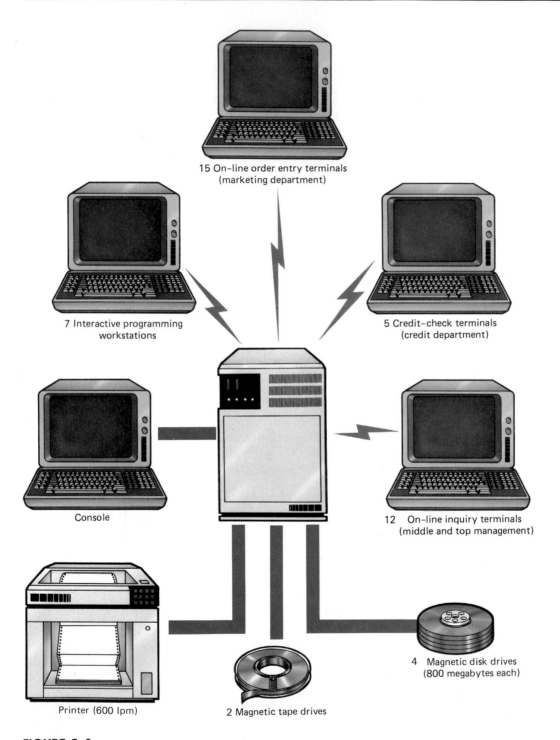

15 On-line order entry terminals
(marketing department)

7 Interactive programming
workstations

5 Credit-check terminals
(credit department)

Console

12   On-line inquiry terminals
(middle and top management)

Printer (600 lpm)

2 Magnetic tape drives

4   Magnetic disk drives
(800 megabytes each)

FIGURE 5–3
A Minicomputer System
This system supports a mail order sporting goods retailer with $40 million
in sales and is representative of a midsize minicomputer.

- *Processing*. It is premature to give you a technical description of processing capabilities. That will be done in Chapter 6, "Inside the Computer." We can, however, give you a feel for the relative processing capabilities of a minicomputer by comparing it to one with which most of us have at least a casual familiarity—the microcomputer. The processor in the minicomputer system of Figure 5–3 has about ten times the processing capability of a state-of-the-art single-user micro.

- *Storage*. An organization's storage-capacity requirements increase even faster than their processing requirements. Typically, the first major upgrade from a microcomputer is away from diskette data storage. The "hard" disk alternative has a much greater capacity than the diskette or microdisk. The minicomputer system in Figure 5–3 has four *disk drives* (discussed in Chapter 7, "Data Storage Devices and Media"), each capable of storing 800 megabytes (million characters) for a total capacity of 3,200 megabytes. The system also has a magnetic *tape drive*, capable of 200 megabytes of on-line sequential storage. Disk data files are periodically dumped, or loaded, to tape for backup.

- *Input*. The primary means of data input to the system are the 20 VDTs installed in the marketing and credit departments. The **operator console** in the machine room is also used to communicate instructions to the system. Seven workstations are used by programmers to enter, debug, and test their programs.

- *Output*. A 1,200-line-per-minute (lpm) printer provides hard copy output. The VDTs in the departments of marketing, credit, programming, and the console in the machine room provide soft copy output. Twelve VDTs are made available to middle and top management for on-line inquiry.

It is unlikely that you would find two minicomputers configured exactly the same way. A company that prefers to use disk, rather than tape, backup

(By permission of Anthony Cresci)

would not need a magnetic tape drive. Another may have a substantial volume of printed output and require two 2,000-line-per-minute printers. Figure 5–3 is an example of one possible configuration.

As the definition of a minicomputer becomes more obscure, the term "minicomputer" will take its place beside "electronic brain." But for now, it remains a commonly used term, even though it lacks a commonly accepted definition.

5–3 MAINFRAME COMPUTER SYSTEMS

Besides the obvious difference in the speeds at which they process data, the major difference between minicomputers and other mainframe computers is the number of remote workstations that they can service. As a rule of thumb, any computer that services more than 100 remote workstations can no longer be called a minicomputer. Some supercomputers, the fastest and most powerful of mainframes, service over 10,000 remote workstations.

The speed at which medium and large mainframe computers can perform operations allows more input, output, and storage devices with greater capabilities to be configured in the computer system. The computer system in Figure 5–4 is used by the municipal government of a city of about a million people. This example should give you an appreciation for the relative size and potential of a medium-sized mainframe computer system. The hardware devices illustrated will be explained in detail in subsequent chapters. The components are briefly described below.

- *Processing*. Mainframe computer systems, including some minis, will normally be configured with the mainframe or *host processor* and several other processors. A typical configuration would have a host processor, a *front-end processor*, and perhaps a *back-end processor*. The host is the main computer and is substantially larger and more powerful than the other *subordinate* processors. The front-end and back-end processors control the data flow in and out of the host processor. Although the host could handle the entire system without the assistance of the front-end and back-end processors, overall system efficiency would be drastically reduced without them. The different types of processors are described in more detail in Section 5–4.

- *Storage*. All mainframe computer systems use similar direct and sequential storage media. The larger ones simply have more of them and they usually work faster. In Figure 5–4 there are four magnetic tape drives and ten magnetic disk drives. The disk drives are *dual density* and can pack twice the data in the same amount of physical storage space as the disks shown in Figure 5–3. The total data storage capacity in the example is 800 megabytes of sequential storage (tape) and 16,000 megabytes of direct-access storage (disk).

- *Input*. The primary means of entering data to the system is the same, no matter what the size of the computer system. The only difference between a large and a small system is the number and location of the workstations. In the example of Figure 5–4, 150 workstations are dedi-

The processing component of this large mainframe computer system (shown in background) can perform 800 million calculations each second. It would require 150 people working around the clock for an entire year to complete the calculations that this computer does in a single second.
(Control Data Corporation)

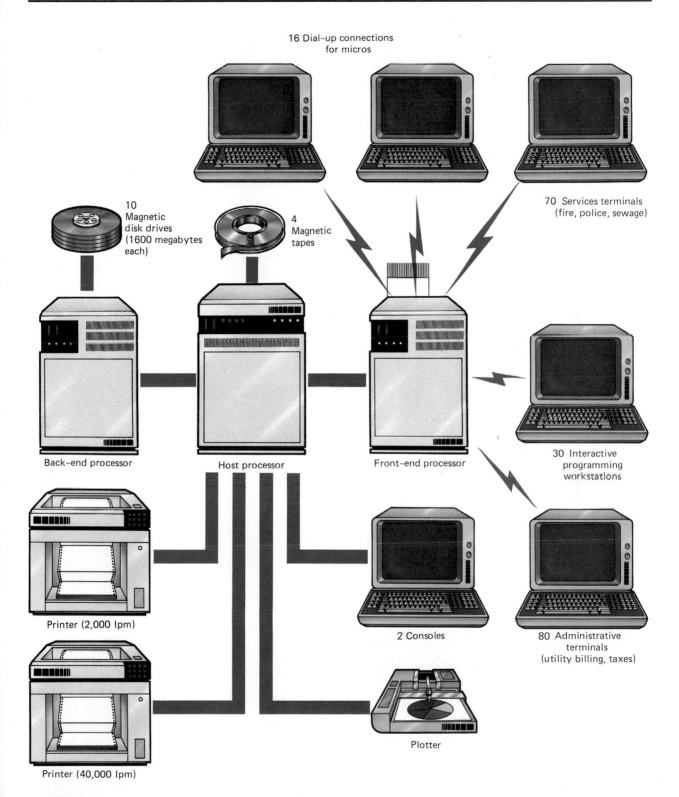

16 Dial-up connections
for micros

70 Services terminals
(fire, police, sewage)

10 Magnetic disk drives (1600 megabytes each)

4 Magnetic tapes

Back-end processor

Host processor

Front-end processor

30 Interactive programming workstations

Printer (2,000 lpm)

2 Consoles

80 Administrative terminals (utility billing, taxes)

Printer (40,000 lpm)

Plotter

FIGURE 5–4
A Mainframe Computer System
This midsize mainframe computer system supports the administrative
processing needs for the municipal government of a city with a population
of about one million.

COMPUTERS IN PERSPECTIVE

1. **Their ability to process and manipulate data at tremendous speeds without error boggles the mind.**

   Before you reach the end of this sentence, a large computer could:

   - process 1,000 airline reservations,
   - calculate the payroll for a company of 1,000,
   - validate the accuracy of 1,000 IRS-1040 forms, *and still have time to*
   - schedule classes for 1,000 students.

2. **Their rate of technological achievement** has surpassed that of all other innovations in history.

   You can carry, in a briefcase, a computer with 40 times the power of the 30-ton ENIAC, the world's first large-scale computer.

3. **They offer more for less money each year.**

   - In 1957, a medium-sized mainframe computer cost about $250,000.
   - Today's microcomputers offer greater memory and processing capability for under $5,000.

cated to service and administrative functions, 30 are used for programming, and 16 **ports** are available for those who might wish to use their PCs to dial-up and log-on to the mainframe computer. A port is an access point in a computer system that permits data to be transmitted between the computer and a peripheral device.

- *Output*. As in the minicomputer system in Figure 5–3, the hard copy is produced on high-speed printers and the soft copy on workstations. In the example there are two printers: a line printer with a speed of 2,000 lines per minute and a page printer that uses electrophotographic printing technology to achieve printing speeds of over 40,000 lines per minute. The plotter, also pictured in the configuration, is used by city engineers to produce hard copies of graphs, charts, and drawings.

5–4 A "HOST" OF COMPUTERS

Ten years ago most processors were simply called *central processing units*, or *CPUs* for short; today, however, not all processors are "central." Figure 5–4 demonstrates how a computer system can have three processors: a host, a front-end, and a back-end processor. Figure 5–5 illustrates an even greater variety of subordinate processors, each one performing a different function.

These special-function processors are strategically located throughout a computer system to increase efficiency and **throughput**, or the rate at which work can be performed by a computer system. A computer system can be configured with the host plus none or all of the subordinate processors shown in Figure 5–5 and micros. Circumstances dictate which, if any, of these subordinate processors and/or micros should be included.

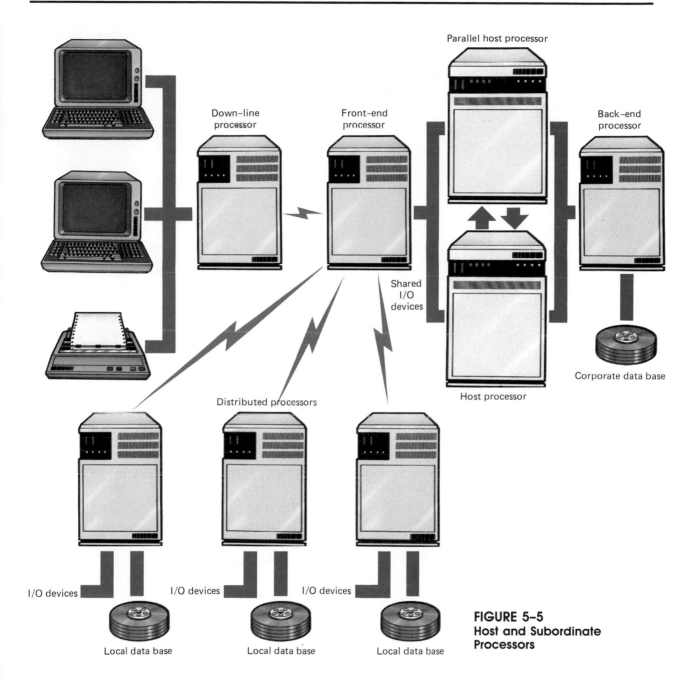

Parallel host processor

Down-line processor

Front-end processor

Back-end processor

Shared I/O devices

Corporate data base

Distributed processors

Host processor

I/O devices   **I/O devices**   **I/O devices**

Local data base   **Local data base**   **Local data base**

**FIGURE 5–5
Host and Subordinate
Processors**

The Need for Special-Function Processors

A processor executes only one instruction at a time, even though it appears
to be handling many tasks simultaneously. A **task** is the basic unit of work
for a processor. At any given time, several tasks will compete for processor
time. For example, one task might involve printing sales reports and another
calculating finance charges.

NASA's Mission Control Center tracks space shuttle flights with the aid of two large mainframe computers. Tracking stations around the world gather data directly from the computers on-board the space shuttle. These data are transmitted to the Mission Control Center via satellite where a host mainframe computer provides position reports and makes trajectory predictions. A parallel host provides backup. (NASA)

Since a single processor is capable of executing only one instruction at a time, one task will be given priority and the others will have to wait. The processor rotates between competing tasks so quickly, however, that it appears as if all are being executed at once. Even so, this rotation eventually takes its toll on processor efficiency. To improve the overall efficiency of a computer system, the *processing load* is *distributed* among several other special-function processors.

The *host* or *mainframe* processor is responsible for overall control of the computer system and for the execution of applications programs. Other processors in the computer system are under the control of and subordinate to the host. The function and relationship of the host and its subordinate processors are discussed below.

The Host Processor.   The **host processor** has direct control over all the other processors, storage devices, and input/output devices. The other processors relieve the host of certain routine processing requirements, such as locating a particular record on a data storage device. In this way, the host can concentrate on overall system control and the execution of applications software.

Figure 5–5 includes a **parallel host**. A parallel host is necessary where **downtime** (host not operational) is unacceptable. For example, in an airline reservation system, thousands of reservations are made and cancelled each hour, 24 hours a day, seven days a week. If the host fails, the parallel host takes over and provides **backup** to keep the system in continuous operation. Most computer systems will not need a parallel host.

The Front-End Processor.   A **front-end processor** relieves the host processor of communications-related processing duties (discussed in more detail in Chapter 9, "Data Communications"). All data being transmitted *to* the host processor *from* remote locations or *from* the host processor *to* remote locations are handled by the front-end processor.

MEMORY BITS

SPECIAL-FUNCTION PROCESSORS

- *Host processor or mainframe*: computer system control and applications software
- *Parallel host processor*: backup
- *Front-end processor*: data communications (host site)
- *Back-end processor or data base machine*: data retrieval (secondary storage)
- *Down-line processor*: data communications (remote site)
- *Distributed processor*: decentralized host
- *Device processor*: microprocessor in hardware devices

The Back-End Processor.   The **back-end processor** or **data base machine** handles tasks associated with the retrieval and manipulation of data stored on secondary storage devices. For example, suppose a program that is executing in the host requires Sally Smith's record from the personnel master file. The host processor issues a request to the back-end processor to retrieve the record of Sally Smith. It is then the responsibility of the back-end processor to issue the commands necessary to retrieve the record and transmit it to the host for processing. By handling the logic and the mechanics of tasks involving the data base, the back-end processor substantially reduces the processing load of the host, thereby speeding the execution of applications programs.

Down-Line Processor.   The **down-line processor** is an extension of the front-end processor. Its name is derived from its physical location. It is located "down-line"—at or near a remote site. The down-line processor formats and prepares the input of several remote workstations for transmission over a *communications link* (line over which data are transmitted). It then transmits the data to the front-end processor. The down-line processor also receives and distributes host output to the appropriate remote terminals or workstations.

The Distributed Processor.   The **distributed processor** is an extension of the host. A distributed processor is the "host" processor system that is "distributed" or physically located in a functional area department (such as accounting, marketing, or manufacturing). These microcomputer and minicomputer systems have their own input/output (I/O), workstations, and storage capabilities and can operate as a stand-alone (i.e., independent of the host) or as a distributed system (i.e., an extension of the host). See Section 5–5 for more information.

Device Processors.   Virtually every hardware device (e.g., printers, workstations, disk drives, and so on) will have at least one embedded microprocessor. These device processors are there to relieve the host and other subordinate processors of the routine tasks associated with hardware operation. For example, in a printer, a microprocessor formats and readies all text for print, then it activates the appropriate mechanisms to feed the paper and do the actual printing.

This newspaper subscribes to a hotline service that provides a variety of worldwide news and financial information. They have three workstations like this one and each is linked to a down-line processor. A single communications link connects the down-line processor with the news service's central computer system in New York City.
(RCA)

The Cray X-MP mainframe computer, which is one of the world's fastest computers, is sometimes called a supercomputer. The people at Cray Research are said to be motivated not so much by a business philosophy as by a belief in creativity. The Cray style is apparent in the written corporate philosophy: "At Cray Research, we take what we do very seriously, but don't take ourselves very seriously."
(Cray Research, Inc.)

Processor Summary

As you can see, a mainframe computer system is not just one processor. Researchers are continuously seeking new ways to introduce more and more processors into a computer system. If four processors are better than one, then 50 must be better than four, and so on. Some large computer systems already have more than 100 processors! In fact, computer designers are thinking in terms of linking *millions* of chip-size processors in a single computer system! This kind of *parallel processing* is expected to result in enormous improvements in throughput.

5–5 INTEGRATED COMPUTER NETWORKS: COMPUTERS WORKING TOGETHER

Centralization versus Decentralization. Through the mid-1970s, the prevailing thought was to take advantage of the economy of scale and *centralize* all information processing in an organization. At the time, an organization could get more computing capacity for its dollar by purchasing larger and larger computer systems. This is no longer true.

Some centralized computer centers have grown so big and complex that they have lost their ability to be responsive to the organization's information needs. This lack of responsiveness was a major factor in reversing the trend from centralization to *decentralization* or **distributed processing**. The growth in the number of distributed processors (see Figure 5–6) is fueling the trend to decentralization.

Distributed Processing. Distributed processing is both a technological and an organizational concept. Its premise is that information processing can be more effective if computer *hardware* (usually micros and minis), *data*, *software*, and, in some cases, *personnel* are moved physically closer to the people who use these resources. That is, if the public relations people need access to a computer and information, these resources are made available to them in their work area. They don't need to go to the information services department for every request. You might say that in distributed processing, users control their "information" destiny.

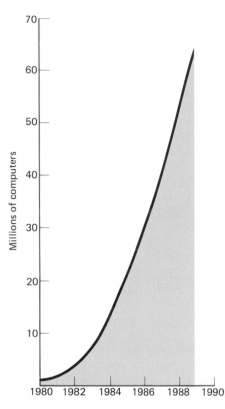

FIGURE 5–6
Growth in the Number of Computers
Microcomputers and the trend to distributed processing have caused a dramatic increase in the number of computers installed in the United States (figures are estimated).

The distributed computer system at this west coast textile warehouse helps administrative personnel keep track of orders and shipping information. Two other warehouses in the midwest and on the east coast have similar distributed systems, and all are linked to the company's headquarters mainframe computer in North Carolina.
(Courtesy of NEC Information Systems, Inc.)

In distributed processing, computer systems are arranged in a **computer network**, with each system connected to one or more other systems. A distributed processing network of computer systems is usually designed around a combination of geographical and functional considerations. In Figure 5–7, for example, a distributed processing network is illustrated for the American Video Games Company. At the headquarters location in Kansas City, American Video has *functionally* distributed processing systems in the account-

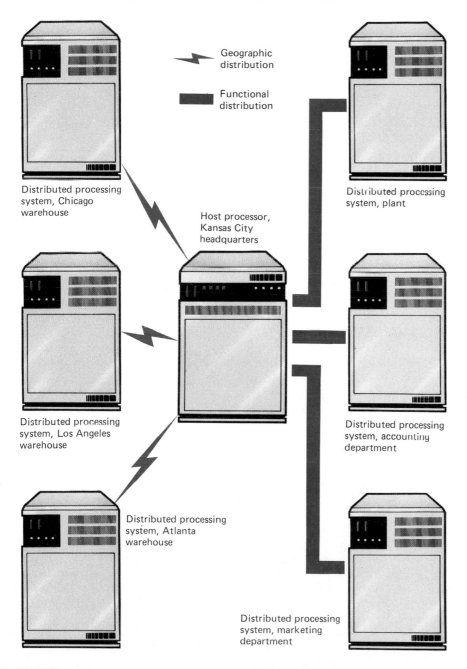

Distributed processing system, Chicago warehouse

Geographic distribution

Functional distribution

Host processor, Kansas City headquarters

Distributed processing system, plant

Distributed processing system, Los Angeles warehouse

Distributed processing system, accounting department

Distributed processing system, Atlanta warehouse

Distributed processing system, marketing department

FIGURE 5–7
A Distributed Processing Network
The distributed processing network of the American Video Games Company (a fictitious name) demonstrates both geographic and functional distribution of processing.

ing department, the marketing department, and the home office plant. *Geo-graphically* distributed processing systems are located at each of three warehouses in Chicago, Los Angeles, and Atlanta.

The host computer system at Kansas City maintains the corporatewide data base and services those departments that do not have their own computer system. Even though the distributed processing systems are part of the computer network, they are entirely self-contained and can operate as stand-alone systems.

5-6 SPECIAL-PURPOSE COMPUTER SYSTEMS

So far, our Chapter 4 (micros) and Chapter 5 (mainframe) discussions have centered around computer systems with the flexibility to do a variety of tasks, such as computer-assisted instruction, payroll processing, and climate control. These are called **general-purpose computers**. Now let's turn our attention to those computers that are designed for a specific application. These are called **special-purpose computers**.

A special-purpose computer is just another micro or mainframe computer system, but it is *dedicated* to a single application and may have special requirements for input/output connections. Special-purpose computers could be installed in aircraft to aid in navigation and in general flight control. They are the violins, clarinets, and drums of music synthesizers. They are also used for materials handling in warehouses to select and move containers without human intervention. Several common applications for special-purpose computers are described below.

Video Games

Certainly one of the most visible special-purpose uses of the computer can be observed at any video arcade. *Video* games are *computer* games. Sometimes we get carried away with shooting at invading starships and forget that we are competing against a cleverly programmed special-purpose computer.

Computer-Aided Design

Computer-aided design (CAD) has revolutionized the way in which engineers and scientists design, draft, and document a product. A CAD computer system includes a graphics workstation, disk storage, and a plotter. An engineer can design a part at the workstation and produce the blueprint automatically on a plotter. By working in two or three dimensions, an engineer can manipulate the design to the desired specifications. Many CAD systems provide the added benefit of color graphics.

With CAD, most of the bugs can be worked out of a design before a prototype is built. Take as an example the design of an automobile. At the stage where it is no more than an idea in an "electronic data base," an automobile design can be put through the paces in a simulated wind tunnel and on a simulated test track. It can even be crashed into a brick wall. It's

A multifunction display panel, like the one shown in the foreground, provides pilots with tactical and navigational information during flight training. A special-purpose computer can take pilots on a simulated trip from Atlanta to Las Vegas without burning a drop of fuel.
(William Rivelli for Allied Corporation)

CAD/CAM GIVES SURGEONS A HAND . . . A FOOT . . . AN ARM

Computer-aided design and manufacturing (CAD/CAM) has given new hope to biomechanical engineers, surgeons, and recipients of artificial joints in hips, legs, and arms.

Before CAD/CAM, surgeons basically had to choose the best-fitting prosthesis item from a catalog, then modify the patient's bone structure during the implant operation.

Now, by using the patient's x-ray data, a biomechanical engineer can use an interactive graphics systems to sketch a rough design of the prosthesis right on the screen. Next, patient data, such as height, weight, and age, are entered and the system goes to work. The result is the design of a prosthesis that is right for a particular person. The prosthesis is then produced on a computer-controlled machine tool from the design specifications.

It's much easier to do test fitting electronically via a graphics system than on the operating table (especially from the patient's perspective!). In essence, this application of computers permits surgeons to design the prosthesis for the patient, and not the other way around.

a lot less expensive to crash an electronic image than the real thing! All of this is made possible with computer-aided design computers.

A CAD system is both a design tool and a laboratory. Just as the automobile design is created electronically, a wind tunnel can be created that simulates the effects of an actual wind tunnel. As an engineer alters the speed and direction of the "wind," the CAD system provides continuous feedback on drag and stability. Based on this feedback, an engineer might wish to alter the design and run the test again.

Robotics

Rudimentary Robotics.   Special-purpose computers control industrial **robots**. The integration of computers and industrial robots is called **robotics**. Contrary to what some might believe, robots are quite different in appearance and function from R2/D2 and C-3PO of *Star Wars*. The most common industrial robot is a single mechanical arm that is controlled by a computer. The arm, called a manipulator, is capable of performing the motions of a human arm. The manipulator is fitted with a "hand" that is designed for each specific task, such as painting, welding, moving parts, and so on.

A computer program is written to control the robot just as a program is written to print payroll checks. The program includes such commands as when to reach, in which direction to reach, how far to reach, when to grasp, and so on. Once programmed, robots don't need much attention. One plant manufactures vacuum cleaners 24 hours a day, seven days a week, *in total darkness*! Since the entire workforce is robots, there is no need to turn on the lights and run up the electricity bill.

An industrial robot is best at repetitive tasks, moving heavy loads, and working in hazardous areas. These types of tasks exist in virtually every kind of industry, from hospitals to cannery row. During the next decade we can anticipate that many less-desirable jobs will be relegated to robots. This concerns and affects a great many people.

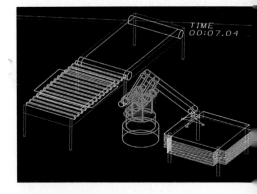

Prior to installation, the work of industrial robots is sometimes simulated on a computer-aided design system to work out the exact timing and sequencing of arm movements.
(Calma Company)

Concerns about Robots.

Few people, even robotics experts, anticipated the explosion of interest of the industrial community in robots. Most attribute this interest to the economy and to management's attempt to remain competitive by reducing cost wherever possible.

Robots will eliminate between one and two million blue collar jobs during the 1980s. However, robots are expected to create a net plus in jobs by 1995. In the meantime, unions are challenging the wisdom of replacing their workers with robots. On the other hand, management reminds workers that robots can do the same repetitive task for one-sixth of the cost. Unions cite social responsibility. Management cites competitive strategy.

As we discussed in Chapters 1 and 2, we are in transition from an industrial society to an information society. Opponents of robots may slow the pace at which workers in repetitive and hazardous tasks are replaced, but we can only conclude that robots will eventually replace human labor wherever their doing so is cost effective. We have only to review recent history to confirm this conclusion. Today's earth movers do the work of a hundred nineteenth-century laborers with shovels. In the nineteenth century, people were convinced that mechanization would eliminate needed jobs and have a negative effect on the quality of life. Today, instead, we enjoy higher employment and a higher quality of life.

A realization of the inevitable has spawned new partnerships between management, labor, and the government. For example, a research venture is underway to develop robotics devices to replace sewing machines in the garment industry. The research is sponsored by a textile workers union, private enterprise, and the U.S. Department of Commerce. They recognize that United States enterprises have traditionally flourished through technological innovation and that it is difficult for U.S. workers to compete with foreign suppliers of labor-intensive consumer goods. Perhaps all garment jobs will be lost if nothing is done. Or perhaps many jobs will be saved if high technology can be introduced into the traditionally labor-intensive garment industry.

Personal Robots.

Some manufacturers believe that robots can be just as valuable in the home as they are in industry. Several companies manufacture and sell "personal robots" that are mobile, have limited speech capability, and have arm movements similar to those of industrial robots. Personal robots will not be washing windows and doing the laundry in the immediate future, but current research by manufacturers and backyard inventors should result in some kinds of affordable and useful personal robots by 1990.

Robots in the Future.

It will be a very long time before our companions and workmates are robots. Before that happens, scientists must overcome several formidable technological hurdles. The first of these is "vision." In the present state of the art of vision systems, distinguishing between a scalpel and a band-aid would be a real challenge for a robot. Most robots are programmed to reach to a particular location and find a particular item. If robots could "see," there would be greater flexibility in the tasks they could be programmed to do.

Once robots achieve some vision capabilities, researchers will begin working on "navigation." Most robots are stationary, and those that aren't can

The HERO JR robot can speak English and "roblish" (a robot's version of English), play games, explore, wake you in the morning, and act as a security guard. HERO JR's greeting is, "I am HERO JR, your personal robot. I am your friend, companion, and security guard." Thousands of preprogrammed activities shape HERO JR's "personality." (Heath Company)

detect the presence only of an object in their path, or they are programmed to operate within a well-defined work area where the position of all obstacles is known.

Computer-Aided Manufacturing

Computer-aided manufacturing (CAM) is a term that was coined to highlight the use of computers in the manufacturing process. There are literally thousands of uses for special-purpose computers in the manufacturing environment. Robots and computer-aided design are typical CAM applications. The movements of machine tools, such as lathes and milling machines, are also controlled by a computer. Other CAM applications for special-purpose computer systems include automated materials handling and assembly-line control.

The integration of the computer with manufacturing is called **integrated CAD/CAM**. In integrated CAD/CAM, the computer is used at every stage of the manufacturing process, from the time a part is conceived until it is shipped. The various computer systems are connected and feed data to one another. An engineer uses a CAD system to design the part. Then, the design specifications are produced and stored on a magnetic disk. The specifications, now in an "electronic data base," become input to another computer system that generates programs to control the robots and machine tools, which handle and make the part. The special-purpose process-control computers are even linked to the company's general-purpose information systems computers to provide data for order processing, inventory management, shop floor scheduling, and general accounting.

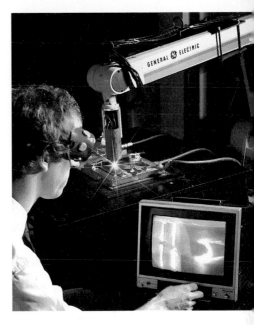

This robot has "eyes." The TV monitor in the foreground shows what is seen by the robot. This welding robot uses its sight to steer itself along irrgularly-shaped joints as it makes the weld.
(General Electric Company)

This computer-controlled materials distribution system is an example application of computer-aided manufacturing. The system helps in the handling and transportation of parts to production sites. Data gathered from this system are transmitted to another computer that monitors all manufacturing processes.
(Courtesy of International Business Machines Corporation)

5–7 COMPUTER SYSTEMS SUMMARY

There has never been a common definition for terms such as microcomputer, minicomputer, and supercomputer. Consequently, their meanings become even more obscure with each leap in technological innovation. Nevertheless, people still use these terms to refer to general classes of computers. Just remember that one person's microcomputer may be another's minicomputer.

Perhaps the most important point to be made in this chapter is this: Whether we talk about a special-purpose computer, a mainframe, a mini, or any other kind of computer system, they differ only in size and how they are applied.

SUMMARY OUTLINE AND IMPORTANT TERMS

5–1 COMPUTER SYSTEM CONCEPTS. Micros and mainframes are both computer systems, but they differ greatly in processing capabilities and in how they are used.

AUTO AUTOMATION

a.

a. Automobile designers use CAD to visualize a three-dimensional cross-section of a design from any visual perspective. They created this solid model to see how a car will look under different lighting conditions. (General Motors Corporation)

b. During testing, computers control the environment in a wind tunnel. After the test, data are analyzed to provide automobile designers with information that can lead to improvements in the aerodynamics of the test automobile. (General Motors Corporation)

c. Robots apply spotwelds to car bodies in this automobile assembly plant. They then paint every nook and crevice of the body. (GM Assembly Division, Warren, Michigan)

b.

c.

Data or hardware devices are said to be **on-line** if they are directly accessible to, and under the control of, the computer. Other data and hardware are said to be **off-line**. In **batch processing**, transactions are grouped before they are processed.

5–2 MINICOMPUTERS. The term **minicomputer**, or **mini**, emerged about 20 years ago as a name for small computers. The name has stuck, even though some of today's minis are more powerful than any computer of the 1960s. Minis now accomplish processing tasks that have been traditionally associated with mainframe computers. There is no generally accepted definition of a minicomputer.

5–3 MAINFRAME COMPUTER SYSTEMS. Besides the obvious differences in processing speed, the major difference between minicomputers and medium-to-large mainframes is the number of remote workstations that can be serviced. A computer servicing more than 100 workstations is no longer a minicomputer.

5–4 A "HOST" OF COMPUTERS. Processors used to be called central processing units, or CPUs; but today, computer systems, even micros, will normally have several processors to increase **throughput**. A

d. Engineers use thermographic tire test procedures to analyze heat buildup on tire surfaces. This enables them to design tires that resist heat, the greatest enemy of tire life. (GenCorp (formerly The General Tire & Rubber Company))

e. A navigation system pinpoints a car's location within a city block, anywhere in the world. To use the system, the driver recalls the applicable map from the car's optical laser disk storage and displays it on the tripmonitor. The car's location is then highlighted on the display. (Ford Motor Company)

f. Automated diagnostic systems are needed to help mechanics service increasingly sophisticated automobiles. (Chevron Corporation)

e.

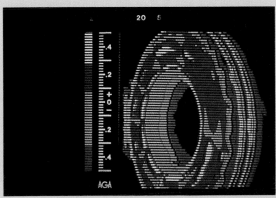
d.

f.

typical configuration might have a **host processor**, or mainframe, a **front-end processor**, and perhaps a **back-end processor** (or **data base machine**). Other special-function processors include **down-line processors**, **distributed processors**, and device processors.

5–5   INTEGRATED COMPUTER NETWORKS: COMPUTERS WORKING TOGETHER.   The trend through the 1970s was toward large centralized information services departments. The current trend is toward decentralizing people, hardware, and information systems through **distributed processing**. Distributed processing is the implementation of a **computer network** of geographically and functionally distributed computers. Distributed processing can result in more effective information processing because hardware, data, software, and personnel are closer to the people who use them.

5–6   SPECIAL-PURPOSE COMPUTER SYSTEMS. **Special-purpose computers** are designed for and usually dedicated to a specific application. Video games, **computer-aided design (CAD)**, **robotics**, and **computer-aided manufacturing (CAM)** are a few of the hundreds of applications for special-purpose computers. The social concern about the widespread implementation of industrial **robots** has spawned a partnership between management, labor, and government.

5–7   COMPUTER SYSTEMS SUMMARY.   A computer is a computer, whether it is called a PC, a mainframe, or a desktop computer. It differs only in size and how it is applied.

REVIEW EXERCISES

Concepts

1.   Give two examples each of both input hardware and output hardware.
2.   In distributed processing, what is distributed?
3.   What is meant by parallel processing?
4.   In the field of robotics, to what does "navigation" refer?
5.   Under what circumstances would it be necessary to install a parallel host?
6.   Give two examples of where a device processor would be installed.
7.   What is a dual-density disk drive?
8.   Contrast general-purpose computer systems to special-purpose computer systems.
9.   What is the purpose of the operator console in a machine room?
10. Distinguish between on-line operation and off-line operation.
11. Contrast the processing environment for mainframe computers to that of a microcomputer.

Discussion

12. Ask two people who know and have worked with computers for at least three years to describe a minicomputer. What can you conclude from their responses?
13. Discuss centralization and decentralization as they are applied to computers and information processing.
14. Discuss how special-function processors can enhance the throughput of a computer system.
15. A company retained a computer consultant to determine if they should computerize certain aspects of corporate operation. The consultant's response was, "You can't afford not to." What is the implication of the consultant's assessment?
16. Management, labor, and government are cooperating to develop robots that will surely eliminate some jobs. Why are they doing this?
17. Explain the rationale for distributed processing.

SELF-TEST (by section)

5-1. A device is said to be _____ when it is accessible to, or under the control of, the processor.
5-2. A minicomputer is the same as a personal computer. (T/F)
5-3. Each peripheral device is connected to a mainframe computer through a port. (T/F)
5-4. The data base machine or _____ processor handles tasks associated with the retrieval and manipulation of data stored on secondary storage.
5-5. The trend in organizations is to centralize all information processing activities. (T/F)
5-6. The integration of the computer with manufacturing is called integrated _____ .
5-7. There is no commonly accepted definition for a supercomputer. (T/F)

Self-Test answers. 5–1, on-line; 5–2, F; 5–3, T; 5–4, back-end; 5–5, F; 5–6, CAD/CAM; 5–7, T.

STUDENT LEARNING OBJECTIVES

- To describe how data are stored in a computer system.
- To demonstrate the relationships between bits, bytes, characters, and encoding systems.
- To translate alphanumeric data to a format for internal computer representation.
- To know why and when to use a particular numbering system.
- To explain and illustrate the principles of computer operations.
- To identify and describe the relationships between the internal components of a computer.

STUDENT LEARNING OBJECTIVES (Appendix to Chapter 6)

- To perform rudimentary arithmetic operations in the binary, octal, and hexadecimal numbering systems.

CHAPTER

6

Inside
the Computer

6-1 DATA STORAGE

In Chapter 1 we learned that *data*, not *information*, are stored in a computer system. *Data are the raw material from which information is derived, and information is data that have been collected and manipulated into a meaningful form*. To manipulate data, we must have a way to store and retrieve it.

It is easy to understand data storage in a manual system. When a customer's address changes, for example, we pull the folder, erase the old address, and write in the new one. We can see and easily interpret data that are manually kept. We cannot see or easily interpret data stored in a computer. This, of course, comes as no surprise. Data are represented and stored in a computer system to take advantage of the physical characteristics of electronics and computer hardware, not humans.

Data are stored *temporarily* during processing in a section of the computer system called **primary storage** or **main memory**. Data are stored for *permanent* storage on **secondary storage** devices, such as magnetic tape and disk drives. We discuss primary storage in detail later in this chapter. Secondary storage is covered in Chapter 7, "Data Storage Devices and Media." In this chapter we focus on the details of how data are represented internally in both primary and secondary storage, and on the internal workings of a computer.

Data are stored temporarily in primary storage during processing and permanently in secondary storage, such as magnetic tape and disk drives.

(Gerber Scientific, Inc.)

(Tandon Corporation)

6-2 A BIT ABOUT THE BIT

The computer's seemingly endless potential is, in fact, based on only two electrical states—*on* and *off*. The physical characteristics of the computer make it possible to combine these two electronic states to represent letters and numbers. An "on" or "off" electronic state is represented by a **bit**. Bit is short for *b*inary dig*it*. The presence or absence of a bit is referred to as *on-bit* and *off-bit*, respectively. In the **binary** numbering system (base 2) and in written text, the on-bit is a 1 and the off-bit is a 0.

Remember from Chapter 3 that the generations of computers were characterized by vacuum tubes, transistors, and integrated circuits. These electronic components enabled computers to distinguish between "on" and "off" and, therefore, to use binary logic.

Physically, these states are achieved in a variety of ways. In primary storage the two electronic states are represented by the direction of current flow. Another approach is to turn the circuit on or off. In secondary storage the two states are made possible by the magnetic arrangement of the ferrous oxide coating on magnetic tapes and disks.

Bits may be fine for computers, but humans are more comfortable with letters and decimal numbers (the base-10 numerals 0–9). Therefore, the letters and decimal numbers that we input to a computer system must be translated to 1s and 0s for processing and storage. The computer translates the bits back to letters and decimal numbers on output. This translation is performed so that we can recognize and understand the output, and it is made possible by encoding systems.

6-3   ENCODING SYSTEMS: COMBINING BITS TO FORM BYTES

EBCDIC and ASCII.   Computers do not talk to each other in English, Spanish, or French. They have their own languages, which are better suited to electronic communication. In these languages, bits are combined according to an **encoding system** to represent letters (**alpha** characters), numbers (**numeric** characters), and special characters (such as *, $, +, and &). For example, in the eight-bit **EBCDIC** encoding system (*E*xtended *B*inary-*C*oded *D*ecimal *I*nterchange *C*ode—pronounced EBB see dik), 11000010 represents the letter B, and 11110011 represents a decimal number 3. In the eight-bit **ASCII** encoding system (*A*merican *S*tandard *C*ode for *I*nformation *I*nterchange—pronounced AS key), a B and a 3 are represented by 01000010 and 00110011, respectively. Letters, numbers, and special characters are collectively referred to as **alphanumeric** characters.

Alphanumeric characters are *encoded* to a bit configuration on input so that the computer can interpret them. The characters are *decoded* on output so that we can interpret them. This coding, which is based on a particular encoding system, equates a unique series of bits and no-bits with a specific character. Just as the words "mother" and "father" are arbitrary English-language character strings that refer to our parents, 11000010 is an arbitrary EBCDIC code that refers to the letter B. The combination of bits used to represent a character is called a **byte** (pronounced bite). Figure 6–1 shows

DIDI DIT   DAH DAH DAH   DIDI DIT

Samuel F. B. Morse (1791–1872) recognized that two types of signals could be sent over a telegraph line. The signals were generated by pressing the transmitter lever down to close the circuit, then releasing it to break the circuit. A quick tap closed the circuit to produce a "dot"; a longer tap produced a "dash." This technique was developed into what we now call the Morse code, which combines dots and dashes to represent alphabetic and numeric characters. The EBCDIC and ASCII codes are similar in the way they combine on-bits and off-bits (1s and 0s).

The big difference between the Morse code and computer codes is the way in which they are interpreted. One is interpreted by humans and the other by computers.

Morse code is still used for wireless communication. Every seafarer knows what to do when an SOS (. . . — — — . . .) comes over the wire.

On May 24, 1844, Samuel Morse tapped out his first telegraphic message: "What Hath God Wrought!"
(Western Union Corporation)

Character	EBCDIC Code Binary Value	EBCDIC Decimal Value	ASCII Code Binary Value	ASCII Decimal Value
A	1100 0001	193	0100 0001	65
B	1100 0010	194	0100 0010	66
C	1100 0011	195	0100 0011	67
D	1100 0100	196	0100 0100	68
E	1100 0101	197	0100 0101	69
F	1100 0110	198	0100 0110	70
G	1100 0111	199	0100 0111	71
H	1100 1000	200	0100 1000	72
I	1100 1001	201	0100 1001	73
J	1101 0001	209	0100 1010	74
K	1101 0010	210	0100 1011	75
L	1101 0011	211	0100 1100	76
M	1101 0100	212	0100 1101	77
N	1101 0101	213	0100 1110	78
O	1101 0110	214	0100 1111	79
P	1101 0111	215	0101 0000	80
Q	1101 1000	216	0101 0001	81
R	1101 1001	217	0101 0010	82
S	1110 0010	226	0101 0011	83
T	1110 0011	227	0101 0100	84
U	1110 0100	228	0101 0101	85
V	1110 0101	229	0101 0110	86
W	1110 0110	230	0101 0111	87
X	1110 0111	231	0101 1000	88
Y	1110 1000	232	0101 1001	89
Z	1110 1001	233	0101 1010	90
a	1000 0001	129	0110 0001	97
b	1000 0010	130	0110 0010	98
c	1000 0011	131	0110 0011	99
d	1000 0100	132	0110 0100	100
e	1000 0101	133	0110 0101	101
f	1000 0110	134	0110 0110	102
g	1000 0111	135	0110 0111	103
h	1000 1000	136	0110 1000	104
i	1000 1001	137	0110 1001	105
j	1001 0001	145	0110 1010	106
k	1001 0010	146	0110 1011	107
l	1001 0011	147	0110 1100	108
m	1001 0100	148	0110 1101	109
n	1001 0101	149	0110 1110	110
o	1001 0110	150	0110 1111	111
p	1001 0111	151	0111 0000	112
q	1001 1000	152	0111 0001	113
r	1001 1001	153	0111 0010	114
s	1010 0010	162	0111 0011	115
t	1010 0011	163	0111 0100	116
u	1010 0100	164	0111 0101	117
v	1010 0101	165	0111 0110	118
w	1010 0110	166	0111 0111	119
x	1010 0111	167	0111 1000	120
y	1010 1000	168	0111 1001	121
z	1010 1001	169	0111 1010	122

FIGURE 6-1
EBCDIC and ASCII Codes
This figure contains the binary and decimal values for the EBCDIC and ASCII codes for commonly used alphanumeric and special characters.

Character	EBCDIC Code Binary value	EBCDIC Decimal value	ASCII Code Binary value	ASCII Decimal value
0	1111 0000	240	0011 0000	48
1	1111 0001	241	0011 0001	49
2	1111 0010	242	0011 0010	50
3	1111 0011	243	0011 0011	51
4	1111 0100	244	0011 0100	52
5	1111 0101	245	0011 0101	53
6	1111 0110	246	0011 0110	54
7	1111 0111	247	0011 0111	55
8	1111 1000	248	0011 1000	56
9	1111 1001	249	0011 1001	57
Space	0100 0000	64	0010 0000	32
.	0100 1011	75	0010 1110	46
<	0100 1100	76	0011 1100	60
(	0100 1101	77	0010 1000	40
+	0100 1110	78	0010 1011	43
&	0101 0000	80	0010 0110	38
!	0101 1010	90	0010 0001	33
$	0101 1011	91	0010 0100	36
*	0101 1100	92	0010 1010	42
)	0101 1101	93	0010 1001	41
;	0101 1110	94	0011 1011	59
,	0110 1011	107	0010 1100	44
%	0110 1100	108	0010 0101	37
—	0110 1101	109	0101 1111	95
>	0110 1110	110	0011 1110	62
?	0110 1111	111	0011 1111	63
:	0111 1010	122	0011 1010	58
#	0111 1011	123	0010 0011	35
@	0111 1100	124	0100 0000	64
'	0111 1101	125	0010 0111	39
=	0111 1110	126	0011 1101	61
''	0111 1111	127	0010 0010	34

the binary value (the actual bit configuration) and the decimal equivalent of commonly used characters in both EBCDIC and ASCII.

ASCII and EBCDIC can represent up to 256 characters (2^8). Even though the English language has considerably fewer than 128 alphanumeric characters, the extra bit configurations are needed to communicate a variety of activities, from ringing a bell to signaling the computer to accept a piece of datum.

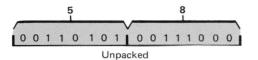 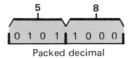

5	8
Unpacked	Packed decimal

FIGURE 6–2
Decimal 58 in ASCII
Since all numeric codes in ASCII have 0011 in the first four positions, the 0011 can be eliminated and two numeric digits can be "packed" into one byte. EBCDIC numbers are packed in a similar manner.

The Nibble.   The eight-bit structure gives these encoding systems an interesting and useful quality. Only four bit positions are needed to represent the ten decimal digits. Therefore, a single numeric digit can be stored in a half-byte, or a *nibble*, as it is sometimes called. This enables us to store data more efficiently by "packing" *two* decimal digits into one eight-bit byte (see Figure 6–2).

Since two decimal digits can be packed into one byte, a byte is not always the same as a character. Even so, the terms "byte" and "character" are often used interchangeably, with an implied understanding that some bytes may contain two numeric characters.

Parity Checking.   Within a computer system, data in the form of coded characters are continuously transferred at high rates of speed between the computer, the input/output (I/O) and storage devices, and the remote workstations. Each device uses a built-in checking procedure to help ensure that the transmission is complete and accurate. This procedure is called **parity checking**.

Logically, a byte is eight bits, but physically there are actually *nine* bits transmitted between hardware devices. Confused? Don't be. The extra **parity bit**, which is not part of the byte, is used in the parity-checking procedure to detect whether a bit has been accidentally changed, or "dropped," during transmission. A dropped bit results in a **parity error**.

To maintain *odd parity* (see Figure 6–3), the extra parity bit is turned *on* when the eight-bit ASCII byte has an *even* number of on-bits. When the ASCII byte has an *odd* number of on-bits, the parity bit is turned *off*. The receiving device checks for this condition. A parity error occurs when an even number of on-bits is encountered. Some computer systems are designed to maintain *even parity*, but both odd and even parity work in the same way.

An eight bit encoding system, with its 256 unique bit configurations, is more than adequate to represent all of the alphanumeric characters used in the English language. The Japanese, however, need a 16-bit encoding system to represent their 50,000 Kanji characters. In the photo, a Japanese journalist is using a Kanji keyboard to enter a story. (Courtesy of International Business Machines Corporation)

FIGURE 6–3
Parity Checking
The letter B is entered and transmitted to the computer for processing. Since the ASCII "B" has an even number of bits, an on-bit must be added to maintain odd parity.

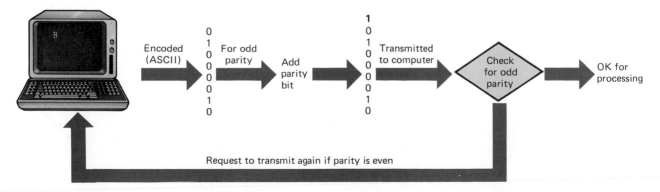

6-4   NUMBERING SYSTEMS AND COMPUTERS: WHY FOUR NUMBERING SYSTEMS?

We humans use a **decimal**, or base-10, numbering system, presumably because people have ten fingers. If we had three fingers and a thumb on each hand, as does "the Extra Terrestrial," E.T., from the popular movie, then in all probability we would be using the **octal** numbering system, which has a base of 8.

Early computers were designed around the decimal numbering system. This approach made the design of the computer logic capabilities unnecessarily complex and did not make efficient use of resources. For example, ten vacuum tubes were needed to represent one decimal digit. In 1945, as computer pioneers were struggling to improve this cumbersome approach, John von Neumann suggested that the numbering system used by computers should take advantage of the physical characteristics of electronic circuitry. To deal with the basic electronic states, "on" and "off," von Neumann suggested the use of the *binary* numbering system. His insight has vastly simplified the way that computers handle data.

Computers *operate* in binary and *communicate* to us in decimal. A special program translates decimal to binary on input, and binary to decimal on output. Under normal circumstances, a programmer would see only decimal input and output. On occasion, though, we must deal with long and confusing strings of 1s and 0s in the form of a **dump**. A dump is like a snapshot of the contents of primary storage (on-bits and off-bits) at a moment in time. To reduce at least part of the confusion of seeing only 1s and 0s on the output, the octal or the **hexadecimal** (base-16) numbering system is used as a shorthand to display the binary contents of both primary and secondary storage (see Figure 6–4).

The decimal equivalents for binary, octal, and hexadecimal numbers are shown in Figure 6–5. We know that in decimal, any number greater than 9 is represented by a sequence of digits. When you count in decimal, you "carry" to the next position in groups of 10. As you examine Figure 6–5, notice that you carry in groups of 2 in binary, in groups of 8 in octal, and in groups of 16 in hexadecimal. Also, note that *three* binary bits can be represented by one octal digit and that *four* bits can be represented by one "hex" digit.

Octal and hexadecimal numbering systems are used only for the convenience of the programmer when reading and reviewing the binary output of a dump (see Figure 6–4). Computers *do not operate or process* in these numbering systems. During the 1960s and early 1970s, programmers often had to examine the contents of primary storage to debug their programs

FIGURE 6-4
A Hexadecimal Dump
Each of the lines contains a hexadecimal representation of the contents of primary storage. The leftmost column of numbers are storage addresses. Each pair of hexadecimal digits represents the eight bits of an EBCDIC byte. The address of the first byte in the dump (29) is 0038C070 in hexadecimal or 00000000001110001100000001110000 in binary. You can see how much space is saved by displaying dumps in "hex" rather than binary.

```
38C070   29306294 4580623F D20DD0AA 62A29640   8CECCC04 88F00010 80000004 88100010   41110003 5010D064 94FCD067 D703D06C
38C0A0   D06E0610 12114770 6202D203 D09F629D   4120D121 45B06236 5820D120 413062C4   477061A6 4810D06E 41110001 4010D06E
38C0D0   1A2C44E0 60701A1E 41818001 44F06076   9640D112 455062DA 94BFD112 4810D06C   02FF1302 FFC3C9D5 C5E240E2 C1D4C540
38C100   FF0098E0 D08012EE 47806310 D27CF000   48A0D06A 4BA0D06C 88A00002 45B0623E   D12094FC D1235B00 D1201A10 5800D120
```

Binary (base 1)	Octal (base 8)	Decimal (base 10)	Hexadecimal (base 16)
000	0	0	0
001	1	1	1
010	2	2	2
011	3	3	3
100	4	4	4
101	5	5	5
110	6	6	6
111	7	7	7
1000	10	8	8
1001	11	9	9
1010	12	10	A
1011	13	11	B
1100	14	12	C
1101	15	13	D
1110	16	14	E
1111	17	15	F
10000	20	16	10

FIGURE 6–5
Numbering-System Equivalence Table

(that is, to eliminate program errors). Today's programming languages have sophisticated **diagnostics** (called error messages) and computer-assisted tools that aid programmers during program development. These diagnostics and development aids have minimized the need for applications programmers to convert binary, octal, and hexadecimal numbers to their decimal equivalents. However, if you become familiar with these numbering systems, you should achieve a better overall understanding of computers.

An appendix to this chapter, *Working with Numbering Systems*, presents the principles of numbering systems, discusses numbering-system arithmetic, and illustrates how to convert a value in one numbering system to its equivalent in another.

Each light on the console of this early third-generation computer represents a bit. A combination of four lights represents a hexadecimal character. Computer operators used these hex characters to decipher computer-generated messages and diagnose machine errors. Today's computers don't have all of the blinking lights because messages are displayed on the operator's console in plain English.
(Courtesy of International Business Machines Corporation)

MEMORY BITS			
NUMBERING SYSTEMS			
Name	**Base**	**Digits**	**Use**
Binary	2	0, 1	Computer processing
Octal	8	0–7	Programmer convenience
Decimal	10	0–9	Human input/output
Hexadecimal (hex)	16	0–9, A–F	Programmer convenience

6–5 COMPONENTS OF A COMPUTER SYSTEM: A CLOSER LOOK AT THE PROCESSOR AND PRIMARY STORAGE

Let's review. We have learned that all computers have similar capabilities and perform essentially the same functions, though some might be faster than others. We have also learned that a computer system has input, output, storage, and processing components, that the *processor* is the "intelligence" of a computer system, and that a single computer system may have several processors. We have discussed how data are represented inside a computer system in electronic states called bits. We are now ready to expose the inner workings of the nucleus of the computer system—the processor.

The internal operation of a computer, or processor, is interesting, but there really is no mystery about it. The mystery is in the minds of those who listen to hearsay and believe science fiction writers. The computer is a nonthinking electronic device that has to be plugged into an electrical power source, just like a toaster or a lamp.

Literally hundreds of different types of computers are marketed by scores of manufacturers. The complexity of each type may vary considerably, but in the end, each processor has only two fundamental sections: the *control unit* and the *arithmetic and logic unit*. *Primary storage* also plays an integral part in the internal operation of a processor. These three—primary storage, the control unit, and the arithmetic and logic unit—work together. Let's look at functions and the relationships between them.

Modern technology has taken away some of the romance associated with the computer mystique. Today's computers don't have hundreds of multicolored blinking lights and swirling tapes. The processing component of this medium-sized mainframe computer system is the box just to the left of the operator console. It has only one switch—on/off.
(Courtesy of International Business Machines Corporation)

Primary Storage

The Technology.   Unlike magnetic secondary storage devices, such as tape and disk, primary storage has no moving parts. With no mechanical movement, data can be accessed from primary storage at electronic speeds, or close to the speed of light. Most of today's computers use CMOS (*C*omplementary *M*etal *O*xide *S*emiconductor) technology for primary storage. A CMOS memory chip that is about one-fourth inch square can store about 1,000,000 bits, or over 100,000 characters of data!

But there is one major problem with semiconductor storage. When the electrical current is turned off or interrupted, the data are lost. Researchers are working to perfect a primary storage that will retain its contents after an electrical interruption. Several "nonvolatile" technologies, such as *bubble memory*, have emerged, but none has exhibited the qualities necessary for widespread application. However, bubble memory is superior to CMOS for use in certain computers. Bubble memory is highly reliable and is not susceptible to environmental fluctuations, and it can operate on battery power for a considerable length of time. These qualities make bubble memory a natural for use with industrial robots and in portable computers.

Function.   Primary storage, or main memory, provides the processor with *temporary* storage for programs and data. *All programs and data must be transferred to primary storage from an input device (such as a VDT) or from secondary storage (such as a disk) before programs can be executed or data can be processed.* Primary storage space is always at a premium; therefore, after a program has been executed, the storage space occupied by it is reallocated to another program that is awaiting execution.

Figure 6–6 illustrates how all input/output (I/O) is "read to" or "written from" primary storage. In the figure, an inquiry (input) is made on a VDT. The inquiry, in the form of a message, is routed to primary storage over a **channel** (such as a coaxial cable). The message is interpreted, and the processor initiates action to retrieve the appropriate program and data from secondary storage. The program and data are "loaded" or moved to primary storage from secondary storage. This is a *nondestructive* read process. That is, the program and data that are read reside both in primary storage (temporarily) and secondary storage (permanently). The data are manipulated accord-

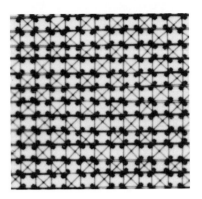

Magnetic core memory was the state of the art for primary storage during the first and second generation of computers. Each "core" in this photo could be magnetized electronically to represent a bit. Today, 16K bits of semiconductor primary storage fit in the same space as one bit of core memory. (Courtesy of International Business Machines Corporation)

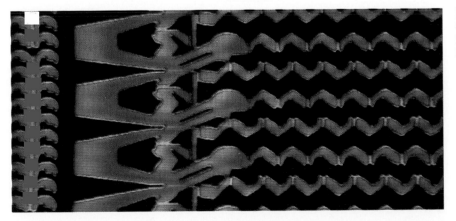

Bubble memory is magnified 5,000 times so that we can see its physical structure. (AT&T Technologies)

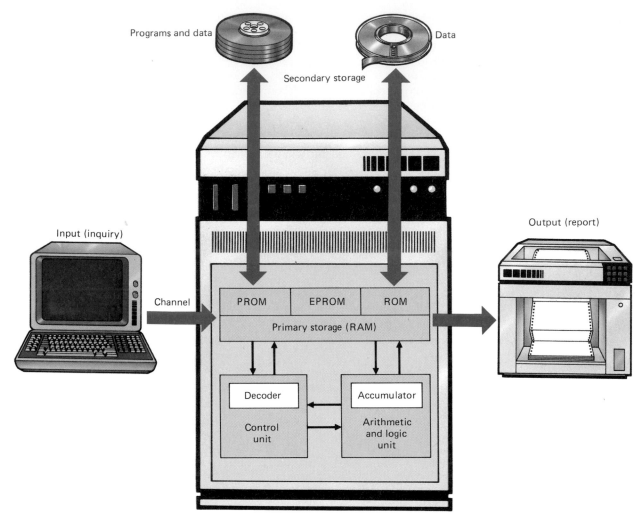

FIGURE 6-6
Interaction Between Primary Storage and Computer System Components
All programs and data must be transferred from an input device or from secondary storage before programs can be executed and data can be processed. Output is transferred to the printer from primary storage.

ing to program instructions, and a report is written from primary storage to a printer.

A program instruction or a piece of data is stored in a specific primary storage location called an **address**. These addresses permit program instructions and data to be found, accessed, and processed. The content of each address is constantly changing as different programs are executed and new data are processed.

RAM, ROM, PROM and EPROM. Another name for primary storage is **random-access memory (RAM)**. A special type of primary storage, called **read-only memory (ROM)**, cannot be altered by the programmer. The contents of the ROM are "hard-wired" (designed into the logic of the memory chip) by the manufacturer and can be "read only." When you turn on a microcomputer system, a program in ROM automatically readies the computer system for use. Then, the ROM program produces the initial display screen prompt.

A variation of ROM is **programmable read-only memory (PROM)**. PROM is ROM into which you, the user, can load "read-only" programs and data. Some microcomputer software packages, such as electronic spreadsheets, are available as PROM units as well as on diskette. Once a program is loaded to PROM, it is seldom, if ever, changed. However, if you need to be able to revise the contents of PROM, there is **EPROM**, erasable PROM.

(By permission of Anthony Cresci)

The Control Unit

Just as the processor is the nucleus of a computer system, the **control unit** is the nucleus of the processor. The control unit has three primary functions:

1. To read and interpret program instructions.
2. To direct the operation of internal processor components.
3. To control the flow of programs and data in and out of primary storage.

A program must first be loaded to primary storage before it can be executed. During execution, the first in a sequence of program instructions is moved from primary storage to the control unit where it is **decoded** and interpreted. The control unit then directs other processor components to carry out the operations necessary to execute the instruction.

The control unit contains high-speed working storage areas called **registers** that can store no more than a few bytes. They are used for a variety of processing functions. For example, registers store status information, such as the *address* of the next instruction to be executed. Because of their high speed, registers facilitate the movement of data and instructions between primary storage, the control unit, and the arithmetic logic unit.

Arithmetic and Logic Unit

The **arithmetic and logic unit** performs all computations (addition, subtraction, multiplication, and division) and all logic operations (comparisons).

Examples of *computations* include the payroll deduction for social security, the day-end inventory, the balance on a bank statement, and the like. A *logic* operation compares two pieces of data; then, based on the result of the comparison, the program "branches" to one of several alternative sets of program instructions. Let's use an inventory system to illustrate the logic operation. At the end of each day the inventory level of each item in stock is compared to a reorder point. For each comparison indicating an inventory level that falls below ($<$) the reorder point, a sequence of program instructions is executed that produces a purchase order. For each comparison indicating an inventory level at or above ($=$ or $>$) the reorder point, another sequence of instructions is executed.

The arithmetic and logic unit also does alphabetic comparisons. For example, when comparing Smyth and Smith, Smyth is evaluated as being alphabetically greater, so it is positioned after Smith.

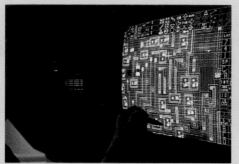

1. (TRW Inc.)

2. (Sperry Corporation)

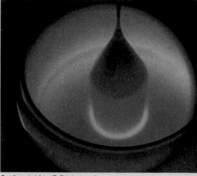

3. (© M/A-COM, Inc.)

7. (Courtesy of International Business
Machines Corporation)

8. (Courtesy of International
Business Machines Corporation)

9. (National Semiconductor Corporation)

DESIGN

1. Chips are designed and made to accomplish a particular function. One chip might be a microprocessor for a personal computer. Another might be primary storage. Another might be the logic for a talking vending machine. Chip designers use computer-aided design (CAD) systems to create the logic for individual circuits. A chip will have from one to 30 layers of circuits. In this multilayer circuit design, each layer is color coded so that the designer can distinguish between the various layers.

2. An electron-beam exposure system etches the circuitry into a glass stencil called a mask. A mask, such as this one, is produced for each circuit layer. The number of layers depends on the complexity of the chip's logic.

FABRICATION

3. Molten silicon is spun into cylindrical ingots. Because silicon, the second most abundant substance, is used in the fabrication of integrated circuits, chips are sometimes referred to as "intelligent grains of sand."

4. The ingot is shaped and prepared prior to being cut into silicon wafers. Once the wafers are cut, they are polished to a perfect finish.

5. Silicon wafers that will eventually contain several hundred chips are placed in an oxygen furnace at 1200°C. When in the furnace, the wafer is coated with other minerals to create the physical properties needed to produce transistors and electronic switches on the surface of the wafer.

6. The mask is placed over the wafer and both are exposed to ultraviolet light. In this way the circuit pattern is transferred to the wafer. Plasma technology (superhot gases) is used to permanently etch the circuit pattern into the wafer. This is one of several techniques used in the etching process. The wafer is returned to the furnace and given another coating on which to etch another circuit layer. The procedure is repeated for each circuit layer until the wafer is complete.

The 1879 invention of the light bulb symbolized the beginning of electronics. Electronics then evolved to the use of vacuum tubes, to transistors, and to integrated circuits. Today's microminiaturization of electronic circuitry is continuing to have a profound effect on the way we live and work.

These relatively inexpensive "computers on a chip" have thousands of uses, many of which we now take for granted. They are found in almost every type of modern machine, from computers to robots, from "smart" home appliances to "talking" cash registers, from car dashboards to high-flying spaceships.

Current technology permits the placement of hundreds of thousands of transistors and electronic switches on a single chip. Chips already fit into wristwatches and credit cards, but electrical and computer engineers want them even smaller. In electronics, smaller is better.

. (© M/A-COM, Inc.)

5. (Gould Inc.)

6. (AT&T Technologies)

0. (Cray Research, Inc.)   11. (Courtesy Intel Corporation)   12. (Courtesy of International Business Machines Corporation)

7. The result of the coating/etching process is a silicon wafer that contains from 100 to 400 integrated circuits.

8. It takes only a second for this instrument to drill 1,440 tiny holes in a wafer. The holes enable the interconnection of the layers of circuits. Each layer must be perfectly aligned (within a millionth of a meter) with the others.

TESTING

9. The chips are tested while they are still part of the wafer. Each integrated circuit on the wafer is powered up and given a series of tests. Fine needles make the connection for the computer-controlled tests. The precision demands are so great that as many as half of the chips are found to be defective. A drop of ink is deposited on defective chips.

PACKAGING

10. A diamond saw separates the wafer into individual chips in a process called "dicing."

11. The chips are packaged in protective ceramic or metal carriers. The carriers have standard-sized electrical pin connectors that permit the chip to be conveniently plugged into circuit boards. Because the pins tend to corrode, the pin connections are the most vulnerable part of a computer system. To avoid corrosion and a bad connection, the pins on some carriers are made of gold.

12. The completed circuit boards are installed in computers and thousands of other computer-controlled devices.

The ENIAC, first full-scale digital electronic computer weighed 50 tons and occupied an entire room. Today, a complete computer is fabricated within a single piece of silicon the size of a child's fingernail.

Chip designers think in terms of nanoseconds (1/1,000,000,000 of a second) and microns (1/1,000,000 of a meter). They want to pack as many circuit elements as they can into the structure of a chip. High-density packing re-

duces the time required for an electrical signal to travel from one circuit element to the next—the result is faster computers. Current research indicates that chips will eventually be produced that contain millions of circuit elements!

The fabrication of integrated circuits involves a multistep process using various photochemical etching and metallurgical techniques. This complex and interesting process is illustrated here with photos, from silicon to the finished product.

6-6 COMPUTER OPERATION: FITTING THE PIECES TOGETHER

Some automobiles have the engine in the front, some have it in the rear, and a few have it in the middle. It's the same with computers. Computer architecture—the way in which they are designed—varies considerably. For example, one vendor's computers might have separate primary storage areas for data and programs. In some microcomputers the *motherboard*, a single circuit board, holds the electronic circuitry for the processor, memory, and the input/output interface with the peripheral devices. A knowledge of these idiosyncrasies is not required of the user; therefore, the following example focuses on the *essentials* of computer operation.

The BASIC program in Figure 6–7 computes and displays the sum of any two numbers. BASIC is a popular programming language. Figure 6–8 illustrates how a processor works by showing the interaction among primary storage, the control unit, and the arithmetic and logic unit during the execution of the BASIC program in Figure 6–7. Primary storage in Figure 6–8 has only ten primary storage locations, and these are used only for data. In practice, both program and data would be stored in primary storage, which usually has a minimum of 64,000 storage locations.

During execution of the BASIC program, one of the numbers (5, in the example) is loaded to a register called an **accumulator**. The other number in primary storage (2, in the example) is added to the 5 in the accumulator, and the value in the accumulator becomes 7. The following statement-by-statement discussion of the BASIC program of Figure 6–7 illustrates exactly what happens as each instruction is executed.

- *Statement 10* (INPUT "INPUT NO."; X) permits the terminal operator to enter any numeric value. The control unit arbitrarily assigns the value to primary storage location *six*. In Figure 6–8, the value entered is 5. Future program references to X recall the content of the storage location whose address is *six*.

FIGURE 6–7
A BASIC Program
This program, written in the BASIC programming language, adds any two numbers and displays the sum.

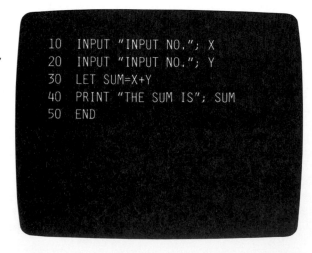

```
10   INPUT "INPUT NO."; X
20   INPUT "INPUT NO."; Y
30   LET SUM=X+Y
40   PRINT "THE SUM IS"; SUM
50   END
```

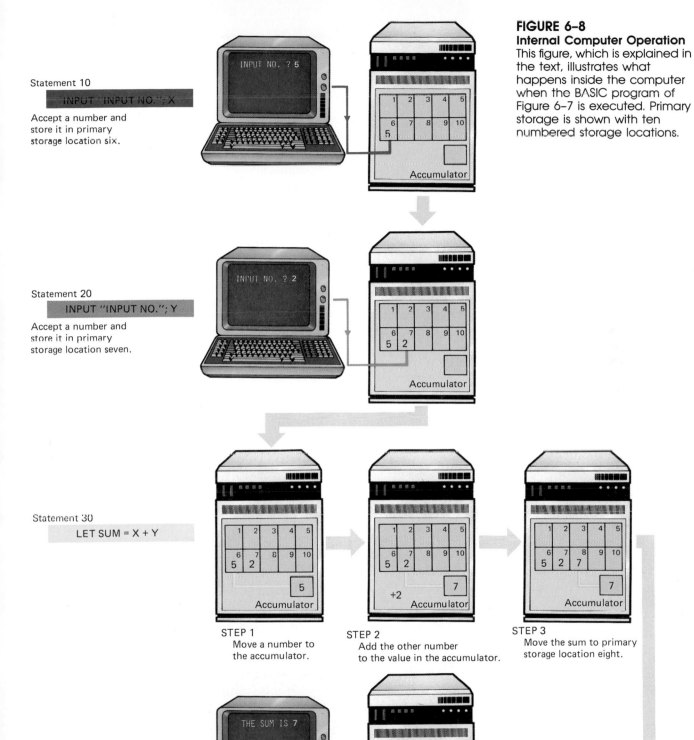

FIGURE 6–8
Internal Computer Operation
This figure, which is explained in the text, illustrates what happens inside the computer when the BASIC program of Figure 6–7 is executed. Primary storage is shown with ten numbered storage locations.

Statement 10

INPUT "INPUT NO."; X

Accept a number and store it in primary storage location six.

Statement 20

INPUT "INPUT NO."; Y

Accept a number and store it in primary storage location seven.

Statement 30

LET SUM = X + Y

STEP 1
Move a number to the accumulator.

STEP 2
Add the other number to the value in the accumulator.

STEP 3
Move the sum to primary storage location eight.

Statement 40

PRINT "THE SUM IS"; SUM

Display sum.

Statement 50

END

Terminate execution.

137

- *Statement 20* (INPUT "INPUT NO."; Y) permits the terminal operator to enter any numeric value. The control unit arbitrarily assigns the value to primary storage location *seven*. In the figure, the value entered is 2.
- *Statement 30* (LET SUM = X + Y) adds the content of location *six* to that of location *seven*. The sum is then stored in location *eight*. This addition is accomplished in three steps.

    Step 1. The 5 in location *six* is moved to the *accumulator*. The 5 remains in location *six* and the value of the *accumulator* becomes 5.

    Step 2. The content of location *seven* (value = 2) is added to the content of the *accumulator* (value = 5). The addition changes the content of the *accumulator* to 7.

    Step 3. The 7 cannot be outputted directly from the *accumulator*; therefore, the content of the *accumulator* (value = 7) is moved arbitrarily to location *eight*. The value of the *accumulator* is unchanged.
- *Statement 40* (PRINT "THE SUM IS   "; SUM) displays, on the workstation screen, "THE SUM IS " and the result of the addition (content of location *eight*), or 7 in the figure.
- *Statement 50* (END) signals the end of the program.

More complex arithmetic and I/O tasks involve further repetitions of these fundamental operations. Logic operations are similar, with values being compared between primary storage locations and registers.

6-7 DESCRIBING THE PROCESSOR: DISTINGUISHING CHARACTERISTICS

People are people, and computers are computers, but how do we distinguish one from the other? We describe people in terms of height, build, age, and so on. We describe computers or processors in terms of *speed*, the *capacity* of their associated primary storage, and the *word length*. For example, a computer might be described as a 1 MIP, 1M, 32-bit micro. Let's see what this means.

Processor Speed.   Processor speed is often measured in **MIPS**, or millions of instructions per second. The processing speed of today's large computers is in the 20 to 100 MIPS range. We even have 1 MIP micros.

Processor speed is also measured in timed intervals called **machine cycles**. Normally, several machine cycles are required to *retrieve*, *interpret*, and *execute* a single program instruction. The shorter the machine cycle, the faster the processor. Machine cycles are measured in milliseconds, microseconds, and nanoseconds—or thousandths, millionths, and billionths of a second. As technology advances, machine cycles will eventually be measured in picoseconds—or trillionths of a second.

We seldom think in time units smaller than a second; consequently it is almost impossible for us to think in terms of computer speeds. Imagine: Today's minicomputers can execute more instructions in a minute than you have had heartbeats since the day you were born!

K—MORE THAN A LETTER BETWEEN J AND L

The letter K is widely used to represent the quantity 1,000. K is an abbreviation for *kilo*, a word element meaning 1,000 (from the Greek *chilioi*, a thousand).

Some unknown person observed that 2 to the tenth power (1,024), a handy number for computer specialists, is approximately equal to 1,000. Before we knew it, 4,096 bytes became 4K bytes—and the rest is history. From that moment on, the letter K became part of comput-

erese. When a microcomputer is configured with 512K bytes of random access memory (RAM), it actually has 524,288 bytes (512 times 1024).

The use of K was picked up by the user community. Having little need for an abbreviation for 1,024, users adopted the original meaning (1,000). Company controllers often quote profits in terms of K dollars—$500K is $500,000.

Capacity of Primary Storage. The capacity of primary storage is stated in terms of the number of bytes that can be stored. As we learned earlier in this chapter, a byte is roughly equivalent to a character (such as A, 1, &).

The memory capacity of microcomputers is usually stated in terms of **K**, a convenient designation for 1024 (2^{10}) bytes of storage. The memory capacity of mainframe computers is stated in terms of millions of bytes (**megabytes or M**). Memory capacities range from 64K bytes in small micros to 128M bytes in supercomputers.

Word Length. A **word** is the number of bits that are handled as a unit for a particular computer system. The word size of modern microcomputers is normally 16 bits or 32 bits. Supercomputers have 64-bit words. Other common word lengths are 8 and 36 bits.

Now, if anyone ever asks you what a 1 MIP, 1M, 32-bit micro is, you've got the answer!

MEMORY BITS

PROCESSOR DESCRIPTION
Speed: MIPS and machine cycle
Capacity: K or M bytes
Word length: bits handled as a unit

The Cray X-MP supercomputer series has a word size of 64 bits and offers up to 1,024 megabytes of primary storage. (Cray Research, Inc.)

APPENDIX: WORKING WITH NUMBERING SYSTEMS

Section 6–4 discusses the relationships between computers and the binary, octal, decimal, and hexadecimal numbering systems. This appendix is included for those who would like to learn how to work with these numbering systems.

Principles of Numbering Systems

Binary.   The binary numbering system is based on the same principles as the decimal numbering system, with which we are already familiar. The only difference between the two numbering systems is that binary uses only two digits, 0 and 1, and the decimal numbering system uses ten digits, 0 through 9.

The value of a given digit is determined by its relative position in a sequence of digits. Consider the example in Figure 6–9. If we want to write the number 124 in decimal, the interpretation is almost automatic because of our familiarity with the decimal numbering system. To illustrate the underlying concepts, let's give Ralph, a little green eight-fingered Martian, a bag of 124 (decimal) marbles and ask him to express the number of marbles in decimal. Ralph, who is more familiar with octal, would go through the following thought process (see Figure 6–9).

- *Step One*. Ralph knows that the relative position of a digit within a string of digits determines its value, whether the numbering system is binary, octal, or decimal. Therefore, the first thing to do is to determine the value represented by each digit position.
- *Step Two*. Ralph knows that, as in any numbering system, the rightmost position has a value of the base to the zero power, or one ($10^0 = 1$). The second position is the base to the first power, or ten ($10^1 = 10$). The third position is the base squared, or 100, and so on.
- *Step Three*. Since the largest of the decimal system's ten digits is 9, the greatest number that can be represented in the *rightmost position* is 9 (9×1). The greatest number that can be represented in the *second position*, then, is 90 (9×10). In the *third position*, the greatest number is 900, and so on. Having placed the marbles in stacks of ten, Ralph knows immediately that there will be no need for a fourth-position digit (the thousands position). It is apparent, however, that a digit must be placed in the third position. Since placing a 2 in the third position would be too much ($200 > 124$), Ralph places a 1 in the third position to represent 100 marbles.
- *Step Four*. Ralph must continue to the second position to represent the remaining 24 marbles. In each successive position, Ralph wants to represent as many marbles as possible. In this case, a 2 placed in the second position would represent 20 of the remaining marbles ($2 \times 10^1 = 20$).
- *Step Five*. There are still four marbles left to be represented. This can be done by inserting a 4 in the rightmost, or "1s" position.
- *Step Six*. The combination of the three numbers in their relative position represents 124 (decimal).

In some programming languages, programmers display special characters that do not appear on the keyboard by entering the hexadecimal equivalent of their ASCII or EBCDIC code.
(Dataproducts Corporation)

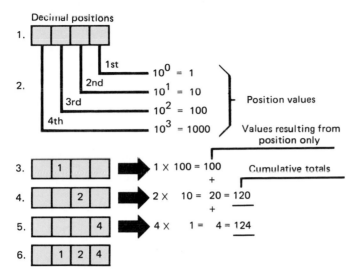

FIGURE 6–9
Numbering-System Fundamentals
Ralph, our eight-fingered Martian, who is used to counting in octal, might go through the thought process illustrated here when counting 124 marbles in decimal. Ralph's steps are discussed in the text.

Ralph would go through the same thought process if asked to represent the 124 (decimal) marbles using the binary numbering system (see Figure 6–10). To make the binary conversion process easier to follow, the computations in Figure 6–10 are done in the more familiar decimal numbering system. See if you can trace Ralph's steps as you work through Figure 6–10.

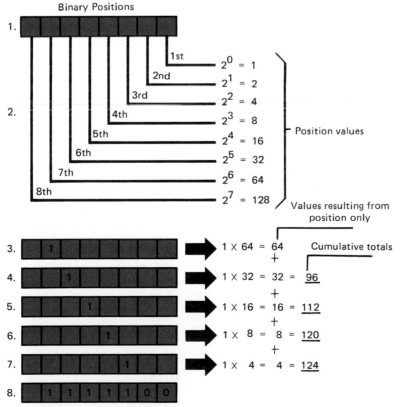

FIGURE 6–10
Representing a Binary Number
To represent 124 marbles in binary, we would follow the same thought process as we would in decimal (see Figure 6–9), but this time we have only two digits (0 and 1). For ease of understanding, the arithmetic is done in decimal.

Octal and Hexadecimal. Perhaps the biggest drawback to using the binary numbering system for computer operations is that programmers may have to deal with long and confusing strings of 1s and 0s. To reduce the confusion, octal (base-8) and hexadecimal (base-16) numbering systems are used as a shorthand to display the binary contents of primary and secondary storage.

Notice that the bases of the binary, octal, and hex numbering systems are multiples of 2: 2, 2^3, and 2^4, respectively. Because of this, there is a convenient relationship between these numbering systems. The numbering-system equivalence table of Figure 6–5 illustrates that a single hexadecimal digit represents four binary digits (e.g., $0111_2 = 7_{16}$, $1101_2 = D_{16}$, $1010_2 = A_{16}$, where subscripts are used to indicate the base of the numbering system). Notice that in hexadecimal, *letters* are used to represent the six higher-order digits.

An octal digit represents three binary digits (e.g., $111_2 = 7_8$, $010_2 = 2_8$, $101_2 = 5_8$). Two hexadecimal digits can be used to represent the eight-bit byte of an EBCDIC equals sign (=) (e.g., $01111110_2 = 7E_{16}$). Figure 6–11 illustrates how a string of EBCDIC bits can be reduced to a more recognizable form using hexadecimal.

We will examine next how to convert numbers of one numbering system to an equivalent number of another numbering system. For example, there are occasions when we might wish to convert a hexadecimal number to its binary equivalent. We shall also learn the fundamentals of numbering-system arithmetic.

FIGURE 6–11
"System" Expressed in Different Ways
The word "System" is shown as it would appear in input/output, internal binary notation, and hexadecimal notation.

Input/output (alphanumeric)	S		y		s		t		e		m	
Internal representation (binary)	1110	0010	1010	1000	1010	0010	1010	0011	1000	0101	1001	0100
Hexadecimal equivalent	E	2	A	8	A	2	A	3	8	5	9	4

Converting Numbers from One Base to Another

Decimal to Binary, Octal, or Hexadecimal. A decimal number can be easily converted to an equivalent number of any base by the use of the *division/ remainder* technique. This two-step technique is illustrated in Figure 6–12. Follow these steps to convert *decimal to binary*.

- *Step 1.* Divide the number (19, in this example) repeatedly and record the remainder of each division. In the first division, 2 goes into 19 nine times, with a remainder of 1. The remainder will always be one of the binary digits, 0 or 1. In the last division, you will be dividing 1 by the base (2) and the remainder will be 1.
- *Step 2.* Rotate the remainders as shown in Figure 6–12; the result (10011) is the binary equivalent of a decimal 19.

Figure 6–13 illustrates how the same division/remainder technique is used to convert a decimal 453 to its hexadecimal equivalent (1C5). In a *decimal-to-hex* conversion, the remainders will always be one of the 16 hex digits. In *decimal-to-octal* conversion, the divisor is 8.

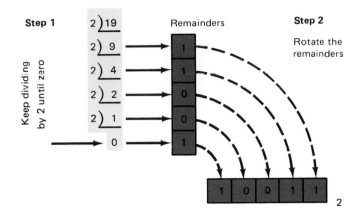

FIGURE 6–12
Converting a Decimal Number to Its Binary Equivalent
Use the two-step division/remainder technique to convert a decimal number to an equivalent number of any base.

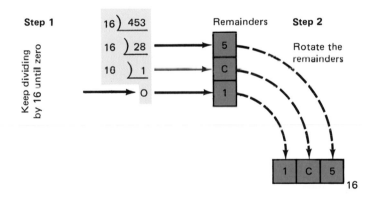

FIGURE 6–13
Converting a Decimal Number to Its Hexadecimal Equivalent
The two-step division/remainder technique is used to convert a decimal number to its hex equivalent.

Binary to Decimal, Octal, and Hexadecimal. To convert from *binary to decimal*, multiply the 1s in a binary number by their position values, then sum the products (see Figure 6–14). In Figure 6–14, for example, binary 11010 is converted to its decimal equivalent.

The easiest conversions are *binary to octal* and *binary to hex*. To convert binary to octal, simply begin with the 1s position on the right and segment the binary number into groups of three digits each, as shown in Figure 6–15. Then refer to the equivalence table of Figure 6–5 and assign each group of three binary digits an octal equivalent. Combine your result, and the conversion is complete. Go through the same procedure for binary-to-hex conversions, except segment the binary number into groups of four digits each.

Octal and Hexadecimal to Binary. Perform the above procedure in reverse to convert octal and hex numbers to binary (see Figure 6–15).

The problem:

The procedure:

FIGURE 6–14
Converting a Binary Number to Its Decimal Equivalent
Multiply the 1s in a binary number by their position values.

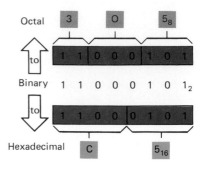

Octal

Binary

Hexadecimal

FIGURE 6–15
Converting a Binary Number to Its Octal or Hexadecimal Equivalent
Place the binary digits in groups of three or four, then convert the binary number directly to octal or hexadecimal.

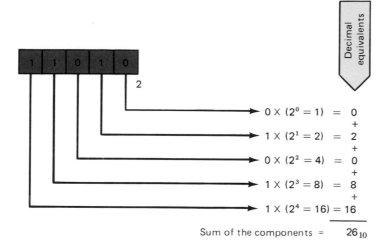

Decimal equivalents

$0 \times (2^0 = 1) = 0$
+
$1 \times (2^1 = 2) = 2$
+
$0 \times (2^2 = 4) = 0$
+
$1 \times (2^3 = 8) = 8$
+
$1 \times (2^4 = 16) = 16$

Sum of the components = 26_{10}

Hexadecimal and Octal to Decimal. Use the same procedure used for binary-to-decimal conversions (see Figure 6–14) to convert *hex to decimal* and *octal to decimal*. Figure 6–16 demonstrates the conversion of a hex 3E7 to its decimal equivalent of 999.

Arithmetic in Binary, Octal, and Hexadecimal. The essentials of decimal arithmetic operations have been drilled into us so that we do addition and subtraction almost by instinct. We do binary arithmetic, as well as that of other numbering systems, in the same way we do decimal arithmetic. The only difference is that we have fewer (binary) or more (hexadecimal) digits to use. Figure 6–17 illustrates and compares addition and subtraction in decimal with that in binary, octal, and hex. Notice in Figure 6–17 that you carry to, and borrow from, adjacent positions just as you do in decimal arithmetic.

FIGURE 6–16
Converting a Hexadecimal Number to Its Decimal Equivalent
Multiply the digits in a hexadecimal number by their position values.

The problem: $3E7_{16} = ?_{10}$

The procedure:

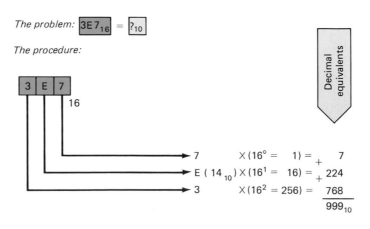

Decimal equivalents

$7 \qquad \times (16^0 = 1) = 7$
+
$E\ (14_{10}) \times (16^1 = 16) = 224$
+
$3 \qquad \times (16^2 = 256) = 768$
$\overline{\qquad\qquad 999_{10}}$

	Binary	Octal	Decimal	Hexadecimal
Addition	1111100 + 10010 10001110	174 + 22 226	124 + 18 142	7C + 12 8E
Subtraction	1111100 - 10010 1101010	174 - 22 152	124 - 18 106	7C - 12 6A

FIGURE 6–17
Binary, Octal, Decimal, and Hexadecimal Arithmetic Comparison
As you can see, the only difference in doing arithmetic in the various numbering systems is the number of digits used.

SUMMARY OUTLINE AND IMPORTANT TERMS

6–1 DATA STORAGE. Data, not information, are stored in a computer system. Data are stored temporarily during processing in **primary storage** or **main memory** and permanently on **secondary storage** devices, such as magnetic tape and disk drives.

6–2 A BIT ABOUT THE BIT. The two electronic states of the computer are represented by a **bit**, short for **binary** digit. Letters and decimal numbers are translated to bits for storage and processing on computer systems.

6–3 ENCODING SYSTEMS: COMBINING BITS TO FORM BYTES. **Alphanumeric** characters are represented in computer storage by combining strings of bits to form unique bit configurations for each character. Characters are translated to these bit configurations, also called **bytes**, according to a particular coding scheme, called an **encoding system**. Popular encoding systems include **ASCII** and **EBCDIC**.

Parity-checking procedures ensure that data transmission between hardware devices is complete and accurate.

6–4 NUMBERING SYSTEMS AND COMPUTERS: WHY FOUR NUMBERING SYSTEMS?. The two primary numbering systems used in conjunction with computers are binary and **decimal**. Decimal is translated to binary on input and binary is translated to decimal on output. The **octal** and **hexadecimal** numbering systems are used primarily as a programmer convenience in reading and reviewing binary output.

6–5 COMPONENTS OF A COMPUTER SYSTEM: A CLOSER LOOK AT THE PROCESSOR AND PRIMARY STORAGE. The processor is the "intelligence" of a computer system. A processor has two fundamental sections, the **control unit** and the **arithmetic and logic unit**, which work together to execute programs. The control unit interprets instructions and directs the arithmetic and logic unit to perform computation and logic operations.

Primary storage, or **RAM**, provides the processor with temporary storage for programs and data. All input/output, including programs, must enter and exit primary storage. Other types of internal storage are **ROM**, **PROM**, and **EPROM**.

6–6 COMPUTER OPERATION: FITTING THE PIECES TOGETHER. Data are passed between primary storage and the **accumulator** of the arithmetic and logic unit for both computation and logic operations.

6–7   DESCRIBING THE PROCESSOR: DISTINGUISHING CHARACTERIS-
      TICS. A processor is described in terms of its speed and primary
      storage capacity. There are no standard measures for speed or pri-
      mary storage capacity; therefore, general computer descriptions must
      be kept in perspective. Speed is measured in **MIPS** and by timed
      intervals called **machine cycles**. Memory capacity is measured in
      K or **M** bytes.
          The **word** size of computers ranges from 16 bits for the smaller
      micros to 64 bits for supercomputers.

APPENDIX: WORKING WITH NUMBERING SYSTEMS

The only difference between the decimal numbering system and the
other numbering systems that are associated with computers is the
number of digits each numbering system has.

Use the division/remainder technique to convert decimal to binary, octal, or hexadecimal. Convert binary, hex, and octal to decimal
by summing the decimal equivalent of the respective position values.
Convert octal and hex to binary and the reverse by working with
binary digits in groups of three and four, respectively. The mechanics
of arithmetic operations is the same for all numbering systems.

REVIEW EXERCISES

Concepts

1. What is the base of the following numbering systems: Binary? Octal?
   Hexadecimal? Decimal? What is the significance of each with respect
   to computers?
2. Distinguish between RAM, ROM, PROM, and EPROM.
3. How many EBCDIC bytes can be stored in a 32-bit word?
4. Which two functions are performed by the arithmetic and logic unit?
5. List examples of alpha, numeric, and alphanumeric characters.
6. Write your first name as an ASCII bit configuration, first in binary,
   then in hexadecimal. Do it again in binary, but this time include
   parity bits where appropriate to maintain an odd parity.
7. What are the functions of the control unit?
8. What advantage does the use of a nibble offer when using the ASCII
   or EBCDIC encoding system?
9. We describe computers in terms of what three characteristics?
10. (Appendix exercise) Convert the following binary numbers to their
    decimal, octal, and hexadecimal equivalents.

    a. 1001   **d.**   1110   **g.**   111   **j.** 110110110
    b. 11100 **e.** 110101 **h.**   10   **k.** 11111111
    c. 101   **f.**   11   **i.** 110001   **l.** 10000001

11. (Appendix exercise) Convert the following octal and hexadecimal
    numbers to their binary equivalents.

Octal		Hexadecimal	
a.	2	**e.**	A
b.	47	**f.**	2E
c.	651	**g.**	389
d.	22	**h.**	CB

12. (Appendix exercise) Express the number of people in your class in binary, octal, decimal, and hexadecimal.

13. (Appendix exercise) Write the numbers expressing 25_{10} to 35_{10} in binary, octal, and hexadecimal.

14. (Appendix exercise) Perform the following arithmetic operations:

   a. $101_2 + 11_2$
   b. $734_8 - 6_8$
   c. $A1_{16} + BC_{16} + 10_{16}$
   d. $60_{10} + F1_{16} - 1001001_2$
   e. $11_2 + 27_8 + 93_{10} - B_{16}$

Discussion

15. The letter K is used to represent 1,024 bytes of storage. Would it not have been much easier to let K represent 1,000 bytes? Explain.

16. Millions of bytes of data are transferred routinely between computing hardware devices without any errors in transmission. Very seldom is a parity error detected. In your opinion, is it worth all the trouble to add and check parity bits every time a byte is transmitted from one device to another? Why?

17. Create a five-bit encoding system that is used for storing upper-case alpha characters, punctuation symbols, and the apostrophe. Discuss the advantages and disadvantages of your encoding system relative to the ASCII encoding system.

SELF-TEST (by section)

6-1. _____ are the raw material from which _____ is derived.

6-2. Bit is the singular for byte. (T/F)

6-3. The combination of bits used to represent a character is called a

   _____ .

6-4. A dump is a snapshot of the contents of primary storage at a moment in time. (T/F)

6-5. Data are loaded from secondary to primary storage in a nondestructive read process. (T/F)

6-6. A single BASIC program instruction can cause several internal operations to take place. (T/F)

6-7. The word length of most microcomputers is 64 bits. (T/F)

App. A decimal 92 is the equivalent of an octal 5C. (T/F)

Self-Test answers. 6–1, Data, information; 6–2, F; 6–3, byte; 6–4, T; 6–5, T; 6–6, T; 6–7, F; App., F.

STUDENT LEARNING OBJECTIVES

- To distinguish between primary and secondary storage.
- To distinguish between secondary storage devices and secondary storage media.
- To describe the principles of operation, methods of data storage, and use of magnetic disk drives.
- To describe the principles of operation, methods of data storage, and use of magnetic tape drives.
- To discuss the applications and use of optical laser disk storage.

CHAPTER 7

Data Storage Devices and Media

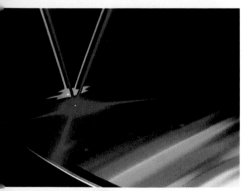

(Storage Technology Corporation)

The most common secondary storage devices are the magnetic disk drive and magnetic tape drive. However, for certain applications, optical laser disk storage technology is emerging as a viable alternative to disk and tape storage.

7-1 SECONDARY STORAGE: PERMANENT DATA STORAGE

Within a computer system, programs and data are stored in *primary storage* and in *secondary storage* (see Figure 7–1). Programs and data are stored *permanently* for periodic retrieval in **secondary storage**, also called **auxiliary storage**. Programs and data are retrieved from secondary storage and stored *temporarily* in high-speed primary storage for processing. If an employee's address is updated during processing, the personnel master file on secondary storage is updated to reflect the change.

You might ask, why two types of storage? Remember from Chapter 6, "Inside the Computer," that most primary storage is semiconductor memory, and the data are lost when the electricity is interrupted. Primary storage also is expensive and has a limited capacity. Even a small company would require many times the capacity of the largest available primary storage (128M) for permanent storage of their programs and data. Secondary storage, however, is relatively inexpensive and has an enormous capacity.

Over the years, manufacturers have developed a variety of devices and media for the permanent storage of data and programs. *Paper tape*, *punched cards*, the *data cell*, and a variety of others have become obsolete. Today, the various types of **magnetic disk drives** and their respective storage media are the state of the art for on-line storage of programs and data. **Magnetic tape drives** complement magnetic disk storage by providing inexpensive backup capability and off-line storage. In this chapter we focus on the terminology, principles, operation, and trade-offs of these secondary storage devices. We will also discuss the potential and applications of the emerging **optical laser disk** technology.

FIGURE 7-1
Primary and Secondary Storage
Programs and data are stored permanently in secondary storage and temporarily in primary storage.

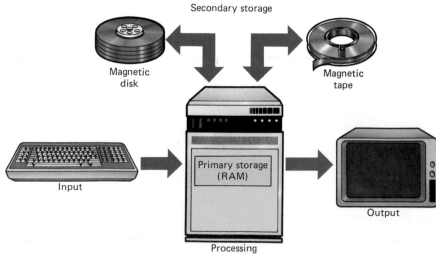

ANNUAL REPORT TAKES NEW TWIST

Intelligent Systems Corporation of Norcross, Georgia, tried something new with its annual report to shareholders. The shareholders received not only a printed annual report, but also a software diskette. The diskette supplements the traditional report by providing text and color graphics—and it's interactive and user friendly!

The program provides a menu of items and presents financial data in spreadsheet and graphic formats. The diskette report is divided into three main sections: financial, which includes graphs and statistical highlights of the written report; operations, which displays facts about the company's organizations and products; and research, which gives information on the company's products.

This concept could eventually lead to the transmission of annual reports and financial updates via data communications directly to shareholders' home computers.

Annual report with supplemental software diskette.
(Intelligent Systems Corporation)

7-2 SEQUENTIAL AND DIRECT ACCESS: NEW TERMS FOR OLD CONCEPTS

An important consideration in both the design of an information system and the purchase of a computer system is the way that data are accessed. Magnetic tape is for **sequential access** only. Magnetic disks have **random-** or **direct-access** capabilities as well as sequential access capabilities. You are quite familiar with these concepts, but you may not realize it. The magnetic tape is operationally the same as the one in home and car tape decks. Let's use a phonograph record as the basis of comparison for the magnetic disk.

Suppose you have the Beatles' classic record album *Sgt. Pepper's Lonely Hearts Club Band*. The first four songs from this record are: (1) "Sgt. Pepper's Lonely Hearts Club Band," (2) "With a Little Help from My Friends," (3) "Lucy in the Sky with Diamonds," and (4) "Getting Better." Now suppose you also have this Beatles' album on a tape cassette. To play the third song on the cassette, "Lucy in the Sky with Diamonds," you would wind the tape forward and search for it "sequentially." To play "Lucy in the Sky with Diamonds" on the phonograph record, all you would have to do is move the needle "directly" to the track containing the third song. This simple analogy demonstrates the two fundamental methods of storing and accessing data—*sequential* and *random*. Both methods are discussed in detail in the pages that follow.

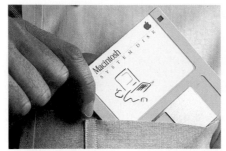

There are four types of interchangeable magnetic disk storage media. (a) The rigid $3\frac{1}{2}$ inch microdisks can fit in a shirt pocket. (b) Diskettes, also called floppy or flexible disks, come in two sizes: $5\frac{1}{4}$ inch and 8 inch. (c) Disk cartridges, which come in a variety of shapes and sizes, normally have a single disk and two recording surfaces. (d) These magnetic disk packs have 11 disks with 20 recording surfaces.

a. (Courtesy of Apple Computer, Inc.)   b. (AT&T Technologies)

c. (BASF Systems Corporation)   d. (BASF Systems Corporation)

7–3 MAGNETIC DISKS

Hardware and Storage Media

Magnetic disk drives are secondary storage devices that provide a computer system with **random** *and* **sequential processing** capabilities. In random processing, the desired programs and data are accessed *directly* from the storage medium. In sequential processing, the computer systems must search through the storage medium to find the desired programs or data.

Since magnetic disk storage is used almost exclusively for direct access, and magnetic tape storage is only sequential access, random processing is discussed in this section with magnetic disks, and sequential processing is discussed in the next section with magnetic tape.

Because of its random and sequential processing capabilities, magnetic disk storage is the overwhelming choice of both micro and mainframe users. A variety of magnetic disk drives (the hardware device) and magnetic disks (the media) are manufactured for different business requirements. The different types of *interchangeable* magnetic disks are shown in the accompanying photographs. In order of increasing storage capacity, they are the $3\frac{1}{2}$-inch **microdisk**, the $5\frac{1}{4}$-inch **diskette**, the 8-inch diskette, the **disk cartridge**, and the **disk pack**. In contrast to the flexible diskettes, or "floppies," the microdisk, disk cartridge, and disk pack are hard or rigid disks.

Not all disk storage media are interchangeable. In fact, the trend is to permanently installed or *fixed* disks (see photos). All fixed disks are rigid. Today, integrated software and data bases require all data and programs to be on-line at all times. In the past, interchangeable disks containing certain files and programs were taken from the shelf and loaded to the disk drives as needed.

Random Processing

ALL↓

Magnetic disks are used for information systems where the data must be accessed directly or where the data are on-line. An airline reservation system provides a good example of this need. Direct-access capability is required to retrieve the record for any flight at any time from any reservations office. The data must be current, or flights may be overbooked or underbooked. Because of the random nature of the reservations data, magnetic tape cannot be used as a storage medium for this type of system.

File and data base organization for random processing, also called **direct processing**, and sequential processing are discussed in detail in Chapter 11, "Data Organization and File Processing."

Principles of Operation

Disk Organization. The manner in which data are organized is similar for interchangeable and fixed hard disks. First we'll focus on hard disks, then discuss how floppy disks differ from hard disks. The hard-disk storage medium for a single drive may consist of one or a stack of several metal platters, each with a thin film coating of cobalt or iron oxide. The thin film coating on the disk can be electronically magnetized by the *read/write* head to represent the absence or presence of a bit (0 or 1). Data are recorded **serially** in concentric circles called *tracks* by magnetizing the surface to represent bit configurations (see Figure 7–2).

The disk spins continuously at a high speed, typically 3,600 revolutions per minute. The rotational movement of the disk passes all data under/over

"20 megabyte hard disk? Yeah, that'd be nice but we'd have to invent the wheel first."
(By permission of Brian Hansen)

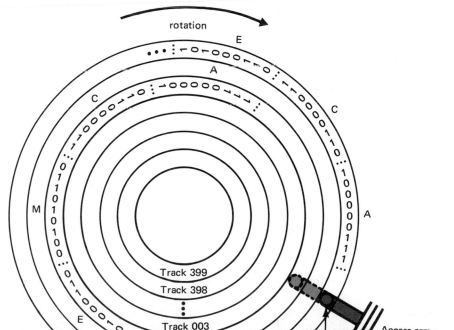

FIGURE 7–2
Top View of a Magnetic Disk with Cylinder Organization
Data are read or written serially in tracks. In the figure, the read/write head is first positioned over cylinder 000, then moved to cylinder 002 to access the record for the ACME company.

The trend in disk storage is toward permanently-installed storage media. The access arms for this fixed disk move the read/write heads to the appropriate track to retrieve the data.
(International Memories, Inc.)

a read/write head, thereby making all data available for access on each revolution of the disk.

Disk drives contain a rigid disk with one to 20 metal platters. To illustrate, we will use 11 platters, a common number. Data are stored on all *recording surfaces* except for those surfaces on the top and bottom of the stack. For a disk with 11 platters, this makes 20 recording surfaces on which data can be stored. A disk drive will have at least one read/write head for each recording surface. The heads are mounted on **access arms** that move in tandem and, literally, float on a cushion of air over the spinning recording surfaces. The tolerance is so close that a particle of smoke from a cigarette will not fit between the read/write head and the recording surface. This is reason number one why computer operators display "No Smoking" signs in the machine room.

To read or write a record, the access arms are moved under program control to the appropriate *cylinder*. Collectively, the cylinder references all *tracks* of the same number. For example, each recording surface has a track numbered 002 and the disk has a cylinder numbered 002. If the record to be accessed is on recording surface 03, track 002, then the access arm and the read/write heads for all 20 recording surfaces are moved to cylinder 002.

In Figure 7–2, the access arm is positioned over track 000 (cylinder 000). In this position, the ACE Company record or any other record on cylinder 000 can be accessed without further movement of the access arm. If the ACME Company record is to be read, the access arm must be positioned over track 002 (cylinder 002) until the ACME record passes under the read/ write head.

Fortunately, the software automatically monitors the location or **address** of our files and programs. We need only enter someone's name to retrieve his or her personnel record. The computer system locates the record and

NO SMOKING!

"No Smoking" signs are commonplace in computer-center machine rooms, and for good reason. The average smoke particle is approximately 250 millionths of an inch in diameter. For rigid disks, the head flying distance (the distance between the read/write head and the disk surface) is usually less than half the diameter of an average smoke particle. A simple comparison reconfirms one of the first rules of data processing: Don't smoke in the machine room.

Smoke and other such foreign matter on the surface of a disk may result in a disk "crash." After a disk crash, data on the disk are extremely difficult, and sometimes impossible, to retrieve.

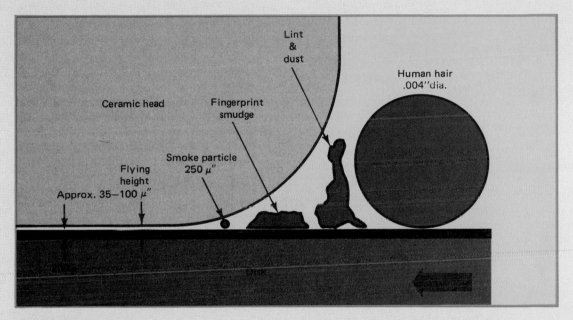

Head Flying Distance. When the disk is spinning at 3,600 rpm (revolutions per minute), the surface of the disk travels across the read/write head at approximately 140 mph (miles per hour).
(© 1982 by Digital Equipment Corporation)

loads it to primary storage for processing. Although the addressing schemes vary considerably between disks, the address will normally reference the *cylinder*, the *recording surface*, and the *relative position* of a record on a track (e.g., the fourth record).

Access Time. The **access time** is the interval of time between the instant when a computer makes a request for a transfer of data from a secondary storage device and the instant when this operation is completed. The access of data from primary storage is at electronic speeds, or approximately the speed of light. But the access of data from secondary storage depends on mechanical apparatus. Any mechanical movement significantly increases the access time.

MEMORY BITS

DISK ACCESS TIME =
- Seek time +
- Rotational delay time +
- Transmission time

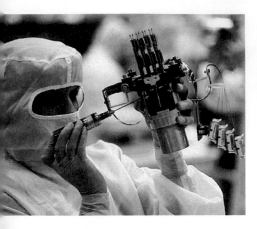

Magnetic disk drives are manufactured in clean rooms that are 1000 times cleaner than operating rooms in hospitals. This technician is making final adjustments to the access arm mechanism before it is installed in the disk drive.
(Courtesy of International Business Machines Corporation)

FIGURE 7–3
Top View of a Magnetic Disk with Sector Organization
Photoelectric cells sense light as it passes through the index hole in sector 0. This feedback enables the computer to monitor which sector is over the read/write head at any given time. The number of sectors that a disk has varies from 1 to 32, depending on the computer system. As in cylinder organization, data are read or written serially in tracks, within a given sector.

The *seek time*, which comprises the greatest amount of the total access time, is the time it takes the mechanical access arm to move to the desired cylinder. Some disk drives have two access arms, one for reading and writing on the inside tracks and another for the outside tracks. With two access arms the average seek time is significantly reduced, because the access arms have less distance to move, and one can move while the other is reading or writing.

The *rotational delay time* is the time it takes for the appropriate record to be positioned under the read-write head. On the average, this would be half the time it takes for one revolution of the disk, or about 8 milliseconds at 3,600 rpm. The *transmission time*, or the time that it takes to transmit the data to primary storage, is negligible. The average access time for most hard-disk drives is less than 20 milliseconds—still very slow when compared with the microsecond-to-nanosecond processing speeds of computers.

Sector Disk Organization

Floppy disks and some rigid disks use **sector organization** to store and retrieve data. Sector organization is similar to the cylinder-type organization, except that each recording surface is divided into sectors, often 16 (see Figure 7–3). Each sector is assigned a unique number; therefore, the *sector number* and *track number* are all that is needed to comprise an address. Again,

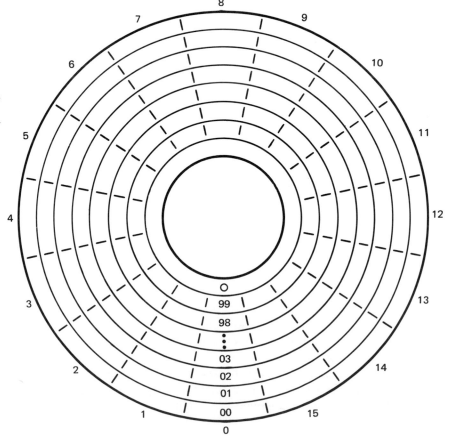

Each of these Winchester disks, a name given to disk drives containing a small fixed disk for low-volume data storage, has two read/write heads for each surface. The smaller one is called a half-height Winchester because two of them can fit into the standard-sized space (3.25 × 5.75 × 8 inches) allotted for a floppy or Winchester drive. The Winchester drive, which is very popular in microcomputers, is named after the 30-30 Winchester rifle. The early drives had two 30 megabyte disks—thus the nickname, Winchester. (Seagate Technology)

you need not be concerned about a file or program's physical address. The system handles all the details for you.

Unlike rigid disks, which are constantly spinning, the floppy is set in motion only when a command is issued to read or write to disk. Rigid disks are preferred for applications that demand frequent disk activity.

Disk Summary

As you can see from this discussion and the accompanying photos, disks come in a wide variety of shapes and storage capacities. The type used would depend on the volume of data that you have and the frequency with which those data are accessed. All types of disks are available for both micros and mainframes; however, most micros use microdisks, floppies, or small fixed disks, called *Winchester disks*. To facilitate system design and to increase throughput, most computer systems, small and large, will have two or more disk drives.

Magnetic disks range in storage capacity from low-capacity floppy disks that can store about 320,000 characters to very high-density rigid disks that can store over 30 million characters on one square inch of recording surface. That's the text of this and 30 other books on a space the size of a postage stamp!

The traditional 10½ inch tape reel is contrasted with the high-density tape cartridge. The much smaller cartridge can store 200 million characters, about 20% more than the reel! (Courtesy of International Business Machines Corporation)

7-4 MAGNETIC TAPE

Hardware and Storage Media

The device on which a **reel** or **cassette** of magnetic tape (the storage medium) is mounted and processed is known as a tape drive. The mechanical operation of a magnetic tape drive is similar to that of a reel-to-reel or cassette audio tape deck. A thin mylar tape passes under a **read/write head** and the data are either (1) read and transmitted to primary storage or (2) transmitted from primary storage and written to the tape.

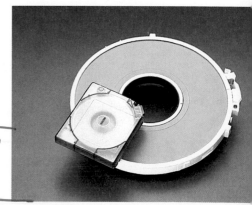

In most data centers, magnetic tapes are manually mounted. The alternative is an automated tape library. Under computer control, the automated tape library retrieves the appropriate tape from the library and mounts it on a tape drive for processing. The tape is automatically returned to the library at the end of the job.
(Braegen)

A tape drive is rated by the **density** at which the data can be stored on a magnetic tape as well as by the speed of the tape as it passes under the read/write head. Combined, these determine the **transmission rate**, or the number of characters per second that can be transmitted to primary storage. Tape density is measured in **bytes per inch (bpi)** or the number of bytes (characters) that can be stored per linear inch of tape. Tape density varies from 1,600 bpi to 20,000 bpi. A 6,250-bpi tape, a common density, traveling under the read/write head at 300 inches per second is capable of a transmission rate of 1,875,000 characters per second.

The $\frac{1}{2}$-inch wide tape reel comes in a variety of lengths, the most common being 2,400 feet. The capacity of a tape is equal to the tape density (bpi) times the length of the tape (in inches). A 6,250-bpi, 2,400-foot (28,800-inch) tape has a capacity of approximately 180 megabytes (million bytes). One hundred and eighty megabytes sounds like ample storage for just about anything, but this is not the case. For example, over 100 such tapes would be required to store just the names and addresses of people in the United States. The tape library at the U.S. Internal Revenue Service contains over 500,000 reels!

Sequential Processing

Magnetic tape storage is used primarily as a backup medium for magnetic disk. A reel or cassette tape can be conveniently mounted to a tape drive for processing, then removed for off-line storage. A cassette is also called a **cartridge**. For backup, a tape is taken from off-line storage, mounted to a tape drive, and the contents of a disk file are "dumped" from the disk to the tape. The tape is removed and placed in off-line storage as a backup to the operational disk master file. Details of backup procedures are discussed and illustrated in Chapter 11, "Data Organization and File Processing."

Although disk storage is the choice of most users for data storage and information processing activities, some mainframe users prefer magnetic tape files for some *sequential processing* jobs because it is conceptually simple and an inexpensive storage medium. Because of the physical nature of magnetic tapes, files must be processed sequentially from beginning to end for each computer run. For example, payroll checks are often processed sequentially. The hours-worked data are entered and stored on magnetic tape, then sorted by employee number. The "transaction tape" is processed sequentially against a sorted employee master file to produce the payroll checks.

On any given computer run, a *single* tape is either input or output, not both. One tape, however, can be just an input tape and another just an output tape. Sequential processing is discussed in detail in Chapter 11, "Data Organization and File Processing."

Principles of Operation

The principles of tape data storage are illustrated in Figure 7–4. The thin film coating of the tape is electronically magnetized by the read/write head to form bit configurations. In EBCDIC, eight bits (the EBCDIC code) plus the parity bit are needed to represent a character. Each of the nine bits is

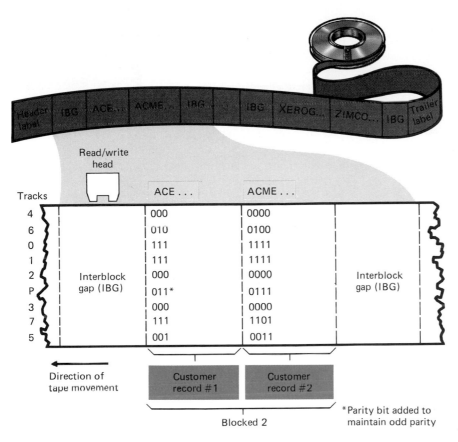

FIGURE 7–4
Cross Section of a Magnetic Tape
This cross section of magnetic tape contains two records from a customer master file. Those tracks in which an "on" bit appears most often (0, 1, 2, P, 3) are clustered in the center of the tape. Those tracks that are least likely to be magnetized to an "on" bit (4, 6, 7, 5) are placed toward the outside so that the data on a tape with damaged edges are less likely to be affected. The tape travels past the write head, then the read head. This enables the computer to read and check the data immediately after they are written to the tape.

stored in one of nine *tracks* that run the length of the tape. In the nine-track tape of Figure 7–4, characters are represented by parallel EBCDIC bit configurations. This method of storing data in adjacent bit configurations is known as **parallel representation**. Compare this parallel representation with the serial representation of magnetic disks in Figure 7–2.

Figure 7–4 portrays a cross section of a magnetic tape that contains a *customer master file*. The data relating to each customer are grouped and stored in a *customer record*. The records are stored *alphabetically by customer name* (from ACE, ACME, . . . , to ZEROG, ZIMCO).

Records are usually grouped in blocks of two or more, separated by an **interblock gap (IBG)**. The IBGs not only signal a stop to the reading process but also provide some margin for error in the rapid *start/stop* operation of the tape drive.

Blocking permits additional records to be transmitted with each "read" or "write." Each time the computer is instructed to read from a magnetic tape, all data between adjacent interblock gaps are transmitted to primary storage for processing. The next read transmits the next **block** of records to primary storage. When the computer is instructed to write to a tape, the data are transmitted from primary storage to the tape drive. Then, a block of data and an IBG are written to the tape.

In Figure 7–4, the records have a blocking factor of two and are said to be "blocked two." Figure 7–5 shows how the same file would appear

Photomicrography techniques are used to show how bits are recorded in parallel on a nine-track magnetic tape.
(AT&T Technologies)

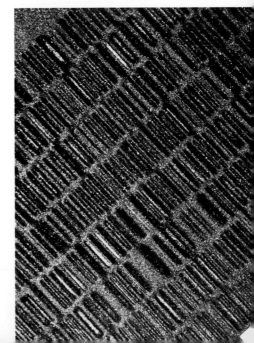

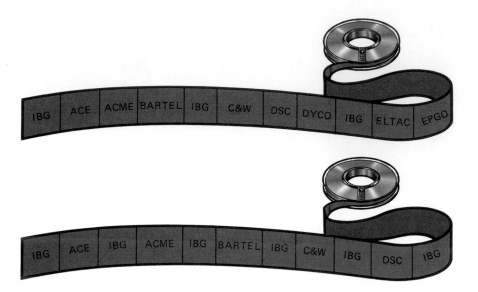

FIGURE 7–5
Customer Records Blocked Three (top) and Unblocked (bottom)

blocked three and unblocked. Notice how the tape blocked three contains more records per linear length of the tape.

To signal the beginning and end of a particular tape file, the computer adds a **header label** and a **trailer label**, respectively. The header label contains the name of the file and the date it was created. The trailer label is written at the end of the data file and contains the number of records in the file (see Figure 7–4).

Streamers: Writing on the Fly

In the past, the simplicity and lower cost of magnetic tape processing often made it preferable to magnetic disk processing. This is no longer true, and today, for the most part, magnetic tape is used for backup. During backup or recovery runs, backup tapes are processed continuously from beginning to end. Since there is seldom a requirement for selective access of records from magnetic tape, there is no reason to start and stop the tapes.

Streamer tape drives record data in a continuous stream, thereby eliminating the need for the start/stop operation of earlier tape drives. Having no start/stop mechanisms, streamer tape drives can store data much more effi-

A tape librarian selects the appropriate tape cartridges from the tape library and delivers them to a computer center. A computer operator inserts the tape cartridges in one or several of the eight tape drives (foreground) for processing.
(Courtesy of International Business Machines Corporation)

An alternative to disk and tape storage is the mass storage device. Mass storage devices are used when on-line access is required for very large data bases. A half trillion characters of data can be stored in this mass storage device. Inside, data cartridges are retrieved from honeycomb-like storage bins and loaded to the read/write station for processing. (Courtesy of International Business Machines Corporation)

ciently than the traditional tape drives that stop, then start the tape's movement over the read/write head at each IBG. Because streamer tape drives store IBGs on the fly, an IBG occupies only $\frac{1}{100}$ inch, as compared to over $\frac{1}{2}$ inch for start/stop tape drives. Streamer tape drives use that "extra" $\frac{1}{2}$ inch to store as many as 10,000 more characters of data. Streamer tape drives use 97% of the tape for data storage, whereas traditional start/stop tapes use only 35% to 70%, depending on the blocking factors.

MEMORY BITS

CHARACTERISTICS OF MAGNETIC TAPE AND DISK

	Tape	Disk
Type access	Sequential	Direct (random) or sequential
Data representation	Parallel	Serial
Storage scheme	IBG separation	Cylinder, sector

7-5 VIDEODISKS: A PICTURE IS WORTH 1K WORDS

By permitting people to watch first-run movies at home, **videodisk** technology has gained wide recognition, but not necessarily wide acceptance. However, the marriage between emerging videodisk technology and computers is expected to have a substantial impact on information systems and our way of interacting with computers. Videodisks have opened the door for new computer applications.

Like music on a phonograph record and data on a magnetic disk, *video* "information" can be stored on-line on videodisks and accessed directly. Approximately 50,000 individual pictures or 30 minutes of moving pictures can be stored on a single 12-inch read-only videodisk. A picture or a sequence of pictures can be accessed directly by frame number(s).

When buyers hold their annual spring pilgrimage to New York's Seventh Avenue garment district, videodisks are used to make buying fashions for the fall season a lot easier. Rather than having to search through scores of showrooms and thumb through thousands of garments, buyers have only to sit at a workstation and enter their fashion needs in terms of size, cost, fabric, and style. The garments that meet their specifications are retrieved

Videodisk technology is an integral part of a computerized fabric and apparel design system. (Cromemco, Inc.)

161

from videodisk under computer control and displayed, along with the location and seller for each garment. The garments were photographed and recorded on videodisk before the buyers arrived.

7-6 OPTICAL LASER DISKS: FROM MEGABYTES TO GIGABYTES

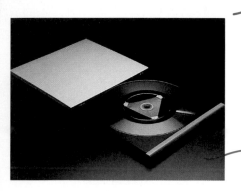

We may be approaching the technological limits of magnetic data storage. When this happens, sophisticated optics and lasers (light amplification by stimulated emission of radiation) may help to take up the slack. When this 14-inch platter is loaded to an optical laser disk drive, four billion characters (four gigabytes) of data are available for on-line access.
(Storage Technology Corporation)

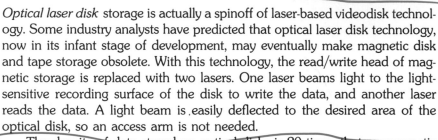

Optical laser disk storage is actually a spinoff of laser-based videodisk technology. Some industry analysts have predicted that optical laser disk technology, now in its infant stage of development, may eventually make magnetic disk and tape storage obsolete. With this technology, the read/write head of magnetic storage is replaced with two lasers. One laser beams light to the light-sensitive recording surface of the disk to write the data, and another laser reads the data. A light beam is easily deflected to the desired area of the optical disk, so an access arm is not needed.

The density of data stored on optical disks is 20 times that on magnetic disks. To put this into perspective, a single 12-inch optical disk can store up to 4 **gigabytes** (billion bytes) of data. That is the equivalent of the text for the entire *Encyclopaedia Britannica*! Moreover, optical disks are less sensitive to environmental fluctuations, store *images* as well as *digital* data, and cost less per megabyte of storage than magnetic disks.

By now you are probably off to purchase some optical laser disks—but perhaps you should reconsider. Most optical laser disks are *read only*. That is, once the data have been written to the medium, they can only be read, not updated or changed. However, erasable optical laser disks with read/write capabilities are beginning to be available commercially.

Optical disk storage is a viable alternative to magnetic tape for archival storage. For example, a company might wish to keep a permanent record

MEMORY BITS

STORAGE

Primary Storage	Secondary Storage
Also known as main memory or RAM	Also known as auxiliary storage
Temporary data and program storage during processing	Permanent on-line and off-line storage of data and programs
Semiconductor and bubble technology	Devices and media:
ROM: read-only RAM	Magnetic tape drive
PROM: programmable ROM	Reel
EPROM: erasable PROM	Cassette
	Magnetic disk drive
	Interchangeable media
	Microdisk
	Diskette
	Cartridge
	Disk pack
	Fixed disk media: called hard or rigid disks
	Videodisks: video information
	Optical laser disks: high-density read-only

of all financial transactions during the last year. Another popular application of optical disks is in information systems that require the merging of text and images that do not change for a period of time. A good example is a "catalog." A customer can "thumb through the pages" of a retailer's electronic catalog on a VDT, or perhaps a PC, and view the item while reading about it. With a few keystrokes the customer can order the item as well.

As optical laser disk technology matures to reliable, cost-effective read/write operation, it may eventually dominate secondary storage in the future as magnetic disk and tape do today.

7-7   WHAT'S NEXT IN DATA STORAGE? _____

The growth in the number of on-line systems has established a need for devices that will permit storage of greater amounts of data that can be retrieved more quickly. Today, the trade-off is between *speed of access* and *volume of storage*. Data access rates are thousands of times faster with primary storage, but the cost of state-of-the-art primary storage is prohibitive for high-volume storage.

We can expect at least one more leap in magnetic disk technology before it gives way to another technology, such as optical laser disks. The new magnetic disk technology will probably permit data to be stored vertically, or perpendicular to the disk face surface, thereby increasing the density tenfold. Once read/write optical laser disks are perfected, look for the usage of these high-density disks to soar.

Eventually, a solid-state primary storage technology will be invented that will permit the cost-effective temporary *and* permanent storage of data and programs, thus eliminating the need for rotating memory such as magnetic and optical laser disks. When this happens, primary and secondary storage will be one and the same. However, don't hold your breath. This may not happen until the end of the 1990s.

High density storage media have made It possible to maintain readily-accessible "electronic libraries." A trust officer of a savings and loan is browsing through the earnings reports of various companies before investing her company's funds.
(Mead Data Central)

SUMMARY OUTLINE AND IMPORTANT TERMS _____

7-1   SECONDARY STORAGE: PERMANENT DATA STORAGE.   Data and programs are stored on **secondary** or **auxiliary storage** for permanent storage. The **magnetic disk drives** and **magnetic tape drives** are the state of the art for both on-line and off-line storage. **Optical laser disk** technology is emerging as an alternative to magnetic disk.

7-2   SEQUENTIAL AND DIRECT ACCESS: NEW TERMS FOR OLD CONCEPTS.   Data are stored sequentially on magnetic tape; they are stored randomly on magnetic disks. **Sequential access** requires the file to be searched record by record until the desired record is found. **Random access** enables the desired record to be retrieved directly from its storage location.

7-3   MAGNETIC DISKS.   The different types of interchangeable magnetic disks are the **microdisk**, the **diskette**, the **disk cartridge**, and the **disk pack**. The trend is away from interchangeable disks to fixed disks.

Magnetic disk drives provide the computer system with direct-access and **random processing** capabilities. Data are stored serially on each recording surface by tracks. Each record that is stored on a disk is assigned an **address** that designates the physical location of the record. An **access arm**, with read/write heads for each recording surface, is moved to the appropriate track or cylinder to retrieve a record.

In **sector organization**, each disk recording surface is divided into sectors.

7-4   MAGNETIC TAPE.   A thin mylar tape is spun on a **reel** or encased in a **cassette** or **cartridge**. This magnetic tape is loaded to a tape drive, where data are read or written as the tape is passed under a **read/write head**. The physical nature of the magnetic tape results in data being stored and accessed sequentially. Data are stored using **parallel representation**, and they are **blocked** to minimize the start/stop movement of the tape. The standard nine-track 2,400-foot tape stores data at a density of 6,250 **bpi**.

Streamer tape drives, which record data in a continuous stream, use available tape storage very efficiently and are used primarily for backup.

7-5   VIDEODISKS: A PICTURE IS WORTH 1K WORDS.   **Videodisk** technology allows video "information" to be stored on-line and accessed directly. This new dimension in on-line storage will have a significant effect on current and future information systems.

7-6   OPTICAL LASER DISKS: FROM MEGABYTES TO GIGABYTES.   **Optical laser disk** storage, now in its infant stage of development, has the capability to store data at 20 times the density of magnetic disks.

7-7   WHAT'S NEXT IN DATA STORAGE?   The trade-off in data storage is between speed of access and volume of storage. Disk data storage technology will continue to improve in the foreseeable future, but eventually disk technology will give way to solid-state high-volume data storage.

REVIEW EXERCISES

Concepts

1.   What are alternative names for flexible disks? Auxiliary storage? Direct processing?
2.   Optical laser disks are a spinoff from what technology?
3.   What is the purpose of the interblock gap?
4.   What information is contained on a magnetic tape header label?
5.   How many megabytes does it take to make a gigabyte?
6.   A program issues a "read" command for data to be retrieved from a magnetic tape. Describe the resulting movement of the data.

7. Using the initials of your name and EBCDIC, graphically contrast parallel and serial data representation.

8. A company's employee master file contains 120,000 employee records. Each record is 1,800 bytes in length. How many 2,400-foot, 6,250-bpi magnetic tapes (interblock gap = .6 inch) will be required to store the file? Assume records are blocked five. Next, assume records are unblocked, and perform the same calculations.

9. A disk pack has 20 recording surfaces and 400 cylinders. If a track can store 10,000 bytes of data, how much data can be stored on eight such disk packs?

Discussion

10. If increasing the blocking factor for a magnetic tape file improves tape utilization, why not eliminate all IBGs and put all the records in one big block? Explain.

11. A floppy disk does not move until a read or write command is issued. Once the command is issued, the floppy begins to spin, and it stops spinning after the command is executed. Why is a disk pack not set in motion in the same manner? Why is a floppy not made to spin continuously?

12. Every Friday night, a company makes backup copies of all master files and programs. Why is this necessary? The company has both tape and disk drives. What storage media would you suggest for the backup? Why?

13. Discuss the application of optical laser disk technology to videotext applications, such as home shopping.

SELF-TEST (by section)

7-1. Data are retrieved from temporary auxiliary storage and stored permanently in main memory. (T/F)

7-2. Magnetic disks have both _____ and _____ access capabilities.

7-3. In a disk drive, the read/write heads are mounted on an access arm. (T/F)

7-4. Tape density is based on the linear distance between IBGs. (T/F)

7-5. _____ technology permits the on-line direct access of both still and moving pictures.

7-6. All optical laser disk technology is read-only. (T/F)

7-7. Rotating data storage devices will be obsolete by 1990. (T/F)

Self-Test answers. 7–1, F; 7–2, direct, sequential; 7–3, T; 7–4, F; 7–5, Videodisk; 7–6, F; 7–7, F.

STUDENT LEARNING OBJECTIVES

- To describe the use and characteristics of the different types of workstations.
- To explain alternative approaches and devices for data entry.
- To describe the operation and application of common output devices.

CHAPTER

8

Input/Output Devices

8

8-1   I/O DEVICES: OUR INTERFACE WITH THE COMPUTER

Data are created in many places and many ways. Before data can be processed and stored, they must be translated to a form that the *computer* can interpret. For this, we need *input* devices. Once the data have been processed, they must be translated back to a form that we can understand. For this, we need *output* devices. These **peripheral** input/output (I/O) devices enable communication between us and the computer.

The diversity of computer applications has encouraged manufacturers to develop and market a variety of I/O methods and hardware. Innovative I/O devices are being continuously introduced to the marketplace. For example, voice recognition devices accept data (input) through simple verbal communication. Speech synthesizers permit verbal communication in the other direction (output).

This chapter is divided into three parts. In the first part, the focus is on the variety of workstations available, most of which are both input and output. The second part presents devices that are used primarily for entering data. The last part describes devices that are strictly output.

This department provides administrative support to three regional insurance claims offices. Because each of these "knowledge workers" routinely deals with computer-generated information, each person needs a workstation to interact with the computer. (Courtesy Burroughs Corporation)

8-2   WORKSTATIONS

A **workstation** is a device that allows us to interact with a computer from just about anywhere. A workstation's primary input mechanism is usually a *keyboard*, and the output is usually a televisionlike display screen called a *monitor*. Workstations, sometimes called **terminals**, come in all shapes and sizes and have a variety of input/output capabilities.

Even the telephone is a workstation. On a push-button telephone, you can enter alphanumeric data from its keypad (keyboard) and by speaking (voice input). Output is computer-generated voice output. Salespersons use telephones as workstations to enter orders and inquire about the availability of certain products while linked to their company's mainframe computer.

Although telephones are the most familiar workstations, the *video display terminal* (*VDT*) and the *microcomputer* are the ones most commonly used for computer interaction. The VDT is affectionately known as the "tube," short for **cathode-ray tube**. From our past discussions (Chapter 4, "Computer Systems—Micros"), we know that a microcomputer can serve as a stand-alone computer or as a workstation linked to a mainframe.

The Keyboard.   Just about all workstations come equipped with a keyboard for input. The typical key-driven data entry device will have a standard *alphanumeric keyboard* with an optional numeric keyboard, called a *ten-key pad*. Some keyboards will also have *special-function keys*, which can be used to instruct the computer to perform a specific operation that may otherwise require several keystrokes.

Workstations in the factory are becoming as common as steel-toed shoes. This one is designed to withstand the heat, humidity, and dust that accompany shop activity.
(Courtesy of International Business Machines Corporation)

FINGER-TANGLING QWERTY VS. USER-FRIENDLY DVORAK

The QWERTY keyboard design that you see on most typewriters and keyboards derived its name from the first six letters on the top row. Patented in the 1890s, it was designed to slow down fast typists, who would otherwise get slow-moving type bars entangled.

The Dvorak keyboard layout, named after its inventor August Dvorak, places the most frequently used characters in the center. You can enter nearly 4,000 different words from the home row on the Dvorak keyboard, as opposed to 100 with the traditional QWERTY layout.

Professor Dvorak invented this keyboard arrangement in 1932. Through ergonomic studies of typists, he noticed that with the QWERTY layout, the majority of the work is done by the weakest fingers, the fourth and fifth fingers of the left hand. The stronger, quicker right hand and middle fingers are used only for the least frequently typed characters.

On Dvorak's keyboard, the most frequently used keys are on the home row (the vowels plus d, h, t, n, and s). The next most frequently used characters are placed up one row, because it is easier to reach up than down. Because this layout distributes the typing workload among the fingers according to their strengths, awkward strokes are reduced by 90 percent. Word processing operators who have switched to

This is the Dvorak keyboard. Notice how the letter "E," the most used character, is positioned directly under the left hand's most powerful finger on the home row.
(Key Tronic)

Dvorak are experiencing as much as a 75% improvement in productivity.

With computers, you can electronically change a QWERTY keyboard to a Dvorak keyboard, and back again to QWERTY, by simply pressing a couple of keys. With the widespread availability of the Dvorak keyboard, look for it to grow in popularity in the coming years.

An engineer uses a light pen to add and delete connections in a circuit design.
(Courtesy of International Business Machines Corporation)

There are two mice in this photo. Both move freely about the desktop. Both have tails. But only one eats cheese.
(Summagraphics Corporation)

Some keyboards are designed for a specific application. The cash-register-like workstations at most fast-food restaurants have special-purpose keyboards. Rather than type in the name and price of an order of French fries, attendants need only press the key marked "French fries" to record the sale.

Other Input Devices. For some applications the keyboard is too cumbersome. For example, a computer artist may need to enter curved lines to create an image. A physician may need to outline the exact shape of a tumor. Such applications call for devices that go beyond the capabilities of keyboards. These devices permit random movement of the **cursor** to create the image. A cursor, or blinking character, always indicates the location on the screen of the next input. The light pen, joy stick, track ball, digitizing tablet and pen, and mouse are among the most popular cursor movement and input mechanisms.

The *light pen* detects light from the cathode-ray tube when it is moved close to the screen. The cursor is automatically locked on to the position of the pen and tracks the movement of the pen over the screen. An engineer may create or modify images directly on the screen with a light pen. A city planner can select from a menu of possible computer functions by simply pointing the light pen to the desired function.

Video arcade wizards are no doubt familiar with the *joy stick* and *track ball*. The joy stick is a single vertical stick that moves the cursor in the direction that the stick is pushed. The track ball is a ball that is inset in the work table in front of the screen. The ball is "rolled" to move the cursor. The *digitizing tablet and pen* is a pen and a pressure-sensitive tablet with the same *X-Y* coordinates as the screen. The outline of an image drawn on a tablet is reproduced on the display screen.

The *mouse*, sometimes called the "pet peripheral," is now standard equipment for some workstations and micros. The mouse, attached to the computer by a cable, is a small device that, when moved across a desktop, moves the cursor. The mouse is used for quick positioning of the cursor over a graphic image, called an *icon* (e.g., a file cabinet or a diskette) or a phrase that depicts some action (e.g., store file on disk). The action is initiated when a button on the mouse is pushed. Also, holding the button down and moving the mouse cause objects on the screen to be moved.

The Monitor. Alphanumeric and graphic output are displayed on the workstation's monitor. The three primary attributes of monitors are the *size* of the display screen, whether the display is *color or monochrome*, and the *resolution* or detail of the display. The size of the screen varies, the most common being that which displays up to 25 lines of 80 characters each. Other common screen sizes are 32 by 80 and 25 by 132. The diagonal dimension of the display screen varies from 5 to 25 inches. Output on a monitor, called **soft copy**, is temporary and is available to the end user only until another display is requested. Contrast this to the permanent **hardcopy** output of printers.

Monitors are either monochrome or color. Monochrome monitors display images in a single color, usually white, green, or amber. Color monitors add the dimension of color, which highlights various aspects of the output. For example, an engineer designing pipelines for an oil refinery can use colors

This CAD system illustrates the difference between a low-resolution monochrome monitor (left) and a high-resolution color monitor. A security specialist is using a digitizing board, a keyboard, and a joy stick (above keyboard) to design the layout of an airport security checkpoint.
(CalComp)

to highlight such things as the direction and type of fluid flow, the size of the pipes, and so on.

Workstations with color monitors can also be used to present alphanumeric information efficiently and effectively. For example, problem cases for a social worker can be highlighted—red for those needing immediate attention and yellow for those with less serious problems. At a glance, the social worker can evaluate the situation and make workload adjustments as appropriate.

Some monitors have a much higher **resolution**, or quality of output. Resolution refers to the number of addressable points on the screen—that is, the number of points to which light can be directed under program control. A strictly alphanumeric workstation has about 65,000 such points. A workstation used primarily for computer graphics and computer-aided design may have over 16 million points. The high-resolution monitors project extremely clear images that look almost like photographs (see the chapter-opener photographs of computer graphics images).

Portable Workstations: Computers to Go

A *portable* workstation has a built-in **modem** (discussed in Chapter 9, "Data Communications") that permits the use of a regular telephone line to transmit and receive data from the host computer. The same features and combinations of I/O found on regular desktop workstations or microcomputers are available on portable workstations. Input is usually done on a keyboard, and output is either printed or displayed on a small screen. Portable workstations weigh from 5 to 12 pounds and are packaged in containers that look like briefcases.

To use a portable workstation, you simply dial the number of the computer on a telephone. Upon hearing the computer's high whistle "greeting," you insert the telephone handset into the modem—this makes the connection between the workstation and the mainframe computer.

This advertising executive's portable workstation helps him keep in touch with office activities and retrieve critical information wherever he travels.
(Copyright 1984 GTE Telenet Communications Corporation)

Portable workstations are used at home by programmers to take advantage of computer time on second and third shifts. Salespersons use portable workstations to make inquiries or to log a sale while in a customer's office. Executives use portable workstations to make the corporate information resources available to them wherever they may travel.

Since most portable workstations are microcomputers, programmers, salespersons, executives, and others can do spreadsheet analysis, word processing, and many other applications while in stand-alone mode. An executive might compose several memos while on a flight, then, upon landing, upload the memos to the headquarter's mainframe for distribution via electronic mail.

Workstation Summary

Workstations of every size and shape are used by secretaries for word processing, by programmers for interactive program development, by clerks for recording transactions, by commercial artists for creating ad pieces, by management for making decisions, by engineers for computer-aided design (CAD), by computer operators to communicate with the computer (via the **operator console**), by shop supervisors for line scheduling, and by thousands of other people for hundreds of applications.

The trend in workstations is to provide processing as well as I/O capability. This, in effect, means that by the second edition of this book, virtually all workstations will be microcomputers with stand-alone processing capability. Microcomputers are becoming so powerful that users are no longer completely dependent on mainframe capabilities for complex processing jobs. With these "intelligent" workstations, users can conduct interactive sessions with mainframe computers or download data for stand-alone processing. Data processed in stand-alone mode can also be uploaded to the mainframe such that they can be shared with users at other workstations.

The computer is playing an ever-increasing role in how we do our jobs. Since the workstation is the means by which we communicate with the computer, it is fast becoming a companion to workers in most fields of endeavor.

MEMORY BITS

WORKSTATION

Input
    Keyboard
    Light pen
    Joystick
    Track ball
    Digitizing tablet and pen
    Mouse
Output
    Monitor (soft copy)
      Monochrome or color
      Low or high resolution
    Printer (hard copy)

The computer operators in this data center interact with the computer through one of the operator consoles.
(Courtesy Burroughs Corporation)

8-3 DATA ENTRY: GETTING DATA INTO THE COMPUTER SYSTEM

Data Entry Concepts

Source Data. Most data do not exist in a form that can be "read" by the computer. Consider the following example. A supervisor uses a pencil and paper to manually complete a time sheet, recording the hours worked by the staff. Before the payroll checks can be computed and printed, the data on their time sheets must be *transcribed* (converted) into a *machine-readable format* that can be interpreted by a computer. The time sheet is known as the **source document**, and, as you might expect, the data on the time sheet are the **source data**.

Not all source data have to be transcribed. For example, the numbers imprinted on the bottom of your bank checks indicate your individual account number and bank. These numbers are already machine readable, so they can be "read" directly by an input device.

Approaches to Data Entry. The term **data entry** is used to describe the process of entering data into a computer system. Computers are programmed to provide operators with display-screen "prompts" to make data entry easy. The display on the operator's screen, for example, may be the image of the source document (such as a time sheet). A **prompt** is a brief message to the operator that describes what should be entered (e.g., "INPUT HOURS WORKED ____").

Data can be entered on a workstation in the following ways:

1. Batch: transactions are grouped, or *batched*, and entered consecutively, one after the other.
2. Transaction-oriented: transactions are recorded and entered as they occur.

To illustrate the difference between batch and transaction-oriented data entry, consider the following example. A mail order merchandiser accepts orders by both mail and phone. The orders received by mail are accumulated, or batched, for data entry—usually at night. But for phone orders there are no handwritten source documents; persons taking the phone orders interact with the computer via workstations to enter the order data while talking with the customer (see Figure 8-1).

On-Line Data Entry. Most data entry to mainframe computer systems, both batch and transaction-oriented, is done on-line. Workstation operators enter data *directly* to the host computer system for processing, as shown in Figure 8-2. The primary advantage of transaction-oriented data entry is that records on the data base are updated immediately, as the transaction occurs. This is quite different from batch data entry, where records are batched periodically. Another advantage of transaction-oriented data entry is that operators can make inquiries to the system. In the example above, a salesperson can check the availability of an item and tell the customer when to expect delivery.

On-line data entry is critical to organizations whose data base must be current every minute of the day. Hotel reservation systems provide excellent examples of on-line data entry. All the major hotel chains have similar reserva-

Each day, this government office receives thousands of student financial aid applications. The applications are batched and the data from these source documents are entered and verified at these workstations.
(National Computer Systems)

FIGURE 8-1
Batch and Transaction-Oriented Data Entry
Mail order merchandisers accept orders by mail and by phone.

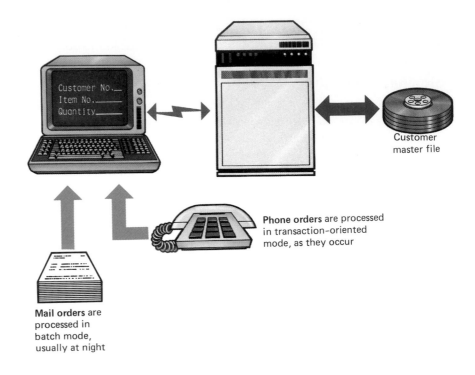

Customer master file

Phone orders are processed in transaction-oriented mode, as they occur

Mail orders are processed in batch mode, usually at night

Data-entry workstations

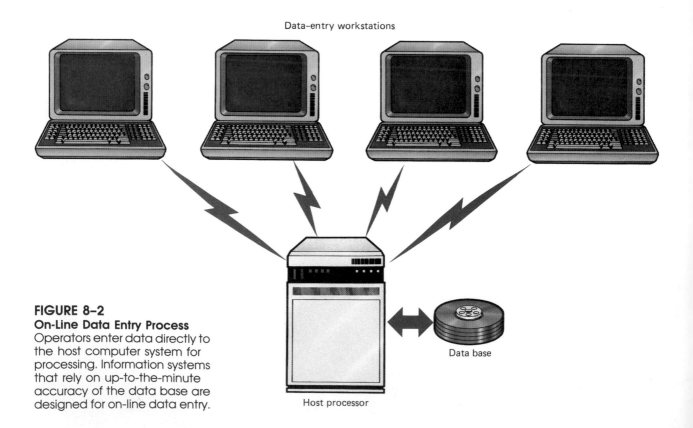

Data base

Host processor

FIGURE 8-2
On-Line Data Entry Process
Operators enter data directly to the host computer system for processing. Information systems that rely on up-to-the-minute accuracy of the data base are designed for on-line data entry.

tion systems. Someone wishing to make a reservation may do so at any hotel or by calling his or her toll-free reservation number. Reservation clerks enter the following data:

1. Name of guest
2. Location (city and particular hotel)
3. Date of reservation
4. Type of room desired
5. Number of nights
6. Number of persons
7. Hold for late arrival (yes or no)
8. Credit card number and type
9. Phone number of guest
10. Organization or person making reservation
11. Address of guest (if written confirmation is requested)

On-line data entry is critical to the routine operation of all hotel chains. Since each hotel has a limited number of rooms, once they are all taken for a particular night, no more reservations can be accepted. So, as soon as an operator receives a call for a room reservation, the operator checks the data base to make sure that rooms are still available. As the reservation is made, the central data base is updated to reflect that one less room is available on certain nights at a particular hotel.

Trends in Data Entry.   The trend in data entry has been toward decreasing the number of transcription steps. This is accomplished by entering the data as close to the source as possible. For example, in sales departments, orders are input directly to the system by salespersons. In accounting departments, financial transactions are recorded and entered into the system by bookkeepers and accountants.

Until recently, data entry has been synonymous with *keystrokes*. The keystroke will be the basic mode of data entry for some time to come, but recent innovations have eliminated the need for key-driven data entry in certain applications. For example, you have probably noticed the preprinted **bar codes** on grocery products. At some supermarket checkout counters these bar codes have eliminated the need for most key entry. Checkers need only pass the product over the *laser scanner* and the price is entered—and the shelf inventory is updated as well.

Data entry is an area where enormous potential exists for increases in productivity. The technology of data entry devices is constantly changing. New and improved methods of transcribing raw data are being invented and put on the market each month. These data entry methods and associated devices are discussed next.

Optical Scanning

Optical character recognition (OCR) provides a way to encode (write) certain data in machine-readable format on the original source document. For example, the International Standard Book Number (ISBN) on the back

In this on-line, transaction-oriented dispatch system, service coordinators take calls from customers with malfunctioning computers and assign service engineers to handle the problems. Service engineers carry hand-held terminals that enable them to transmit service status and parts orders directly to the system.
(Courtesy of International Business Machines Corporation)

The trend in data entry is to minimize keystrokes and capture data as close to the source as possible in machine-readable form. For example, supermarket checkout systems use laser scanners to read the bar codes that identify each item. Price and product description are retrieved from a data base and recorded on the sales slip.
(Courtesy of International Business Machines Corporation)

cover of this book is written in machine-readable OCR. This eliminates the need for publishers and bookstore clerks to key these data manually. OCR equipment consists of a family of devices that encode and read OCR data.

OCR Scanners.   OCR characters are identified through light-sensitive devices called **OCR scanners.** Both scanner technologies, *contact* and *laser*, bounce a beam of light off an image, then measure the reflected light to determine the value of the image. Hand-held *wand scanners* make contact as they are brushed over the printed matter to be read. Stationary *laser scanners* are more versatile and can read data passed near the scanning area. Both can recognize printed characters and various types of codes.

OCR devices can "learn" to read almost any typeface, including this book! The "learning" takes place when the structure of the character set is described to the OCR device. Special OCR devices can even read hand-printed letters if they are recorded on a standard form and written according to specific rules.

OCR scanners can be classified into the following five categories:

- *Label scanners*. These devices read data on price tags, shipping labels, and the like. A hand-held wand scanner is a label scanner.
- *Page scanners*. These devices scan regular typewritten pages.
- *Document scanners*. Document scanners are capable of scanning documents of varying sizes (e.g., utility-bill invoice stubs and sales slips from credit card transactions).
- *Continuous-form scanners*. These devices read data printed on continuous forms, such as cash register tapes.
- *Optical mark scanners*. Optical mark scanners scan preprinted forms, such as multiple-choice test answer forms. The position of the "sense marks" indicates a particular response or character. Optical mark scanning is somewhat dated but still applicable where handwritten data entry is impractical.

This optical page scanner enables the full range of everyday printed materials to be directly entered into a computer system. Publishers use such systems to enter typewritten manuscripts into a computer system for typesetting. Manual keyboarding of the text would take a week or more, but the page scanner converts typewritten text to computer format in a few hours.
(Sperry Corporation)

Hospitals use hand-held wand scanners to automatically update patient records. Nurses scan preprinted labels on medicines and supplies that are to be used by a particular patient. By using optical scanners, hospitals simplify record keeping while maintaining tight control over inventory.
(CAERE Corporation)

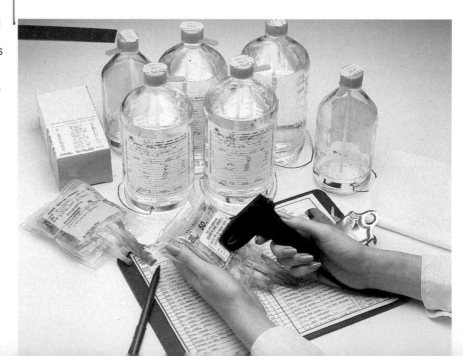

XYZ AIRFREIGHT CO.

* SEA 5794 4PCS 86.4KG *

data recording, data transmission.

0123456789
ABCDEFGHIJ

8151-054100

FIGURE 8-3
Various Codes That Can Be Interpreted by Scanners

Applications of Optical Scanners

Bar Codes. The stationary scanners, such as those in supermarkets, use lasers to interpret the bar codes printed on products. Bar codes represent alphanumeric data by varying the width and combination of adjacent vertical lines. Just as there are a variety of internal bit encoding systems, there are a variety of bar coding systems (see Figure 8–3). One of the most visible of these systems is the Universal Product Code (UPC). The UPC, originally used for supermarket items, is gaining momentum and is now being printed on other consumer goods. The advantage of bar codes over characters is that the position or orientation of the item being read is not as critical to the scanner. In a supermarket, for example, the data can be recorded even if a bottle of ketchup is rolled over the laser scanner!

Wand Scanners. The hand-held wand scanner is now common in point-of-sale (POS) systems in retail stores throughout the world. Clerks need only brush the wand over the price tag to record the sale. Since the POS terminal is on-line, the inventory is also updated as each item is sold.

Wand scanners are also used to read package labels in shipping and receiving and in inventory management. Passport inspection is even being automated with the use of wand scanners. Customs officials enter passport numbers via wand scanners to help speed the processing of international travelers.

OCR Turnaround Documents. OCR devices are custom made for situations where data can be encoded by the computer system on a **turnaround document** and when visual recognition is important. A turnaround document is computer-produced output that is ultimately returned as *machine-readable input* to a computer system. The utility billing system of an electric company is a good example of this OCR application.

The utility billing system procedures may be seen in Figure 8–4.

1. The invoices (turnaround documents) shown in Figure 8–5 are generated from the customer master file and the electricity usage file. Data on the invoice are printed in a format that can be read by an OCR document scanner. Therefore, no data entry is required unless the amount of the payment is less than the amount due.

FIGURE 8–4
Electricity Utility Billing System
This system invoices customers with OCR turnaround documents, thereby minimizing the amount of key entry required. The five steps are discussed in the text.

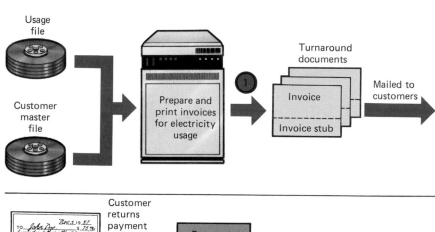

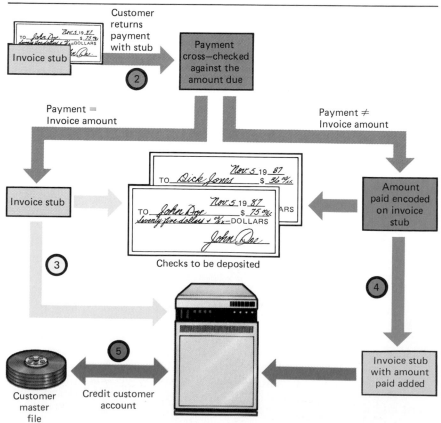

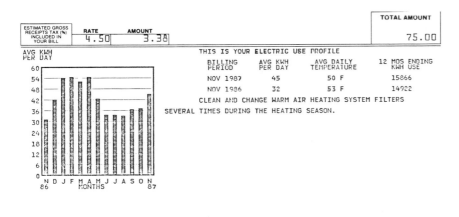

Pennsylvania Power & Light Company
TWO NORTH NINTH STREET, ALLENTOWN, PA. 18101

FIGURE 8–5
An Invoice for Electricity Usage
The top portion of this invoice is an OCR turnaround document that is used to record an incoming payment. The electric use profile at the bottom of the invoice graphically illustrates the customer's electricity usage over the past year. Notice the three different sizes and styles of print.

2. The customers return the OCR-readable invoice stubs (turnaround documents) with the payment. Clerks cross-check the payment amount against the amount due. Partial payments are separated out from full payments.

3. An OCR scanner reads the original turnaround document of full-payment customers to acknowledge receipt of payment.

4. The only data entry required is on partial payments. The amount of the payment is encoded on the partial-payment invoice stubs, and these are read by the OCR device.

5. The customer's account is credited by the amount of the payment.

In an attempt to cut cost and speed tax-return processing, the Internal Revenue Service is already distributing the short form as a turnaround document—next, the long form!

Original Source Data Collection.   Optical character recognition is also used for original source data collection. An example is data collection for credit card purchases (by VISA, MasterCard, and the like). When you make a credit card purchase, your card, a multicopy form, and a portable imprint device are used to record the sales data in machine-readable OCR format. On the form, the data recorded for most credit card purchases include the *account number of the buyer*, the *account number of the merchant*, and the *amount of the purchase*. One copy of the form is given to the customer as a record of purchase, one copy is retained by the merchant, and the third copy, a stiffer card, is sent to the bank that issued the credit card. With the data already in OCR format, no further data entry is required. During processing, the charged amount is recorded as a debit to the buyer's account and a credit to the merchant's account.

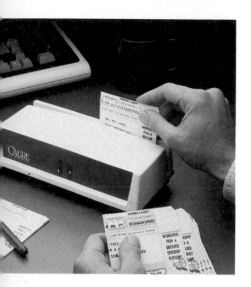

An electric utility company uses a slot scanner to process remittances more quickly and accurately. When the payment and turnaround stub are received, a clerk verifies that the payment and invoice match, then runs the stub through the scanner to update the customer's record.
(CAERE Corporation)

The telephone in this clothing store is actually a combination phone and terminal. Clerks get confirmation on credit purchases by sliding the credit card's magnetic stripe through the slot. The customer's account number and the amount of the purchase (entered by the clerk) are transmitted to a central computer for processing and a confirmation (or rejection) number is returned and displayed.
(Copyright 1984 GTE Telenet Communications Corporation)

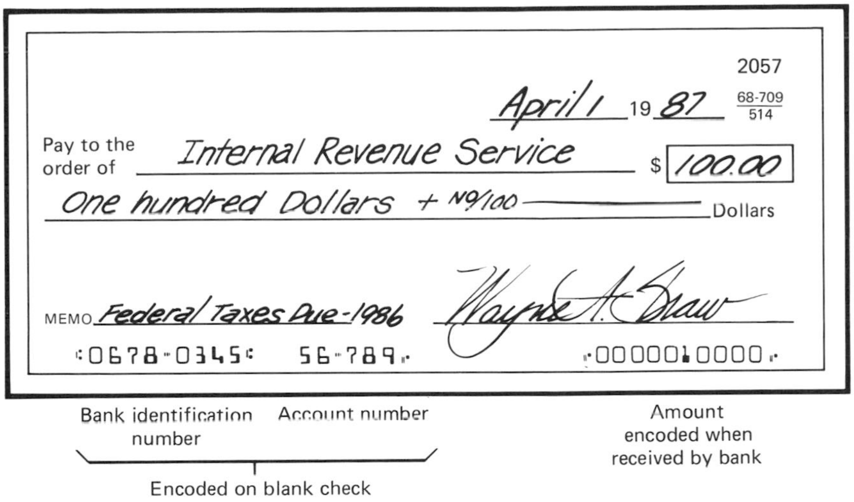
2057
April 1 19 87
68-709
514
Pay to the order of
Internal Revenue Service
$ 100.00
One hundred Dollars + NO/100
Dollars
MEMO Federal Taxes Due-1986
⑆0678-0345⑆ 56-789⑈ ⑈0000010000⑈
Bank identification number
Account number
Encoded on blank check
Amount encoded when received by bank

FIGURE 8–6
A Magnetic Ink Character Recognition (MICR) Encoded Check
Notice that the amount is entered on the check when it is received by the bank.

Magnetic Ink Character Recognition

Magnetic ink character recognition (MICR) is similar to optical character recognition and is used exclusively by the banking industry. MICR readers are used to read and sort checks and deposits. You have probably noticed the *account number* and *bank number* encoded on all your checks and personalized deposit slips. The *date* of the transaction is automatically recorded for all checks processed that day; therefore, only the *amount* must be keyed in (see Figure 8–6).

Magnetic ink character recognition devices are used instead of OCR because of the increased speed and accuracy of MICR. The special magnetic characters permit the processing speeds that banks need to sort and process thousands of checks each day.

Automatic teller machines (ATM) and electronic funds transfer (EFT) permit funds to be "electronically" transferred from one account to another without the need to produce a hard-copy source document, such as a check or a deposit slip. As EFT grows, look for a diminished need for MICR equipment. With the cost of processing a check or deposit slip now in excess of $1, the banking industry will do everything possible to eliminate the need for hard-copy checks and deposits, including offering home banking services for PC owners.

In the near future, OCR data entry for credit card transactions may be replaced with electronic funds transfer. With EFT, your transactions are recorded on-line, thereby eliminating the need for mailings and subsequent OCR processing operations.

People naturally point at what they want. With this system you don't have to worry about buttons or moving a mouse around. All you do is point to the desired options on a touchscreen display, and the computer does the rest.
(Photo courtesy of Hewlett-Packard Company)

Magnetic Stripes and Smart Cards

The **magnetic stripes** on the backs of charge cards and badges offer another means of data entry. The magnetic stripes are encoded with data appropriate for the application. For example, the account number and privacy code are encoded on cards for automatic teller machines.

Magnetic stripes contain much more data per unit space than do printed characters or bar codes. Also, since they cannot be read visually, they are excellent for storing confidential data, such as the privacy code. Employee cards and security badges often contain authorization data for access to physically secured areas, such as the computer center. To gain access, an employee inserts a card or badge into a **badge reader**. The authorization code is read and checked before the individual is permitted into a secured area. The badge reader may also be on-line to the computer. On-line badge readers maintain a chronological log of those persons entering or departing secured areas.

The enhanced version of cards with a magnetic stripe is the **smart card**. The smart card, similar in appearance to other cards, contains a microprocessor that retains certain security and personal data in its memory at all times. Because the smart card can contain more information, has some processing capability, and is almost impossible to duplicate, it may be that, in the future, cards with magnetic stripes will be replaced with the smart card.

Time consuming check authorizations at grocery stores may be a thing of the past with the introduction of cash dispensing systems. This customer uses her bank card (with magnetic stripe) and a keyboard to withdraw cash from her bank account.
(Diebold, Incorporated)

Voice Data Entry

Computers are great talkers, but they are not very good listeners. It is not uncommon for a **voice data entry** system to misinterpret the slamming of a door for a spoken word. Voice data entry, or **voice recognition**, devices can be used to enter limited kinds and quantities of data. Despite its limitations, voice data entry has a number of applications. Salespersons in the field can enter an order simply by calling the computer and stating the customer number, item number, and quantity. Quality control personnel, who must use their hands, call out defects as they are detected. Baggage handlers at airports simply state the three-letter destination identifier, and luggage is routed to the appropriate conveyer system. Physicians in the operating room can request certain information on a patient while operating. A computer-based audio response unit or a voice synthesizer (both covered later in this chapter) make the conversation two-way.

"Oh, your daughter's computer is darling. And what adorable peripherals!"
(By permission of Anthony Cresci)

Quality control inspectors in this refrigerator assembly plant record defects through voice data entry. The system enables interactive communication with the computer and frees the inspector's hands for other activities.
(Texas Instruments, Inc.)

Here is how it works. When you speak into a microphone, each sound is broken down and examined in several frequencies. Then, the sounds in each frequency are digitized (1s and 0s) and matched against similarly digitized words in a data base. In voice data entry, the creation of the data base is called *training*. Most voice data entry systems are *speaker dependent*; that is, they respond to the speech of a particular individual. Therefore, a data base of words must be created for each person using the system. When creating the data base, persons using the system must repeat each word that is to be interpreted by the system up to 20 times—thus the "training." This is necessary because we seldom say words in the same way every time. There will probably be a different inflection or nasal quality even if we say the word twice in succession.

State-of-the-art *speaker-independent* systems have a very limited vocabulary, perhaps the numbers, "yes," and "no." Though the vocabulary is limited, they do not require training and can be used by anyone. However, they do require a very large data base in order to accommodate anyone's voice pattern.

Researchers are developing speaker-independent data bases of several thousand words that will enable the transcription of complete spoken sentences with a high degree of accuracy. It is only a matter of time before programmers can enter their programs in spoken English rather than through time-consuming keystrokes, and managers can dictate their correspondence directly to the computer. For those of us who type poorly or not at all, this will be a most welcome technological breakthrough.

Vision Systems

To give computers eyesight, a camera provides the input needed to create the data base. First a vision system, complete with camera, digitizes the images of all objects to be interpreted. The digitized form of each image is then stored in the data base. When in operation, the vision inputs are digitized; then the computer interprets them by matching the structure of the input with those in the data base.

As you can imagine, **vision input systems** are best suited to tasks where only a very few images will be encountered. These tasks are usually simple, monotonous ones, such as inspection and item selection. For example, a robot on an assembly line might perform several functions, depending on which one of three parts is coming down the line and whether it meets certain quality control specifications. A vision system can determine which part it is, perform rudimentary gauging inspections, then signal the robot's computer to take appropriate action.

Portable Data Entry

Portable data entry devices are hand held and usually off-line. The typical portable data entry device would have a limited keyboard and a magnetic cassette tape on which to "capture" the data. After the data have been entered, they are batched to the host computer for processing.

One portable data entry device combines a hand-held optical wand with a keyboard. Stock clerks in department stores routinely use such devices to

Industrial vision input systems are used to "visually" inspect parts as they roll along a conveyer. The image of a part is entered and digitized so that it can be matched against an electronic image in the data base. Mismatches, or flawed parts, are kicked out for closer human inspection.
(Analog Devices, Inc., Two Technology Way, Norwood, MA 02062)

Customer names and addresses are stored in the proper sequence in the memory of this portable data entry device. Therefore, the only piece of datum entered at each location is the meter reading. At the end of the day, the meter reader transmits the data to the company's host computer via a telephone hookup.
(MSI Data Corporation)

collect and enter reorder data. As clerks check the inventory level visually, they identify the items to be restocked. First the price tag is scanned by the wand, then the number to be ordered is entered on the keyboard.

Another portable data entry device contains a pressure-sensitive writing pad that recognizes hand-printed alphanumeric characters.

8-4   OUTPUT DEVICES

Output devices translate bits and bytes to a form that we can understand. Workstations are both input and output devices. The most common "output only" devices (printers, computer-output microfilm/microfiche, voice response units, and plotters) are discussed in this section.

Printers

Printers produce **hard-copy** output, such as management reports, payroll checks, and program listings. Printers are generally classified as **serial printers**, **line printers**, or **page printers**. Printers are rated by their print speed. Print speeds for serial printers are measured in *characters per second* (*cps*), and for line and page printers they are measured in *lines per minute* (*lpm*). The print-speed ranges for the three types of printers are 40–450 cps, 1,000–3,600 lpm, and 500–40,000 lpm, respectively.

Printers are further categorized as impact or nonimpact. An impact printer uses some type of hammer or hammers to "impact" the ribbon and the paper, much as a typewriter does. Nonimpact printers use chemicals, lasers, and heat to form the images on the paper. Only nonimpact printers can achieve print speeds in excess of 3,600 lpm.

Serial Printers.   Serial printers are the primary hard-copy output unit for microcomputers, and they are often used in conjunction with one or several workstations to provide hard-copy capability. Impact serial printers rely on **dot-matrix** and **daisy-wheel** technology. Nonimpact serial printers employ **ink-jet** and **thermal** technology. Regardless of the technology, the images are formed *one character at a time* as the print head moves across the paper.

The Dot-Matrix Printer.   The dot-matrix printer configures printed dots to form characters and all kinds of images in much the same way as lights display time and temperature on bank signs. One or several vertical columns of small print hammers are contained in a rectangular "print head." The hammers are activated independently to form a dot character image as the print head moves horizontally across the paper. The characters in Figure 8–7 are formed within a 7×5 dot matrix. The number of dots within the matrix varies from one printer to the next.

The quality of the printed output is directly proportional to the density of the dots in the matrix. High quality dot-matrix printers form characters that appear solid, and they can be used for business letters as well as for routine data processing output. Figure 8–8 illustrates how the dots can be overlapped to create a letter-quality appearance. These printers are called *dual-mode* because of their dual-function capabilities.

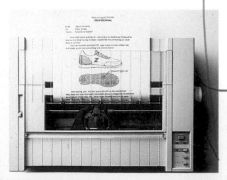

This graphics and text output shows the versatility of a dot-matrix printer. A dot-matrix printer can produce hard copies of graphic images (as they would appear on a screen) just as easily as it prints letters and reports.
(Courtesy of Apple Computer, Inc.)

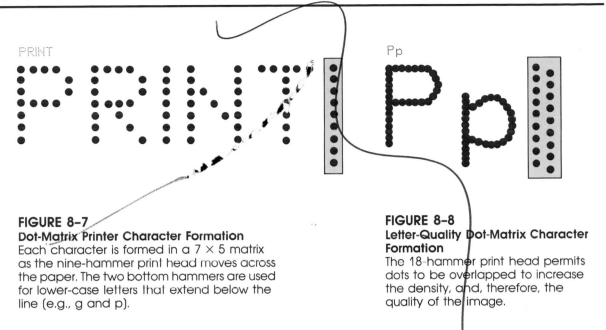

FIGURE 8–7
Dot-Matrix Printer Character Formation
Each character is formed in a 7 × 5 matrix as the nine-hammer print head moves across the paper. The two bottom hammers are used for lower-case letters that extend below the line (e.g., g and p).

FIGURE 8–8
Letter-Quality Dot-Matrix Character Formation
The 18-hammer print head permits dots to be overlapped to increase the density, and, therefore, the quality of the image.

Dot-matrix printers are more flexible than printers of fully formed characters. Depending on the model, dot-matrix printers can print a variety of sizes and types of characters (even old English and script characters), print in colors, print graphics, and print bar codes.

The Daisy-Wheel Printer.   The daisy-wheel printer produces high-quality output for word processing applications. An interchangeable daisy wheel containing a set of fully formed characters is spun to the desired character. A print hammer strikes the embossed character on the print wheel to form the image. The print quality is at least equal to that of the best electric typewriters.

Although daisy-wheel printers have the highest-quality text output, they are the slowest of the serial printers and cannot produce graphic output.

The Ink-Jet Printer.   Ink-jet printers squirt "dots" of ink on the paper to form images in a manner similar to that of the dot-matrix printer. The big advantage that ink-jet printers have over dot matrix printers is that they can produce *multicolor* output. Sales of color ink-jet printers are expected to increase substantially as users, accustomed to color output on their video monitors, come to want color on their hard-copy outputs.

The nozzles on the print head of a color ink-jet printer expel thousands of droplets per second to produce many different colors. The principle of ink-jet printing is illustrated as high-speed photography catches airborne droplets in flight. The results are often amazing—especially this elaborate design for an oriental rug.
(Courtesy of International Business Machines Corporation)
(Advanced Color Technology)

The daisy-wheel printer is so named because its print mechanism resembles the shape of a daisy. Each of the "petals" of the daisy-wheel contains a fully-formed impression of a character. The interchangeable daisy-wheels are available in a wide variety of character sets.
(SCM Corporation)

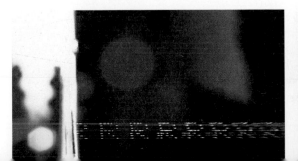

The Thermal Printer. The thermal printer is an alternative to the other serial printers. Heat elements are activated to produce dot-matrix images on heat-sensitive paper. The major disadvantage is the cost of the heat-sensitive paper. The advantages include compactness, limited noise, and low purchase price. Some thermal printers are capable of color output.

Line Printers. Line printers are impact printers that print *a line at a time*. The two most popular types of line printers are the band printer and the matrix line printer.

Band and Chain Printers. Band and chain printers have a print hammer for each print position in the line of print (usually 132). On a band printer, several similar character sets of fully formed characters are embossed on a horizontal band that is continuously moving in front of the print hammers. On a chain printer, the characters are embossed on each link of the print chain. On both types, the paper is momentarily stopped and, as the desired character passes over a given column, the hammer is activated and the image is formed on the paper.

Band and chain printers are capable of printing on continuous-feed paper, as well as on cards and documents of varying sizes (even on mailing labels). Interchangeable bands and chains make it easy for operators to change the style of print (the typeface).

The Matrix Line Printer. Matrix line printers print a line of *dots* at a time. Needlelike hammers are lined up across the width of the paper. Like serial matrix printers, the characters are formed in rectangular dot configurations. Matrix printers are much more flexible than band printers are, and they can perform the same types of print operations as serial matrix printers do (see above), including graphic output.

This line printer uses an operator-changeable steel band and prints 1,500 lines per minute. To load the continuous-feed paper, the acoustical enclosure is raised and the "gate" containing the band and ribbon is swung open.
(Storage Technology Corporation)
(Courtesy of International Business Machines Corporation)

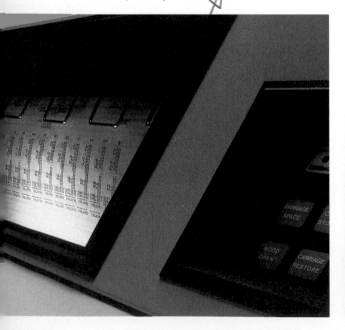

Inside this page printer, laser beams scan across the print drum to create text and graphics at speeds of over 20,000 lines per minute.
(Sperry Corporation)
(Courtesy of International Business Machines Corporation)

Page Printers.   Page printers are of the nonimpact type and use electrophotographic and laser printing technology to achieve high-speed hard-copy output by printing *a page at a time*. Operating at peak capacity during an eight hour shift, a page printer can produce almost a quarter of a million pages—that's 50 miles of output. This enormous output capability is normally directed to persons outside an organization. For example, large banks use page printers to produce statements for checking and savings accounts; insurance companies print policies on page printers; and electric utility companies use them to bill their customers.

Page-printer technology provides the capability to superimpose preprinted forms on continuous-feed stock paper. This eliminates a company's need to purchase expensive preprinted forms. Page printers have the capability to print graphs and charts, and they offer considerable flexibility in the choice of size and style of print.

Printer Summary.   Hundreds of printers are produced by dozens of manufacturers. There is a printer manufactured to meet the hard-copy output requirements of any company or individual. Almost any combination of features can be obtained. You can specify the speed, quality of output, color requirements, flexibility requirements, and even noise level. Printers sell for as little as a good pair of shoes or for as much as a small office building.

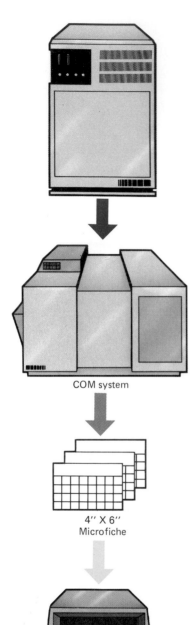

COM system

4″ X 6″
Microfiche

Microform viewer

FIGURE 8–9
**The Computer Output
Microfilm/Microfiche (COM)
Process**
In the on-line COM process,
data are routed directly from
the computer to the COM
system.

The trend in computer centers is toward producing less printed output. If a permanent hard copy is not needed, a soft copy is less expensive and easier to obtain. Look for the requirements for printed output to diminish as more and more on-line workstations are installed. As an example: A computer center in a large midwestern company delivered a truckload of printed output to the personnel department every Thursday night for almost ten years. Now, 20 on-line terminals allow people in the personnel department to interact directly with the computer and with the personnel data base.

In a few years, printers will be used almost exclusively for "external" output, such as bank statements and utility bills. In a few more years, even external output will be soft copy. Our utility bills will be delivered by *electronic mail* to our personal computers and paid by *electronic funds transfer* from our account to that of the utility company.

Computer Output Microfilm/Microfiche

Computer output microfilm/microfiche (COM) devices prepare microfilm and microfiche that can be read on microfilm viewers. Each COM device contains an image-to-film recorder and a duplicator for making multiple copies of a microfiche.

In the COM process (see Figure 8–9), the images (output) to be miniaturized are prepared, as if to be printed, on a computer system. This output is then sent to the COM device. Here the images are miniaturized for microform viewers.

In the miniaturization process, images are displayed on a small high-resolution video display. A camera exposes a small segment of the microfilm for each display, thereby creating a grid pattern of images, or frames. The microfilm is then developed and cut into 4- by 6-inch sheets of microfiche, each containing up to 270 frames. The duplicator section makes multiple copies of the microfiche. Each sheet of microfiche is titled and indexed so that the appropriate frame or "page" can be retrieved quickly on a viewer.

This COM system can operate independently as an off-line system, or it can be linked to the host computer for on-line processing.
(NCR Corporation)

COM is an alternative to an on-line computer-based system when up-to-the-minute information is not critical. COM is also used extensively instead of hard copy for archival storage (e.g., old income tax records).

COM equipment can produce in minutes what may take hours to produce on a printer. But the real advantage of COM is the elimination of cumbersome volumes of printed output. These advantages are nevertheless overshadowed by the potential of on-line systems. As terminals and on-line systems become commonplace, a trend is emerging to replace COM applications with on-line systems. On-line systems offer the added advantages of direct access and immediate update to the data base.

Voice Response Units

There are two types of **voice response units**: one uses a *recording* of a human voice and other sounds, and the other uses a *speech synthesizer*. The first type of voice response unit selects output from user-recorded words, phrases, music, alarms, or anything that you might record on tape, just as a printer would select characters. Most of us have probably heard, "The number you have dialed has been changed to eight-six-one-four-zero-three-eight." The initial phrase and the numbers are "outputted" using a voice response unit.

In "recorded" voice response units, the actual analog recordings of sounds are converted to digital data, then permanently stored in a memory chip. On output, the selected sound is converted back to analog before being routed to a speaker. These chips are mass-produced for specific applications, such as output for ATMs, microwave ovens, smoke detectors, elevators, alarm clocks, automobile warning systems, video games, and vending machines, to mention a few.

Speech synthesizers convert raw data to electronically produced speech. To do this, these devices combine sounds resembling the phonemes (basic sound units) that make up speech. A speech synthesizer is capable of producing at least 64 unique sounds. The existing technology produces synthesized speech with only limited vocal inflections and phrasing. Still, the number of applications is growing. In one application, an optical-character reader scans books to retrieve the raw data. The speech synthesizer then translates the

An interior view of this reading machine shows an optical scanner reading a typewritten letter. The scanner's output is automatically converted to computer signals which in turn are converted to full-word English speech using a speech synthesizer. This machine can even read novels to blind persons.
(Kurzweil Computer Products)

printed matter into spoken words for blind persons. In another application, the use of speech synthesizers is opening a new world to speech-impaired children who were once placed in institutions because they could not communicate verbally. As the quality of the output improves, speech synthesizers will enjoy a broader base of applications. Speech synthesizers are relatively inexpensive and are becoming increasingly popular with many personal computer owners.

Today, we must see and touch our workstations to interact with a computer, but in a few years, we'll be talking with computers as we move about our homes and offices.

Plotters

A **pen plotter** is a device that converts computer-generated graphs, charts, and line drawings to high-precision hard-copy output. There are two basic types of pen plotters: the *drum plotter* and the *flatbed plotter*. Both types have one or more pens that move over the paper to produce the image. Several pens are required to vary the width and color of the lines. Pens are selected and manipulated under computer control. On the drum plotter, the pens and the drum move concurrently to produce the image. On the flatbed plotter, only the pen moves.

Electrostatic plotter/printers produce a "quick and dirty" hard copy of graphic images for plot previewing. The final plot is completed on the high-precision drum or flatbed plotters.

An architect uses a graphics workstation to create a likeness of a house, then uses a 14-pen plotter to create the hard copy blueprint drawing.
(Houston Instrument)

A research economist uses this eight-pen flatbed plotter to draw a map of the United States that is divided into economic regions.
(Houston Instrument)

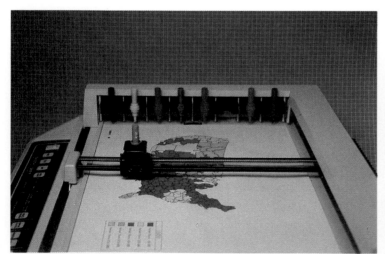

SUMMARY OUTLINE AND IMPORTANT TERMS

8-1 I/O DEVICES: OUR INTERFACE WITH THE COMPUTER. A variety of **peripheral** input and output devices complement the computer system to provide the interface between us and the computer system.

8-2. WORKSTATIONS. We interact with a computer system through a **workstation** or **terminal**. VDTs and micros are the most common workstations. The input mechanism is usually a keyboard, and the output is normally a display screen, called a monitor. Other input devices associated with workstations include the light pen, the joy stick, the track ball, the digitizing tablet and pen, and the mouse.

A **soft copy** (as opposed to **hard copy**) of alphanumeric and graphic output is displayed on the monitor. The three attributes of monitors are size (diagonal dimension 5 to 25 inches), color (monochrome or color), and **resolution** (quality of output).

Portable workstations are packaged for ease of movement and handling and have a built-in **modem** that enables connection to a telephone line for remote transmission of data.

Workstations are quickly becoming companions to workers in most fields of endeavor.

8-3 DATA ENTRY: GETTING DATA INTO THE COMPUTER SYSTEM. **Source data** are transcribed to a machine-readable format or read directly by data entry devices. In batch **data entry**, source data are entered consecutively as a group. In transaction-oriented data entry, the operator interacts directly with the data base and updates the data base as the transaction occurs. The trend in data entry is to minimize the number of transcription steps by entering data on-line, at the source.

Optical character recognition eliminates the need for some manual data entry by encoding certain data in machine-readable format. **OCR scanners** recognize printed characters and certain coded symbols, such as **bar codes**. OCR scanners are used for original source data collection and with **turnaround documents**. **Magnetic ink character recognition** devices, which are used almost exclusively in banking, are similar to OCR in function but have increased speed and accuracy.

Magnetic stripes and **smart cards** provide input to **badge readers**. **Voice data entry** or **voice recognition** devices can be used to enter limited kinds and quantities of data. **Vision input systems** are best suited for tasks that involve only a few images. **Portable data entry** devices are hand held and are normally used to collect data off-line.

8-4 OUTPUT DEVICES. Output devices translate data stored in binary to a form that can be interpreted by the end user. Workstations are both input and output devices. Printers prepare hard-copy output at speeds of 40 to 40,000 lines per minute. **Serial printers** are both impact and nonimpact, where **line printers** are impact only and **page printers** are nonimpact only. The technologies used to produce the image vary widely from one printer to the next.

Computer output microfilm/microfiche (COM) devices prepare microfilm and microfiche as a space- and time-saving alternative to printed output. **Voice response units** provide recorded or synthesized voice output. **Pen plotters** and **electrostatic plotter/printers** convert stored data to hard-copy graphs, charts, and line drawings.

REVIEW EXERCISES

Concepts

1. Which has greater precision, a pen plotter or an electrostatic plotter?
2. What is meant when someone says that voice data entry systems are speaker dependent?
3. List devices, other than key-driven, that are used to input source data to a computer system.
4. What is the purpose of having a computer console?
5. Which types of printers print fully formed characters?
6. What is a turnaround document? Give two examples.
7. Identify all input and output methods used by an automatic teller machine.
8. What is a smart card?
9. What is the relationship between a light pen and a cursor?
10. What advantages does on-line data entry have over off-line data entry?
11. Give three example applications for bar codes.
12. Give three examples of how a police department would use computer output.
13. Why do banks use MICR rather than OCR for data entry?

Discussion

14. Describe the input/output characteristics of a workstation that would be used by engineers for computer-aided design.
15. Department stores use hand-held wands to interpret the bar codes imprinted on the price tags of the merchandise. Why do they not use slot scanners as supermarkets do?
16. Suppose the company you work for batches all sales data for data entry each night. You have been asked to present a convincing argument to top management on why funds should be allocated to convert the current system to transaction-oriented data entry. What would you say?
17. What input/output capabilities are available at your college?
18. Compare today's vision input systems with those portrayed in such films as *2001* and *2010*. Do you believe that we will have a comparable vision technology by the year 2001?

SELF-TEST (by section)

8-1 (a) Input devices translate data to a form that can be interpreted by a computer. (T/F)

(b) The primary function of I/O peripherals is to facilitate computer-to-computer data transmission. (T/F)

8-2 (a) All keyboards have special-function keys. (T/F)

(b) The quality of output on a workstation's monitor is determined by its _____ .

8-3 (a) Optical character recognition is a means of original source data collection. (T/F)

(b) A _____ is a brief message to an operator that describes what data are to be entered.

8-4 (a) Ink-jet printers are classified as impact printers. (T/F)

(b) Dot-matrix printer technology is available in serial and line printers. (T/F)

Self-Test answers.   8–1 (a), T; (b), F; 8–2 (a), F; (b), resolution; 8–3 (a), T; (b), prompt; 8–4 (a), F; (b), T.

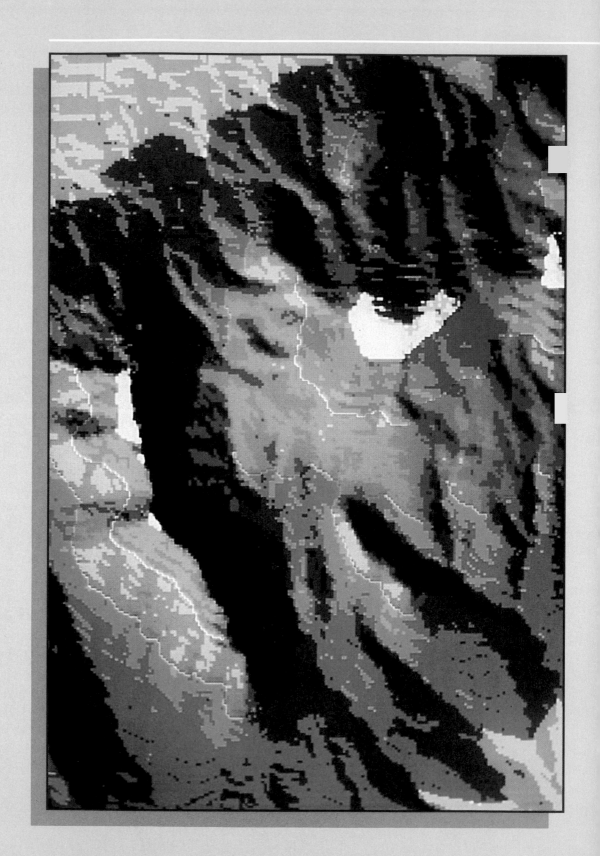

STUDENT LEARNING OBJECTIVES

- To demonstrate an understanding of data communications terminology and applications.
- To detail the function and operation of data communications hardware.
- To describe the alternatives and sources for data transmission services.
- To illustrate the various types of computer networks.

CHAPTER

9

Data
Communications

9

A traveling government official uses the data communications capabilities of a public telephone and his pocket computer to send an arrival message to his staff in Washington, D.C.
(RCA)

9–1 DATA COMMUNICATIONS: FROM ONE ROOM TO THE WORLD

For many years we have depended on telephone conversations and the postal service to communicate data and information from one location to another. Now, thousands of memos and charts can be sent to locations around the world in a matter of seconds. This is possible because of **data communications** capabilities. Data communications is, very simply, the collection and distribution of "electronic" data from and to remote facilities. Data are transmitted from computers to workstations and other computers over land, in the air, and under the sea. Telephone lines, satellites, and coaxial cable on the ocean floor are a few of the many ways that data are transmitted.

Our society is becoming more dependent on data communications capabilities. Government, business, and individuals have an increased need to communicate with one another. You might even say that our society is shrinking (figuratively, of course), for between data communications and computer technology, it is just as easy to communicate with someone in another state as it is with someone in the next building.

Through the 1960s, a company's computing hardware was located in a single room, called the machine room. Since that time, microcomputers, workstations, and data communications have made it possible to move hardware and information systems "closer to the source" and to the people who use them. Before long, workstations will be as much a part of our work environment as desks and telephones are now.

Several other terms describe the general area of data communications. **Telecommunications** encompasses not only data communications, but any type of remote communication, such as the transmission of a television signal. **Teleprocessing**, or **TP**, is the combination of *tele*communications and data *processing* and is often used interchangeably with the term data communications. The integration of computer systems, workstations, and communications links is referred to as a **computer network**.

9–2 WHY "GO ON-LINE"?

Easily accessible data communication facilities and the widespread availability of workstations just about signal the end of the batch processing era. In batch processing, transactions are periodically batched for processing, and reports are generated and distributed daily or weekly. Today, people want information *now*, and they want it to be *current*. These demands cannot be met with batch information systems.

Organizations use communications-based information systems—that is, they "go on-line"—to get an *immediate response* to an inquiry from an *up-to-the-minute data base*. For example, in a department store, a sale is recorded immediately on a POS terminal. With an up-to-the-minute data base, an illegal charge card or a customer's exceeding the charge limit can be detected before the sale is completed. In a batch system, an illegal charge card could be used all day before being detected.

WE'VE COME A LONG WAY

After driving the invading Persian forces to the sea, the Greek general Miltiades sent Pheidippides, his swiftest runner, to warn Athens of a possible sea attack. Pheidippides ran from the plains of Marathon to Athens, a distance of 26 miles, shouted "Rejoice, we conquer," and then died.

Sending a message 26 miles or around the world is not nearly so dramatic today. The speed at which we send messages has evolved from Pheidippides, to the Pony Express, to the telegraph, to the telephone. Now we can send a message the length of this book via communications satellites anywhere in the world in a couple of seconds.

Without Pheidippides' news of victory, the Athenians would have assumed defeat by the much larger Persian army and surrendered the city. Today's long-distance messages are more routine but no less important—and timeliness is still a critical factor.

Farmers at this cotton cooperative have an on-line hookup to a computer network that provides them with up-to-the-minute commodities prices. (Courtesy of International Business Machines Corporation)

Increased capability and *flexibility* are important features of on-line systems. Business executives have the corporate data base at their fingertips. Before leaving home in the morning, a company president can use a PC to review a list of slow-selling products, then inform all vice-presidents, via electronic mail, of a meeting to address these problem areas.

9–3 APPLICATIONS FOR DATA COMMUNICATIONS ____

The applications for on-line communications-based systems are limited only by the imagination. The descriptions that follow should give you an idea of the variety of data communications applications that already exist.

Electronic Mail. Computer networks enable us to route messages to each other. A message can be a note, letter, report, chart, or even the manuscript of a book. Each person in an organization can be assigned an "electronic

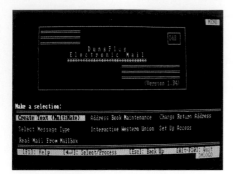

To send a message via electronic mail, the user initiates the "E-mail" software, then works from a menu to produce and send the message.
(DunsPlus, a company of The Dun & Bradstreet Corporation)

mailbox" in which messages are received and stored on secondary storage. To "open" and "read" your **electronic mail**, or "E-mail," you simply go to the nearest workstation and recall the message from storage.

A national sales manager can inform regional sales managers of a price reduction via electronic mail and avoid the time-consuming ritual of "telephone tag." The message would originate on a workstation at the national headquarters. It would then be routed to the electronic mailboxes of the regional managers. Each manager "opens the mail" by displaying the message on a workstation.

Electronic mail is a common application at many colleges. An instructor can route assignments to students. Students can arrange project meetings. If you have any mail, you are told to check your mail when you "log on" at your workstation.

 Information Networks and Videotext.   Information networks and videotext (see Chapter 4, "Computer Systems—Micros") make a wide variety of services available through data communications. You can use your home or office workstation to do your banking, catch up on the stock prices, check out the menu at a local restaurant, or do your grocery shopping.

Inquiry/Response.   An on-line information system will let you make an inquiry at a workstation and receive a response. For example, an attorney

ELECTRONIC CONVERSATIONS

Computerized bulletin boards and electronic mail have opened new channels of communication for those who want to communicate electronically.

If someone wants to call a bulletin board system, or BBS, to post a message or look for information, they will need a modem (to make the telephone-line connection) and the BBS phone number. Electronic mail, or E-mail, works much the same way.

Behavioral scientists at Carnegie-Mellon University are now studying how this new medium of communication affects the content and tone of the message. Do people relate differently through electronic conversations than through face-to-face conversations? The answer is a very strong Yes!

Researchers say that use of the electronic language is informal and uninhibited, sometimes to the point of rudeness. In addition, one person generally does not dominate the conversation. Because of this, some companies are finding that more people are participating in

This touchscreen display illustrates the use of a software product designed specifically for writing memos.
(Photo courtesy of Hewlett-Packard Company)

a decision-making process because they have a chance to "talk."

Electronic conversations do not convey the nonverbal cues of personal conversation, which can encourage social feedback or inhibit extreme behavior. The messages, they find, focus on the text itself rather than the audience.

A waitress in a Tokyo restaurant enters a credit card account number into a nationwide credit verification system. (Courtesy of International Business Machines Corporation).

might request a listing of precedent-setting cases involving computer fraud; the director of personnel might wish to see the training record of an employee; or a salesperson in a department store might inquire about a customer's credit limit.

A user making an inquiry is always concerned about the system's **response time**, which is the elapsed time between when a message is sent and when a response is received. Response time is an important consideration in the design of an on-line information system. As a rule of thumb, the average response time should be less than 1 second, except during peak periods. A high response time is an indication of a poorly designed system or a lack of computing capacity. Figure 9–1 shows how operator productivity decreases as the response time increases.

The response time will vary considerably, depending on the complexity of the inquiry, the number of workstations, the capacity of the host, and the capacity of the channel. In college computer centers, for example, the response time inevitably increases as the due date for a big programming assignment approaches and students begin to jam the system.

Transaction Processing/Data Entry.   Data can be entered on-line, directly from the source location. For example, telephone marketers at mail order houses can enter order data while talking with customers, as can reservations clerks for airlines and hotels.

Data Collection.   Computer networks can be used to collect data from remote locations. Some organizations, such as the federal government's Central Intelligence Agency (CIA), control access to certain sections of the headquarters building by installing badge readers at the entrances to secured areas. Each badge reader is linked to the computer; it collects data that logs when a person enters and exits each secured area and who that person is.

Process Control.   Data communications systems are also used to control processes. A city can continuously monitor the direction and volume of traffic

FIGURE 9–1
Response Time Versus Operator Productivity
Higher response times not only result in nonproductive wait times, but they also cause operators to lose their interactive momentum with the computer.

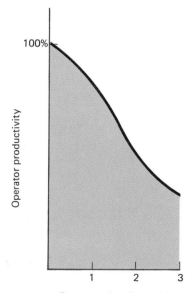

by accepting input from sensors located in the streets. These data are fed to a central computer system that coordinates traffic signals to optimize the flow of traffic.

Remote Processing.   Computer networks provide the capability for anyone in an organization to use the mainframe computer and a variety of software for computational purposes. Engineers, clergy, actuaries, loan officers, scientists, and others need only swivel their chairs to the nearest workstation to solve their computational problems.

Interactive Programming.   Programmers write their programs at workstations while in direct communication with the computer. This mode of program development is known as *interactive programming*. Interactive program development is an enormous improvement over the punched-card program development of the 1950s and 1960s where the **turnaround time**, or the elapsed time between submitting the program and receiving the results, could be as much as a day! On-line debugging aids, immediate **diagnostics** (error messages), and the elimination of turnaround time have greatly reduced the aggravation and the time required to develop and test a program.

Data communications and interactive programming have made it possible for programmers to work at home on their own workstations. Employers have encouraged this "electronic cottage" concept by permitting some programmers to spend some of their working time at home. With the elimination of travel time, coffee breaks, idle conversations, and numerous office distractions, companies have found that some conscientious, self-motivated programmers can be more productive at home—although others are more productive when surrounded by a work environment where household and family distractions fade into the distance.

A computer system maintains efficient control over the processing of 900,000 pounds of oranges per day. In this process control application, the system monitors the data gathered from remote sensors at the feed, extraction, and finishing stations.
(Gould Inc.)

9-4   DATA COMMUNICATIONS HARDWARE _____

Data communications hardware is used to transmit data in a computer network between workstations and computers and between computers. This hardware includes modems, down-line processors, front-end processors, and data PBXs. The integration of these devices with workstations and computer systems is illustrated in Figure 9–2 and discussed below.

The Modem

Telephone lines were designed for voice communication, not data communication. The **modem** (*mo*dulator/*dem*odulator) converts computer-to-workstation electrical *digital* signals to *analog* signals so that the data can be transmitted over telephone lines (see Figure 9–3). The digital electrical signals are "modulated" to make sounds similar to those you hear on a touch-tone telephone. Upon reaching their destination, the analog signals are "demodulated" by another modem to computer-compatible electrical signals for processing. The process is done in reverse for workstation-to-computer communication.

On most workstations, the modem is an optional device that is contained on a circuit board and simply plugged into an empty slot in the workstation.

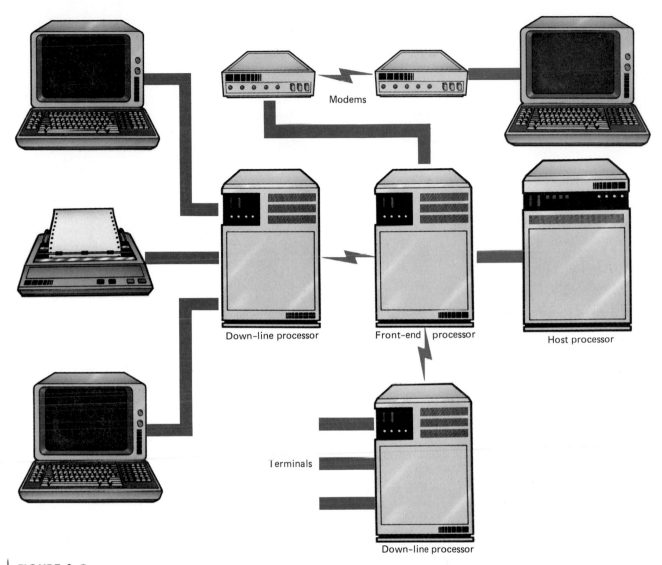

FIGURE 9–2
Hardware Components in Data Communications
Devices that handle the movement of data in a computer network are the
modem, down-line processor, front-end processor, and host processor.

To make the connection with a telephone line, you simply plug the telephone
line into the modem, just as you would if connecting a telephone. Modems
are "intelligent" devices that provide some processing capability. For instance,
the modem can automatically dial-up the computer (*auto-dial*), then establish
a link (*log on*), and even answer incoming calls from other computers (*auto-
answer*).

    For transmission media other than telephone lines, the modulation/de-
modulation process is not required. A modem is always required when you
"dial-up" the computer on a telephone line. If you need a telephone hookup
(for a voice conversation) on the same line and do not want to hassle with

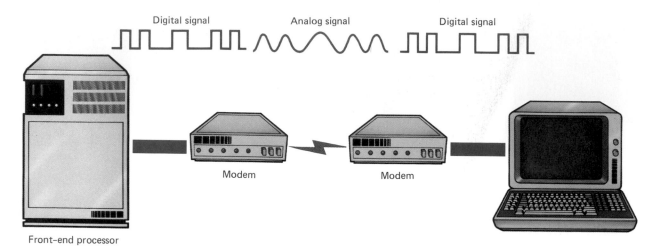

Digital signal   Analog signal   Digital signal

Modem   Modem

Front-end processor

FIGURE 9-3
The Modulation/
Demodulation Process
Electrical digital signals are
modulated to analog signals
for transmission over telephone
lines, then demodulated for
processing at the destination.

If every desk is expected to
have a telephone, a personal
computer, and a modem, why
not combine them into a single
unit? Some manufacturers
have: This voice/data
workstation permits
communication with other
people and other computers.
(AT&T Information Systems)

disconnecting the phone with each use, you can purchase a modem with
an **acoustical coupler**. To make the connection, you mount the telephone
handset directly on the acoustical coupler. Some workstations have not only
a built-in modem but a built-in telephone as well.

The Down-Line Processor

The **down-line processor**, discussed briefly in Chapter 6, is remote from
the host processor. It collects data from a number of low-speed devices,
such as workstations and serial printers. The down-line processor then transmits "concentrated" data over a *single* communications channel (see Figure
9–4).

The down-line processor, also called a **concentrator** or **multiplexor**,
is an economic necessity when several low-speed workstations are located
at one remote site. One high-speed line connecting the down-line processor
to the host is considerably less expensive than several low-speed lines connecting each workstation to the host. An airport airline reservations counter might
have four workstations. Each workstation is connected to a down-line processor, which in turn is connected to a central host computer. An airport
might have one or several down-line processors, depending on its size.

The Front-End Processor

The workstation or computer sending a **message** is the *source*. The workstation or computer receiving the message is the *destination*. The **front-end
processor** (described briefly in Chapter 6) establishes the link between source
and destination in a process called **handshaking**.

If you think of messages as mail to be delivered to various points in a
computer network, then the front-end processor is the post office. Each computer system and workstation is assigned an **address**. The front-end processor
uses these addresses to route messages to their destination(s). The content
of a message could be anything from a program instruction to an "electronic"

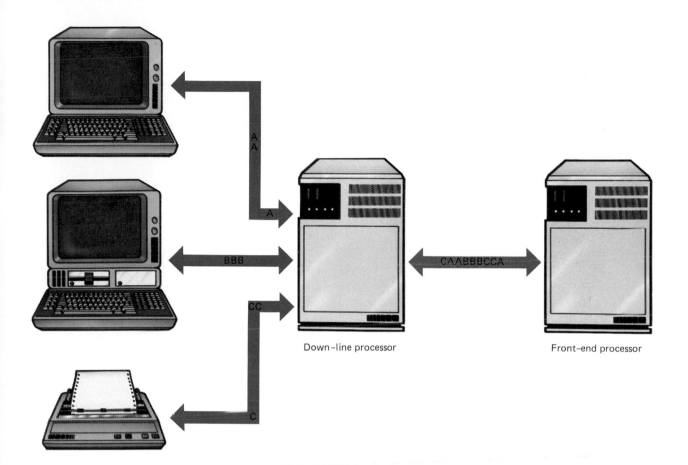

FIGURE 9–4
"Concentrating" Data for Remote Transmission
The down-line processor "concentrates" the data from several low-speed
devices for transmission over a single high-speed line. Data received from
a front-end processor are interpreted by the down-line processor and routed
to the appropriate device.

This office is one of 27 regional
customer support centers. Each
workstation is connected to a
concentrator (foreground) that
is connected via a high-speed
communications line to the
company's headquarters office
in Columbus, Ohio.
(© MICOM Systems, Inc., 1983)

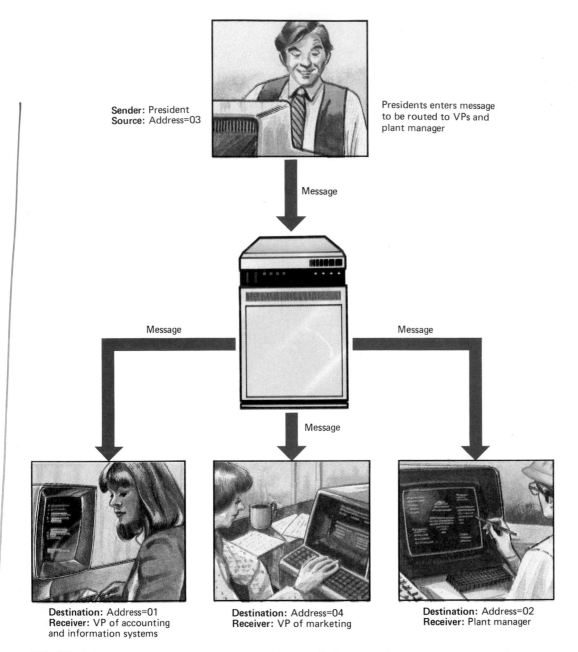

Sender: President
Source: Address=03

Presidents enters message
to be routed to VPs and
plant manager

Message

Message   Message

Message

Destination: Address=01
Receiver: VP of accounting
and information systems

Destination: Address=04
Receiver: VP of marketing

Destination: Address=02
Receiver: Plant manager

FIGURE 9–5
Message Routing
In the illustration, the president
sends a message to two VPs
and the plant manager.

memo. Figure 9–5 illustrates how a memo would be sent from the president
of a company to two vice-presidents and the plant manager. It is not uncommon for a front-end processor to control communications between a dozen
down-line processors and a hundred or more workstations.

The front-end processor relieves the host processor of communications-
related tasks, such as message routing, parity checking, code translation, editing, and cryptography (the encryption/decryption of data). This processor
"specialization" permits the host to operate more efficiently and to devote
more of its resources to processing applications programs.

The Data PBX

The old-time telephone PBX (private branch exchange) switchboard has given its name to a new generation of devices for **data PBX** switching. The data PBX is actually a computer that electronically connects computers and workstations much as telephone operators manually connected people on the old PBX switchboards.

With the trend to distributed processing, a single organization is likely to have more than one mainframe computer and a bunch of workstations. The data PBX, serving as the hub of data activity, permits these computers and workstations to talk to one another. Figure 9–6 illustrates how several mainframe computer systems can be linked via a data PBX.

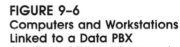

MEMORY BITS

HARDWARE FOR DATA COMMUNICATIONS
- Modem
- Down-line processor (concentrator or multiplexor)
- Front-end processor
- Data PBX

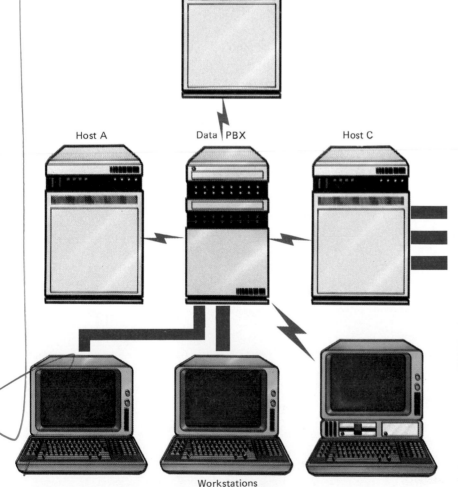

Workstations

FIGURE 9–6
Computers and Workstations Linked to a Data PBX
Any two of the host computers or workstations can be linked together for data transmission by the data PBX.

A data PBX connects computing devices for data communication in a manner similar to the way operators used to connect telephones for voice communication. With the data PBX, however, it's all automatic.
(AT&T Technologies)

9-5 THE DATA COMMUNICATIONS CHANNEL: DATA HIGHWAYS

Transmission Media

A **communications channel** is the facility by which data are transmitted between locations in a computer network. Data are transmitted as combinations of bits (0s and 1s). A channel's *capacity* is rated by the number of bits that can be transmitted per second. A regular telephone line can transmit up to 9,600 bits per second (bps), or 9.6K bps (thousands of bits per second). Under normal circumstances, a 9.6K bps line would fill a video monitor in 1 or 2 seconds. Data rates of 1,500K bps are available through common carriers, such as American Telephone and Telegraph (AT&T). The channel, also called a **line** or a **data link**, may be comprised of one or a combination of the transmission media discussed below.

Telephone Lines.   The same transmission facilities that we use for telephone conversations can also be used to transmit data. This capability is provided by communications companies throughout the country and the world.

Optical Fiber.   Very thin transparent fibers have been developed that will eventually replace the copper wire traditionally used in the telephone system. These hairlike fibers carry data faster and are lighter and less expensive than their copper-wire counterpart.

The differences in the data transmission rates of copper wire and optical fiber are tremendous. In the time it takes to transmit a single page of Webster's *Unabridged Dictionary* over copper wire (about 6 seconds), the entire dictionary could be transmitted over a single optical fiber.

The majority of remote data communications is still carried via the network of copper telephone lines. The telephone system, originally set up for voice communication, is being updated (e.g., optical fiber) to better handle data communications.
(© M/A-COM, Inc.)

Copper wire in the telephone network is being replaced by the more versatile optical fiber. This cable, seen in cross-section, contains flat ribbons, each with a dozen glass fibers. Laser-generated light pulses are transmitted through these ultrathin glass fibers. A pair of optical fibers can simultaneously carry 1,344 voice conversations and interactive data communications sessions.
(Courtesy of AT&T Bell Laboratories)

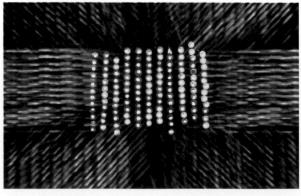

An astronaut in a manned maneuvering unit is preparing to dock with a Westar VI communications satellite. The astronaut later docked with the satellite and moved it near the end of the remote manipulator system so that it could be loaded in the bay of the space shuttle and brought back to earth for repair.
(NASA)

In satellite communications, data are first transmitted to an earth station, where giant antennas route signals to another earth station via a communications satellite. The signals are then transmitted to their destination over another type of communications channel.
(TRW Inc.)

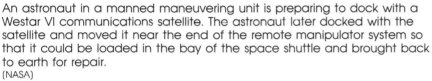

    Another of the many advantages of optical fiber is its contribution to data security. It is much more difficult for a computer criminal to intercept a signal sent over optical fiber (via a beam of light) than it is over copper wire (an electrical signal).

Coaxial Cable.   Coaxial cable contains electrical wire and is constructed to permit high-speed data transmission with a minimum of signal distortion. Coaxial cable is laid along the ocean floor for intercontinental voice and data transmission. It is also used to connect workstations and computers in a "local" area (from a few feet to a few miles).

Microwave repeater stations, such as these atop the Haleakala Crater in Maui, Hawaii, relay signals to transceivers or other repeater stations.
(Long and Associates)

Satellites.   Communications channels do not have to be wires or fibers. Satellites are routinely launched into orbit for the sole purpose of relaying data communication signals to and from earth stations. A satellite is launched and set in a geosynchronous orbit 22,300 miles above the earth. A geosynchronous orbit permits the communications satellite to maintain a fixed position relative to the surface of the earth. Each satellite can receive and retransmit signals to slightly less than half of the earth's surface; therefore, three satellites are required to effectively cover the earth (see Figure 9–7). The big advantage of satellites is that data can be transmitted from one location to any number of other locations anywhere on (or near) our planet.

Microwave.   Transmission of microwave radio signals is line-of-sight; that is, the radio signal travels in a direct line from one repeater station to the next until it reaches its destination (see Figure 9–8). Because of the curvature of the earth, microwave repeater stations are placed on the tops of mountains and towers, usually about 30 miles apart.

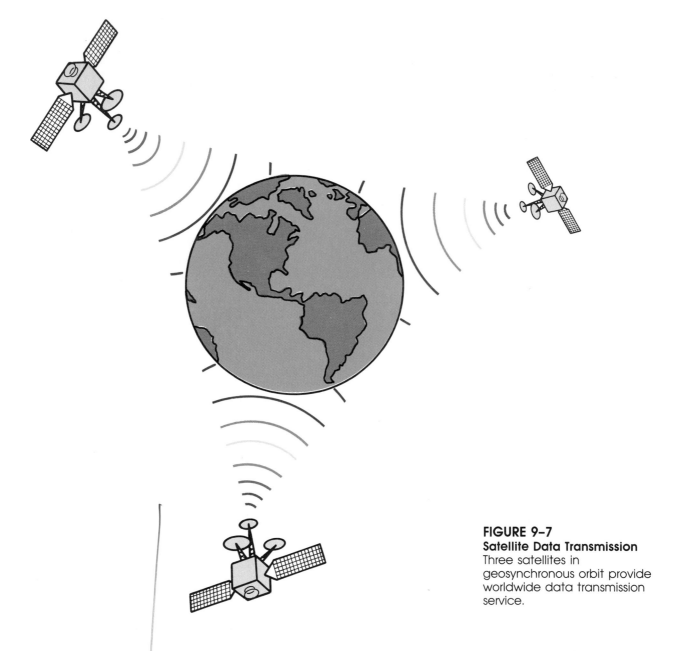

FIGURE 9-7
Satellite Data Transmission
Three satellites in
geosynchronous orbit provide
worldwide data transmission
service.

Data Transmission in Practice

A communications channel from computer A in Seattle, Washington, to computer B in Orlando, Florida (see Figure 9–9), would usually consist of several different transmission media. The connection between computer A and a workstation in the same building is probably coaxial cable. The Seattle company might use a communications company, such as AT&T, to transmit the data. The company would then transmit the data through a combination of transmission facilities that might include optical fiber, microwave, and satellite.

FIGURE 9–8
Microwave Data Transmission
The curvature of the earth requires that line-of-sight microwave signals be
carried via microwave repeater stations.

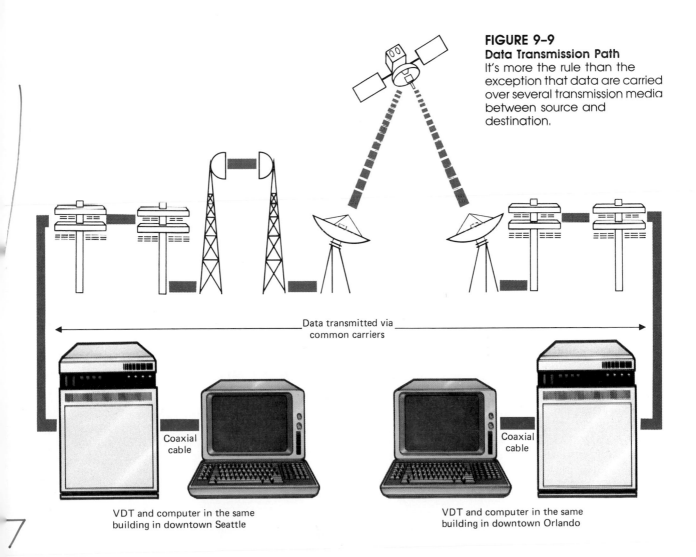

FIGURE 9–9
Data Transmission Path
It's more the rule than the
exception that data are carried
over several transmission media
between source and
destination.

Data transmitted via
common carriers

Coaxial
cable

Coaxial
cable

VDT and computer in the same
building in downtown Seattle

VDT and computer in the same
building in downtown Orlando

9–6 DATA TRANSMISSION SERVICES _____

Common Carriers

It is impractical, not to mention illegal, for companies to string their own coaxial cables between Philadelphia and New York City. It is also impractical for them to set their own satellites in orbit. Therefore, companies turn to **common carriers**, such as AT&T and Western Union, to provide channels for data communications. Data communications common carriers, which are regulated by the Federal Communications Commission (FCC), offer two basic types of service: private lines and switched lines.

A **private line** (or **leased line**) provides a dedicated data communications channel between any two points in a computer network. The charge for a private line is based on channel capacity (bps) and distance (air miles).

QUESTIONS AND ANSWERS ABOUT SATELLITES

WHY SATELLITES? Through earthstation-to-satellite communication, people around the world can communicate via telephone or telex, through electronic data transfer, by facsimile, and by teleconferencing. Satellite communication permits live television broadcasts to be transmitted around the globe. The beauty of satellite communication is that it permits communication from any point on earth to any other point. Satellite communication is not bound by the constraints of physical media, such as coaxial cable.

HOW ARE THEY PUT INTO ORBIT? Satellites launched from the United States are shot into space by multistage rockets from Cape Canaveral in Florida or Vandenberg Air Force Base in California. Ninety-eight percent of the satellites are launched from the U.S.A. or Russia.

WHO PLACES THEM IN ORBIT? Organizations such as the National Aeronautics and Space Administration (NASA), the Communications Satellite Corporation (COMSAT), the International Telecommunications Satellite Organization (Intelsat), and others are responsible for placing satellites in orbit.

NASA's Space Shuttle is now delivering and repairing many satellites. COMSAT, created by Congress in 1962, provides satellite-based services and products to the international, maritime, and U.S. domestic markets. Intelsat, a consortium of over 100 countries, operates satellites that provide about two-thirds of all intercontinental telecommunications.

HOW DO THEY STAY IN ORBIT? The pull of gravity is the key. Satellites must be traveling at just the right speed to go into orbit. If their speed is too slow, they fall toward earth and burn up. If they travel too fast, they are flung into outer space. A typical orbital speed is around 17,000 miles per hour.

WHAT ARE THE TYPES OF ORBITS? A variety of orbits are possible, depending on what part of the earth or space the satellite is to cover or avoid. Elliptical orbits permit satellites to come closer to earth twice during each orbit. In circular orbits, the satellite is approximately the same distance from earth throughout each orbit. Some are placed in a "geosynchronous" orbit 22,300 miles over the equator where they are synchronized with the spin of the earth. In this way they have a fixed relationship with the earth.

HOW MANY AND HOW LONG? According to NASA, over 3,000 have been put into orbit since Sputnik in 1957. Of those, about 300 remain.

Some are made to last a few weeks or months, and others for many years. A few fall out of orbit and disintegrate when they reach the earth's atmosphere.

This common carrier's earth station control console in New Jersey monitors video and data communications traffic between satellites and earth. (RCA)

You can use the rule of thumb of *$1 per mile per month* to get a rough estimate of the cost of an interstate 4.8K bps private line. For example, a company might expect to pay about $1,000 per month for a private line between Denver and Houston (the distance is about 1,000 miles).

A **switched line** (or **dial-up line**) is available strictly on a time-and-distance charge, similar to a long-distance telephone call. You make a connection by "dialing-up" the computer; then a modem sends and receives data.

As a rule of thumb, a private line is the least expensive alternative if you expect to use the channel more than three hours per day and you do not need the flexibility to connect with several different computers.

Specialized Common Carriers

During the early years of computer networks and data communications, "Ma Bell" had a virtual monopoly on providing data communications services. Monopolies have never inspired innovation, and the FCC opened the door for competition in the form of **specialized common carriers**. The net result of the FCC decision was improved service from common carriers and expanded capabilities from specialized common carriers.

One type of specialized common carrier is known as a **value-added network (VAN)**. A VAN may or may not use the transmission facilities of a common carrier, but, in each case, it "adds value" to the transmission service. The value added over and above the standard services of the common carriers may include electronic mail and code conversion for communication between noncompatible computers. Not only does a VAN offer expanded services, but the total service cost may be less than that of the basic service from a common carrier.

To illustrate how a VAN can offer the same or better service at a reduced rate, consider the following (see Figure 9–10). The Ace Corporation wishes

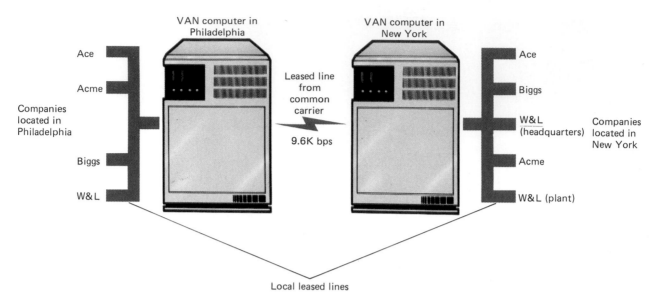

VAN computer in
Philadelphia

VAN computer in
New York

Ace

Acme

Companies
located in
Philadelphia

Biggs

W&L

Leased line
from
common
carrier

9.6K bps

Ace

Biggs

W&L
(headquarters)

Companies
located in
New York

Acme

W&L (plant)

Local leased lines

FIGURE 9-10
Part of a Value-Added Network (VAN)
A VAN uses transmission media more efficiently and is, therefore, able to offer transmission service at a reduced rate.

to lease a 9.6K bps private line between New York and Philadelphia from a common carrier. Ace is likely to use only 15 percent of the capacity of the line. A VAN could lease the same line from the same common carrier (or use their own) and use the line to capacity by combining the New York/ Philadelphia data transmission requirements of Ace Corporation with those of several other companies. The VAN uses computers on each end of the line to collect the data and redistribute them to appropriate destinations. In effect, several corporations share the same line and its cost with little or no loss in performance.

9-7 NETWORKS: LINKING COMPUTERS AND WORKSTATIONS

Computer Networks

Network Configurations.   Each time you use the telephone, you use the world's largest computer network—the telephone system. A telephone is an end point, or a **node**, that is connected to a network of computers that route your voice signals to another telephone, or node. The node in a computer network can be a workstation or another computer. Computer networks are configured to meet the specific requirements of an organization. The basic computer network configurations—star, ring, and bus—are illustrated in Figure 9-11.

The **star configuration** involves a centralized host computer that is connected to a number of smaller computer systems. The smaller computer systems communicate with one another through the host and usually share the host computer's data base. Both the central computer and the distributed computer systems are connected to workstations (micros or VDTs). Any workstation can communicate with any other workstation in the network. Banks

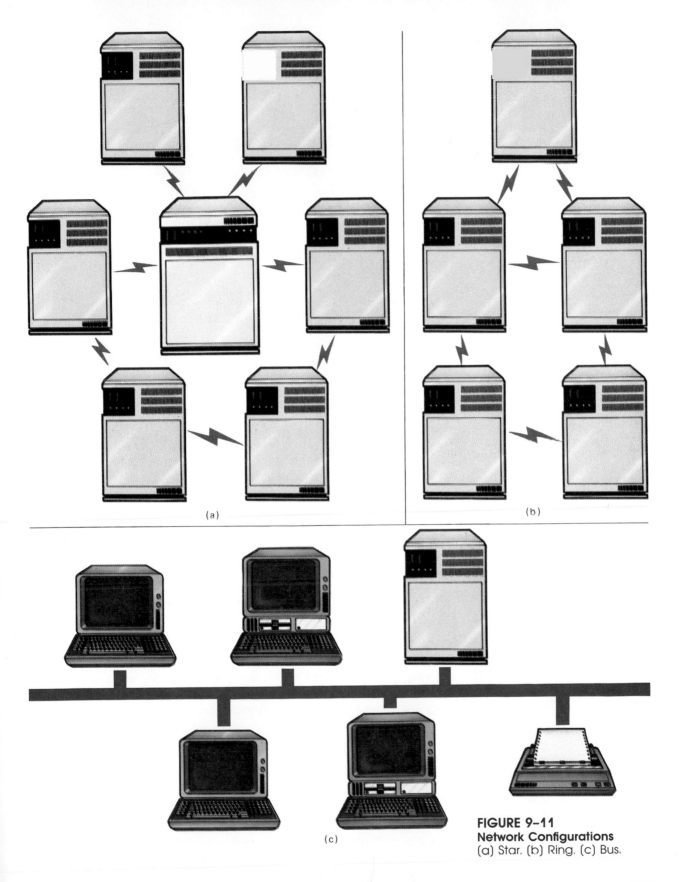

(a)

(b)

(c)

FIGURE 9–11
Network Configurations
(a) Star. (b) Ring. (c) Bus.

These operators monitor the operation of a computer network that interconnects hundreds of computers and workstations.
(Copyright 1984 GTE Telenet Communications Corporation)

At the end of each month, this plant manager downloads cost data from the company's mainframe computer to his microcomputer (see modem under the phone). He then uses micro-based graphics software to compare expenditures for the Boston plant with those of the Phoenix and Indianapolis plants.
(Management Science America, Inc. (MSA))

usually have a large home-office computer system with a star network of minicomputer systems in the branch banks.

The **ring configuration** involves computer systems that are approximately the same size, and no one computer system is the focal point of the network. Each intermediate computer system must read a message and pass it along to the destination computer system.

The **bus configuration** permits the connection of workstations, peripheral devices, and microcomputers along a central cable. Devices can be easily added to or deleted from the network. Bus configurations are most appropriate when the devices linked are close to one another (see the discussion of local area networks that follows).

A pure form of any of these three configurations is seldom found in practice. Most computer networks are *hybrids*—that is, combinations of these configurations.

The Micro/Mainframe Link.   Micros, initially designed for use by a single individual, have even greater potential when they can be linked with mainframe computers. To give micros this dual-function capability, vendors developed the necessary hardware and software to have **micro/mainframe links**. There are three categories of micro/mainframe links:

1. The microcomputer serves as a dumb terminal.
2. Data are requested from a micro, then downloaded from a mainframe to the micro for processing.
3. Both work together to process data and produce information.

Micro/mainframe links of the first two types are well within the state of the art, but achieving the third is no easy task. The tremendous differences in the way computers and software are designed make complete micro/mainframe integration of activities difficult and, for some combinations of micros and mainframes, impossible.

Gateways. **Gateways** are helping to alleviate the problems associated with linking noncompatible micros, minis, and mainframes. A gateway is software that permits computers of different design architectures to "talk" to one another. For example, there is a gateway that permits Wang mainframe computers to communicate with IBM mainframe computers.

Local Networks

A **local area network (LAN)**, or a **local net**, for short, is a system of hardware, software, and communications channels that connects devices on the same premises, such as a college campus or a cluster of office buildings. A local net permits the movement of data (including text, voice, and graphic images) between mainframe computers, personal computers, workstations, I/O devices, and even data PBXs. For example, your micro can be connected to another micro, to mainframes, and to shared resources, such as printers and disk storage. The distance separating devices in the local net may be a few feet to a few miles.

(By permission of Michael Artell)

The unique feature of a local net is that a common carrier is not required to transmit data between computers, workstations, and shared resources. Because of the proximity of devices in local nets, a company can install its own communications channels (such as coaxial cable or optical fiber).

Like computers, cars, and just about everything else, local nets can be built at various levels of sophistication. At the most basic level they permit the interconnection of PCs in a department so that users can send messages to one another and share files and printers. The more sophisticated local nets permit the interconnection of mainframes, micros, and the gamut of peripheral devices throughout a large, but geographically constrained, area, such as a cluster of buildings.

In the near future, you will be able to plug a workstation into a communications channel just as you would plug a telephone line into a telephone jack. This type of data communications capability is being installed in many new office buildings and even in some hotel rooms.

For intracity data communications, many companies are installing their own private microwave system. These miniature microwave stations provide an inexpensive alternative to the more costly coaxial cable systems.
(© M/A-COM, Inc.)

Local nets are often integrated with "long-haul" networks. For example, a bank will have home-office teller workstations linked to the central computer via a local net. But for long-haul data communication, the bank's branch offices must rely on common carriers.

9–8 LINE CONTROL: RULES FOR TRANSMITTING DATA ___

Polling and Contention

When a workstation or a microcomputer is connected to a computer over a single communications channel, this is a **point-to-point** connection. When more than one workstation or micro is connected to a single communications

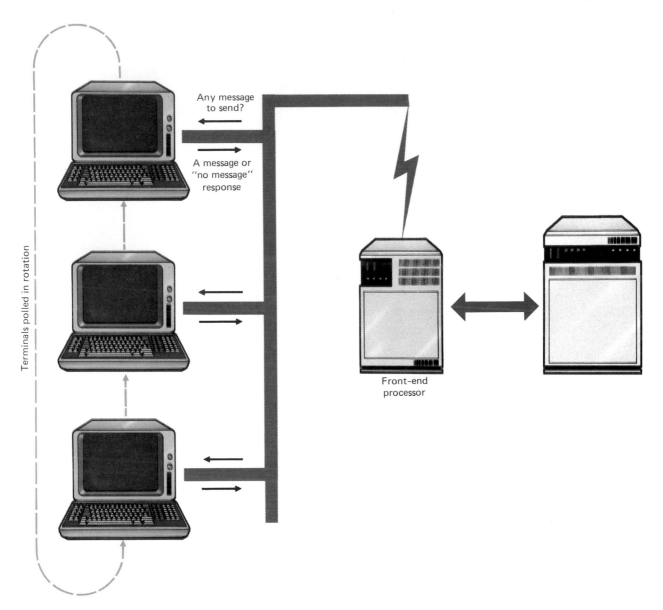

FIGURE 9–12
The Polling Process
Each terminal is polled in rotation to determine if a message is ready to be sent.

channel, the channel is called a **multidrop** line. Workstations on a multidrop line must share the data communications channel. Since all workstations cannot use the same channel at once, line-control procedures are needed. The most common line-control procedures are **polling** and **contention**.

In polling, the front-end processor "polls" each workstation in rotation to determine whether a message is ready to be sent (see Figure 9–12). If a particular workstation has a message to be sent and the line is available, the front-end processor accepts the message and polls the next workstation.

Programmers can adjust the polling procedure so that some workstations are polled more often than others. For example, tellers in a bank are continu-

The 48 data entry workstations shown here are part of a local area network that includes 200 other workstations located in the same building.
(Computer Consoles Inc.)'

ously interacting with the system. A loan officer, however, may average only two inquiries in an hour. In this case, the teller workstations might be polled four times for each poll of a loan-officer workstation.

In contention, a workstation with a message to be sent automatically requests service from the host processor. A request might result in a "line busy" signal, in which case the workstation waits a fraction of a second and tries again, and again, until the line is free. Upon assuming control of the line, the workstation sends the message and then relinquishes control of the line to another workstation.

Communications Protocols

Communications **protocols** are rules established to govern the way that data are transmitted in a computer network. The two general classifications of protocols, **asynchronous** and **synchronous**, are illustrated in Figure 9–13.

In asynchronous data transmission, data are transferred at irregular intervals on an as-needed basis. *Start/stop bits* are appended to the beginning and end of each message. The start/stop bits signal the receiving workstation/computer at the beginning and end of the message. Asynchronous transmission, sometimes called start/stop transmission, is best suited for data communication involving low-speed I/O devices, such as VDTs and serial printers.

In synchronous transmission, the source and destination operate in timed synchronization to enable high-speed data transmission. Start/stop bits are not required in synchronous transmission. Data transmission between computers and between cluster controllers and front-end processors normally is synchronous.

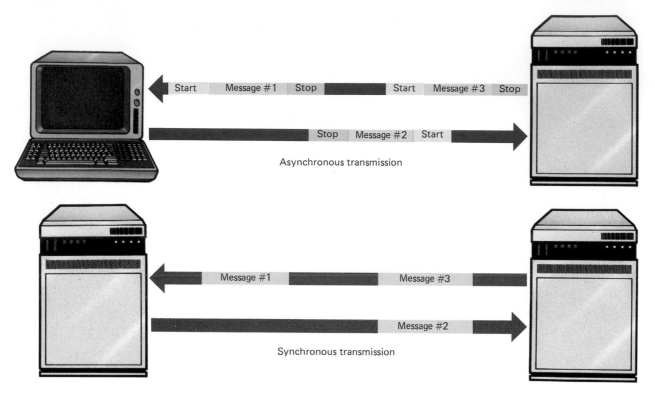

FIGURE 9-13
Asynchronous and Synchronous Transmission of Data
Asynchronous data transmission takes place at irregular intervals, where synchronous data transmission requires timed synchronization.

SUMMARY OUTLINE AND IMPORTANT TERMS _____

9-1 DATA COMMUNICATIONS: FROM ONE ROOM TO THE WORLD. Modern businesses use **data communications** to transmit data and information at high speeds from one location to the next. Data communications, or **teleprocessing (TP)**, makes an information system more accessible to the people who use it. The integration of computer systems via data communications is referred to as a **computer network**.

9-2 WHY "GO ON-LINE"? Companies are converting existing batch systems to on-line systems for a variety of reasons: to get a faster response to inquiries, to keep the data base current at all times, and to get more capability and flexibility in the system design.

9-3 APPLICATIONS FOR DATA COMMUNICATIONS. A given computer network will support at least one and probably four or more of the following types of communications-based applications: **electronic mail**, information networks and videotext, inquiry/response, transaction processing/data entry, data collection, process control, remote processing, and interactive programming.

9-4 DATA COMMUNICATIONS HARDWARE. The data communications hardware used to facilitate the transmission of data from one remote location to another includes **modems**, **down-line processors**, **front-end processors**, and **data PBXs**. Modems modulate and demodulate signals so that data can be transmitted over telephone lines. The latter three are special-function processors; they not only convert the signal to a format compatible with the transmission facility but also relieve the host processor of a number of processing tasks associated with data communications. One of the duties of the front-end processor is to establish the link between the source and the destination in a process called **handshaking**.

9-5 THE DATA COMMUNICATIONS CHANNEL: DATA HIGHWAYS. A **communications channel** (**line**, or **data link**) is the facility by which data are transmitted between locations in a computer network. A channel may be composed of one or more of the following transmission media: telephone lines, optical fiber, coaxial cable, satellites, and microwave. A channel's capacity is rated by the number of bits that can be transmitted per second.

9-6 DATA TRANSMISSION SERVICES. **Common carriers** provide communications channels to the public, and lines can be arranged to suit the application. A **private**, or **leased**, **line** provides a dedicated communications channel. A **switched**, or **dial-up**, **line** is available on a time-and-distance charge basis. **Specialized common carriers**, such as **value-added networks**, offer expanded transmission services.

9-7 NETWORKS: LINKING COMPUTERS AND WORKSTATIONS. Computer systems are linked together to form a computer network. The basic patterns for configuring computer systems within a computer network are **star**, **ring**, and **bus**. In practice, most networks are actually hybrids of these configurations.

The connection of microcomputers to a mainframe computer is called a **micro/mainframe link**. **Gateways** help to alleviate the problems associated with linking noncompatible computers in a computer network.

9-8 LINE CONTROL: RULES FOR TRANSMITTING DATA. A communications channel servicing a single workstation is a **point-to-point** connection. A communications channel servicing more than one workstation is called a **multidrop** line. The most common line-control procedures are **polling** and **contention**.

Data communications **protocols** are rules for transmitting data. The **asynchronous** protocol begins and ends each message with start/stop bits and is used primarily for low-speed data transmission. The **synchronous** protocol permits the source and destination to communicate in timed synchronization, for high-speed data transmission.

REVIEW EXERCISES

Concepts

1. What is meant by geosynchronous orbit and how does it relate to satellite data transmission?

2. What is the purpose of a multiplexor?

3. What is the relationship between teleprocessing and a computer network?

4. What device converts digital signals to analog signals for transmission over telephone lines? Why is it necessary?

5. Why is it not advisable to spread microwave relay stations 200 miles apart?

6. Construct a diagram illustrating the activities of the punched-card program-development process. Which of these activities are eliminated in interactive program development?

7. Briefly describe the function of a data PBX.

8. Briefly describe several hospital applications for data communications.

9. Describe circumstances for which a leased line would be preferred over a dial-up line.

10. Find out how to use your college's electronic mail system. The computer center should have literature explaining its use. If you are doing any programming, you have authorization for file space and you will probably have an electronic mailbox. Send an intriguing message to one of your classmates to set up a rendezvous to study computers.

11. Consider this situation: A remote line printer is capable of printing 800 lines per minute (70 characters per line average). Line capacity options are 2.4K, 4.8K, or 9.6K bps. Data are transmitted according to the ASCII encoding system. What capacity would you recommend for a communications channel to permit the printer to operate at capacity?

Discussion

12. Suppose you are a systems analyst for a municipal government. You have been asked to justify the conversion from a batch to an on-line incident-reporting system to the city council. What points would you make?

13. How is a specialized common carrier, such as a value-added network, able to improve on the services offered by a common carrier and offer these services at a reduced cost?

14. Discuss the difference between turnaround time and response time.

15. List and briefly describe all of the data communications applications in Section 9–3 that are implemented at your college.

16. How could you, as a student, benefit from using your college's data communications capabilities for word processing?

SELF-TEST (by section)

9–1. The general area of data communications encompasses telecommunications. (T/F)

9-2.   Getting an immediate response to an inquiry is one of several reasons to "go on-line." (T/F)

9-3.   _____ is the elapsed time between submitting a program and receiving the results.

9-4.   Another name for a front-end processor is multiplexor. (T/F)

9-5.   It is more difficult for a computer criminal to tap into an optical fiber than a copper telephone line. (T/F)

9-6.   The two basic types of service offered by common carriers are private line and leased line. (T/F)

9-7.   A LAN is designed for "long-haul" data communications. (T/F)

9-8.   In asynchronous data transmission, start/stop bits are appended to the beginning and end of each message. (T/F)

Self-Test answers.   9–1, F; 9–2, T; 9–3, Turnaround time; 9–4, F; 9–5, T; 9–6, F; 9–7, F; 9–8, T.

SOFTWARE AND
DATA MANAGEMENT

STUDENT LEARNING OBJECTIVES

- To discuss the terminology and concepts associated with programming languages and software.
- To distinguish between and give examples of applications software and systems software.
- To characterize each generation of programming languages.
- To categorize programming languages by generation.
- To describe the function of compilers and interpreters.
- To detail the purpose and objectives of an operating system.

CHAPTER

10

Programming Languages and Software Concepts

In Chapters 4 through 9, we discussed the operation and application of computer hardware. Most of us will agree that computers have become an integral part of society. We can touch them and see the results of their seemingly endless capabilities. But the computer-literate person recognizes that hardware is useless without **software**, and software is useless without hardware.

A computer system does nothing until directed to do so. A **program**, which consists of instructions to the computer, is the means by which we tell a computer to perform certain operations. These instructions are logically sequenced and assembled through the act of **programming**. **Programmers** use a variety of **programming languages**, such as COBOL and BASIC, to communicate instructions to the computer.

We use the term software to refer to the programs that direct the activities of the computer system. Software falls into two general categories: applications and systems. **Applications software** is designed and written to perform specific personal, business, or scientific processing tasks, such as payroll processing or statistical analysis. Other examples include the programs for claims processing (insurance), tax collection (local government), registration (university), order entry processing (manufacturing), and satellite trajectory tables (NASA).

Systems software is more general than applications software and is usually independent of any specific application area. Systems software programs support *all* applications software by directing the basic functions of the computer. For example, when the computer is turned on, an initialization

Below left. Programs written to address a specific business processing task, such as a point-of-sale system, are called applications software.
(Courtesy of International Business Machines Corporation)

Below right. At the end of each day, the operator calls a program that copies critical magnetic disk files to magnetic tape for backup. Such general software is referred to as systems software.
(Cullinet Software, Inc.)

MEMORY BITS	
SOFTWARE	
Applications	**Systems**
Claims processing (insurance)	Programming language compilers/ interpreters
Tax collection (local government)	Operating systems
Order entry processing (manufacturing)	Utility programs
Registration (university)	Communications software
Satellite trajectory tables (NASA)	Database management systems

program prepares and readies all devices for processing. Software that permits us to write programs in COBOL and BASIC is also systems software. The operating system, too, discussed later in this chapter, is classified as systems software.

10-2 GENERATIONS OF PROGRAMMING LANGUAGES

We "talk" to computers within the framework of a particular programming language. There are many different programming languages, most of which have highly structured sets of rules. The selection of a programming language depends on who is involved and the nature of "conversation." The president of a company may prefer a different type of language than a professional programmer; languages used for payroll processing may not be appropriate for ad-hoc (one time) inquiries. The use and application of the more common programming languages is discussed in Sections 10–3 and 10–8.

Like computers, programming languages have evolved in generations. With each new generation, fewer instructions are needed to instruct the computer to perform a particular task. That is, a program written in a first-generation language that computes and prints student grade averages may require 100 or more instructions; the same program in a fourth-generation language may have fewer than ten instructions.

The hierarchy of programming languages, shown in Figure 10–1, illustrates the relationships between the six generations of programming languages.

FIGURE 10-1
The Hierarchy of Programming Languages
As you progress from one generation of programming languages to the next, fewer instructions are required to perform a particular programming task.

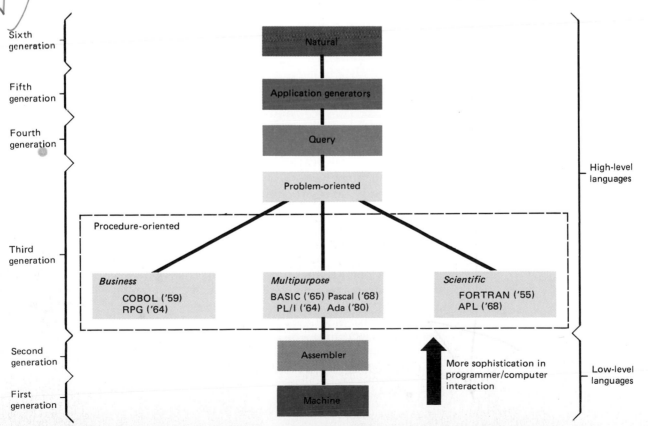

The later generations do not necessarily provide us with greater programming capabilities, but they do provide a *more sophisticated programmer/computer interaction*. In short, each new generation is easier to understand and use. For example, in the fourth, fifth, and sixth generations, we need only instruct the computer system *what to do*, not necessarily *how to do it*. When programming in one of the first three generations of languages, you have to tell the computer what to do *and* how to do it.

The ease with which the later generations can be used is certainly appealing, but the earlier languages also have their advantages. All six generations of languages are in use today.

10-3 THE FIRST AND SECOND GENERATIONS: "LOW-LEVEL"

Machine Language

Each computer has only *one* programming language that can be executed—the **machine language**. We talk of programming in COBOL, Pascal, and BASIC, but all of these languages must be translated to the machine language of the computer on which the program is to be executed. These and other high-level languages are simply a convenience for the programmer.

Machine-language programs, the *first generation*, are written at the most basic level of computer operation. Because their instructions are directed at this basic level of operation, machine language and assembler language (see below) are collectively called **low-level languages**. In machine language, instructions are coded as a series of 1s and 0s. As you might expect, machine-language programs are cumbersome and difficult to write. Early programmers had no alternative. Fortunately, we do.

Assembler Language

A set of instructions for an **assembler language** is essentially one-to-one with those of machine language. Like machine languages, assembler languages are unique to a particular computer. The big difference between the two types is the way the instructions are represented by the programmer. Rather than a cumbersome series of 1s and 0s, assembler languages use easily recognized symbols, called **mnemonics**, to represent instructions (see Figure 10–2). For example, most assembler languages use the mnemonic "A" to represent an "Add" instruction. The assembler languages ushered in the *second generation* of programming languages.

Prior to 1970, machine- and assembler-level languages were often used for applications program development and were always used for systems software development. Although it took longer, many programmers preferred assembler programming because they believed it used the computer system more efficiently. Since then, the power and flexibility of new generations of languages have put them beyond low-level languages in terms of both human and computer efficiency. Consequently, most programming is now done in **high-level languages** (third through sixth generations).

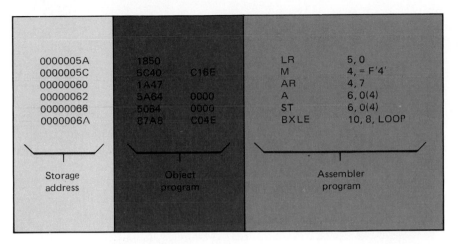

FIGURE 10-2
Part of an Assembler-Language Program
Even relatively simple assembler-language programs may contain a hundred or more instructions. The machine-language equivalent (object program) is shown in hexadecimal. The leftmost column contains the primary storage addresses for each machine-language and assembler-language instruction.

10-4 COMPILERS AND INTERPRETERS: PROGRAMS FOR PROGRAMS

No matter which language a high-level program is written in, it must be translated to machine language before it can be executed. This conversion of high-level instructions to machine-level instructions is done by systems software programs called compilers and interpreters.

Compilers

The **compiler** program translates the instructions of a high-level language, such as COBOL, to machine-language instructions that the computer can interpret and execute. A separate compiler (or an interpreter, discussed in the next section) is required for each programming language intended for use on a particular computer system. That is, to execute both COBOL and Pascal programs, you must have a COBOL compiler and a Pascal compiler. High-level programming languages are simply a programmer convenience; they cannot be executed in their source, or original, form.

The actual high-level programming-language instructions, called the **source program**, are translated or **compiled** to machine-language instructions by a compiler. The circled numbers in Figure 10–3 cross-reference the following numbered discussion of the compilation process.

1. Suppose you want to write a COBOL program. You first enter the instructions into the computer system through an on-line workstation. Having done so, you identify the language (COBOL) in which you wrote the program and request that the program be compiled.

2. The COBOL compiler program is called from secondary storage and loaded to primary storage along with the COBOL source program. [*Note:* Step 3 will be attempted but not completed if the source program has errors or **bugs** (see Step 4).]

3. The COBOL compiler translates the source program to a machine language program called an **object program**. The object program is the

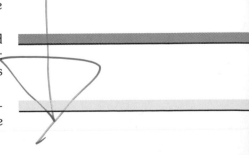

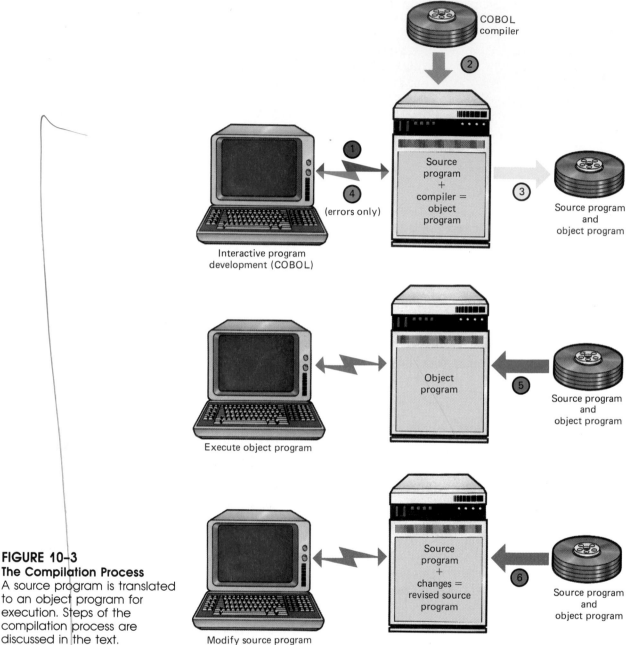

FIGURE 10-3
The Compilation Process
A source program is translated to an object program for execution. Steps of the compilation process are discussed in the text.

output of the compilation process. At this point, the object program resides in primary storage and can be executed upon your command.

The compilation process can be time consuming, especially for large programs. Therefore, if you intend to execute the program at a later time, perhaps during another session, you should store the object program on secondary storage for later recall. On most mainframe computer systems this is done automatically.

4. If the source program contains a **syntax error** (e.g., an invalid instruction format), the compiler will display an error message, or diagnostic, on the workstation screen, then terminate the compilation process. A diagnostic identifies the program statement or statements in error and the cause of the error. Syntax errors usually involve invalid instructions. Consider the following COBOL statement: DISPLY "WHOOPS". The statement is invalid because DISPLAY is misspelled.

    As a programmer, you will make the necessary corrections and attempt the compilation over, and over, and over again, until the program compiles and executes. Don't be discouraged. Very few programs compile on the first, second, or even third attempts. When your program finally compiles and executes, don't be surprised if the output is not what you expected. A "clean," or error-free, compilation is likely to surface undetected **logic errors**. For example, your program logic might result in an attempted division by zero; this is mathematically and logically impossible and will result in a program error. In most cases, you will need to remove a few such bugs in the program logic and in the I/O formats before the program is finished.

5. Suppose you come back the next day and wish to execute your COBOL program again. Instead of repeating the compilation process of Step 2, you simply call the object program from secondary storage and load it to primary storage for execution. Since the object program is already in machine language, no compilation is necessary.

COMMODORE GRACE MURRAY HOPPER: THE MOTHER OF SOFTWARE

Commodore Grace Hopper (1906–   ) of the U.S. Navy has made life a lot easier for many programmers. As a mathematician at Remington Rand in 1951, she conceived a new type of internal program that could perform certain computer tasks automatically. The program, called a *compiler*, was designed to scan a programmer's instructions and produce (or compile) these into machine-readable binary instructions. Her reason: Why start from scratch with every program you write when a compiler could be developed to do a lot of the basic work for you over and over again? Dr. Hopper's "automatic programming" technique was later perfected by others in the field.

The U.S. Navy recalled Commodore Hopper from retirement to become its spokesperson on the subject of computers. To say that Commodore Hopper has spunk is an understatement. In fact, she hopes to be celebrating New Year's Eve in 1999 so that she can look back and say, "See, we told you the computer could do that!"

Commodore Grace Murray Hopper, USNR, Ret.
(Sperry Corporation)

6. If you want to make any changes to the original source programs, you will: recall the original source code from secondary storage, make the changes, recompile the program, and create an updated object program (repeat Steps 1–4).

Programs that are run frequently are stored and executed as object programs. Recompilation is necessary only when the program is modified.

Interpreters

An **interpreter** is a system software program that ultimately performs the same function as a compiler—but in a different manner. Instead of translating the entire source program in a single pass, an interpreter translates *and* executes each source program instruction before translating and executing the next.

The obvious advantage of interpreters over compilers is that an error in instruction syntax is brought to the attention of the programmer immediately, thereby prompting the programmer to make corrections during program development. This is a tremendous help.

As we know, advantages are usually accompanied by disadvantages. The disadvantage of interpreters is that they do not use computing resources as efficiently as a program that has been compiled. Since the interpreter does not produce an object program, it must perform the translation process each time a program is executed.

For programs that are to be run often, programmers take advantage of the strengths of both interpreters and compilers. First, they develop and debug their programs using an interpreter. Then, they compile the finished program to create a more efficient object program that can be used for routine processing.

10–5 THE THIRD GENERATION: FOR PROGRAMMER CONVENIENCE _____

A quantum leap in programmer convenience accompanied the introduction of the *third generation* of programming languages. A third-generation language is placed in one of two categories: **procedure-oriented languages** or **problem-oriented languages** (review Figure 10–1).

Procedure-Oriented Languages

The flexibility of procedure-oriented languages permits programmers to model almost any scientific or business procedure. Instructions are **coded**, or written, sequentially and processed according to program specifications.

Unless triggered by program logic to do otherwise, the processor selects and executes instructions in the sequence in which they are written. In a production payroll system, for example, a particular sequence of program instructions is executed for salaried employees; another sequence is executed for hourly employees. The same sequence of program instructions is repeated for each salaried employee, however, and the other sequence of instructions is repeated for each hourly employee.

Procedure-oriented languages are classified as *scientific*, *business*, or *multipurpose*. These are illustrated in Figure 10–1 and discussed below.

Scientific Languages. Scientific languages are algebraic/formula-type languages. These are specifically designed to meet typical scientific processing requirements, such as matrix manipulation, precision calculations, iterative processing, the expression and resolution of mathematical equations, and so on. For example, engineers and actuaries turn to scientific languages when writing programs for statistical analysis.

FORTRAN. **FORTRAN** (*For*mula *Tran*slator), the first procedure-oriented language, was developed in 1955. It was, and it remains, the most popular scientific language (see Figure 10–4). However, the rise in the popularity of BASIC, Pascal, APL, and PL/I has begun to chip away at FORTRAN's hold on first place.

APL. **APL** (*A P*rogramming *L*anguage) is a *symbolic interactive* programming language used primarily by engineers, mathematicians, and scientists. APL, introduced in 1968, is unique in that a special workstation is required for writing APL programs. Its keyboard has a special character set that includes the symbols for writing APL instructions. These symbols provide programmers with a "shorthand" that speeds up the process of coding a program.

APL's limited-output formatting capability has not concerned engineers and scientists. Their concern is primarily the solution and not the manner in which the information is displayed (see Figure 10–5).

This metalurgist is using a scanning electron beam microscope to gather data for the analysis of engine valves. She wrote the programs to do the statistical analysis of the data in FORTRAN.
(TRW Inc.)

FIGURE 10–4
A FORTRAN Program
This program computes the economic order quantity (EOQ).

```
00100        INTEGER EOQ
00200   10   TYPE 100
00300  100   FORMAT(/,1X, 'ENTER COST/ITEM, NO. REQUIRED/YEAR, AND ITEM',
00400        1'STORAGE COST')
00500        ACCEPT *, COST, NUMBER, STCOST
00600        EOQ=SQRT((2*COST*NUMBER)/STCOST)
00700        TYPE 200, EOQ
00800  200   FORMAT(/, 1X, 'THE ECONOMIC ORDER QUANTITY IS ', I6)
00900        TYPE 300
01000  300   FORMAT(/, 1X, 'DO YOU WISH TO CALCULATE ANOTHER EOQ? (Y OR N)')
01100        ACCEPT 400, MORE
01200  400   FORMAT(A1)
01300        IF (MORE.EQ.'Y') THEN GO TO 10
01400        END
```

```
ENTER COST/ITEM, NO. REQUIRED/YEAR, AND ITEM STORAGE COST
?22.5, 5000, 2.15

THE ECONOMIC ORDER QUANTITY IS 323

DO YOU WISH TO CALCULATE ANOTHER EOQ? (Y OR N)
? N
```

```
             ∇AVG[□]∇
             ∇ AVG QUIZSCORES;NRSCORES;MEAN
  [1]    ⍝    DESCRIPTION OF FUNCTION 'AVERAGE'
  [2]    ⍝      ACCEPTS ANY NUMBER OF QUIZ SCORES THEN COMPUTES AND DISPLAYS
  [3]    ⍝        THE AVERAGE ROUNDED TO ONE DECIMAL PLACE
  [4]    NRSCORES←ρ,QUIZSCORES
  [5]    MEAN←(+/,QUIZSCORES)÷NRSCORES
  [6]    'THE AVERAGE OF THE ',(▼NRSCORES),' QUIZ SCORES IS ',(5 1 ▼MEAN)
             ∇
```

```
              AVG 94 83 88
     THE AVERAGE OF THE 3 QUIZ SCORES IS 88.3
```

FIGURE 10-5
An APL Program
This program accepts any
number of quiz scores, then
computes and displays the
average, which is rounded to
one decimal place.

Business Languages.   Business programming languages are designed to
be effective tools for developing business information systems. The strength
of business-oriented languages lies in their ability to store, retrieve, and manipulate alphanumeric data.

The arithmetic requirements of most business systems are minimal. Although sophisticated mathematical manipulation is possible, it is cumbersome
to achieve, so it is best left to scientific languages.

COBOL.   **COBOL**, the first business programming language, was introduced in 1959. It remains the most popular. The original intent of the developers of COBOL (*Co*mmon *B*usiness *O*riented *L*anguage) was to make its
instructions approximate the English language. Although COBOL is a very
powerful language, many programmers consider it to be excessively wordy.
Here is a typical COBOL *sentence*: "IF SALARY-CODE IS EQUAL TO
'H' MULTIPLY SALARY BY HOURLY-RATE GIVING GROSS-PAY ELSE
PERFORM SALARIED-EMPLOYEE-ROUTINE." Note that the sentence contains several instructions and even a period.

Professional programmers have a love/hate relationship with COBOL.
It is not uncommon for one programmer's opinion of COBOL to be 180
degrees out of phase with that of a colleague. Personal opinions notwithstanding, COBOL has over 20 years of momentum and acceptance, and it will
probably be a mainstay of business systems programming for years to come.
Over half of all production programs for currently running business systems
are written in COBOL.

The American National Standards (ANS) Institute has established standards for COBOL and other languages. The purpose of these standards is
to make COBOL programs *portable*. A program is said to be portable if it
can be run on a variety of computers. Unfortunately, the ANS standards
are only casually followed; consequently, it is unlikely that a COBOL program
written for a Burroughs computer, for example, can be executed on a Honeywell computer without some modification.

COBOL programs are divided into the following four *divisions* (see Figure
10-6):

- *Identification Division*. Identifies general information, such as program name, programmer, date written, and so on.

- *Environment Division*. Identifies the type of computer system (manufacturer and model) on which the program is to be run as well as the data storage and I/O devices to be used.

- *Data Division*. Describes the format of all data elements, internal variables, records, and files used by the program.

- *Procedure Division*. Contains the logic of the program and the sequence of instructions to be executed. Within the procedure division, instructions are written as sentences and logically combined to form *paragraphs*.

RPG. **RPG** (*R*eport *P*rogram *G*enerator) was originally developed in 1964 for IBM's entry-level punched-card business computers and for the express purpose of generating reports. As punched cards went the way of vacuum

FIGURE 10-6
A COBOL Program
This program computes gross pay for hourly wage earners.

```
0100 IDENTIFICATON DIVISION.
0200 PROGRAM-ID.            PAYPROG.
0300 REMARKS.               PROGRAM TO COMPUTE GROSS PAY.
0400 ENVIRONMENT DIVISION.
0500 DATA DIVISION.
0600 WORKING-STORAGE SECTION.
0700 01 PAY-DATA.
0800       05 HOURS         PIC 99V99.
0900       05 RATE          PIC 99V99.
1000       05 PAY           PIC 9999V99.
1100 01 LINE-1.
1200       03 FILLER        PIC X(5)       VALUE SPACES.
1300       03 FILLER        PIC X(12)      VALUE "GROSS PAY IS  ".
1400       03 GROSS-PAY     PIC $$$$9.99.
1500 01 PRINT-LINE          PIC X(27).
1600 PROCEDURE DIVISION.
1700 MAINLINE-PROCEDURE.
1800       PERFORM ENTER-PAY.
1900       PERFORM COMPUTE-PAY.
2000       PERFORM PRINT-PAY.
2100       STOP RUN.
2200 ENTER-PAY.
2300       DISPLAY "ENTER HOURS AND RATE OF PAY".
2400       ACCEPT HOURS, RATE.
2500 COMPUTE-PAY.
2600       MULTIPLY HOURS BY RATE GIVING PAY ROUNDED.
2700 PRINT-PAY.
2800       MOVE PAY TO GROSS-PAY.
2900       MOVE LINE-1 TO PRINT-LINE.
3000       DISPLAY PRINT-LINE.
```

```
Enter hours and rate of pay
43, 8.25
    Gross pay is $354.75
```

Children at a summer
computer camp are busy
learning and creating with
LOGO, a language designed
specifically as an interactive
learning tool. LOGO enables
students to do more than add
and subtract—they can also
draw geometric shapes by
instructing an imaginary "turtle"
to walk around the screen.
(ExperCamp)

tubes, RPG remained—evolving from a special-purpose problem-oriented language to a general-purpose procedure-oriented language. Its name has made RPG the most misunderstood of the programming languages. People who do not know RPG still associate it with report generation when, in fact, it has become a powerful programming language that matured with the demands of RPG users.

RPG has always differed somewhat from other procedure-oriented languages in that the programmer specifies certain processing requirements by selecting the desired programming options. That is, during a programming session, the programmer is presented with *prompting formats* at the bottom of the workstation screen. The programmer requests the prompts for a particular type of instruction, then responds with the desired programming specifications (see Figure 10–7).

Smaller computer installations may use RPG exclusively as the programming language for all their information processing needs. In larger installations, RPG is still used primarily for the preparation of reports.

Multipurpose Languages.   Multipurpose languages are equally effective for both business and scientific applications. These languages are an outgrowth of the need to simplify the programming environment by providing programmers with one language that is capable of addressing all of a company's programming needs.

BASIC.   **BASIC**, developed in 1964, is the primary language supported by millions of personal computers. BASIC is also used extensively on mainframe computer systems, primarily for one-time "quick and dirty" programs.

BASIC is perhaps the easiest language to learn and use (see Figure 10–8). It is commonly used for both scientific and business applications—and even for developing video games. The widespread use of BASIC attests to the versatility of its features. In fact, BASIC is the only programming language that is supported on virtually every computer.

The special section, "BASIC Programming," at the back of the book contains more background information and a comprehensive tutorial on the BASIC programming language.

PL/I.   **PL/I** (*P*rogramming *L*anguage/*I*), introduced in 1964, was hailed as the answer to many of the shortcomings of existing programming languages,

FIGURE 10–7
Interactive RPG Programming
Shown here is an interactive
specification menu used in the
preparation of an RPG
program.

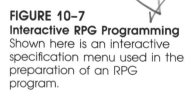

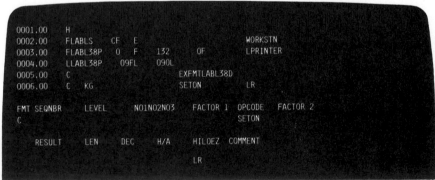

```
100  REM   <<<< Start Main >>>>
110  REM
120  REM   Call Module 1.1 - Accept Number
130  GOSUB 1000
140  REM   Begin loop to be executed 'NUMBER' times
150  COUNT = 1
160  WHILE COUNT <= NUMBER
170    REM   Call Module 1.2 - Accept Grades
180    GOSUB 2000
190    REM   Call Module 1.3 - Compute Average
200    GOSUB 3000
210    REM   Call Module 1.4 - Display Results
220    GOSUB 4000
230  WEND
240  END
250  REM   <<<< End Main >>>>
999  REM
1000 REM   ==== Module 1.1 - Accept Number
1010 PRINT "Enter total number of students";
1020 INPUT NUMBER
1030 PRINT
1999 RETURN
2000 REM   ==== Module 1.2 - Accept Grades
2010 REM   Input student grades and add one to loop counter 'COUNT'
2020 PRINT "Enter three quiz scores separated by commas";
2030 INPUT Q1, Q2, Q3
2040 REM   Increment loop counter
2050 COUNT = COUNT + 1
2999 RETURN
3000 REM   ==== Module 1.3 - Compute Average
3010 AVERAGE = (Q1 + Q2 + Q3) / 3
3999 RETURN
4000 REM   ==== Module 1.4 - Display Results
4010 PRINT "The average grade is "; AVERAGE
4020 PRINT
4999 RETURN
```

```
run
Enter total number of students? 3

Enter three quiz scores separated by commas? 73,91,85
The average grade is  83

Enter three quiz scores separated by commas? 86,88,99
The average grade is  91

Enter three quiz scores separated by commas? 66,84,75
The average grade is  75

Ok
```

FIGURE 10-8
A BASIC Program
This program averages three quiz scores for any number of students. This and fourteen other example BASIC programs are discussed in the special section, "BASIC Programming," at the back of the book.

such as COBOL and FORTRAN. It has not, however, won the widespread acceptance that was originally anticipated. The slow acceptance of PL/I is due, not to lack of quality or capability, but to the substantial investment and commitment that companies already had in COBOL and FORTRAN. A PL/I example is shown in Figure 10-9.

Four computer systems on-
board the space shuttle
simultaneously execute
identical programs during
ascent and reentry. The
programs are written in HAL/S,
a language similar to PL/I.
(NASA)

FIGURE 10-9
A PL/I Program
This program computes the
future value of an investment,
given the interest rate and the
number of years the investment
is held.

```
0001   FUTVAL: PROCEDURE OPTIONS (MAIN);
0002   DECLARE (INVESTMENT, FUTUREVALUE) FIXED DECIMAL (7,2);
0003   DECLARE (YEARS, INTEREST) FIXED DECIMAL (2,1), DECLARE DUMMY CHAR(72);
0004   DISPLAY ('ENTER INITIAL INVESTMENT ')REPLY(DUMMY);
0005   INVESTMENT = DUMMY;
0006   DISPLAY ('ENTER NUMBER OF YEARS ')REPLY(DUMMY);
0007   YEARS = DUMMY;
0008   DISPLAY ('ENTER INTEREST RATE ')REPLY(DUMMY);
0009   INTEREST = DUMMY;
0010   FUTUREVALUE = INVESTMENT*(1.0 + INTEREST/100.)**YEARS;
0011   DISPLAY('THE FUTURE VALUE OF $'  INVESTMENT  ' COMPOUNDED');
0012   DISPLAY('ANNUALLY FOR ' YEARS ' YEARS AT '  INTEREST  '% IS $'
0013     FUTUREVALUE;
0014   END;
```

```
ENTER INITIAL INVESTMENT
5500
ENTER NUMBER OF YEARS
5
ENTER INTEREST RATE
12.5
THE FUTURE VALUE OF $ 5500.00 COMPOUNDED
ANNUALLY FOR 5.0 YEARS AT 12.5% IS $ 9911.18
```

```
 1  PROGRAM MEANDEV(INPUT, OUTPUT);
 2  CONST
 3     MAX = 100;  YES = 'Y';  NO = 'N';  BLANK = ' ';
 4  VAR
 5     COUNT, I: INTEGER;  VALUE: ARRAY [1..MAX] OF REAL;
 6     MEAN, SUM, SD, SDEVIATION, NUM: REAL;  RESPONSE: CHAR;
 7  BEGIN
 8     WRITELN('COMPUTE MEAN AND STANDARD DEVIATION FOR UP TO 100 VALUES');
 9     WRITELN;
10     REPEAT
11        WRITELN('ENTER OBSERVATION VALUES.  END INPUT WITH -999.9');
12        AD := 0.0;  COUNT := 0; SUM : 0.0;        (*  INITIALIZE VARIABLES  *)
13        READ(NUM);                                 (*  READ IN VALUES  *)
14        WHILE(NUM <> -999.9) AND (COUNT < MAX) DO BEGIN
15           COUNT := COUNT + 1;
16           VALUE[COUNT] := NUM;
17           SUM := SUM + NUM;
18           READ(NUM)
19        END;                                       (*  WHILE  *)
20        IF COUNT > 0 THEN
21           MEAN := SUM/COUNT;                      (*  COMPUTE MEAN  *)
22        FOR I := 1 TO COUNT DO
23           SD := SD + SQR(VALUE[I] - MEAN);
24        SDEVIATION := SQRT(1 / (COUNT - 1) * SD);  (*  COMPUTE STANDARD DEVIATION *)
25        WRITELN('NUMBER IN SAMPLE = ', COUNT: 1);
26        WRITELN('MEAN = ', MEAN: 6: 2);
27        WRITELN('STANDARD DEVIATION = ', SDEVIATION: 6: 5);
28        REPEAT
29           WRITELN('ANOTHER SAMPLE (Y OR N)?');
30           REPEAT                                  (*  READ PAST LEADING BLANKS  *)
31              READ(RESPONSE)
32           UNTIL RESPONSE <> BLANK
33        UNTIL (RESPONSE = YES) OR (RESPONSE = NO)
34     UNTIL RESPONSE = NO
35  END.                                             (*  PROGRAM  *)
```

```
COMPUTE MEAN AND STANDARD DEVIATION FOR UP TO 100 VALUES

ENTER OBSERVATION VALUES. END INPUT WITH -999.9
128 99.2 136.4 114 108.3 100.6 92.8 124 -999.9
NUMBER IN SAMPLE = 8
MEAN = 112.91
STANDARD DEVIATION = 15.44034
ANOTHER SAMPLE (Y or N)?
N
```

Pascal. During the last decade **Pascal**, named after the seventeenth-century French mathematician Blaise Pascal, has experienced tremendous growth. Introduced in 1968, Pascal is considered the state of the art among widely used procedure-oriented languages (see Figure 10–10).

Although only 1% to 2% of business-system programs are now written in Pascal, its power, flexibility, and self-documenting structure are factors that cannot be overlooked for long. Many college and university computer science and information systems programs are advocating Pascal. With students graduating and carrying their expertise into the business world by the thousands, it stands to reason that in the future, Pascal will attain growing acceptance in the business community.

FIGURE 10–10
A Pascal Program
This program computes the mean and standard deviation of any number of observations.

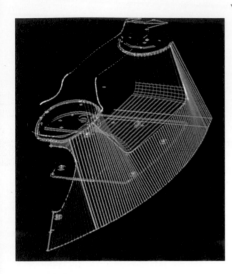

Computer-aided design enables engineers to see, test, and modify a design from any viewpoint. Pascal, a multipurpose programming language, is often used to develop software for computer-aided design (CAD).
(Calma Company)

LISP, a *list p*rocessing language, is well suited to applications of artificial intelligence because it can link up lists and discern complex objects. This LISP programmer is developing an expert system that will help individuals to invest their money more wisely.
(Symbolics, Inc.)

C. The results of a recent employment survey showed **C** programmers to be in the greatest demand. Developers of proprietary software are very interested in C because it is considered more transportable than other languages. That is, it is relatively machine independent: a C program written for one type of computer can be run on another type with little or no modification. When faced with the time-comsuming and expensive task of translating programs to run on a dozen micros and mainframes, C becomes an inviting option.

Another inviting quality of C is that it can be used for developing both systems and applications software. Traditionally, systems software has been written in an assembler language and applications software in a procedure-oriented language.

Ada. **Ada** is a multipurpose language developed for the U.S. Department of Defense. The language was named to honor the nineteenth-century pioneer, Lady Augusta Ada Lovelace, considered by some to be the first programmer. Although Ada has been selected to replace COBOL as a standard for the U.S. Department of Defense, relatively few programmers know and understand Ada. Its developers are, however, optimistic that as more people begin to study it, Ada will gain momentum and widespread acceptance not only in the military but in the private sector as well. Ada is the most recent and, perhaps, the most sophisticated procedure-oriented language.

Problem-Oriented Languages

A problem-oriented language is designed to address a particular application area or to solve a particular set of problems. Problem-oriented languages do not require the programming detail of procedure-oriented ones. The emphasis of problem-oriented languages is more on *input and the desired output* than on the *procedures or mathematics involved*.

Problem-oriented languages have been designed for scores of applications: simulation (e.g., GPSS, SLAM); programming machine tools (e.g., APT); analysis of stress points in buildings and bridges (e.g., COGO); and word processing (e.g., Wordstar).

Programs for computerized machine tools are written in problem-oriented languages.
(Cromemco, Inc.)

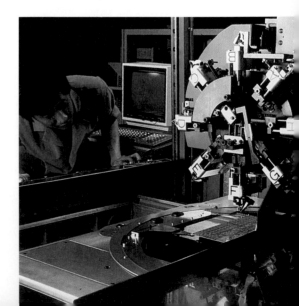

Although simulation problems can be programmed in FORTRAN, Pascal, and other procedure-oriented languages, the same problems can be programmed much more easily in SLAM, a problem-oriented language. Problem-oriented languages do not have the flexibility of procedure-oriented languages; they are limited to the application for which they are designed.

10-6 THE FOURTH GENERATION: QUERY LANGUAGES

Query Languages

Over the years, most organizations accumulated large amounts of computer-based data that only the professional programmer could access. Prior to *fourth-generation* languages (mid-1970s), users had to describe their information needs to a professional programmer, who would then use procedure-oriented languages to supply the information. Fulfilling a typical user request would take at least a couple of days and as much as two weeks. By then, the information might no longer be timely. With fourth-generation **query languages**, these same ad-hoc requests, or *queries*, can be completed in minutes by the user, without involving computer professionals!

Principles and Use.   Query languages use high-level Englishlike instructions to retrieve and format data for user inquiries and reporting. Most of the procedure portion of a query-language program is generated automatically by the computer and the language software. As a programmer in query languages, you need only specify "what to do," *not* "how to do it"; a programmer using a procedure-oriented language would have to write instructions depicting "what to do" *and* "how to do it." Thus, the use of query languages for certain information needs yields substantial improvements in programming productivity. The features of a query language include Englishlike instructions, limited mathematical manipulation of data, automatic report formatting, sequencing (sorting), and record selection by criteria.

With four to eight hours of training and practice, you can learn to write query-language programs, make inquiries, and get reports—without the assistance of a professional programmer. With query languages, it may be easier and quicker to sit down at the nearest workstation and write a program than it is to relate inquiry or report specifications to a programmer. Now managers can attend to their own seemingly endless numbers of ad-hoc requests. Query languages benefit everyone concerned. Users get the information that they need quickly, and programmers can devote their time to an ever-increasing backlog of information systems projects. Professional programmers use query languages to increase their productivity as well.

Query-Language Example.   The *query-language* example presented here will give you a feel for the difference between a procedure-oriented language, such as COBOL, and a query language. About 20 query languages are commercially available, such as NOMAD2 and EASYTRIEVE Plus. The example shows how a representative query language can be used to generate a management report. Suppose a personnel manager wanted the report shown in Figure

PAYROLL FOR DEPARTMENTS 991, 914

DEPARTMENT	EMPLOYEE NAME	EMPLOYEE NUMBER	SEX	NET PAY	GROSS PAY
911	ARNOLD	01963	1	356.87	445.50
911	LARSON	11357	2	215.47	283.92
911	POWELL	11710	1	167.96	243.20
911	POST	00445	1	206.60	292.00
911	KRUSE	03571	2	182.09	242.40
911	SMOTH	01730	1	202.43	315.20
911	GREEN	12829	1	238.04	365.60
911	ISAAC	12641	1	219.91	313.60
911	STRIDE	03890	1	272.53	386.40
911	REYNOLDS	05805	2	134.03	174.15
911	YOUNG	04589	1	229.69	313.60
911	HAFER	09764	2	96.64	121.95
DEPARTMENT TOTAL				2,522.26	3,497.52
914	MANHART	11602	1	250.89	344.80
914	VETTER	01895	1	189.06	279.36
914	GRECO	07231	1	685.23	1,004.00
914	CROCI	08262	1	215.95	376.00
914	RYAN	10961	1	291.70	399.20
DEPARTMENT TOTAL				1,632.83	2,403.36
FINAL TOTAL 17 RECORDS TOTALED				4,155.09	5,900.88

FIGURE 10–11
A Payroll Report

10–11. To obtain the report, the manager wrote the query-language program in Figure 10–12:

- *Instruction 1* specifies that the payroll data are stored on a FILE called PAYROLL. Although the data of only one file are needed in this example, requests requiring data from several files are no more difficult.
- *Instruction 2* specifies that the information in the report is to be *sorted* (department 911 before 914) and LISTed BY DEPARTMENT. It also specifies which data elements within the file are to be included in the report of Figure 10–11. If the instruction had been LIST BY DEPARTMENT BY NAME, then the employee names would be listed in alphabetical order for each department.
- *Instruction 3* specifies the criterion by which records are SELECTed. The personnel manager is interested only in those employees from DEPARTMENTs 911 and 914. Other criteria could be included for further record selections. For example, the criterion "GROSS > 400.00" could be added to select only those people (from departments 911 and 914) whose gross pay is greater than $400.00.
- *Instruction 4* causes SUBTOTALS to be computed and displayed BY DEPARTMENT.

```
1.  FILE IS PAYROLL
2.  LIST BY DEPARTMENT NAME ID SEX NET GROSS
3.  SELECT DEPARTMENT = 911, 914
4.  SUBTOTALS BY DEPARTMENT
5.  TITLE: "PAYROLL FOR DEPARTMENTS 911, 914"
6.  COLUMN HEADINGS:  "DEPARTMENT", "EMPLOYEE, NAME";
    "EMPLOYEE, NUMBER"; "SEX"; "NET, PAY"; "GROSS, PAY"
```

FIGURE 10–12
Query-Language Program to Produce Report of Figure 10–11
Each instruction is discussed in detail in the text.

- *Instructions 5 and 6* allow the personnel manager to improve the appearance and readability of the report by including a title and labeling the columns. Instruction 5 produces the report title, and instruction 6 specifies descriptive column headings.

The COBOL equivalent of this request would require over 150 lines of code!

Query languages are effective tools for generating responses to a variety of requests for information. Short query-language programs, similar to the one in Figure 10–12, are all that is needed to respond to the following typical management requests:

- Which employees have accumulated over 20 sick days since January 1?
- Are there any deluxe single hospital rooms to be vacated by the end of the day?
- What is a particular student's average in all English courses taken?
- List departments that have exceeded their budget alphabetically by the department head's name.

Entrepreneurial Innovation

Procedure-oriented languages, such as FORTRAN and COBOL, were designed by volunteer committees and individuals, primarily for the public domain. Companies, such as CDC and IBM, then developed compilers and interpreters to support these languages. The fourth-, fifth-, and sixth-generation languages are products of entrepreneurial innovation. That is, these languages (e.g., NOMAD2, EASYTRIEVE Plus) are developed to be marketed and sold. The demand for very high-level languages is so great that many entrepreneurs have produced products for this highly competitive market. Each of the last three generations may have a dozen or more equally popular languages. Customers will, of course, purchase a language that will best meet their information processing needs.

10-7 THE FIFTH GENERATION: APPLICATION GENERATORS

Principles and Use. **Application generators** are designed primarily for use by computer professionals. The concept of an application generator is not well defined, nor will it ever be, as entrepreneurs are continually working to provide better ways to create information systems. In contrast to the *ad-*

Systems development with application generators is somewhat of a "cut and paste" job; that is, modules of reusable code are linked together to perform specific tasks. Once users and analysts create the desired screens (see photo) and establish certain design specifications, an applications generator does the rest—automatically. In this example, a language called CAP (computer-aided programming) selects and links appropriate program segments to accomplish the maintenance of a vendor file. (Netron Inc.)

hoc orientation (one-time information requests) of fourth-generation query languages, application generators are designed to assist in the *development* of full-scale information systems.

During the development of an information system with an application generator, also called a code generator, programmers specify, through an interactive dialogue with the system, what information processing tasks are to be performed. This is essentially a fill-in-the-blank process. After programmers enter their specifications, the actual procedure-level instructions are automatically generated. In the creation of an information system, you would describe the data base, then specify screen layouts for file creation and maintenance, data entry, management reports, and menus. The application generator software consists of modules of **reusable code** that are pulled together and integrated automatically to complete the system.

Improved Productivity.   Application generators are currently in the infant stage of development. Existing application generators do not have the flexibility of procedure-oriented languages; therefore, the generic reusable code of application generators must occasionally be supplemented with *custom code* to handle unique situations. Normally, about 10% to 15% of the code would be custom code. Application generators provide the framework by which to integrate custom code with generated code.

When used for the purposes intended, application generators can increase programmer and systems analyst productivity by as much as 500%. As they mature, application generators will play an ever-increasing role in information systems development.

10-8   THE SIXTH GENERATION: NATURAL LANGUAGES

The next step in the sophistication of programming languages is the **natural language**: the sixth generation. The premise behind a natural language is that the programmer or user needs little or no training. He or she simply writes, or perhaps verbalizes, specifications without regard for instruction format or syntax. To date, there is no such language. Researchers are currently working to develop pure natural languages that will permit an unrestricted dialog between us and a computer. Although the creation of such a language is difficult to comprehend, it is probably inevitable.

In the meantime, natural languages with certain syntax restrictions are available. And for limited information processing tasks, such as ad-hoc inquiries and report generation for a specific application area, existing natural languages work quiet well. With certain limitations, existing natural languages permit users to express queries in normal, everyday English. You can phrase a query any way you want. For example, you could say, "Let me see the average salaries by job category in the marketing department." Or you would get the same results if you said, "What is the average salary in the marketing department for each job classification?" If your query is unclear, the natural-language software might ask you questions that will clarify any ambiguities.

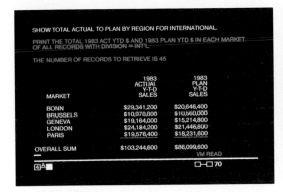
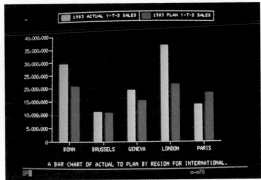

When using a natural language, all you have to do is ask. The top line on the first photo is a query entered by a user. The tabular and graphic summary are generated automatically in response to the request.
(© Artificial Intelligence Corporation)

A natural language interprets many common words, but other words peculiar to a specific application or company would have to be added by the user. All common and user-supplied words comprise the **lexicon,** or the dictionary of words that can be interpreted by the natural language. The sophistication of the types of queries that can be accepted are very much dependent on the comprehensiveness of the lexicon. In the above inquiry, the words "Let," "me," and "see," their meaning, and the context in which they are used would have to be entered into the lexicon before the phrase "Let me see" could be interpreted by the natural-language software. Also, in the above example, "category" and "classification" must be defined in the lexicon to mean the same thing.

A natural-language equivalent of the query-language program of Figure 10–12 would be: "Show me a report of employee payroll data for departments 911 and 914." Department and overall summary data are automatically generated. Usually, state-of-the-art natural-language software can interpret no more than a one-sentence query at a time. Other typical natural-language queries might be:

- Are there any managers between the ages of 30 and 40 in the northwest region with MBA degrees?
- Show me a pie chart that compares voter registrations for the southern states.
- What are the top ten best-selling fiction books in California?

10-9   THE OPERATING SYSTEM: THE BOSS

Just as the processor is the nucleus of the computer system, the **operating system** is the nucleus for all software activity. The operating system is a family of *systems software* programs that are usually, though not always, supplied by the computer system vendor.

Mainframe Operating Systems

Design Objectives.   All hardware and software, both systems and applications, are under the control of the operating system. You might even call the operating system the "boss." The logic, structure, and nomenclature of the different operating systems vary considerably. However, each is designed with the same three objectives in mind:

1. Minimize turnaround time [elapsed time between submittal of a job (e.g., print payroll checks) and receipt of output].
2. Maximize throughput (amount of processing per unit time).
3. Optimize the use of the computer system resources (processor, primary storage, and peripheral devices).

The Supervisor.   One of the operating system programs is always *resident* in primary storage (see Figure 10–13). This program, called the **supervisor**,

FIGURE 10–13
Software, Storage, and Execution
The supervisor program is always resident in primary storage and calls other programs, as needed, from secondary storage. All programs must be in object format to be executed. Applications programs rely on data base management system software to assist in the retrieval of data from secondary storage. Software in the front-end processor handles data communications-related tasks.

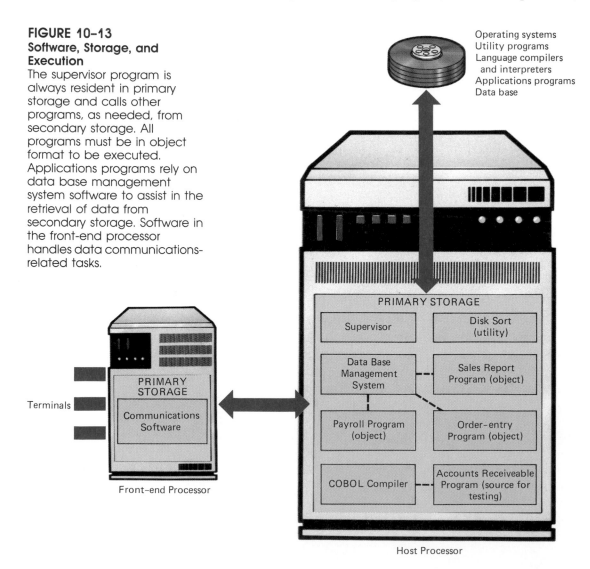

loads other operating system and applications programs to primary storage as they are needed. For example, when you request a COBOL program compilation, the supervisor loads the COBOL compiler to primary storage and links your source program to the compiler to create an object program. In preparation for execution, another program, the **linkage editor**, assigns a primary storage address to each byte of the object program.

Allocating Computer Resources.   In a typical computer system, several jobs will be executing at the same time. The operating system determines which computer system resources are allocated to which programs. As an example, suppose that a computer system with only one printer has three jobs whose output is ready to be printed. Obviously two must wait. The operating system continuously resolves this type of resource conflict to optimize the allocation of computer resources.

Operator Interaction.   The operating system is in continuous interaction with computer operators. The incredible speed of a computer system dictates that resource-allocation decisions be made at computer speeds. Most of these decisions are made automatically by the operating system. For decisions requiring human input, the operating system interrogates the operators through the operator console. The operating system also sends messages to the operator. A common message is "Printer no. 1 is out of paper."

(By permission of Michael Artell)

Compatibility Considerations.   There are usually several operating system alternatives available for medium and large computers. The choice of an operating system depends on the processing orientation of the company. Some operating systems are better for *timesharing*, others for *batch processing*, and others for *distributed processing*.

Applications programs are not as portable between operating systems as we would like. An information system is designed and coded for a specific *compiler*, *computer*, and *operating system*. This is true for both micros and mainframes. Therefore, programs that work well under one operating system may not be compatible with a different operating system.

Microcomputer Operating Systems

The objectives and functions of microcomputer operating systems are similar to mainframe operating systems. Although some vendors of microcomputers supply their own operating systems, many use **MS DOS**, **CP/M**, or **UNIX**. MS DOS, developed by Microsoft Corporation, CP/M, developed by Digital Research Corporation, and UNIX, developed by AT&T, have become the unwritten standards for the microcomputer industry. MS DOS and CP/M have a long tradition of acceptance in the single-user microcomputer environment. UNIX has a similar tradition of acceptance in the multiuser mainframe environment.

Some of today's micros are more powerful than the UNIX-based mainframe computers of the early 1980s. This increased capacity enabled micro vendors and AT&T to adapt the very popular UNIX operating system for *multiuser*, *multitasking* (able to handle different processing tasks at the same time) microcomputers. Of course, MS DOS and CP/M have been upgraded to handle the multiuser, multitasking environment also. You may encounter

Although some personal computers can service several workstations, the operating systems for most personal computers are oriented to servicing a single user. (Courtesy of Apple Computer, Inc.)

spinoffs of these operating systems. For example, PC DOS for the IBM PC is based on Microsoft's MS DOS, and XENIX is a spinoff of UNIX.

Because these operating systems are so widely used, hundreds of software vendors have developed systems and applications software that are compatible with them.

Before you can use a microcomputer, you must "**boot** the system." The procedure for booting the system on most micros is to simply load the operating system from the disk into primary storage, then flip the "on" switch. A few seconds later, with the operating system in memory, you are ready to begin processing.

Other System Software Categories

In this chapter we have discussed two system software categories: *programming-language compiler/interpreters* and *operating systems*. In this section we discuss three more: *utility programs*, *communications software*, and *data base management system software*.

Utility Programs. **Utility programs** are service routines that make life easier for us. They eliminate the need for us to write a program every time we need to perform certain computer operations. For example, with the help of utility programs, an employee master file can be easily "dumped" or copied from magnetic disk to magnetic tape for backup, or the employee master file can be sorted by social security number.

Communications Software. **Communications software** controls the flow of traffic (data) to and from remote locations. In small computers this is an operating system function, but in mainframe computer systems the communications software is usually separate (see Figure 10–13). Communications software is executed on the front-end processor, the down-line processor, and the host processor. Functions performed by communications software include: preparing data for transmission (i.e., inserting start/stop bits in messages), polling remote terminals for input, establishing the connection between two terminals, encoding and decoding data, and parity checking.

Data Base Management Systems (DBMS). **Data base management system (DBMS)** software provides the interface between application programs and the data base. If you want to write a program to update employee records, the only instructions that you will need to retrieve a record are those required to accept the employee's name at a workstation. Once the employee's name is entered, the data base management system software does the rest. The employee record is retrieved from secondary storage and moved to primary storage for processing. Control is then returned to your application program to complete the update.

In effect, a programmer does not have to be concerned with finding or retrieving data. This is handled by the data base management system software and is transparent to the programmer; that is, it is done automatically without programmer intervention. DBMS concepts are discussed in greater detail in Chapter 11, "Data Organization and File Processing."

10-10 SOFTWARE CONCEPTS

Multiprogramming

All computers, except small micros, have **multiprogramming** capability. Multiprogramming is the *seemingly simultaneous execution* of more than one program at a time. In Section 10–3 we learned that a computer can execute only one program at a time. But the internal processing speed of a computer is so fast that several programs can be allocated a "slice" of computer time in rotation; this makes it appear to us that several programs are being executed at once.

The great difference in processor speed and the speeds of the peripheral devices makes multiprogramming possible. A 40,000-line-per-minute printer cannot even challenge the speed of an average mainframe processor. The processor is continually waiting for the peripheral devices to complete such tasks as retrieving a record from disk storage, printing a report, or copying a backup file onto magnetic tape. During these "wait" periods, the processor just continues processing other programs. In this way, computer system resources are used efficiently.

In a multiprogramming environment, it is not unusual for several programs to require the same I/O device. For example, two or more programs may be competing for the printer. Rather than hold up the processing of a program by waiting for the printer to become available, both programs are executed and the printer output for one is temporarily loaded to magnetic disk. As the printer becomes available, the output is called from magnetic disk and printed. This process is called **spooling**.

Virtual Memory

We learned in Chapter 6, "Inside the Computer," that all data and programs must be resident in primary storage to be processed. Therefore, primary storage is a critical factor in determining the *throughput*, or how much work can be done by a computer system per unit of time. Once primary storage becomes full, no more programs can be executed until a portion of primary storage is made available.

The operating system of this large host computer system is the nerve center of a network of distributed computer systems. The system services hundreds of on-line users in a multiprogramming environment.
(Borden Inc.)

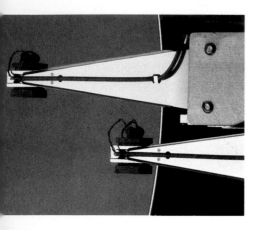

Virtual memory is created by storing programs on disk storage, then rolling pages into the main memory as they are needed.
(Seagate Technology)

Virtual memory is a systems software addition to the operating system that effectively expands the capacity of primary storage through the use of software and secondary storage. This allows more data and programs to be resident in primary storage at any given time.

The principle behind virtual memory is quite simple. Remember, a program is executed sequentially—one instruction after another. Programs are segmented into **pages**, so only that portion of the program being executed is resident in primary storage. The rest of the program is on disk storage. Once the instructions have been executed in the page that is resident in primary storage, or control is passed to an instruction in another page, the appropriate page is *rolled* (moved) into primary storage from disk storage. This page replaces the previous page, and program execution continues.

The advantage of virtual memory is that primary storage is effectively enlarged, giving programmers greater flexibility in what they can do. For example, some applications require several large programs to be resident in primary storage at the same time (for example, order-processing and credit-checking programs). If the size of these programs exceeds the capacity of "real" primary storage, then virtual memory can be used as a supplement to complete the processing.

The disadvantage of virtual memory is the cost in efficiency during program execution. A program that has many branches to many pages will execute slowly because of the time required to roll pages from secondary to primary storage. Excessive page movement results in too much of the computer's time being devoted to page handling and not enough to processing. This excessive data movement is appropriately named *thrashing* and can actually be counterproductive.

SUMMARY OUTLINE AND IMPORTANT TERMS _____

10-1 PROGRAMMING AND SOFTWARE.   A **program** directs a computer to perform certain operations. The program is produced by a **programmer**, who uses any of a variety of **programming languages** to communicate with the computer. Programs are referred to as **software**.

Software is classified as either **applications software** or **systems software**. Applications software is designed to perform certain personal, business, or scientific processing tasks. Systems software is more general and supports the basic functions of the computer.

10-2 GENERATIONS OF PROGRAMMING LANGUAGES.   Like computers, programming languages have evolved in generations. With each new generation comes a more sophisticated programmer/computer interaction.

10-3 THE FIRST AND SECOND GENERATIONS: "LOW-LEVEL."   The first two generations of programming languages are **low-level languages**; that is, the programmer must identify each fundamental operation that the computer is to perform. The **machine language** is the only language that can be executed on a particular computer. **High-level languages** have surpassed machine language and **assembler language** in terms of human efficiency.

10-4 COMPILERS AND INTERPRETERS: PROGRAMS FOR PROGRAMS. High-level languages must be translated to machine language to be executed. High-level languages are a programmer convenience and facilitate the programmer/computer interaction. A **compiler** is needed to translate a **source program** in a high-level language to an **object program** in machine language for execution. An **interpreter** performs a function similar to a compiler, but it translates one instruction at a time.

10-5 THE THIRD GENERATION: FOR PROGRAMMER CONVENIENCE. Third-generation languages are either **procedure-oriented languages** or **problem-oriented languages**. Procedure-oriented languages are classified as scientific (**FORTRAN** and **APL**), business (**COBOL** and **RPG**), or multipurpose (**BASIC**, **PL/I**, **Pascal**, **C**, and **Ada**). Problem-oriented languages are designed for a particular application.

10-6 THE FOURTH GENERATION: QUERY LANGUAGES.   In fourth-generation **query languages**, the programmer need only specify "what to do," not "how to do it." The features of query languages include Englishlike instructions, limited mathematical manipulation of data, automatic report formatting, sequencing, and record selection by criteria.

10-7 THE FIFTH GENERATION: APPLICATION GENERATORS. **Application generators**, the fifth generation, are designed to assist in the development of full-scale information systems. Application generators consist of modules of **reusable code** that are pulled together and integrated automatically to complete the system.

10-8 THE SIXTH GENERATION: NATURAL LANGUAGES.   The sixth-generation **natural language** will someday enable programmers to write or verbalize program specifications without regard to instruction format or syntax. In current natural languages, the sophistication of the queries is very much dependent on the **lexicon** supplied by the user.

10-9 THE OPERATING SYSTEM: THE BOSS.   The design objectives of an **operating system**, the nucleus of all software activity, are to minimize turnaround time, maximize throughput, and optimize the use of computer resources. Operating systems are oriented to a particular type of processing environment, such as timesharing, batch, or distributed processing.

   MS DOS, **CP/M**, and **UNIX** are popular operating systems for microcomputers. Until recently, micro operating systems were oriented to servicing a single user. Today, the more sophisticated micro operating systems support the multiuser, multitasking environment.

   Systems software categories include programming-language compilers/interpreters, operating systems, **utility programs**, communications software, and **data base management systems**.

10-10 SOFTWARE CONCEPTS. **Multiprogramming** is the seemingly simultaneous execution of more than one program at a time on a single computer. **Virtual memory** effectively expands the capacity of primary storage through the use of software and secondary storage.

REVIEW EXERCISES

Concepts

1. Associate each of the following with a particular generation of languages: lexicon, mnemonics, and Ada.

2. What are the four divisions in a COBOL program? Which one contains the program logic?

3. Program diagnostics identify what two types of program errors?

4. Name two procedure-oriented programming languages in each of the three classification areas—business, scientific, and multipurpose.

5. What are the programs called that translate source programs to machine language? Which one does the translation on a single pass? Which one does it one statement at a time?

6. Which programming language must be entered on specially designed terminals? Why?

7. Contrast fourth-generation to fifth-generation languages.

8. Why is it necessary to spool output in a multiprogramming environment?

9. Give two examples each of applications and systems software.

10. Name the systems software category associated with: (a) the organization's data base, (b) file backup, and (c) overall software and hardware control.

11. Modify the query-language program in Figure 10–11 to display the following report.

PAYROLL FOR DEPARTMENT 911

SEX	EMPLOYEE NAME	EMPLOYEE NUMBER	DEPT	NET PAY	GROSS PAY
1	ARNOLD	01963	911	356.87	445.50
1	POWELL	11710	911	167.96	243.20
1	POST	00445	911	206.60	292.00
1	SMOTH	01730	911	202.43	315.20
1	GREEN	12829	911	238.04	365.60
1	ISAAC	12641	911	219.91	313.60
1	STRIDE	03890	911	272.53	386.40
1	YOUNG	04589	911	229.69	313.60
SEX TOTAL				1894.03	2675.10
2	LARSON	11357	911	215.47	283.92
2	KRUSE	03571	911	182.09	242.40
2	REYNOLDS	05805	911	134.03	174.15
2	HAFER	09764	911	96.64	121.95
SEX TOTAL				628.23	822.42
FINAL TOTALS				2522.26	3497.52

Discussion

12. Discuss the difference between a program and a programming language.

13. If each new generation of languages enhances interaction between programmers and the computer, why not write programs using the most recent generation of languages?

14. Which generations of languages would a public relations manager be most likely to use? Why?

15. Suppose you are a programming manager and find that 12 of the 16 programmers would prefer to switch to COBOL from RPG. Would you support the switch, given that all 600 existing programs are written in RPG and only three programmers are proficient in CO-BOL? Why or why not?

16. How would your college use multiprogramming for administrative purposes? For educational purposes? Discuss, giving examples.

SELF-TEST (by section) _____

10-1. _____ software is more general than _____ software.

10-2. When programming in one of the first three generations of languages, you tell the computer "what to do," not "how to do it." (T/F)

10-3. Assembler-level languages use mnemonics to represent instructions. (T/F)

10-4. An object program is always free of logic errors. (T/F)

10-5. A COBOL program has _____ (how many) divisions.

10-6. A fourth-generation program will normally have fewer instructions than the same program written in a third-generation language. (T/F)

10-7. Application generators are used almost exclusively for ad-hoc requests for information. (T/F)

10-8. An individual must undergo extensive training before he or she can write programs in a natural language. (T/F)

10-9. The operating system program that is always resident in main memory is called the supervisor. (T/F)

10-10. Programs are segmented into pages before they are spooled. (T/F)

Self-Test answers.   10–1, Systems, applications; 10–2, F; 10–3, T; 10–4, F; 10–5, four; 10–6, T; 10–7, F; 10–8, F; 10–9, T; 10–10, F.

STUDENT LEARNING OBJECTIVES

- To identify sources of data.
- To describe and illustrate the relationships between the levels of the hierarchy of data organization.
- To describe how data are stored, retrieved, and manipulated in computer systems.
- To demonstrate an understanding of the principles and use of sequential and random processing.
- To demonstrate an understanding of the principles and use of data base management systems.
- To discuss the differences between file-oriented and data base organization.

CHAPTER 11

Data Organization and File Processing

11–1 DATA: THE KEY TO INFORMATION _____

Data Management

Data management encompasses the storage, retrieval, and manipulation of data. In this chapter we will discuss the concepts and methods involved in computer-based data management. We will discuss first the traditional methods of data organization, then data base management systems.

Your present or future employer will probably use both the traditional and the data base approaches to data management. Many existing information systems were designed using traditional approaches to data management, but the trend now is to use the data base approach to develop new information systems.

Sources of Data

So far, we have discussed data with respect to information and computer hardware. But where do data come from? And how are data compiled?

Obtaining the data necessary to extract information and generate output is always one of the more challenging tasks in information processing. Data have many sources. They can be compiled as a result of a *telephone call*; received in the form of *letters* and *turnaround documents*; and collected on *remote workstations*, perhaps as part of a point-of-sale and airline reservation system. Some data are *generated outside of the company* (e.g., when a customer submits an order specifying type and quality of products). Most data, however, are *generated internally* (e.g., expenses, inventory activity, hours worked, and so on).

Data can come from strange places. For example, metal sensors in the streets relay data to a central computer that controls traffic. Long-distance telephone calls generate destination and duration data for billing purposes.

"He said his first word today— DA-TA!"
(By permission of Anthony Cresci)

The floor of the Chicago Mercantile Exchange is the source of thousands of pieces of trading data. An information system continually updates a securities data base so that stock brokers in offices all over the country have access to up-to-the-minute quotations on stocks, bonds, and commodities.
(Cromemco, Inc.)

The digitizing of an image, perhaps an x-ray, creates data. Even hardware errors provide a source of data.

The data that we need are not always readily available. Existing data are usually not in the proper format, or they are not complete or up to date. Once consistent and reliable sources of data have been identified for a particular application, procedures must be established to obtain these data. To do this, users and computer specialists work together to establish a scheme of data organization and a method by which to manage the data. The material in this chapter will provide some insight into how this is done.

11–2 THE HIERARCHY OF DATA ORGANIZATION: WHICH COMES FIRST—THE BIT OR THE BASE? _____

In this section we will expand on the *hierarchy of data organization*, a concept that was introduced in Chapter 1. Recall that each information system has a hierarchy of data organization, and that each succeeding level in the hierarchy is the result of combining the elements of the preceding level (see Figure 11–1). Data are logically combined in this fashion until a data base is achieved. The six levels of the hierarchy are *bit*, *character*, *data element*, *record*, *file*, and *data base*. The first level, bits, is handled automatically, without action on the part of either the programmer or the end user. The other five levels are important design considerations for any information processing activity.

Data are the foundation of any information system. A programmer's, analyst's, or user's knowledge of data organization and the alternative approaches to processing these data are critical to the success of an information system. In the following sections we discuss each level of the hierarchy and how each relates to the succeeding level.

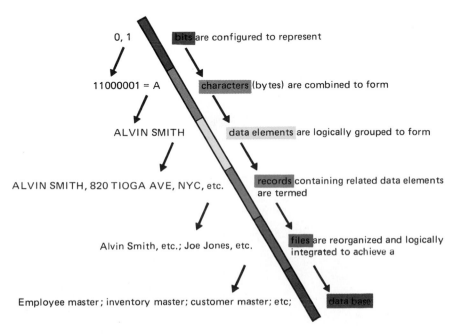

0, 1   bits are configured to represent

11000001 = A   characters (bytes) are combined to form

ALVIN SMITH   data elements are logically grouped to form

ALVIN SMITH, 820 TIOGA AVE, NYC, etc.   records containing related data elements are termed

Alvin Smith, etc.; Joe Jones, etc.   files are reorganized and logically integrated to achieve a

Employee master; inventory master; customer master; etc;   data base

**FIGURE 11–1
The Hierarchy of Data
Organization**

Bits and Characters

A **character** is represented by a group of **bits** that are configured according to an encoding system, such as ASCII or EBCDIC. Whereas the bit is the basic unit of primary and secondary storage, the character is the basic unit for human perception. When we enter a program instruction on a workstation, each character is automatically encoded to a bit configuration. The bit configurations are decoded on output so that we can read and understand the output. In terms of data storage, a character is usually the same as a **byte** (see Chapter 6, "Inside the Computer").

Data Elements

The **data element** is the lowest-level *logical* unit in the data hierarchy. For example, a single character (e.g., "A") has little meaning out of context. But when characters are combined, they form a logical unit, such as a name (e.g., "Alicia" or "Alvin"). A data element is best described by example: social security number, first name, street address, marital status—all are data elements. A data element is also called a **field**.

A "date" is not necessarily *one* element, but *three* data elements—day, month, and year. The same is true for "address." The data elements in an address are street address, city, state, and zip code. If we treated the entire address as one data element, it would be cumbersome to print, since the street address is normally placed on a line separate from city, state, and zip code. Also, since name-and-address files are often sorted by zip code, it is a good idea to store the zip code as a separate data element.

When it is stored on secondary storage, a data element is allocated a certain number of character positions. The number of positions allocated is the *field length*. The field length of a telephone area code is 3. The field length of a telephone number is 7.

Data Items.   Whereas data elements are the general, or generic, reference, the specific "value" of a data element is called the **data item**. For example, a social security number is a data element, but "445487279" and "440214158" are data items. Street address is a data element, but "1701 El Camino" and "134 East Himes Street" are data items.

Coding of Data Elements.   Many data elements can be coded. The aim in doing so is to save data entry keystrokes and storage space. For example,

When you travel by air and check your luggage through to your destination, a three-character destination tag (e.g., CHI is Chicago, OKC is Oklahoma City) is attached to each piece of luggage. At some airports, this coded data element (destination) is read by an optical scanner and your luggage is automatically routed, via conveyor, to the appropriate pick-up station. (AT&T Technologies)

Position	A/N	Code	Description
1	Alpha	G E R	General Educational Research
2–3	Alpha	BI CE CH EE FA ZY	Biology Civil Engineering Chemical Engineering Electrical Engineering Fine Arts Zoology
4–6	Numeric	not applicable	Unique numerical project identifier

Examples:

RBI001 — Research project #001, biology
ECH022 — Educational project #022, chemical engineering
GFA306 — General project #306, fine arts

FIGURE 11–2
Coded Data Elements
The figure illustrates the coding scheme for a six-position university account number. Example coded data elements are shown at the bottom.

the "sex" data element on the employee record is usually coded. The data entry operator simply enters "M" or "F" instead of "male" or "female". Any time a coded "sex" data item is printed or displayed, the code is translated to "male" or "female". It's interesting to note that the "sex" data element is not always so simple to code. Some organizations have four (that's right, four!) codes for sex: male, female, unidentified, and indeterminate.

Data elements can be designed so that a coded data item, such as an account number, can have special meaning and provide information to the user. For example, a six-position account number for a university might be coded as shown in Figure 11–2. RBI001 would designate the account number for research project (R) number 1 (001) in the Biology Department (BI).

Records

A **record** is a description of an event (e.g., a sale, a hotel reservation) or a thing (e.g., a person or a part). Related data elements describing an event or a thing are logically grouped to form a record. For example, Figure 11–3 contains a partial list of data elements for a typical employee record—

DATA ELEMENTS	DATA ITEMS
Employee/social security number	445447279
Last name	SMITH
First name	ALVIN
Middle initial	E
Department (coded)	ACT
Sex (coded)	M
Marital status (coded)	S
Salary (per week)	800.00

FIGURE 11–3
A Portion of an Employee Record
The data elements listed are commonly found in employee records. Example data items appear next to each data element.

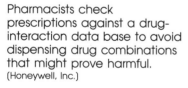

it also shows the data items for an *occurrence* of a particular employee record: "Department," "Sex," and "Marital status" are coded for ease of data entry and to save storage space.

The record is the lowest-level logical unit that can be accessed from a file. For example, if the personnel manager needs to know just the marital status of Alvin E. Smith, his entire record will be retrieved from secondary storage and transmitted to primary storage for processing.

Files

A **file** is a collection of related records. The employee master file contains a record for each employee. An inventory file contains a record for each inventory item. The accounts receivable file contains a record for each customer. The term "file" is also used to refer to a named area on a secondary storage device that contains a *program* or *textual material* (such as a letter).

The traditional approach to data organization revolves around the file. Certain inherent redundancies are built into this approach; that is, data elements must be repeated in several files for processing purposes. In a university, for example, student files are likely to be maintained by placement, residence operations, financial aids, and the registrar. Certain data, such as student name, campus address, and so on, are duplicated in each file. In one case, analysts at a large southwestern university uncovered 75 separate computer-based files that maintained basic student data!

Data Base

The **data base** is the data resource for all computer-based information systems. In a data base, the data are integrated and related so that data redundancy is minimized. In the university example above, if a student moves,

Pharmacists check prescriptions against a drug-interaction data base to avoid dispensing drug combinations that might prove harmful. (Honeywell, Inc.)

the address must be changed in 75 separate files. In a data base, student data are stored only *once* and made available to all departments. Therefore, only one update is needed.

Data base management system (DBMS) software (discussed in Sections 11–6 through 11–9) has enabled many organizations to move from traditional file organization to data base organization, thereby enjoying the benefits of a higher level of data management sophistication.

11–3 TRADITIONAL APPROACHES TO DATA MANIPULATION AND RETRIEVAL

In traditional file processing, files are sorted, merged, and processed by a **key data element**. For example, in a student file the key would probably be "student name," and in an inventory file the key would be "part number."

When you write programs based on the traditional approaches, data are manipulated and retrieved either *sequentially* or *randomly*. You might recall that sequential and random (or direct) access were discussed briefly in Chapter 7, "Data Storage Devices and Media." Remember, an analogy was made between sequential processing and cassette tapes, and between random processing and phonograph records. Sequential and random processing are presented in detail in the sections that follow.

11–4 SEQUENTIAL PROCESSING: ONE AFTER ANOTHER

Sequential files, used for **sequential processing**, contain records that are ordered according to a key data element. The key, also called a **control field**, in an employee record might be social security number or employee name. If the key is social security number, the employee records are ordered and processed *numerically* by social security number. If the key is employee name, the records are ordered and processed *alphabetically* by last name. *A sequential file is processed from start to finish. The entire file must be processed, even if only one record is to be updated.*

The principal storage medium for sequential files is magnetic tape. Direct-access storage devices (DASD), such as magnetic disks, can be used also for sequential processing (see Section 11–5).

Principles of Sequential Processing

Sequential processing procedures for updating an inventory file are illustrated in Figures 11–4, 11–5, and 11–6. Figure 11–4 lists the contents of an inventory *master file*, which is the permanent source of inventory data, and a *transaction file*, which reflects the daily inventory activity.

Prior to processing, the records on both files are sorted and arranged in ascending sequence by part number (the key). A utility sort program takes

At this medical instrumentation company, the record of any fixed inventory item (e.g., a desk, a push cart) can be retrieved by keying in the item's inventory control number, which is the key data element. (Management Science America, Inc. (MSA))

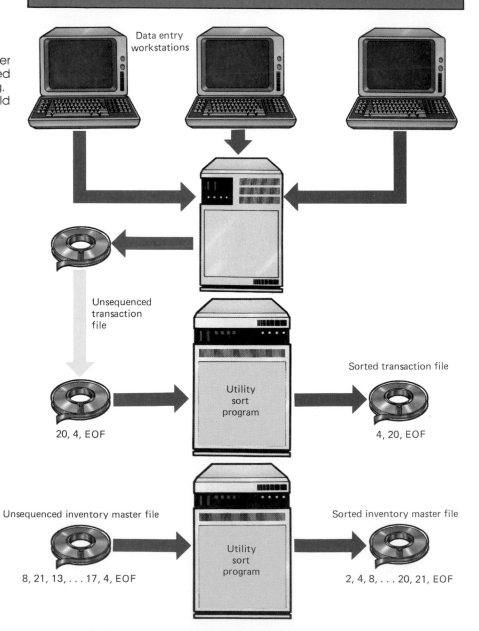

FIGURE 11-4
Inventory Master and Transaction Files
Both files are sorted by part number. The numbers in [ ]s reflect the inventory master file after the update. Figures 11-6 and 11-7 graphically illustrate the update process.

FIGURE 11-5
Sorting
Unsequenced inventory master and transaction files are sorted prior to sequential processing. Normally, the master file would be sorted as a result of prior processing.

Inventory master file (sorted by part number)

Part no.	Price	No. used to date	No. in stock
2	.25	40	200
4	1.40	100 [106] *	100 [94]
8	.80	500	450
•	•	•	•
•	•	•	•
•	•	•	•
20	4.60	60 [72]	14[2]
21	2.20	50	18

One record →

Transaction file (sorted by part number)

Part no.	No. used today
4	6
20	12

* [ ] reflects updated values

Data entry workstations

Unsequenced transaction file

20, 4, EOF

Utility sort program

Sorted transaction file

4, 20, EOF

Unsequenced inventory master file

8, 21, 13, . . . 17, 4, EOF

Utility sort program

Sorted inventory master file

2, 4, 8, . . . 20, 21, EOF

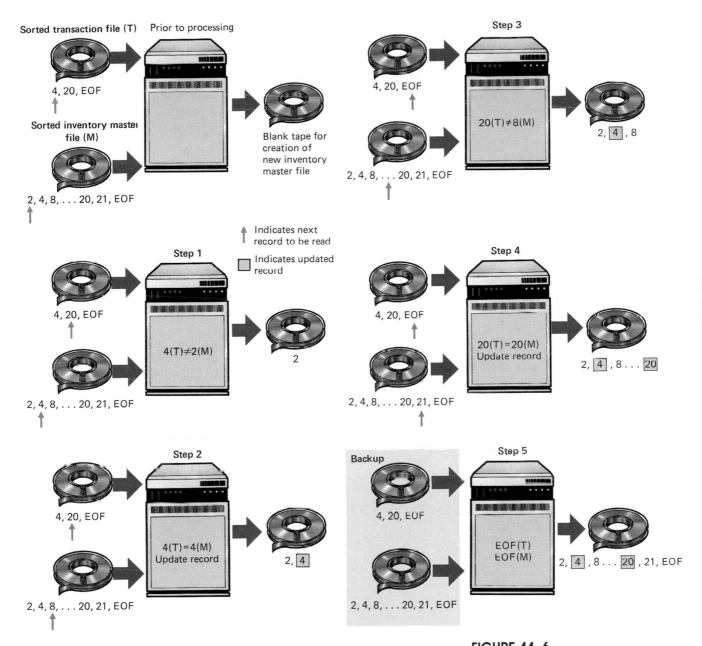

Sorted transaction file (T)   Prior to processing

4, 20, EOF

Sorted inventory master file (M)

2, 4, 8, . . . 20, 21, EOF

Blank tape for creation of new inventory master file

↑ Indicates next record to be read

☐ Indicates updated record

Step 1

4, 20, EOF

4(T)≠2(M)

2, 4, 8, . . . 20, 21, EOF

2

Step 2

4, 20, EOF

4(T)=4(M)
Update record

2, 4, 8, . . . 20, 21, EOF

2, 4

Step 3

4, 20, EOF

2, 4, 8, . . . 20, 21, EOF

20(T)≠8(M)

2, 4, 8

Step 4

4, 20, EOF

20(T)=20(M)
Update record

2, 4, 8, . . . 20, 21, EOF

2, 4, 8 . . . 20

Backup

4, 20, EOF

2, 4, 8, . . . 20, 21, EOF

Step 5

EOF(T)
EOF(M)

2, 4, 8 . . . 20, 21, EOF

**FIGURE 11-6
Sequential Processing**
An inventory master file is updated using sequential processing and magnetic tapes. Processing steps are discussed in the text. Notice in Step 5 that the backup is a by-product of sequential processing.

a file of unsequenced records and creates a new file with the records sorted according to the values of the key. The sort process is illustrated in Figure 11–5.

Figure 11–6 shows both the inventory master and transaction files as input and the *new inventory master file* as output. Since the technology does not permit records to be "rewritten" on the master file, a new master file tape is created to reflect the updates to the master file. *A new master file is always created in sequential processing for master file updates*. The processing steps are illustrated in Figure 11–6 and explained as follows:

- *Prior to processing*. If the two input tapes are *not sorted* by part number, they must be sorted as shown in Figure 11–5. The sorted tapes are then mounted on the tape drives. A blank tape, mounted on a third tape drive, will ultimately contain the updated master file. The arrows under the part numbers in Figure 11–6 indicate which records are positioned before the read/write heads on the respective tape drives. These records are the *next* to be read. Each file has an **end-of-file marker (EOF)** that signals the end of the file.

- *Step 1*. The first record (4) on the transaction file (T) is read and loaded to primary storage. Then the first record (2) on the master file (M) is loaded to primary storage. A comparison is made of the two keys. Because there is not a match [4 ≠ (is not equal to) 2], the first record on the master file is written to the new master file tape without being changed.

- *Step 2*. The next record (4) on the master file is read and loaded to primary storage. After a positive comparison (4 = 4), the record of part number 4 is updated (see Figure 11–4) to reflect the use of 6 items and then written to the new master file. In Figure 11–4 note that the "number in stock" data item is reduced from 100 to 94 and the "number used to date" is increased from 100 to 106. Updated records in Figure 11–6 are enclosed in boxes.

- *Step 3*. The next record from the transaction file (20) and the next record from the master file (8) are read and loaded to primary storage. A comparison is made. Since the comparison is negative (20 ≠ 8), the record for part number 8 is written to the new master file without being changed.

- *Step 4*. Records from the master file are individually read and loaded, and the part number is compared to that of the transaction record (20). With each negative comparison (e.g., 20 ≠ 17), the record from the old master file is written, without change, to the new master file. The read-and-compare process continues until a match is made (20 = 20). Record 20 is then updated and written to the new master file.

- *Step 5*. A read is issued to the transaction file and an end-of-file marker is found. All records on the master file following the record for part number 20 are written to the new master file, and the end-of-file marker is recorded on the new master file. All tapes are then automatically rewound and removed from the tape drives for off-line storage and processing at a later time. The transaction file and old master file are retained as *backup* to the new master file. Fortunately, *backup is a by-product of sequential processing*. After the new master file is created, the old master file and the transaction file become the backup. If the new master is destroyed, the transaction file can simply be run against the old master file to recreate the new master file.

    Backup files are handled and maintained by *generation*, with the up-to-date master file being the current generation. This tape cycling procedure is called the **grandfather-father-son method** of file backup. The "son" file is the up-to-date master file. The "father" generation is noted in Step 5 of Figure 11–6. Most computer centers maintain a grandfather file (from the last update run) as a backup to the backup.

Magnetic tape is currently the preferred medium for archival storage, but optical recording disk technology is advancing rapidly. This single optical disk stores as much information as 20 reels of magnetic tape. (3M)

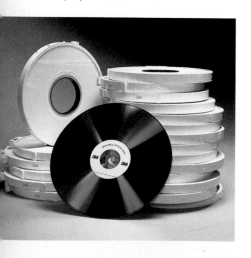

11-5 RANDOM OR DIRECT-ACCESS PROCESSING: PICK AND CHOOSE

A **direct-access file**, or a **random file**, is a collection of records that can be processed randomly (in any order). This is called **random processing**. Only the value of the record's key field is needed in order for a record to be retrieved or updated. More often than not, magnetic disks are the primary storage medium for random processing.

You can access records on a direct-access file by more than one key. For example, a salesperson inquiring about the availability of a particular product could inquire by *product number* and, if the product number is not known, by *product name*. The file, however, must be created with the intent of having multiple keys.

Random-Access Methods

Indexed Sequential-Access Method.   The procedures and mechanics of the way a particular record is accessed directly are, for the most part, transparent to users, and even to programmers. However, some familiarity will help you understand the capabilities and limitations of direct-access methods. The **indexed sequential-access method**, or **ISAM** (pronounced EYE sam) is a popular method that permits both sequential and random processing.

An ISAM file is actually two files: the *data file* contains the records (e.g., for each student, for each inventory item); the smaller *index file* contains the key and disk address of each record on the data file. A request for a particular record is first directed to the index file, which, in turn, "points" to the physical location of the desired record.

Direct Access.   Another method of accessing records randomly applies a formula, called a *hashing algorithm*, to the record key. The disk address is arithmetically calculated from the key. The advantage of this method, sometimes called **hashing**, is that usually only one disk access is needed to retrieve a record. In contrast, ISAM requires several disk accesses.

The address of a record is derived from the key field. For example, to obtain the record of part number 6173 in an inventory master file, the key value (6173) is input to a formula that yields a disk address (i.e., cylinder, recording surface, and record). A wide variety of hashing algorithms are used for accessing records directly.

The limited number of disk accesses permits records to be retrieved more quickly with direct access than with ISAM. ISAM, however, permits records to be accessed sequentially as well as randomly. These are the basic trade-offs between the two random-access methods.

Principles of Random Processing

In Figure 11–7, the inventory master file of Figure 11–4 is updated from an *on-line* workstation to illustrate the principles of random processing. The following activities take place during the update:

A commercial information service maintains a random access file that contains the price histories on over 600,000 pieces of art by over 30,000 artists. Before buying a piece of art, prospective buyers use the service to see if the asking price is consistent with the actual sale price of the artist's other works. To make the inquiry, the user need only enter the artist's name.
(Courtesy of International Business Machines Corporation)

Magnetic disks are the principle data storage medium for information systems that require random processing.
(TRW Inc.)

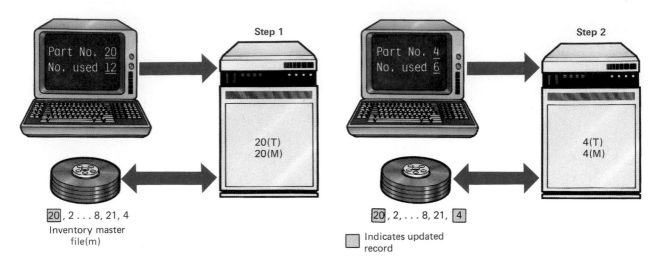

20, 2 . . . 8, 21, 4
Inventory master
file(m)

20, 2, . . . 8, 21, 4

☐ Indicates updated
   record

FIGURE 11-7
Random Processing
An inventory master file is
updated using random
processing and magnetic disks.
Processing steps are discussed
in the text.

- *Step 1*. The first transaction (for part no. 20) is entered into primary storage from an on-line workstation. The computer issues a read for the record of part number 20 on the inventory master file. The record is retrieved and transmitted to primary storage for processing. The record is updated and written back to the *same* location on the master file. The updated record is simply written over the old record.

- *Step 2*. A second transaction (for part no. 4) is entered into primary storage. The computer issues a read for the record of part number 4 on the inventory master file. The record is retrieved and transmitted to primary storage for processing. The record is then updated.

Since only two updates are to be made to the inventory master file, processing is complete. However, unlike sequential processing where the backup is built-in, random processing requires a special run to provide backup to the inventory master file. In the backup activity illustrated in Figure 11–8, the master file is "dumped" from disk to tape at frequent intervals, usually daily. If the inventory master file is destroyed, it can be recreated by dumping the backup file (on tape) to disk (the reverse of Figure 11–8).

As you can see, random processing is more straightforward than sequential processing, and it has those advantages associated with on-line processing (see Chapter 9, "Data Communications"). Figure 11–9 summarizes the differ-

FIGURE 11-8
Backup Procedure for Random Processing
Unlike sequential processing, a separate run is required to create the backup for random processing.

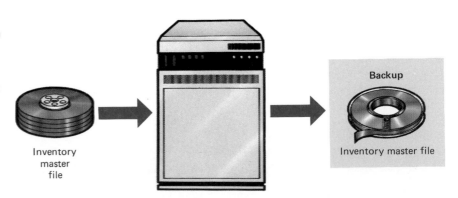

Inventory
master
file

Backup

Inventory master file

	Sequential Processing	Random Processing
Primary Storage Medium		
Preprocessing	Files must be sorted	None required
File Updating	Requires complete processing of file and creation of new master file	Only active records are processed, then rewritten to the same storage area
Data Currency	Batch (at best, data are a day old)	On-line (up-to-the-minute)
Backup	Built-in (old master file and transaction file)	Requires special provisions

FIGURE 11-9
Differences Between Sequential and Random Processing

ences between sequential and random processing. The special section, "BASIC Programming" (Module VII), at the end of the book demonstrates the programming required for the sequential and random processing of files.

11-6 DATA INTEGRATION: SOLVING THE DATA PUZZLE

Our discussion thus far has focused on traditional file processing. These files are usually designed to meet the specific requirements of a particular functional-area department, such as the registrar's office or the financial aid office. Consequently, very similar, but different, files are created to support the registration and financial aid systems.

Earlier we mentioned a university that maintained over 75 separate computer-based files containing student data. The registrar maintains grades, the financial aid office maintains data on student scholarships, and the placement office maintains data on career interests. At least half the data elements on each of these student files are common (e.g., student name, marital status, street address, sex, and so on), and each file must be updated separately when a student marries or moves.

Data redundancy is costly, but it can be minimized by designing an *integrated data base* to serve the organization as a whole, not just one specific department. The integrated data base is made possible by **data base management system (DBMS)** software. Some of the DBMS software packages on the market include IMS, dBASE III, TOTAL, IDMS, IDMS/R, DL1, System 2000, RAMIS, ADABAS, Ingress, SQL/DS, and Encompass.

DBMS technology was introduced in the early 1970s, but it did not gain widespread acceptance until late in the decade. Early data base management systems were inefficient and required substantially more hardware capacity than traditional file processing. Now, hardware requirements have been

A WORLD OF INFORMATION AT YOUR FINGERTIPS

A microcomputer offers more than stand-alone capability for programming, word processing, and spreadsheet analysis—much more. A number of commercially available information networks offer entertainment, information, and a variety of services to owners of microcomputers. Besides a micro, all you would need in order to take advantage of these information networks is a modem, a telephone line, and a few dollars. You would normally pay a one-time fee. For the fee, you get an account number that will permit you to establish a link with the network. You are then billed based on your usage of the information network. Most networks have a monthly minimum charge.

The following list summarizes the types of entertainment, information, and services available through information networks.

HOME BANKING. Check your account balances, transfer money, and pay bills in the comfort of your home or office.

NEWS, WEATHER, SPORTS. Get the latest releases directly from the wire services.

GAMES. Hundreds of single and multiplayer games are available. You can even play games with friends in other states!

FINANCIAL INFORMATION. Get up-to-the-minute quotes on stocks, securities, bonds, options, and commodities.

BULLETIN BOARDS. Special-interest bulletin boards offer users a forum for exchange of ideas and information. Besides those offered by information networks, thousands of bulletin board systems (BBS) are made available free of charge by individuals and computer clubs.

ELECTRONIC MAIL. Send and receive mail to and from other network users. Each network subscriber is assigned an ID and an electronic mailbox. To retrieve mail, a subscriber must enter a secret password.

SHOP AT HOME. Select what you want from a list of thousands of items offered at discount prices. Payment is made via electronic funds transfer (EFT) and your order is delivered to your doorstep.

REFERENCE. Look up items of interest in an electronic encyclopedia. Scan through various government publications. Recall articles on a particular subject.

EDUCATION. Choose from a variety of educational packages, from learning arithmetic to preparing for the Scholastic Aptitude Test (SAT). You can even determine your own IQ!

REAL ESTATE. Moving? Check out available real estate by scanning the listings for the city to which you are moving.

TRAVEL. Plan your own vacation or business trip. You can check airline schedules and make your own reservations. You can even charter a yacht in the Caribbean or rent a lodge in the Rockies.

An information network includes such services as news, games, and electronic shopping.
(Copyright Viewdata Corporation of America 1984)

reduced and hardware capacity has increased to the point where DBMS software is available even on personal computers.

11-7 WHAT'S TO BE GAINED FROM A DATA BASE ENVIRONMENT?

Greater Access to Information. Most organizations have accumulated a wealth of data, but translating these data to meaningful information has, at times, proven difficult, especially in a traditional file environment. Under these circumstances, an organization may be *data rich* but *information poor*. A DBMS can turn a wealth of data into a wealth of information.

The structure of an integrated data base provides enormous *flexibility* in the types of reports that can be generated and the types of on-line inquiries that can be made. This expanded scope of available information has enabled management to make more informed and, therefore, better decisions than they might have without it.

Minimizing of Data Redundancy. A data base management system minimizes data redundancy through advanced *data structures*, or the manner in which the data elements and records are related to each other. To enhance processing efficiency, some data redundancy must be built into the data base. This *controlled data redundancy* is minuscule when compared to the costly redundancy of a traditional file environment. By minimizing data redundancy, data collection and update procedures are simplified. *Data integrity*, or the accuracy of the data, is enhanced because, if a student moves, for example, the street address is updated in only *one* place—the data base.

Software Development Made Easier. The data base environment opens new doors for programmers and systems analysts. It provides information that would be too time consuming or too impractical to obtain using traditional file organization. The programming task is simplified with a data base management system because data are more readily available.

In a data base, data are *independent* of the applications programs. That is, data elements can be added, changed, and deleted from the data base, and this does not affect existing programs. Adding a data element to a record of a traditional file may require the modification and testing of dozens, and sometimes hundreds, of programs. Other significant technical advantages to data base management systems exist, but they are beyond the scope of this introductory text.

Approaches to Data Base Management. The processing constraints of traditional files are overcome by data base management systems software. To do this, data base management systems rely on sophisticated data structures. The examples presented in Sections 11-8 and 11-9 should help you to better understand the principles and advantages of data base management systems. The examples present two types of data base management systems that are commonly found in practice. The first example illustrates the principles of *CODASYL* (*Co*nference for *D*ata *Sy*stems *L*anguages) DBMSs, sometimes called *network* DBMSs, and the second example illustrates the principles of *relational* DBMSs.

An information service makes the full text of newspapers (including *Computerworld*), wire services, magazines, newsletters, and government publications available for immediate on-line access. Subscribers to this service, called NEXIS, use key words to enter the data base and zero in on a particular topic (e.g., computer crime, earthquakes). (Mead Data Central)

A CODASYL DBMS Example. Consider the following situation. A library currently maintains a file that contains the following data elements on each record:

- Title
- Author(s)
- Publisher
- Publisher's address
- Classification
- Publication year

The head librarian wants more flexibility in obtaining decision-making information. Many of the librarian's requests would be impractical with the existing traditional file (see Figure 11–10). A data base administrator recommended restructuring the file for a CODASYL data base management system. The data base administrator is a computer specialist who designs and maintains the data base.

Not surprisingly, the analysts found certain data redundancies in the existing file. Since each book or title has a separate record, the *name* of an author who has written several books is repeated for each book written. A given publisher may have hundreds, even thousands, of books in the library—but in the present file, the *publisher* and *publisher's address* are repeated for each title.

To eliminate these data redundancies, the data base administrator suggested the records shown in Figure 11–11. The **data base record** is similar to the record of a traditional file in that it is a collection of related data elements and is read from, or written to, the data base as a unit.

Next, the data base administrator establishes the relationships between the records. There is a *one-to-many* relationship between the publisher and title records. That is, one publisher may publish any number of titles. The publisher-title relationship is represented in Figure 11–11 by a connecting line between the two records. A double arrow toward the title record represents the possibility of more than one title per publisher. The publisher-title combination is called a **set**. Other sets defined by the data base administrator are title-author and author-title. Figure 11–11 is a graphic representation of the logical structure of the data base, called a **schema** (pronounced SKEE muh).

In the data base schema of Figure 11–11, a particular author's name appears only once. The author's name is then linked to the title records of those books he or she has authored. The publisher record is linked to all of the titles that it publishes. When accessing a record in a program, you simply request the record of a particular title, author, or publisher. Once you have the author's record, then you can use the links between records to retrieve the titles of the books written by that author. Similarly, if you

Libraries are converting their cumbersome card catalogs to computer data base systems. These systems almost eliminate data redundancy and provide library patrons with immediate on-line access to subject, title, and author information. Publishers are already supplying libraries with "index card" data in machine-readable format.
(Courtesy of International Business Machines Corporation)

FIGURE 11–10
Record Layout
This record layout is for a traditional book inventory file in a library.

Title	ISBN number	Publication year	Publisher	Publisher's address	Author 1	Author 2	Author 3	Author 4

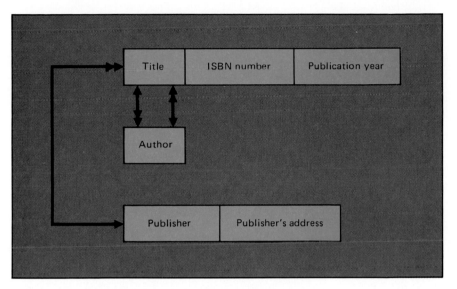

FIGURE 11-11
A Data Base Schema
The record layout of the
traditional book inventory file in
Figure 11-10 is reorganized into
data base records and
integrated into a data base
schema to minimize data
redundancy. Relationships are
established among the data
base records so that authors,
titles, and publishers can be
linked as appropriate.

request the record of a particular publisher, you can obtain a list of all titles
published by that publisher.

Occurrences.   Figure 11-11 is a representation of the schema, and Figure
11-12 is an *occurrence* of the data base structure. The schema and the

FIGURE 11-12
**An Occurrence of the Data
Base Structure**
Notice that publishers can be
linked to authors via the title
record and vice versa.

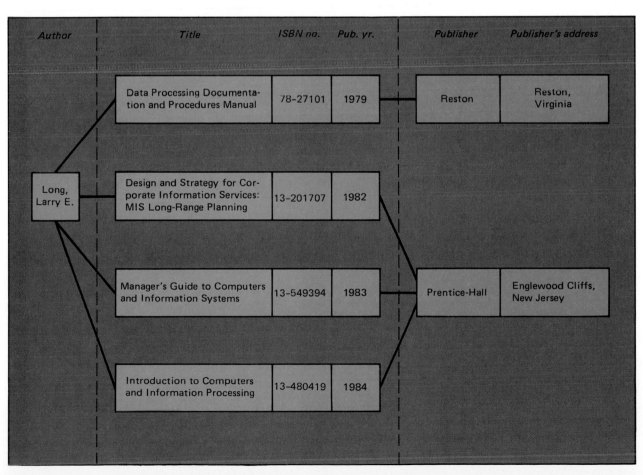

occurrence are analogous to the data element and the data item (e.g., publisher; Prentice-Hall). One is the definition—the category or abstract—and the other is the actual value or contents.

Queries to the Data Base.   This data base design eliminates, or at least minimizes, data redundancy and permits the head librarian to make a wide range of inquiries. For example:

- What titles were written by Mark Twain?
- List those titles published in 1986 by Prentice-Hall (alphabetically by title).
- What authors have published with the Brady Publishing Company since December 1985?

These and other similar inquiries are relatively easy to obtain with a data base management system. Similar inquiries to the library's existing file would require not only the complete processing of the file, but perhaps several data preparation computer runs for sorting and merging.

If the head librarian decides after a year to add, for example, the Library of Congress number to the title record, the data base administrator can make the revision without affecting existing programs.

11-9   RELATIONAL DATA BASE MANAGEMENT SYSTEMS

Relational versus CODASYL DBMSs.   The relational approach to data base management systems has been gaining momentum through the 1980s. In contrast to the CODASYL DBMS, data are accessed by *content* rather than by *address*. That is, the relational approach uses the computer to search the data base for the desired data rather than accessing data through a series of indices and physical addresses, as with CODASYL DBMSs. In relational DBMSs, the data structures, or relationships between data, are defined in *logical*, rather than physical, *terms*. That is, the relational data base has no predetermined relationship between the data, such as the one-to-many sets in the CODASYL schemas (see Figure 11–11). In this way, data can be accessed at the *data element* level. In CODASYL structures, the entire record must be retrieved to examine a single data element.

The trend is to relational DBMSs for small data bases, but its requirement for time-consuming sequential searches leaves open the question of which type is best for large data bases.

A Relational DBMS Example.   Let's stay with library applications for our relational DBMS example, but let's shift emphasis from book inventory to book circulation. The objective of a circulation system is to keep track of who borrows which books, then monitor the timely return of the books. In the traditional file environment, the record layout might appear as shown in Figure 11–13. In the record shown, a library patron can borrow from one to four books. Precious storage space is wasted for patrons that borrow infrequently, and the four-book limit may force prolific readers to make more frequent trips to the library.

MEMORY BITS

APPROACHES TO DATA MANAGEMENT
- Sequential processing
- Random (or direct) processing
  Indexed sequential-access method (ISAM)
  Direct access
- Data base management systems (DBMS)
  CODASYL
  Relational

Card No.	First Name	Last Name	Address				Book #1 (ISBN)	Due Date	Book #2 (ISBN)	Due Date	Book #3 (ISBN)	Due Date	Book #4 (ISBN)	Due Date
			Street	City	ST	ZIP								

FIGURE 11-13
Record Layout
This record layout is for a traditional book circulation file in a library.

The data base administrator recommended the relational DBMS organization shown in Figure 11–14. The data base contains two *tables*, each containing rows and columns of data. A row is roughly equivalent to the occurrence of a CODASYL record. The column headings, called *attributes*, are analogous to data elements.

The first table contains patron data and the second table contains data relating to books out on loan. Each new patron is assigned a number and issued a library card with a number that can be read with an optical wand scanner. The patron's card number, name, and address are added to the data base. When the patron borrows a book, the librarian at the circulation desk uses a wand scanner to enter the card number and the book's ISBN number. These data and the due date, which are entered on a keyboard, become a row in the "on loan" table. Notice that by using a relational DBMS there is no limit to the number of borrowed books that the system can handle for a particular patron.

Queries to the Data Base. Suppose the circulation librarian wanted a report of overdue books as of April 8 (4/8). The query would be: "List all books overdue" (query date is 4/8). The search criteria of "due date < (before) 4/8" is applied to the "due date" column in the "on loan" table (see Figure 11–15). The search surfaces two overdue books; then the system uses the

FIGURE 11-14
A Relational Data Base Organization
The record layout of the traditional book circulation file record of Figure 11–13 is reorganized and integrated into a relational data base with a "Patron Data" table and a "Books-on-Loan Data" table.

Patron Data

Card No.	First Name	Last Name	Address			
			Street	City	ST	ZIP
1243	Jason	Jones	18 W. Oak	Ponca City	OK	74601
1618	Kay	Smith	108 10th St.	Newkirk	OK	74647
2380	Heather	Hall	2215 Pine Dr.	Ponca City	OK	74604
2644	Brett	Brown	1700 Sunset	Ponca City	OK	74604
3012	Melody	Beck	145 N. Brook	Ark. City	KS	67005
3376	Butch	Danner	RD#7	Tonkawa	OK	74653
3859	Abe	Michaels	333 Paul Ave.	Kaw City	OK	74641

Books-on-Loan Data

Card No.	Book No. (ISBN)	Due Date
1618	89303-530	4/7
1243	13-201702	4/20
3859	13-48049	4/9
2644	18-23614	4/14
2644	71606-214	4/14
2644	22-68111	4/3
1618	27-21675	4/12

Card No.	Book No. (ISBN)	Due Date		Overdue? (Due Date < 4/8)
1618	89303-530-0	4/7	→	Yes
1243	13-201702-5	4/20	→	No
3859	13-48049-8	4/9	→	No
2644	18-23614-1	4/14	→	No
2644	71606-214-0	4/14	→	No
2644	22-68111-7	4/3	→	Yes
1618	27-21675-2	4/12	→	No

FIGURE 11-15
Queries to a Relational Data Base
The figure graphically illustrates the resolution and output of an April 8th query to the data base: "List all books overdue."

Overdue Books (4/8)			
Card No.	Name	Due Date	ISBN Number
1618	Kay Smith	4/7	89303-530-0
2644	Brett Brown	4/3	22-68111-7

MICROELECTRONICS + PHOTOGRAPHY = PHOTOMICROGRAPHY

The microscopic world of electronics has been magnified by a number of photographic techniques. These techniques have been used during the chip manufacturing process to capture the beauty of the shapes and materials in these high-technology products.

Optical photomicrography is the process of producing greatly magnified photographs of a minute subject with the use of a compound microscope. *Photomacrography*, on the other hand, makes moderately magnified pictures of small objects. *Thermography* is used to catch the amount of radiation or heat emitted by an object. *Interferometry* enables density variations in the subject to be illustrated in the photograph.

AT&T Technologies has been a leader in this growing field of photomicrography through its traveling photo exhibit called "Microscapes: The Hidden Art of High Technology." Let your imagination go as you view the innovative photos from the "Microscapes" exhibit.

Processor board.
(AT&T Technologies)

Connector pins of a plug-in circuit board.
(AT&T Technologies)

Computer-generated temperature pattern.
(AT&T Technologies)

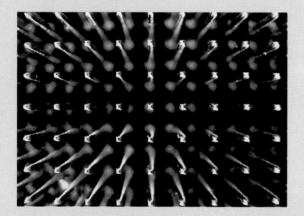

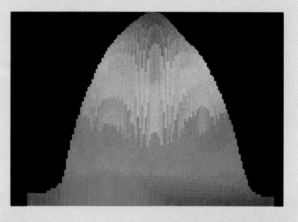

card numbers to cross-reference delinquent patrons in the "patron" table to obtain their names and addresses. The report at the bottom of Figure 11–15 is produced in response to the librarian's query. Data on each book, including publisher, author, and ISBN number, might be maintained in another table in the relational data base.

We all keep data, both at our place of business and at home. DBMS software and the availability of computing hardware make it easier for us

A Canadian fishery uses a microcomputer and a relational data base management system to record the catch for the day. In a relational DBMS, the determination of the relationships between the data are dynamic; that is, the data relationships are assigned automatically to meet a user's information needs.
(Courtesy of International Business Machines Corporation)

to extract meaningful information from these data. In time, working with data bases will be as much second nature as reaching in a desk drawer for a file folder.

SUMMARY OUTLINE AND IMPORTANT TERMS

11-1 DATA: THE KEY TO INFORMATION.   Most organizations use both the traditional and data base approaches to data management. The trend is to the data base approach.

Data come from many sources. The source and method of data entry are important considerations in information processing. Some data are generated outside the organization, but most are generated as a result of internal operations.

11-2 THE HIERARCHY OF DATA ORGANIZATION: WHICH COMES FIRST—THE BIT OR THE BASE?   The six levels of the hierarchy of data organization are **bit**, **character** (or **byte**), **data element**, **record**, **file**, and **data base**. The first level is transparent to the programmer and end user, but the other five are integral to the design of any information processing activity. A string of bits is combined to form a character. Characters are combined to represent the values of data elements. Related data elements are combined to form records. Records with the same data elements combine to form a file. The data base is the company's data resource for all information systems.

11-3   TRADITIONAL APPROACHES TO DATA MANIPULATION AND RETRIEVAL.   In traditional file processing, files are sorted, merged, and processed by a **key data element**. Data are retrieved and manipulated either sequentially or randomly.

11-4   SEQUENTIAL PROCESSING: ONE AFTER ANOTHER.   **Sequential files**, used for **sequential processing**, contain records that are ordered according to a key, also called a **control field**. A sequential file is processed from start to finish, and a particular record cannot be updated without processing the entire file.

In sequential processing, the records on both the transaction and the master file must be sorted prior to processing. A new master file is created for each computer run in which records are added or changed.

11-5   RANDOM OR DIRECT-ACCESS PROCESSING: PICK AND CHOOSE.   The **direct-access** or **random file** permits **random processing** of records. The primary storage medium for direct-access files is magnetic disk.

The **indexed sequential-access method (ISAM)** is one of several access methods that permit a programmer random access to any record on the file. In ISAM, the access of any given record is, in effect, a series of sequential searches through several levels of an index file. This search results in the disk address of the record in question.

Direct access of a particular record can also be achieved using a **hashing** algorhithm. With this method of random access, the disk address is arithmetically calculated from the key.

In random processing, the unsorted transaction file is run against a random master file. Only the records needed to complete the transaction are retrieved from secondary storage.

11-6   DATA INTEGRATION: SOLVING THE DATA PUZZLE.   A traditional file is usually designed to meet the specific requirements of a particular functional-area department. This approach to file design results in the same data being stored and maintained in several separate files. Data redundancy is costly and can be minimized by designing an integrated data base to serve the organization as a whole and not any specific department. The integrated data base is made possible by **data base management system (DBMS)** software.

11-7   WHAT'S TO BE GAINED FROM A DATA BASE ENVIRONMENT?   The benefits of a data base environment have encouraged many organizations to convert information systems that use traditional file organization to an integrated data base. Data base management systems permit greater access to information, minimize data redundancy, and provide programmers and analysts more flexibility in the design and maintenance of information systems.

Data base management systems rely on sophisticated data structures to overcome the processing constraints of traditional files. Two common types of DBMSs are CODASYL and relational.

11–8 CODASYL DATA BASE MANAGEMENT SYSTEMS. In CODASYL data bases, data links are established between **data base records**. One-to-one and one-to-many relationships between data base records are combined to form **sets**. The data base **schema** is a graphic representation of the logical structure of these sets.

11–9 RELATIONAL DATA BASE MANAGEMENT SYSTEMS. In relational DBMSs, data are accessed by content rather than by address. There is no predetermined relationship between the data; therefore, the data can be accessed at the data element level. The data are organized in tables in which each row is roughly equivalent to an occurrence of a CODASYL record.

REVIEW EXERCISES

Concepts

1. What are the six levels of the hierarchy of data organization?
2. What is the lowest-level logical unit in the hierarchy of data organization?
3. Name two possible key data elements for a student file. And name two for an inventory file.
4. In the grandfather-father-son method of file backup, which of the three files is the most current?
5. What is the purpose of an end-of-file marker?
6. Under what circumstances is a new master file created in sequential processing?
7. What is meant when someone says that data are program-independent?
8. Use the technique of Figure 11–6 to graphically illustrate the sequential processing steps required to update the inventory master file of Figure 11–4. The transaction file contains activity for part numbers 8 and 21. Assume the transaction file is unsequenced.
9. Use the technique of Figure 11–7 to graphically illustrate the random processing steps required to update the inventory master file of Figure 11–4. The transaction file contains activity for part numbers 8 and 21. Provide for backup.
10. The attribute of a relational DBMS is analogous to which level of the hierarchy of data organization?
11. A company manufactures screws. They make all screws of both brass and steel. Currently the screw lengths range from $\frac{1}{4}$ inch to 2 inches

in $\frac{1}{4}$-inch increments, but plans are being made to increase the product line to $3\frac{1}{2}$ inches. Each length of screw is manufactured with three types of heads—round, hex, and flat. The president wants to be able to look at the screw number on a report and be able to know which screw is referenced without including a description of the screw. You have been asked to set up a coding scheme to do this. The screw number should be coded within a minimum of positions to save disk storage.

12. The registrar's office maintains a course file that contains pertinent data about each section of each course. List the data elements that you think would be included on each section record and underline those that should be coded. What field length would you recommend for each data element? Would you recommend that the file be sequential or random? Why?

Discussion

13. How can an organization be data rich but information poor?

14. Contrast the advantages and disadvantages of sequential and random processing. Do you feel there will be a place for sequential processing in 1990? If so, where?

15. Assume that the registrar, housing office, and placement service at your college all have computer-based information systems that rely on traditional file organization. Identify possible redundant data elements.

16. Identify the sources of data that eventually become input to the student information system at your college.

17. The author contends that a fundamental knowledge of the capabilities and limitations of ISAM is important, even though ISAM storage and search procedures are transparent to the programmer. Do you agree or disagree? Why?

18. What do you feel is the most significant advantage to using a data base management system? Why?

SELF-TEST (by section)

11-1. Since a turnaround document is machine readable, it is not considered a source of data. (T/F)

11-2. _____ is another name for field.

11-3. A key data element is not needed for sequential processing. (T/F)

11-4. The entire sequential file must be processed if only one record is to be updated. (T/F)

11-5. ISAM organization is based on direct access via hashing algorithms. (T/F)

11-6. Integrated data bases are made possible by DBMS software. (T/F)

11-7. One of the disadvantages of DBMS software is that applications programs must be modified when the data base design is changed. (T/F)

11-8. The logical structure of a CODASYL data base is called a schema. (T/F)

11-9. The trend is to relational DBMSs for small data bases. (T/F)

Self-Test answers.   11-1, F; 11-2, Data element; 11-3, F; 11-4, T; 11-5, F; 11-6, T; 11-7, F; 11-8, T; 11-9, T.

IV

INFORMATION
SYSTEMS

CHAPTER 12

Information Systems in Business and Industry

12–1 OUR THIRST FOR INFORMATION _____

Part IV, "Information Systems" (Chapters 12–15), will acquaint you with the concepts, applications, and people associated with computer-based information systems. The focus of the present chapter and Chapter 13 is on the variety of information systems. Also covered are what and how much information to provide at different levels of management, how to justify the cost of an information system, proprietary information systems (i.e., systems for sale), and system security. Chapter 14 describes the process by which information systems are developed. Chapter 15 addresses the programming activity.

Information Systems

We combine *hardware*, *software*, *people*, *procedures*, and *data* to create an **information system**. A computer-based information system provides both a *data processing* capability and *information* to help people make better decisions. The data processing capability, or the handling and processing of data, is only one facet of an information system. A complete information system provides decision makers with on-demand reports and inquiry capabilities, as well as routine periodic reports. Because an information system aids management in making business decisions, it is sometimes called a **management information system**, or **MIS** for short.

Until recently, most payroll systems were data processing systems that did little more than process time sheets, print payroll checks, and keep running totals of annual wages and deductions. The demand for more and better personnel information resulted in an upgrade of payroll systems such that they can predict the average number of worker sick days, monitor salary equality between minority groups, make more effective use of available skills, and so on. As a result, payroll *data processing systems* have evolved to human resource *information systems*.

A **decision support system (DSS)** is a sophisticated information sys-

A wheat cooperative operates an information system that services over 50,000 farmers and 120 grain elevators. Farmers make on-line inquiries to obtain up-to-the-minute wheat prices. Inventory and sales accounting transactions are batched and recorded daily.
(Sperry Corporation)

Decision support systems provide these land developers with direct access to the information they need to make critical decisions about the ecological and economic consequences of developing certain parcels of land. A DSS can supply the information when they want it and in the form they want it.
(Cullinet Software, Inc.)

tem that uses the latest technological innovations (e.g., color graphics, data base management systems), planning and forecasting models, and query languages to produce and present information to support management in the decision-making process. Managers spend much of their day requesting and analyzing information before making a decision. Decision support systems help close the information gap and improve the quality of management decisions.

User-Developed Information Systems

Information systems are developed to meet information demands, which, in today's businesses, are almost endless. To give you an idea of just how much managers want support information, the average information services department carries a $3\frac{1}{2}$-year backlog of requests for the development of information systems. We have heard that "time is money"; it is also true that "information is money." Users cannot wait three or four years for the information they need, so many of them are taking matters into their own hands. With the help of user-friendly software tools such as fourth-generation languages, electronic spreadsheets, and decision support systems, they are doing it themselves.

The combination of distributed processing, powerful micros, and user-friendly software has resulted in rapidly expanding the base of computer-wise users. These users have the tools and knowledge to meet many of their own information processing needs. In fact, a greater percentage of an organization's ever-growing information processing needs are being met with little or no involvement on the part of an information services department. This trend is illustrated in Figure 12–1. Notice that each year a growing percentage of an organization's information processing needs are being met by the user community.

User-developed information systems are usually *function based*; that is, they are designed to support an individual's or a department's information needs. In contrast, information systems developed by the information services department usually are *integrated* and are designed to support several departments, or the organization as a whole.

Systems Ripe for Computerization

A manual system has the same components as a computer-based system—input, processing, output, and storage. If we were to talk in terms of numbers of systems, the overwhelming majority in both government and industry are still manual. This is true of large companies with complex computer networks as well as of small companies without computers. Tens of thousands of manual systems have been approved to be upgraded to computer-based information systems. Ten times that many are awaiting tomorrow's talented and creative people, perhaps you, to identify their potential for computerization.

As in a computer-based system, a manual system has an established pattern for work and data flow. For example, a payroll clerk receives the time sheets from supervisors; the individual employee's records are retrieved from folders stored alphabetically in a file cabinet; the payroll clerk uses a calculator to compute gross and net pay, then manually types the payroll check and stub. Finally, the payroll register, a listing of the amount paid and the deductions for each employee, is compiled on a tally sheet with

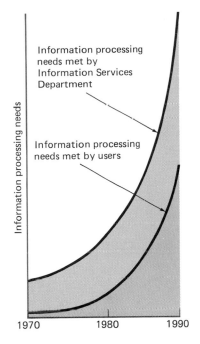

Information processing needs met by Information Services Department

Information processing needs met by users

Information processing needs

1970   1980   1990

FIGURE 12–1
Meeting Information Processing Needs
Each year a greater percentage of an organization's total information processing needs are being met by the user community.

In the construction business, the accuracy of cost estimates may mean the difference between making or losing money. These engineers developed an information system that uses historical data and updated cost data to produce reliable estimates of project costs. (Honeywell, Inc.)

column totals. About the only way to obtain information in a manual system is to painstakingly thumb through employee folders to find and extract what we need.

Today, most payroll systems have been automated. But look in any office in almost any organization and you will find rooms full of filing cabinets, tabbed three-ring binders, and drawers filled with 3- by 5-inch name-and-address cards. These manual files are symbols of opportunities to improve an organization's profitability and productivity through computerization—a type of automation intended to *improve* jobs, *not to eliminate* jobs.

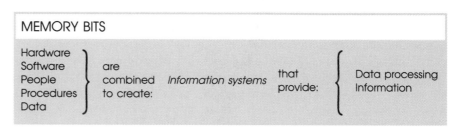

MEMORY BITS

Hardware
Software
People   are combined   *Information systems*   that provide: Data processing
Procedures   to create: Information
Data

12-2 LEVELS OF ORGANIZATIONAL ACTIVITY: WHO GETS WHAT INFORMATION

An organization has four levels of activity—*clerical*, *operational*, *tactical*, and *strategic*. Information systems process data at the clerical level and provide information for managerial decision making at the other three levels.

The quality of an information system is judged by its output. A system that generates the same 20-page report for personnel at both the clerical and strategic levels is defeating the purpose of an information system. The information needs at these two levels of activity are substantially different: a secretary has no need, or desire, for such a comprehensive report; the president of the company would never use the report because it would take too long to extract the few pieces of important information.

Programmers, systems analysts, and users must determine the specific informational needs at each level of organizational activity during the system design process. The key to developing quality information systems is to "filter" information so that the people at the various levels of activity receive the information they need to accomplish their job function—no more, no less. The quality of an information system depends very much on getting the *right information* to the *right people* at the *right time*.

Clerical Level.   Clerical-level personnel, those involved in repetitive tasks, are concerned primarily with transaction handling. You might say they process data. At the end of each term in a college or university grade-reporting system, for example, the secretaries of each academic department enter the grades into the system.

Operational Level.   Personnel at the operational level have well-defined tasks that might span a day, a week, or as much as three months, but their tasks are essentially short-term. Their information requirements are directed at operational feedback. In the grade-reporting system, for example, the chair-

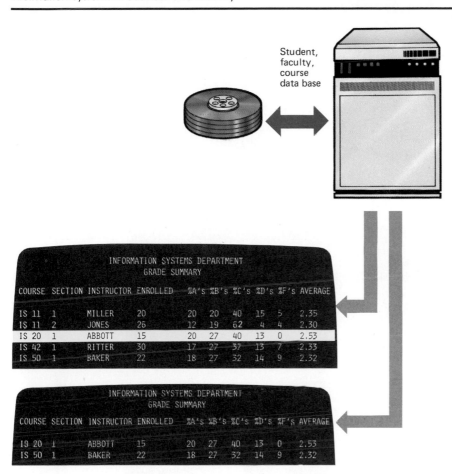

FIGURE 12–2
An Operational-Level Grade-Summary Report and Exception Report
These grade summary reports are prepared in response to inquiries from operational-level personnel. Contrast this figure with Figures 12–3 and 12–4.

man of the information systems department might want a report showing the average grade awarded for each course and any inconsistency in grading. In Figure 12-2, Professor Abbott's course is highlighted because the grades were somewhat higher than those of other instructors.

Managers at the operational, tactical, and strategic levels often request **exception reports** that highlight critical information. Such requests can be made to the information system department, or managers can make inquiries directly to the system, using a query language. For example, the chairman of the department might request an exception report listing only those instruc-

This regional sales staff works primarily at the operational level of activity. Their information horizon is normally less than three months: If they can't get their product to their customer in this time span, a competitor will.
(Bethlehem Steel Corporation)

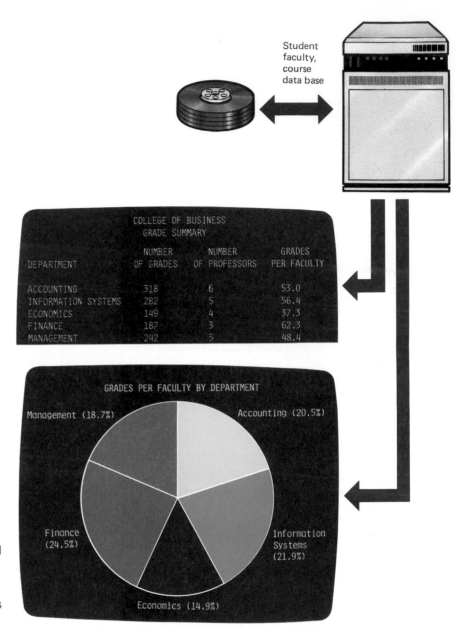

FIGURE 12-3
A Tactical-Level Grade-Summary Report shown in Tabular and Graphic Form
The grade summary report and pie chart are prepared in response to inquiries from tactical-level personnel. Contrast this figure with Figures 12-2 and 12-4.

tors who awarded As or Bs to 45 percent or more of their students. For the information systems department, only Professors Abbott and Baker would appear on the report (see Figure 12-2).

Tactical Level.   At the tactical level, managers concentrate on achieving that series of goals required to meet the objectives set at the strategic level. The information requirements are usually periodic, but on occasion, managers require "what if" reports. Tactical managers are concerned primarily with operations and budgets from year to year. In the grade-reporting system, the dean of the college of business might want to know the number of grades given per professor for each department in the college (see Figure 12-3).

To get a better feel for the relative workloads of the five departments, the dean requested that grades-per-faculty be graphically presented in a pie chart (see Figure 12–3).

Strategic Level.   Managers at the strategic level are objective minded. Their information system requirements are often one-time reports, "what if" reports, and trend analyses. For example, the president of the college might ask for a report showing the five-year trend for grade averages by college (Figure 12–4). Knowing that it is easier to detect trends in a graphic format than a tabular listing, the president requested that the annual grade data be summarized in a bar graph (Figure 12–4).

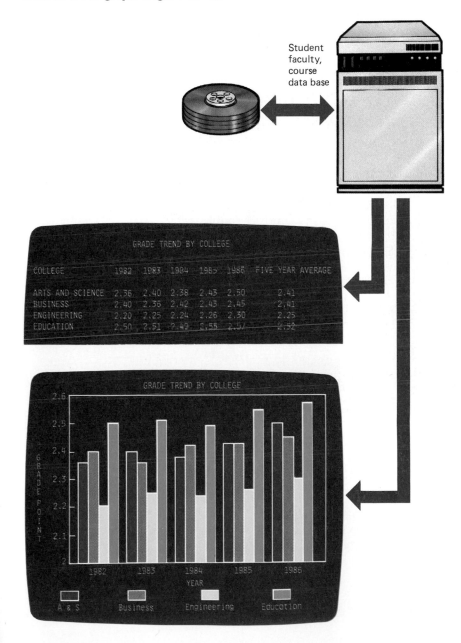

Student faculty, course data base

FIGURE 12–4
A Strategic-Level Grade-Trend-by-College Report shown in Tabular and Graphic Form
The grade-trend report and bar chart are prepared in response to inquiries from strategic-level personnel. Contrast this figure with Figures 12–2 and 12–3.

MEMORY BITS

INFORMATION REQUIREMENTS

▪ Clerical level	→	Primarily transaction handling
▪ Operational level	→	Short-term operational feedback
▪ Tactical level	→	Long-term operational feedback
▪ Strategic level	→	"What if" and trend analysis

12-3 USER-FRIENDLY SOFTWARE AND SYSTEMS

Within a few years the majority of professional people, and virtually all office workers, will spend some portion of their day interacting with a computer system. In a few more years almost everybody, including blue collar workers, will use the computer regularly. Interacting with workstations will become part of the daily routine of musicians, lawyers, shop foremen, children, housewives, architects, clerks, teachers, artists, physicians, and choreographers. In anticipation of this upswing in the number and variety of computer users, systems are being designed to be more *user friendly*. A system is said to be user friendly when someone with relatively little computer experience has no difficulty using it.

User-friendly systems simplify user interaction by communicating easily understood words, phrases, and even pictographs, called *icons*, to the end user. If confusion arises, the end user simply issues a "HELP" command to request more detailed instructions about how to proceed. Programmers occasionally insert humor into system responses to maintain the "user-friendly" philosophy and to break the monotony. For example, instead of responding "TRANSACTION COMPLETE," one programmer designed the information

A user-friendly micro software package lets users "paint" pictures on the screen. The user can pick any of several "pull down" menus (File, Edit, Mode, Tools, etc.) by using a mouse to move the arrow over the desired menu ("Tools" in the photo). The menu is then "pulled down" and temporarily superimposed over the drawing. The "painter" selects activities from the menu, then picks the appropriate icon or color (left and right of drawing) to fill the screen with the skyline of lower Manhattan.
(Courtesy of International Business Machines Corporation)

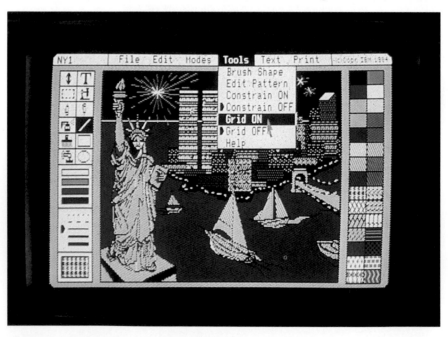

system to respond randomly with one of twenty responses such as "LOOKING GOOD," "NICE GOING," or "JOLLY GOOD SHOW." An input error resulted in "WHOOPS," or "YOU GOTTA BE KIDDING!"

User-friendly systems not only assist the user while interacting with the system, but they also present information in a format that can be more readily understood. For example, user-friendly systems provide the facility to present tabular data as bar charts, pie charts, and line drawings. We can absorb a graphic summary of information more quickly than a screen full of numbers.

12-4 INFORMATION SYSTEMS COMMON TO MOST BUSINESSES

Certain computer applications and information systems are universal and are equally appropriate at a manufacturing company, a university, a hospital, or even a cottage industry (people working out of their home). These applications normally involve *personnel* and *monetary* accounting, but they also include several other common application areas, such as inventory control and office automation. Each of these application areas can be, and usually is, integrated to some extent.

Payroll.   Having already read several payroll-related examples earlier in the text, you should be somewhat familiar with payroll systems. The two primary outputs of a payroll system are the payroll check and stub, which are distributed to the employees, and the payroll register, which is a summary report of payroll transactions.

Accounts Receivable.   The accounts receivable system keeps track of money owed the company on charges for goods sold or services rendered. When a customer purchases goods or services, the customer record is updated to reflect the charge. An invoice, bill, or statement reflecting the balance due is periodically sent to active customers. Upon receipt of payment, the amount due is decreased by the amount of the payment.

Management relies on the accounts receivable system to identify overdue accounts. Reports are generated that "age" accounts to identify those customers whose accounts are overdue by more than 30 days, 60 days, or 90 days.

Accounts Payable.   Organizations purchase everything from paper clips to bulldozers on credit. So the accounts payable system is the other side of the accounts receivable system. An invoice from a creditor company's accounts receivable system is input to the accounts payable system. When a company receives an invoice, the system generates a check and adjusts the balance. Most companies design their accounts payable system to take advantage of discounts for prompt payment.

General Ledger.   Every monetary transaction that occurs within an organization must be properly recorded. Payment of a bill, an interdepartmental transfer of funds—both are examples of monetary transactions. The general ledger system keeps track of these transactions and provides the input necessary to produce an organization's financial statement. A financial statement includes the *profit and loss statement* and the *balance sheet*.

This portable computer has more power than some mainframes of a decade ago. This supervisor is entering data that reflect the receipt of certain building materials. The data are downloaded to the company's mainframe computer system as input to the accounts payable system. (GRiD Systems Corporation)

The Securities Exchange Commission (SEC) requires publicly held companies to file quarterly financial statements. In the past, this requirement has resulted in 6 million pages of reports being sent to the SEC every three months. Now, each report is transmitted to the SEC electronically via data communications. With the current system, stock brokers and investors can look through thousands of financial statements from their workstations, whereas in the past they had to wait several weeks before they could see the reports.

In the not too distant past, accountants manually posted debits and credits for each account in a ledger book, thus the name general ledger for today's electronic system. Other "account" systems (accounts receivable, accounts payable, payroll, and so on) are sources of financial transactions and feed data to the general ledger system.

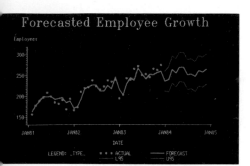

A human resource development system produced this graph that plots employee growth over a four-year period. (SAS Institute Inc., Cary, NC)

(By permission of Anthony Cresci)

Inventory Management and Control. Walk into most organizations and you see desks, file cabinets, and even computers; these items are called fixed assets. A fixed-asset inventory record is maintained for each item and includes such data as date purchased, cost, and inventory item number. These records are maintained for asset-control and tax purposes.

Manufacturing companies must also manage in-process and finished-goods inventories. These inventory systems monitor the quantity on hand and the location of each inventory item. Figure 12–5 illustrates a few of the menus and input/output displays in a typical on-line inventory system.

Human-Resource Development. Human resource development systems are essentially personnel accounting systems, which maintain pertinent data on employees. Besides routine historical data (e.g., educational background, salary history, and so on), the system would include data on performance reviews, skills, and professional development.

Budgeting. Each year, managers spend months preparing their department budgets for the coming fiscal year. To aid in this task, the budget system provides each manager with historical information on past line item expendi-

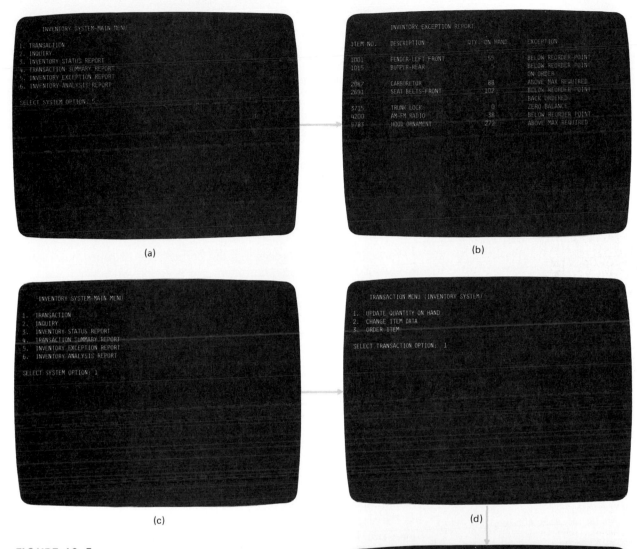

(a)

(b)

(c)

(d)

FIGURE 12–5
Interactive Session with an On-Line Inventory System
(a) The main menu presents the user with six processing
options. The user enters option "5" to obtain an inventory
exception report. (b) This exception report is produced
when main menu option "5" is selected. Only those
inventory items whose quantity on hand is too high or
too low are listed. (c) From the main menu, the user selects
option "1" to get the transaction menu. (d) This screen
is produced when main menu option "1" is selected.
Desiring to update quantity on hand, the user selects
transaction option "1". (e) From this transaction display
screen, the user enters *item number*, *number received*,
and *number used* to update quantity on hand.

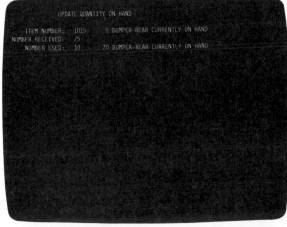

(e)

tures (e.g., salaries, office equipment, office supplies, and so on). Based on this information and projected budget requirements, each manager can make budget requests for the next fiscal year. The budget system matches these requests against projected revenues. The process is repeated until the coming year's budget is established.

Office Automation.   During the last ten years, much has been said and written about **office automation**. The term refers collectively to those computer-based applications associated with general office work. Companies using office automation extensively have experienced productivity increases of 50% to 100%, yet less than 15% of the companies can claim extensive use of office automation applications. So we have a long way to go before office automation is fully implemented. Office automation applications include word processing, data entry, electronic mail, image processing, voice processing, and office information systems. Each of these applications is discussed below.

Word Processing.   Word processing, the cornerstone of office automation, revolves around written communication and is found wherever there is an office with a computer. Word processing means using the computer to enter, store, manipulate, and print text in letters, memos, reports, books, and so on. Like accounting and grade reporting, word processing is just another application for computers and is available for virtually every micro and mainframe computer.

Your college computers probably have word processing software that can make preparing reports and term papers much easier and neater than writing them out by hand or by typing them. With word processing, you will have to key in only the initial draft; then you can make revisions and corrections to the disk-based draft until it is ready to be printed in final form.

The fundamental concepts of word processing are discussed briefly below. These concepts are discussed in more detail in the special section, "Integrated Microcomputer Software," that follows Chapter 17.

- *Formatting a Document.* When you *format* a document, you are describing the size of the print page and how you want the document to look when printed. As with the typewriter, you must set the left and right margins, the tab settings, line spacing, and character spacing. You can even justify on both the left and the right margins, such as in newspapers and books. Depending on the software, some or all of these specifications are made in a *layout line*.

- *Entering Text.* To begin preparation of the document, all you have to do is start typing. Text is entered in **replace mode** or **insert mode**. When in replace mode, the character that you enter *overstrikes* the character at the cursor position.

  When in insert mode, you can enter *additional* text. For example, suppose you entered "To: Sharon Rasley" and would like to add the title "Dr." Simply select insert mode, place the cursor on the "S" in "Sharon", and enter "Dr. ". The text will then read "To: Dr. Sharon Rasley."

  Word processing permits *full-screen editing*. That is, you can move the cursor to any position in the document to insert or replace text.

Dr. An Wang founded Wang Laboratories, Inc. in Boston, MA in 1951. Wang Labs has been a major contributor of innovations in the field of office automation. Dr. Wang invented the principle upon which magnetic core memory is based. He also introduced a desktop computer, named LOCI, in 1965.
(Courtesy of Wang Laboratories, Inc.)

When you enter text, you press the carriage return key only when you wish to begin a new line of text. As you enter text in replace mode, the computer automatically moves the cursor to the next line. When in insert mode, the computer manipulates the text such that it *wraps around*, sending words that are pushed past the right margin into the next line, and so on to the end of the paragraph.

- *Features*. Word processing features presented here are common to most word processing software packages. Two of the handiest features are the *copy* and *move* commands. With the copy feature, you can select a word, a phrase, or as much contiguous text as you desire, and copy it to another portion of the document. To do this, you simply issue the copy command, then tell the computer what to copy and where to put it. At the end of the copy procedure, two exact copies of the text are present in the document. The move command works in a similar manner, except the text that you select is moved to the location that you designate and the original text is deleted (see Figure 12–6).

Right. With word processing systems, changes to reports and letters can be made quickly and easily.
(Photo courtesy of Hewlett-Packard Company)

FIGURE 12-6
The Move Command in Word Processing
In the first screen, the text to be moved is identified. The cursor is then positioned at the "move to" location—in our example, after the first sentence. In the second screen, the move command is issued and the designated text is "moved" to a location following the first sentence.

```
To:        Field Sales Staff
From:      G. Brooks, Regional Sales Manager
Re:        Weekly Briefing Session

     The Sales Department's weekly briefing session will be
held at 9:00 a.m. this Thursday.  Last month's sales figures
and new sales strategies will be discussed.  See you
Thursday! We'll meet in the second floor conference room.
```

```
To:        Field Sales Staff
From:      G. Brooks, Regional Sales Manager
Re:        Weekly Briefing Session

     The Sales Department's weekly briefing session will be
held at 9:00 a.m. this Thursday.  We'll meet in the second
floor conference room.  Last month's sales figures and new
sales strategies will be discussed.  See you Thursday!
```

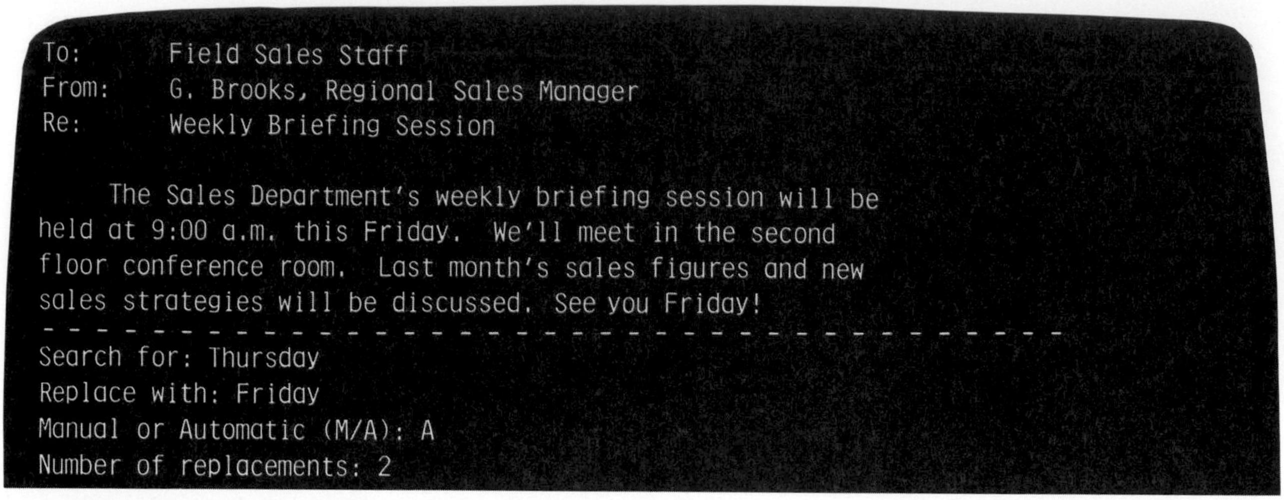

```
To:       Field Sales Staff
From:     G. Brooks, Regional Sales Manager
Re:       Weekly Briefing Session

     The Sales Department's weekly briefing session will be
held at 9:00 a.m. this Friday.  We'll meet in the second
floor conference room.  Last month's sales figures and new
sales strategies will be discussed.  See you Friday!
- - - - - - - - - - - - - - - - - - - - - - - - - - - - - - - - - -
Search for: Thursday
Replace with: Friday
Manual or Automatic (M/A): A
Number of replacements: 2
```

FIGURE 12-7
The Global Search and Replace Command in Word Processing
All occurrences of the word "Thursday" in the memo of Figure 12-6 are replaced with "Friday" when a global search and replace command is issued.

The *search* or *find* feature permits you to search through the entire document and identify all occurrences of a particular character string. For example, suppose the meeting announced in the memo of Figure 12–6 is switched from Thursday to Friday. If you wanted to search the memo for all occurrences of "Thursday", you would simply initiate the search command and type in "Thursday". The cursor would be immediately positioned at the first occurrence of "Thursday". You can also *search and replace*. For example, you can selectively replace "Thursday" with "Friday". Or, you can *replace* all occurrences instantly with a *global search and replace* (see Figure 12–7).

If spelling is a problem, then word processing is the answer. Once you have entered the text and formatted the document the way you want it, you can call on the *spell* feature. The spell feature checks every word in the text against an electronic dictionary (usually from 75,000 to 150,000 words), then alerts you if a word is not in the dictionary.

Other word processing features, such as *centering* of titles, *indenting*, *boldface*, *underline*, *header* and *trailer labels*, and *pagination* (numbering of pages), are discussed in the special section, "Integrated Microcomputer Software," that follows Chapter 17.

■ *Merging Text with a Data Base*. Besides providing a faster and easier way to type, the text generated by word processing can be merged with data from a data base. For example, a typical word processing application could involve the preparation of the same letter that is to be sent to a number of people. Suppose an art studio wanted to invite 100 preferred customers to a private art showing. The secretary with a regular typewriter has two choices: either type 100 separate letters or type one letter and photocopy it 100 times. In the business world, the latter is not acceptable. Using word processing, a secretary can type the letter once, store it on the disk, then simply merge the customer name-and-address file (also stored on the disk) with the letter. The letters are then printed with the proper addresses and salutations. Figure 12–8 illustrates how a standard letter is merged with a name-and-address file to produce a "personalized" letter.

Data Entry. The data entry function is usually part of a more encompassing

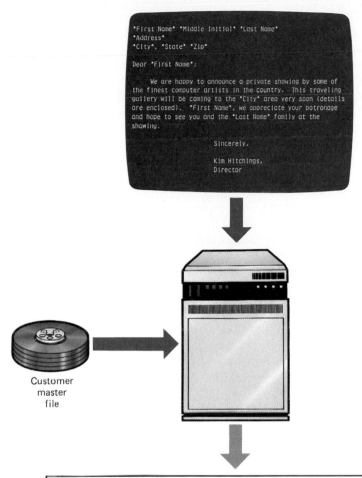

First Name *Middle Initial* *Last Name*
Address
City, *State* *Zip*

Dear *First Name*:

   We are happy to announce a private showing by some of
the finest computer artists in the country. This traveling
gallery will be coming to the *City* area very soon (details
are enclosed). *First Name*, we appreciate your patronage
and hope to see you and the *Last Name* family at the
showing.

                    Sincerely,

                    Kim Hitchings,
                    Director

Customer
master
file

                    The Contemporary Art Gallery   C A G
                         1791 Brookhaven Avenue
                         Baltimore, MD 21233

Marty E. Chambers
115 Vista Drive
Walla Walla, WA 99362

Dear Marty:

   We are happy to announce a private showing by some of
the finest computer artists in the country. This traveling
gallery will be coming to the Walla Walla area very soon
(details are enclosed). Marty, we appreciate your patronage
and hope to see you and the Chambers family at the showing.

                    Sincerely,
                    Kim Hitchings,
                    Director

FIGURE 12-8
Merging Data with Word Processing
The names and addresses from a customer master file are retrieved from secondary storage and merged with the text of a letter. In the actual letter, the appropriate data items are inserted for *First Name*, *Address*, *City*, and so on. In this way, a "personalized" letter can be sent to each customer.

information system, but since it is a traditional office function, data entry is sometimes associated with office automation. Data entry hardware and techniques are presented in Chapter 8, "Input/Output Devices."

Electronic Mail. The electronic mail, or E-mail, application, which is discussed in Chapter 9, "Data Communications," lets us send messages to people in the next office, in Japan, or anywhere in the "data communications" world.

Computers are revolutionizing legal practices. Rather than spending days researching related cases in legal casebooks, this attorney uses key words to search a massive full-text data base containing more cases than any law office's library. A search of applicable "computer negligence" cases was completed in 20 minutes.
(Mead Data Central)

Image Processing.   Image processing involves the creation, storage, and distribution of pictorial information. There are two levels of image processing sophistication.

At the first level, *facsimile* equipment, which has been around since the 1960s, transfers hard-copy documents via telephone lines to another office. The process is similar to making a copy on a copying machine, except that the original is inserted in a facsimile machine at one office and a hard copy is produced on another facsimile machine in another office.

Recent technological innovations have expanded the scope of image processing. An *image processor* uses a camera to scan and digitize the image; then the digitized image is stored on a disk. The image can be handwritten notes, photographs, drawings, or anything that can be digitized. In digitized form, the image can be retrieved, displayed, altered, merged with text, stored, and sent via data communications to one or several remote locations.

Overnight mail services use image processing to provide two-hour delivery service. The customer simply brings the documents to be sent to a local distribution facility; the documents are digitized and sent via data communications to the destination distribution facility. Hard copies are made from the digitized images, then delivered to their destination, all in less than two hours—guaranteed!

Voice Processing.   Voice processing includes *voice message switching* and *teleconferencing*. The workstation for voice message switching (a store-and-forward "voice mailbox" system) is a touch-tone telephone. Voice message switching accomplishes the same function as electronic mail, except the hard copy is not available. When you send a message, your voice is digitized and stored on a magnetic disk for later retrieval. The message is routed to the destination(s) you designate (using the telephone's keyboard); then it is heard upon request by the intended receiver(s). A voice store-and-forward system permits you to send one or many messages with just one phone call.

Teleconferencing enables people in different locations to see and talk to each other and to visually share charts and other meeting materials. The voice and video of teleconferencing are supported by the telephone network. The idea behind teleconferencing is that people who are geographically scattered can meet without the need for time-consuming and expensive travel.

The use of teleconferencing has fallen short of initial expectations because people have found out that electronic interaction is not a substitute for direct human interaction. The controlled teleconferencing environment does not transmit subtle nonverbal communication, which is so important to human understanding.

Office Information Systems.   Several small information systems address traditional office tasks. For example, one system allows people to keep their personal *calendars* on-line. As workers schedule activities, they block out times in their electronic calendars. There are definite advantages to having a central data base of personal calendars. Let's say that a public relations manager wants to schedule a meeting to review the impact of some unfavorable publicity. To do this, the manager enters the names of the participants and the expected duration of the meeting. The *conference scheduling* system searches the calendars of affected people and suggests possible meeting times. The

The "calendar" is one of many timesaving office
information systems.
(GRiD Systems Corporation)

manager then selects a meeting time, and the participants are notified by
electronic mail. Of course, their calendars are automatically updated to reflect
the meeting time.

Another common office application is the company *directory*. The directory contains basic personnel data: name, title, department, location, and phone
number. To "look up" someone's telephone number, all you have to do is
enter the person's name on your workstation, and the associated data are
displayed. The beauty of the directory data base is that it is always up to
date, unlike hard-copy directories which never seem to have the current titles
or phone numbers.

Other systems permit you to organize *personal notes*, keep *diaries*, document ideas in a *preformatted outline*, and keep a *tickler* file. When you
log-on in the morning, the tickler file automatically reminds you of "things
to do" for that day.

12–5   HOW DIFFERENT BUSINESSES
USE THE COMPUTER

Information systems are part of the everyday routine in every *functional area*
in every *type of organization*. Application areas that are normally computerized
within the various industry groups are listed in Figure 12–9 and briefly discussed in the following sections. Each of these application areas can be,
and usually is, integrated (e.g., it shares a data base) to some extent.

The following is not an exhaustive treatment of computer applications
in business and industry—that would take many books. These applications
are presented to illustrate and acquaint you with some of the ways computers
are used in a variety of industries. Computer applications in government,
health, and education are presented in Chapter 13.

Manufacturing

The *order-entry and processing* system accepts and processes customer orders.
The system then feeds data to the warehouse or plant, depending on whether
the order is for stock items or special order, and to the accounts receivable

APPLICATIONS OF COMPUTER GRAPHICS: BUSINESS AND INDUSTRY

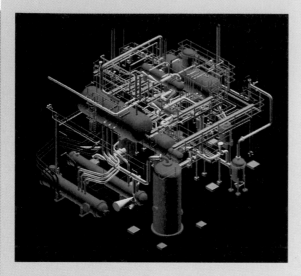

Once chemical engineers construct a three-dimensional model, they can look at their plant design from different angles. With this background work done in the office, the chance of on-site construction difficulties are lessened.
(Reprinted with permission from Computervision Corporation, Bedford, MA)

Cutting and pasting is passé with graphics systems. Once text and illustrations have been merged, composed pages can be previewed on a graphics workstation. Seen here is the screen image of a Yellow Pages format.
(Intergraph Corporation)

Color computer graphics are used by architects to produce realistic interior and exterior models. This graphic three-dimensional model of a building lobby even depicts shadows.
(Intergraph Corporation)

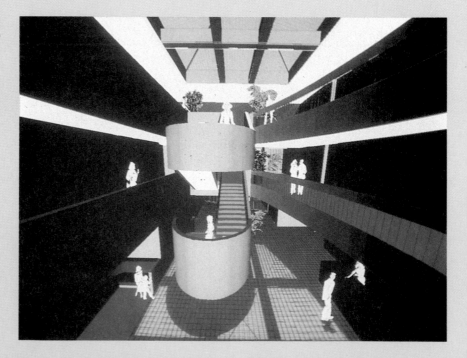

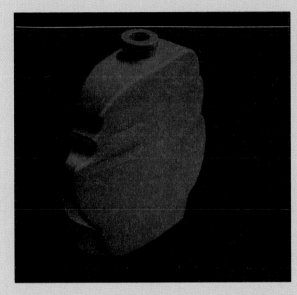

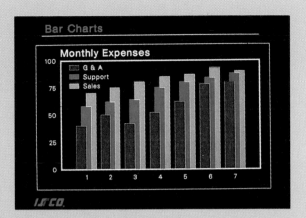

CAD systems are used to design consumer goods, such as this perfume bottle.
(Reprinted with permission from Computervision Corporation, Bedford, MA)

Computer graphics is a natural for the preparation of exciting presentation graphics. This bar chart vividly contrasts expenses associated with G & A (general and administrative categories), support, and sales for seven products.
(ISSCO)

This tactical screen display is visible from the flight deck of the starship Enterprise in the motion picture "Star Trek: The Wrath of Khan."
(Evans & Sutherland)

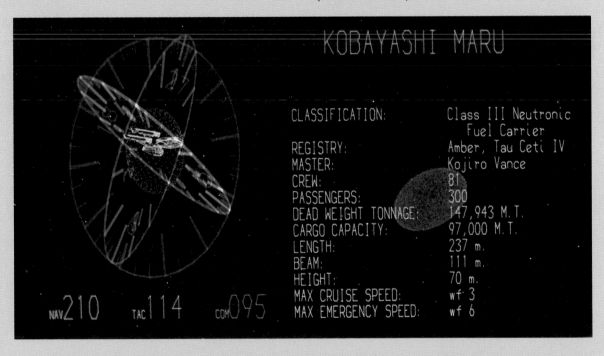

GENERAL
Payroll
Accounts receivable
Accounts payable
General ledger
Inventory management and control
Human resource development
Budgeting
Office automation
  Word processing
  Data entry
  Electronic mail
  Image processing
  Voice processing
  Office information systems

MANUFACTURING
Order-entry and processing
Production scheduling
Market analysis
Project management and control
Standard costing
Manufacturing resource planning (MRP)
CAD/CAM
Robotics

RETAIL SALES
Point of sale (POS)
Intercompany networking

FINANCIAL SERVICES
Electronic funds transfer (EFT)
Automatic teller machines (ATM)
Home banking
Financial planning

PUBLISHING
Word processing
Typesetting
Graphics design
Page formatting
Educational support software
Customized printing on demand
Magazines on a disk

TRANSPORTATION
Reservations
Fleet maintenance
Satellite monitoring systems

INSURANCE
Policy administration
Claims processing
Actuarial accounting

ENTERTAINMENT
Professional sports systems
Television news (video composition)
Video games
Film industry

THE ARTS
Computer art
On-line script development
Theater set design
Dance choreography
Musical composition
Musical synthesizers

FIGURE 12-9
Summary of Computer Applications by Industry
These are but a few of the many computer applications for any given industry.

system for billing. The system also tracks orders and provides order status information from the time the order is received until it is delivered to the customer.

Production scheduling systems allocate manufacturing resources in an optimal manner. A well-designed system will minimize idle time for both workers and machines and ensure that needed materials are at the right place at the right time.

This shop supervisor relies on a production scheduling system to help him make the best possible use of expensive computer-controlled machine tools.
(Sperry Corporation)

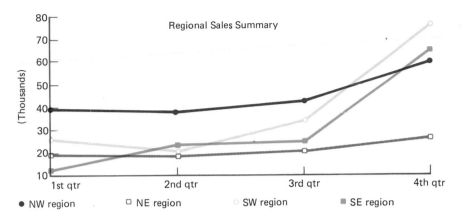

FIGURE 12–10
Scatter Plot of Regional Sales
Quarterly sales figures from four regions are plotted to aid in market analysis.

Market analysis systems rely on historical and current data to identify fast- and slow-moving products, to pinpoint areas with high sales potential, to make forecasts of production requirements, and to plan marketing strategy. For example, in Figure 12–10, the scatter plot of regional sales over the last four quarters demonstrates clearly that fourth-quarter sales in the northeast region did not keep pace. Based on this finding, management might elect to focus more attention on the northeast region during the coming quarter.

Project management and control systems provide management with the information necessary to keep projects within budget and on time. Periodic reports would present actual versus anticipated project costs and the number of days ahead or behind schedule.

Other information systems commonly found in manufacturing companies include *standard costing, manufacturing resource planning* (*MRP*), and *CAD/ CAM* (computer-aided design/computer-aided manufacturing). Robotics is also an application of computers in manufacturing (see Chapter 5, "Computer Systems—Mainframes").

Retail Sales

The most prominent system in the retail sales industry is the *point-of-sale* (*POS*) system. The cash-registerlike POS workstation logs the transaction of the sale (see the example and illustration in Chapter 2, Figure 2–3), and the sale also updates the inventory status of the item sold. This immediate feedback is valuable input to marketing strategy. For example, a department store chain relies on its POS system to identify fast-selling items so that they can be reordered before the stock is depleted. This system also identifies slow-moving items so that management can reduce the price accordingly.

Traditionally, orders for shelf items are computer generated in hard-copy format, then sent by mail to wholesale distributors. It is not unusual for a single order from a department store chain to list thousands of items. When the wholesaler receives the order, key-entry operators enter the orders. The trend today is to use *intercompany networking* (linking of the computers of different companies). The orders are sent from the retailer to the distributor via data communications, thereby eliminating the need for hard-copy orders and redundant key data entry.

With the prospect of increased productivity, manufacturing companies have been rushing to install more and more applications of computer-aided design (CAD) and robotics. In the photo, a keyboard in production is put through its paces by a robotic tester.
(Courtesy of International Business Machines Corporation)

Point-of-sale workstations are a convenience to both customers and retailers. With the implementation of each new POS workstation, we are inviting greater use of EFT and moving closer to a "cashless society." (Courtesy of International Business Machines Corporation)

The banking industry would prefer that their customers use ATM's for banking transactions rather than tellers. The average ATM transaction takes less time, but most importantly, it costs less than half that of a teller transaction. We can expect the cost of banking services to drop as more and more people use ATMs. (Courtesy of International Business Machines Corporation)

Before long, POS systems will be integrated with EFT (electronic funds transfer) systems, so that what is now a *credit* transaction will be a *cash-transfer* transaction. That is, when a customer purchases an item, the amount of the sale is debited, via EFT, from the customer's checking account and credited to the account of the retail store. No further funds transfer is needed. Of course, credit purchases will still be possible.

Financial Services

The financial services industries, which include banking, savings and loan, and brokerage firms, are entering an exciting era. The computer is the impetus behind some radical and progressive changes in the way these money brokers do business. For example, financial services organizations serve as a money "buffer" between buyer and seller. The traditional approach to money exchange has been for the seller to bill the buyer, the buyer to write a check for the amount of the bill, the seller to deposit the check, and the bank to transfer the funds from the buyer's to the seller's account. Throughout the remainder of the 1980s we can expect to see this traditional approach give way to more and more EFT.

In electronic funds transfer, the amount owed is transferred "electronically" from one account to another (in a bank, savings and loan, or brokerage firm). For example, rather than sending out thousands of statements that require each customer to pay the bill in his or her own way, some utility companies are cooperating with customers and banks so that payments are transferred electronically at the end of each billing period. As another example, some employers are bypassing the printing of payroll checks. Based on data supplied to the banks, pay is electronically transferred from employer to employee accounts.

Automatic teller machines (ATMs) are the most visible symbol of EFT. In over 100 banks, however, EFT has been extended to the home in the form of *home banking* systems. Subscribers to a home banking service use their personal computers as workstations to pay bills, transfer funds, and inquire about account status. Some systems also provide subscribers with other services, such as "electronic" shopping, electronic mail, and up-to-the-minute stock market quotations. Other financial services organizations offer similar systems. For example, several brokerage firms permit clients to use their PCs to tap into a data base that contains their account data as well as timely information about the securities market.

All financial institutions offer *financial planning* services. Part of the service involves a computer-based analysis of a customer's investment portfolio. Input to the system includes current and anticipated income, amount and type of investments, assets and liabilities, and financial objectives (e.g., minimize taxes, pension level at age 65). The output from the analysis is recommendations aimed at optimizing the effectiveness of a particular person's investment portfolio.

Futurists are predicting that the current system of currency exchange will gradually be replaced by EFT. By the end of the decade, the corner drugstore will probably have a POS workstation that will allow you to buy even a candy bar through EFT.

Publishing

Word processing, computerized *typesetting*, computer-aided *graphics design*, and *page formatting* have revolutionized the way newspapers, books, and magazines are produced. Reporters and writers enter and edit their stories on their portable micros or on-line workstations. Once all copy is on-line, pages are automatically formatted, according to type and spacing specifications. All these steps were traditionally handled with pencils, paper, and typewriters. The document then went on to editing, retyping, composing, proofreading, cutting, pasting, and photographing of the final page format before plates could be made for the presswork.

Publishers of books have traditionally produced hard-copy products, but more and more they will also be involved in the production of *educational support software*. For example, within a few years, most introductory textbooks will be accompanied by educational software (e.g., this book has a software supplement). The interactive nature of software adds a new dimension to the learning process.

Eventually, *customized printing on demand* will be available at bookstores. Instead of making a selection from available books, you will make a selection from a list of virtually any current book. The book will then be printed (figures and all) and bound while you wait. This approach will provide a greater selection for the customer and vastly reduce costly inventory for both bookstore and publisher.

Although customized printing on demand is a few years away, *magazines on a disk* are here today. These magazines are distributed in diskette format for display on home PCs. In the same vein, as optical laser technology moves into the home, dictionaries and encyclopedias will be sold in the form of high-density laser disks.

An information system at this newspaper handles news editing, classified advertising, page formatting, and numerous other related tasks.
(Courtesy of International Business Machines Corporation)

Transportation

Airline *reservation* systems, discussed on several occasions in previous chapters, are among the most sophisticated of information systems. Airline and travel agents have workstations on which they can make reservations for any U.S.-based airline. The tickets are even printed at the travel agents' workstations. The same is true for rail and bus services and for auto rentals.

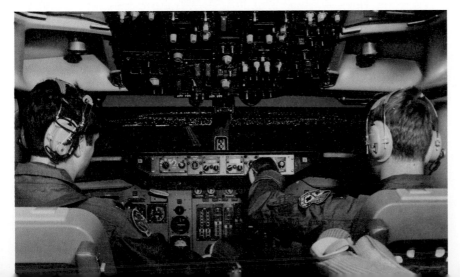

These Air Force pilots are looking out the window of a simulated aircraft into a computer-generated scene. Pilots practice flight control and emergency procedures while a variety of flight conditions are shown visually and simulated with the instruments. These pilots are "flying" a low-level training mission over Bakersfield, California at night.
(Evans & Sutherland and Rediffusion Simulation)

```
              MAY MAINTENANCE SCHEDULE - - FIRST WEEK
 VEHICLE NO.          DESCRIPTION               MAINTENANCE ACTIVITY
 7                    EXECUTIVE LIMO            SEMI-ANNUAL PM
 12                   1-TON TRUCK              OIL CHANGE AND FILTER
                                               LUBE
 22                   1-TON TRUCK              ROTATE TIRES
 33                   9-PASSENGER VAN          REPLACE TIRES
                                               REPLACE WATER HOSES
```

FIGURE 12–11
Fleet Maintenance Report
This report is produced periodically to alert maintenance personnel to fleet maintenance requirements.

A major concern of airlines, railroads, and bus lines is the periodic upkeep of their fleet of transport vehicles. With hundreds, and even thousands, of vehicles, it is difficult for maintenance crews to keep track of when to change the oil, when to replace a particular part, and many other routine preventive maintenance tasks. A *fleet maintenance* system (see Figure 12–11) periodically prompts maintenance personnel to perform these routine tasks, vehicle by vehicle.

A *satellite monitoring system* uses satellite communications to monitor the status of trucks. The system detects when a truck is idle or moving, the weight of the truck's contents, and the speed of the truck. As anticipated, truckers are resisting the implementation of this "spy in the sky."

Insurance

The information systems of an insurance company have more external interaction, or communication with people outside the company, than do other businesses. Most of the external communication is with customers. The volume of transactions makes computer-based *policy administration* and *claims processing* systems a necessity. Insurance agents hook up to headquarters computers so they can quote, write, and deliver insurance policies while customers wait.

An insurance company makes or loses money on the basis of the accuracy of its *actuarial accounting* system. This system maintains countless statistics that serve as the basis for the rate structure. An actuarial system provides the following kinds of information: the probability that a 20-year-old Kansas City resident with no automobile accident history will have an accident; or the life expectancy of a 68-year-old female whose parents died of natural causes.

Entertainment

The computer is now an integral part of the entertainment industry. *Pro football* coaches rely heavily on feedback from their computer systems to call plays and set defenses during a game. The system predicts what the opposing team is expected to do based on statistics of what they have done in the past. In fact, the computer is becoming the deciding factor between evenly matched opponents in many sports. In *professional tennis*, specially designed portable computers are used to keep statistics on stroke effectiveness

Coaches in many sports, including swimming, have turned to computers to help provide them with better information about the performance of their athletes. (Courtesy of International Business Machines Corporation)

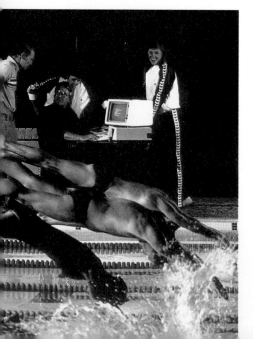

and strategies. Pro tennis players analyze the results; then, during play, they emphasize their strengths and attack an opponent's weaknesses.

The computer has made it possible for *television network news* teams to compose video pictures of key persons and locations (e.g., the President and the White House) that otherwise could not be made available because of time constraints. Also, instead of sending researchers to libraries to cull the relevant facts, reporters tap into a data base and have the facts they need in seconds.

Then, of course, there are *video*, or should we say "computer," *games*. Interest in video games seems to be lessening as people realize that what they have is a computer with a seemingly infinite number of practical applications. The computer games industry, however, is anticipating a resurgence of interest with the introduction of videodisk technology in games. With video-disk-based games (e.g., the "Dragon's Lair" game), the images are lifelike color motion pictures instead of computer graphics.

Computers have had quite an impact on the *film industry*. Many special effects and even the sets for some movies are generated with computer graphics. Cartoons and animated movies are no longer drawn one frame at a time. The scenes and characters are drawn, by hand or with a computer, then manipulated with computer graphics to create the illusion of motion. Computer graphics has even made it possible to revive old black-and-white movies—in color!

BLACK-AND-WHITE CINEMA COMES ALIVE WITH COLOR

Laurel and Hardy in living color! Now, through an innovative use of computer technology, it is possible to change the old black-and-white films to color.

This colorizing process uses an electronic scanner that breaks each frame of the film into an array of 525,000 separate dots. Each dot is stored and manipulated by the computer. An art director reviews the frames at the beginning, middle, and end of a scene and selects a specific color for every object in the scene (e.g., a coat, a chair, and so on). The computer operator, with a digital graphics table and electronic palette as tools, "hand paints" the images according to the art director's color specifications, much like paint-by-the-numbers. Then a specially designed, high-speed computer colors the remainder of the frames in a scene by comparing every new frame with the preceding one. Since the colors of less than 4% of the dots will change from frame to frame, the computer is able to keep track of moving objects.

This process can be used on today's color films, too. For example, a facial flaw can be retouched, or a day sky can be changed to a night sky.

At present, there is a debate as to whether colorization will improve or harm the movie classics. Movie purists would never consider watching *Casablanca* in color! Many people today, however, have come to expect color.

A colorized version of a black and white Laurel and Hardy movie.
(Mobile Image Canada Limited)

The Arts

In the arts, the computer is being welcomed with open arms, but only after a long wait-and-see period. Artists and performers now realize that the computer is a human creation and it enhances our human abilities to be creative. *Computer art* is now a recognized art form, just like water colors and oils. Traditional painters use computers to experiment with colors on a display screen before committing them to canvas. Sculptors use computer graphics capabilities to generate three-dimensional sketches.

In the *theater*, playwrights use word processing systems that are especially designed for the theater environment. Besides the obvious benefits of word processing, there are side benefits to having the script "on-line." Actors can learn their lines while interacting with a computer that "reads" the lines of other actors; that is, only the lines of other actors are displayed on the screen, unless the actor requests that all lines be displayed. Using computer graphics, set designers lay out the backdrops and props before they are built. Again, there are side benefits to having the set design "on-line." The director can work out and document the stage movements of all actors before the start of rehearsals.

In *dance*, as in sports, computer graphics are used to refine dance movements through biomechanical analysis. Also, computers have proved handy tools by which to document the choreography of dances.

Music composition software is to composers as word processing software is to authors. This software relieves composers of much of the burden of documenting their compositions in music notation, thereby allowing them to concentrate on the more creative aspects of composing. Those who make the music are also benefitting from computers. Musicians can create a variety of new sounds with computer-based *music synthesizers*.

Certainly, many new applications will emerge as computers begin to play a more active role in the arts.

The set of S.M. Synge's "The Playboy of the Western World" was designed with the help of a computer-aided design (CAD) system.
(Allentown College of St. Francis de Sales, directed by Gerald J. Schubert, O.S.F.S., photo by Lee Butz)

This music synthesizer produces musical sounds that are indistinguishable from those produced by conventional, accoustical instruments: piano, brass, strings, woodwinds, percussion, vocal chorus, and even sound effects. This revolutionary new synthesizer opens new doors for performers, composers, and music educators. To hear is to believe!
(Kurzweil Music Systems)

COMPUTER ARTISTS CHOOSE FROM 16.8 MILLION COLORS

The color workstation is playing a more significant role in a growing number of applications. It is required in architecture for producing realistic interior and exterior models. People in energy exploration use it for evaluating seismic information that describes formations below the earth's surface. Engineers use it in modeling, plant design, and electronics. And it is used in the field of art.

Computer artists can mix, erase, change color schemes, or produce an amazing array of tints at the touch of a button. On some systems, 256 distinct grades of reds, greens, and blues can be mixed to produce 16.8 million different colors. With this range of tones and intensities, even the most intricate, delicately shaded patterns and shapes can be displayed accurately.

Whether the artist uses a palette and easel or a graphics workstation, it still takes a creative mind and a keen eye to produce "good" art. The computer is just another tool of creativity.

Computer art.
(Mindset Corporation)

Just as photography has never replaced painting, the computer will never replace the brush. The computer is just another medium of artistic expression.

SUMMARY OUTLINE AND IMPORTANT TERMS _____

12-1 OUR THIRST FOR INFORMATION   An **information system** is a computer-based system that provides both a data processing capability and information to help managers make decisions. An information system is also called a **management information system**, or **MIS**, because of its orientation to management. A **decision support system** is a sophisticated information system that uses the latest hardware and software technologies to provide better, more timely information.

Each year, a growing percentage of an organization's information processing needs are being met by the user community.

12-2 LEVELS OF ORGANIZATIONAL ACTIVITY: WHO GETS WHAT INFORMATION.   The four levels of organizational activity are strategic, tactical, operational, and clerical. Information must be filtered at the various levels of activity to ensure that the intended end user receives that information necessary to accomplish his or her job function. Too much information will be confusing, and too little information will not allow end users to accomplish their jobs effectively.

12-3 USER-FRIENDLY SOFTWARE AND SYSTEMS.   User-friendly systems permit end users who have very little computer experience to interact easily with a computer system. Icons and "HELP" commands contribute to a system's user friendliness.

12–4   INFORMATION SYSTEMS COMMON TO MOST BUSINESSES.
Computer applications found in most organizations include payroll,
accounts receivable, accounts payable, general ledger, inventory management and control, human resource development, budgeting, and
office automation.

Office automation refers collectively to computer-based applications associated with general office work. These include word processing, data entry, electronic mail, image processing, voice processing,
and office information systems.

12–5   HOW DIFFERENT BUSINESSES USE THE COMPUTER.   Some computer applications are unique to a particular type of organization,
such as production scheduling (manufacturing), point-of-sale (retail),
electronic funds transfer (financial services), typesetting (publishing),
reservations (transportation), actuarial accounting (insurance), special
effects (entertainment), and music composition (the arts).

REVIEW EXERCISES

Concepts

1.   Software for music composition is to composers as what is to authors?
2.   How do computers help professional tennis players?
3.   What is "wraparound" in word processing?
4.   Electronic funds transfer is associated with what industry?
5.   Which information system produces invoices? Purchase orders? Bal-
     ance sheets?
6.   What differentiates a decision support system from an information
     system?
7.   Distinguish between replace mode and insert mode in word process-
     ing.
8.   List and briefly describe three manual systems with which you are
     familiar and that you feel are prime candidates for computerization.
9.   Name three office information systems.
10. What are the levels of organizational activity, from specific to general?

Discussion

11. Would you buy a "magazine on a disk"? Why or why not?
12. Movie purists abhor the thought of great black-and-white classics,
     such as *Casablanca*, being changed to color with the aid of computer
     technology. What do you think?
13. Would it be possible for a medium-sized insurance company to main-
     tain a skeleton information systems department and use proprietary
     software for all of their computer application needs? Explain.
14. Why do you suppose truckers are resisting the implementation of
     satellite monitoring systems when they know that such a system will
     provide management with better control information?

15. Has the application of computer technology to the arts in any way stifled artistic creativity? Has it enhanced creativity? Explain.

16. Discuss the emerging role of personal computers in electronic funds transfer.

SELF-TEST (by section)

12-1 (a) We combine hardware, software, people, procedures, and data to create an _____ .

    (b) A manual system has the same components as a computer-based system. (T/F)

12-2 (a) Operational-level personnel are concerned primarily with transaction handling. (T/F)

    (b) Exception reports are produced for managers at the operational, tactical, and strategic levels. (T/F)

12-3 (a) Pictographs, called _____ , help systems to be more user friendly.

    (b) Trends are more easily recognized when data are presented in tabular rather than graphic format. (T/F)

12-4 (a) The balance sheet is a by-product of a general ledger system. (T/F)

    (b) Accounts payable is generally associated with office automation applications. (T/F)

12-5 (a) Automatic teller machines are an implementation of EFT. (T/F)

    (b) Claims processing systems are associated with the _____ industry. (T/F)

Self-Test answers.   12–1(a), information system; (b), T; 12–2(a), F; (b), T; 12–3(a), icons; (b), F; 12–4(a), T; (b), F; 12–5(a), T; (b), insurance.

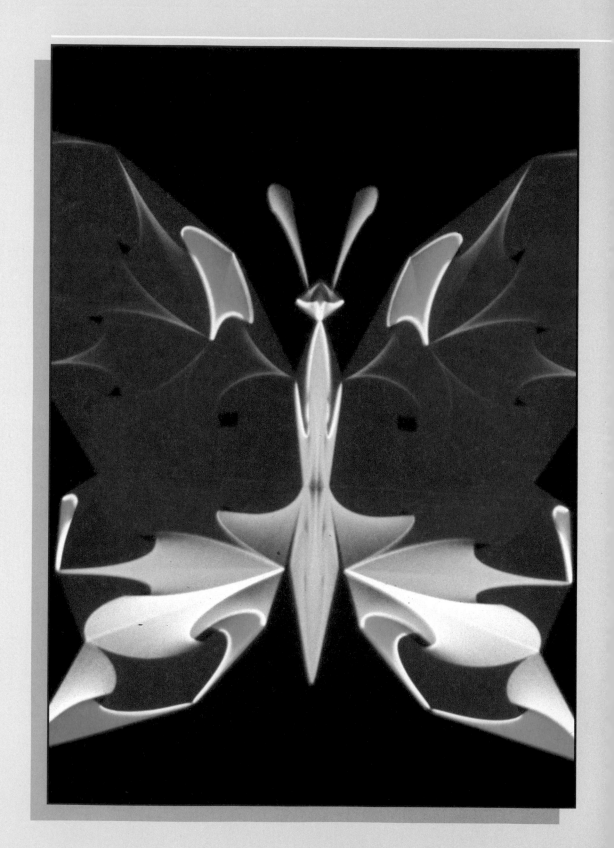

STUDENT LEARNING OBJECTIVES

- To discuss a variety of computer-based applications in government, health, and education.
- To present benefits and costs associated with the justification of the implementation of computer technology.
- To list the advantages and disadvantages of using proprietary software.
- To identify points of security vulnerability for the computer center and for information systems.

CHAPTER 13

Information Systems in Government, Health, and Education

13

13–1 INFORMATION SYSTEMS IN GOVERNMENT

Local Government

Local governments use a wide variety of information systems (see Figure 13–1). Most cities supply and bill citizens for at least one of the three major utility services: water, refuse, and electricity. Besides these *utility billing* systems, a *tax collection* system periodically assesses citizens for income, school, and real estate tax.

FIGURE 13–1
Summary of Computer Applications for Government, Health, and Education
These are but a few of the many computer applications in these areas.

GOVERNMENT
- Local
  - Utility billings
  - Tax collection
  - Police reporting
  - Fire incident reporting
  - Census and urban planning
  - Election reporting
  - License and permit administration
  - Traffic control
  - Parking meter systems
- State
  - Welfare
  - Employment security
  - Highway patrol
  - Revenue
  - Education
  - Lottery
  - Crime bureau
- Federal
  - National crime information system
  - Grant administration
  - Filing of tax returns
  - Treasury's Executive Information System
  - Military (guidance systems)
  - Congressional computer network
  - Space programs (NASA)

HEALTH CARE
- Hospitals
  - Room census
  - Patient accounting
  - On-line patient information
  - CAT and MR scanners
  - Diagnosis systems
  - Physician's accounting
- Private practice
- Pharmacy (drug interaction)
- Medical research

EDUCATION
- Primary and Secondary
  - Courseware
  - Computer-assisted instruction (CAI)
  - Student record-keeping
- Higher Education
  - Administrative
    - Student information systems
    - Alumni
  - Research
  - Education (use of computer as teaching tool)
- Continuing education

The local fire and police departments fight crime and fires and attend to other emergencies with the help of an information system. In seconds, dispatchers can select which squad car or fire station would be the most responsive to a given emergency.
(Courtesy of International Business Machines Corporation)

A city planner uses a plotter to produce a hard copy drawing that illustrates recent zoning changes to a city suburb.
(CalComp)

Cities also have *police* systems which are used for incident reporting, inquiry, and dispatching. Many police departments even have workstations mounted in their cruisers. From these workstations, officers can view the arrest record of an individual, request a "rundown" on an auto's license number, or check out what other officers are doing. Police detectives can search data bases for suspects by matching modus operandi, nicknames, body marks, physical deformities, locations, time of day, and even footwear.

Some *fire* departments are electronically informed of the location of a fire. Here's how it works. Someone at the site of the fire calls a three-digit "fire reporting" number. In a split second, a computer system searches its data base for the address of the calling phone (therefore, the location of the fire), then automatically dispatches vehicles from the nearest fire station.

Other systems that are typically supported by local governments include *census and urban planning*, *election reporting*, *license and permit administration*, *traffic control*, and even *parking meters* systems. In one case, a large city implemented a parking meter system that resulted in tens of thousands of dollars of delinquent fines being collected. The system paid for itself in the first month of operation!

State Government

At the state level of government, each major agency has its own information systems department. *Welfare*, *employment security*, *highway patrol*, *revenue*,

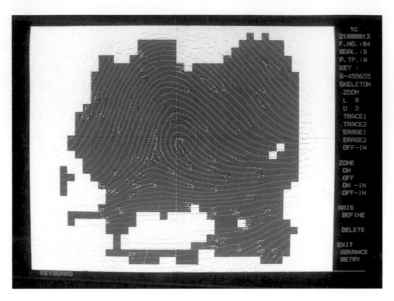

Above. In the past, a manual search through a fingerprint file could take a detective months—often without success. Today, computers take only a few minutes to check fingerprints from the scene of a crime against a large data base of fingerprints—often with great success.
(Courtesy of NEC Information Systems, Inc.)

and *education* are only a few of the many state agencies that have information systems departments. In some states, one of the most visible systems is the *lottery* agency. A bet is registered immediately at any of thousands of on-line workstations located in stores and restaurants throughout the state. The on-line lottery systems have made it possible for people to be "instant" winners (or losers).

Several state *crime bureaus* are using computers for fingerprint identification. Once the millions of fingerprints have been converted to digital data and stored on disk, the system can check up to 650 prints per second. In a manual search, an investigator would take hours to do what a computer can do in a single second. This new technology doesn't give criminals much of a head start!

Federal Government

The federal government has thousands of computer systems scattered throughout the world. The Federal Bureau of Investigation (FBI) has its *national crime information system* (*NCIS*) to help track down criminals. The National Science Foundation (NSF) has a *grant administration* system that enables it to monitor the progress and budgets for research projects. The Internal Revenue Service (IRS) now permits on-line *filing of tax returns* from our

Left. Lottery patrons are issued tickets at this workstation. Thousands of similar workstations are located throughout the state and linked to a central computer system in the state capital.
(General Instrument Corporation)

home PCs. This service saves us and the IRS a lot of time and money. For us, the on-line system performs all of the necessary table searches and computations, and it even cross-checks the accuracy and consistency of the input data. For the IRS, no further data entry or personal assistance is required.

The Treasury Department maintains the *Treasury's Executive Information System*. This system provides up-to-the-minute information on the foreign currency exchange rates and stock quotes. The Secretary of the Treasury carries a portable computer so that he can tap the system for information. The timely information provided by the system is critical to the effective functioning of the Treasury Department. Each day, the Secretary makes decisions that affect the world money market.

National defense systems are becoming more "high tech." Missiles use computer-controlled *guidance systems* to travel thousands of miles and land on or within feet of their targets. Some aircraft are equipped with sophisticated computer-controlled autopilots that can be activated to actually land an aircraft, even on moving aircraft carriers. Intelligence photos, taken at high altitudes, can be computer enhanced to show incredible detail—would you believe the headlines of a newspaper? The Aegis System can track hundreds of approaching missiles and aircraft and, based on system input, determine the best defense strategy, then select and activate defensive weapons systems. Controversial proposals for so-called "star wars" systems are based on sophisticated computer technology.

Computer technology has caused Congress to take on a new look. Senators and representatives have workstations in their offices that permit them to scan proposed legislation, send electronic mail, vote on legislation from their offices, do research, and correspond with constituents. The system also allows lobbyists, reporters, and other interested persons to monitor voting

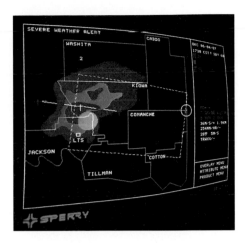

The Next Generation Weather Radar System (Nexrad) is being developed by the U.S. Department of Commerce. The display improves severe weather forecasting by color coding varying weather conditions in a geographical area (southern Oklahoma in photo).
(Sperry Corporation)

This programmer is making modifications to the NORAD (North American Aerospace Defense) early warning system. The system alerts military forces of an air attack so they can take defensive action.
(TRW Inc.)

Offices in the legislative branch of government are interconnected with a local area network (LAN) which integrates voice, data, and video communication. A computer-based information system records each vote registered by a senator or congressperson. Legislators make inquiries to this data base to determine which of their colleagues are sympathetic to their special interests. Lobbyists also take advantage of this information.
(AT&T Technologies)

The nurse's station is the hub of hospital activity and the source of information for both nurses and doctors. They use the terminals at the nurse's station to retrieve information from the hospital's information system.
(Texas Instruments, Inc.)

records, session attendance, and other matters of public interest. Another benefit of the *congressional computer network* is that it lets congressional committees poll members of congress for their feedback while legislation is still in draft form, instead of waiting until the legislation is put to a vote.

The most sophisticated government computer systems are associated with *NASA* and the space program. A mind-boggling network of ground and on-board computers must work together, without malfunction, to take people to the moon and shuttle people between the earth and orbit about the earth.

13-2 INFORMATION SYSTEMS IN HEALTH CARE _____

Hospitals

In health care, the computer is a constant companion to both patients and medical personnel. This is especially so in hospitals, where at the beginning of each day the status of each room is updated in the *room census* data base (see Figure 13–2). The *patient accounting* system updates patient records to reflect lab tests, drugs administered, and visits by a physician. This system also handles patient billing.

In the *operating room*, surgeons have on-line access to the patient's medical records. Some of these interactive systems are even voice activated to free the surgeon's hands for more critical tasks. Computers have taken some of the risk out of complex surgical procedures by warning surgeons of life-threatening situations. For example, during brain surgery, a computer monitors the patient's blood flow to the brain. Once discharged to an *intensive care*

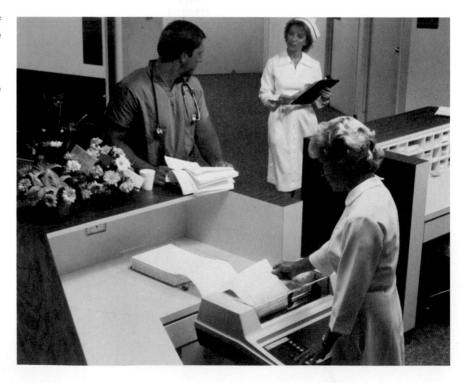

```
              ROOM CENSUS REPORT (BY ROOM NUMBER)
                          FIRST FLOOR


   ROOM NO.            PATIENT NAMES
              BED 1                      BED 2


   101S      MARK MILLS
   102D      JAMES FLOYD                 LARRY SMITH
   103D      ELLEN MOREL                 -----------
   104W4     JANE WEAR                   SALLY ABLE
             NANCY YOUNG                 -----------
   105S      FRED KENT
   106S      -----------
   107D      MATT KENNEDY                HANK OREM


    S-SINGLE      D-DOUBLE    W-WARD (NO. OF BEDS)
```

```
              ROOM CENSUS REPORT (BY LAST NAME)
                          FIRST FLOOR



   PATIENT NAME                          ROOM NO.


   SALLY ABLE                            104
   JAMES FLOYD                           102
   MATT KENNEDY                          107
   FRED KENT                             105
   MARK MILLS                            101
   ELLEN MOREL                           103
   HANK OREM                             107
   LARRY SMITH                           102
   JANE WEAR                             104
   NANCY YOUNG                           104
```

FIGURE 13-2
Hospital Room Census Reports
Room census reports are compiled by room number (soft copy) and patient name (hard copy).

Computer-controlled intensive
care units provide nurses and
physicians with a continuous
graphic display of patient
cardiac activity. A warning is
sounded when patient data
exceed acceptable limits.
(Advanced Devices, Inc., Two
Technology Way, Norwood, MA 02062)

unit, computers continue to monitor a patient's vital signs and alert attending
personnel of danger situations. Most life-support systems (e.g., artificial lungs)
are also computer controlled.

Computer-controlled devices provide physicians and surgeons with information that simply was not available a few years ago. Because surgeons
can "see" more clearly into a person's body with *CT* or *CAT* (computer
tomography) *scanners* and *MR* (magnetic resonance) *scanners*, medical procedures may be less drastic owing to improved information. For example, a
surgeon may not have to amputate an entire limb to eliminate the spread
of bone cancer if an MR scan detects the cancer only in a limb's extremities.
CAT scanners permit the results of several scans to be combined, then forged
into three-dimensional images. MR scanners, the most recent technology for
viewing inside the body, combine computers and a large doughnut-shaped
magnet to produce video images of a cross section of a body. MR scanners
permit internal "pictures" that, before, could be obtained only through exploratory surgery. Physicians view and analyze the images from CAT and MR
scanners on color graphics monitors.

"Expert" *diagnosis* systems (discussed in Chapter 2) help physicians identify diseases and isolate problems. The physician enters the patient's symptoms
and the system queries an expert system data base to match symptoms with
possible illnesses. The system will request more information from the doctor
if the illness cannot be diagnosed with existing information.

In recent years the cost of a hospital room has soared, and still some
hospitals operate in the red. To get back in the black, hospitals are implementing procedures to better control costs. For the first time, they are implementing
systems that optimize the use of their resources, while maximizing revenue.
A *physician's accounting* system provides hospital administrators with information about how each physician is using hospital facilities. For example,
such systems identify physicians who tend to admit patients who could just
as well be treated as outpatients. These patients typically generate less revenue
for the hospital and take up a bed that could best be used by a seriously ill
patient.

Data obtained during scanning
by magnetic resonance (MR)
diagnostic equipment are
computer-reconstructed to
form cross-sectional images of
the body's tissues and organs.
This technology enables
doctors to distinguish between
benign and malignant tumors,
and to detect conditions that
could lead to heart attacks.
(General Electric Company)

Private Practice

Why does a physician or dentist need a computer in *private practice*? That answer is simple—private practice is a business that necessitates the handling of many administrative functions, such as patient record keeping, billing and collections, appointment scheduling, and insurance processing. Of course, physicians can also use computers to improve their delivery of patient care. Doctors can tap into a variety of medical information services from their office workstations: expert diagnosis systems, medical data bases (for researching an illness), prescription data bases, and drug-interaction data bases. A physician can even link to a hospital's mainframe computer system to check patient status.

Pharmacy

The *drug-interaction* system was discussed as an example in Chapter 2. With thousands of drugs on the market, it is too time consuming for a pharmacist to manually check the drug interactions for each drug pair prescribed for each patient. Therefore, the speed of the computer is used to query a "drug-interaction" data base to ensure that a patient is not prescribed drugs that may cause an adverse reaction when combined with other drugs.

Medical Research

The microprocessor has opened new vistas for *medical research*. Our body is an electrical system that is very compatible with these tiny computers. Researchers have made it possible for paraplegics to pedal bicycles and take crude steps under the control of external computers. In the system, various muscle groups in the legs are excited electronically to cause the legs to perform a walking motion. The system has given new hope to paraplegics who were told they would never walk again. To be sure, much remains to be done, but researchers insist that someday, computer implants will enable paraplegics to walk.

Specimens are sent to this medical laboratory for analysis. Computer controlled instruments analyze the specimens and produce reports which are distributed to the attending physicians.
(William Revelli for Allied Corporation)

Dental groups use this OCR system for centralized record keeping and billing. Following each patient visit, a dental assistant scans each patient's account number and preset codes for each service provided.
(CAERE Corporation)

COMPUTERS AND THE PHYSICALLY CHALLENGED

Computer technology is having a profound effect on the physically challenged. Computers not only help repair malfunctioning muscles and nerve pathways, but they are enabling physically challenged people to take control of their environments.

The use of portable terminals and communication links helps many physically challenged users telecommute to work. For the blind and the deaf, there are products that can translate the words on a monitor into a tactile display. Braille keyboards and Braille word processing software have opened up new worlds to the blind. There are even products that scan hardcopy printed material via optical character recognition and translate the words to synthesized speech. In essence, the computer can now read books and magazines to the blind. For those who cannot speak, computer-produced synthesized speech has allowed communication that was never before possible.

Some day the hope is to pick up impulses directly from the central nervous system. These electrical signals become input to a computer system, which can control muscle groups that are no longer under the control of the nervous system. Researchers have already experienced

This blind person is using an optical scanner (right hand) that converts printed matter into digitized images of characters. These images are interpreted by the computer and translated into a tactile form that a blind person can feel with a finger (left hand).
(Telesensory Systems, Inc.)

some success in this area, and they are optimistic about prospects for the future.

This sports physician is conducting research in the area of exercise physiology. In the photo, he is measuring the peak oxygen consumption of a sprint cyclist in a computerized pulmonary monitoring exercise laboratory.
(Gould Inc.)

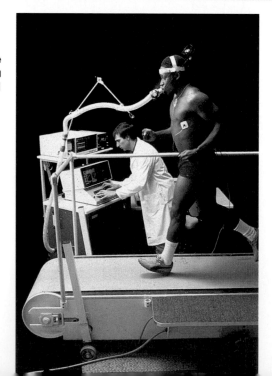

In the past, artificial organs have been impractical because they required bulky external control mechanisms. Now, powerful computers, no larger than your fingernail, have the capabilities to control complex mechanical devices that can be implanted to replace malfunctioning organs. Little or no external apparatus is required. Again, this research is in the infant stages, but early limited success with artificial hearts has been encouraging.

13-3 INFORMATION SYSTEMS IN EDUCATION

Primary and Secondary Education

The computer has added a new dimension to the educational process. A computer can give "individual" attention to a student. This is a welcome relief to overcrowded classrooms. It is interactive and is quick to respond to a student's input. The use of software allows for a variety of approaches to different learning styles: it incorporates the visual, the auditory, and the kinesthetic learning styles. The use of dynamic graphics and the interactive nature of software (i.e., immediate feedback) has "turned on" many students to the learning process.

Educational software, often referred to as *courseware*, is not limited to the sequential format of books. *Computer-assisted instruction* (*CAI*) can demonstrate and present material, provide opportunities for drill and practice, test for understanding of the material, evaluate the test results, and provide follow-up instruction based on test results. Educational software packages have been developed that reinforce and complement virtually every subject covered in kindergarten through high school—helping students learn everything from the alphabet to calculus. Moreover, many educational software packages have taken on an entertainment quality that enables students to

Thirty percent of all educational software is developed for use by children under seven years of age—but parents have fun with it too!
(Photo supplied courtesy of Epson America)

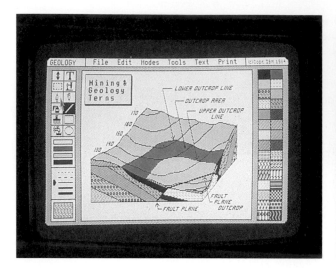

This screen, taken from an earth sciences educational software series, is representative of computer-assisted instruction (CAI).
(Courtesy of International Business Machines Corporation)

These children are at a summer camp enjoying hiking and canoeing while learning about computers. "Computer" camps give children an opportunity to get a more in-depth exposure to the concepts and applications of computers.
(ExperCamp).

enjoy the learning process. And on the flip side, educators are encouraging the use of some entertainment-oriented software packages because of their educational value.

Computers are a tool for both teacher and student. *Student record-keeping systems* help teachers keep up-to-the-minute data on each student and provide current information for parent/teacher conferences. Word processing software has been used in grammar and composition classes and to help children learn to read through writing. Computer literacy is begun in the early grades, where languages such as LOGO and PILOT are being used to teach logic and problem solving.

The use of the computer is allowing the handicapped to be more readily mainstreamed into the classroom. Speech synthesizers allow those who have not been able to "talk" to take part for the first time. For visually impaired students, written text is "read" (using optical scanning), then displayed a word at a time in print large enough for the students to read.

Computers are expanding the capabilities of this student and his classmates in special education classes. Computers open up new horizons in communication for students with special needs due to a disability, such as cerebral palsy.
(Courtesy of International Business Machines Corporation)

ACADEMIC PROGRAM			**STUDENT ROSTER**	

ACADEMIC PROGRAM	
COLLEGE :	College of Business
CLASS :	Second Semester Sophomore
DEGREE :	B.S. Computer Information Systems
MAJOR 1 :	Information Systems
MAJOR 2 :	Accounting
MINOR 1 :	Drama
MINOR 2 :	
ADVISOR :	Prof. M. Holland

STUDENT NUMBER	TERM	DATE
461-37-4188	1987 SPRING	02/03/87

STUDENT NAME
Salash, Sandy S.

COURSE SECTION NUMBER			SUBJECT ALPHA	COURSE TITLE	CREDIT HOURS	GRADE TYPE	MEETS		
COLLEGE	SUBJ.	SECTION					DAYS	TIME	* BLDG/ROOM
218-264-03			HIST	American, 1865 to Present	3.0		M W F	08:10 – 9:00	MG 202
301-108-04			ACCT	Fundamentals of Accounting	3.0		M W F	09:10 – 10:00	WL 430
225-307-02			CIS	Structured Design Techniques	3.0		T R	09:10 – 10:00	PA 502
225-307-03			CIS	Laboratory	0.0	CR	T	13:10 – 16:00	PA 501
225-310-01			CIS	COBOL II	3.0		T R	10:10 – 11:00	PA 360
225-310-04			CIS	Laboratory	0.0	CR	R	13:10 – 16:00	PA 501
270-001-01			DRA	Improvisation	3.0		M W F	11:10 – 12:00	DH 312
150-012-06			MATH	Business Statistics	2.0		T R	08:10 – 09:00	XS 401
				Hours Rostered: 17.0					

Higher Education

In colleges and universities, computer uses can be placed into three categories: *administration*, *research*, and *education*. The *student information system* is the focus of administrative computing. At the center of the student information system is the registration subsystem. Within registration are grade reporting, transcript maintenance, and class scheduling (Figure 13–3). Other student-related subsystems include job placement, housing, admissions, and financial aid.

Upon graduation, your name will surely become a permanent entry in the alumni data base. Many college and university development offices use computer-based systems to obtain information on how they can best direct their campaigns for alumni contributions and endowments.

There are as many research uses for the computer as there are professors. Sociologists analyze large amounts of demographic data in an attempt to draw conclusions about societal trends. Psychologists employ a variety of computer-based testing techniques to prove or disprove behavioral theories. Literature professors use text processing to analyze and compare the styles of authors. Human-factors engineers "wire" subjects directly to a computer to collect data during experiments.

In most colleges, either computer literacy has been made a general education requirement for all students, or such a requirement is being seriously considered. Dozens of colleges now require their students to own computers. In these colleges, professors in every discipline are encouraged to design their assignments to take advantage of a "computerized" student body. To get their assignments or messages from their classmates, students "log on" to the college's central mainframe computer system.

FIGURE 13–3
Student Roster of Classes
A student roster is generated and distributed to each student who preregisters for the term.

An authoring system can help writers and poets to bring their words alive on a computer screen with the use of color, animation, and interesting graphics. According to Edmund Skellings, a Florida poet laureate and developer of an authoring system called *The Electronic Poet,* a professor can "show the intricate patterning and texturing of sound embedded in the work of the great poets of the past." The photo shows how Robert Browning's poem, "Meeting at Night," can be highlighted to demonstrate the concept of rhyme.
(Control Color Corporation)

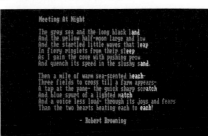

Professors often use computers
as a tool to illustrate a particular
concept to a student.
(TRW Inc.)

Continuing Education

Correspondence courses have been integral to the continuing-education effort
for many years. Now, some colleges are offering continuing-education courses
with a twist: "*correspondence computing*." Student and instructor communicate with one another, not through the postal system, but via electronic mail.
For standard courses, much of the student interaction is automatic (preset
assignments and testing) and does not require instructor participation. If a
student has a question, it is routed to the instructor's "electronic" mailbox.
The instructor answers in a similar manner. Students prepare reports and
instructors grade them at their respective workstations—no hard copy is required!

13–4 JUSTIFYING THE EXPENSE OF IMPLEMENTING COMPUTER TECHNOLOGY

Whether in industry, government, health care, or education, you don't decide
to use the computer just because it sounds like a good idea or it might be
fun. An information system, CAD/CAM, robotics, CAI, or any other use of
the computer is like any other investment opportunity—it must be justified.
In the final analysis, uses of the computer are normally approved if, and
only if, *the benefits are greater than the costs*.

Benefits.   The benefits of a computer system are either *tangible* or *intangible*.
The tangible benefits result in monetary savings or earnings. For example,
a plant production scheduling system saves a company money by providing
information that helps its managers use resources more efficiently than they
might without one.

Intangible benefits are difficult to quantify, but they are a major consideration when justifying expenditures for computing hardware and software.
For example, it is difficult to measure the economic worth of a CAI system
that helps a child to learn, but there is no denying that there is an intangible
value. As another example, the prestige and convenience associated with a
bank's automatic teller machines may lure customers from other banks. Intangible benefits cannot be readily translated into earnings or savings, but they
are real benefits, and so they must be considered when making a decision
to automate.

The intangible benefits were an
important consideration when
evaluating the implementation
of this PC- and laser-based
system to verify blood types. The
system has little economic
value, but it helps to minimize
the risk of mismarking the blood
or administering the wrong
blood type.
(Courtesy of International Business
Machines Corporation)

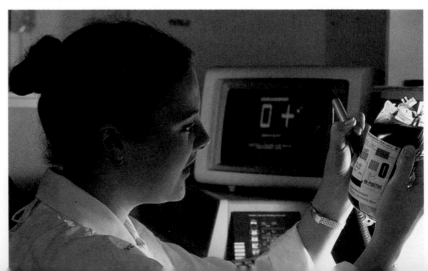

Costs.   The two types of costs associated with the purchase of computer hardware and software are *one-time* costs and *recurring* costs. The one-time costs include all expenses associated with the development and implementation of a particular use of computer technology. The biggest share of the one-time costs are usually personnel, hardware, and software.

Sometimes in our evaluation we overlook the recurring costs. These are costs that are incurred after implementation. For example, the cost of production and ongoing system maintenance must be considered when evaluating the merits of an on-line student information system. Depending on the system being evaluated, recurring costs could include the programmers' time for systems maintenance, data entry, computer time and data storage, paper and other consumable materials, hardware upgrades, and charges for data communications services.

Benefit/Cost Analysis.   Managers weigh benefits against costs by using what is called **benefit/cost analysis**. Simply stated, if the tangible benefits outweigh the cost, the system is normally approved.

You might be faced with evaluating a proposal where the estimated costs are greater than the estimated savings. In these cases, you must subjectively weigh the anticipated loss against the intangible benefits. If the intangible benefits appear to be greater than the loss, the system is usually given the go-ahead.

MEMORY BITS	
BENEFIT/COST ANALAYSIS	
IF	$\dfrac{\text{Benefits}}{\text{Costs}} > 1$
THEN	Approve proposal for new system
ELSE	Reject proposal

13-5 TECHNOLOGY TRANSFER: WHY REINVENT THE WHEEL?

Undoubtedly, you are aware that there is an enormous demand for computer-related services within virtually every organization. There is so much to be done that sometimes it seems that everything must be done by yesterday!

Since most computer centers suffer from a shortage of human resources, managers are turning to *technology transfer* as a solution. Technology transfer is a buzz word that means applying existing technology to a current problem or situation. In all probability, some organization has, at one time or another, addressed the same problem or system on which you might be working.

All colleges, for example, need registration and class scheduling systems. All manufacturing companies need inventory management systems. All organizations use electronic spreadsheets and word processing software. These and many other application-specific and generalized systems have been developed and "packaged" for sale by software vendors. These systems are called **proprietary software**, or **packaged systems**. The "package" sold by the software vendors consists of the programs (software) and their associated documentation. For larger, more complex packaged systems, vendors also offer training and consultation on how to use the systems.

You might ask, "Why not buy all needed software and eliminate the need for programmers and systems analysts?" It's not that simple. Proprietary software systems, especially information systems, are not always implemented as they are designed. Often substantial in-house modification is needed to fit local circumstances. Depending on the information system, it may be easier to start from scratch than to purchase and modify a packaged system.

PAPER PUSHERS! MAKE WAY FOR THE PAPERLESS SOCIETY

What does a "paperless society" mean to you? To some, it might imply that we will be reading less. Such is not the case. In fact, we may be reading more, but not necessarily from hard-copy documents, such as letters, magazines, and books. As we evolve in the direction of a paperless society, we are sending and receiving more information in the form of computer-generated soft-copy output.

We have been a society oriented to paper—the more the better. But sometimes too many reports and reams of paper can be more confusing than informing. With the use of computers and on-line systems, we can get the information we want without sorting through stacks of reports.

In the "paperless" approach to information flow, decision makers not only are defining what information they want, but they are active participants in retrieving this information. With on-line systems, they are no longer dependent on someone else, nor do they have to wait several days to get information that they need now.

It is unlikely that we will ever be a totally paperless society, but as we evolve to a greater reliance on and use of on-line capabilities, more memos and letters will be sent via electronic mail, magazines may be sent in the form of diskettes, and the information on hard-copy reports will, instead, be generated from on-line inquiries. As an alternative to newspapers, some people may prefer to tap into an information network from their home computers to get the daily news.

The Internal Revenue Service distributes over 14,000 different forms, and taxpayers return hundreds of millions of completed forms. For officials at the IRS, the emergence of the paperless society may be a blessing. The IRS is hoping to elimate much of the paper flow by permitting taxpayers to file their returns electronically directly from their home or office computers.

Computers have provided an alternative to the paper-proliferation problem, but what is to become of the professional paper pusher?

Fifteen years ago computer specialists had at least a passing familiarity with most of the major software packages. As people began to recognize the benefits of software technology transfer, the development of proprietary software accelerated. Personal computers then opened up a whole new market and fueled the further growth of proprietary software. Now, thousands of software vendors are producing tens of thousands of software packages from which to choose. You can purchase personal computer software that will help you with home finances for less than $100. The software for a sophisticated corporate financial planning system may cost as much as $100,000.

13–6 SECURITY: WALK SOFTLY BUT CARRY A BIG STICK

Any information system has points of vulnerability. Too much is at stake to overlook these threats to the security of a computer center and an information system. These threats take many forms: white collar crime, natural disasters (e.g., earthquakes, floods), vandalism, and carelessness.

White collar crime is real and exists undetected in some of the most unlikely places. It is sophisticated crime with sophisticated criminals. And it is more widespread than estimates would lead us to believe. Most computer crimes are undetected; others are unreported. A bank may prefer to write off a $100,000 embezzlement rather than publicly announce to its depositors that its computer system is vulnerable.

This section is devoted to discussing the security measures needed to neutralize threats to computer-center and information systems security (see Figure 13–4).

Computer-Center Security

The vulnerable points of computer centers are the *hardware*, *software*, *files/ data bases*, *data communications*, and *personnel*. Each is discussed separately below.

Hardware.   If the hardware fails, the system fails. The threat of failure can be minimized by implementing security precautions that prevent access by unauthorized personnel and by taking steps to keep all hardware operational.

Common approaches to securing the premises from unauthorized entry include closed-circuit TV monitors, alarm systems, and computer-controlled devices that check employee badges, fingerprints, or voice prints before unlocking doors at access points. Also, computer centers are usually isolated from

FIGURE 13–4
Security Precautions
Some, or all, of the security measures noted in the figure are implemented in most computer centers. Each precaution helps to minimize the risk of a computer system's vulnerability to crime, disasters, and failure.

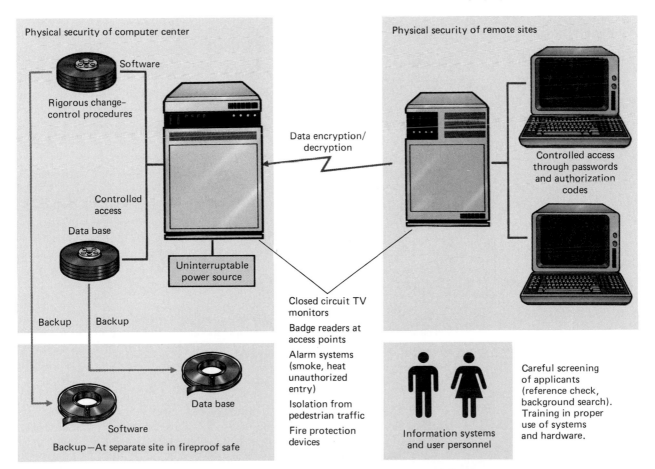

Physical security of computer center

Software

Rigorous change-control procedures

Controlled access

Data base

Backup   Backup

Data encryption/decryption

Uninterruptable power source

Data base

Software

Backup—At separate site in fireproof safe

Physical security of remote sites

Controlled access through passwords and authorization codes

Closed circuit TV monitors
Badge readers at access points
Alarm systems (smoke, heat unauthorized entry)
Isolation from pedestrian traffic
Fire protection devices

Information systems and user personnel

Careful screening of applicants (reference check, background search). Training in proper use of systems and hardware.

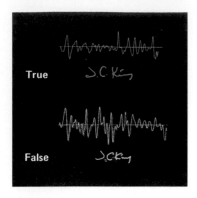

Biometric identification systems are beginning to replace systems that use the plastic card (badge) as a "key" for entry to secured areas, such as computer centers. One such system asks users for their signature before permitting entry to a secured area or access to a sensitive data base. If the digitized image of the signature does not match that of the authorized signature, then entry or access is denied. (Courtesy of International Business Machines Corporation)

(By permission of Michael Artell)

pedestrian traffic. Machine-room fires are extinguished by a special chemical that douses the fire but does not destroy the files or equipment.

Computers, especially mainframe computers, must have a "clean," continuous source of power. To minimize the effects of "dirty" power or power outages, many computer centers have installed an **uninterruptible power source (UPS)**. Dirty power, such as sags and surges in power output or brownouts (low power), cause parity errors and program execution errors. An UPS system serves as a control buffer between the external power source and the computer system. In an UPS system, the computer is powered by batteries (which deliver clean power), which in turn are regenerated by an external power source. If the external power source fails, the UPS system permits operation to continue for a period of time after an outage. This allows operators to either "power-down" normally or switch to a backup power source, normally a diesel generator.

With more and more on-line systems and the improvements in computer reliability, there has been a reversal in traditional hardware maintenance strategy. For many years, *customer engineers* (hardware repairpersons) followed a schedule of routine, usually weekly, *preventive maintenance*. When they arrived at the site, the computer was shut down, even if it was working fine, and all systems were checked out. With almost all systems going on-line, shutting a system down may cause hundreds of workers to remain idle during preventive maintenance activities. Today, the most popular maintenance strategy, for both micros and mainframes, is to *wait until it breaks, then fix it*.

Software.   Unless properly controlled, software can be modified for personal gain. Thus, close control over software development and documentation is needed to minimize the opportunity for computer crime. Operational control procedures that are built into the system design will constantly monitor processing accuracy. These controls are discussed in Chapter 14, "The System Development Process." Unfortunately, cagey programmers have been known to get around some of these controls. Perhaps the best way to safeguard programs from unlawful tampering is to use rigorous change-control procedures. Such procedures make it difficult to modify a program for purposes of personal gain.

Bank programmers certainly have opportunities for personal gain. In one case, a couple of programmers modified a savings system to make small deposits from other accounts to their own accounts. Here's how it worked: The interest for each savings account was compounded and credited daily; the calculated interest was rounded to the nearest penny before being credited to the savings account; programs were modified to round down on all interest calculations and put the "extra" penny in one of the programmer's savings accounts. It may not seem like much, but a penny a day from thousands of accounts adds up to big bucks. The "beauty" of the system was that the books balanced and depositors did not miss the 15 cents (an average of $\frac{1}{2}$ cent per day for 30 days) that was judiciously taken from each account each month. Even the auditors have difficulty detecting this crime because the total interest paid out for all accounts is correct. However, the culprits slipped up and were apprehended when someone noticed that they repeatedly withdrew inordinately large sums of money.

Unfortunately, other enterprising programmers in other industries have been equally imaginative.

Files/Data Bases.   The data base contains the raw material for information. In some cases, the files/data bases are the life blood of an organization. For example, how many companies can afford to lose their accounts receivable file that documents who owes what? Having several generations of backups to all files is not sufficient insurance against loss of files/data bases. The backup and master files should be stored in fireproof safes in separate rooms, preferably in separate buildings.

One company's file security procedures were well documented but not adhered to in practice. Machine-room operators opened the doors to the fireproof safe in the morning and did not close them until night. Backup and master files were stored side-by-side in the safe. When a raging fire destroyed the computer center and the contents of the safe, the company was forced into bankruptcy.

Data Communications.   The mere existence of a data communications network poses a threat to security. A knowledgeable criminal can tap into the system from a remote location and use the system for personal gain. In a well-designed system, this is not an easy task. But it can be and has been done! When one criminal broke a company's security code and tapped into the communications network, he was able to order certain products without being billed. He filled a warehouse before eventually being caught. Another tapped into an international banking exchange system to "reroute" funds to an account of his own in a Swiss bank. In another case, an oil company was able to consistently outbid a competitor by "listening in" on their data transmissions. On several occasions, overzealous young "hackers" have tapped into sensitive defense computer systems; fortunately, no harm was done.

Some organizations use *cryptography* to scramble messages sent over data communications channels. Someone who unlawfully intercepted such a message would find meaningless strings of characters. Cryptography is analogous to the "code book" used by intelligence people during the cloak-and-dagger days. Instead of a code book, however, a "key" is used in conjunction with *encryption/decryption* hardware to unscramble the message. Both sender and receiver must have the key, which is actually an algorithm that rearranges the bit structure of a message. Companies that routinely transmit sensitive data over communications channels are moving to data encryption as a means to limit access to the system and its data.

Personnel.   Managers are paying close attention to who gets hired for positions that permit access to computer systems and sensitive data. Someone who is grossly incompetent can cause just as much harm as one who is inherently dishonest.

Information Systems Security

Information systems security is classified as physical or logical. *Physical security* refers to hardware, facilities, magnetic tapes, and other things that could be illegally accessed, stolen, or destroyed.

These photos illustrate how cryptography works. The original employee assessment is produced by a manager using word processing. The second photo shows the encrypted text as it is sent to company headquarters via data communications. At headquarters, the assessment is decrypted to its original form for viewing.
(Jones Futurex, Inc.)

Logical security is built into the software by permitting only authorized persons to access and use the system. Logical security for on-line systems is achieved primarily by **passwords** and **authorization codes**. Only those persons with a "need to know" are told the password and given authorization codes. On occasion, however, these security codes fall into the wrong hands. When this happens, an unauthorized person can gain access to programs and sensitive files by simply dialing-up the computer and entering the codes. To thwart this, some computer systems have implemented another level of security in the form of a *dial-back* procedure. With this procedure, you dial-up the computer, hang up, then the computer dials-back your workstation to make the contact. The dial-back procedure deters some unlawful entry, but you lose some flexibility in that each person can access the computer only from a particular workstation.

Keeping passwords and authorization codes from the computer criminal is not easy. One computer criminal took advantage of the fact that a bank's automatic teller machine (ATM) did not "time out" for several minutes. That is, the authorization code could be entered without reinserting the card to initiate another transaction. Using high-powered binoculars, he watched from across the street as the numeric code was being entered. He then ran over to the ATM and was waiting when the customer left. He quickly entered the code and made withdrawals before the machine timed out. Needless to say, this design flaw has been eliminated in existing ATM systems.

Level of Risk

No amount of security measures will completely remove the vulnerability of a computer center or an information system. Security systems are implemented in degrees. That is, an information system can be made marginally secure or very secure, but never totally secure. Each organization must determine the level of risk that it is willing to accept. Unfortunately, some corporations are willing to accept an enormous risk and hope that these rare instances of crime and disaster do not occur. Some corporations have found out too late that *rarely* is not the same as *never*!

Contingency Planning

Most organizations maintain a **contingency plan** that details what to do if there is an environmental disaster, sabotage, gross negligence, or any other extraordinary event that drastically disrupts the operation of a computer center. A contingency plan describes duties and responsibilities, alternative hardware sites, and the logistics for recovering from such disasters.

SUMMARY OUTLINE AND IMPORTANT TERMS _____

13-1   INFORMATION SYSTEMS IN GOVERNMENT.   Some of the computer applications found in local government include utility billing, tax collection, police and fire incident reporting, and urban planning. State governments use computers for everything from fingerprint

APPLICATIONS OF COMPUTER GRAPHICS: GOVERNMENT, HEALTH, AND EDUCATION

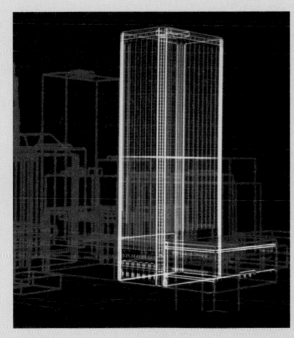

This graphic perspective illustrates how the skyline of a large city will be changed with the addition of another skyscraper.
(Evans & Sutherland and Skidmore, Owings & Merrill)

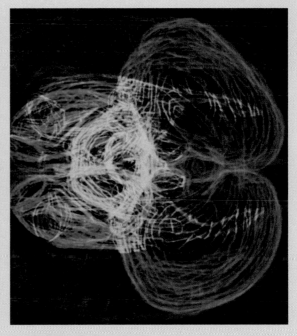

This frontal perspective of the human brain graphically illustrates the relationship between the cerebellum, brain stem, cerebral cortex, ventricles, and basal ganglia.
(Evans & Sutherland and the University of California at San Diego)

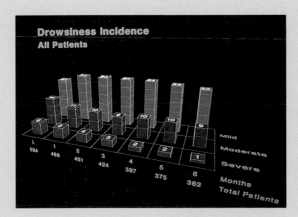

Computer graphics can be used to display the results of medical research. The results of a study on how each of six drugs affect drowsiness are portrayed in this graphic illustration.
(ISSCO)

Dynamic graphics can simulate a variety of weather patterns as case studies for meteorology students.
(Cromemco, Inc.)

analysis to running statewide lotteries. The federal government has thousands of computer systems throughout the world that are used in a wide variety of computer applications.

13-2   INFORMATION SYSTEMS IN HEALTH CARE.   In a hospital, computers help administrative personnel with billing; they help nurses to monitor patients; and they help doctors to diagnose illnesses. Physicians in private practice tap into a variety of medical information services. Pharmacists rely on computers to identify potentially harmful drug interactions. The computer has enabled medical research to advance in leaps and bounds.

13-3   INFORMATION SYSTEMS IN EDUCATION.   Courseware and CAI now play an important role in primary and secondary education. In colleges and universities, new computer applications are being implemented in the administrative, research, and education areas each day.

13-4   JUSTIFYING THE EXPENSE OF IMPLEMENTING COMPUTER TECHNOLOGY.   An information system is just like any other investment opportunity in that it must be cost justified. In essence, this means that the benefits, both tangible and intangible, should be greater than the cost of a proposed system.

13-5   TECHNOLOGY TRANSFER: WHY REINVENT THE WHEEL? Technology transfer is the application of existing technology to a current problem or situation. A common approach to technology transfer is to purchase and install **proprietary software**, or **packaged systems**, as an alternative to in-house software development.

13-6   SECURITY: WALK SOFTLY BUT CARRY A BIG STICK.   The threats to the security of computer centers and information systems call for precautionary measures. A computer center can be vulnerable in its hardware, software, files/data bases, data communications, and personnel. Information systems security is classified as physical security or logical security. Security systems are implemented in degrees, and no system or computer center can be made totally secure.

REVIEW EXERCISES _____

Concepts

1.   What is the purpose of a "key" in cryptography?
2.   Describe the dial-back security procedure.
3.   How do computers help surgeons in an operating room?
4.   Name four applications of the computer in a municipal government.
5.   What is "correspondence computing"?
6.   Describe the contents of a contingency plan.
7.   Describe the most popular maintenance strategy for computers.
8.   What precautions can be taken to minimize the effects of hardware failure?

9. The mere fact that a system uses data communications poses a threat to security. Why so?

10. Name two medical information services that are available to physicians in private practice.

11. What computer-based applications are unique to hospitals?

12. Identify the recurring costs of an on-line student information system.

Discussion

13. Identify the tangible and intangible benefits of an automated traffic control system.

14. In a federal agency, passwords are given to people who need access to confidential information. A new set of passwords are issued every other month. Is this extra work of issuing new passwords really necessary? Discuss.

15. Evaluate your college's computer center with respect to security. Identify areas where you think it is vulnerable and discuss ways to improve its security.

16. Physician's accounting systems have been implemented under a cloud of controversy. Why?

17. Discuss the short- and long-term benefits of designing an information system to be user friendly.

SELF-TEST (by section)

13-1. Timely information is so valuable to the Secretary of the Treasury that the Secretary carries a portable computer. (T/F)

13-2. The primary use of computers in hospital intensive care units is to collect patient billing information. (T/F)

13-3. Educational software is sometimes called _____ .

13-4. A proposed system is normally given the go-ahead if the intangible benefits are greater than the cost. (T/F)

13-5. Proprietary software is software that has been packaged for sale to the general public. (T/F)

13-6. Cryptography is the study of the assignment of security codes. (T/F)

Self-Test answers.   13–1, T; 13–2, F; 13–3, courseware; 13–4, F; 13–5, T; 13–6, F.

STUDENT LEARNING OBJECTIVES

- To describe the four stages of the system life cycle.
- To discuss the characteristics and benefits of a systems development methodology.
- To describe and order the systems development activities for:
  - Phase I—Prototyping
  - Phase II—Systems Analysis and Design
  - Phase III—Programming
  - Phase IV—Conversion and Implementation
  - Phase V—Post-Implementation Evaluation
- To explain the concept of prototyping.
- To demonstrate a knowledge of several system design techniques.
- To place the programming task in perspective with respect to the systems development process.
- To distinguish between the different approaches to system conversion.
- To know what to look for during the post-implementation evaluation.

CHAPTER 14

The Systems Development Process

14

14-1 THE SYSTEM LIFE CYCLE

An information system is analogous to the human life form. It is born, grows, matures, and eventually dies. The **system life cycle** has four stages, as shown in Figure 14–1.

Birth Stage.   In the *birth stage* of the system life cycle, someone has an idea as to how the computer can assist in providing better and more timely information.

Development Stage.   The idea becomes a reality during the *development stage* of the system life cycle. During the development stage, systems analysts, programmers, and users work together to analyze an organization's information processing needs and design an information system. The design specifications are then translated into programs, and the system is implemented.

Production Stage.   Upon implementation, the information system enters the *production stage* and becomes operational, serving the information needs of the organization. The production stage is the longest of the four stages and will normally last from four to seven years. During the production stage, information systems are continuously modified, or "maintained," to keep up with the changing needs of the organization.

Death Stage.   The accumulation of system modifications to a dynamic information system eventually takes its toll on system efficiency. The *death stage* arrives when an information system becomes so cumbersome to maintain that it is no longer economically or operationally effective. At this time, the system is discarded and the system life cycle is repeated.

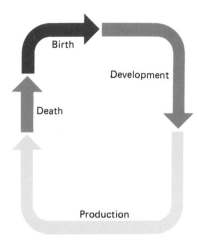

FIGURE 14-1
The System Life Cycle
A system is not immortal. It is born, grows, matures, and eventually dies.

An idea often signals the birth of an information system. These supervisors at a chemicals plant are discussing the possibility of designing a system that will help them in scheduling shutdowns for routine equipment maintenance. (Honeywell, Inc.)

14-2 TURNING AN IDEA INTO AN INFORMATION SYSTEM

In this chapter we will present the state of the art in systems development, which is currently a combination of the traditional approach and the latest technological tools and design aids. Since systems development is a *team* effort, most organizations have adopted a standardized **systems development methodology** that provides the framework for cooperation. This step-by-step approach to systems development is essentially the same, whether it be for an airline reservation system or a personnel system.

An organization's methodology is usually presented in a manual and depicts the following:

1. Activities to be performed.
2. The relationship and sequence of these activities.
3. The key evaluation and decision **milestones** [significant points in the development process (e.g., programming is completed)].

In recent years, methodologies have encouraged greater user involvement, emphasized the design aspects, and relied more on fourth- and fifth-generation languages to generate the software. These trends are included in the methodology presented in this chapter.

Information is critical to sociologists, teachers, engineers, nurses, and people in scores of other professions. In the search for better and more timely information, these people often find themselves working closely with programmers and systems analysts in the development of an information system. Because users are taking on a more active role in systems development, it is important that the user community have a solid understanding of their role in the system development process.

The Service Request: Lights, Camera, Action!

The **service request**, which is normally compiled by the user, gets the ball rolling. When user departments do not have the technological expertise or resources to meet certain information needs, then they submit a service request to the information services department to request that a *new information system be developed* or that *an existing system be enhanced*. Because the extent of the requests usually exceeds the available personnel and computer resources, each request must be evaluated relative to its contribution to the organizational need. A completed service request for a college residence operations system is shown in Figure 14–2.

Based on a benefit/cost analysis (see Chapter 13) of the service request, a decision is made to either *table* the project or *approve* it. Approval triggers one of two activities: the purchase and implementation of a proprietary software package (see Chapter 13) or the beginning of the systems development methodology. A five-phase methodology is the focus of the remainder of this chapter.

OBJECTIVES FOR PROPOSED SYSTEM

Primary Objectives:
1. To automate the room assignment procedure.
2. To automate the inventory record keeping task.

Supporting Objectives:
1. To provide the staff of Residence Operations with an instrument to use in making more efficient and effective decisions.
2. To integrate existing procedures.

FUNDAMENTAL OPERATION OF PROPOSED SYSTEM

The basic work flow of the present system will be followed. Areas to be computerized include:

1. Freshmen roommate and room assignment procedure
2. Inventory control
3. Student billing to include damage billing
4. File updates (to be on-line)
5. Report generation including:
   On campus population by building and room number
   Off campus population
   Home address labels
   Statistical reports of residence halls population
   Room assignment notification

SCOPE OF PROPOSED SYSTEM

Other Organizational Interfaces:
1. Bursar and Registrar — to supply student information
2. Campus Maintenance — for general repairs and upkeep on residence halls
3. Dining Service — to inform them of the number of students on the various meal plans
4. Admissions Office — to handle housing assignments

Volumes

The proposed system must be able to process approximately 2100 students in the residence halls. The general student files will include approximately 4000 students.

PRESENT SYSTEM PROBLEMS

There are a number of problems with the present system:

1. Excessive paper work.
2. Time–consuming procedures for assigning rooms and roommates.
3. No cross reference between room inventory and occupancy (i.e., lack of inventory control).
4. No way to systematically isolate recurring maintenance problems.

JUSTIFICATION

The proposed system should eliminate those problems noted above, as well as provide information for better decisions. Service to the student will be improved through more responsive procedures.

LONG-RANGE OBJECTIVES

The proposed system will ultimately be incorporated into the proposed student information system, scheduled for implementation in three years.

FIGURE 14–2
A Service Request
This service request was completed for a college residence operations system.

A Five-Phase Systems Development Methodology

The five-phase systems development methodology discussed in this chapter should give you an overview of what is involved in developing and implementing an information system. The phases are:

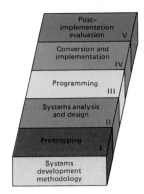

- *Phase I—Prototyping*. During Phase I, information requirements are identified and a **prototype system** is developed that serves as a model for the development of the full-scale system.
- *Phase II—Systems Analysis and Design*. During Phase II, systems analysts and users work together to compile detailed system specifications. These specifications are submitted to programmers for coding in Phase III.
- *Phase III—Programming*. During Phase III, the software needed to support the system is developed.
- *Phase IV—Conversion and Implementation*. During Phase IV, data files are created, and the new system is implemented and put into operation.
- *Phase V—Post-Implementation Evaluation*. Phase V begins the *production stage* of the life cycle (see Figure 14–1). During this stage the system is periodically evaluated to ensure that it continues to meet the information processing needs of the organization.

These five phases are equally applicable to systems development in small, one-person businesses and in large organizations with several layers of management. In practice, the systems development process may be divided into three, five, or even ten phases, but the chronology of the activities remains essentially the same.

A Responsibility Matrix: Defining Who Does What, and When

We are about to discuss the information systems development process in the context of the above five-phase systems development methodology. In

At the start of a project, it is always a good idea for the project team leader to assemble the team, go over the system development methodology, and make sure responsibility areas are clearly understood.
(Living Videotext, Inc.)

Key: **A** = Approval **C** = Consultation **R** = Primary responsibility **P** = Participating responsibility	Individuals and groups involved		
	Project team	IS management	User management
Phase I — Prototyping			
I-1. Appoint project team and establish project schedule		R	P
I-2. Document present system	R		C
I-3. Interview users	R		C
I-4. Complete general system design of the proposed system	R		C
I-5. Develop prototype system	R		P/A
Phase II — Systems Analysis and Design			
II-1. Specify data base requirements	R		
II-2. Establish controls	R		
II-3. Complete detailed system design	R		C
II-4. Conduct structured walkthrough	P	R	A
II-5. Prepare layouts	R		C
Phase III — Programming			
III-1 Review systems specifications	R		
III-2. Identify and describe programs to be written	R		
III-3. Write, Test, and document programs	R		
Phase IV — Conversion and Implementation			
IV-1. Conduct system test	R		P
IV-2. Convert to new system	R		P
Phase V — Post-Implementation Evaluation			
V-1. Conduct post-implementation evaluation	R		C
V-2. System maintenance		P	R

FIGURE 14-3
Systems Development Responsibility Matrix
The project team has direct responsibility for most systems development activities,
but information services and user managers have participating responsibilities
and are called upon for consultation and approval.

this way, you can more easily identify *who* does *what*, and *when*. To help you, the methodology is graphically illustrated in the form of a *responsibility matrix* in Figure 14–3.

The major activities for each of the five phases are listed along the left-hand side of the responsibility matrix. Although some of the activities are accomplished at the same time, they are generally presented in the order in which they are begun. The phases and numbered activities in the responsibility matrix are the basis for our discussion of the systems development process.

TOO MANY PEOPLE ON THE TEAM

The size of the project team varies with the complexity and scope of the project. Each project has a different optimal number of members. The figure illustrates what happens when the size of the project team is increased. Up to a certain number, each additional person assigned to the project team makes a positive contribution. After that, each additional member actually reduces the per-person contribution to the project effort.

The point to be made is that some information systems projects are very complex and cannot be hurried to completion, no matter how many people are working on them. A project that would take three people ten months

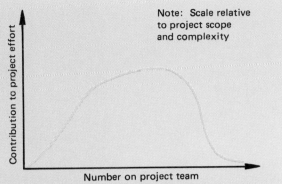

Note: Scale relative to project scope and complexity

The Effect of Project Team Size on Work Output.

cannot be done by 30 people in one month. It just doesn't work that way.

The individuals and groups directly involved in the development of an information system are listed across the top of the matrix. Each is described as follows:

- *Project Team*. The project team will normally consist of systems analysts, programmers, perhaps the data base administrator, and one or two people who will eventually use the system (users). Systems analysts design the system and develop the system specifications. The programmers use these "specs" as guidelines to write the programs. The data base administrator assists the team in designing and creating the data base. These and other computer specialist positions are discussed in detail in Chapter 16, "Jobs and Career Opportunities."

- *Information services management*. This group includes the director and other managers in the information services department (introduced in Chapter 1).

- *User Management*. This group encompasses all user managers (e.g., director of personnel, VP of marketing) who affect or are affected by the proposed development project.

The entries in the matrix reflect the extent and type of involvement for each of the above individuals and groups.

- A   Denotes *approval* authority.
- C   Denotes that the individual/group may be called in for *consultation*.
- R   Denotes who has primary *responsibility* for a particular activity.
- P   Denotes that although the individual or group does not have primary responsibility, they have *participating responsibility*.

Not all information systems are developed in cooperation with the information services department. Some systems, especially micro-based systems, are developed entirely by users.
(SCM Corporation)

For years, automobile manufacturers have built prototype models that could be tested for aerodynamics, aesthetics, and functionality. Only recently has prototyping become popular with information systems development. Now, over 70% of all new information systems emerge from a prototype system and the percent is increasing each year. (Ford Motor Company)

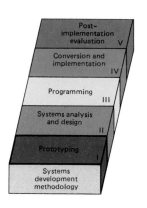

14-3   PHASE I—PROTOTYPING

The objective of Phase I—Prototyping is to analyze the current situation, identify information needs, and develop a prototype system. A prototype system is a scaled-down model of the proposed system. The prototype system would normally handle the main transaction-oriented procedures, produce the critical reports, and permit rudimentary inquiries. In effect, the prototype system permits users a "sneak" preview of the completed system. Having gained some hands-on experience, users can better relate their exact information processing needs to the project team.

Until about 1982, it was not economically feasible to develop a prototype system. In fact, it would probably have cost almost as much to do a prototype as it would to develop the entire system. But today the project team can use fourth- and fifth-generation languages to create a subset of the proposed system that, to the user at a workstation, appears and acts very much like the finished product.

The following numbered activities for Phase I correspond to the responsibility matrix of Figure 14–3.

I-1. Appoint Project Team and Establish Project Schedule

A project team is appointed by managers of the information services department and the affected user departments. One member of the team is appointed the **project leader**.

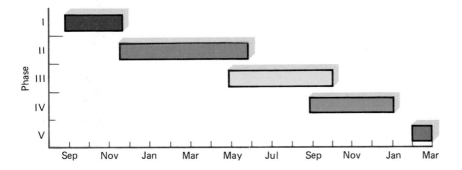

FIGURE 14-4
Bar Chart of a Project Schedule
Systems development project teams often use bar charts to schedule activities and track progress toward implementation.

Every information system project has a deadline. The project team leader is assigned so many programmers, systems analysts, and users. Based on the deadline and the resources available, the project leader establishes an implementation schedule.

A typical project schedule is illustrated in the **bar chart** of Figure 14-4. A *start date* and a *completion date* are estimated for each phase. Figure 14-5 is presented to give you a feel for how much of the project team's effort is spent on each of the five phases. A range of "percent effort" is presented to reflect the variations in emphasis between companies.

I-2. Document Present System

Before you can design a new system, you must have a good grasp of the existing flow of information, be it manual or computer-based. If the existing system is computer-based, it is usually accompanied by some type of documentation. If the existing system is manual, the project team may need to compile a basic documentation package that includes a list and examples of all reports and documents, system data elements and files, and a graphic illustration of the information and work flow of the present system.

The information and work flow of the present system is documented by reducing the system to its basic component parts: *input*, *processing*, and *output*. A variety of design techniques can be used to graphically depict

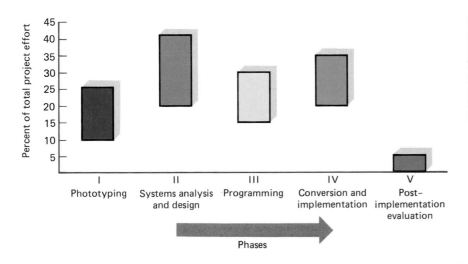

FIGURE 14-5
Relative Project Effort
Programming is usually no more than 15% to 30% of the total project effort. The bulk of a project team's effort is devoted to analysis, design, and implementation.

the logical relationship between these parts. Perhaps the most popular, although not necessarily the best for all situations, is **flowcharting**. Other more "structured" techniques include **data flow diagrams** and **hierarchical plus input-processing-output (HIPO)**. These techniques are discussed briefly in Phase II, Activity II–5, Complete Detailed System Design.

I–3. Interview Users

One of the first activities for project team members is to exercise their communicative skills and talk with the people who are going to use the system. User feedback is the basis for the project team's specifications for system input, processing, and output requirements (information needs). The evaluation of the existing system (I–2) also provides valuable input to the specifications or **specs**.

At this point, the emphasis turns toward *output requirements*. In the system design process, you begin with the desired output and work back to determine input and processing requirements. Outputs are printed reports, workstation displays (e.g., graphic art for an ad piece), or some kind of transaction (e.g., purchase order, payroll check).

I–4. Complete General System Design of the Proposed System

From the information gathered thus far, the project team analyzes the existing system and assesses information needs, then develops a *general system design* of the proposed system. The general system design, and later the detailed design (in Phase II), involves continuous communication between members of the project team and all levels of users. After evaluating several alternative approaches, the project team translates the system specs into a general system design.

The general design of the proposed system is documented both by a graphic illustration (e.g., data flow diagrams), showing the fundamental operation of the proposed system, and by a supporting written description.

"Bad news, boss. All the systems analysts are out with the systemic flu!"
(By permission of Fred Jackson III)

I-5. Develop Prototype System

Throughout the twentieth century, manufacturers have built prototypes of everything from toasters to airplanes. Automobile manufacturers build a prototype car according to original design specifications. Every aspect of the prototype is tested and—if engineers see possibilities for improvement—it is modified. Prototyping now is becoming SOP (standard operating procedure) for software development.

Defining System Specifications. Traditionally, a rough spot in the systems development process has been defining the systems specifications. In the past this activity was usually done in cooperation with users and was done as soon into the project as possible. The reason for defining specifications so quickly was this: Once the design and programming were begun, the technology (primarily third-generation languages and traditional file processing) did not permit much flexibility to make design changes.

Design changes were costly and, if possible, were avoided. When users failed to relate all of their information requirements to the project team, the system specifications often were ill defined and incomplete. Eventually these information oversights caused the project team to backtrack and make costly modifications. To avoid this, the project team at a certain point would "freeze" the specs, after which no more changes could be made before the system was implemented. Well, frozen specs are like ice cubes—when enough heat is applied, they melt!

With the current fourth- and fifth-generation languages and data base management systems, the specs are only cooled, not frozen. These tools make it possible to develop a working prototype system, which is usually a subset of the proposed system. Even though it is a subset, the prototype system will have menus, reports, various input/output screens, and a data base. To the user, the prototype version will look very much like the real thing. Depending on the complexity of the system, the prototype can be completed with a minimum of programming effort.

Creating the Prototype System. To create a prototype system, project team members first rough-out the logic of the system and how the elements fit together, then suggest to the user the I/O interfaces (system interaction with user). The project team members sit down with users to create and modify whatever interactive display screens are required to meet their information processing needs. Remember, with fifth-generation languages, called application generators (see Chapter 10), all you have to do is describe the screen image (menus, reports, inquiries, etc.) and the programming code is automatically generated for you. If a data base, other than the existing one, is needed, perhaps a new data base will have to be created.

Users can actually sit down at a workstation and test out the prototype system. As they do so, new information needs usually surface and they find better ways to do certain activities. In effect, the prototype is the beginning. From here, the system is expanded and refined to meet the users' total information needs. Fifth-generation languages are limited in what they can do, so the system may require a certain amount of **custom coding**, probably in third- and fourth-generation languages. Sometimes, if no expansion or refinement is needed, the prototype becomes the operational system, and Phases II–IV are not required!

With application generators and other very high-level languages, a prototype system can actually be developed in interactive consultation with the user.
(Photo courtesy of Hewlett-Packard Company)

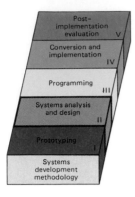

14-4 PHASE II—SYSTEMS ANALYSIS AND DESIGN _____

Once the prototype system is in operation, Phase II—Systems Analysis and Design is begun. The prototype forms the foundation. In Phase II, the format and content of *all* input and output are described, the prototype system is refined, the data base specifications are prepared, and the detailed system design is completed.

To this point, little or no custom code for detailed programs has been written. The majority of the programming code has been *automatically generated* by fifth-generation languages. Much remains to be done before the system is fully conceptualized and detailed programming can begin. Doing detailed programming now is like beginning the construction of a skyscraper without a blueprint. Programming is the brick, mortar, and steel of an information system and should not be started until the detailed system design (the blueprint) is completed.

The following numbered activities for Phase II correspond to the responsibility matrix of Figure 14–3.

II-1. Specify Data Base Requirements

The data base is the common denominator in any system. It contains the raw material (data) necessary to produce the output (information). In manufacturing, for example, you decide what you are going to make, then you order the raw material. In the process of developing an information system, you decide what your output requirements are, then you determine which data are needed to produce the output. In a sense, the output requirements can be thought of as input to data base design.

With the trend to integrated on-line systems and DBMS technology, at least part, and perhaps all, of the data base may already exist. Creation of

These financial analysts rely on historical data as well as up-to-the-second stock trading information to advise their clients. The need for historical information demands that the data dictionary for this financial information system include such historical data elements as the year-to-date highs and lows for each stock.
(Quotron Systems, Inc.)

No.	Name	Description	Format	Coded	Responsibility	Best sellers list (R)	Over due report (R)	On-loan report (R)	Patron data base (D)	Book data base (D)	Checkout display (S)	Acq. data entry (S)	Data base update (S)
1	TITLE	Complete title of book	X(150)	No	Acquisitions	X	X	X		X	X	X	X
2	ISBN	ISBN number	9(13)	No	Acquisitions			X	X	X	X	X	
3	PUBYR	Year of publication	9(2)	No	Acquisitions	X				X		X	X
4	AUTHOR	Name of an author	X(25)	No	Acquisitions	X				X		X	X
5	PUBL	Name of publisher	X(25)	No	Acquisitions					X		X	X
6	DUE	Due date of book	9(6)	No	Circulation		X		X		X		
7	CARDNO	Patron card number	9(4)	Yes	Circulation				X		X		
8	FNAME	First name of patron	X(10)	No	Circulation			X	X		X		

Report (R)   Data base (D)   Display screen (S)

the data base may not be necessary; however, it is likely that a few data elements will need to be added.

The first step in data base design is to compile a **data dictionary**. A data dictionary, illustrated in Figure 14–6, is simply a listing of all data elements in the data base. An existing data base will already have a data dictionary. The data elements, along with certain descriptive information, are listed along the left-hand side of the data dictionary "matrix."

The matrix portion of Figure 14–6 is completed *after* the data base organization has been determined and *after* the reports and input screens are designed. The data elements are then cross-referenced to reflect their occurrence in data base records, reports, and input screens.

FIGURE 14–6
Data Dictionary
Companies maintain an up-to-date data dictionary with descriptive information for all data elements. The use or occurrence of these data elements is cross-referenced to appropriate files, reports, and source documents. The entry in the "Format" column describes the data element's length and whether it is numeric (9) or alphanumeric (X).

II–2. Establish Controls

An information system should run smoothly under normal circumstances. But, as Murphy has taught us, "If anything can go wrong, it will." We, as users, programmers, and operators, make oversights and errors in judgment. But, to err is human. Computers may not be human, but they are machines and machines sometimes fail.

Because of the ever-present potential for human and hardware errors, coupled with the threat of computer crime, it is important that we build in controls to ensure the accuracy, reliability, and integrity of the system. Without controls, an enterprising computer criminal might be able to supplement his or her checking account without making a deposit. An erroneous data entry error could result in the delivery of a red car instead of a blue one. Someone expecting a monthly pay check of $2,500 might receive $250,000. A computer operator could cause chaos by forgetting to do the daily audit run. This activity (II–2) is conducted to prevent these, and any of a thousand other, undesirable events from happening.

Many information systems call for hard copy output on preprinted forms. These forms are designed during Phase II— Systems Analysis and Design. (SCM Corporation)

Information system controls minimize or eliminate errors before, during, and after processing so that the data entered and the information produced are complete and accurate. Controls also minimize the possibility of computer fraud. There are four types of controls: *input controls*, *processing controls*, *output controls*, and *procedural controls*.

Input Controls.   Data are checked for accuracy when entered into the system. In on-line data entry, the data entry operator verifies the data by sight checks. Also, a variety of checking procedures are designed into the software. Two of these software control procedures are discussed below.

■ *Reasonableness check*. Suppose ZIMCO Enterprise's maximum order to date is 250 farkles, and an order is entered for 2,000 farkles. Since an order of 2,000 is much greater than the maximum order to date of 250, the entry is historically unreasonable, and the probable error is brought to the attention of the data entry operator (see Figure 14–7).

■ *Limits check*. A limits check assesses whether the value of an entry is out of line with that expected. For example, ZIMCO Enterprise's policy guarantees 40 hours of work per week for each employee and limits overtime to 15 hours per week. A limits check on the "hours-worked" entry guarantees that a value between 40 and 55, inclusive, is entered.

FIGURE 14–7
Reasonableness Check
The data entry operator is given an opportunity to rekey an "unreasonable" entry. In this instance, 2000 is historically unreasonable.

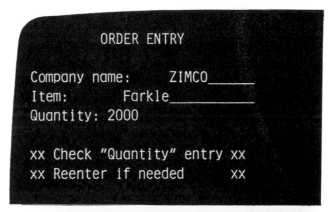

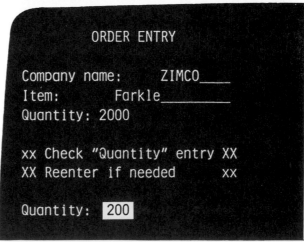

Processing Controls. Systems analysts and programmers use a variety of techniques to validate that processing is complete and accurate. Control totals and consistency checks are a few of the many techniques that can be built into the software.

- *Control total.* A control total, or hash total, is a value that is known to be the accumulated sum of a particular data element. Control totals are used primarily to verify that processing is complete. For example, when payroll checks are printed, the employee numbers are added together and compared to a known value. If the accumulated control total is not equal to the known value, then the computer operator knows immediately that some checks were not processed or that some checks were processed that should not have been.
- *Consistency check.* The consistency check compares like data items for consistency of value. For example, if a customer's kilowatt-hour usage is 300 percent higher for March of this year than for March of last year, the invoice would not be processed without the electric utility company's checking the accuracy of the meter reading.

Output Controls. Some people take for granted that any computer-produced output is accurate. Such is not always the case. There are too many things that can go wrong. One of many methods of output control is *crossfoot checking*. This technique is used in reports, such as the one in Figure 14–8, that have column and row totals with some arithmetic relationship to one another. A beverage distributor, for example, displays a daily delivery report that contains the number of cases of each beverage loaded on each of four delivery trucks. As each truck departs from the warehouse, a physical count is made of its cases. The column totals for each beverage type should equal the total for all delivery routes.

Procedural Controls. In an information system, the work is done either by the computer system or by people. Programs tell the computer what to do. People are guided by procedures. Some procedures are built into the system for control purposes. For example, many organizations subscribe to the *separation-of-duties* procedure. The theory behind this procedure is that

The opportunity for any wrongdoing is diminished when operators are not involved in programming and programmers are not involved in operations.
(Management Science America, Inc. (MSA))

FIGURE 14–8
Crossfoot Checking
The sum of the row totals equals the sum of the column totals.

QUERY: Let me see the daily delivery report.

ROUTE NO.	COLA	FIZZ	BURP	ROUTE TOTAL
1	41	68	32	141
2	29	18	64	111
3	71	65	48	184
4	67	58	56	181
TOTAL	108	209	200	617

if responsibilities for input, processing, and output are assigned to different people, most attempts to defraud the system will be foiled. It is unlikely that would-be computer criminals could solicit that much cooperation.

II–3. Complete Detailed System Design

The *detailed system design* is the result of analysis of feedback from users of the prototype system, and of detailed input/output, processing, and control requirements. The *general system design* of Phase I depicts the relationship between major processing activities and has enough detail for development of a prototype system. The detailed design includes *all* processing activities and the input/output associated with them.

The detailed design is the cornerstone activity of the system development process. It is here that the relationships between the various components of the system are defined. The system specifications and the prototype system are integrated with the project team's imagination and skill to create an information system. The detailed system design is the culmination of all previous work. Moreover, it is the *blueprint* for all project team activities that follow.

A number of techniques aid programmers and analysts in the design process. Each of these techniques permits the design of the system to be graphically illustrated. Two of these techniques—HIPO and data flow diagrams—are briefly discussed below. Flowcharting and several other techniques are discussed in Chapter 15, "Programming Concepts."

Hierarchy Plus Input-Processing-Output. **Hierarchy plus input-processing-output**, or **HIPO** (pronounced HI poe), is a top-down design technique that permits the project team to divide the system into independent modules for ease of understanding and design. HIPO follows the "divide and conquer" line of reasoning.

HIPO has several standard forms. A *structure chart* breaks a system down into a hierarchy of modules. For example, a structure chart for a payroll system is shown in Figure 14–9. Each module is then broken into finer levels on input-processing-output detail in an *overview diagram*. In Figure 14–10, an overview diagram is shown for module 1.3.1 of Figure 14–9, weekly payroll processing.

The primary advantage of HIPO is that it encourages analysts and programmers to examine the system from the top, down (i.e., from the general to the specific). The result is a more structured design. This advantage is, to some extent, offset by the cumbersome volume of paperwork required to document the system.

Data Flow Diagrams. Like HIPO charts, **data flow diagrams**, or **DFDs**, document the system at several levels of generality. Only four symbols are needed for data flow diagrams: *entity*, *process*, *flow line*, and *data store*. The symbols are summarized in Figure 14–11 and their use is illustrated in Figure 14–12. The entity symbol ☐ , a square with a darkened border, is the source or destination of data or information flow. An entity can be a person, a group of persons (e.g., customers or employees), a department, or even a place (e.g., warehouse). Each process symbol ☐ , a rectangle with rounded corners, contains a description of a function to be performed.

Some systems are designed with a windowing feature that lets users view several outputs on the screen at the same time. With this kind of design, the user is not limited to viewing only text or only graphics output.
(Courtesy of International Business Machines Corporation)

FIGURE 14-9
HIPO Structure Chart
This structure chart breaks a payroll system
down into a hierarchy of modules.

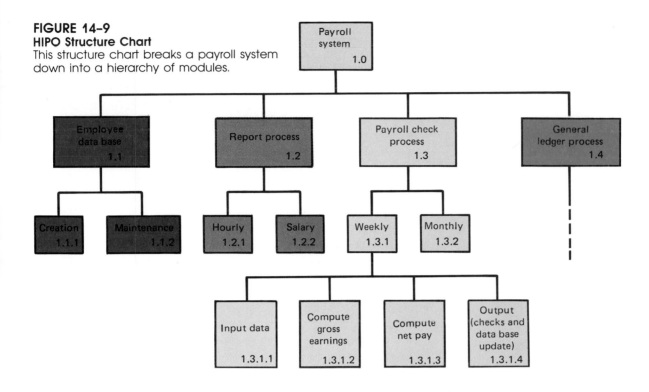

FIGURE 14-10
HIPO Overview Diagram
The example overview diagram illustrates the input, processing,
and output components of Module 1.3.1 of Figure 14-9.

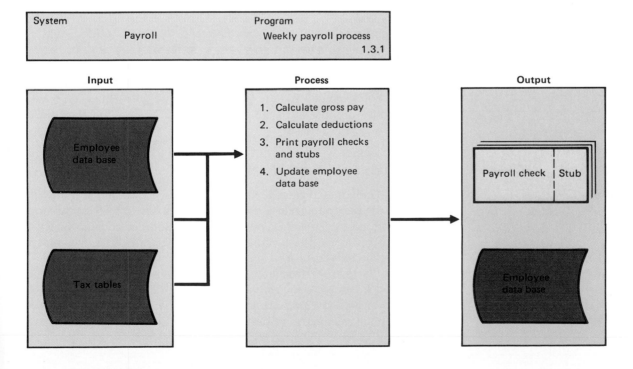

ID

Description

Process

An <u>entity</u> that
is source or
destination of
data/information

Direction of
<u>flow</u> of data/
information

<u>Data storage</u>

FIGURE 14–11
Data Flow Diagram Symbols

Typical processes include "enter data," "calculate," "store," "create," "produce," and "verify." Process symbol identification numbers are assigned in levels, similar to HIPO structure charts (e.g., 1, 1.1). The flow lines ⟶ indicate the flow and direction of data or information. Data storage symbols ⬛, open-ended rectangles, identify storage locations for data. A storage location could be a file drawer, a shelf, a data base on magnetic disk, and so on.

In the example of Figure 14–12, a data flow diagram documents that portion of a personnel system that produces payroll checks. Processes 1 and 2 deal with the employee data base, but in Process 3 the actual payroll checks are produced. In the bottom portion of Figure 14–12, Process 3 is *exploded* to show greater detail. Notice that the *second-level* processes within the explosion of Process 3 are numbered 3.1, 3.2, 3.3, and 3.4. Process 3.1 could be exploded to third level of processes to show even greater detail (e.g., 3.1.1, 3.1.2, etc.).

Design Technique Summary.   There is no one best analytical or design technique. If you elect to take more advanced courses, you will gain a deeper understanding of these and other techniques. The best approach is to use a combination of techniques that fits the circumstances for a particular company, system, or program.

The principles of HIPO, data flow diagrams, flowcharting (discussed in Chapter 15), or any of a dozen other design techniques are not difficult to learn. But applying these techniques to the design of information systems requires practice, practice, and more practice. You can learn how to type, but that does not mean that you are going to write the great American novel. These techniques are just tools. It's your skill and imagination that make an information system a reality.

During a structured walkthrough, the logic of a proposed system design is carefully examined by a peer group. In the photo, two project team members are "walking through" the specs for a proposed system that will help government officials monitor the effectiveness of government grants for education.
(Intergraph Corporation)

II–4. Conduct Structured Walkthrough

We are human beings, and we make mistakes. We overlook things and don't always select the best way to design a program or a system. To do the best job possible, project team members often ask other interested and knowledgeable persons to review and evaluate what they have done. This peer-review procedure is called a **structured walkthrough**.

The procedures of a structured walkthrough are simple. The material to be reviewed (a system design in our example) is distributed several days in advance to appropriate persons. During the actual walkthrough, the person(s) who did the work explains the design and the accompanying documen-

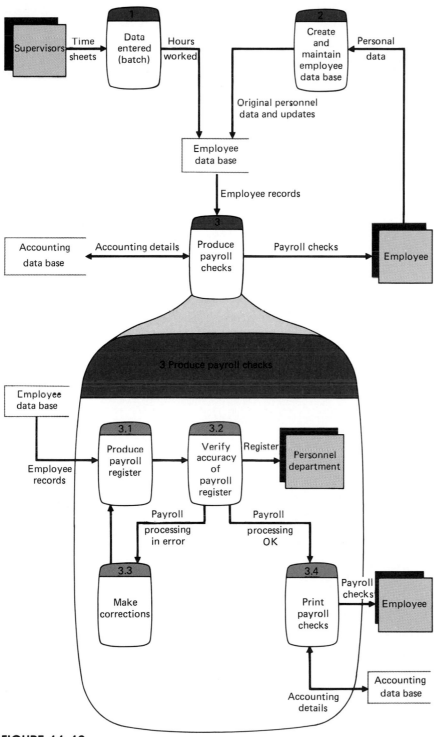

FIGURE 14-12
Data Flow Diagram
In the example data flow diagram of a personnel system,
process 3 is exploded to show greater detail.

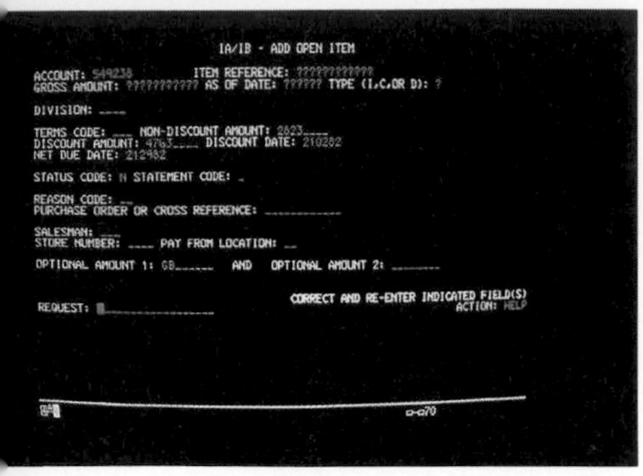

The screen layout for this accounts receivable system makes good use of color to help the user distinguish between input prompts, user-supplied input, system-supplied customer data, and messages to the user.
(Management Science America, Inc. (MSA))

tation. This is done by "walking through" the system, step by step, perhaps with the aid of one of the design tools (e.g., HIPO charts). After the walkthrough, the project team evaluates all recommendations and incorporates the good ideas into the system design.

Several structured walkthroughs are scheduled for most system development projects, and they have proven to be a very effective tool. When project team members know their work is going to be scrutinized by their colleagues, they try hard to do a good job. Wouldn't you?

II–5. Prepare Layouts

So far, except for the screen displays designed in the prototype system, most of the output requirements have only been identified and briefly described. The programmer, however, needs specifics. So, detailed output specifications, called **layouts**, are prepared. These layouts show programmers exactly where

FIGURE 14–13
Screen Layout
Detailed layouts are prepared for each hard- and soft-copy output.

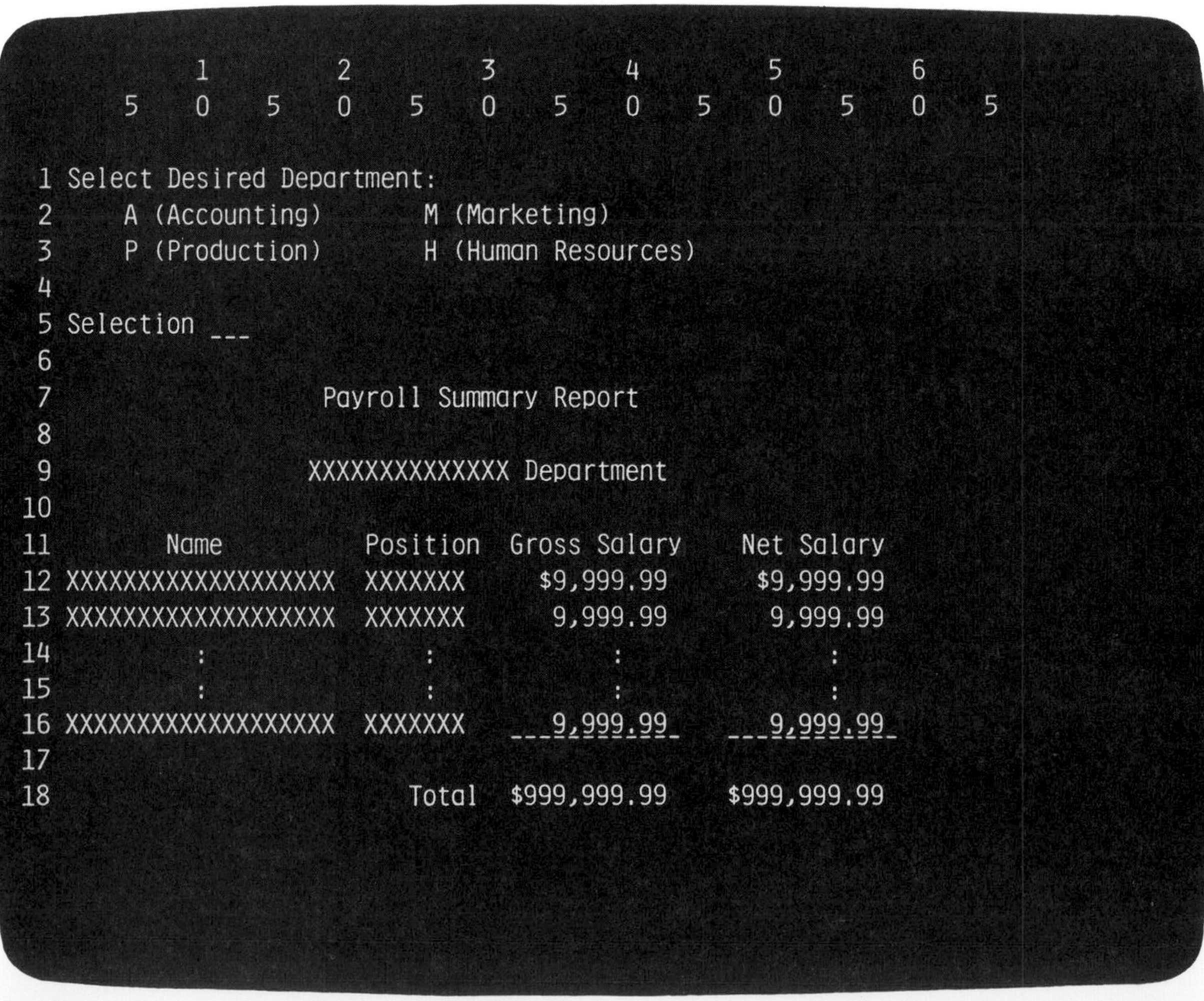

the output information should be placed on printed reports and workstation screen displays. The layout shows the specific location of such items as *report title*, *column headings*, and, in the case of workstation screens, *input formats* for data entry.

Figure 14–13 illustrates a screen layout for a departmental payroll summary report. All of the example reports and interactive screen displays pictured in photographs throughout this book were produced from a layout similar to that of Figure 14–13.

14-5   PHASE III—PROGRAMMING

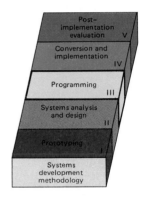

With detailed specifications in hand, we are now ready to write the programs needed to make the proposed system operational. Some of the program code was generated when we used fifth-generation languages (i.e., applications generators) to develop and refine the prototype system. During Phase III the remainder of the programs are written. The four major activities of this phase (see Figure 14–3) are discussed below.

III-1. Review System Specifications

During Phase III, programming becomes the dominant activity, and the programmers really go to work. The system specifications completed in Phase II—Systems Analysis and Design are all that is needed for programmers to write, or "code," the programs to implement the information system. Before getting started, programmers review the following system specifications:

■ Printer output layouts of reports and transactions
■ Workstation input/output screen layouts
■ Data dictionary
■ Files and data base design
■ Controls and validation procedures
■ Data entry specifications
■ General and detailed systems design

Once programmers have reviewed and understood the above specs, the programming task is begun. A superior programming effort will go for naught if the system specifications are incomplete and poorly written. As the saying goes, "Garbage in, garbage out."

III-2. Identify and Describe Programs to Be Written

An information system needs an array of programs to create and update the data base, print reports, permit on-line inquiry, and so on. Depending on the scope of the system and how many programs can be generated with fifth-generation languages, as few as three or four or as many as several hundred programs may need to be written before the system can be implemented. At this point all programs needed to make the system operational are identified and described. Each program description includes the following:

■ Type of programming language (e.g., COBOL, BASIC, Pascal)

DO IT RIGHT THE FIRST TIME

A system development methodology provides a framework through which the many people involved can coordinate their activities. It also encourages project team members to produce up-to-date and complete documentation (e.g., data base design, program logic diagrams, and so on) so that everyone on the project team understands *what has been done* and *what is being done*.

Because a methodology identifies and sequences development activities, the project can be planned, monitored, and controlled. Project teams that do not use a methodology of some kind tend to rush through a development project, bypassing important steps along the way. As a result, they tend to overlook impor-

tant design consideration and avoid documentation. Their rush to finish the system inevitably reduces the overall quality of the end product. A poor-quality system may result in *lower development costs*, but it requires considerably *more maintenance* after implementation. In the long run, a poorly designed system will always cost more than a high-quality system.

The figure highlights the economics of *doing it right the first time*. An oversight left undetected becomes more and more difficult to correct as the project progresses from one phase to the next. A logic error that would take one hour to correct in Phase II would take nine days to correct in Phase V!

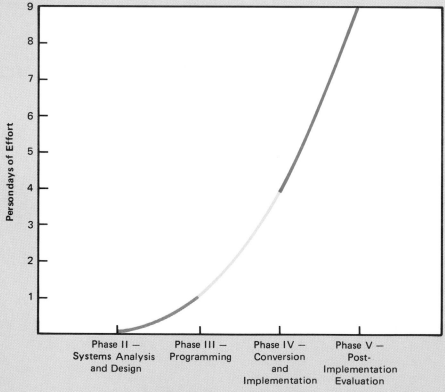

The Cost of an Error. This chart depicts the relative personnel time required to correct a logic error when first detected in the different phases of development.

- A narrative of the program, describing the tasks to be performed
- Frequency of processing (e.g., daily, weekly, on-line, and so on)
- Input to the program
- Output produced by the program
- Limitations and restrictions (e.g., sequence of input data, response-time maximums, and so on)
- Detailed specifications (e.g., specific computations and logical manipulations, any tables, and so on).

III-3. Write, Test, and Document Programs

Armed with systems specifications and program descriptions, we are now ready to write the programs. The development of a program is actually a *project within a project*. Just as there are certain steps that the project team takes to develop an information system, there are certain steps a programmer takes to write a program. Each of the following program development steps is described in greater detail in Chapter 15, "Programming Concepts."

1. Describe the problem to be addressed by the programmer
2. Analyze the problem.
3. Design the general logic of the program.
4. Design the detailed logic of the program.
5. Code the program.
6. Test and debug the program.
7. Document the program.

Once all programs are written, Phase III is complete and we are ready to go on to Phase IV—Conversion and Implementation. In Phase IV all the work comes together, and the information system becomes a reality.

In programming, two heads are sometimes better than one. A programmer can become so close to a program that he or she may overlook obvious errors in logic. These errors often shine as bright as a neon light when the program design is discussed with a colleague.
(General Electric Company)

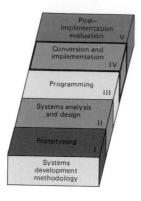

14-6 PHASE IV—CONVERSION AND IMPLEMENTATION _

During Phases I, II, and III the information system is designed and the programs are written and individually tested. But we're not home free yet—much remains to be done before the system becomes operational. The primary objective of Phase IV—Conversion and Implementation is to install the information system and make it operational.

Even though the programs of the system have been individually or *unit tested* (Phase III), there is no guarantee that the programs will work as a system. Therefore, integrated *systems testing* is accomplished in Phase IV. In addition, the project team provides user training on the operation of the information system and creates (or revises) the data base. At the completion of Phase IV, the system is turned over to the users as an operational information system.

In Phases I, II, and III the project team integrates input, output, processing, and storage requirements to design and code an information system. In Phase IV the project team is confronted with a different challenge. They must now integrate *people*, *software*, *hardware*, *procedures*, *and data*. The four major activities of Phase IV are described briefly below and illustrated in the responsibility matrix, Figure 14–3.

IV-1. Conduct System Test

During system testing, systems analysts are constantly gathering feedback from users. Analysts are especially interested in hearing about errors and parts of the system where interaction is cumbersome or slow.
(National Computer Systems)

The individual programs were tested and debugged in Phase III, but they have not been integrated and tested as a system. An information system for inventory management and control may have a hundred programs and a comprehensive data base; these must be tested together to ensure harmony of operation. The purpose of the system test is to validate all software, input/output, procedures, and the data base. It is a safe bet that a few design errors, procedural errors, or oversights will surface during system testing. Minor modifications in design and programming may be required to complete the system test to the satisfaction of the users.

IV-2. Convert to New System

Now we are ready to implement the system; this normally involves a "conversion" from the existing system to the new one. An organization's approach to system conversion depends on their *willingness to accept risk* and the *amount of time available* for the conversion. Four common approaches are parallel conversion, direct conversion, phased conversion, and pilot conversion. These approaches are graphically illustrated in Figure 14–14 and discussed below.

Parallel Conversion. In **parallel conversion**, the existing system and the new system operate simultaneously, or in parallel, until the project team is confident that the new system is working properly. The two key advantages of parallel conversion are that (1) the existing system serves as backup, in case the new system fails to operate as expected, and (2) the results of the new system can be compared to the results of the existing system.

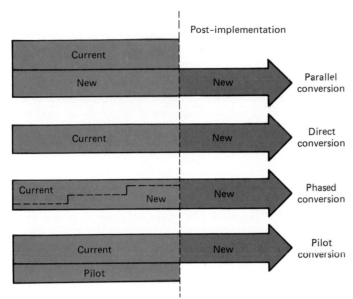

FIGURE 14-14
Common Approaches to System Conversion

There is less risk with this strategy because the present system provides backup, but it also imposes a double workload on personnel and hardware resources during the conversion. The duration of parallel conversion is usually one month or a major system cycle. For a public utility company, this might be one billing cycle, which is usually a month.

Direct Conversion.   As companies improve their system testing procedures, they begin to gain confidence in their ability to implement a working system. Some companies forego parallel conversion for a **direct conversion.** A greater risk is associated with direct conversion because there is no backup in case the system fails.

Companies select this "cold turkey" approach when there is no existing system or when the existing system is substantially different. For example, most on-line student registration systems are implemented cold turkey.

System conversion may mean double work for some users. Organizations selecting the parallel approach to system conversion will need to maintain the existing system until all are satisfied that the new system is working properly. (TRW Inc.)

Phased Conversion.   In **phased conversion**, an information system is implemented one module at a time by either parallel or direct conversion. For example, in a point-of-sale system, the first phase might be to convert the sales accounting module. The second phase could be the inventory management module. The third might be the credit check module.

Phased conversion has the advantage of spreading out the demand for resources so that the demand is not as heavy as it might be at any one time. The disadvantages are that the conversion takes longer, and there must be a system interface between the existing and new system after each new module is implemented.

Pilot Conversion.   In **pilot conversion**, the new system is implemented by parallel, direct, or phased conversion as a "pilot" system in only one of the several areas for which it is targeted. For example, suppose a company wanted to implement a manufacturing resources planning system in its eight plants. One plant would be selected as a *pilot* and the new information system would be implemented there first.

The advantage of pilot conversion is that the inevitable bugs in a system can be removed before the system is implemented at the other locations. The disadvantage is that the implementation time for the total system takes longer than if the entire system were implemented at one time.

The User Takes Control.   Once the conversion has been completed, the information system enters the *production* stage of the system life cycle, and the system is turned over to the users.

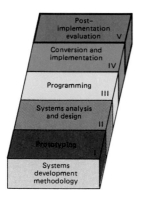

14–7   PHASE V—POST-IMPLEMENTATION EVALUATION

Just as a new automobile will need some screws tightened after a few hundred miles, an information system will need some "fine tuning" just after implementation. Over the production stage of the system life cycle, the system will be modified many times to meet the changing needs of the organization. The two activities of Phase V—Post-Implementation Evaluation (see Figure 14–3), which are discussed below, deal with what takes place after implementation.

V–1. Conduct Post-Implementation Evaluation

The **post-implementation evaluation** is a critical examination of the system after it has been put into production. The evaluation is conducted three to six months after implementation. This waiting period allows several factors to stabilize: the resistance to change, the anxieties associated with change, and the learning curve. It also allows time for unanticipated problems to surface.

The post-implementation evaluation focuses on the *actual* versus the *anticipated* performance objectives. Each facet of the system is assessed with respect to present criteria. If any part of the system is judged deficient, plans are made to correct the problems.

Three to six months after the hardware, software, people, procedures, and data have been integrated into an operational information system, key members of the project team are conducting a post-implementation evaluation to assess the overall effectiveness of an aircraft maintenance system.
(Courtesy of International Business Machines Corporation)

Also, it is a good idea to document what went wrong. No information system has ever been developed without mistakes being made. The best way to avoid making the same mistakes again is to identify the mistakes, then write them down.

V-2. System Maintenance

Once an information system is implemented and "goes on-line," the emphasis is switched from *development* to *operations*. In a payroll system, supervisors begin to enter hours-worked on their workstations, and the computer center produces and issues payroll checks. Once operational, an information system becomes a cooperative effort between the users and the information services department.

An information system is dynamic and must be responsive to the changing needs of the company and those who use it. The process of modifying an information system to meet changing needs is known as *system maintenance*.

There are two approaches to system maintenance. The first, and least desirable, is the "reactive" approach. That is, *do nothing unless requested to do so* by the people who use it. The more effective, "proactive" approach requires the project team to *review the system* once or twice a year to see where it can be improved. During this review, they look into such things as the following:

- Effectiveness of the system
- Turnaround time
- Response time

- Relevance of information
- Input/output formats and content
- File and data base organization
- Update, control, and backup procedures
- Currency of system documentation

The results of periodic system reviews, service requests, and, occasionally, a bug in the system are what prompt system maintenance activities.

An information system cannot live forever. The accumulation of modifications and enhancements will eventually make any information system cumbersome and inefficient. Minor modifications are known as **patches**. Depending on the number of patches and enhancements, an information system will remain operational, or in the production stage, from four to seven years.

Toward the end of the useful life of an information system, it is more trouble to continue patching the system than it is to redesign the system from scratch. The end of the production stage signals the "death" stage of the information system life cycle (see Figure 14–1). A new system is then "born" of need, and the system development process is repeated.

SUMMARY OUTLINE AND IMPORTANT TERMS

14–1 THE SYSTEM LIFE CYCLE. The four stages of a computer-based information system comprise the **system life cycle**. They are birth, development, production, and death.

14–2 TURNING AN IDEA INTO AN INFORMATION SYSTEM. The process of developing a computer-based information system is essentially the same, regardless of the information system being developed. Some organizations follow a **systems development methodology** that provides the framework for cooperation between the various people involved in a development project.

A **service request**, which is usually prepared by the user, signals the beginning of a systems development project. The service request is for an enhancement to an existing system or for a development of a new system. A decision, based on a benefit/cost analysis, is made to either approve or table the project.

Systems development methodologies vary in scope, complexity, sophistication, and approach. A five-phase methodology is presented in a responsibility matrix to help you understand the activities and responsibilities for the development of an information system. The matrix shows when and to what extent individuals and groups are involved in each activity of the systems development process.

14–3 PHASE I—PROTOTYPING. The objective of Phase I is to analyze the current situation, identify information needs, and develop a **prototype system**, or a subset of the proposed system. A **project leader's** first activity is to establish a project schedule and graphically illustrate it in a **bar chart**.

After familiarizing themselves with the existing system, the project team completes a general system design so that they can better understand the scope of the system. To do this, they use design techniques, such as **flowcharting**, **data flow diagrams**, and **HIPO**.

A prototype system is created, primarily with fifth-generation languages, that will enable users to test out the fundamental operation of the proposed system prior to full implementation.

14-4 PHASE II—SYSTEMS ANALYSIS AND DESIGN.   During Phase II the format and content of all input and output are described, the prototype system is refined, the data base specifications are prepared, and the detailed system design is completed.

After the **data dictionary** has been compiled, controls are built into the system to ensure the accuracy, reliability, and integrity of the information system. Input, processing, output, and procedural controls are designed to detect system errors so that corrective action can be taken as quickly as possible.

A detailed system design is completed which integrates feedback from the prototype system with a synthesis of the input/output, processing, and control requirements. At this point in the system development process the project team integrates the system specifications with their own technical and procedural innovations to create an information system. To do this they use any of a number of helpful design techniques.

To insure that something was not overlooked or designed incorrectly, a **structured walkthrough** is conducted. The project team then completes Phase II with the input/output **layouts** and the data entry specifications.

14-5 PHASE III—PROGRAMMING.   During Phase III of the systems development methodology, programs are written, creating the software necessary to make the information system operational.

Programmers review the system specifications (from Phase II) with systems analysts and users on the project team. Each program to be written is identified and described. For each program, the programmer does the following: describes the problem; analyzes the problem; designs the general, then the detailed logic; then codes, tests, and documents the program.

14-6 PHASE IV—CONVERSION AND IMPLEMENTATION.   In Phase IV the work of Phases I, II, and III is integrated with people, software, hardware, procedures, and data, and the information system becomes operational.

A system test is conducted to ensure that the various components of the system work correctly and in harmony. After a satisfactory system test, the system is converted. Approaches to the conversion of a system are **parallel**, **direct**, **phased**, and **pilot conversion**.

14-7 PHASE V—POST-IMPLEMENTATION EVALUATION.   In Phase V the system is fine tuned shortly after implementation; then it is modified as needed to meet the changing needs of the organization.

About three to six months after implementation, a **post-implementation evaluation** is conducted. This evaluation is a critical examination of the information system after it becomes operational.

An information system is dynamic and must be responsive to the changing needs of the company. The process of adjusting information systems to meet these needs is known as systems maintenance. An information system can be revised only so many times before it becomes too cumbersome to use and maintain. This signals the "death" of the information system and the "birth" of its successor. The system life cycle is then repeated.

REVIEW EXERCISES

Concepts

1. What is the objective of prototyping?
2. Draw and identify the four symbols used in data flow diagrams.
3. What are patches?
4. What advantage does direct conversion have over parallel conversion? Parallel over direct conversion?
5. In which stage of the information system life cycle are systems "conceived"? "Maintained"?
6. What are the consequences of omitting a structured walkthrough of a detailed system design?
7. Name three system design techniques.
8. What is a structure chart and how is it used?
9. What is the purpose of a bar chart?
10. Give two examples of uses of a control total.
11. Design a screen layout for an on-line course registration system. Design only that screen with which the student would interact to register for courses. Distinguish between input and output by underlining the input.

Discussion

12. Why is it important to spend time documenting and understanding the existing system if it is to be discarded after a new system is developed?
13. What dangers are involved in developing an information system without following a methodology?
14. Would it be easier for one person or five people to do a relatively simple program? Draw a parallel to the size of a project team.
15. Some managers consider it a waste of time for two programmers to be familiar with each program. Argue for *or* against this attitude.
16. A bank programmer developed an algorithm to determine the check digit for the bank's credit card numbers. The programmer sold the algorithm to an underground group that specialized in counterfeit credit cards. A year later the programmer was caught and pleaded guilty. What do you feel is a just sentence for this crime?

17. Do you feel that operator sight checks are a valid approach to data entry verification? Why or why not?

18. Discuss specific input, processing, output, and procedural controls that could be built into a payroll system.

SELF-TEST (by section)

14-1. The system becomes operational in the _____ stage of the system life cycle.

14-2. The service request is normally compiled by programmers. (T/F)

14-3. A prototype system is developed in Phase _____ of the system development process.

14-4. The limits check is a procedural control. (T/F)

14-5. Phase III—Programming is the only phase that can be completed out of sequence. (T/F)

14-6. Greater risk is associated with direct conversion than with phased conversion. (T/F)

14-7. The post-implementation evaluation is normally conducted one year after system implementation. (T/F)

Self-Test answers. 14–1, production; 14–2, F; 14–3, I; 14–4, F; 14–5, F; 14–6, T; 14–7, F.

STUDENT LEARNING OBJECTIVES

- To identify approaches to solving a programming problem.
- To describe the concept of structured programming.
- To demonstrate an understanding of the principles and use of flowcharting and other program design techniques.
- To classify the different types of program instructions.
- To describe the steps and approaches to program development.

CHAPTER 15

Programming Concepts

15-1 PROGRAMMING IN PERSPECTIVE _____

A computer is not capable of performing calculations or manipulating data without exact step-by-step instructions. These instructions take the form of a computer program. Five, fifty, or even several hundred programs may be required for an information system. Electronic spreadsheet software is made up of dozens of programs that work together so that you can perform spreadsheet tasks. The same is true of word processing software.

Most of the programs that you develop while you are a student will be independent of those developed by your classmates and, more often than not, independent of one another. In a business environment, programs are often complementary to one another. For example, you might write a program to collect the data and another program to analyze the data and print a report.

There is no such thing as an "easy" program. A programming task, whether it be in the classroom, in business, or at home, should challenge your intellect and logic capabilities. As soon as you develop competence at one level, your instructor will surely assign you a program that is more difficult than anything you have done in the past. Even when doing recreational programming on your personal computer, you won't be satisfied with an "easy" program. You will probably challenge yourself with increasingly complex programs.

Programming can be enormously frustrating, especially at first. *Don't despair!* Just when you think that the task confronting you is impossible, a little light will turn on and open the door to the joy of learning to program. That light has turned millions of people on to programming, and it will turn you on, too (if it hasn't already).

Programming has come a long way since the late 1940s when programmers set electrical switches to create programs. Today programming is done interactively at sophisticated programmer workstations. This programmer is creating a program that monitors and controls a coal-gasification facility.
(Dahlgren Museum, Naval Surface Weapons Center)
(General Electric Company)

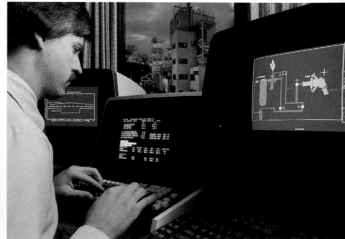

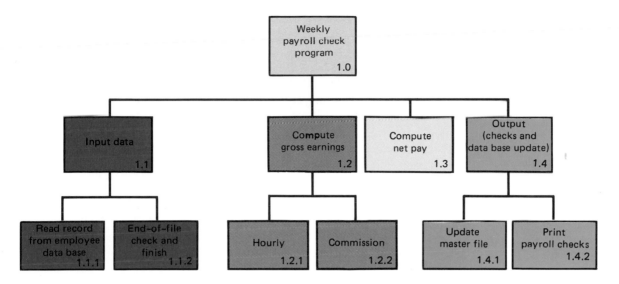

FIGURE 15-1
Program Structure Chart
The logic of a payroll program to print weekly payroll checks can be broken into modules for ease of understanding, coding, and maintenance.

15-2 PROBLEM SOLVING AND PROGRAMMING LOGIC

A single program addresses a particular problem: to define dance movements, to compute and assign grades, to permit an update of a data base, to monitor a patient's heart rate, to analyze marketing data, and so on. In effect, when you write a program, you are solving a *problem*. To solve the problem you must derive a *solution*. And to do that, you must use your powers of *logic*.

A program is like the materials used to construct a building. Much of the brainwork involved in the construction of a building goes into the blueprint. The location, appearance, and function of a building are determined long before the first brick is laid. And so it is with programming. The design of a program, or its programming logic (the blueprint), is completed before the program is written (or the building is constructed). This section and the next discuss approaches to designing the logic for a programming task. Later in this chapter we'll discuss the program and the different types of program instructions.

Structured Program Design: Divide and Conquer

Figure 15-1 illustrates a *structure chart* for a program to print weekly payroll checks. Hourly and commission employees are processed weekly. A structure chart for a program to print monthly payroll checks for salaried employees would look similar, except that task 1.2, compute gross earnings, would not be required. The salary amount can be retrieved directly from the employee data base.

The structure chart permits a programming problem to be broken down into a hierarchy of tasks. A task can be broken down into subtasks, as long

A team of Federal Aviation Administration (FAA) programmers were recently faced with the problem of developing a system that could handle the rapid increase in air traffic. To solve the problem, they developed a more highly automated air traffic control system that relieves these Air Force controllers of certain time-consuming manual tasks. With the new system, they are able to keep pace with an ever-increasing number of flights.
(Sanders Associates, Inc.)

as a finer level of detail is desired. The most effective programs are designed so they can be written in **modules**, or independent tasks. It is much easier to address a complex programming problem in small, more manageable modules than as one big task. This is done using the principles of **structured programming**.

In structured programming, the logic of the program is addressed hierarchically in logical modules (see Figure 15–1). In the end, the logic of each module is translated into a sequence of program instructions that can be executed independently. By dividing the program into modules, the structured approach to programming reduces the complexity of the programming task. Some programs are so complex that, if taken as a single task, they would be almost impossible to conceptualize, design, and code. Again, we must "divide and conquer."

15–3 PROGRAM DESIGN TECHNIQUES _____

A number of techniques are available to help programmers analyze a problem and design the program. HIPO and data flow diagrams, presented briefly in Chapter 14, "The Systems Development Process," can be used as *program* design aids as well as *system* design aids. Both can graphically capture the logic of systems (the general level) or programs (the detailed level). The process symbol in a *system* data flow diagram might represent one or several programs (e.g., print payroll checks), whereas a process symbol in a *program* data flow diagram might represent a computation (e.g., compute federal tax deduction). In this section, three more design techniques—*flowcharting*, *pseudocode*, and *decision tables*—are presented as they would be used in the design of a program's logic. These techniques can also be used as system design tools.

Every other workstation in this college computer laboratory is a microcomputer. The other workstations are linked to the mainframe in the background. The techniques used in designing computer programs are the same for both micros and mainframes.
(Control Data Corporation)

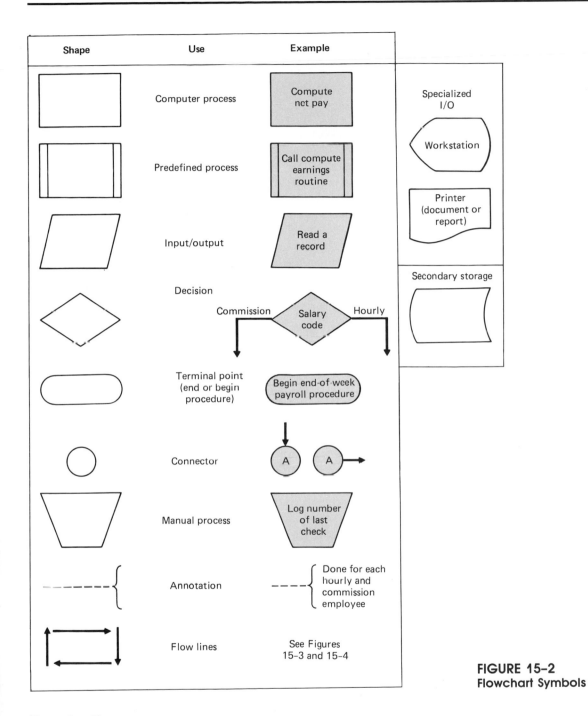

FIGURE 15-2
Flowchart Symbols

Flowcharting

One of the most popular design techniques is **flowcharting**. **Flowcharts** illustrate data, information, and work flow through the interconnection of *specialized symbols* with *flow lines*. The combination of symbols and flow lines portray the logic of the program or system. The more commonly used flowchart symbols are shown in Figure 15–2.

Flowcharting Symbols.   Each symbol indicates the *type of operation to be performed*, and the flowchart graphically illustrates the *sequence in which the operations are to be performed*. *Flow lines* ⟶ depict the sequential flow of the program logic. A rectangle ▭ signifies some type of *computer process*. The process could be as specific as "compute an individual's grade average" (in a program flowchart) or as general as "prepare class schedules for the fall semester" (in a system flowchart). The *predefined process* ▯, a special case of the process symbol, is represented by a rectangle with extra vertical lines. The predefined process refers to a group of operations that may be detailed in a separate flowchart. The parallelogram ▱ is a generalized *input/ output* symbol that denotes any type of input to, or output from, the program or system. The diamond-shaped symbol ◇ marks the point at which a *decision* is to be made. In a program flowchart, a particular set of instructions is executed based on the outcome of a decision. For example, in a payroll program, gross pay is computed differently for hourly and commission employees; therefore, for each employee processed, a decision is made as to which set of instructions are to be executed.

Each flowchart must begin and end with the oval *terminal point* symbol ⬭. A small circle ○ is a *connector* and is used to break and then link flow lines. The connector symbol is often used to avoid having to cross lines. The trapezoid ⬭ indicates that a *manual process* is to be performed. Contrast this to a computer process represented by a rectangle. The bracket ⎯{ permits descriptive notations to be added to flowcharts.

The *on-line data storage symbol* ▭ represents a file or data base. The most common *specialized input/output* symbols are the *workstation* ⬭ and the *printer* (hard copy) ⌐ symbols.

These symbols are equally applicable to system and program flowcharting and can be used to develop and represent the logic for each. A *system* flowchart for a payroll system is illustrated in Figure 15–3. Contrast this system flowchart to the *program* flowchart of Figure 15–4. The program flowchart portrays the logic for the structure chart of Figure 15–1. The company in the example of Figure 15–1 processes hourly and commission employee checks each week (salary employee checks are processed monthly). Gross earnings for hourly employees are computed by multiplying hours-worked times the rate of pay. For salespeople on commission, gross earnings are computed as a percentage of sales.

If you'll remember from Chapter 14, "The Systems Development Process," we discussed a HIPO example for a payroll system. The structure chart of Figure 15–1 and the flowchart of Figure 15–4 represent the *program* logic to accompany module 1.3.1 of the Chapter 14 *system* structure chart (Figure 14–9).

The Driver Module.   In structured programming, each program has a **driver module** that causes other program modules to be executed as they are needed. The driver module for our example payroll program (see Figure 15–4) is a **loop** that "calls" each of the subordinate modules, or **subroutines**, as they are needed for the processing of each employee. The program is designed such that when the payroll program is initiated, the "input data" module (1.1) is executed, or "performed" first. After execution, control is then returned to the driver module, unless there are no more employees to

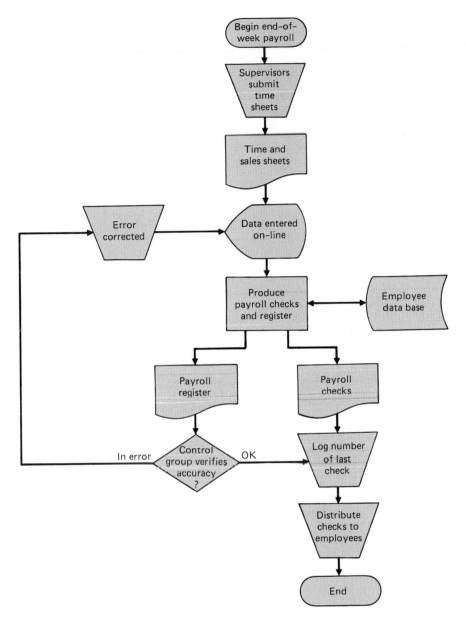

FIGURE 15-3
General Systems Flowchart
This flowchart graphically illustrates the relationship between I/O and major processing activities in a payroll system.

be processed, in which case execution is terminated (the "Finish" terminal point). For each hourly or commission employee, Modules 1.2, 1.3, and 1.4 are performed, and at the completion of each subroutine, control is passed back to the driver module.

When dividing the logic of a program into modules, a good guideline to follow is that each module should have a *single entry point* and a *single exit point*. That is, a program module should begin and end with the same instructions each time it is executed. Thus, transfer of control into and out of a particular program module occurs only at the entry and exit points. The single-entry/single-exit-point guideline encourages good program logic, because it does not permit multiple branches to other modules. An excess

FIGURE 15–4
Program Flowchart
This flowchart portrays the logic of a program to compute and print payroll checks for commission, hourly, and salaried employees (see the structure chart of Figure 15–1). The logic is designed so that a driver module calls subroutines as they are needed to process each employee.

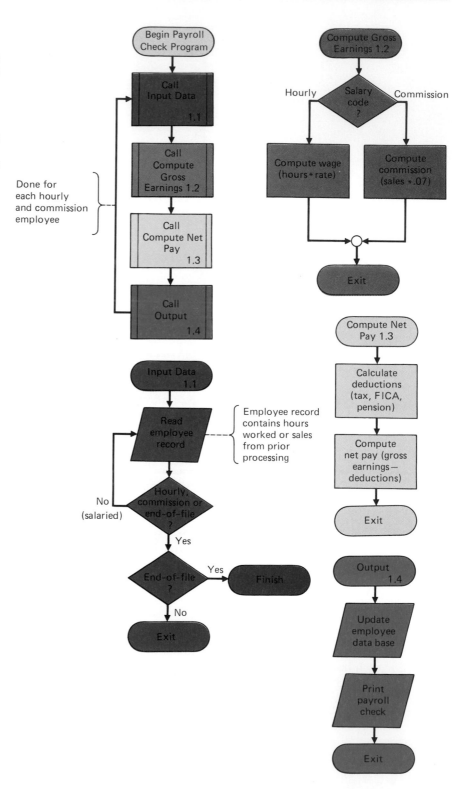

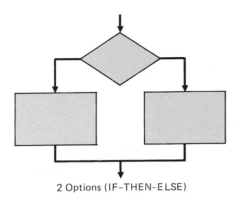

2 Options (IF-THEN-ELSE)

FIGURE 15-6
Selection Control Structures
Any number of options can result from a decision in a selection control structure.

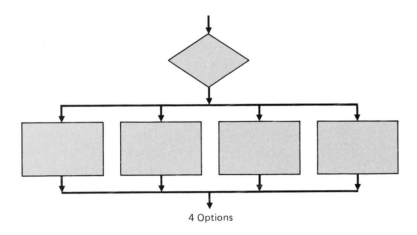

4 Options

FIGURE 15-5
Sequence Control Structures

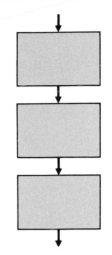

FIGURE 15-7
Loop Control Structures
The two types of loop structures are DOWHILE and DOUNTIL.

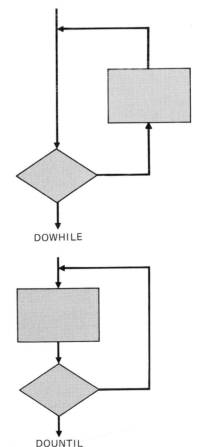

DOWHILE

DOUNTIL

of branches tends to confuse the logic of the program. The modules that begin or end a program may have an extra entry/exit point to begin or end program execution.

Programming Control Structures. Through the 1970s, programmers unknowingly wrote what is now referred to as "spaghetti code." It was so named because their program flowcharts appeared more like a plate of spaghetti than a logical analysis of a programming problem. The redundant and unnecessary branching (jumps from one portion of the program to another) of a spaghetti-style program resulted in confusing logic, even to the person who wrote it. These programs were difficult to write and debug, and even harder to maintain.

Computer scientists thwarted this dead-end approach to developing program logic by identifying three basic *control structures* into which any program, or subroutine, can be segmented. By conceptualizing the logic of a program in these three structures—*sequence*, *selection*, and *loop*—programmers can avoid writing spaghetti code and thus produce programs that can be more easily understood and maintained. The use of these three basic control structures has paved the way for a more rigorous and scientific approach to solving a programming problem. These three control structures are illustrated in Figures 15-5, 15-6, and 15-7, and their use is demonstrated in the payroll example of Figure 15-4.

Sequence Structure. In the sequence structure (Figure 15–5), the processing steps are performed in sequence, one after another. Modules 1.3 and 1.4 in Figure 15–4 are good examples of sequence structures.

Selection Structure. The selection structure (Figure 15–6) depicts the logic for selecting the appropriate sequence of statements. In Figure 15–4, our example payroll program, the selection structure is used to illustrate the logic for the computation of gross pay for hourly and commission employees (Module 1.2). In the selection structure, a decision is made as to which sequence of instructions is to be executed next. In Module 1.2, is the salary code for an employee record "hourly" or "commission"? In the actual payroll program, a different sequence of instructions is executed for hourly and commission employees. The two-option selection structure is sometimes referred to as *IF-THEN-ELSE*. For example, *IF* the salary code is hourly, *THEN* compute wages, *ELSE* compute commission (employee pay type is commission by default).

The selection structure of Module 1.2 presents two decision options: hourly or commission. Other circumstances might call for three or more decision options. For example, suppose part-time hourly employees are treated differently than full-time hourly employees, and salary employees are also paid weekly. In this case, there would be four decision options: hourly (full-time), hourly (part-time), commission, and salary.

Loop Structure. The loop structure (Figure 15–7) is used to represent the program logic when a portion of the program is to be executed repeatedly until a particular condition is met. There are two variations of the loop structure (see Figure 15–7): when the decision, or *test-on-condition*, is placed at the beginning of the statement sequence, it becomes a *DOWHILE loop*; when placed at the end, it becomes a *DOUNTIL loop* (pronounced doo while and doo until). Notice that the leading statements in a DOUNTIL structure will always be executed at least once. In the example payroll flowchart of Figure 15–4, that portion of the input data module (1.1) that reads an employee record is illustrated in a DOUNTIL loop. Employee records, containing

THE TEN COMMANDMENTS FOR FLOWCHARTING

1. Organize flowchart in modules.
2. Use standardized symbols only.
3. Vary symbol size, but do not change the shape.
4. Maintain consistent spacing between symbols.
5. Illustrate interaction between all inputs, processing steps, outputs, and files/data bases.
6. Compile with the general sequence of flow from upper left to lower right.
7. Minimize use of connectors.
8. Do not cross flow lines.
9. Print text.
10. Use a pencil (with a BIG eraser).

hours-worked and sales data, are read sequentially. Since only hourly or commission employees are processed weekly, the loop is repeated until the record of an hourly or commission employee is read, or until the end-of-file marker is reached. When an hourly or commission employee record is read, control is returned to the driver module, which in turn passes control to Module 1.2.

Level of Flowchart Detail.   The example program flowchart of Figure 15–4 is made somewhat general so that the concepts can be demonstrated more easily. A flowchart showing greater detail could be compiled, if desired. For example, Figure 15–8 illustrates how Module 1.3, Compute Net Pay, can be expanded to show more detail.

In program flowcharting, the level of detail is a matter of personal preference. Some programmers complete a general flowchart that outlines the overall program logic, then flesh it out with a more detailed flowchart. Many other examples of program flowcharting can be found in the special section, "BASIC Programming," at the end of the book.

Pseudocode

Another design technique that is used almost exclusively for program design is called **pseudocode**. While the other techniques represent the logic of the program graphically, pseudocode represents the logic in programlike statements written in plain English. Since pseudocode does not have any syntax guidelines (i.e., rules for formulating instructions), you can concentrate on developing the logic of your program. Once you feel that the logic is sound, the pseudocode is easily translated to a procedure-oriented language that can be executed. In Figure 15–9, the logic of a simple program is represented in pseudocode and with a flowchart.

Decision Tables

The **decision table** is a handy tool that analysts and programmers use to graphically depict what happens in a system or program for occurrences of various circumstances. The decision table is based on "IF . . . THEN" logic. IF this set of conditions is met, THEN take this action. Decision tables are divided into quadrants (see Figure 15–10). Conditions that may occur are listed in the *condition stub* (the upper left quadrant). The possible occurrences for each condition type are noted in the *condition entries* (the upper right quadrant). Each possible set of conditions, called a *rule*, is numbered at the top of each column. Actions that can result from various combinations of conditions, or rules, are listed in the *action stub* (the lower left quadrant).

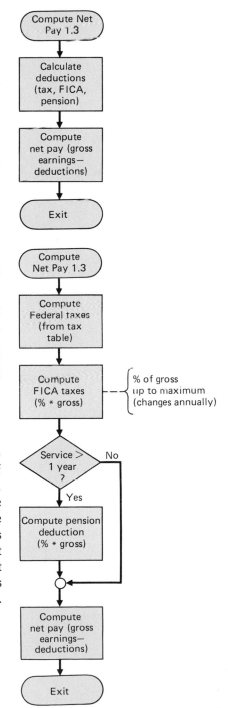

FIGURE 15–8
Level of Detail in Flowcharts
The logic of Module 1.3, Compute Net Pay, of Figures 15–1 and 15–4 is depicted in a general and a more detailed flowchart.

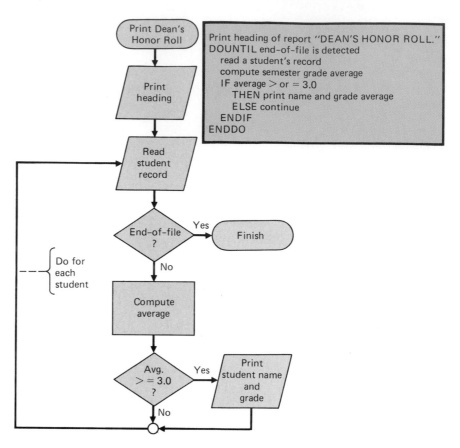

FIGURE 15–9
Pseudocode Example with Flowchart
This pseudocode program depicts the logic of a program to compile
a list of students who have qualified for the dean's honor roll. The same
logic is shown in a flowchart.

FIGURE 15–10
Decision-Table Format
Decision tables are divided into
four quadrants: condition stub,
condition entries, action stub,
and action entries.

	Heading	*Rules*
"IF"	Condition stub	Condition entries
"THEN"	Action stub	Action entries

For each rule, an action-to-be-taken entry is made in the *action entries* (the lower right quadrant).

The decision table in Figure 15–11 illustrates what action is taken for each of several sets of conditions. For example, *IF* the employees to be processed are salaried and it is the end of the month (rule 1), *THEN* both paychecks and a payroll register are printed. *IF* the employees to be processed are on a commission and it is the end of the week (rule 4), *THEN* paychecks only are printed.

The decision table is not a good technique for illustrating work flow. It is, however, very helpful when used in conjunction with flowcharts, data flow diagrams, and HIPO charts. The major advantage of decision tables is that a programmer or analyst must consider *all* alternatives, options, conditions, variables, and so on. With decision tables, the level of detail is dictated by the circumstances. With flowcharts and other design techniques, the level of detail (contrast Figures 15–4 and 15–8) is more a matter of personal preference.

Payroll type/output chart	Rules				
	1	2	3	4	5
Salaried employee	Y	N	N	N	N
Hourly employee	N	Y	Y	N	N
Commission employee	N	N	N	Y	Y
End of week	N	Y	N	Y	N
End of month	Y	N	Y	N	Y
Print paychecks	X	X		X	X
Print payroll register	X	X	X		X

FIGURE 15–11
Decision Table
This decision table depicts what payroll outputs would be generated for various payroll types and conditions.

Egoless Programming

On occasion, a programmer might choose to write a program that will forever stand as a monument to how clever he or she can be. Unfortunately, "clever" programs detract from the effectiveness of a system. They may be clever to their author, but to the person who has to maintain the program, the logic may be indecipherable. To encourage teamwork and quality information systems, some companies have asked their programmers to adopt the principle of **egoless programming**. In short, this means that programs are developed for the team and the project, and not for the individual and his or her ego.

There is no substitute for good sound logic in programming. If you follow the guidelines of structured programming and make judicious use of program design techniques, your program will be easier to write, use, and maintain.

Automated Design Tools

Software packages are now available that permit you to interactively create flowcharts, structure charts, and data flow diagrams on a display screen. For example, with data flow diagrams, you simply designate the type of symbol, where you want it to go, and its caption. The symbol and its caption are then displayed on the screen. You can create as many symbols as needed to depict the program or system logic. The symbols and flow lines can be moved, added, deleted, and revised as you test out various solutions to the problem.

Software packages are also available that automatically generate flowcharts directly from program code. The use of these generators is not recommended for original program development, but they may be useful when redocumenting programs whose documentation is out of date.

As for pseudocode, you probably already have access to all the software you need. Since pseudocode is simply text, any good word processing package will do nicely.

Such automated design tools are a welcome relief to the time-consuming task of manually documenting the logic of a program or system. And they sure save on erasures!

More than half of a programmer's time is spent on program maintenance, that is, the modification of existing programs to meet the changing needs of the organization. The program maintenance task is much easier if the program logic is well documented with a flowchart, pseudocode, or some other design technique. (Honeywell, Inc.)

MEMORY BITS

SYSTEM AND PROGRAM DESIGN TECHNIQUES
- Flowcharting
- Data flow diagrams (DFD)
- Hierarchical plus input-processing-output (HIPO)
- Pseudocode
- Decision tables

15-4   SO WHAT'S A PROGRAM?: CONCEPTS AND PRINCIPLES OF PROGRAMMING

A computer program is made up of a sequence of instructions that are executed one after another. These instructions, also called **statements**, are executed in sequence unless the order of execution is altered by a "test-on-condition" instruction or a "branch" instruction.

The flowchart of our example payroll program (Figure 15–4) is recreated in Figure 15–12, along with a sequence of language-independent instructions. Except for the computation of gross earnings, the processing steps are similar for both types of employees. Two sequences of instructions are needed to compute gross earnings for *hourly* and *commission* employees. We can also see from the flowchart that the sequence in which the instructions are executed may be altered at three places (decision symbols), depending on the results of the test-on-condition. In Module 1.2, for example, the sequence of instructions to be executed depends on whether the test-on-condition detects an hourly or commission employee.

To the right of the flowchart in Figure 15–12 is a representation of a sequence of language-independent instructions and the order in which they are executed. *Statement numbers* are included, as they are in most program listings. This program could be written in any procedure-oriented language. The purpose of the discussion below is to make you familiar with general types of programming instructions, and not those of any particular programming language. Each language has an instruction set with at least one instruction in each of the following *instruction classifications:* input/output, computation, control, data transfer and assignment, and format.

These programmers write programs in COBOL, BASIC, and C. Although these programming languages are substantially different in their capabilities and uses, the concepts embodied in these languages are similar enough that these programmers have no trouble writing in one language in the morning and another in the afternoon. (Cromemco, Inc.)

Input/Output.   Input/output instructions direct the computer to "read from" or "write to" a peripheral device (e.g., printer, disk drive). *Statement 50* of Figure 15–12 requests that an employee record, including pay data, be read from the data base. *Statement 320* causes a payroll check to be printed.

Computation.   Computation instructions perform arithmetic operations (add, subtract, multiply, divide, and raise a number to a power). *Statement 160* (PAY = HOURS * RATE) computes gross earnings for hourly employees. *Statement 190* (PAY = SALES * .07) computes gross earnings for commission employees, where the commission is 7% of sales.

Control (Decision and/or Branch).   Control instructions can alter the sequence of the program's execution. *Unconditional* and *conditional* instructions prompt a decision and, perhaps, a branch to another part of the program or to a subroutine. In Figure 15–12, *statements 10–40, 80, 110, 130, 140, 210, 270,* and *340* are control instructions.

Unconditional Instructions.   Statements 10 through 40 are unconditional branch instructions. An unconditional branch instruction disrupts the normal sequence of execution by causing an unconditional branch to another part of the program or to a subroutine. In *statements 10–40*, the branch is from the driver module to a subroutine. The CALL statement works in conjunction with the RETURN statement to branch to another location, then RETURN control back to the statement following the CALL. For example, the CALL at *statement 10* passes control to the "Input Data" module (1.1) at *statement 50*, then the RETURN at *statement 120* passes control back to the driver module at *statement 20*.

Another unconditional branch instruction, very popular before structured programming, is the GOTO (pronounced, go too) instruction. The GOTO statement causes control of execution to "go to" another portion of the program. A GOTO instruction is placed at *statement 170* so that once the hourly pay is calculated, control is passed directly to the RETURN statement in order to bypass that portion of module 1.2 that deals with commission employees.

The GOTO at *statement 170* was included for demonstration purposes, but in an actual program it should have been avoided when possible. Programming gurus advocate that the GOTO statement be used sparingly. Excessive use of GOTOs destroys the logical flow of the program and makes it difficult to divide the program into modules. Some companies simply do not permit the use of GOTO statements at all, thus the term **GOTO-less programming**. The theory behind GOTO-less programming is that programmers tend to use GOTOs to get out of a "programming corner" instead of applying good sound logic. If GOTOs are not allowed, then programmers are encouraged to divide the program into modules and to make judicious use of the three control structures in Figures 15–5, 15–6, 15–7. For example, to avoid the GOTO statement (160) in the example, the "compute gross earnings" module (1.2) could have been subdivided into Modules 1.2.1 (hourly computation) and Module 1.2.2 (commission computation).

The END instruction at *statement 130* terminates program execution. Control is passed to the END instruction from *statement 110* when the end-of-file marker is detected.

FIGURE 15–12
Program Flowchart with Language-Independent Instructions
The flowchart (same as Figure 15–4) presents the logic of a payroll program to compute and print payroll checks for commission, hourly, and salaried employees. The accompanying "program" has a few language-independent instructions to help illustrate the concepts and principles of programming. A detailed discussion of this figure is presented in the text.

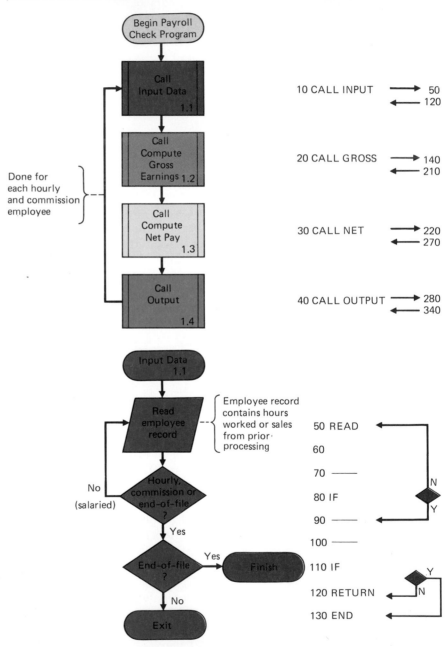

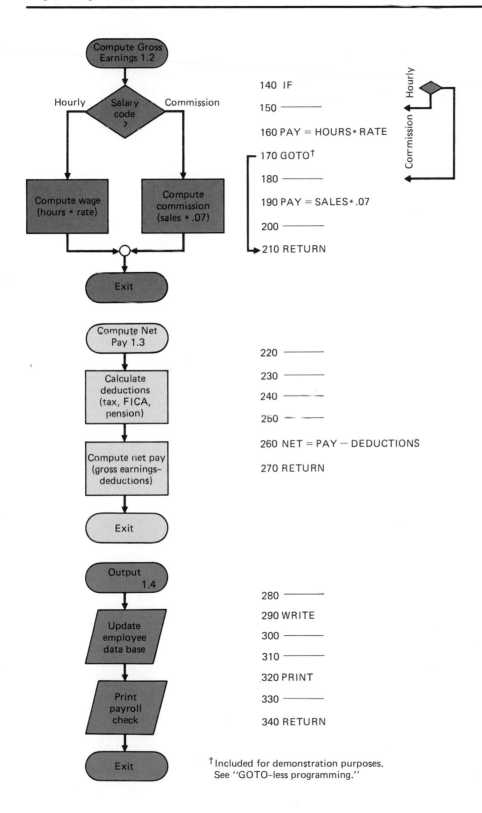

140 IF

150 ————

160 PAY = HOURS * RATE

170 GOTO†

180 ————

190 PAY = SALES * .07

200 ————

210 RETURN

220 ————

230 ————

240 ————

250 ————

260 NET = PAY — DEDUCTIONS

270 RETURN

280 ————

290 WRITE

300 ————

310 ————

320 PRINT

330 ————

340 RETURN

† Included for demonstration purposes.
  See "GOTO-less programming."

Most programs that we write today evaluate precise data. For example, your bank account is either overdrawn or it isn't. As the field of artificial intelligence grows, programming logic must begin to mirror the human thinking process. These programmers are learning about "fuzzy logic." Applications of artificial intelligence must cope with such "fuzzy" concepts as "close," "almost," and "big." (LISP Machine Inc.)

Conditional Instructions. Statements *80* and *110* are conditional branch instructions and are generally referred to as IF statements: If certain conditions are met, then a branch is made to a certain part of the program. The conditional branch at *statement 80* causes the program to "loop" until the employee record read is for either an hourly or a commission employee, or the end-of-file marker is reached. The sequence of instructions, *statements 50 through 80*, comprise a DOUNTIL loop. The IF at *statement 110* causes the program to terminate if there are no more employees to be processed. Each programming language offers one or more specialized instructions for the express purpose of creating loops.

In *statement 140*, the salary code is checked. IF the salary code is "commission," then a branch is made to *statement 180* and processing is continued.

Data Transfer and Assignment.   Data can be transferred internally from one primary storage location to another. In procedure-oriented languages, data are transferred or "moved" by *assignment instructions*. These instructions permit a *string constant*, also called a *literal value*, such as "The net pay is", or a *numeric value*, such as 234, to be assigned to a named primary storage location.

In a program, a primary storage location is represented by a **variable name** (e.g., PAY, HOURS, NET). A variable name in a program statement refers to the *contents* of a particular primary storage location. For example, a programmer may use the variable name HOURS in a computation statement to refer to the numeric value of the *hours worked* by a particular employee.

Data are transferred internally by simply equating the contents of two variables. In Figure 15–13, for example, an employee's salary is read into primary storage and stored in a location named SALARY. A program statement, PAY = SALARY, then transfers the contents of the primary storage location named SALARY (3000) to the primary storage location named PAY. The previous contents of PAY (2550) is destroyed and replaced with the contents of SALARY. The contents of SALARY, though, remains the same.

FIGURE 15–13
Internal Data Transfer
An employee's salary is read into memory and stored in a location named SALARY. When PAY is equated to SALARY in a data transfer and assignment instruction (PAY = SALARY), the value currently in the memory location named PAY (2550) is replaced with the value of SALARY (3000).

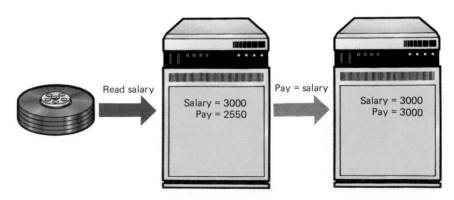

In *statement 260* of Figure 15–12, NET = PAY − DEDUCT, the arithmetic result of subtracting DEDUCT from PAY is stored in NET.

Format.   Format instructions are used in conjunction with input and output instructions; they describe how the data are to be entered or outputted from primary storage. When the READ at *statement 50* retrieves an employee's record from secondary storage, it is loaded to primary storage as a string of characters. The format instruction enables the program to distinguish which characters are to be associated with the variables EMPLOYEE-NAME, SAL-ARY-CODE, and so on.

On output, format instructions print headings on reports and present data in a readable format. For example, PAY may be computed to be 324750; however, on output, you would want to "edit" 324750 and insert a dollar sign, a decimal point, and perhaps a comma, for readability ($3,247.50). This is called *editing* the output.

With these few types of instructions, you can model almost any business or scientific procedure, whether it be sales forecasting or guiding rockets to the moon. This discussion is paralleled in the special section, "BASIC Programming," at the end of the book, with actual BASIC examples being given for each instruction type.

> **MEMORY BITS**
>
> **PROGRAM INSTRUCTION CLASSIFICATIONS**
> - Input/output
> - Computation
> - Control
>   Unconditional branch
>   Conditional branch
> - Data transfer and assignment
> - Format

15–5 WRITING PROGRAMS

If you are writing programs to implement an information system, then any programming assignment would be accompanied by the systems specifications and program descriptions from Phase II—Systems Analysis and Design. The contents of the specifications and descriptions are summarized in Chapter 14, "The Systems Development Process," activities III–2 and III–3. If you are writing a single program, then you may need to do some analytical work that might otherwise have been done in Phase II.

Remember, writing a program is a project within itself. The following steps, first listed in Chapter 14, are followed for each programming project.

- Step 1.   Describe the problem.
- Step 2.   Analyze the problem.
- Step 3.   Design the general logic of the program.
- Step 4.   Design the detailed logic of the program.
- Step 5.   Code the program.
- Step 6.   Test and debug the program.
- Step 7.   Document the program.

Step 1.   Describe the Problem.   The "problem" is described in the program descriptions completed in activity III–3 (see Chapter 14). For example, a problem might be to write a program that accepts numeric quiz scores and assigns a letter grade. Another problem might be to write a program that identifies and prints the names of customers whose accounts are delinquent. Your instructor will probably define the problem for programs that you might do as class assignments.

Programming is no longer limited to technical specialists. End users in marketing, entertainment, and a hundred other fields are acquiring their own micros and learning to program. For short programs, it may take less time for end users to write their own programs than to describe the problem to a programmer.
(Seagate Technology)

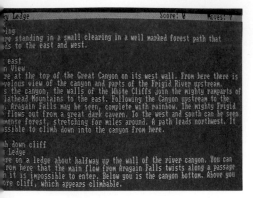

Not all programming problems are information related. The problem confronting the programmers of Zork I was to introduce surprising twists, challenging situations, and unique characters from which a user can create and participate in a story. With interactive fiction software such as Zork I, the user gives directions such as "walk east" or "climb down cliff." Zork I responds with a new situation. (Infocom)

Step 2. Analyze the Problem. In this step, you break the problem into its basic components for analysis. Remember, "Divide and conquer." Although different programs have different components, a good place to start with most programs is to analyze the *output*, *input*, *processing*, and *file-interaction* components. You would then identify important considerations in the design of the program logic. At the end of the problem analysis stage, you should have a complete understanding of what needs to be done and a good idea of how to do it.

Steps 3 and 4. Design the General and Detailed Logic of the Program. Next you have to put the pieces together in the form of a logical program design. Like the information system, the program is also designed in a hierarchical manner, or from the general to the specific.

The General Design (Step 3). The *general* design of the program is oriented primarily to the major processing activities and the relationships between these activities. The structure chart of Figure 15–1 and the flowchart of Figure 15–4, both discussed earlier in this chapter, illustrate the general design of a weekly payroll program to compute and print pay checks. By first completing a general program design, you make it easier to investigate alternative design approaches. Once you are confident of which approach is best, a more detailed design may be completed.

The Detailed Design (Step 4). The *detailed* design results in a graphic representation of the program logic that includes *all* processing activities and their relationships, calculations, data manipulations, logic operations, and all input/output. Figure 15–8, discussed earlier, contrasts general and detailed program design.

It is best to test the logic of a program in graphic format (e.g., flowchart or data flow diagram) before you code the instructions. If you rush into Step 5 (Code the Program), you will spend a lot of unnecessary time backtracking to fix the things you overlooked. Resist the urge to start coding before you have the logic of the program firmly fixed in your mind—and on paper. After all, if you don't have time to do it right the first time, how could you possibly have time to do it over?

Peer Review of Design. More often than not, programming is a team effort. In programming, it is true that "two heads are better than one." For this reason, programmers often ask their colleagues to evaluate their logic before proceeding to code the program. This can be done formally, through a *structured walkthrough* (see Chapter 14), or informally.

Whether you are reviewing the design of your own program or somebody else's, you would look for such attributes as ease of understanding, soundness of logic, and attainment of the required objectives.

A completed program is more a beginning than an end. Once the program goes into production, it must be constantly revised to meet the changing needs of the company. A poorly designed program can be a nightmare to the programmers who inherit the maintenance responsibility for it over the life of the system. A peer review, such as a structured walkthrough, is a good way to eliminate bad programs and make long-term maintenance a more enjoyable task.

A team of programmers is usually assigned to work on big projects. The programming team meets as a group at least once per week to coordinate efforts, discuss problems, and report on individual and team progress.
(Management Science America, Inc. (MSA))

Step 5.   Code the Program.   Whether you "write" or "code" the program is a matter of personal preference. In this context, the terms are the same. In Step 5, the graphic and narrative design of program development Steps 1 to 4 is translated into machine-readable instructions, or programs. If the logic is sound and the design documentation (e.g., flowcharts, pseudocode, and so on) is thorough, then the coding process is relatively straightforward.

The best way to write a program is to work directly from the design documentation and compose the program interactively at a workstation or PC. Remember, programs are much easier to write when broken down into several small and more manageable modules. Programmers have shown time and time again that it takes less time to code ten 50-line modules than it does to code a single 500-line program.

When you write a program, you should have appropriate documentation on hand. This documentation may consist of some or all of the following:

- The data dictionary (with standardized names for variables, e.g., NET, HOURS)
- The coding scheme for coded data elements
- The file layouts and data base schemas
- Printer and video display layouts
- Data entry specifications
- The program design documentation (e.g., HIPO charts, flowcharts, program descriptions, and so on)

You may not need to write original code for every programming task. Many organizations maintain libraries of frequently used program modules, called **reusable code**. For example, several programmers might use the same reusable code for an input subroutine.

"I've gone over this program five times, but I still feel like I've forgotten something."
(By permission of Anthony Cresci)

The debugging of a program may take more time than the coding. In this photo, a professor is helping a student programmer search for a logic error by checking the output against expected results.
(The DeVry Institutes)

Step 6. Test and Debug the Program. Once the program has been entered into the system, it is likely that you will encounter at least one of those cantankerous **bugs**. A bug is an error in program syntax and logic. Ridding a program of bugs is the process of **debugging**.

Syntax Errors. Debugging a program is a repetitive process, whereby each successive attempt gets you one step closer to a working program. The first step is to eliminate *syntax errors* or **diagnostics**; you get a syntax error when you violate one of the rules for writing instructions (e.g., placement of parentheses, spelling of commands, and so on). The diagnostics on the first run are mostly typos (e.g., REED instead of READ). Most compilers and interpreters identify the number of the statement causing the diagnostic and give you an **error message**. As you will quickly find out, if you haven't already, error messages are not always totally explanatory. The error message points you in the right direction, but some extra effort may be required to isolate the exact cause of the error.

Logic and I/O Errors. Once the diagnostics have been removed, the program can be executed. A diagnostic-free program is not necessarily a working program. You now have to debug the *logic of the program* and the *input/output formats*. To do this, you need to create *test data* and, perhaps, a *test data base* so you know what to expect as output. For example, suppose you write a program to average three grades and assign a letter grade. If your test data are 85, 95, and 75, then you would expect the average to be an 85 and the letter grade to be "B." If the output is not 85 and "B," then there is a bug in the program logic.

A program whose logic is sound might have input or output formats that need to be "cleaned up" to meet layout specifications. Suppose your output looked like this:

THE LETTER GRADE ISB

and the layout specs called for this:

THE LETTER GRADE IS B

Then you would need to modify the output format to include a blank space between IS and the letter grade.

Most of the interactive programming languages have software debugging aids. One of the most helpful aids, especially for finding logic errors, is the *trace*. When you ask for a trace, you get a sequential log of the order in which statements or sections of the program are executed (see trace example in the special section, "BASIC Programming," Learning Module II). The trace also shows you which branches were taken during execution. By comparing the *actual* sequence of execution against the *expected* sequence, you can usually isolate the error.

Test Data. Test data are an integral part of the test procedure. Test data are made up so that all possible circumstances or branches within the program are tested. Good test data contain both valid and erroneous data. It's always a good idea to deliberately introduce erroneous data to see if error routines are working properly. For example, in a program that averages grades, you might wish to include an error routine that questions grades greater than 100. To test this routine, you simply enter a grade of, say, 108. If the program works properly, the error routine will detect the erroneous data and display an error message. A good programmer lives by Murphy's Law, which assumes that if it can happen, it will! Don't assume that whoever uses your program will not make certain errors in data entry.

A program may be bug-free after *unit testing*, but eventually it will have to pass *systems testing*, where all programs are tested together. Thorough testing is essential to quality information systems, otherwise a "bug" might fly up and "byte" you at the worst possible time. It has happened before.

Step 7. Document the Program.

When you write a program in a college course, you turn it in, it's graded, and then it's returned. Your effort contributes to your knowledge and expertise, but in all probability the program you wrote will not be used again. In a business environment, however, a program that you write may be used every day—for years!

Over the life of the system, procedures and information requirements change. For example, because the social security tax rate is revised each year, certain payroll programs must be modified. To keep up with these changes, programs must be periodically updated, or maintained. Program maintenance can be difficult if the program documentation is not complete and up to date.

The programs you write in college are not put into production and are, therefore, not maintained. You may ask, "Why document them?" The reason is simple. Good documentation now helps to develop good programming habits that will undoubtedly be carried on in your future programming efforts. *Documentation* is part of the *programming process*. It's not something you do after the program is written.

In business, you may or may not be responsible for maintaining your own programs. In all probability, other programmers will eventually be given maintenance responsibility for your programs. A well-documented program will make life much easier for those who must maintain it. You might say, "Well, I know the program backward and forward and don't really need much documentation." You might be intimately familiar with a program that you have just completed, but what about six months and 20 programs from now? You would be surprised at how much we humans forget about our own creative work. A good program documentation package includes the following items:

- *Program Title.* A brief descriptive title (e.g., PRINT_PAYROLL _CHECKS).
- *Language.* Language in which program is written (e.g., COBOL, BASIC).
- *Narrative Description.* A word description of the functions performed.
- *Variables List.* A list containing the name and description of each variable used in the program.
- *Source Listing.* A hard-copy listing of the source code.
- *Detailed Program Design.* The flowcharts, decision tables, and so on.

Getting all of the bugs out of your program is reason enough for a small celebration.
(Photo supplied courtesy of Epson America)

The tools of a programmer are always changing. This new display screen uses a mixture of neon and argon gas to create sharp graphic images. Programmers use graphics capabilities to achieve a more effective display of information. A realtor could not describe this house to a client as well as this display does.
(Courtesy of International Business Machines Corporation)

A COSTLY BUG

We remember the Mariner 2 spacecraft for its historic probe into deep space in 1963. But what happened to Mariner 1 launched a year earlier? Mariner 1 went deep all right, but not into space. It went deep into the Atlantic Ocean.

The guidance program that was used successfully on previous Atlas missions was also used for Mariner 1. An investigation into the crash of the Mariner 1 surfaced the cause of the crash: a program error. A curious set of circumstances caused the program to take branches not taken in the Atlas flights. As a result, a program instruction with a logic error was executed. Because a programmer inadvertently omitted one character from an equation, Mariner 1 "turned left, then nosed down."

This multimillion-dollar oversight serves to highlight two important programming principles. First, a computer does exactly what a program tells it to do, nothing less and nothing more. Second, program testing must be comprehensive so that all possible circumstances are examined.

The first computer "bug."
(Dahlgren Museum, Naval Surface Weapons Center)

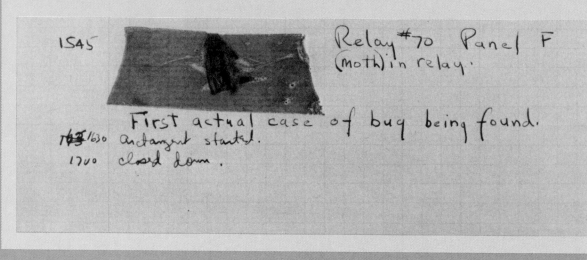

- *Input/Output Layouts.* The printer and workstation display layouts; examples of hard-copy output (e.g., payroll check).
- *Frequency of Processing.* How often the program is run (e.g., daily, weekly, on-line).
- *Detailed Specifications.* The arithmetic computations, sorting and editing criteria, tables, control totals, and so on.
- *Test Data.* A test package that includes test data and expected results. The test data are used to test and debug the program after each program change.

Some of these documentation items can be included in the actual program as *internal* documentation. Descriptive programmer remarks throughout the program make a program easier to follow and to understand. Typically, the program title, a narrative description, and the variables list would also be included as internal documentation. All of the example BASIC programs in the special section, "BASIC Programming," at the back of the book illustrate internal documentation.

A programmer on a project team might be responsible for one or a dozen programs. However, each program evolves through this seven-step process.

SUMMARY OUTLINE AND IMPORTANT TERMS _____

15-1 PROGRAMMING IN PERSPECTIVE.   We direct computers to perform calculations and manipulate data by describing step-by-step instructions in the form of a program. Learning to program can be somewhat frustrating at first, but with a little practice, programming is just plain fun.

15-2 PROBLEM SOLVING AND PROGRAMMING LOGIC.   Programs can provide solutions to particular problems. The creativity in programming is in the application of logic to problem solving.

The most effective programs are designed so that they can be written in **modules**. Addressing a programming problem in logical modules is known as **structured programming**.

15-3 PROGRAM DESIGN TECHNIQUES.   Data flow diagrams and HIPO (see Chapter 14) can also be applied to programming logic. Design techniques such as **flowcharting**, **pseudocode**, and **decision tables** are commonly used to represent systems and programming logic.

Flowcharts illustrate data, information, and work flow through the interconnection of specialized symbols with flow lines. In structured programming, each program is designed with a **driver module** that calls **subroutines** as they are needed.

Program logic can be conceptualized in three basic control structures: sequence, selection, and **loop**. There are two variations on the loop structure: DOWHILE and DOUNTIL.

Pseudocode represents program logic in programlike statements that are written in plain English. There are no syntax guidelines for formulating pseudocode statements.

Decision tables are used by both programmers and analysts to depict what happens for occurrences of various circumstances.

15-4 SO WHAT'S A PROGRAM?: CONCEPTS AND PRINCIPLES OF PROGRAMMING.   A computer program is made up of a sequence of instructions or **statements**. There are five classifications of instructions.

- Input/output instructions direct the computer to read or write to a peripheral device.
- Computation instructions perform arithmetic operations.
- Control instructions can alter the sequence of a program's execution.

■ Data transfer and assignment instructions permit data to be transferred internally.

■ Format instructions describe how data are to be entered or outputted from primary storage.

15–5   WRITING PROGRAMS.   The writing of a program is a project within itself and follows the following seven steps:

■ Step 1.   Describe the problem.
■ Step 2.   Analyze the problem. Examine the output, input, processing, and file-interaction components.
■ Step 3.   Design the general logic of the program.
■ Step 4.   Design the detailed logic of the program.
■ Step 5.   Code the program. Use appropriate documentation and **reusable code**.
■ Step 6.   Test and debug the program. Programs are **debugged** to eliminate **diagnostics** and logic errors and to clean up the input/output.
■ Step 7.   Document the program. Once the program has been thoroughly tested, the program documentation is updated and a program documentation package is compiled.

REVIEW EXERCISES

Concepts

1. Draw the flowcharting symbols for manual process, terminal point, workstation, and decision.

2. Where is the test-on-condition placed in a DOWHILE loop? In a DOUNTIL loop?

3. Assign meaningful variable names to at least six data elements that you might expect to find in a personnel record.

4. Write a pseudocode program that represents the logic of Module 1.1 (Input Data) in Figure 15–4.

5. Give an original example of a computation instruction.

6. Name and illustrate the three basic program control structures.

7. What common program instructions are associated with conditional and unconditional statements?

8. What is the purpose of a test-on-condition instruction?

9. Describe the characteristics of good test data.

10. What are the benefits of structured programming?

11. What is meant by the remark "garbage in, garbage out" as applied to systems specifications and programming?

12. Complete a bar chart depicting your study and preparation for all of your quizzes, papers, and programming assignments in all classes through the remainder of the term.

13. In a decision table, in which quadrant is the condition stub? The action entries?

Discussion

14. Discuss how a "team effort" relates to egoless programming.
15. Discuss the rationale for the "divide and conquer" approach to programming.
16. What is the rationale for completing a general design of a program's logic before completing a detailed design?
17. Break up into groups of four so that each group can conduct several structured walkthroughs. Rotate the role of presenter so that each member has a chance to walkthrough the logic and I/O of a recent programming assignment.
18. Discuss the justification for the extra effort required to fully document a program.

SELF-TEST (by section)

15-1 (a) The software for an electronic spreadsheet is contained in a single program. (T/F)
   (b) Computer programs direct the computer to perform calculations and manipulate data. (T/F)
15-2 (a) Programs are written in_____ , or independent tasks.
   (b) The effectiveness of structured programming is still a matter of debate. (T/F)
15-3 (a) Flowcharting is used primarily for program design and rarely for systems design. (T/F)
   (b) IF-THEN-ELSE logic is associated with the selection structure. (T/F)
15-4 (a) There is a direct relationship between the number of GOTO instructions in a program and how well the program's design is structured. (T/F)
   (b) "Subtotal Amount" is a_____ constant.
15-5 (a) Frequently used program modules are called reusable code. (T/F)
   (b) Once a program has been unit tested, no further testing is required. (T/F)

Self-Test answers. 15–1 (a), F; (b), T; 15–2 (a), modules; (b), F; 15–3 (a), F; (b), T; 15–4 (a), F; (b), string; 15–5 (a), T; (b), F.

GENIGRAPHICS
Houston, Texas

- To identify computer specialist positions in information services departments and in user departments.
- To describe the functions, responsibilities, and organization of an information services department.
- To identify job opportunities in organizations that provide computer-related products or services.
- To become aware of the relationship between career mobility and computer knowledge.

CHAPTER

16

Jobs and Career
Opportunities

16

Whether you are seeking employment (or perhaps a promotion) as a teacher, an accountant, a writer, a fashion designer, a lawyer, or in any of a hundred other jobs, one question is frequently asked: "What do you know about computers?" Already, well over half of all white collar workers routinely work with computers. By 1990, virtually all white collar workers and a good portion of the blue collar workers will spend a significant portion of their day interacting with a computer.

Upon completion of this course, you will be part of the computer-literate minority and able to respond affirmatively to this inquiry. But what about that 95% of our society that must answer "nothing" or "very little"? These people will find themselves at a disadvantage.

If you are planning a career as a computer specialist, opportunity abounds. Almost every organization, no matter how small or large, employs computer specialists. And most of those companies are always looking for qualified people.

For the last decade, people with computer/information systems education have been at or near the top of the "most wanted" list. With millions (yes, millions!) of new computers being purchased and installed each year, it is a good bet that this trend will continue. Of course, the number of people being attracted to the booming computer fields is also increasing. Even so, the most pessimistic forecasters predict a doubling of the demand for computer specialists during the next decade.

This chapter should give you some insight into career options and opportunities in the computer areas. Today, the majority of computer specialist positions, such as operators, programmers, or systems analysts, are in an organization's information services department. But with the trend to dis-

A product manager for a soft drink company monitors the success of marketing campaigns by gathering and analyzing data from regional distribution offices. Computer specialists at a regional office develop and maintain a variety of administrative information systems. Both need a solid foundation of computer knowledge to accomplish their jobs effectively.
(Copyright 1984 GTE Telenet Communications Corporation)
(Sperry Corporation)

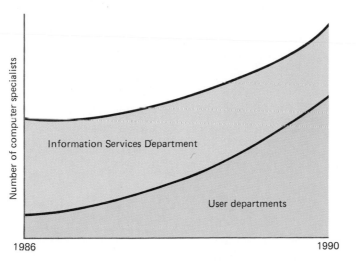

FIGURE 16–1
Computer Specialist Positions in Transition
The trend to distributed processing has increased the number of computer specialists in the user areas.

tributed processing, we are seeing a movement of computer specialists to the user departments. Some people are predicting that as many as 75% of the computer specialist positions will be in the user groups by 1990 (see Figure 16–1). Even now, virtually every type of user group is vigorously recruiting people with computer expertise. Job opportunities in the information services department and in the user areas are discussed in the sections that follow.

16–2 THE INFORMATION SERVICES DEPARTMENT

If you are pursuing a career as a computer specialist, then the material in this section will familiarize you with some of the opportunities in an organization's information services department. If you are pursuing a noncomputer career, then this section will give you some insight as to whom to contact when you have a computer-related question or request. It is not uncommon for computer users to have daily contact with people in the information services department. Besides helping in the development of information systems, computer specialists in an information services department routinely respond to user inquiries on micro/mainframe links, hardware evaluation, and use of software packages, to mention a few.

Responsibility

The information services department is the data and information "nerve center" of an organization. Most organizations—hospitals, insurance companies, universities, and so on—have an information services department. The *data* are supplied by the various user groups. In return, the information services department provides the software and operational support needed to produce *information*. The basic responsibility of an information services department is to be responsive to the organization's information processing needs.

To meet this responsibility, information services departments offer the following services:

Programmers, systems analysts, and other computer specialists in an information services department work together to meet an organization's data processing and information needs.
(Courtesy of International Business Machines Corporation)

- They develop, implement, and maintain information systems throughout the organization.
- They handle the ongoing operation of information systems.
- They maintain the data base.
- They maintain information-related standards, procedures, and policies.
- They provide computer-center and information systems security.
- They advise users on issues involving computers and the use of computers.

Centralized and Decentralized Organization

Most information services departments evolved as part of the accounting/finance function. As accounting systems, such as payroll and accounts receivable, proved the worth of the computer, other departments, such as personnel and marketing, began to request that systems be developed for them. Information services departments, then called data processing or DP departments, grew rapidly. As a result, these departments were centralized to take advantage of the economies of scale. But rapid growth caused some information services departments to become cumbersome and unnecessarily complex.

By the late 1970s, a *lack of responsiveness* to user needs and the *availability of small, cost-effective computers* had reversed the trend toward centralization. Many companies are now decentralizing the information services function through *distributed processing* (see Chapter 5). However, even in a distributed processing environment, a central information services department is needed

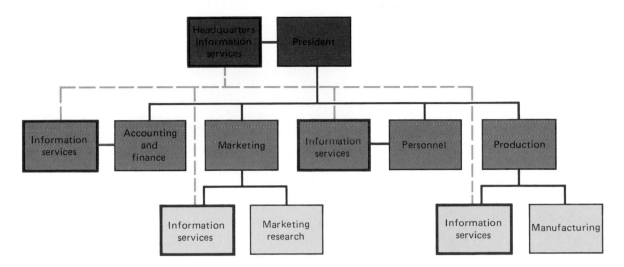

FIGURE 16–2
Distributed Processing Organization
In distributed processing, the computer and information resources are moved closer to the people who use them.

to coordinate all the activities involving information resources, such as hardware acquisition, information planning, and so on.

In effect, distributed processing is moving hardware, software, data, and computer specialists closer to where they are needed—the user areas. For example, in a distributed processing environment, user groups, such as accounting and marketing, have their own computer systems and computer specialists. These "distributed" computer systems are usually linked to a centralized host computer that is supported by the information services department. Figure 16–2 illustrates a company organized for distributed processing operation.

The trend is away from further centralization of information services and toward distributing processing capabilities closer to the people who use them. This distributed computer system, which is part of a network of computers, is on a truck in the middle of an oil field. You can't get much closer than that.
(Chevron Corporation)

Computer Specialist Positions in the Information Services Department

Most of the career fields in an information services department can be divided into seven groups. These are *management*, *systems analysis*, *programming*, *technical support*, *data communications*, *operations*, and *education*. Figure 16–3 gives a brief explanation of each group.

Position descriptions in each of these seven major groups are presented in the sections that follow. These should give you a feeling for the scope of computer-related job opportunities. Keep in mind that the number and type of career paths open to someone entering the computer fields is expanding each year. In a few years, there will be even more career options at each job level.

To allow for professional growth and promotions, most companies usually have several levels for each position. For example, if you take a job in a large company and continue in the programming field, you might begin as

The Information Services Department	
Management	Managers in each of the groups that follow perform the traditional management functions: planning, organizing, staffing, directing, and controlling.
Systems analysis	The systems analysis group analyzes, designs, and implements computer-based information systems.
Programming	The programming group translates system design specifications produced by systems analysts into programs.
Technical support	The technical support group designs, develops, maintains, and implements systems software (i. e., generalized software, such as the operating system and data base management system).
Data communications	The data communications group designs computer networks and implements hardware and software that permits data transmission among computers and workstations.
Operations	The operations group performs those machine room activities associated with the running of operational information systems (e.g., loading tapes, scheduling, and running jobs). Operations also includes control functions and data entry. The trend to on-line data entry is causing the data entry function to be "distributed" to the user areas.
Education	The education group is responsible for the continuing education of computer specialists and for training users in the operation of hardware and information systems.

FIGURE 16-3
Groups in an Information Services Department

an *assistant programmer*, with promotions to *programmer*, *senior programmer*, *chief programmer*, and *programming manager*. A small company may have only two levels. As you would expect, your assignments become more complex and demanding with each promotion.

Management

Director of Information Services. The **director of information services** is the chief information officer (CIO) and has responsibility for all computer and information systems activity in the organization. At least half of the director's time is spent interacting with user managers and executives. In this capacity, the director coordinates the integration of data and information systems and serves as the catalyst for new systems development. The remainder of the director's time is devoted to managing the information services department. In medium and large information services departments, each group has a manager. The managers of systems analysis, programming, operations, and the other groups would normally report to the director of information services.

Systems analysts work with users to ensure that they get the information they need in a format that they can easily understand. This analyst recommended presenting productivity data in the form of a color coded pie chart. (Dataproducts Corporation)

Systems Analysis Group

Systems Analyst.   The function of a **systems analyst**, or simply "analyst," is the analysis, design, and implementation of information systems. Systems analysts work closely with users to design information systems that meet their data processing and information needs. Specific development tasks are discussed in detail in Chapter 14.

The role of these "problem solvers" is expanding with the technology. For example, with fifth-generation languages (see Chapter 10) users and analysts can work together at a workstation to design *and* implement certain systems—without programmer involvement!

Systems analysts are also assigned a variety of other tasks. These might include feasibility studies, system reviews, security assessments, MIS long-range planning, or perhaps serving on a hardware selection committee.

Programming Group

Applications Programmer.   The **applications programmer**, or simply programmer, translates analyst-prepared system and input/output specifications into programs. Programmers design the logic, then code, debug, test, and document the programs, as described in Chapter 15. The programs that are written by an applications programmer are designed for a certain application, such as market analysis or inventory management.

Sometimes called "implementors" or "miracle workers," programmers are charged with turning specifications into an information system. To do this, they must exhibit logical thinking and overlook nothing. A good programmer is *perceptive*, *patient*, *persistent*, *picky*, and *productive*: the 5 Ps of programming.

The nature of the work and the availability of specially designed workstations has made computer careers particularly inviting to the physically challenged. The man in the photo works as a programmer/analyst at a computer services company. (Boeing Computer Services)

Some companies distinguish between *development* and *maintenance* programmers. Development programmers create *new* systems. Maintenance programmers enhance *existing* systems by *modifying* programs to meet changing needs. On the average, about 50% of the applications programming tasks are related to maintenance and 50% to new development.

A distinction is also made between *business systems* programmers and *scientific* programmers.

Programmer/Analyst.   A person holding a **programmer/analyst** position performs the functions of both a programmer and a systems analyst. In some companies, you are either a programmer or an analyst. In others, you are both and are part of a combined systems analysis and programming group.

Technical Support Group

Systems Programmer.   **Systems programmers** develop and maintain systems software. Remember from Chapter 10, "Programming Languages and Software Concepts," that systems software is fundamental to the general operation of the computer; that is, it does not address a specific business or scientific problem. Systems software includes operating systems, utility programs, data base management systems, and language compilers.

Data Base Administrator (DBA).   The **data base administrator** position evolved with data base management systems software and the need to integrate information systems (as discussed in Chapter 11, "Data Organization and File Processing"). The data base administrator designs, creates, and maintains the organization's data base. The DBA coordinates discussions between user groups to determine the content and format of the data base so that data redundancy is kept to a minimum. Accuracy and security of the data base are also responsibilities of the data base administrator. An in-depth knowledge of data base management systems is a prerequisite to obtaining a DBA position.

Data Communications Group

Data Communications Specialist.   The **data communications specialist** designs and maintains computer networks that link computers and workstations for data communications. This involves selecting and installing appropriate hardware, such as modems, data PBXs, and front-end processors, as well as selecting the transmission media (see Chapter 9, "Data Communications"). Data communications specialists also develop and implement the software that controls the flow of data between computing devices.

Operations Group

Computer Operator.   The **computer operator** performs those hardware-based activities that are needed to keep production information systems operational. An operator works in the machine room, initiating software routines and mounting the appropriate tapes, disks, and preprinted forms. The operator

The large computer systems run by these operators support an information network that offers a variety of information services to more than 60,000 people throughout the country. (Quotron Systems, Inc.)

is in constant communication with the computer while monitoring the progress of a number of simultaneous production runs, initiating one-time jobs, and trouble shooting. If the computer system fails, the operator initiates restart procedures to "bring the system up."

Librarian.   The **librarian** selects the appropriate magnetic tapes and disks from off-line storage and delivers them to the operator. The operator mounts the tapes and disks on the secondary storage devices for processing, then returns them to the librarian for storage. The librarian maintains a status log on each tape and disk. It is not unusual for a computer center to have hundreds, and even thousands, of tapes and disks.

The librarian is also charged with maintaining a reference library filled with computer books, periodicals, and manuals, as well as internal system and program documentation (i.e., data flow diagrams, program listings).

Control Clerk.   The **control clerk** accounts for all input to and output from the computer center. The control clerk follows standard procedures to validate the accuracy of the output before it is distributed to the user department. For example, a control clerk will check the employee number control total (see Chapter 14, "The Systems Development Process") before releasing the payroll checks for distribution.

Data Entry Operators.   The **data entry operator**, sometimes called the key operator, uses key entry devices to transcribe data into machine-readable format. Although most information services departments have a small data entry group, the majority of the data entry operators are "distributed" to the user areas.

Education Group

Education Coordinator.   The **education coordinator** coordinates all computer-related educational activities. Anyone selecting a computer-related

Education coordinators plan and conduct seminars to acquaint both users and computer specialists with the latest software and hardware products.
(Courtesy of International Business Machines Corporation)

career also adopts a life of continuing education. Computer technology is changing rapidly, and you have to run pretty fast just to stand still! The education coordinator schedules computer specialists for technical update seminars, video training programs, computer-assisted instruction, and others, as needed. Often, the education coordinator conducts the training sessions.

Education coordinators are also involved with the development and delivery of user training programs. As systems go on-line and the number of workstations grows, more and more users must be trained in the use of their workstations and systems.

Education and Experience Requirements for Employment in the Computer Fields

The education and experience requirements for employment vary, depending on the employer's needs. However, the majority of people now entering the programmer or analyst career fields have degrees in data processing, information systems, or computer science. Entry-level systems programmers and data base administrators usually have degrees in computer science or engineering. Operations personnel, except for data entry operators, will need a technical school diploma or an associate degree in information systems or data processing. Keyboarding skills and some familiarity with computers are sufficient for most data entry jobs.

These are the educational backgrounds most common among people seeking jobs in the computer field. But the fact remains—you will find people with backgrounds in everything from accounting to zoology seeking and holding computer-related jobs.

Organization of an Information Services Department

In some information services departments, one person is the chief cook and bottle washer. Other departments have several thousand people. Both small and large "shops" (a slang term for information services departments) must accomplish the functions of systems analysis, programming, technical support, data communications, operations, and education. Differences in the way they are organized are due primarily to the degree of specialization.

Figure 16–4 illustrates how an information services department in a medium-to-large corporation might be organized. This chart illustrates a traditional organizational structure that could vary, depending on circumstances.

A typical organizational structure for a small company is illustrated in Figure 16–5. Some specialty areas are not noted in the chart. Personnel in small companies double-up on duties. For example, a programmer might also be the data base administrator.

Taking a Job in an Information Services Department

If you have completed an associate or bachelor's degree and seek entry-level employment in an information services department, you will probably begin as a programmer. Technical school graduates and some associate degree holders accept employment as *operators*, *control clerks*, *librarians*, and *data*

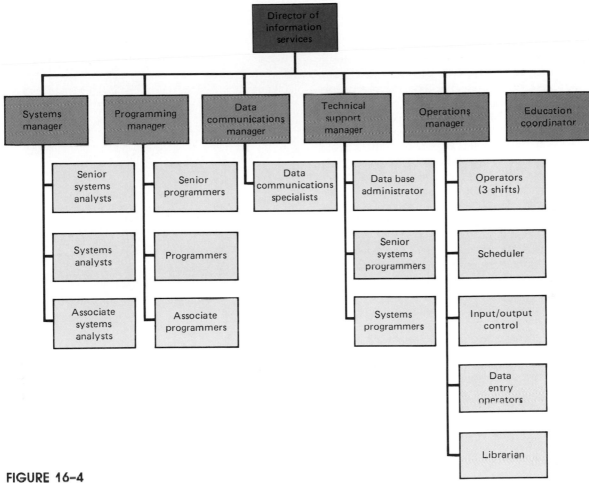

FIGURE 16–4
Organization Chart—Medium and Large Information Services Departments
No two information services departments are organized the same way, but the above example is, in general, representative.

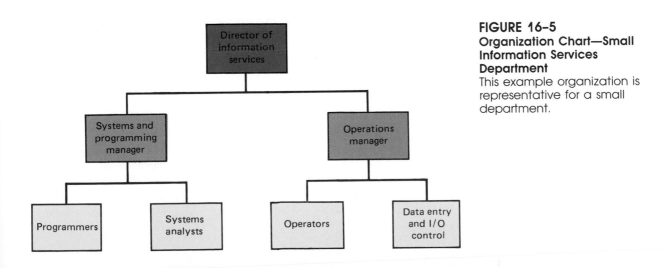

FIGURE 16–5
Organization Chart—Small Information Services Department
This example organization is representative for a small department.

THE 94% SOLUTION

What do computer specialists think about their profession? According to Dewar's Career Profile research, there is a high degree of job satisfaction among computer professionals. Ninety-four percent of the people sampled were "satisfied" with their jobs. Seventy percent were "very satisfied." For the purposes of the survey, job satisfaction is defined as experiencing meaningfulness and responsibility in one's work, and also having a knowledge of results.

The profile notes the main reasons people choose the computer field: they have a strong personal interest and they seek personal growth. A chance to be creative and the opportunity to learn new skills were the top rewards for those choosing the computer field. The survey results indicated that financial remuneration is of little importance to the computer professional.

Over 90% of those surveyed felt that the computer careers offered greater opportunities for women and minorities than other fields.

Would those surveyed consider leaving the computer field? Not on your life, say 94% of the respondents.

A programmer/analyst speaks enthusiastically about her career opportunities.
(Photo courtesy of Hewlett-Packard Company)

entry operators. After gaining operations experience, those with associate degrees and programming education often are promoted to programming positions.

Relatively few companies recruit recent graduates to fill *systems analyst* positions. Most companies prefer their analysts to have programming experience. You might be hired as a *programmer/analyst*, but assignments for a rookie programmer/analyst are usually programming tasks for the first couple of years.

The rationale behind starting people as programmers is well founded. Programming not only develops logic and design skills but also provides "real-world" insight into the capabilities and limitations of a computer system. A programmer learns what a computer system can and cannot do. This knowledge is valuable in virtually every computer specialist position.

Once you have a solid foundation in programming (18 months to three years), you can pursue a career as a programmer or branch out into other information systems careers. There is no traditional career path; two people would rarely advance through the ranks in the same manner. You will probably be faced with the luxury of having several promotion alternatives at each level.

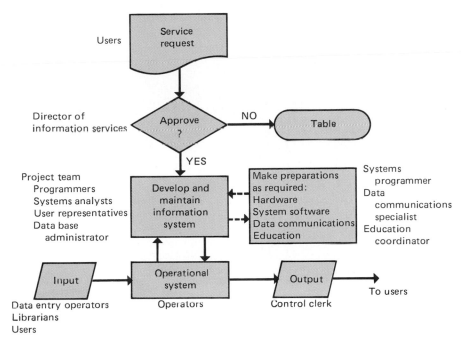

FIGURE 16-6
Position Functions and Information Systems
This chart summarizes the relationship between the various information services positions and user personnel in the development and operation of an information system.

Organization Summary

Figure 16–6 graphically summarizes the relationship between the positions that have been described and the development and operation of an information system. A *user* request for a computer-related service, called a service request, is compiled and submitted to the information services department. Because resources are limited, the *director of information services* approves those requests that appear to offer the greatest benefits to the organization.

A project team made up of *systems analysts*, *programmers*, *user representatives*, and possibly the *data base administrator* is formed to develop and implement the information system. *Systems programmers* and *data communications specialists* make changes to the hardware configuration, data communications network, and systems software, as required. The *education coordinator* schedules needed training sessions for both computer specialists and users. Once the system is implemented and becomes operational, operations people handle the routine input, processing, and output activities. *Data entry operators* transcribe the raw data to machine-readable format. The *librarian* readies magnetic storage media for processing. *Operators* initiate and monitor computer runs and distribute the output to *control clerks*, who then check the output for accuracy before delivering it to the *users*.

16–3 COMPUTER SPECIALISTS IN THE USER AREAS: INFORMATION CENTERS AND USER LIAISONS

As we discussed earlier, more and more computer specialists are migrating to the user areas (see Figure 16–1). Today it's not just the information services department that has computers. Computers are found in every area. Organiza-

Information center specialists assist users in the use and application of hardware and software until they can become self sufficient.
(Cullinet Software, Inc.)

tions that had *one mainframe* computer in 1975 may have several mainframes plus *100 micros* today. Besides the computer specialists in the traditional areas (e.g., programming, systems analysis), a new breed of computer specialists is emerging in the user areas. These include *information center specialists*, *user liaisons*, *office automation specialists*, and *microcomputer specialists*.

Information Center Specialists.   An **information center** is a facility in which computing resources are made available to various user groups. The computing resources might include workstations that are linked to a mainframe, microcomputers, printers, and plotters (for preparation of presentation graphics). The information center would also have a variety of software available for use, such as micro applications software (spreadsheet, data base), query languages, word processing, and decision support software.

Perhaps the most important component of an information center is the people who assist users. These people, called **information center specialists**, conduct training sessions, answer questions, and help users to help themselves.

Office Automation Specialists.   Office automation encompasses those computer-based applications generally associated with office work, such as word processing, image processing, and electronic mail (see Chapter 12, "Information Systems in Business and Industry," for details). **Office automation specialists** are being hired to help with the growing demand for automating office activities. These specialists know the operation of the hardware and the use of the software associated with each of the office automation applications. They help users to implement, then make effective use of office systems.

User Liaisons.   In some user groups, the intensity of computer and information processing activity is so heavy that a full-time, "live-in" specialist is needed to coordinate these activities. This person, often called the **user liaison**, serves as the technical interface between the information services department

User liaisons foster improved communication between computer specialists and users. The better the communication, the better the resulting information systems.
(Bethlehem Steel Corporation)

and the user group. Being part of the user group, the user liaison becomes extremely familiar with their information processing problems and needs and is, therefore, in a better position to explain these problems and needs to systems analysts. The user liason coordinates system conversions and is the catalyst for new systems development.

Microcomputer Specialists.   From the popularity of microcomputers has emerged a new career path, sometimes referred to as **microcomputer specialist**. Users do not always have the time to learn the details of using microcomputers and their software. Rather than have each person in an office learn micros and micro software packages (e.g., electronic spreadsheet) inside out, a firm can have a micro specialist help users over the rough spots, as well as develop new systems. In this way, users can focus their attention on applying micros to their immediate information needs rather than on system quirks.

These specialists also keep abreast of the changes in technology, both in general and as these changes relate to their application area. Since microcomputer specialists are continuously attentive to an evolving technology, the departments in which they work are in a better position to take advantage of new innovations in microcomputer hardware and software.

Computerologists
(By permission of Bob Glueckstein)

16-4   OTHER CAREER OPPORTUNITIES: SERVICES, HARDWARE, SOFTWARE, AND EDUCATION _____

In the last two sections our discussion has focused on jobs typically found in an organization's information services department or in a user group. There are also a host of computer specialist career opportunities in organizations that provide computer-related products or services. For ease of discussion, let's divide these organizations into four groups: services, hardware vendors, software vendors, and education. A particular organization may fit into two,

These programmers work for a service bureau and are under contract to an import/export firm. They will work on-site until their current project is completed, then they probably will be assigned to another project at another company. (Dataproducts Corporation)

three, or even all four of these groups. For example, Control Data Corporation markets computers and software, and it provides consulting and education services as well.

Service Vendors

The computer revolution is creating a tremendous demand for computer-related services. In response to this demand, a number of service organizations have emerged. These include *service bureaus*, *facilities management companies*, *turnkey companies*, *consulting firms*, and *computer repair stores*, to mention a few.

Service Bureaus.   Service bureaus provide almost any kind of information processing services. These services include, but are not limited to, developing and implementing information systems, providing computer time (timesharing), and transcribing source data. A service bureau is essentially a public computer center. Therefore, it needs people in most of the traditional computer career specialities.

Service bureau employees who work under contract to develop information systems for a client company are referred to as *contract programmers* and *contract systems analysts*. Some contract programmers and analysts are not associated with a service bureau. They usually work alone or in small groups of two or three. To get contracts, they either solicit their own or work through a broker who provides them with names of potential clients. Drawn by the lure of being one's own boss, the number of contract programmers and analysts working on their own has increased tenfold since the late 1970s.

Facilities Management Companies.   Facilities management companies offer an alternative for firms that would like to have an internal information services department but do not want the responsibility of managing it. If you work for a facilities management company, you would physically move into a client company's computer center and, along with your colleagues, take over all facets of the center's operation.

Turnkey Companies.   A turnkey company contracts with a client to install a complete system, both hardware and software. One of the major selling points of a turnkey company is that the hardware and/or software are installed with minimum personnel involvement from the purchasing company. Rather than purchase the hardware and software separately and install an information system themselves, a company may contract with a turnkey company to handle everything.

Consulting Firms.   Consulting firms provide advice relating to the use of computers and the information resource. Consultants usually have specialized expertise that is otherwise not available to clients.

Computer Repair Stores.   One of the fastest growing service groups is computer repair stores. There weren't very many TV repair shops in 1950, but look at them now. History is repeating itself with micros. Ten years ago, microcomputers were somewhat novel, not to mention expensive. Today they

Computer consultants rely on their specialized expertise to help clients in a variety of areas. These consultants are designing computer work areas that will be aesthetically pleasing while providing comfort and efficiency. (TRW Inc.)

The rapid growth in the number of computers has resulted in the emergence of a new industry— computer repair. Fortunately, computers are much more reliable today. Hourly charges for computer repair are ten times what they were 20 years ago.
(Courtesy of International Business Machines Corporation)

are a common consumer item, and they "get sick" and need repair. Appropriately, one computer repair chain is called the "Computer Doctor."

As a rule, microcomputers are very reliable and seldom need repair. However, a buyer usually has the option to pay for each service or take out a maintenance contract.

Hardware Vendors

Computer Systems Manufacturers.   The most visible hardware vendors are the computer system manufacturers, such as Digital Equipment Corporation (DEC), Apple, IBM, and Hewlett-Packard (HP). Twenty years ago, there were less than a dozen companies manufacturing computer systems. Today there are hundreds. These companies manufacture the processor and usually some or all of the peripheral equipment (disk drives, printers, workstations, and so on).

Manufacturers "burn in" microcomputers for several days before shipment to lower the probability that a system will fail on delivery.
(Cromemco, Inc.)

The competition in the high-technology field of computer hardware is fierce. Manufacturers routinely purchase the competition's processors and peripheral equipment, then disassemble them in search of technological innovations that can be applied to their own product line. This practice has become so widespread that a term was coined to describe it: "reverse engineering."

Leasing Companies.   Most computers are available for purchase or for lease. The monthly charge for leasing a computer system is based roughly on what the monthly payments would be if the computer were purchased over a four-year period. Leasing companies purchase computers, often from manufacturers, then lease them for less than the manufacturer does. A leasing company, referred to as the "third party," makes a profit by keeping its computers under contract for five or more years.

Plug-Compatible Manufacturers.   Plug-compatible manufacturers (PCMs) make peripheral devices that can be attached directly to another manufacturer's computer. A PCM might manufacture disk drives and tape drives that operate, and sometimes look like, those of the original computer system manufacturer. These devices are called "plug-compatible" because a PCM disk drive need only be "plugged" into the computer to become operational.

Original Equipment Manufacturers.   Original equipment manufacturers, or *OEMs*, do not actually manufacture hardware. Therefore, the term "OEM" is somewhat misleading. OEMs typically integrate the hardware and software of several vendors with their own software, then sell the entire package. For example, one OEM integrates one vendor's microcomputer, another's electronic spreadsheet software, and yet another's voice input device to create a system on which spreadsheet applications can be run without a keyboard. Since OEMs "add value" to each component of the system, they are sometimes called value-added dealers.

Computer Stores.   Until the late 1970s, computer systems were sold exclusively in the customer's office. Computer retail outlets, such as Computerland, which opened its doors in 1976, have made it possible for customers to shop for computers in much the same way they would shop for stereo components. Because the price of a computer has been so drastically reduced, computer retail outlets and most department store chains now carry a wide variety of small computer systems, including minicomputers.

A used-computer market has given birth to a growing number of used-computer dealers. It seems as if individuals and companies are always "trading up" to computers with greater processing capabilities. This puts a lot of "pre-owned" computers on the market.

Jobs with Hardware Vendors.   Hardware vendors market and service hardware. To do so, they need *marketing representatives* to sell the products and *systems engineers* to support them once they have been installed. Marketing representatives hold a technical sales position that requires a broad knowledge of the company's products and their capabilities. They normally spend time with customers assessing their information processing needs, then submit proposals for their review. Marketing reps in retail outlets spend little time

Thousands of retail stores specialize in the sale of hardware and software for small computer systems. (Computerland)

VALLEY OF THE CHIP MAKERS

In Silicon Valley, California, jobs are growing twice as fast as the population. Street names like Semiconductor Drive give you a hint as to what this northern California industrial center is all about.

This area, sometimes called a "magnet of creative minds," has spawned many billion-dollar companies from garages and two-room offices.

Silicon Valley is the first major electronics center, but competition is evolving throughout the country. Boston is fast becoming "Silicon Valley East." Newcomers such as the Research Triangle Park in North Carolina and the Austin, Texas area are poised to make a significant impact on the chip industry.

To say that the lifestyles of the chip makers are different is an understatement. They thrive on the element of risk associated with the industry. One product may be the talk of the industry today and obsolete tomorrow. Workers at these high-tech companies share ideas as they share beer at a local pub. The proximity of the companies makes intercompany movement easy. A

The Silicon Valley in California.
(Photo courtesy of Hewlett-Packard Company)

management style of strict dress codes, little flex time, and "do this" and "don't do that" will not work, because the people in this industry have so many other job alternatives. Labor unions, as well, have not penetrated this market. As one manager was quoted as saying, "You're promoted by working smarter, not harder."

with customers and seldom prepare written proposals. A systems engineer has more technical knowledge and is schooled in the details of the company's hardware and software operation. The systems engineer is the technical "expert" and is often called on by customers for advice on technical matters. Behind the scenes, programmers and analysts develop software for the computer systems they sell.

Software Vendors

Companies that produce and market software are called *software vendors* or "software houses." What you buy from a software house is a **software package** for a particular computer-based system or application. The software package contains the software, on a magnetic tape or disk, and its accompanying documentation. The software could be an expert system for archeologists, an authoring system just for poets, a data base management system, or any of thousands of other proprietary software packages. Software vendors copyright proprietary software by registering their creation with the Copyright Office in Washington, D.C.

Copyright software is protected from unlawful duplication and use. When you purchase or lease a software package, you receive a *license agreement*

Several software vendors specialize in developing and marketing computer-aided design software for architects. (Harris Corporation, Computer Systems Division)

to use it. Typically, this agreement limits the use of the software to one computer system at a time. It is a violation of copyright laws to duplicate proprietary software for use on several computer systems unless permission is granted by the vendor in a *site license agreement*. Software prices range from about $30 to hundreds of thousands of dollars.

Organizations and individuals buy software packages for two reasons. First, they do not have to wait for the software for a system to be developed. Second, it is usually less expensive than developing software themselves. The problem with software packages is "what you see is what you get." A package may have too few or too many features for a particular organization. In these cases, the organization has three choices: change whatever it is doing to accommodate the package, modify the package, or develop custom software.

Many stories are told about successful software entrepreneurs who turned an idea into millions of dollars. These opportunities still exist today, and thousands of aspiring entrepreneurs are creating companies and placing their software on the market each year. Some struggle to marginal success and some fail, but a few make it big—real big!

Education

The computer explosion in the last few years has created an insatiable demand for computer-related education. People in the workforce and those preparing to enter it need to be computer literate to be effective in this age of information. In essence, this means that every student and virtually every person in the workforce wants an opportunity to achieve computer literacy. Many of those taking computer-literacy courses are catching the bug and are pursuing advanced computer education in parallel with their chosen fields.

This demand for computer education is taxing the resources of our educational institutions and has given rise to a tremendous demand for *professors*

CW COMMUNICATIONS/INC.: SERVING MORE THAN NINE MILLION COMPUTER-INVOLVED PEOPLE AROUND THE WORLD

In 1967, Pat McGovern started the first newsweekly for the computer community called *Computerworld*. Unlike other computer periodicals at the time, *Computerworld* was weekly instead of monthly and a newspaper instead of a magazine. By covering many things quickly rather than a few things in depth, and by being weekly, it was designed to help those in the computer community keep abreast of a rapidly changing industry.

The idea worked, and today *Computerworld* has become the largest specialized business publication in the United States (as measured by advertising revenue). It has become the flagship publication of CW Communications/Inc., which now publishes nearly five dozen computer-related periodicals in over 25 countries.

People in the computer businesses have taken a fancy to slogan buttons. *Computerworld* has come up with some real winners in its "ridiculous button" contests. How about some of these: "Equal Bytes for Women," "A Rolling Disk Gathers No MOS," "NANO, NANO," "Fiche or Cut Byte," "My Company Is MIS Managed," "IS MS DOS A FEMINIST?" Oh, well, "Disk, too, shall pass."

and *instructors*. The fastest-growing curriculums on most campuses are those in computer science and information systems. But the demand for computer-related education is so great that professors and instructors are being recruited to teach computer applications in a variety of curriculums. Art professors teach computer graphics; physiology professors teach computer instrumentation for ergonomics experiments; sociology professors teach data base concepts as applied to the analysis of demographic trends; and music professors teach synthesized music and the use of the computer as a tool for composition.

Instructors are needed in industry as well. Programmers, analysts, and users are forever facing the announcement of a new technological innovation or the installation of a new system. In-house education is focused on the specific educational needs of the organization. Without instructors to direct

The growing demand for computer-related education has created more job opportunities in education than there are instructors to fill them. The demand for instructors in the computer areas is strong in both colleges and industry. (AT&T Technologies)

this effort, a hundred new workstations may end up as bulky paperweights if people are not trained in how to use them.

The delivery of computer education can take on many forms. Several firms specialize in the development of self-paced instructional videos and CAI courses. Such courses cover everything from computer literacy to advanced data communications. The courses are normally accompanied by a support text and workbooks. Educators that develop these self-paced courses do not have the direct student contact that instructors have, but they need similar skills plus a sensitivity to the challenge of self-paced learning.

If you wish to pursue a career in the field of computer education, you will need a solid educational foundation and several years of field experience.

16-5 CAREER MOBILITY AND COMPUTER KNOWLEDGE

Computer literacy is already a prerequisite to employment in some professions, such as business and engineering. Within a few years, computer literacy may well be a prerequisite for success in most professions. Career mobility is becoming forever intertwined with an individual's current and future knowledge of computers.

Just as advancing technology is creating new jobs, it is changing old ones. Some traditional jobs will change, or even disappear. For example, office automation is radically changing the function and role of secretaries and office managers. With computer-aided design (CAD), draftspersons are learning new ways to do their jobs.

Career advancement, of course, ultimately depends on your abilities, imagination, and performance. Your understanding of computers can only enhance your opportunities. If you cultivate your talents and you aspire to leave your mark on your chosen profession, the sky is the limit.

SUMMARY OUTLINE AND IMPORTANT TERMS

16-1 THE JOB OUTLOOK FOR THOSE WITH COMPUTER KNOWLEDGE. People who can claim computer knowledge on their resumes will have an advantage over those who cannot. This is true in a great many professional disciplines.

Virtually every organization employs or is considering employing computer specialists. More and more of these computer specialist positions are being filled in user groups.

16-2 THE INFORMATION SERVICES DEPARTMENT.   The information services department is the data and information "nerve center" of an organization. Its responsibilities include development, implementation, maintenance, and ongoing operation of information systems;

maintenance of the data base and standards; security of information systems; and serving as internal advisor on computer-related affairs.

The trend toward distributed processing has caused previously centralized information services departments to "distribute" some of their activities to the functional areas.

The career fields in an information services department can be divided into seven groups: management, systems analysis, programming, technical support, data communications, operations, and education.

The number and type of career paths open to someone entering the computer/information systems field is expanding each year. Some of the most visible career paths are **systems analyst**, **programmer** (applications and systems), **programmer/analyst**, **data base administrator**, **data communications specialist**, **computer operator**, **librarian**, **control clerk**, **data entry operator**, and **education coordinator**.

The actual organizational structure of an information services department will vary considerably from one organization to the next. Individuals in smaller companies will normally perform several functions. Large companies have enough people to specialize.

16-3 COMPUTER SPECIALISTS IN THE USER AREAS: INFORMATION CENTERS AND USER LIAISONS. A new breed of computer specialists is emerging in the user areas. **Information center specialists** work in an **information center** and help users to help themselves. **Office automation specialists** help users make effective use of office systems. The **user liaison** serves as the technical interface between the information services department and the user groups. The **microcomputer specialist** stays on top of the latest micro hardware and software technology and helps implement this technology in a user area.

16-4 OTHER CAREER OPPORTUNITIES: SERVICES, HARDWARE, SOFTWARE, AND EDUCATION. There are a host of career opportunities that are not in an information services department or a user group. These opportunities are found with vendors of computer services, hardware, and software and in the area of computer education.

The different types of service organizations include service bureaus, facilities management companies, turnkey companies, consulting firms, and computer repair stores. Hardware vendors include computer systems manufacturers, leasing companies, plug-compatible manufacturers (PCMs), original equipment manufacturers (OEMs), and computer stores. Software vendors produce **software packages** that are leased or sold under a license agreement. The computer explosion has created a tremendous demand for qualified instructors at all levels.

16-5 CAREER MOBILITY AND COMPUTER KNOWLEDGE. Computer literacy is a prerequisite to employment in some professions, and in a few more years it may well be a prerequisite in most professions.

REVIEW EXERCISES

Concepts

1. What type of hardware would be needed in an information center?
2. What is the difference in the job functions of development and maintenance programmers?
3. People of what job function would be involved in the selection and implementation of data PBXs and front-end processors?
4. What type of programmer is usually associated with the technical support group? With the programming group?
5. What is the function of a user liaison?
6. Which job function accounts for all input to and output from a computer center?
7. Name four positions in the operations area.
8. Would every company with an information services department have a data base administrator? Why or why not?
9. Describe the business of OEMs.
10. Contrast the jobs of systems engineer and marketing representative. How do they complement each other?
11. Distinguish between a turnkey company and a facilities management company.

Discussion

12. Of the job functions described in this chapter, which would you prefer? Why?
13. Discuss the advantages of distributed processing from the standpoint of career mobility.
14. Some companies will have only one level of programmer or systems analysts, where other companies will have two, three, and even four levels. Discuss the advantages of having several levels for a particular position (e.g., Programmer I, Programmer II, and so on).
15. Do you feel that programmers and systems analysts should report to the same person, or should they be organized into separate groups? Defend your answer.
16. A company recruits people to become programmer/analysts. All project team members do both programming and analysis. In what ways would this affect the systems development methodology discussed in Chapter 14? Discuss the effects this arrangement would have on career development.
17. Discuss the merit of systems analysts having programming experience.
18. Select five position announcements from the classified ads section of *Computerworld*. Describe what you feel would be appropriate experience and education requirements for each of the positions.

SELF-TEST (by section) _____

16-1. The trend to distributed processing is causing more and more computer specialists to move to the user departments. (T/F)

16-2. The librarian handles most of the training in an information services department. (T/F)

16-3. Office automation specialist is a fancy name for a word processor. (T/F)

16-4. PCM stands for plug-compatible manufacturer. (T/F)

16-5. Computer literacy is not yet a prerequisite for employment in any profession. (T/F)

Self-Test answers.   16–1, T; 16–2, F; 16 3, F; 16–4, T; 16–5, F.

STUDENT LEARNING OBJECTIVES

- To discuss the issue of certification of computer professionals.
- To appreciate the scope and charge of computer-oriented professional societies.
- To explore ethical questions surrounding the use of computers.
- To identify causes of illegal information processing activity.
- To identify possible computer applications of the future.

Computers in Society— Tomorrow

CHAPTER 17

17-1 THE NEW FRONTIER

Computers have created a "new frontier," both in technology and in the way we live our lives. New frontiers possess elements of the unknown that seem to invite exploration and challenge. Perhaps it is the lure of a new frontier that is causing more and more people to make computers an integral part of their daily activities, both at home and at work. Each new innovation and each new product brings about some change in our lives, with a cumulative profound effect on us all.

Are we moving too fast? Should we slow down and step more deliberately into this new frontier? Industry, government, education, and individuals are currently wrestling with these and other tough questions.

Rapid Expansion. The rapid expansion of the computer industry has resulted in uncontrolled and haphazard growth. Researchers and manufacturers have been almost desperate in their attempts to push their technology ahead of the competition's. As a result, even the most basic standards have been ignored until just recently.

This youthful industry is just now beginning to mature. Hardware vendors, software vendors, users, and government are cooperating to set standards on programming languages, data communications, data bases, and so on. We are entering an era of controlled growth in which hardware, software, and data will be more compatible. This compatibility will make it easier for computer systems to "talk" to each other and, therefore, easier for us to obtain information.

Computers and data communications have turned our world into a "global village." This satellite is being launched into geosynchronous orbit above the Atlantic Ocean. It and this earth station will link North America with Europe.

(© M/A-COM, Inc.)

(NASA)

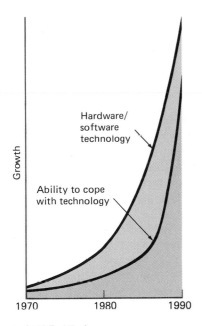

Rapid advances in computer technology have outpaced our ability to apply the full potential of this technology to the needs of society. And the growth of technology is actually accelerating. This experimental silicon wafer contains over 2,000 chips.
(Courtesy of International Business Machines Corporation)

FIGURE 17–1
The Technology Gap

The Technology Gap.   The "technology gap" is a direct result of almost four decades of uncontrolled growth. This gap between *the technology* and *our ability to cope with the technology* is illustrated in Figure 17–1. Hardware and software technology has experienced incredible growth during this period—and the pace of development is quickening. Our ability to cope with this technology and to realize its potential has not kept pace. Because of this technology gap, industry is five to ten years behind in using state-of-the-art technology. For example, technology for the popular automatic teller machines (ATMs) existed almost 15 years ago, yet some banks are only now installing ATM service.

There is strong evidence that the gap is starting to close. Improved management techniques and a more widespread computer awareness are the primary reasons. As the technology gap narrows, organizations will be able to take advantage of all the benefits of a rapidly changing technology. This means even better job opportunities for those who explore this new frontier.

17–2 PROFESSIONALISM AND ETHICS

Licensing and Certification

If your chosen career involves the use of computers, you may be in constant contact with sensitive data and, perhaps, have the power to control events. Accompanying such a job is an implied responsibility to maintain the integrity of the system and its data. Failure to do so could have a disastrous effect on the lives of individuals and on the stability of the organization.

The New Frontier.
(By permission of Bob Glueckstein)

At present, licensing or certification is not a requirement for programmers, operators, or any other computer professional; nor is it required for users of computers. Licensing and certification are hotly debated issues. Many professions require demonstration of performance at a certain level of competence before permission is granted to practice. Through examination, the engineer becomes a registered professional engineer, the attorney becomes a member of the bar, and the accountant becomes a certified public accountant.

Within the computer community, there are several certifications. However, none is a prerequisite to gaining employment. Recruiters may view the holding of certification as favorable, but not a prerequisite to employment. The **Certificate in Data Processing (CDP)** is a general certification in the area of computers and information systems. The **Certificate in Computer Programming (CCP)** is specifically for programmers. The CDP and CCP are administered by the Institute for Certification of Computer Professionals. The **Certified System Professional (CSP)** is a general certification administered by the Association for Systems Management. The **Certified Information Systems Auditor (CISA)** is administered by the EDP Auditor's Association, and the **Certified Data Educator (CDE)** is administered by the Data Education Certification Council. The CDP, CCP, CSP, CISA, and CDE are awarded upon successful completion of an examination.

Professional Societies

Several hundred professional societies have emerged with the information revolution. These societies promote a common bond among professionals with similar interests. This unity of purpose instills a professional attitude among the membership. A few of the more prominent professional societies that are organized primarily for computer specialists include:

- Association for Computing Machinery (ACM)
- Data Processing Management Association (DPMA)
- Society for Information Management (SIM)
- Data Entry Management Association (DEMA)
- Independent Computer Consultants Association (ICCA)
- Association for Systems Managers (ASM)
- Association of Information Systems Professionals (AISP)

The orientation of these societies is implied in their names.

Other professional societies are organized for special-interest groups— those interested in a particular application of the computer. Whatever your chosen profession or special interest, there is probably a computer society for you to join. The following are just a few of several hundred such organizations, and the list is growing each month.

- Association of Rehabilitation Programs in Data Processing (ARPDP)
- Association of Small Computer Users in Education (ASCUE)
- Black Data Processing Associates (BDPA)
- EDP Auditor's Association (EDPAA)
- Health and Beauty Aids Users Society (HABACUS)

Each month professional societies meet to discuss computer-related topics, issues, and trends. At this DPMA meeting, the topic was "The Impact of Artificial Intelligence on Information Systems Development."
(Long and Associates)

- Hospital Information Systems Sharing Group (HISSG)
- Library and Information Technology Association (LITA)
- Life Insurance Systems Association (LISA)
- Society for Computer Applications in Engineering, Planning, and Architecture (CEPA)
- Society for Computer Medicine (SCM)
- Steel Industry Systems Association (SISA)
- Women in Information Processing (WIP)
- Computer Law Association

The American Federation of Information Processing Societies (AFIPS) is an umbrella organization that affords societies with similar goals an opportunity to join forces on certain issues and activities.

The Question of Ethics

One of the largest professional societies adopted a code of ethics over 15 years ago. The code warns members that they can be expelled or censured if they violate the code. However, to date, not one of the society's tens of thousands of members has been expelled or censured for violating the code. Other professional societies publish a code of ethics as well, and they, also, rarely or never take action against delinquent members. Does this mean that there are no violations? Of course not. A carefully drafted code of ethics provides some guidelines for conduct, but professional societies cannot be expected to police the misdoings of their membership. In many instances, a code violation is also a violation of the law.

A code of ethics provides direction for computer professionals and users so that they act responsibly in their application of computer technology. The following code of ethics is in keeping with the spirit of those encouraged by computer societies.

1. Maintain the highest standard of professional behavior.
2. Avoid situations which create a conflict of interest.
3. Do not violate the confidentiality of your employer or those that you service.

It is more the rule than the exception that a computer professional will have ready access to a broad range of sensitive information, both personal and corporate. Because of the potential for the abuse of this information, some professional societies have adopted a code of ethics.
(Phillips Petroleum Company)

4. Continue to learn so that your knowledge level keeps pace with the technology.
5. Use information judiciously and maintain system integrity at all times.
6. Do not violate the rights or privacy of others.
7. Accomplish each task to the best of your ability.
8. Do not break the law.

If you follow this eight-point code, it is unlikely that anyone will question your ethics. Nevertheless, well-meaning people routinely violate this simple code because they are unaware of the tremendous detrimental impact of their actions. With the speed and power of computers, a minor code infraction can be easily magnified to a costly catastrophe. For this reason, computers are raising new questions on ethics. The three case studies that follow illustrate the ethical overtones surrounding the application of computer technology.

Case 1.   Let's take as an example the case of computerized dialers. A computerized dialing system automatically dials a telephone number, then plays a prerecorded message. Telephone numbers are entered into the system, then dialed one after another. If there is no answer, the number is redialed at a later time. Such systems are used for "telemarketing" a variety of products, not to mention politicians and ideologies. Is this an invasion of an individual's privacy?

Consider the company that, for a fee, will use its computerized dialing system to do telemarketing for local merchants. The system contains every telephone number in the city telephone directory. A message announcing a sale, a new service, or whatever is recorded for each client. Each day the system is activated and the "computer" makes calls from 8 A.M. to 10 P.M.

Is this application an ethical use of computers, or is it an invasion of privacy and an abuse of another person's time? During the course of a single day, the system can interrupt the lives of thousands of people. How many of us would welcome the opportunity to listen to a prerecorded commercial when we answer the phone? Is telemarketing in violation of the above code of ethics? How about item 6?

There are, of course, legitimate uses of computerized dialing systems. For example, the IRS uses them to notify delinquent taxpayers; school districts use them to notify parents of truant children; and retailers alert customers that they can pick up the items they ordered.

Case 2.   The vice-president of a sporting goods chain purchased a $500 electronic spreadsheet software package. The purchase agreement permits the use of the software on any micro at the office or at his home. However, the purchase agreement strictly prohibits the reproduction of this copyright software for purposes other than backup. After a week of transporting the software back and forth between his office and home, he decided to make an extra copy so that he would have one for home and one for the office. The VP knew that this act was in violation of the purchase agreement, but he rationalized his actions because he would be the only person to use the software.

Just as office workers of 50 years ago would never have dreamed of electronic mail or fingertip access to billions of characters, it is difficult for us to imagine what the future holds and how new technological innovations will impact society. (Honeywell, Inc.)

Copyright laws protect literature, music, software, and the design of a silicon chip. A sophisticated circuit design, such as the one in the photo, may be the result of a multimillion dollar research effort. (Sperry Corporation)

The VP copied the software as a matter of personal convenience. After all, he could have continued transporting the software between home and work. Did he violate the above code of ethics? What about items 1 and 8?

Case 3.   Members of the United States Congress have franking privileges, or free mail. Before computers, most letters were sent in response to constituent inquiries. Computers and high-speed printers have made it possible to crank out 30,000 "individualized" letters per hour. Some congresspersons have been known to send out millions of letters a year.

Is this massive amount of correspondence an attempt to better inform the constituents, or is it politically motivated and an abuse of the power of the computer? Is this application a violation of the above code of ethics? How about items 2 and 5?

17-3 COMPUTERS AND THE LAW _____

We try to develop systems and use the computer within the limits of any applicable law. Unfortunately, the laws are not always clear, because many legal questions involving computers and information processing are being debated for the first time. To no one's surprise, computer law is the fastest-growing type of law practice.

Laws governing computer and information processing are few, and those that do exist are subject to a variety of interpretations. A few federal laws are in force and most of the states have adopted laws, but these are only the skeleton of what is needed to direct an orderly and controlled growth of automation. Only now are lawmakers beginning to recognize the impact of computers, and legislation is slow in coming. Critics have faulted as the bottleneck our lawmakers' reluctance to become computer literate.

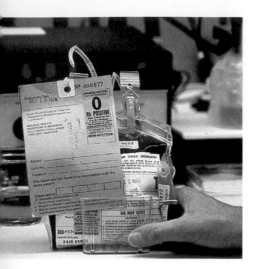

The inventory for most hospital blood banks is maintained on a computer. By mislabelling a quart of blood, a negligent employee could cause the wrong type blood to be administered to a patient. Negligence, one of the two kinds of illegal processing activity, is usually a result of poor input/output control. (Courtesy of International Business Machines Corporation)

Negligence.   The two main causes of illegal information processing activity are negligence and fraud. Let's look at negligence first. *Negligence* causes someone external to the organization to be unnecessarily inconvenienced and is usually a result of poor input/output control. For example, a woman who was essentially communicating with a computer was continually sent dunning notices and visited by collection agencies for not making payments on an automobile. This was after she had completed payment in full. Although the company's records and procedures were in error, the company forcibly repossessed the automobile without thoroughly checking their procedures and the legal implications. The woman had to sue the company for the return of her bought-and-paid-for automobile. The court ordered the automobile returned and the company to pay her a substantial sum as a penalty.

This is a clear case of a misinterpretation of a computer maxim—GIGO (garbage in, garbage out). GIGO does *not* stand for "garbage in, gospel out." Some people take the accuracy of computer output for granted. The company blamed the incident on a mistake by the computer. The court stated that *people* enter data and interpret output and that the people affected should be treated differently than punched cards. *Trust in the infallibility of a computer does not constitute a defense in a court of law*. This incident points out the importance of careful system design and exhaustive testing.

Fraud.   The other area of illegal information processing activity is a premeditated or conscious effort to defraud the system. Remember the bank programmers in Chapter 13 who created an unauthorized savings account into which they placed thousands of "extra" pennies each day. This is an example of *fraud*. Any illegal entry into a computer system for the purpose of personal gain is considered fraud. Over 50% of all computer frauds are internal; that is, they are committed by employees of the organization that is being defrauded. About 30% of those defrauding employees are computer specialists who work in an information services department.

Privacy.   More media and legislative attention has been attracted to the issue of an individual's privacy than to negligence or fraud. The individual must be afforded certain rights regarding the privacy of data or of information relating to him or her. However, these rights have yet to be uniformly defined by our lawmakers. In the absence of legislative guidelines, the following principles are offered for consideration and discussion.

1. People should be made aware that data are being collected about them and aware of how these data are to be used.
2. A person should be permitted to inspect his or her personal data and information.
3. A person should be permitted to supplement or clarify personal data and information.
4. Data and information found erroneous or irrelevant must be removed.
5. Disclosure of personal information should be limited to those with a need to know.
6. A log should be maintained of all persons inspecting any individual's personal information.

SUPERCHIPS ARE CHOCK-FULL OF CHIPS

The concept of a "computer on a chip" is changing every day. The superchip revolution is just part of the push toward mastery of wafer technology. In superchips, scientists are attempting to produce a wafer-sized chip that will hold all the memory and logic they need for a particular processing task. This would eliminate many of the problems associated with the production and integration of silicon chips (e.g., cutting wafers into chips, connecting them together).

When the chips are individually connected, it takes time for electrical signals to travel along the lengths of wire that connect the chips. Computer designers talk in terms of nanoseconds and picoseconds, so speed is a major factor in the development of computer systems. To increase the speed of operation, designers are using lasers to etch the circuitry over the entire silicon wafer, thus creating the superchip.

Superchips, however, do have their problems. One is that the circuitry over the entire wafer must be tested and work properly. This is the equivalent of saying that there can be no defective chips in a wafer. In practice, this is seldom the case. The future of the superchip is very much dependent on the prospect of defect-free production.

With the current chip technology, the equivalent of a superchip is hundreds of chips con-

Superchips.
(General Electric Company)

nected together on circuit boards that would take up many times the space of a superchip. Superchips are, perhaps, the next step in the microminiaturization of electronic circuitry. Within a few years, computers as powerful as today's desk-size mainframe computers will be about the size of a hand calculator.

7. Adequate safeguards must be in place to ensure the security of personal data and information (e.g., locked doors, passwords).

17-4 COMPUTER APPLICATIONS OF THE FUTURE _____

It seems as if the computer is everywhere—yet, in reality, we are only scratching the surface of possible computer applications. The outlook for innovative, exciting, and beneficial computer applications is bright—very bright indeed.

Expectations and Reality

The short-term expectations that the general public have for computer technology are probably excessive. Intense media coverage has given the computer novice the impression that bed-making, dish-washing domestic robots are

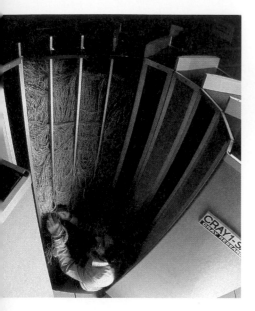

This is one of the largest and fastest computers in the world, but it is still not powerful enough to simulate an airplane in flight. It can simulate a wing or a fuselage, but not the entire aircraft. Of course, aerospace engineers want it all. Their expectations are representative of people in other professions who already have plans for computers that are not even developed.
(Chevron Corporation)

just around the corner; that computer-controlled organ transplants are almost perfected; and that computers have all the answers! To be sure, we are making progress in leaps and bounds, but we have a long way to go before such applications are feasible. Nevertheless, these rising expectations are a challenge to computer professionals to deliver.

Of course, no one can see into the future, but we can extrapolate from trends and our knowledge of current research. This section paints a futuristic picture of some computer applications that are sociologically, economically, and technologically feasible within the next decade.

Videotext

As the percentage of homes with micros increases, so does the potential for **videotext** applications. Videotext systems, a number of which exist today, provide certain services to an end user through a communications link to a workstation. The workstation is normally a microcomputer or a television/microcomputer combination. The two-way system provides the end user with information (e.g., airline flight schedules) and permits the end user to enter data (e.g., reservations for airline flights).

The four components of a videotext system are the central computer, the data base, the network, and the workstations. The central computer system controls all interaction with the videotext system and the data base. The data base contains data and screens of information (e.g., perhaps a graphic display of a refrigerator with price and delivery information) that are presented to videotext users. The transmission media in the network can be the telephone system, two-way cable TV, or any of a variety of digital data transmission media (see Chapter 9, "Data Communications"). As workstations and microcomputers proliferate, a greater variety of videotext systems will be made available to more and more people. Even now, workstations are available in many airplanes and hotel rooms.

These engineers are creating a new "page" of information for a videotext system. The screens, such as the one showing a baseball score, become part of a videotext data base that can be accessed by those who subscribe to an information service.
(RCA)

Hotel guests can communicate with their homes, companies, or virtually anyone else through the use of computers in their rooms. They can obtain theater or airline tickets, shop or order gifts, scan restaurant menus, and even play video games. In a few years, all major hotels will provide videotext service to their guests.

Videotext has an endless number of applications. For example, let's take real estate. Suppose you live in Tuscon, Arizona, and have been transferred to Salt Lake City, Utah. It is only a matter of time before you will be able to gain access to a videotext system that has a national listing of homes for sale. Here is how it will work. You will enter your purchase criteria: Salt Lake City, Utah: $80,000 to $100,000; no more than 1 mile from an elementary school; double garage; and so on. The system will then present pictures and specifications of those homes that meet your criteria.

Retail and entertainment videotext applications are discussed later in this section.

Communications

The telephone as we know it will probably disappear. In the relatively near future, the function of the telephone will be incorporated into our home computers and workstations so that we can not only hear, but see the person on the other end of the line. Moreover, we will be able to pass data and information back and forth as if we were sitting at the same table. We'll be able to operate home appliances, such as answer machines and video recorders, and control environmental conditions, such as temperature and lighting, from remote workstations.

Currently, voice and data are transmitted as both analog and digital signals (see Chapter 9, "Data Communications"). In the future, all communication will be digital, including television. A digital television signal will provide TVs with greater versatility. Our televisions will function much like computer workstations. The display screen will be larger, and each TV will have a keyboard for two-way communication. If you so desire, you can split the screen and watch two, or even three, programs at once. You can continue to watch a program and request that the stock reports be subtitled across the screen. During a news program, newscasters can sample the thinking of tens of thousands of people in a matter of minutes. As they ask the questions, we at home respond on our keyboard. Our responses are immediately sent to a central computer for analysis. The results can be reported almost immediately. In this way, television news programs will keep us abreast of public opinion on critical issues and the feeling toward political candidates on a day-to-day basis.

In the Office

The traditional letter may never become obsolete, but electronic mail will become an increasingly popular alternative, especially since most of us will have our own workstations, both at home and at work. To prepare and send a letter, an executive will dictate, not to a secretary, but to a computer! The executive's words will be transcribed directly into text, without key entry.

The use of voice recognition systems is gaining in popularity, especially in information retrieval environments where "no hands" computer control is useful or required. This system interprets and enters a spoken word to the system in less than one-third of a second.
(Texas Instruments, Inc.)

THE AUTOMATED OFFICE (ACT 1, SCENE 1)

Characters: Sandy Stone, Madison Avenue advertising executive, Lynn Melrose, administrative assistant
Time: A Monday morning in late April
Setting: An office in Manhattan
Sandy: (enters stage left) Good morning Lynn, did you have a nice weekend?
Lynn: (gleefully) Very nice, thank you.
Sandy: Have you finished that report for the ZIMCO account? I'd like to make a few quick changes.
Lynn: Yes . . . I'll call it up on your workstation.
Sandy: I'll make those changes and route it via electronic mail to ZIMCO headquarters.

I see the ad piece is ready for ZIMCO's approval. (enthusiastically) That new presentation graphics equipment has certainly improved the quality of work coming out of the Art Department. Would you send ZIMCO a facsimile copy for approval? We have a noon deadline to meet!

Also Lynn, would you set up an emergency teleconference meeting with my counterparts in Chicago, Houston, and L.A.?
Lynn: (confidently) Consider it done. Each of them will have the message in their electronic mailboxes in a couple of minutes.
Sandy: We'll also need to put a notice on the computer bulletin board about the availability of that new position in market research.

Don't let me forget to sit down this afternoon and run statistical summaries on the BURPO research data. Using our on-line stat package, it shouldn't take more than a few minutes. (sotto voce) I used to spend all day on these summaries.

(leans back in the chair reflectively) You know Lynn, our automated office has sure made life a lot easier.
Lynn: (secure in the fact that the day won't be all memos, calling, adding figures, and paper shuffling) I couldn't agree more.
Sandy: Oh, by the way Lynn, I won't be in the office tomorrow. I'm going to telecommute and finish the BURPO report.
(both take a seat at their workstations)

CURTAIN

The letter will then be routed to appropriate destinations via electronic mail. The recipient of the letter can request that it be displayed at a workstation or read, using synthesized speech.

With professionals spending a greater percentage of their working day interacting with the computer, look for the "electronic cottage" concept to gain momentum. At least a part of the work of most professionals will be done at home. For many professionals, their work is at their fingertips, whether at home or the office.

A Peek at the Crystal Ball: Business, Government, Health Care, and Education

Manufacturing.   In the face of growing competition from international markets, manufacturing companies, especially those that are labor intensive, are being confronted with three choices: "automate, migrate, or evaporate." They can *automate*, thereby lowering cost and increasing productivity. They can *migrate* (move) to countries that offer less expensive labor. Or they can *evaporate*. Most have elected to automate, even with the blessing of organized labor. As one labor leader put it, "If we don't do it, I'm convinced we'll lose the jobs anyway."

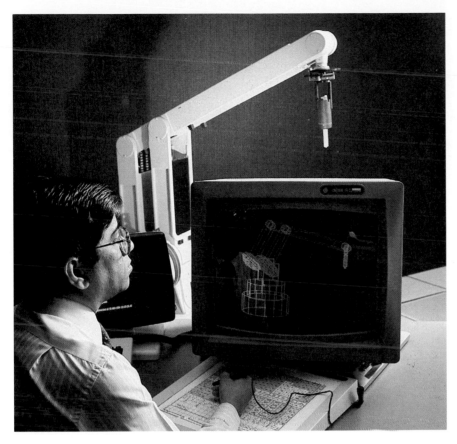

Computer-controlled industrial robots can do certain tasks at less cost than assembly line workers. This engineer is using a robotics simulation software package to put a robot through its paces on a computer screen, rather than through "trial and error" on the factory floor.
(General Electric Company)

With the trend to greater use of automation, we can anticipate an increase in the number of industrial robots (see Chapter 5). As the smokestack industries become more "high tech," the complexion of their workforces will change. There will be a shift of emphasis from brawn to brains. A few unmanned plants already exist: this number will grow. These radical changes are a by-product of our transition from an industrial society to an information society. Traditional jobs will change or be lost forever, but new, and hopefully more challenging, jobs will emerge to replace them.

Retail. Videotext will enable us to do our shopping electronically. Instead of walking through the aisles of a grocery store or thumbing through stacks of shirts, we will be able to use our personal computer and videotext information to select and purchase almost any retail item. The items selected will be automatically picked, packaged, and, possibly, delivered to our doorstep. Videotext will help speed the completion of routine activities, such as grocery shopping, leaving us more time for leisure, travel, and the things we enjoy.

Financial Services. The overwhelming acceptance of automatic teller machines has fueled the trend to more electronic funds transfer (EFT). Over the next decade, transaction documents, such as checks and credit card purchase slips, will begin to disappear. Monies will be electronically transferred at the time of the purchase from the seller's account to the buyer's account.

You can use your personal computer and an information service to send electronic mail or even flowers. To send flowers, you would make a selection from available arrangements, enter the name and address of the receiving party, and enter your credit card number. Your request is routed, via data communications, to the nearest participating florist.
(Texas Instruments, Inc.)

Computer technology is providing new alternatives for the distribution of the "printed" word. This optical laser disk contains the entire set of the *Encyclopaedia Britannica,* and a lot more. Some day soon, library patrons will use one of the patron workstations to look up words in a dictionary and to "thumb through" readers guides and other reference books.
(3M)

Total EFT will require an enormously complex communications network that links the computers of all financial institutions with virtually all businesses. Such a network is technologically and economically feasible today, but sociologically we are a few years away.

Publishing.   Certainly books, magazines, newspapers, and the "printed word," in general, will prevail for casual reading and study. However, it is not unreasonable to expect that publishers will offer *soft-copy* publishing as an alternative to *hard-copy* publishing. We'll be able to receive books, magazines, and newspapers in electronic format, perhaps via data communications on our home computers or on a disk. A few specialized computer trade magazines are available now on disks, but in a few years a wide variety of magazines will be distributed via data communications or disks.

Can you imagine a book store without any books? It's possible! With customized printing on demand, you will be able to browse through virtually any current book from a workstation; then, if you wish to purchase the book, it will be printed and bound while you wait!

Transportation.   Someday soon, computer-based automobile navigation systems will be standard equipment on cars. There are already enough satellites in the sky for an on-board automobile navigation system to obtain a fix. A fix establishes the location of the car. The car's location will be noted on a video display of a road map. You will be able to call up appropriate regional or city maps from an on-board optical laser disk storage, and you will even be able to plot your course and track progress.

By now you are probably saying that this Buck-Rogers-type application is a bit far fetched. Well, prototypes of automobile navigation systems are now being tested—and they work!

Entertainment.   How about videotext and soap operas? Yes, through interactive videotext, you will be an active participant in how a story unfolds. The soaps will be shot so they can be pieced together in a variety of ways. Imagine, you can decide whether Michelle marries Clifton or Patrick!

It won't be long before the rough drafts for television series scripts are written by computers. Many of the weekly television shows have a formula plot. For instance, heroes are presented with a problem situation, they confront the problem, they get in trouble, they get out of trouble, stick the bad guys, and live to do it again next week. Formula plots lend themselves nicely to computer-produced rough-draft scripts. The computer system will already have the names of the key characters on file. The systems will also have dialogues for a variety of situations. The names of nonregulars (e.g., the bad guys) are randomly generated by the computer. The script writers enter a story-line sketch, then the computer pieces together dialogues and scenes within the restrictions of the show's formula plot and the story line. The script writers then refine the draft script.

The Arts.   Computer art has added another dimension to the pictorial art form. Most current computer art is static, but a growing number of artists are creating dynamic computer art. That is, the artist creates a continuously changing image. This type of computer art is usually recorded on video tape for presentation.

A computer artist uses subtle shades of blue to blend the sea and sky with the setting sun.
(Genigraphics Corporation)

The original photo of the San Francisco skyline is of poor quality. It was digitized and computer-enhanced by a feature known as "constrast stretching" to produce a much more vivid photo.
(Photo courtesy of Comtal/3M)

Sculptors may someday become more productive with the aid of computers. For example, a sculptor can create three-dimensional "sketches" on a computer, similar to the way an engineer designs a part using computer-aided design (CAD). The computer activates a robotlike sculpting tool that roughs-out the general shape of the figure. The sculptor then adds the creative touches that make a piece of clay a work of art.

Government.   Computer-enhanced photography will enable us to break out the finer details in photographs. Its immediate application is in the area of military intelligence; with computer-enhanced photography, the headlines in a newspaper can be read from a photograph taken 150 miles above the earth.

Local, state, and federal elections might not require an army of volunteers. Politicians might not have to worry about rain on Election Day. We will eventually record our votes from home or business workstations. Such a system will encourage greater voter participation. Of course, security and voter authenticity will be a concern. One possible solution would be to ask voters to identify themselves with their social security number and a voter registration security code that is known only to the voter. A few years later we won't need to carry cards or remember numbers; each voter's identity will be validated when the system reads our fingerprints and our voiceprint.

The IRS will tighten up on tax cheaters by feeding taxpayer lifestyle data into sophisticated models. Descriptive data, such as neighborhood and automobile type, will be used to predict whether people are underpaying taxes.

Health Care.   Expert systems have already benefitted physicians by helping them diagnose physical illnesses (see Chapter 13, "Information Systems in Government, Health, and Education"). In the near future we can anticipate

Until only recently most medical applications of computer technology were administrative in nature. This physician is requesting a second opinion from an expert system. Expert systems and other computer-based medical innovations are rapidly changing the manner and quality of health care delivery.
(Copyright 1984 GTE Telenet Communications Corporation)

expert systems that help diagnose and treat mental illnesses and emotional problems as well. Psychologists and psychiatrists will continue to work with patients in the classical manner, but with the added advantage of a "partner." This "partner" can tap a vast storehouse of knowledge and recommend everything from lines of questioning to diagnosis and treatment.

The handicapped can look forward to improved mobility and independence. Sophisticated prostheses can be activated by voice, motion, muscle activity, breathing, and even blinking of the eyes. Research is under way that may enable paraplegics to walk by substituting a computer for a nervous system that has ceased to function.

Medical and technical researchers have dared to contemplate the integration of computers with the brain. That is, we will electrically connect tiny computer implants to the brain for the purpose of enhancing the brain's computational and factual-recall capabilities.

Education. Computer systems are revolutionizing the education process. For example, as students learn via computer-assisted instruction (CAI), they can request visual reinforcement from hundreds of still and moving pictures that are stored on optical laser disks. There is truth to the old saying that "one picture is worth a thousand words."

Computers are beginning to play a more active role in the education of learning-disabled children. Current human-resource limitations do not permit the luxury of constant one-on-one attention for these children. However, in between group and one-on-one sessions, a computer system that is capable of responding to a wide variety of inputs can be dedicated to each child. For example, computers complement the kinesthetic (touch and feel) approach to dyslexia (impaired reading ability). Children with dyslexia can engage in interactive reading that offers immediate feedback and reinforcement. At present, we are only beginning to tap the computer as an educational tool.

Computers have the potential to enable nationwide uniform testing for elementary and secondary students. With uniform learning standards for each subject at each level, it will be possible to advance students from one grade to the next on the basis of achievement rather than age.

Artificial Intelligence

We have artificial sweeteners, artificial grass, artificial flowers—why not artificial intelligence? In Chapter 1, "The World of Computers," artificial intelligence (AI) is defined as an expansion of the capabilities of computers to include the ability to reason, to learn, to strive for self-improvement, and to simulate human sensory capabilities. Chapter 1 focuses on state-of-the-art applications of artificial intelligence, but what does the future hold for AI?

Today's computers can produce reams of paper, perform billions of calculations, and control the flow of thousands of messages, but, at the day's end, they know no more than they did at its start. Much of the research in the area of artificial intelligence is aimed at giving computers the ability to emulate human reasoning and, therefore, learn. Now computer "knowledge" is derived from human knowledge. Perhaps, in the future, computers will learn and contribute to their own knowledge base.

Richard Greenblatt, co-founder of LISP Machine Inc., and a colleague are discussing a programming problem. These developers of artificial intelligence applications write programs that deal more with symbols than with bits, bytes, or data elements, because humans think in terms of symbols. For example, when you look for your friend in a classroom, you don't rely on a rigid decision process that entails close examination of characteristics like gender, hair color, and so on. You see your friend in a more general manner. AI systems deal with objects and symbols, just like people do.
(LISP Machine Inc.)

Researchers in artificial intelligence hold out great promise for tomorrow's expert systems, one of several areas of AI research. Crude, but effective, expert systems (see Chapter 1) are now being commercialized for medical diagnosis, oil exploration, and several other areas. An expert system is a knowledge-based system to which preset rules are applied to solve a particular problem, such as determining a patient's illness. Present expert systems are based primarily on factual knowledge—a definite strength of computers. We humans, though, solve problems by combining factual knowledge with our strength—*heuristic knowledge*—that is, intuition, judgment, and inferences.

The really tough decisions involve both factual *and* heuristic knowledge. For this reason, researchers are working to improve the computer's ability to gather and use heuristic knowledge. This formidable technological hurdle stands in the way of humanlike expert systems. However, this hurdle will eventually be cleared, and expert systems will abound for virtually every profession. Attorneys will have mock trials with expert systems to "pre-try" their cases. Doctors will routinely ask a "second opinion." Architects will "discuss" the structural design of a building with an expert system. Military officers can "talk" with the "expert" to plan battlefield strategy. City planners will "ask" an expert system to suggest optimal locations for recreational facilities.

AI research is continually enhancing the abilities of computers to simulate human sensory capabilities. In the not-too-distant future, we will be able to have meaningful verbal conversations with computers. These computers will be able to talk, listen, and even smell the roses!

HISTORY IS MADE: PARAPLEGIC WALKS WITH COMPUTER ASSISTANCE

In the 1700s, Luigi Galvani experimented with electrical current and its ability to make muscles contract. Some 200 years later, that same principle has reached a state of development that even Galvani might not have foreseen: A person with totally paralyzed legs has walked under her own muscle power for the first time, using a computerized electrical stimulation-feedback system.

Following an automobile accident on her high school graduation night, Nan Davis was paralyzed from the waist down. She walked for the first time in four years with the assistance of a small computer, a safety harness, her determination, and the dedicated work of Dr. Jerrold Petrofsky. Petrofsky is the executive director of Wright State University's National Center for Rehabilitation Engineering.

Five years after her accident, she walked outside the laboratory setting to receive her diploma from Wright State University—and she did it on her own two feet, with a small, portable computer, without the aid of a safety harness, and on the arm of Dr. Petrofsky and an assistant.

With the present system, Davis is able to not only stand and walk forward as she did with her first walk, but she can walk backward and sit down as well. The system uses a sensory feedback system that tells the computer the position and movement of the legs, so the computer knows which muscles to electrically stimulate next to achieve coordinated movement.

Eventually, if the experiments go as planned, she may one day walk with considerably less visible assistance. Tiny microprocessors will be implanted under her skin near the paralyzed muscles, doing the work of the surface elec-

With a little computer assistance, paraplegic Nan Davis, shown with Dr. Jerrold Petrofsky, can walk.
(Wright State University, Dayton, Ohio)

trodes and assisted by the sensors and a computer the size of a calculator. These potentially could give her the ability not only to walk forward and backward, sit, and stand, but also to climb stairs.

"While it will be a long time until this system will be on the market," says Petrofsky, "the knowledge of what is happening here will give people hope. What we are working toward is the possibility that someday, a large number of people will stand up and move again."

Source: Courtesy of Wright State University, Dayton, Ohio.

17-5   YOUR CHALLENGE

Having mastered the contents of this book and this course, you are now poised to exploit the benefits of the computer in your personal and business lives. You should also have an appreciation of the scope and impact of computers on society, both now and in the future. This course, however, is only the beginning. The computer learning process is ongoing. The dynamics of a rapidly advancing computer technology demands a constant updating of skills and expertise. Perhaps the excitement of technological innovation and ever-changing opportunities for application is part of the lure of computers.

By their very nature, computers bring about change. With the total amount of computing capacity in the world doubling every two years, we can expect even more dramatic change in the future. The cumulative effects of these changes are altering the basic constructs of society and the way we live, work, and play. Workstations have replaced calculators and ledger books; electronic mail speeds communication; word processing has almost eliminated typewriters; computer-aided design has rendered the T-square and compass obsolete; computer-assisted instruction has become a part of the teaching process; EFT may eventually eliminate the need for money; videotext systems are affecting shopping habits . . . and the list goes on.

We as a society are, in effect, trading a certain level of computer dependence for an improvement in the quality of life. This improvement in the way we live is not a foregone conclusion. It is our challenge to harness the power of the computer and direct it toward the benefit of society. To be an active participant in this age of information, we as a society and as individuals must continue to learn about and understand computers.

Never before has such opportunity presented itself so vividly. This generation, *your generation*, has the technological foundation and capability to change dreams to reality.

SUMMARY AND IMPORTANT TERMS

17–1 THE NEW FRONTIER. Computers have created a "new frontier," both in technology and in the way we live our lives. The rapid growth of computer technology and the use of computers has resulted in a somewhat uncontrolled and haphazard growth. The technology gap, which is the gap between the technology and our ability to cope with the technology, is beginning to close.

17–2 PROFESSIONALISM AND ETHICS. People whose jobs put them in contact with sensitive data can actually control events. This puts even greater pressure on these people and their peers to conduct themselves as professionals. Certification programs, such as the **CDP**, **CCP**, **CSP**, **CISA**, and **CDE**, and professional societies help encourage professionalism.

A code of ethics provides direction for computer professionals and users so that they act responsibly in their application of computer technology.

17–3 COMPUTERS AND THE LAW. An information system should be developed to comply with any applicable law. At present, the laws that govern the privacy of personal data and illegal computer-based activity are inadequate, but these laws are being revised and expanded. Therefore, privacy of data and the possibility of fraud or negligence should be a consideration in the design of every information system.

Albert Einstein said, "Imagination is more important than knowledge, for knowledge is limited while imagination embraces the entire world." You now have a base of computer knowledge. With a computer and a little imagination, you can be very creative.
(Courtesy of Apple Computer, Inc.)

17-4   COMPUTER APPLICATIONS OF THE FUTURE.   The number and variety of computer applications is expected to grow rapidly in the coming years. In the near future, we can anticipate more **videotext** systems, telephones integrated into workstations, the widespread acceptance and use of electronic mail, unmanned manufacturing facilities, electronic shopping, less use of cash, soft-copy publishing, automobile navigation systems, create-your-own-story soaps on television, robot sculptors, computer-controlled artificial limbs, and expert systems that help us with business and domestic decisions.

17-5   YOUR CHALLENGE.   The computer offers us the opportunity to improve the quality of our lives. It is our challenge to harness the power of the computer and direct it to the benefit of society.

REVIEW EXERCISES

Concepts

1. Briefly describe two uses for expert systems.
2. What are the unabbreviated names for the following societies: SIM, DPMA, and EDPAA?
3. What are the uses of a computerized dialing system?
4. Contrast the illegal information processing activities of negligence and fraud.
5. What are some of the problems that must be overcome to improve computer-simulated speech? Computer-simulated sight?
6. Based on your knowledge of the capabilities of computers, now and in the future, speculate on at least three futuristic applications that we can expect within the next five years.
7. Briefly describe a videotext application in the retail industry.

Discussion

8. Why is EFT a controversial issue?
9. Relatively few computer professionals have any kind of certification. Is it really necessary?
10. Why do some more senior managers tend to view unfavorably young people who have computer knowledge?
11. "Automate, migrate, or evaporate." Discuss this statement from the points of view of manufacturing management and of labor.
12. During the implementation of computer applications, managers have traditionally focused on hardware and software. Now they realize that they must pay more attention to the human needs as well. What are these needs?
13. Discuss possible futuristic applications of computers in health care.

14. What specific steps should be taken by the business and computer community to close the "technology gap"?

15. Why do you suppose our laws governing computers and information processing are inadequate?

16. Compare your perspective on computers today with what it was four months ago. How have your feelings and attitudes changed?

SELF-TEST (by section)

17-1 (a) The gap between the technology and our ability to cope with the technology is expanding. (T/F)

    (b) ATMs became technologically feasible about 1980. (T/F)

17-2 (a) _____ is the umbrella organization for computer-oriented societies.

    (b) Professional societies are not legally obligated to expel members for code-of-ethics infractions. (T/F)

17-3 (a) Trust in the infallibility of a computer does not constitute a defense in a court of law. (T/F)

    (b) Computerized dialers are an unethical application of computer technology. (T/F)

17-4 (a) The use of electronic mail is on the rise. (T/F)

    (b) The magazine-on-a-disk has been discussed but is beyond the state of the art. (T/F)

17-5 (a) CAD has rendered the T-square obsolete. (T/F)

    (b) The total computing capacity in the world is increasing at slightly less than 25% per year. (T/F)

Self-Test answers. 17-1(a), F; (b), F; 17-2(a), AFIPS; (b), T; 17-3(a), T; (b), F; 17-4(a), T; (b), F; 17-5(a), T; (b), F.

INTEGRATED
MICROCOMPUTER
SOFTWARE

INTEGRATED MICROCOMPUTER SOFTWARE

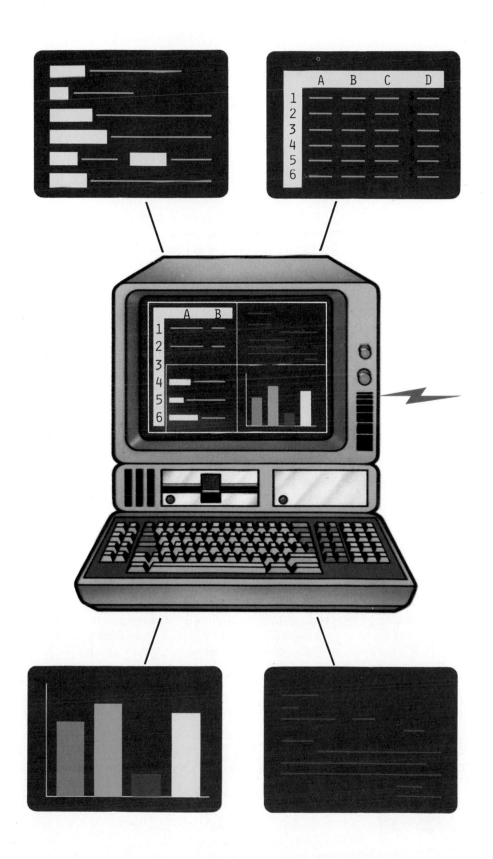

S-1 INTEGRATED MICRO SOFTWARE: A "WINDOW" TO INFORMATION

Picture a large sheet of paper as big as a desktop. On this paper are horizontal and vertical lines that make up thousands of small rectangles in which you can enter data. Now, imagine this large sheet of paper as an electronic **worksheet** in a computer system. This electronic worksheet is the basis for **integrated microcomputer software**, the subject addressed in this special section of the book. In contrast to software that is designed for a *specific* application, integrated microcomputer software is *general-purpose* software and provides the framework for a great number of business and "personal" applications.

In effect, integrated micro software, or simply **integrated software**, permits us to work as we always have—on several projects at a time—but with the assistance of a computer. For example, a professor might create an electronic worksheet in which to handle grades and other related administrative duties. In one corner of the worksheet, a grade-book-like grid could be set up that lists student names in a column and items to be graded as labels for adjacent columns. The grid is completed as grades are awarded throughout the term. In another corner of the worksheet the professor might do the same for another class. At the end of the semester the professor computes and plots the term average for each student, thereby creating a bar chart in another corner of the worksheet. In still another area of the worksheet, the professor might write a memo recommending the top students for special recognition. Another area might contain personal "things-to-do" notes.

A Family of Programs

The term integrated software refers to the *integration* of the following five *software* components.

- **Data Management.** The data management component permits users to create and maintain a data base and to extract information from the data base.

- **Electronic Spreadsheet.** The electronic spreadsheet component permits users to work with the rows and columns of a matrix (or spreadsheet) of data. Several spreadsheets can be contained in a single worksheet.

- **Graphics.** The graphics component permits users to create charts and line drawings which graphically portray the data in a data base or spreadsheet.

- **Word Processing.** The word processing component permits users to enter, store, manipulate, and print text.

- **Communications.** The communications component permits users to send and receive transmissions of data to/from remote computers, and to process and store the data as well.

This family of programs works together so that users can perform a variety of functions involving the *manipulation* and *presentation* of shared alphanumeric data and text. You can choose from over 30 commercially available integrated software packages.

Consider our "integrated" example involving the professor. The professor uses the *data management* component to create a display screen format into which data can be entered for each student. The *electronic spreadsheet* features are used to compute the final term averages. The professor then uses the *graphics* component to produce charts that graphically illustrate the distribution of the grades. Before assigning letter grades at the end of the term, the professor analyzes these charts. Then the spreadsheet "programming" capabilities are used to automatically assign the letter grades. The professor does not actually write programs, but with the spreadsheet software, some functions can be performed that have traditionally required the writing of special programs. The professor uses *word processing* software to write interoffice memos concerning student progress. At the end of the term, the professor calls on the *communications* software to route the machine-readable data (student name and letter grade) directly to the college's central computer system for processing. Student data appear only once in the worksheet, but are accessible by all five software components.

A buyer for a furniture store tracks actual versus planned sales for various classes of furniture with an electronic spreadsheet. This microcomputer permits voice, as well as keyboard, input. (Texas Instruments, Inc.)

In 1980, most word processing was done on computers that were designed specifically for word processing. Now over 70% of all word processing is done on versatile microcomputers. This executive uses word processing software to write and print letters.
(Photo courtesy of Hewlett-Packard Company)

These applications of integrated software are expanded upon in the detailed discussions that follow (Sections S-4 through S-8). Many examples and illustrations are drawn from the professor's worksheet activity. Each of the five integrated software components is discussed with respect to *function*, *concepts*, and *use*.

A Powerful Productivity Tool

"This used to take me over a week, and now I do it in 30 minutes!" Similar statements have been made by thousands of users of integrated software. Integrated software is now a proven productivity tool in any field that requires people to work with text, numbers, or graphics (and that list doesn't leave out many people!). Integrated software is often characterized as a productivity tool because it helps to relieve the tedium of many time-consuming manual tasks.

With data management we can format and create a file in minutes. Electronic spreadsheets permit us to perform certain arithmetic and logic operations without writing programs. Say goodbye to grid paper, plastic templates, and the manual plotting of data: graphics software prepares bar, pie, and line charts without our drawing a single line. No more retyping—thanks to word processing software. And communications software helps to minimize redundant data entry.

Integrated Software Concepts

The example of how a professor maintains grades using integrated software illustrates how data are shared by the five software components. Each of these components is also available commercially as a separate software package. However, the trend is to integration. Besides minimizing redundancy in data and data entry, the capabilities of all five software components are simultaneously available to users.

With integrated software, you can switch from one project to the next with relative ease. When you do this, you are switching from one *working environment* (e.g., spreadsheet) to another working environment (e.g., word processing). Designated areas of a worksheet are called **windows**. A worksheet may have several windows, most of which may be too large to be displayed on a single screen. Depending on the size of the window subarea, you may need to "move" the window around by *scrolling* vertically or horizontally to view all data or text.

You can even "look through" several windows on a single display screen, but you can work only in one window at a time. This is called the "current" window. Figure S-1 shows a screen with three windows for three working environments: spreadsheet (of student data), data management (a data entry form), and word processing (a memo). Windows can overlap one another in the worksheet as well as on the display screen.

You can perform work in one of the windows displayed in Figure S-1, or you can **zoom** in on a particular window. That is, the window you select is expanded to fill the entire screen (see Figure S-2). Press a key and you

FIGURE S-1
Integrated Software Windows
The user of integrated software can select one working environment, such as electronic spreadsheet, while viewing windows of one or more other working environments (e.g., word processing and data management).

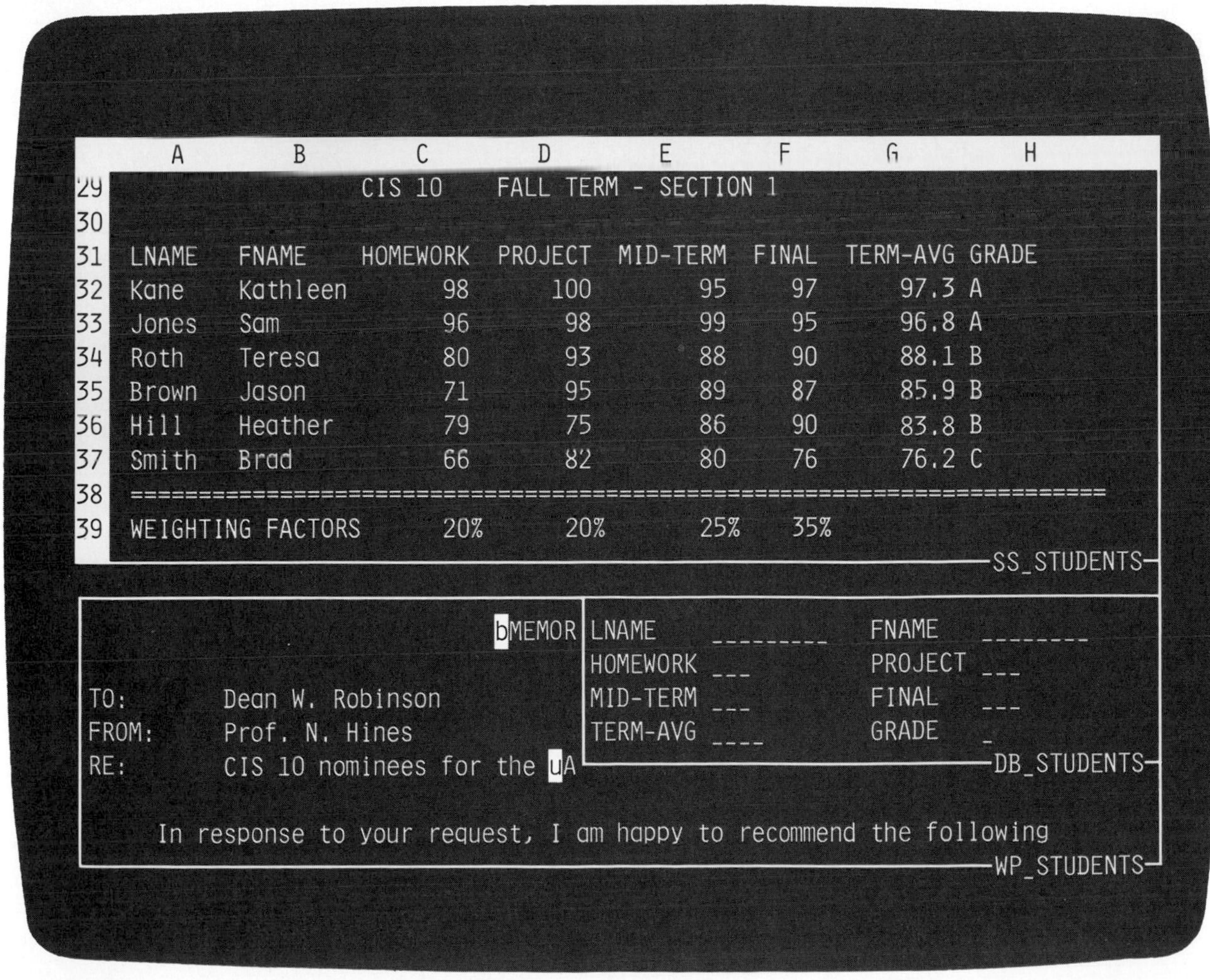

```
C29:   CIS 10     FALL TERM - SECTION 1

           A          B          C          D          E          F          G          H
 29                            CIS 10     FALL TERM - SECTION 1
 30
 31    LNAME      FNAME      HOMEWORK   PROJECT    MID-TERM   FINAL   TERM-AVG  GRADE
 32    Kane       Kathleen        98        100          95      97      97.3  A
 33    Jones      Sam             96         98          99      95      96.8  A
 34    Roth       Teresa          80         93          88      90      88.1  B
 35    Brown      Jason           71         95          89      87      85.9  B
 36    Hill       Heather         79         75          86      90      83.8  B
 37    Smith      Brad            66         82          80      76      76.2  C
 38    ==============================================================================
 39    WEIGHTING FACTORS        20%        20%         25%     35%
 40
 41                        MINIMUM --------- AVERAGE ------- MAXIMUM
 42                           76.2              88.02           97.3
 43
```

FIGURE S-2
Spreadsheet: Student Grades
"Zoom" in on a particular window to fill the screen with that working
environment. The spreadsheet in Figure S-1 is expanded to fill the screen.

can return to a multiwindow display. A multiwindow display permits you
to view how a change in one window affects another window. For example,
as you change the data in a spreadsheet, you can view how an accompanying
pie chart is revised to reflect the new data.

When you switch between different types of tasks, such as word processing
and graphics, you are actually "looking" through different windows of the
electronic worksheet. As we progress through the examples, the tremendous
advantages of integrated micro software will become more and more apparent.
By pushing a single key, you can bounce around the worksheet, selecting
whatever window you wish. Once in a particular window, you can switch
working environments (i.e., one of the five software components) to fit your
needs. For example, it may be better to switch back and forth between spreadsheet and word processing environments to compile a report. In effect, windows are your *visual link* to the worksheet.

You can even create **window panes**! As you might expect, a window
is divided into panes so that you can view several parts of the same window
subarea at a time. For example, suppose you were writing a long report
and were in a word processing working environment; then you might wish
to write the conclusions to a report in one window pane while viewing portions
of the report in another window pane (see Figure S-3).

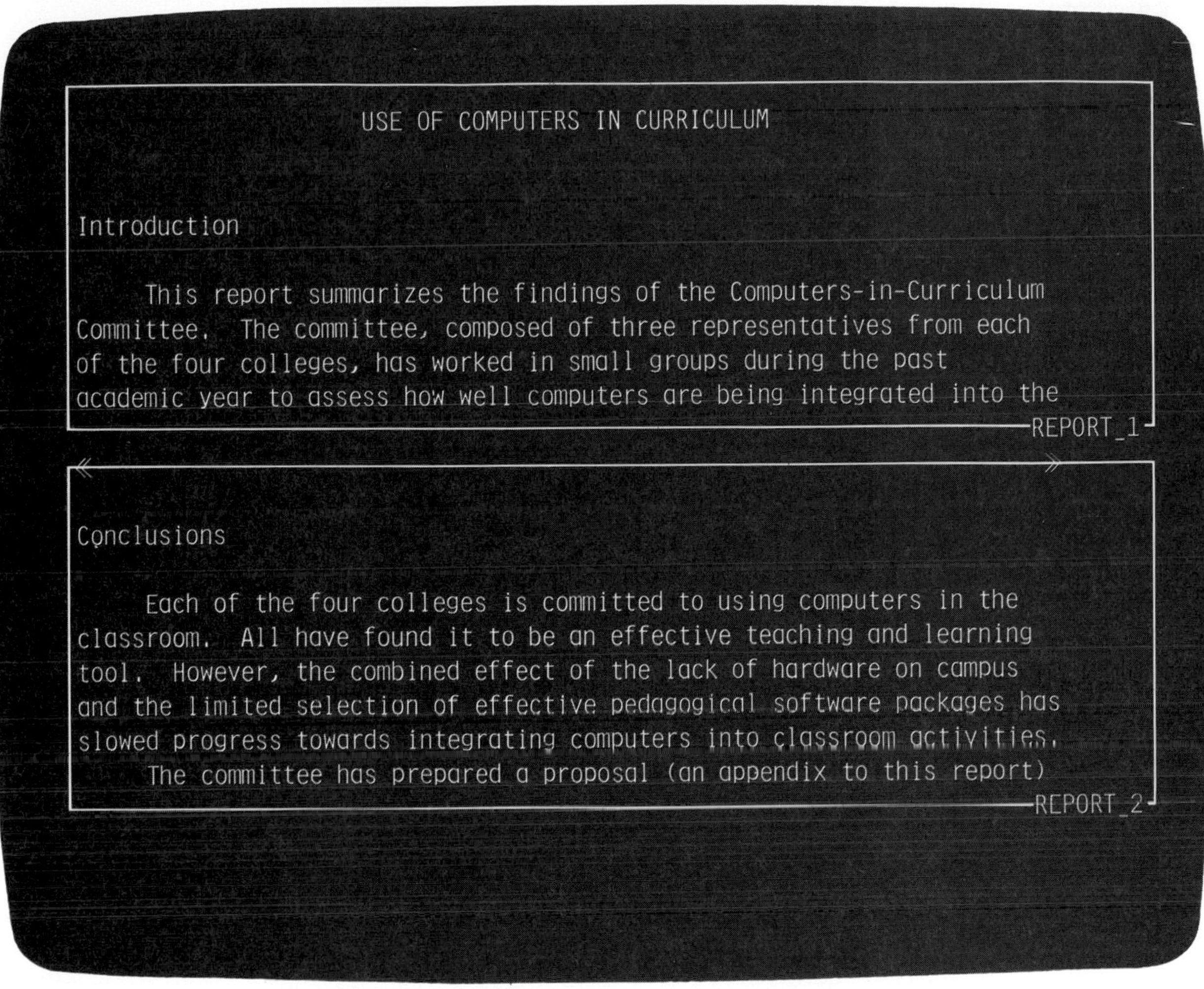

```
                    USE OF COMPUTERS IN CURRICULUM


Introduction

     This report summarizes the findings of the Computers-in-Curriculum
Committee.  The committee, composed of three representatives from each
of the four colleges, has worked in small groups during the past
academic year to assess how well computers are being integrated into the
                                                        ─REPORT_1─
«                                                                        »

Conclusions

     Each of the four colleges is committed to using computers in the
classroom.  All have found it to be an effective teaching and learning
tool.  However, the combined effect of the lack of hardware on campus
and the limited selection of effective pedagogical software packages has
slowed progress towards integrating computers into classroom activities.
     The committee has prepared a proposal (an appendix to this report)
                                                        ─REPORT_2─
```

FIGURE S-3
Word Processing: Window Panes
Two parts of a report can be viewed at the same time through window
panes.

S-2   INTERACTING WITH THE SYSTEM _____

User Friendly.   Software is said to be **user friendly** when someone with
relatively little computer experience has no difficulty using the system. User-
friendly systems communicate easily understood words and phrases to the
end user, thus simplifying the user's interaction with the computer system.
A central focus of the design of integrated software packages is user friendliness.

     There are, of course, degrees of user friendliness. At the first level, it is
assumed that the user has little or no experience and that the user's interaction

DISKETTES: HANDLE WITH CARE

Costing only a few dollars, a blank diskette has a very modest value. But once you begin to use the diskette, its value, at least to you, increases greatly. Its value includes the many hours of work that you have spent entering data and writing programs. Such a valuable piece of property should be handled with care. Here are a few Do's and Don'ts:

Do:

- Label each diskette with a soft-tipped pen.
- Store diskettes in their envelopes so that the exposed surface is covered.
- Store diskettes vertically—or, if flat, place no more than ten to a stack.

- Store at temperatures ranging from 50–125 degrees Fahrenheit.
- Keep a backup of diskettes containing important data and programs.

Don't:

- Fold, spindle, or mutilate.
- Force a diskette into the disk drive (it should slip in with little or no resistance).
- Touch the diskette surface.
- Place near a magnetic field, such as magnetic paper-clip holders, tape demagnetizers, or electric motors.
- Expose diskettes to direct sunlight for a prolonged period.

with the software will be tentative and deliberate. At this level, the system offers some welcome "hand holding." For example, some integrated software packages use **icons** or pictographs, rather than words or phrases, to communicate with the end user. When you wish to issue a file handling command, for example, you position the cursor near the icon representing files (perhaps a file cabinet or a diskette). When you select a particular icon, you are then presented with a menu of file handling choices. Your choices might be to save, retrieve, or delete a file.

The first level of user friendliness may be too friendly, and even cumbersome, for the seasoned user. Too much hand holding forces experienced users to work more slowly than they would like; therefore, integrated software provides alternatives. As you become familiar with the software, you can learn and use techniques that offer a more efficient interaction with the system.

A handy feature available on most integrated software packages is the **help command**. When you find yourself in a corner, you can press the "help" key, and more explanation or instruction is displayed on the screen. When you are finished reading the help information, the system returns you to your work at the same point that you left it.

Input and Control. A microcomputer's *keyboard* is normally the primary input and control device. You enter data and issue commands via the keyboard. It has, besides the standard typewriter keyboard, *function keys*, also called *soft keys*. When pressed, these function keys trigger the execution of software, thus the name "soft" key. For example, pressing a particular function key might call up a menu of possible activities that can be performed. Another function key might rearrange the words in a paragraph for right and left justification. Some keyboards are equipped with a *ten-key pad* (numbers for rapid numeric data entry).

A keyboard also has *cursor control keys*. These "arrow" keys allow you to move the cursor up, down, left, and right. The *HOME* key moves the cursor to the upper left-hand corner of the screen or window area.

Other important keys common to most keyboards are the *backspace* (*BKSP*), *escape* (*ESC*), *control* (*CTRL*), and *alternate* (*ALT*) keys. Press the BKSP key to move the cursor one position to the left and delete the character in that position. The ESC key may have many functions, depending on the integrated software package, but in most situations you can press the ESC key to negate the current command. The CTRL and ALT keys are used in conjunction with another key. You hold down a CTRL or ALT key to give another key new meaning. For example, on some word processing systems you press HOME to move the cursor to the top left corner of the screen. When you press CTRL and HOME together, the cursor is positioned at the beginning of the document.

Another device used for input and control in integrated software is the *mouse*. The hand-held mouse is connected to the computer by an electrical cable (the mouse's tail) and rolled over a desktop to move the cursor. Buttons on the mouse are activated to select a menu item or to perform certain tasks, such as moving blocks of data from one part of the screen to another. Another option with a few integrated software packages is *voice input*. Voice input permits users to enter commands, numbers, and some data verbally. Not all integrated software packages are set up to permit mouse and voice input.

Menus.   When using integrated software, you issue commands and initiate operations by selecting activities to be performed from a *hierarchy of menus*. These hierarchies are sometimes called "menu trees." When you select an item in the *main menu*, you are normally presented with another menu of activities, and so on—thus the "tree." Depending on the items you select, you may progress through as many as eight levels of menus before processing is initiated. The menus appear in a *control panel* that is usually, but not always, located at the bottom or top of the screen. On some integrated software packages the menus are superimposed in a window over whatever is currently on the screen. You select a particular menu item by positioning the cursor over or next to the item with the use of the cursor control keys or a mouse.

The main menu might give you the choice of working environment: *data management*, *spreadsheet*, *graphics*, *word processing*, or *communications*. If you select *graphics*, another menu asks you what type of chart you want produced: *bar chart*, *pie chart*, or *line chart*. If you select *bar chart*, then another menu gives you more choices: do you wish to *create* a new one or *revise* an existing one? If you select *create*, then more menus are presented that permit you to describe the appearance of the chart (e.g., labels) and to identify what data are to be charted.

Learning to Use Integrated Software.   When you purchase integrated software, you will receive at least one manual, the software on diskettes, and a *tutorial disk*. If this is your first exposure to integrated software, it is a good idea to go over the tutorial disk. When you load the tutorial disk on the micro, an instructional program interactively walks you through a simulation (demonstration) of the features and use of the software. Once you have an overview understanding of the features and how the components fit together, the manual makes a lot more sense.

An integrated microcomputer software package, such as Lotus Development Corporation's Symphony, will normally include a set of reference manuals and several diskettes containing the software for data management, electronic spreadsheet, word processing, graphics, communications, and on-line tutorials.
(Lotus Development Corporation)

S-3 HARDWARE CONSIDERATIONS _____

Integrated software evolved as software for microcomputers, but it has become so popular that the inevitable has happened—it is now commercially available for mainframe computers as well. In the mainframe environment, you will probably not be concerned with configuring the hardware or implementing the software, but with micros you might be. Therefore, we'll focus this discussion on microcomputers.

The Microcomputer. Each year, the sophistication of integrated software is growing with the advances in hardware technology. When selecting integrated software, pay particular attention to the minimum hardware requirements needed to realize the full potential of the software. Microcomputer software is designed for use on a specific microcomputer or its compatible companions. Make sure that you are buying the right software for your micro.

How Much RAM? Integrated software packages will also have a minimum RAM (random-access memory) requirement (e.g., 256K or 384K). Vendor-stated RAM requirements do not include the user area, or that portion of memory that stores your data and text. Since the size of the RAM is usually an option at the time of purchase, you may have to decide how much RAM you need. As a rule of thumb, you will need at least 64K of RAM for the user area. To speed interaction with the system, all data and text for a particular worksheet are stored in RAM. If you anticipate working with data bases that have several thousand records or with long reports, then you should probably plan on reserving at least 256K of RAM for the user area.

To determine the minimum RAM requirement, add the minimum RAM requirement for the integrated software to your anticipated user-area requirement. The RAM initially configured with your micro is usually not an irreversible decision. Optional *add-in circuit boards* can be purchased and literally plugged into the micro to increase available RAM. RAM is increased in 64K or 256K increments on most micros.

Optional Add-ins. Other add-in circuit boards are available that permit graphics displays and data communications. Most integrated software is designed to take advantage of color/graphics monitors and graphics printers, if you have them. On some micros, the graphics circuitry is standard; on others you will have to ask for it. The same is true of data communications. Check with your dealer.

The Monitor. Integrated software packages are designed to take advantage of a *high-resolution color monitor*. They will, of course, work with a *monochrome monitor*, but the added dimension of color is lost. High-resolution monitors are available in both monochrome and color. The higher the resolution, the greater the clarity of the image displayed on the screen. Certain graphic images that are generated by the integrated software cannot be displayed on low-resolution monitors. In these cases, the graphic image displayed is a scaled-down version of what would be printed on a graphics printer or displayed on a high-resolution monitor.

The Printer and Plotter.   *Dot-matrix* and *laser printers* with graphics capabilities permit you to take full advantage of the hard copy capabilities of integrated software. Full-font printers produce letter-quality alphanumeric output, such as reports and letters, but they are cumbersome for producing graphs and charts.

A *pen plotter*, an optional device on most microcomputer systems, can produce extremely high-quality graphs and charts. Multipen plotters can produce color charts.

The Keyboard.   Features of keyboards and alternative "input and control" devices are described in Section S-2.

The Secondary Storage.   Integrated software is sold and distributed on several $5\frac{1}{4}$-inch diskettes or microdisks; therefore the microcomputer system should be configured with at least one disk drive. The use of two drives, however, expedites processing activities and backup procedures. Two high-density diskettes provide up to 3 megabytes of on-line storage. A single Winchester hard-disk drive provides from five to 40 megabytes of on-line storage and permits more rapid access to on-line data.

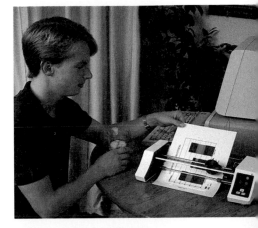

Micro owners use graphics software and their "personal plotters" at home and in the office to produce vibrant multicolor graphics.
(Houston Instrument)

REVIEW EXERCISES (S-1 THROUGH S-3) _____

1. Name and briefly describe the five software components of integrated microcomputer software.
2. What is the function of soft keys? Of cursor control keys?
3. What are designated areas of a worksheet called?
4. Name two microcomputer input devices besides the keyboard.
5. Describe the attributes of user-friendly software.
6. When purchasing a microcomputer system, what are the RAM options? The monitor options? The add-in options?
7. Create a menu tree for an interactive student course registration system. The system permits students to preregister for courses to be taken next term.

S-4 DATA MANAGEMENT _____

Function

With data management software, you can create and maintain a data base and extract information from the data base. The data management software component is sometimes referred to simply as "data base." To use data management software, you first identify the format of the data, then design a display format that will permit interactive entry and revision of the data (see the DB_STUDENTS window in Figure S-1). Once it has become a part of the data base, a *record* (which is related data about a particular event or thing) can be deleted or revised.

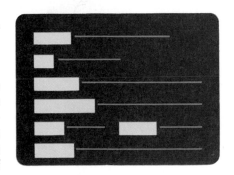

Data management software also permits you to retrieve and view records based on preset criteria. For example, a command might be to find all students in CIS 10 who earned an A for the term. Data can also be sorted for display in a variety of formats. For example, CIS 10 student records can be sorted and presented in descending order (highest grades first) by term average (see the SS_STUDENTS window in Figure S-4).

Most of the functions performed while in the data management work environment can also be performed in the electronic spreadsheet environment. However, the screen formatting capability of data management software makes it the choice for creating and maintaining a data base.

FIGURE S-4
Integrated Software Windows
In the figure, the data for Brad Smith are entered in a data management window that is formatted for input of student data (DB_STUDENTS).

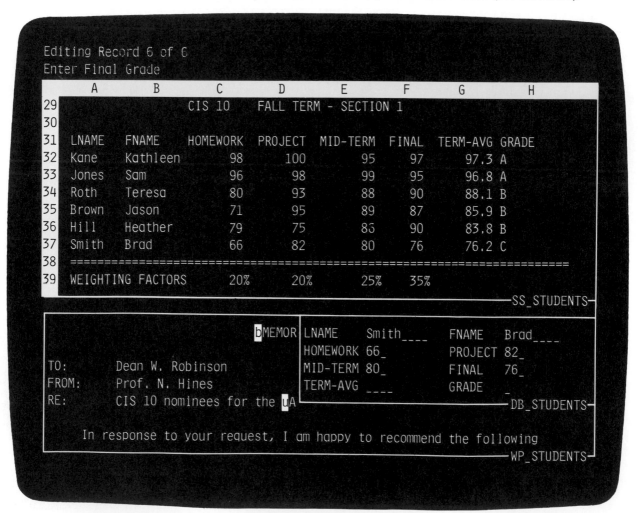

Concepts

Data management concepts are very similar to the traditional hierarchy of data organization. Related **fields**, such as first name, last name, and homework grade, are grouped to form **records**. A collection of related records make up a data **file** or a **data base**. In integrated software terminology, "file" and "data base" are sometimes used interchangeably. However, the more sophisticated integrated software packages do distinguish between the two.

Data are entered in a data entry screen format, such as that shown in the DB_STUDENTS window of Figure S-1. Once entered (see DB_STUDENTS window of Figure S-4), the data are stored automatically in the worksheet as rows (records) and columns (fields) of data. In the SS_STUDENTS window of Figure S-4, the row numbered 32 contains Kathleen Kane's record. The column headings in the worksheet are the data base field names. Notice that all student last names are under the column heading LNAME. Similarly, first names are under the column heading FNAME.

Data are entered as numbers or alphanumeric character strings, also called **labels**. As a user, you would name each field, then describe its size and type. For example, the HOMEWORK grade field in Figure S-4 is a three-digit numeric field. The *field name* is HOMEWORK; the *field size* is three digits; and the *field type* is numeric. A label field can be a single word, such as a last name (e.g., Kane or Jones), or a word phrase of up to several hundred characters in length.

In the screen format of Figure S-4, the TERM-AVG and GRADE fields are computed at the end of the term by the software. No data are entered by the professor in these fields. They are included on the data entry screen to permit data base searches on these fields (e.g., find students whose term average is greater than 95).

Use

Records are easily added, deleted, or edited (revised) in the data management working environment. You can browse through the data base by moving from record to record, or you can specify certain selection criteria and move directly to a particular record. For example, let's say that Heather Hill has just submitted an overdue homework assignment. This changes her overall homework grade from 79 to 83. To edit Ms. Hill's record, the professor must first "find" her record. To do this, he simply sets the LNAME (last name) *criteria*. The software searches for all records where LNAME = "Hill". In our example, there is only one, so Heather Hill's record appears immediately on the screen. If the class had several students named Hill, the professor would "page" through the Hills until Heather Hill's record appeared. If the professor wanted to avoid having to view the records of all students named Hill, the criteria would be further defined to be: LNAME = "Hill" *and* FNAME = "Heather".

When Heather Hill's record appears on the screen (Figure S-5), the professor moves the cursor to the appropriate field (HOMEWORK) and updates the homework grade; that is, 79 is edited to be 83. Had the term average

This interior designer uses data management software to maintain a data base that contains pertinent client information, such as address, type of house, and various preferences (e.g., color schemes, style of furniture). (Courtesy of Apple Computer, Inc.)

```
Editing Record 5 of 6
Enter Homework Grade

LNAME     Hill_____      FNAME    Heather_
HOMEWORK 83_            PROJECT 75_
MID-TERM 86_           FINAL   90_
TERM-AVG _____          GRADE    _
```

FIGURE S-5
Data Management: Editing Existing Data
To change the contents of a field, move the cursor to the appropriate field
and enter the new data. In the example, Heather Hill's homework grade is
changed to 83 (compare with her homework grade in Figure S-4).

already been computed, it would be automatically revised to reflect the new
homework grade.

You can place certain data entry restrictions on fields to help validate
the accuracy of input data. For example, you can specify that any grade
entry not exceed 100 (e.g., HOMEWORK <= 100). As a double check, you
can also specify that grade entries must be numeric. With these input validation
restrictions in place, any entry that is greater than 100 (e.g., 182, 101) or
nonnumeric (e.g., 9B, 8O [eight oh, not zero]) will not be accepted.

With the data base application, you can:

1. Find records that meet certain criteria (e.g., LNAME = "Hill").
2. Extract and list only those records that meet certain criteria.
3. Sort records in ascending or descending sequence by primary, secondary,
   and tertiary fields.
4. Perform "what if" analysis.

These capabilities, also available to you in the electronic spreadsheet application, are discussed and illustrated in the next section.

REVIEW EXERCISES (S-4) _____

1. Describe the capabilities of data management software.
2. What characteristics describe a particular field?
3. What is the purpose of setting criteria for a data base?
4. Give an example (not already discussed) of a field that might be in
   a student data base that would be computed.
5. What is the relationship between a field and a record?
6. Give examples of at least ten fields that might be contained in a
   student record.

HANDS-ON EXERCISES

1. a. Design a data entry screen to accept the following sales data for Diolab, Inc., a manufacturer of a diagnostic laboratory instrument that is sold primarily to hospitals and clinics.

DIOLAB INC. SALES (UNITS)

REGION	QTR1	QTR2	QTR3	QTR4
NE REGION	214	300	320	170
SE REGION	120	150	165	201
SW REGION	64	80	60	52
NW REGION	116	141	147	180

  b. What is the data base record?

  c. Which entries are labels? Numbers?

  d. What are the field names?

2. a. What criteria would be needed to select all Diolab regions that sold more than 200 units in the fourth quarter? More than 150 units in the third quarter?

  b. What regions would be first and last if the records were sorted in decending order by first-quarter sales? In ascending order by fourth-quarter sales?

3. If you have access to data management software, enter the above Diolab data into a data base. Perform the selections and sorts in Hands-on Exercise 2. Revise the NE Region first-quarter sales to 241. Obtain a printout of the data base and store the data on a disk file named DIOLAB.

S-5 THE ELECTRONIC SPREADSHEET

Function

In 1978, a Harvard student convinced a couple of recent MIT graduates to rewrite their new business software to run on a personal computer. The software, called VisiCalc, became the first electronic spreadsheet. The 1979 introduction of VisiCalc revolutionized the way people perceived microcomputers. Suddenly, microcomputers were no longer just for games or education; they could also be a valuable asset for business.

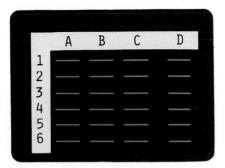

The name "electronic spreadsheet" describes the software's fundamental application. The spreadsheet has been a common business tool for centuries. Before computers, the ledger (a spreadsheet) was the accountant's primary tool for keeping the books. Professors' grade books are set up in spreadsheet format.

Electronic spreadsheets are simply an electronic alternative to thousands of traditionally manual tasks. No longer are we confined to using pencils, erasers, and hand calculators for applications that deal with rows and columns of data. Think of anything that has rows and columns of data and you have identified a use for spreadsheet software. For example, how about profit and loss statements, personnel profiles, demographic data, and budget summaries—to mention a few? Because electronic spreadsheets so closely resemble many of our manual tasks, they are enjoying widespread acceptance.

Concepts

Organization. Electronic spreadsheets are organized in a *tabular structure* with **rows** and **columns**. The intersection of a particular row and column designates a **cell**. As you can see in Figure S-6, the rows are *numbered* and the columns are *lettered*. Single letters identify the first 26 columns and double letters are used thereafter (A, B, . . ., Z, AA, AB, . . ., AZ, BA, BB, . . ., BZ). The number of rows or columns available to you depends on the size of your micro's RAM. Most spreadsheets permit hundreds of columns and thousands of rows.

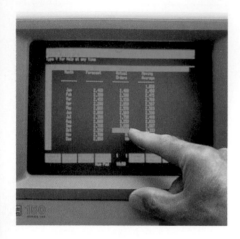

This screen illustrates how VisiCalc, the first spreadsheet program, can be used to portray a month-by-month analysis of forecast versus actual orders.
(Photo courtesy of Hewlett-Packard Company)

FIGURE S-6
Spreadsheet: Organization
Spreadsheets are organized with numbered rows and lettered columns. The pointer is positioned at cell address C32. The cell address of the pointer location and the cell content are shown in the control panel at the top of the screen.

C32: 98

	A	B	C	D	E	F	G	H
29			CIS 10	FALL TERM - SECTION 1				
30								
31	LNAME	FNAME	HOMEWORK	PROJECT	MID-TERM	FINAL	TERM-AVG	GRADE
32	Kane	Kathleen	98	100	95	97	97.3	A
33	Jones	Sam	96	98	99	95	96.8	A
34	Roth	Teresa	80	93	88	90	88.1	B
35	Brown	Jason	71	95	89	87	85.9	B
36	Hill	Heather	83	75	86	90	84.6	B
37	Smith	Brad	66	82	80	76	76.2	C
38	==							
39	WEIGHTING FACTORS		20%	20%	25%	35%		
40								
41			MINIMUM ---------		AVERAGE -------		MAXIMUM	
42			76.2		88.15		97.3	
43								

Data are entered and stored in a cell, at the intersection of a column and a row. During operations, data are referenced by their **cell address**. A cell address identifies the location of a cell in the worksheet by its column and row, with the column designator first. For example, in Figure S-6, C31 is the address of the column heading "HOMEWORK," and C32 is the address of Ms. Kane's homework grade, 98.

A movable highlighted area "points" to the current cell. This highlighted area, which is appropriately called the **pointer**, can be moved around the spreadsheet with the cursor control keys to any cell address. To add, delete, or edit an entry at a particular cell, the pointer must be located at that cell. The contents of the current cell are displayed in reverse video (black on white with monochrome monitors). The pointer in Figure S-6 is at cell C32.

Working with an Electronic Spreadsheet.   Now for the beauty of a spreadsheet: If you change the value of a cell in a spreadsheet, all other affected cells are changed accordingly. For example, if you will remember from the data management section and Figure S-5, Heather Hill's homework grade was originally 79. After grading the late homework, the professor revised her homework grade from 79 to 83. Immediately after the change is made, her term average, grade, and other affected cells are automatically recomputed. Compare cells C36 and G36 in Figures S-4 and S-6.

Cell Entries.   To make an entry in the spreadsheet, simply move the pointer with the cursor control keys to the appropriate cell, and key in the data. To *edit* or replace an existing entry, you also move the pointer to the appropriate cell. The new or revised entry appears first in the *control panel* beside the cell address (see Figure S-6). Once you have completed work on a particular entry, press the carriage return or a cursor control key to make the entry in the actual spreadsheet. For example, let's say that "Kane" in A32 was incorrectly entered initially as "Kand". To make the correction, the professor would move the pointer to A32, indicate that the cell value is to be edited (usually an edit key), then delete the "d", add the "e", and press the carriage return.

Numeric, Label, and Formula Entries.   The value that you enter in a cell is either *numeric*, a *label*, or a *formula*. The values in C32, D32, E32, and F32 are numeric. A label is a word, phrase, or any string of alphanumeric text (spaces included) that occupies a particular cell. In the example of Figure S-6, "LNAME" in cell A31 is a label value, as is "Hill" in A32 and "CIS 10 FALL TERM–SECTION 1" in C29. Notice that the label in C29 extends across columns C, D, E, and F and includes spaces. If an entry were made in D29, only the first eight positions, or the width of column C, would be visible on the spreadsheet (e.g., "CIS 10   ").

Unless otherwise specified, numeric entries are right justified (lined up on the right) and label entries are left justified. However, you can specify that entries be left or right justified, or centered in the column. Note that the column headings in A31, B31, and H31 are left justified and that the column headings in C31, D31, E31, and F31 are right justified to improve the appearance of the spreadsheet.

Cells G32 and H32 contain formulas, but it is the numeric results (e.g., 97.3) and the character-string results (e.g., "A") that are shown in the spreadsheet. A *character string* is a group of one or more alphanumeric characters.

When resolved, the formula in G32 becomes 97.3 and H32 becomes "A". The formula value of G32, which uses weighting factors to compute the overall term average for each student, is shown in the control panel at the top of Figure S-7. With the pointer at G32, the formula appears in the control panel and the actual numeric value appears in the spreadsheet. If the pointer were to be moved one column to the left, F32: 97 would be displayed at the top of the screen.

Spreadsheet formulas use standard notation for **arithmetic operators**: + (add), − (subtract), ∗ (multiply), / (divide), ^ (raising to a power, or exponentiation). The formula contained in G32 (top of Figure S-7) computes the term average for the record in row 32 (Kathleen Kane). Compare this formula:

(C39∗C32)+(D39∗D32)+(E39∗E32)+(F39∗F32)

to the formula in cell G33 (below):

(C39∗C33)+(D39∗D33)+(E39∗E33)+(F39∗F33)

Notice that the first formula references those grades in row 32 and the second formula references those grades in row 33; however, the cells referencing the weighting factors (e.g., C39) in row 39 remain the same for all formulas in column G. This makes sense, because the weighting factors in cells C39, D39, E39, and F39 are applied to the computation of each student's grade.

FIGURE S-7
Spreadsheet: Formulas
The actual content of G32 is the formula in the control panel. The result of the formula appears in G32 in the spreadsheet.

```
G32:  ($C$39*C32)+($D$39*D32)+($E$39*E32)+($F$39*F32)

        A        B         C         D         E        F        G        H
  29                    CIS 10    FALL TERM - SECTION 1
  30
  31  LNAME    FNAME     HOMEWORK  PROJECT  MID-TERM  FINAL  TERM-AVG GRADE
  32  Kane     Kathleen        98      100        95     97     97.3  A
  33  Jones    Sam             96       98        99     95     96.8  A
  34  Roth     Teresa          80       93        88     90     88.1  B
  35  Brown    Jason           71       95        89     87     85.9  B
  36  Hill     Heather         83       75        86     90     84.6  B
  37  Smith    Brad            66       82        80     76     76.2  C
  38  ==================================================================
  39  WEIGHTING FACTORS       20%      20%       25%    35%
  40
  41                  MINIMUM --------- AVERAGE ------- MAXIMUM
  42                     76.2            88.15             97.3
  43
```

The distinction between the way the grades and weighting factors are represented in the formulas highlights a very important concept of electronic spreadsheets, that of **relative cell addressing** and **absolute cell addressing**.

Relative and Absolute Cell Addressing.   The professor entered the term-average formula only once: in G32 (see above). Then, spreadsheet commands were selected that copied the formula into cells G32 through G37. You can see from the above formulas that the exact formula was not copied. Instead, the formula in G33 designates the cells for the record in row *33* (Jones), not *32* (Kane). The same is true of the formulas for rows 34 through 37. The formula in G32 references cells that have a "relative" position to G32, the location of the formula. When the formula in G32 is copied to G33, the electronic spreadsheet software revises these *relative cell addresses* so they apply to a formula that is located in G33. As you can see, the formula in G33 references cells that contain the grades for the second student (row 33).

Since the weighting factors remain the same for each student, the professor assigned each weighting factor an *absolute cell address*. The absolute cell address does not change when a formula in which it appears is copied from row to row or from column to column; therefore, the formulas in the TERM-AVG column will always reference the weighting-factor values in cells C39, D39, E39, and F39. An absolute cell address is denoted by a dollar sign ($) prefix before the column and before the row (e.g., C39).

The relative cell address is based on its position relative to the cell containing the formula. When you copy a formula to another cell, the relative cell addresses are revised to reflect their new position relative to the new location of the formula. The absolute cell addresses remain unchanged. In effect, the formula in G32 multiplies the weighting factors times whatever values occupy the four positions adjacent and to the left of the formula location in G32 (i.e., C32, D32, E32, F32). When the formula is copied to G37, the weighting factors, which remain the same, are multiplied times whatever values occupy the four positions adjacent and to the left of G37 (i.e., C37, D37, E37, F37).

As another example of relative addressing, look at the spreadsheet in Figure S-8. Suppose the formula B3*E1 is in cell A1. B3 is a relative

FIGURE S-8
Spreadsheet: Relative and Absolute Cell Addressing
When the formula in A1 is copied to C2, the formula in C2 becomes D4*E1.

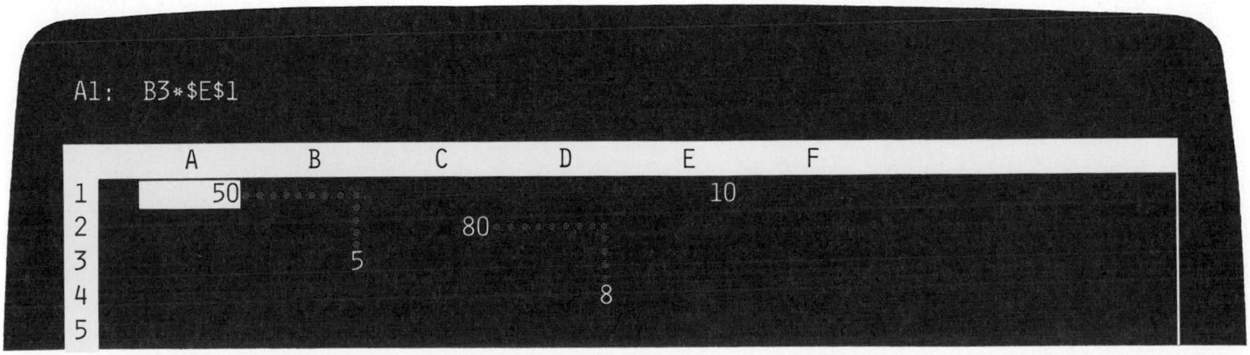

cell address that is 1 column to the right of and 2 rows down from A1. If this formula is copied to C2, then the formula in C2 is D4*E1. Notice that D4 has the same relative position to the formula in cell C2: 1 column to the right and 2 rows down. The absolute cell address remains the same in both formulas.

You might ask, "Why beat around the bush? Why not just enter the numeric weighting factors directly in the formula?" Well, you could, but what if the professor wanted to revise the weighting factors from 20%, 20%, 25%, 35% to 10%, 30%, 25%, 35%; then all the formulas would have to change. By defining the weighting factors in the formula as variables with absolute cell addresses, the professor would change the value of C39 to 10% and D39 to 30% to change the weighting-factor values in all formulas that reference these cells.

Ranges.   Many electronic spreadsheet operations ask you to designate a **range**. The four types of ranges are highlighted in Figure S-9:

1.   A single cell (example range is G32)
2.   All or part of a column of adjacent cells (example range is A32 . . A37)
3.   All or part of a row of adjacent cells (example range is C39 . . F39)
4.   A rectangular block of cells (example range is C32 . . F37)

FIGURE S-9
Spreadsheet: Ranges
The four types of ranges are highlighted: cell, column, row, and block.

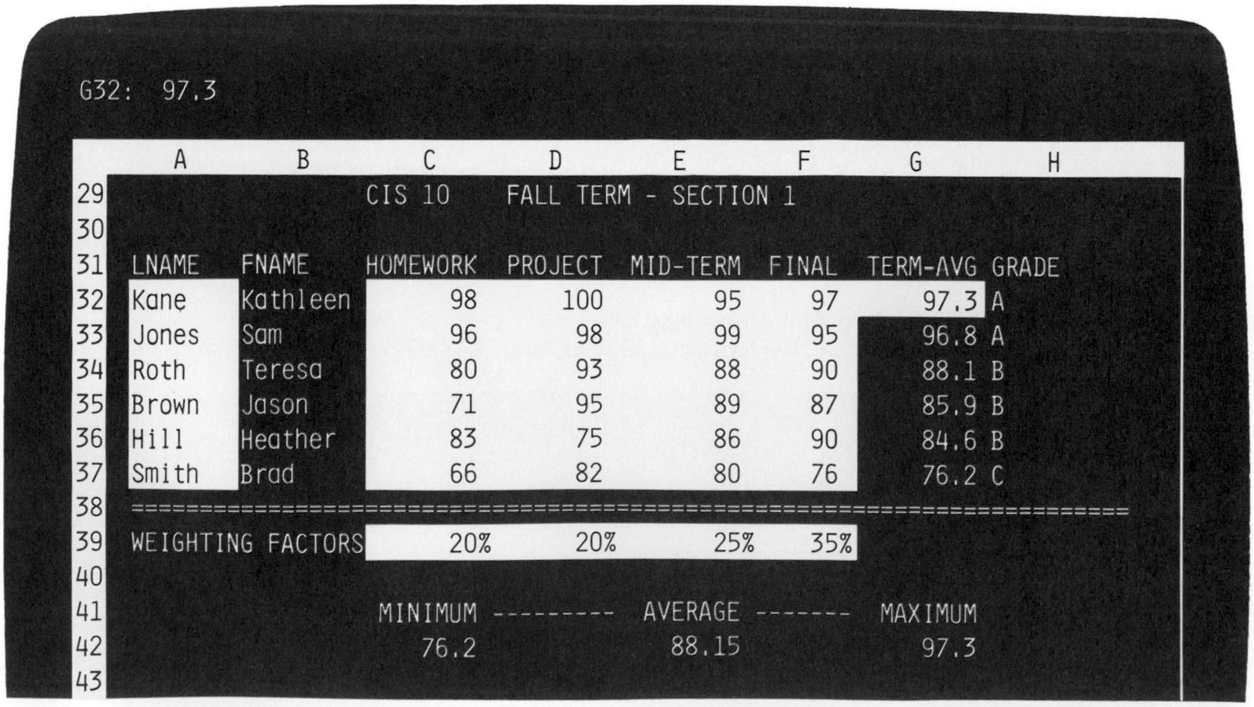

A particular range is depicted by the addresses of the endpoint cells and separated by two periods (some packages use only one period, e.g., C32 . F37). Any cell can comprise a single cell range. The range for the LNAME entries in Figure S-9 is A32 . . A37 and the range for the weighting-factor values is C39 . . F39. The range of grade data entered by the professor is depicted by any two opposite corner cell addresses (e.g., C32 . . F37 or C37 . . F32).

Many spreadsheet operations require users to designate one or several ranges. Do this by moving the pointer to an endpoint cell. Then you *anchor* the pointer by pressing a particular key, often a tab or a period. Once you have set the anchor (e.g., C32), move the pointer to the other endpoint (e.g., F37), press return, and you have defined the range (C32 . . F37). Ranges can also be defined by simply keying in the addresses of the endpoint cells.

The copy operation requires users to define a "copy from" range and a "copy to" range. When the term-average formula in G32 was copied to other cells in the TERM-AVG column, G32 was defined as the "copy from" range, and G33 . . G37 was the "copy to" range. When you want to erase a portion of the worksheet, you first define the range that you wish to erase. For example, if you wish to erase the line separating the data from the weighting factors, you define the range to be A38 . . H38, then issue the erase command.

Creating Spreadsheet Formulas. The three types of cell entries are numbers, labels, and formulas. This section expands on the use and application of formulas: the essence of spreadsheet operations. A formula causes the spreadsheet software to perform numeric and/or string calculations and/or logic operations that result in a numeric value (e.g., 97.3) or an alphanumeric character string (e.g., "A" or "Kathleen Kane"). A formula may include one or all of the following: *arithmetic operations*, *functions*, *logic operations*, and *string operations*. Each is discussed below in more detail.

When you design the spreadsheet, keep in mind where you want to place the formulas and what you want them to accomplish. Since formulas are based on relative position, you will need a knowledge of the layout and organization of the data in the worksheet. When you define a formula, you must first determine what you wish to achieve (e.g., calculate term average). Then select a cell location for the formula (e.g., G32) and create the formula by connecting relative and absolute cell addresses with operators, as appropriate. In many instances, you will copy the formula to other locations (e.g., G32 was copied to G33 . . G37) in Figure S-9.

Spreadsheet applications begin with a blank screen and an idea. The spreadsheet that you create is a product of skill and imagination. What you get out of a spreadsheet is very much dependent on how effectively you use formulas.

Arithmetic Operations. Formulas containing arithmetic operators are resolved according to a hierarchy of operations. That is, when more than one operator is included in a single formula, the spreadsheet software uses a set of rules to determine which operation to do first, second, and so on. In the hierarchy of operations, illustrated in Figure S-10, exponentiation has the highest priority, followed by multiplication-division, and addition-subtrac-

The Hierarchy of Operations	
OPERATION	**OPERATOR**
Exponentiation	^
Multiplication-Division	* /
Addition-Subtraction	+ –

FIGURE S-10
The Hierarchy of Operations

tion. In the case of a tie (e.g., * and /, or + and –), the formula is evaluated from *left to right*. *Parentheses*, however, override the priority rules. Expressions placed in parentheses have priority and are evaluated innermost first, and left to right.

In the formula:

(C39*C32)+(D39*D32)+(E39*E32)+(F39*F32)

the parentheses do not affect the result, since the multiplications would be resolved first anyway. But it is a good idea to use parentheses whenever they help to clarify the formula.

Let's use the spreadsheet in Figure S-11 to further illustrate the use of arithmetic formulas. This spreadsheet is intended to help university administrators plan for increasing enrollment in each college and overall. Column C

FIGURE S-11
Spreadsheet: Formulas and Formatting
Formulas in the range F4 .. H7 calculate the expected annual growth of students. Formulas in the range F11 .. H11 calculate the annual growth rate. Student figures are formatted as fixed, with no decimal places, and percentage figures are formatted as percentages.

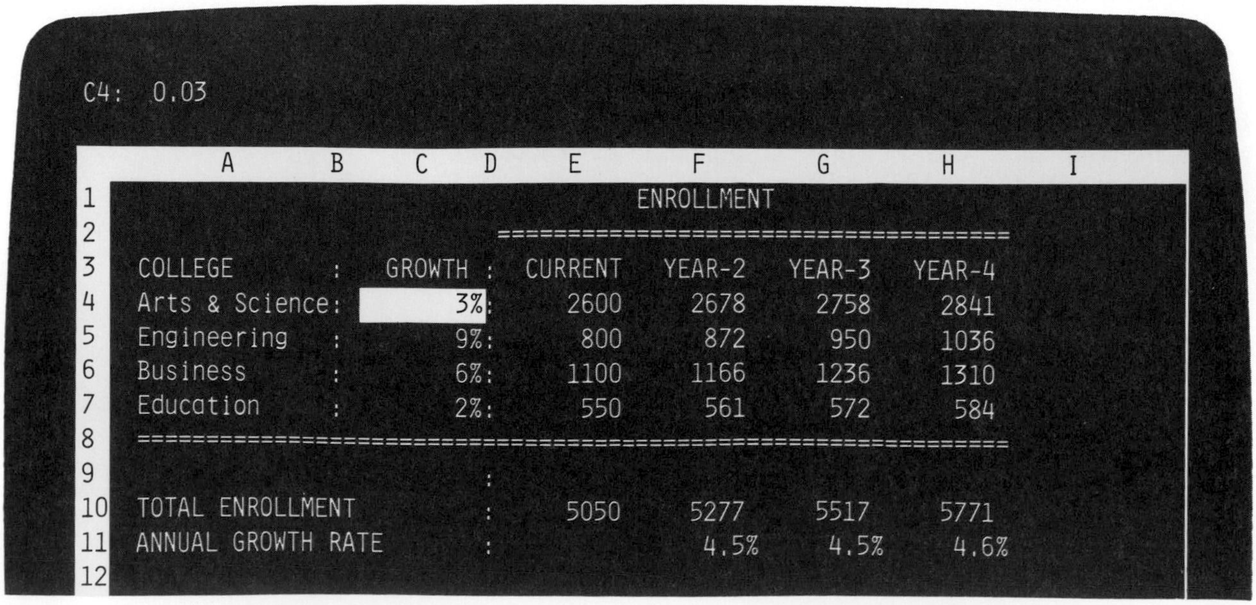

```
C4:  0.03

          A         B      C    D     E         F        G        H        I
 1                                          ENROLLMENT
 2                             =========================================
 3    COLLEGE        :    GROWTH :  CURRENT   YEAR-2   YEAR-3   YEAR-4
 4    Arts & Science:        3%:     2600     2678     2758     2841
 5    Engineering   :        9%:      800      872      950     1036
 6    Business       :        6%:     1100     1166     1236     1310
 7    Education      :        2%:      550      561      572      584
 8                             =========================================
 9                       :
10    TOTAL ENROLLMENT  :              5050     5277     5517     5771
11    ANNUAL GROWTH RATE :                       4.5%     4.5%     4.6%
12
```

contains the projected growth-rate data for each college. The growth-rate entries are *formatted* to appear as percentages for ease of reading. They were actually entered as .03, .09, and so on. Also notice how colons (:) are entered in columns B and D and how the *width* of these columns is adjusted to enhance readability. Column E reflects the current enrollments in each college. All other entries are the results of formulas.

The formulas in the range F4 .. H7 are based on the current enrollments and projected growth rates (percent per year) for each college. Three formulas are required to project enrollments in the second through fourth years. Remember that (1+C4) is (1+.03), or 1.03. For the Arts and Science College, the formulas are:

    F4: E4∗(1+C4)   (for YEAR-2)

    G4: E4∗(1+C4)^2 (for YEAR-3)

    H4: E4∗(1+C4)^3 (for YEAR-4)

Once entered, these formulas are copied to the ranges F5 .. F7, G5 .. G7, and H5 .. H7, respectively. Figure S-12 illustrates the order in which the formula in G4 is evaluated. The result was formatted as *fixed* with *no decimal places* so that the projected enrollment is rounded to the nearest person.

The annual growth rates for years 2 through 4 are calculated by dividing the total enrollment in one year by that of the previous year, then subtracting 1. The formula was entered in F11, then copied to G11 .. H11.

    F11: (F10/E10)−1
    G11: (G10/F10)−1
    H11: (H10/G10)−1

Notice the relative position of the two cells to the location of the formulas. The numerator (e.g., F10) is just above the formula (e.g., F11), and the denominator is one column to the left and one row up (e.g., E10). The result is formatted as a *percentage* and rounded to *one decimal place*. Formatting caused .04495 (the actual arithmetic result of the formula in F11) to appear as 4.5%.

The total enrollment figures in the range E10 .. H10 are calculated by predefined functions. Functions are described in the next section.

Functions. Electronic spreadsheets offer users a wide variety of predefined operations called **functions**. These functions can be used to create formulas that perform mathematical, logical, statistical, financial, and character-string operations on spreadsheet data. To use a function, simply preface the desired function name with a prefix symbol (e.g., "@"; the symbol may vary between software packages), and enter the **argument**. The argument, which is placed in parentheses, is the data to be operated on. The argument can be one or several numbers, character strings, or ranges that represent data.

In the example of Figure S-11, the total enrollment figures can be calculated with arithmetic operators:

    E10: E4+E5+E6+E7

or with a single function and its argument:

    E10: @SUM(E4 .. E7)

The above function computes the sum of the enrollment figures in the range

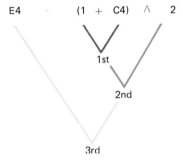

FIGURE S-12
Evaluation of an Arithmetic Expression
The formula in G4 of Figure S-11 is resolved by the computer in stages, according to the hierarchy of operations (see Figure S-10).

E4 .. E7. The use of predefined functions can save a lot of time. What if the range to be summed was E4 .. E600? The formula in E10 was copied to the range F10 .. H10.

In the example of Figure S-13, the professor used functions to calculate the overall class average and to determine the minimum and maximum numeric grades for the term. To do this, the professor entered the following functions in G39, G40, and G41, respectively:

G39: @AVG(G32 .. G37)
G40: @MIN(G32 .. G37)
G41: @MAX(G32 .. G37)

The argument for each of these functions is the range of cells representing the numeric term averages for each student.

Other spreadsheet functions include: trigonometric functions, square root, comparisons of values, manipulations of strings of data, computation of Julian dates, computation of net present value and internal rate of return, and a variety of techniques for statistical analysis. Vendors of spreadsheet software create slightly different names for their functions.

Logic Operations.   Logical operations involve the use of **relational operators** and **logical operators** (see Figure S-14) to compare numeric and

FIGURE S-13
Spreadsheet: Functions and Relational Operators
Summary data in the range C42 .. G42 are computed with functions (e.g., @AVG). The formulas in the range H32 .. H37 use relational operators to assign letter grades.

```
C32:   98

        A          B          C          D          E          F          G          H
29                        CIS 10      FALL TERM - SECTION 1
30
31  LNAME      FNAME      HOMEWORK   PROJECT   MID-TERM   FINAL   TERM-AVG  GRADE
32  Kane       Kathleen         98       100         95      97      97.3 A
33  Jones      Sam              96        98         99      95      96.8 A
34  Roth       Teresa           80        93         88      90      88.1 B
35  Brown      Jason            71        95         89      87      85.9 B
36  Hill       Heather          83        75         86      90      84.6 B
37  Smith      Brad             66        82         80      76      76.2 C
38  =================================================================================
39  WEIGHTING FACTORS        20%       20%        25%     35%
40
41                       MINIMUM ---------- AVERAGE ------- MAXIMUM
42                        76.2                88.15             97.3
43
```

Relational Operators	
COMPARISON	**OPERATOR**
Equal to	=
Less than	<
Greater than	>
Less than or equal to	< =
Greater than or equal to	> =
Not equal to	<>

Logical Operators AND and OR	
OPERATION	**OPERATOR**
For the condition to be true:	
Both sub-conditions must be true	AND
At least one subcondition must be true	OR

FIGURE S-14
Relational and Logical Operators

string values. The result of a logical operation is that an expression is either *true* or *false*.

Logical operations are used to establish criteria for record selection in both data management and spreadsheet software. In Figure S-13, the following relational expressions, or *conditions*, establish criteria that would result in the following record selections:

HOMEWORK<75	Brown and Smith
LNAME="Roth"	Roth
TERM-AVG>=E42	Kane and Jones (E42 is the average, 88.15)

Logical operations are used primarily in criteria definition and in formulas containing an IF function. The format of the IF function is:

IF(*condition*, *result* [*condition true*], *result* [*condition false*])

Suppose the following IF function is placed in I10 in Figure S-15 to determine

FIGURE S-15
Spreadsheet: Logical Operators
See discussion in text.

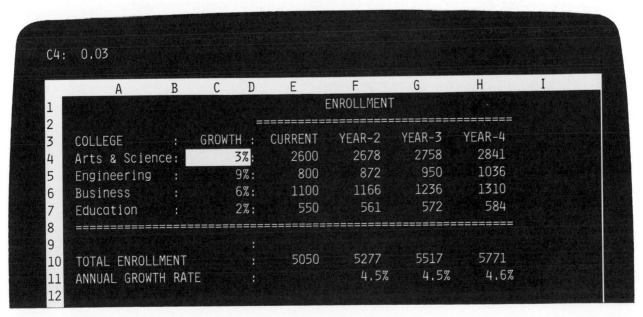

```
C4:   0.03

        A      B     C    D     E        F        G       H          I
1                                     ENROLLMENT
2                              ===================================
3    COLLEGE      :  GROWTH :  CURRENT  YEAR-2   YEAR-3   YEAR-4
4    Arts & Science:    3%:     2600     2678     2758     2841
5    Engineering  :     9%:      800      872      950     1036
6    Business     :     6%:     1100     1166     1236     1310
7    Education     :    2%:      550      561      572      584
8                              ===================================
9                    :
10   TOTAL ENROLLMENT :          5050     5277     5517     5771
11   ANNUAL GROWTH RATE :                 4.5%     4.5%     4.6%
12
```

if the anticipated growth in the student population is "rapid" (greater than 700 through year 4) or "normal."

IF((H10—E10)>700,"Rapid growth","Normal growth")

Since 721 (5771 − 5050) > 700, the condition is true; therefore, the character string "Rapid growth" would be placed in I10. If the data in Figure S-16 are applied, the condition 561 (5611 − 5050) > 700 is false; therefore, "Normal growth" would be the result.

The logical operators AND and OR permit us to combine relational expressions in a single criterion or IF function. For example, let's apply the following formulas to Figures S-15 and S-16:

IF((H10—E10)>700 # AND # @AVG(F11 . . H11) >.03,"Rapid growth",
    "Normal growth")

For the data in Figure S-15, both conditions are true and the result is "Rapid growth." With the AND logical operator, both must be true for the result to be true. For the data in Figure S-16, the first condition is false and the second is true. Therefore, the evaluation is false and the result is "Normal growth."

IF the AND were replaced by an OR as follows:

IF((H10—E10)>700 # OR # @AVG(F11 . . H11)>.03,"Rapid growth",
    "Normal growth")

the evaluation would be true for the data in both Figures S-15 and S-16. Since the second condition is true for Figure S-16, "Rapid growth" would be placed in I10.

FIGURE S-16
Spreadsheet: Logical Operators
See discussion in text.

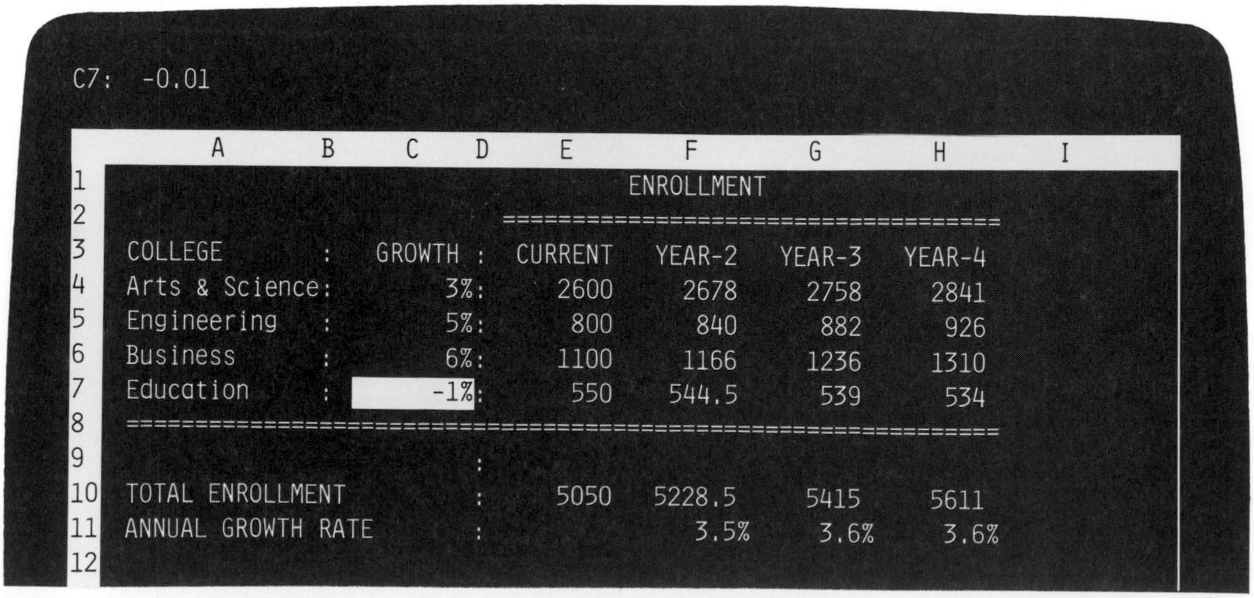

```
C7:  -0.01

            A      B      C     D      E        F         G        H       I
 1                                          ENROLLMENT
 2                              ===================================
 3   COLLEGE          :  GROWTH :  CURRENT   YEAR-2    YEAR-3   YEAR-4
 4   Arts & Science:        3%:     2600      2678      2758     2841
 5   Engineering    :        5%:      800       840       882      926
 6   Business       :        6%:     1100      1166      1236     1310
 7   Education       :       -1%:      550      544.5      539      534
 8                ===================================
 9                          :
10   TOTAL ENROLLMENT        :     5050      5228.5     5415     5611
11   ANNUAL GROWTH RATE      :                 3.5%      3.6%     3.6%
12
```

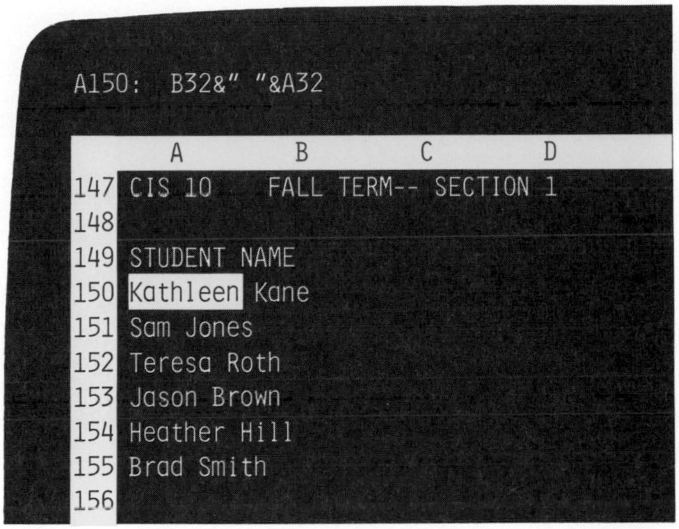

```
A150:  B32&" "&A32

          A        B        C        D
147  CIS 10      FALL TERM-- SECTION 1
148
149  STUDENT NAME
150  Kathleen Kane
151  Sam Jones
152  Teresa Roth
153  Jason Brown
154  Heather Hill
155  Brad Smith
156
```

FIGURE S-17
Spreadsheet: Concatention
The first-name and last-name
fields of Figure S-13 are
concatenated with a blank
(" ") to produce this report.

The result in an IF function can be a number, a character string, or even another formula. The professor in our grade example takes advantage of the formula result option to assign letter grades at the end of the term for the student data in Figure S-13. To do this, the following formula is entered in H32 and copied to H33 . . H37:

H32: @IF(G32>=90,"A",@IF(G32>   =80,"B",@IF(G32>=70,"C",
      @IF(G32 >=60,"D","F"))))

The formulas in the range H32 . . H37 assign the grade "A" to term averages (G32 . . G37) that are greater than or equal to 90, "B" to term averages that are greater than or equal to 80, and so on. Take as an example the evaluation of Teresa Roth's grade. Since the condition 88.1 (in location G32) is false (it is not >=90), the result of the evaluation is another IF. Since the condition 88.1>=80 is true, "B" is the result.

String Operations. A character string can be a label, a user-defined group of alphanumeric characters, part of a label, or the *concatenation* (putting together) of labels and other character strings. For example, the professor might wish to produce a report that lists all students in Figure S-13 with the first name first, then a space, and then the last name. This can be done by concatenating three character strings: the labels in the FNAME and LNAME columns, and a space (" "). Concatenation is denoted by an "and" (&) sign. The results are then placed in another area of the worksheet. The following formula is entered, then copied five times in the same column to create the report in Figure S-17:

A150: B32&" "&A32

The entry in A150 becomes "Kathleen Kane". Notice that the complete report is in column A.

Adding/Deleting Rows/Columns. You can insert or delete entire rows and columns. For example, if Brad Smith in Figure S-18 dropped CIS 10, the professor would simply delete the entire record (row 37). Since deleting

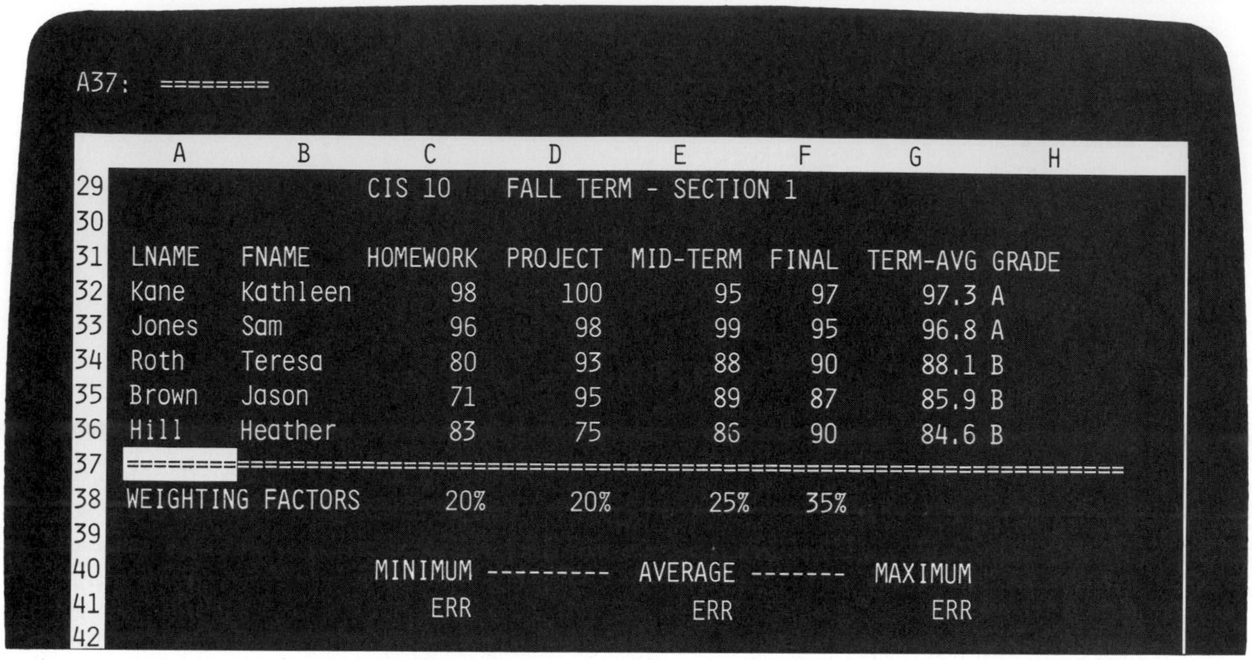

```
A37:    ========

      A          B          C          D          E          F          G          H
29                        CIS 10     FALL TERM - SECTION 1
30
31  LNAME      FNAME      HOMEWORK   PROJECT    MID-TERM   FINAL   TERM-AVG GRADE
32  Kane       Kathleen        98       100          95      97      97.3 A
33  Jones      Sam             96        98          99      95      96.8 A
34  Roth       Teresa          80        93          88      90      88.1 B
35  Brown      Jason           71        95          89      87      85.9 B
36  Hill       Heather         83        75          86      90      84.6 B
37  =================================================================================
38  WEIGHTING FACTORS        20%       20%         25%     35%
39
40                        MINIMUM ---------   AVERAGE -------   MAXIMUM
41                            ERR                  ERR               ERR
42
```

FIGURE S-18
Spreadsheet: Deleting a Row
Row 37 (Brad Smith's record) of Figure S-13 is deleted to produce this
spreadsheet.

row 37 affects the ranges for the minimum, average, and maximum computations, ERR (for error) is displayed in cells C41, E41, and G41 (see Figure
S-18). To correct the error, the professor must revise the ranges.

In Figure S-19, the professor inserted a column for laboratory grades
between the PROJECT and MID-TERM columns. When the LAB column
is inserted, all columns to the right of column D are moved over one column;
that is, the MID-TERM column shifts to column F. Column E becomes the
new LAB column. Notice how the term averages are not affected by the
addition of another column. The spreadsheet software automatically adjusts
the relative cell addresses in the term-average formulas, now in column H.
However, to reflect the addition of a laboratory grade, you have to add a
new weighting factor, then edit the term-average formulas accordingly.

Viewing Data in a Spreadsheet.   What if CIS 10 had 150 students rather
than 6? Since the screen on the monitor can display only a certain amount
of information, the professor would need to *scroll* vertically through the
spreadsheet to view students at the end. To view spreadsheet areas that
extend past the sides of the screen, you would need to scroll horizontally.
Scrolling through a worksheet is much like looking through a magnifying
glass as you move it around a page of a newspaper. You scroll left-right
and/or up-down to view various portions of a large spreadsheet or worksheet
(see Figure S-20).

```
E31:  LAB

         A         B         C         D         E         F         G         H
29                        CIS 10     FALL TERM - SECTION 1
30
31   LNAME     FNAME     HOMEWORK  PROJECT       LAB   MID-TERM  FINAL   TERM-AVG
32   Kane      Kathleen        98       100                95       97       97.3
33   Jones     Sam             96        98                99       95       96.8
34   Roth      Teresa          80        93                88       90       88.1
35   Brown     Jason           71        95                89       87       85.9
36   Hill      Heather         83        75                86       90       84.6
37   Smith     Brad            66        82                80       76       76.2
38   ===========================================       ============================
39   WEIGHTING FACTORS        20%       20%               25%      35%
40
41                       MINIMUM ---------       AVERAGE -------   MAXIMUM
42                           76.2                   88.15              97.3
43
```

FIGURE S-19
Spreadsheet: Inserting a Column
A column for laboratory grades is inserted in the spreadsheet of Figure S-13.

FIGURE S-20
Scrolling
Scroll vertically and horizontally to view those portions of a spreadsheet that
do not fit on a single screen.

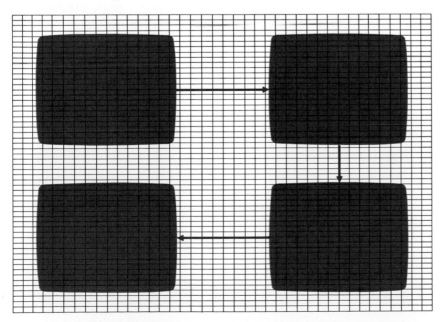

```
A36:  Hill


        A          B          C         D         E        F         G        H
 31  LNAME      FNAME     HOMEWORK   PROJECT   MID-TERM  FINAL   TERM-AVG  GRADE
 35  Brown      Jason          71        95         89      87      85.9  B
 36  Hill       Heather        83        75         86      90      84.6  B
 37  Smith      Brad           66        82         80      76      76.2  C
 38  =========================================================================
 39  WEIGHTING FACTORS         20%       20%        25%     35%
 40
 41                       MINIMUM --------- AVERAGE ------- MAXIMUM
 42                           76.2                 88.15             97.3
```

FIGURE S-21
Spreadsheet: Freeze Column Headings (Rows)
When the column headings are "frozen" at the top of the screen, they are
always visible when scrolling vertically through the student records.

As the professor scrolls down a long list of students, the column headings
(e.g., LNAME, FNAME, etc.) disappear from the screen to make room for
other students. As you can imagine, data without labels can be very confusing.
However, spreadsheet software has a solution to this dilemma: you can *freeze*
selected columns or rows. In the example of Figure S-21, the professor has
frozen row 31, the column headings, at the top of the screen so they are
always visible when scrolling through the student records. When you freeze
a portion of the screen, you are creating a new border with labels, and everything moves on the screen but the labels. Notice in Figure S-21 that the
first three student records are off the screen, but the heading labels remain.
The top three student records are returned to the screen when the professor
scrolls in the other direction. The pointer cannot be positioned in a frozen
area.

You can also freeze the leftmost columns, the ones which usually identify
a record. In Figure S-22, the professor froze the student name (columns A
and B), then scrolled horizontally to place the TERM-AVG and GRADE columns adjacent to the name columns. The freeze feature is particularly helpful
when the spreadsheet contains many columns of data and you want to work
with only a few columns at a time.

Formatting Data for Readability.   The appearance of data in a spreadsheet
can be modified to enhance readability. For example, the value .2 was entered
as a weighting factor in cell C39 (Figure S-23), but it appears in the spreadsheet
display as a percent. This is because the range C39 . . F39 was *formatted*
so that the values are automatically displayed as percents rather than fractions
(i.e., .2 becomes 20%). The methods of formatting data vary considerably
between integrated software packages.

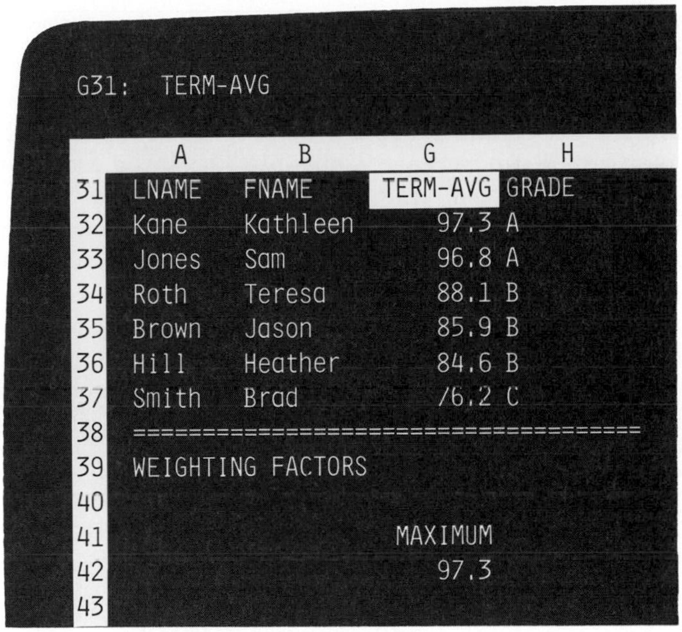

```
G31:  TERM-AVG

         A         B          G        H
   31  LNAME    FNAME      TERM-AVG GRADE
   32  Kane     Kathleen     97.3 A
   33  Jones    Sam          96.8 A
   34  Roth     Teresa       88.1 B
   35  Brown    Jason        85.9 B
   36  Hill     Heather      84.6 B
   37  Smith    Brad         76.2 C
   38  ======================================
   39  WEIGHTING FACTORS
   40
   41                      MAXIMUM
   42                        97.3
   43
```

FIGURE S-22
Spreadsheet: Freeze Columns
When columns A and B are "frozen" at the left of the screen, they are always visible when scrolling horizontally.

Currency amounts can be formatted so that commas and a dollar sign are inserted. For example, if the value 1346.3 is entered in a cell formatted for currency, it would be displayed as $1,346.30.

Numeric data can be defined so they are displayed with a fixed number of places to the right of the decimal point. In Figure S-23, the format of the term average figures is fixed with one decimal position. Numbers with more decimal digits than specified in the format are rounded when displayed.

FIGURE S-23
Spreadsheet: Searches (TERM-AVG<80)
Student records are highlighted when the TERM-AVG is less than 80. For these records, only Brad Smith's data meet this criterion.

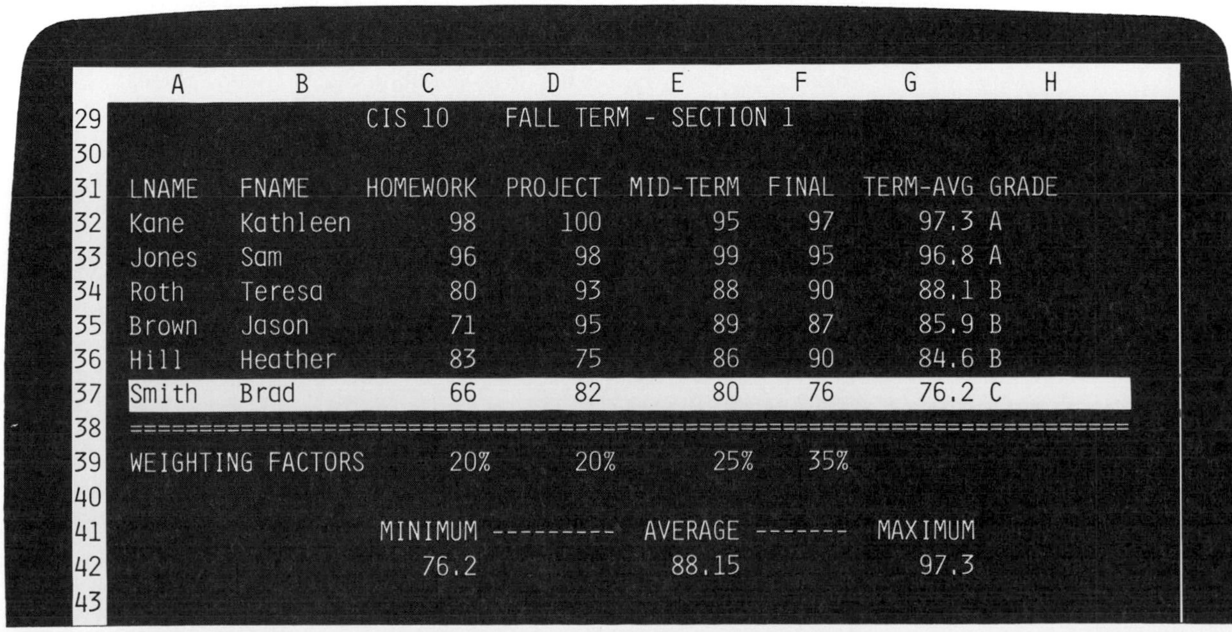

```
         A        B          C         D         E       F        G         H
   29              CIS 10      FALL TERM - SECTION 1
   30
   31  LNAME    FNAME      HOMEWORK  PROJECT  MID-TERM  FINAL  TERM-AVG GRADE
   32  Kane     Kathleen      98       100       95      97      97.3 A
   33  Jones    Sam           96        98       99      95      96.8 A
   34  Roth     Teresa        80        93       88      90      88.1 B
   35  Brown    Jason         71        95       89      87      85.9 B
   36  Hill     Heather       83        75       86      90      84.6 B
   37  Smith    Brad          66        82       80      76      76.2 C
   38  ==============================================================
   39  WEIGHTING FACTORS     20%       20%       25%     35%
   40
   41            MINIMUM --------- AVERAGE ------- MAXIMUM
   42              76.2              88.15           97.3
   43
```

Use

Spreadsheet Templates.   The electronic spreadsheet of Figure S-23 is a **template**, or a model, of a grade book that can be used over and over for different classes and by different professors. A template is analogous to a production program and a data base. It can be used again and again by different people with different sets of data. Another professor may change the title, the weighting factors, and, of course, the student data, but the layout and operations are already in place to calculate and assign grades and to produce summary statistics.

With electronic spreadsheets, a template is easily modified to fit a variety of situations. For example, another professor might add a laboratory grade. To do this, one would simply modify the existing template by adding a "LAB" column (see Figure S-19) and updating the term-average formula to reflect the laboratory grade.

Searches.   Electronic spreadsheet software lets you search for records or entries that meet certain criteria. For example, if the professor wanted to highlight those students with term averages below 80, the criteria would be set to be:

TERM-AVG<80

As shown in Figure S-23, Brad Smith's record would be highlighted because his term average, 76.2, is less than 80. Suppose the criteria were set to:

TERM-AVG<E42 and HOMEWORK<=75

Those students who were below the class average (88.15 in E42) and scored 75 or less on their homework would be highlighted. For these criteria, Brown would be highlighted first, then Smith.

"What If" Analysis.   Spreadsheet software is the perfect tool for "what if" analysis. For example, the professor wanted to ask "what if" the weighting factors for the homework and the project were revised from 20% and 20% to 10% and 30%. Remember, these values are referenced as absolute cell addresses in the formulas for term average. Therefore, any change in the value of a weighting factor will also change the results of all formulas in which it appears. The results of a weighting factor change in cells C39 and D39 are shown in Figure S-24. Compare the results to Figure S-23.

These educators use data management software in conjunction with spreadsheet software to ask "what if" questions concerning student enrollment.
(Dataproducts Corporation)

```
C39:  0.1

        A        B        C        D        E        F        G          H
29                        CIS 10    FALL TERM - SECTION 1
30
31  LNAME    FNAME    HOMEWORK  PROJECT  MID-TERM  FINAL  TERM-AVG GRADE
32  Kane     Kathleen      98      100        95     97      97.5 A
33  Jones    Sam           96       98        99     95      97.0 A
34  Roth     Teresa        80       93        88     90      89.4 B
35  Brown    Jason         71       95        89     87      88.3 B
36  Hill     Heather       83       75        86     90      83.8 B
37  Smith    Brad          66       82        80     76      77.8 C
38  =================================================================
39  WEIGHTING FACTORS      10%      30%       25%    35%
40
41                   MINIMUM ---------  AVERAGE -------  MAXIMUM
42                     77.8              89.0              97.5
43
```

FIGURE S-24
Spreadsheet: "What If" Analysis
This spreadsheet results from the following inquiry: "What if the weighting factors for the homework and project were revised from 20% and 20% to 10% and 30%?" Only cells C39 and D39 are changed. Under the new weighting, the same letter grades are awarded, but Teresa Roth jumped from 88.1 to 89.4 and might be considered for an "A."

In earlier examples (Figures S-15 and S-16), the university provost did some "what if" analysis with the enrollment figures. In Figure S-15 they asked "what if" the projected annual growth rates were 3%, 9%, 6%, and 2% for each college. In Figure S-16 they asked "what if" the projected annual growth rates for engineering and education were less optimistic (i.e., 5% and −2%).

Reporting. You can establish certain criteria, and the software extracts (selects) records that meet these criteria, then lists them in a report (as opposed to highlighting them in a search). For example, if you wanted to produce a report listing all students with term averages of 95 or better, then you set the following criterion:

TERM-AVG>=95

Also, the professor wanted the list sorted in alphabetic sequence by student name. To do this, the LNAME entries are identified as the primary sort key and FNAME entries as the secondary sort key. Only the records of Kathleen Kane and Sam Jones are selected. Their records are then sorted and copied to a report range (K31 .. R33). The report is shown in Figure S-25. This example will be expanded in the word processing section.

```
K31:  LNAME

        K        L         M        N        O        P        Q        R
31  LNAME    FNAME     HOMEWORK  PROJECT MID-TERM    FINAL TERM-AVG GRADE
32  Jones    Sam            96       98       99       95     96.8 A
33  Kane     Kathleen       98      100       95       97     97.3 A
34
```

FIGURE S-25
Spreadsheet: Report Generation
The criterion, TERM-AVG>=95, is applied to the spreadsheet of Figure S-23
to produce this report.

For the criteria:

HOMEWORK<85 and PROJECT<85

Heather Hill and Brad Smith's records are selected and moved to the report
area (see Figure S-26).

```
K31:  LNAME

        K        L         M        N        O        P        Q        R
31  LNAME    FNAME     HOMEWORK  PROJECT MID-TERM    FINAL TERM-AVG GRADE
32  Hill     Heather        83       75       86       90     84.6 B
33  Smith    Brad           66       82       80       76     76.2 C
34
```

FIGURE S-26
Spreadsheet: Report Generation
The criteria, HOMEWORK<85 and PROJECT<85, are applied to the
spreadsheet of Figure S-23 to produce this report.

Spreadsheet Summary

We have really only begun to tap the benefits of spreadsheet software. We've
seen how the data management component of integrated software can be
employed to create a data base and entries for the spreadsheet. Next we
will discuss how these data can be used to create a variety of graphs and
charts. Then we'll see how the spreadsheet data can be integrated with word
processing and sent via data communications. There's more to come!

REVIEW EXERCISES (S-5) _____

1. Describe the layout of an electronic spreadsheet.
2. Give an example cell address. Which portion of the address depicts the row and which portion depicts the column?
3. On what is a relative cell address based?
4. Give an example of each of the four types of ranges.
5. Give examples of the three types of entries that can be made in an electronic spreadsheet.
6. What type of operators are used to compare numeric and string values?
7. Write the equivalent formula for @AVG(A1 .. D1) without the use of functions.
8. If the formula B2*B1 is copied from C1 to E3, what is the formula in E3? If the formula in E3 is copied to D45, what is the formula in D45?
9. What is the difference between the pointer and the cursor?
10. List three alternatives descriptors for the range A4 .. P12.
11. When do you "anchor the pointer"?
12. What would you use in a formula to override the priority rules for arithmetic operators?
13. What formula would be entered in cell C2 to compute GROSS pay?

```
        A       B        C
1 HOURS   RATE      GROSS
2      40     10.50      420.00
```

14. What formula would be entered in A5 to sum all of numbers in the range A1 .. A4?
15. When would you need to scroll horizontally? Vertically?
16. What is a spreadsheet template?

HANDS-ON EXERCISES _____

1. The following data represent the unit sales data for the past year for Diolab, Inc.

DIOLAB INC. SALES (UNITS)

REGION	QTR1	QTR2	QTR3	QTR4
NE REGION	214	300	320	170
SE REGION	120	150	165	201
SW REGION	64	80	60	52
NW REGION	116	141	147	180

If you have not already done so (for Hands-on Exercise 3 in Section S-4), enter the above title, headings, and data in an electronic spreadsheet. Place the title in the range B1, the column headings in the range A2 .. E2, the row headings in the range A3 .. A6, and the sales data in the range B3 .. E6.

If the following assignments are to be handed in, print out the initial spreadsheets, then print them out again for each revision.

2. Add another column heading called SALES/YR in F2 of the Diolab spreadsheet. Enter a formula in F3 that sums the sales for each quarter for the northeast region. Copy the formula to the range F4 .. F6. SALES/YR should be 1004 for the NE Region and 636 for the SE Region.

3. Add average sales per quarter, AVG/QTR, in column G. AVG/QTR should be 251 for the NE Region and 159 for the SE Region.

4. Add two more columns that reflect sales per salesperson. In column H, add number of salespersons, PERSONS: 5, 3, 2, and 4, respectively. In column I, add formulas that compute sales per person, SALES/PER (from the data in SALES/YR and PERSONS columns). SALES/PER should be 200.8 for the NE Region and 212 for the SE Region.

5. In the range B8 .. F8, use functions to total sales for each quarter and for the year. The total sales for all regions should be 2480.

6. Copy the range A2 .. A6 to A12 .. A16 and B2 .. E2 to B12 .. E12. Diolab, Inc., sales are estimated to be 120% of last year's sales. Complete the newly created spreadsheet by multiplying last year's quarterly sales data by 1.2 and placing the result in the spreadsheet. Title this set of data ESTIMATED DIOLAB INC. SALES – NEXT YEAR. The NE Region first-quarter sales should be 257 (rounded) and the SE Region second-quarter sales should be 180.

7. Each of the lab analysis units sells for $2,000. Add formulas in column F to compute estimated GROSS sales ($2,000 times the total of the estimated quarterly sales) for each region. Also format the GROSS sales values as currency with no decimal places such that the NE Region amount appears as $2,409,600 (SE Region is $1,526,400). You may need to expand the width of column F to 11 positions.

8. How would you describe the criteria for selecting records for which the fourth-quarter sales were greater than first-quarter sales? Apply these criteria to the Diolab, Inc., sales data for last year. Use these criteria to "find" and "extract" appropriate records. Only the SE and NW Regions meet these criteria.

9. Sort last year's sales data by SALES/YR (highest sales first). The order of the regions should be NE, SE, NW, and SW after the sort.

10. Change the width of columns B through E to 6 positions.

S-6 GRAPHICS

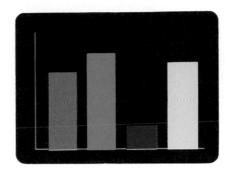

Function

With the graphics component of integrated software, you can create a variety of presentation graphics from data in a data base or a spreadsheet. Among the most popular presentation graphics are **bar charts**, **pie charts**, and **line charts** (see Figure S-27). Other types of charts are possible. Each of these charts can be annotated with chart *titles*, *labels* for axes, and *legends*.

Some graphics software lets you create and store original drawings. To do this, however, your personal computer must be equipped with a mouse, joy stick, digitizing board, or some type of device that permits the input of curved and angular lines. To make drawing easier to do, such software even offers a data base filled with a variety of frequently used symbols, such as rectangles, circles, cats (yes, even cats), and so on. Some companies draw and store the image of their company logo so it can be inserted on memos, reports, and charts.

FIGURE S-27
Graphics: Bar Chart, Clustered-Bar Chart, Pie Chart, and Line Chart

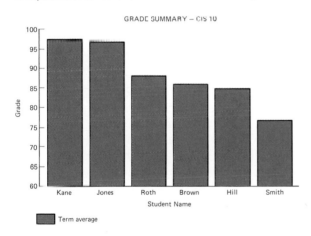

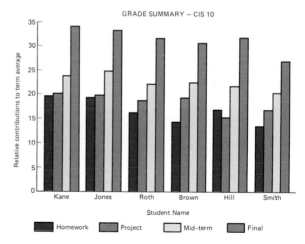

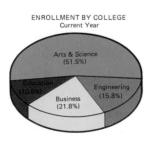

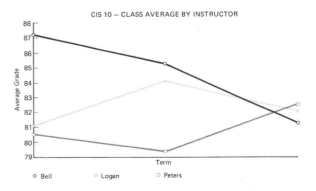

With graphics software, you can prepare professional-looking visuals for presentations. The plotter draws the image directly on a blank acetate. When the acetate is placed on an overhead projector, the graphic image is projected on a large screen.
(Tektronix, Inc.)

Graphic representations of data have proven to be a very effective means of communication. It is easier to recognize problem areas and trends in a chart than it is in a tabular summary of the same data. For many years, the presentation of tabular data was the preferred approach to communicating tabular information. This was because it was simply too expensive and time consuming to manually produce presentation graphics. Today, you can use graphics software to produce perfectly proportioned, accurate, and visually appealing charts in a matter of seconds. Prior to the introduction of graphics software, the turnaround time was at least a day, and often a week.

Concepts

With integrated software, the data needed to produce a chart already exist in a spreadsheet or data base. The graphics software leads you through a series of prompts, the first of which asks you what type of graph is to be produced: bar chart, pie chart, line chart, and so on. You then select the spreadsheet ranges (or data base fields) that are to be plotted. You can also select ranges for the labels. Once you have identified the ranges for the data and labels, and perhaps added a title, you can display, print, or plot the graph.

Since the graphics software component is integrated with the data base and spreadsheet software components, any change in the worksheet data is reflected in the charts as well. When you create "what if" situations, any charts that you have defined are automatically updated each time you change the data.

Use

Bar Charts.   Let's return to the professor and the student data (reproduced in Figure S-28) to demonstrate the use of bar charts. Before assigning grades, professors often plot their grades to see if there are any apparent dividing lines for the As, Bs, and so on. To produce the bar chart in Figure S-29, the professor in our example first used the *sort* feature of the electronic spreadsheet to sort the records by TERM-AVG in descending sequence (highest grade first). Appropriate ranges were then specified; that is, the values in the TERM-AVG column (range G32 . . G37) are to be plotted and the values in the LNAME column (range A32 . . A37) are to be inserted as labels along the *x* axis. The professor also added a title for the chart (GRADE SUMMARY – CIS 10), titles for the *x* axis (STUDENT NAME) and *y* axis (GRADE), and a legend (TERM AVERAGE) to denote the meaning of the bars. The professor set the origin to 60, rather than 0, so that the differences between grades would be more apparent.

The bar chart of Figure S-29 graphically highlights how three groups of students fall neatly within the traditional grade breaks (90, 80, and so on) for assigning letter grades. Had the chart indicated a need for the professor to curve the grades and establish new grade breaks, the grade assignment formulas in the range H32 . . H37 (Figure S-28) could be easily edited to reflect the new grade breaks (e.g., 90 would become 92, 80 would become 84, and so on).

```
C29:  CIS 10    FALL TERM - SECTION 1

      A        B         C         D        E        F        G          H
29                     CIS 10     FALL TERM - SECTION 1
30
31   LNAME    FNAME    HOMEWORK   PROJECT  MID-TERM  FINAL   TERM-AVG GRADE
32   Kane     Kathleen      98       100        95      97      97.3 A
33   Jones    Sam           96        98        99      95      96.8 A
34   Roth     Teresa        80        93        88      90      88.1 B
35   Brown    Jason         71        95        89      87      85.9 B
36   Hill     Heather       83        75        86      90      84.6 B
37   Smith    Brad          66        82        80      76      76.2 C
38   ======================================================================
39   WEIGHTING FACTORS     20%       20%       25%     35%
40
41                     MINIMUM --------- AVERAGE ------- MAXIMUM
42                       76.2              88.15            97.3
43
```

FIGURE S-28
Spreadsheet: Student Data
These data are used to produce the bar charts of Figures S-29 and S-30.

FIGURE S-29
Graphics: Bar Chart
The TERM-AVG for each student in Figure S-28 is graphically represented in
this bar chart.

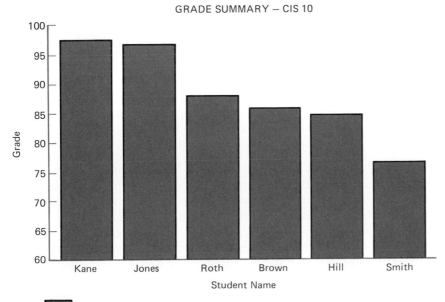

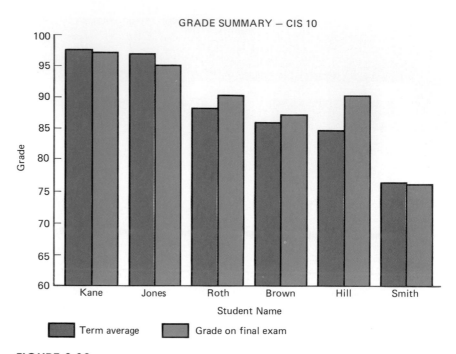

FIGURE S-30
Graphics: Clustered-Bar Chart
The TERM-AVG and FINAL for each student in Figure S-28 are graphically
represented in this clustered-bar chart.

The grades on the final exam (range F32 . . F37) can be plotted alongside
the term average in a *clustered-bar chart*. The resultant chart, shown in Figure
S-30, permits the professor to visually correlate the grade on the final exam
with the term average for each student.

To better assess the strengths and weaknesses of a particular student,
the professor created another spreadsheet in a different area of the worksheet.
This spreadsheet (see Figure S-31) reflects each grade's *contribution* to the
term average. The entries were calculated by multiplying the weighting factors
by the grade. In C92, .2*98 = 19.6. From these data the professor created
the *stacked-bar chart* in Figure S-32. This chart graphically illustrates how
Heather Hill's poor showing on the project probably cost her an "A." An
alternative way to graphically present these same data is illustrated in the
clustered-bar chart in Figure S-33.

Pie Charts.   Pie charts are the most basic of presentation graphics. A pie
chart graphically illustrates each "piece" of data in its proper relationship
to the whole "pie." To illustrate how a pie chart is constructed and used,
refer again to the "enrollment" spreadsheet reproduced in Figure S-34. The
university's provost produced the pie chart in Figure S-35 by specifying the
values in the CURRENT column (range E4 . . E7) to be the "pieces" of the
pie. It was further specified that the values in the COLLEGE column (range
A4 . . A7) be inserted as labels, and a title was added. The numbers in parentheses represent what percent each piece (i.e., college enrollment) is of
the whole (i.e., total enrollment).

```
C96:  0.2*C36

       A        B          C         D        E        F        G          H
88                    CIS 10      FALL TERM - SECTION 1
89         GRADES ARE ADJUSTED TO REFLECT WEIGHTING FACTORS
90
91  LNAME    FNAME     HOMEWORK  PROJECT  MID-TERM  FINAL   TERM-AVG
92  Kane     Kathleen      19.6     20.0     23.8   34.0      97.3
93  Jones    Sam           19.2     19.6     24.8   33.3      96.8
94  Roth     Teresa        16.0     18.6     22.0   31.5      88.1
95  Brown    Jason         14.2     19.0     22.3   30.5      85.9
96  Hill     Heather       16.6     15.0     21.5   31.5      84.6
97  Smith    Brad          13.2     16.4     20.0   26.6      76.2
98  ================================================================
99  POINTS POSSIBLE         20       20       25     35       100
100
```

FIGURE S-31
Spreadsheet: Student Data of Figure S-28 Revised to Reflect Contribution to TERM-AVG
These data are used to produce the bar charts of Figures S-32 and S-33.

FIGURE S-32
Graphics: Stacked-Bar Chart
This stacked-bar chart shows the relative contribution of each grade (in the spreadsheet of Figure S-28) to the TERM-AVG grade. The actual data for the chart come from Figure S-31.

GRADE SUMMARY — CIS 10

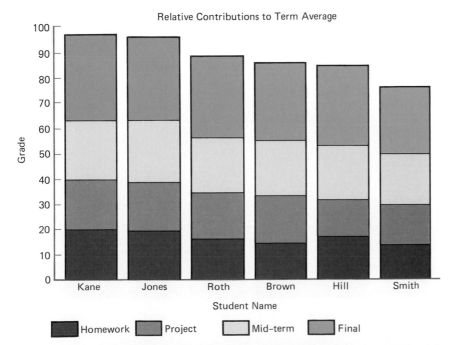

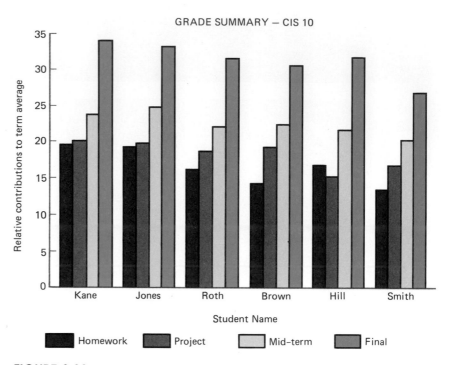

FIGURE S-33
Graphics: Clustered-Bar Chart
This clustered-bar chart is an alternative to the stacked-bar chart of Figure S-32.

FIGURE S-34
Spreadsheet: Student Enrollment Data
These data are used to produce the pie chart of Figure S-35.

```
C7:  -0.01

          A       B    C    D   E       F        G        H        I
 1                                     ENROLLMENT
 2                              ==================================
 3   COLLEGE     :  GROWTH :  CURRENT   YEAR-2   YEAR-3   YEAR-4
 4   Arts & Science:      3%:    2600     2678     2758     2841
 5   Engineering  :       5%:     800      840      882      926
 6   Business     :       6%:    1100     1166     1236     1310
 7   Education    :      -1%:     550    544.5      539      534
 8               ==================================================
 9                      :
10   TOTAL ENROLLMENT   :        5050   5228.5     5415     5611
11   ANNUAL GROWTH RATE :                 3.5%     3.6%     3.6%
12
```

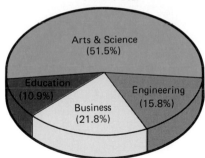

ENROLLMENT BY COLLEGE
Current Year

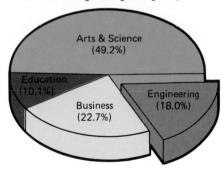

ENROLLMENT BY COLLEGE
4th Year — Engineering College Exploded

FIGURE S-35
Graphics: Pie Chart
The values in the CURRENT column of Figure S-34 are graphically represented in this pie chart.

FIGURE S-36
Graphics: Pie Chart with One Piece Exploded
The values in the YEAR-4 column of Figure S-34 are graphically represented in this pie chart. The Engineering College piece is exploded.

A pie chart reflecting the projected fourth-year enrollment is shown in Figure S-36. The values for this pie chart are taken from the YEAR-4 column (range H4 .. H7). Since Engineering was projected to have the highest rate of growth, the Engineering "piece" was *exploded* (or separated) from the pie for emphasis.

FRAMEWORK, an integrated software package, illustrates how spreadsheet data and the resultant clustered-bar chart can be depicted on the same screen by using windows.
(Copyright © Ashton-Tate 1984, FRAMEWORK ™ is a trademark of Ashton-Tate)

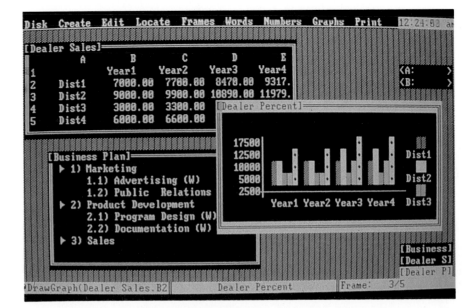

```
A102:

        A          B        C         D         E
102 [        ]  CIS 10 - CLASS AVERAGES BY INSTRUCTOR
103
104 INSTRUCTOR            FALL      SPRING     SUMMER
105 Bell                 87.2       85.2       81.2
106 Logan                80.5       79.3       82.4
107 Peters               81.1       84.1       82.0
108
```

FIGURE S-37
Spreadsheet: Class Averages by Instructor Data
These data are used to produce the line chart of Figure S-38.

Line Charts.   A line chart connects like points on a graph with one or several lines. To illustrate how this is done, consider the data in the spreadsheet of Figure S-37. The spreadsheet contains the CIS 10 class averages by instructor during the last academic year. During the fall term the chairperson of the department asked the instructors to work together to achieve equity in grading. The line chart produced in Figure S-38 shows how they have done. Three ranges of data are plotted and connected with a line, one for each instructor. From the chart, it appears that the instructors finally agreed on an appropriate target for the class average.

FIGURE S-38
Graphics: Line Chart
This line chart shows a plot of the data of Figure S-37. A line connects the class averages for each instructor during the past year.

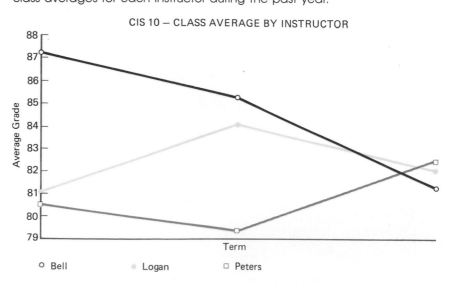

CIS 10 — CLASS AVERAGE BY INSTRUCTOR

INFORMING AND PERSUADING WITH PRESENTATION GRAPHICS

Making a presentation? Want help in getting your point across? According to a study conducted by the University of Pennsylvania, people who use visual aids in their presentations are perceived as being more professional, persuasive, and effective than those who don't. Whether the concepts are simple or complex, the use of graphics make them easier to understand.

Computer-generated graphics software adds another dimension to a presentation. Points can be visually presented with charts and graphs that are highlighted with color, various type fonts, line styles, and fill patterns. You can even create freehand drawings, graphic designs, and animated picture shows to enhance your graphics presentation.

A variety of graphics output hardware can be used with the computer-generated graphics software. Dot-matrix printers and pen plotters produce hard-copy color graphics. You can also produce slides for presentations. With the click of a camera, the computer-generated image is transferred to a high-resolution color slide (well, almost that quickly). And finally, you can use systems that project the image to a large screen to be viewed by a room full of people.

Of course, although a chart or a graph may be visually appealing, its quality is only as good as that of the data upon which it is based.

REVIEW EXERCISES (S-6)

1. Name three types of charts commonly used for presentation graphics.
2. In integrated software, what is the source of the data needed to produce the charts?
3. Name and graphically illustrate (by hand) two variations on the bar chart.
4. What types of input devices enable you to produce original line drawings?
5. Under what circumstances is a graphic representation of data more effective than a tabular presentation of the same data?
6. What is meant when a portion of a pie chart is exploded?
7. Is it possible to present the same information in a stacked bar and a line chart? How about stacked bar and pie charts?

HANDS-ON EXERCISES

1. The following Diolab, Inc., sales data are reproduced from Hands-on Exercises in Sections S-4 and S-5.

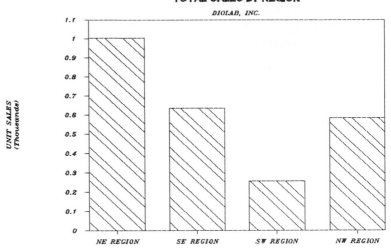

TOTAL SALES BY REGION
DIOLAB, INC.

DIOLAB INC. SALES (UNITS)

REGION	QTR1	QTR2	QTR3	QTR4	SALES/YR
NE REGION	214	300	320	170	1004
SE REGION	120	150	165	201	636
SW REGION	64	80	60	52	256
NW REGION	116	141	147	180	584

Produce the accompanying bar chart showing the total unit sales by region for Diolab, Inc. Label the y and x axes as shown.

2. Produce the accompanying pie chart showing the total unit sales by region for Diolab, Inc. Title the chart and label each piece as shown.

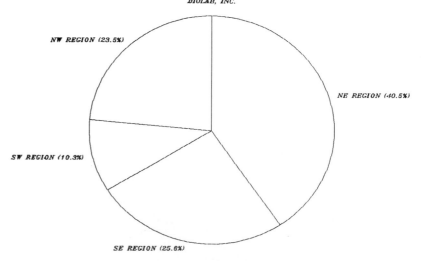

TOTAL SALES BY REGION
DIOLAB, INC.

NW REGION (23.5%)

NE REGION (40.5%)

SW REGION (10.3%)

SE REGION (25.6%)

3. Compare the information portrayed in the bar and pie charts above.

4. Produce the accompanying clustered-bar chart showing quarterly unit sales by region for Diolab, Inc. Title the chart, label the axes, and include a legend as shown.

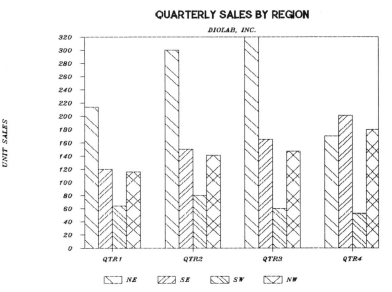

5. Produce the accompanying line chart showing quarterly unit sales by region for Diolab, Inc. Title the chart, label the axes, and include a legend as shown.

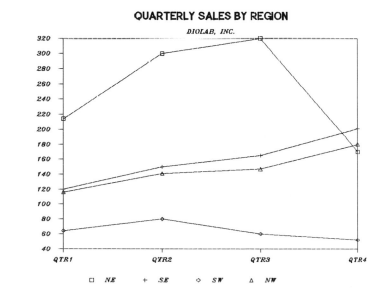

6. Compare the information portrayed in the clustered-bar and line charts above.

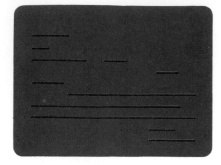

S-7   WORD PROCESSING _____

Function

The "glamor" software of the 70s, word processing, has become a mainstay application of computers in virtually every office. Word processing is using the computer to enter, store, manipulate, and print text in letters, reports, books, and so on. Once you have used word processing, you will probably wonder (like a million others before you) how in the world you ever survived without it!

With the integration of word processing and the other four components of integrated software, the already enormous benefits of word processing are enhanced even further. Besides providing an easier, faster alternative to typing and revising documents, word processing capabilities can now be integrated with other applications. If you think about it, seldom do we produce a report or chart without adding some explanatory text. And with communications capabilities, we may not always need to produce a hard copy of a letter or a memo—we can just send it via electronic mail.

This microcomputer system is configured with a desktop laser printer. The marketing manager uses word processing software to draft memos, letters, and reports. Hard copies can be produced on the laser printer at the rate of eight pages a minute.
(Compugraphic Corporation, Wilmington, MA)

Word processing has virtually eliminated the need for opaque correction fluid and the need to rekey revised letters and reports. Revising a hard copy is time consuming and cumbersome, but revising the same text in electronic format is quick and easy. You simply make corrections and revisions to the text on the computer before the document is displayed or printed in final form.

Figure S-39 reproduces the spreadsheet (the student data) and the word processing windows (a memorandum) that were originally illustrated in Figure S-1. Examples in this word processing section focus on the memo in Figure S-39 and how data from the spreadsheet can be integrated into the memo.

FIGURE S-39
Integrated Software Windows:
Spreadsheet and Word Processing

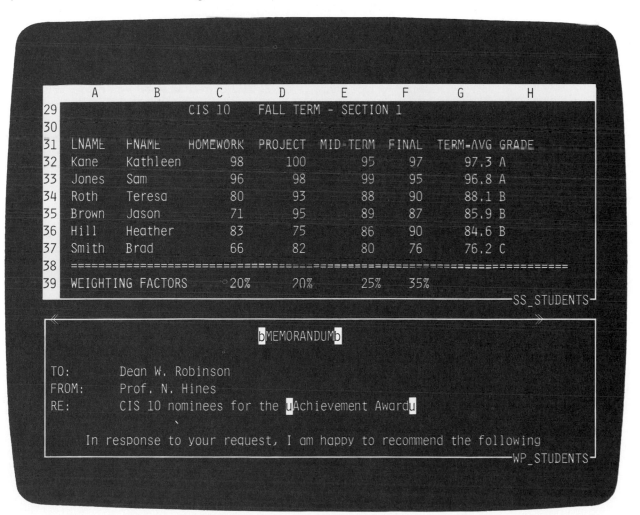

Concepts

Formatting a Document.   When you *format* a document, you are describing the size of the print page and how you want the document to look when it is printed. As with the typewriter, you must set the left and right margins, the tab settings, line spacing (e.g., lines/inch), and character spacing (e.g., characters/inch). Depending on the software package, some or all of these specifications are made in a *layout line*. You can have as many layout lines as you want in a single document. The text following a particular layout line is printed according to its specifications until another layout line is defined.

You must also specify the size of the paper, then set margins for the top and bottom of the text. The default paper size is almost always $8\frac{1}{2}$ by 11 inches.

As an option, you can even *justify* (line up) both the left and the right margins, like the print in newspapers and this book. Word processing software is able to produce "clean" margins on both sides by adding small spaces between characters and words in a line.

Entering Text.   To begin preparation of a document, all you have to do is begin typing. Text is entered in **replace mode** or **insert mode**. When in replace mode, the character that you enter *overstrikes* the character at the cursor position. For instance, suppose you typed the word "the", but you wanted to type "and". To make the correction in replace mode, you would position the cursor at the "t" and type a-n-d, thereby replacing the "the" with "and".

Entry mode is switched between replace and insert mode by pressing a key. When in insert mode, you can enter *additional* text. For example, suppose you entered "the Achievement Award" in the first sentence of the memo of Figure S-40 and would like to add the word "annual" and a space (" ") before "Achievement". Simply select insert mode, place the cursor on the "A" in "Achievement", and enter "annual". After the addition, the sentence will read "the annual Achievement Award" (see Figure S-41).

Word processing permits *full-screen editing*. That is, you can move the cursor to any position in the document to insert or replace text. You can browse through a multiscreen document by *scrolling* a line at a time or a "page" (a screen) at a time. You can edit any part of any screen.

When you enter text, you press the carriage return key only when you wish to begin a new line of text. As you enter text in replace mode, the computer automatically moves the cursor to the next line. In insert mode, the computer manipulates the text such that it *wraps around*, sending words that are pushed past the right margin into the next line, and so on, to the end of the paragraph. In Figures S-40 and S-41, notice how the words "in CIS" (in the second sentence) are wrapped around to the next line when "annual" is inserted.

Common Features.   Features common to most word processing software packages are mentioned and briefly discussed in this section. Two of the handiest features of word processing are the *copy* and *move* commands. With the copy feature, you can select a sentence, a paragraph, a section of

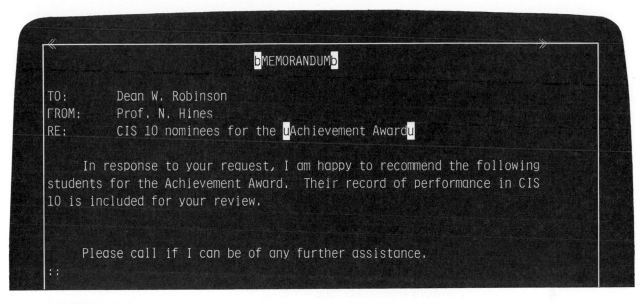

FIGURE S-40
Word Processing: Memorandum
The text material in this memo is revised for illustrative purposes in Figures
S-41 through S-45.

FIGURE S-41
Word Processing: Insert Mode
This memo is the result of the word "annual" being inserted in the first sentence
of the memo in Figure S-40. Notice how the text wraps around to make
room for "annual".

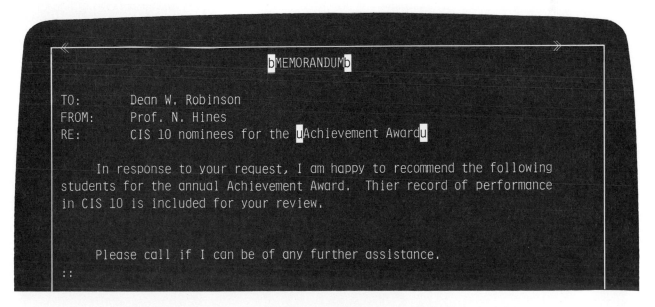

a report, or as much contiguous text as you desire and copy it to another portion of the document. To do this, follow these steps:

1. Issue the copy command.
2. Indicate the start and ending positions of the text to be copied (range).
3. Move the cursor to the beginning location (upper left) of where you wish the text to be copied.
4. Press the carriage return to complete the copy operation.

At the end of the copy procedure, two exact copies of the text are present in the document.

The professor who wrote the memo in Figure S-41 would like to send essentially the same memo for another class that is taught. Rather than reenter the text, the above procedures are followed to produce a copy right below the original (see Figure S-42).

FIGURE S-42
Word Processing: Copy Text
A copy of the memo of Figure S-41 is made just below the original. The copy command steps are listed in the text.

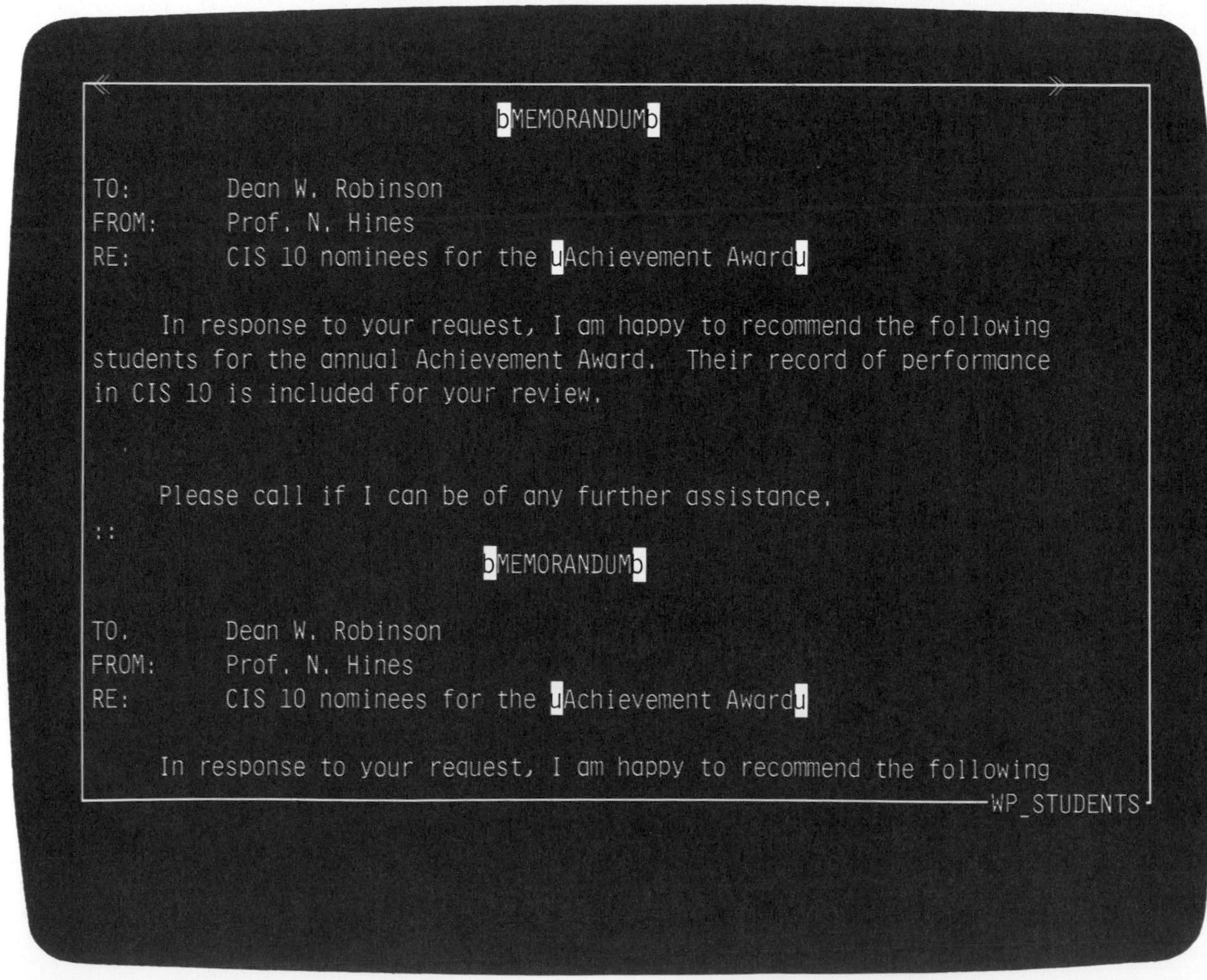

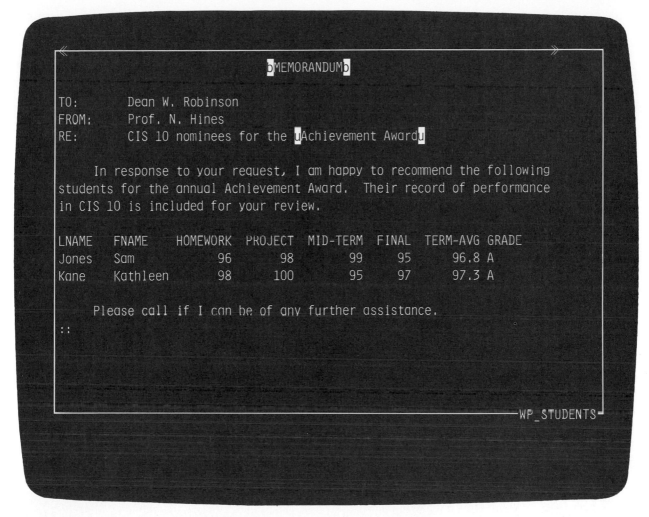

FIGURE S-43
Word Processing: Integration of Spreadsheet and Word Processing
The spreadsheet-generated report of Figure S-25 is moved from a spreadsheet area into the text of the memo of Figure S-41 to produce this memo.

The move command works in a similar manner, except the text that you select is moved to the location that you designate and the original is deleted. The following example demonstrates both the move command and how spreadsheet and word processing applications can be integrated. Rather than reproduce the students' records of performance, the professor moves the report of Figure S-25 (criterion is TERM-AVG $>=$ 95) from one area of the worksheet into the blank space in the memo (see Figure S-43).

The *search* or *find* feature permits you to search through the entire document and identify all occurrences of a particular character string. For example, if you want to search for all occurrences of "CIS 10" in Figure S-43, you simply initiate the search command and type in the desired character string, "CIS 10" in this example. The cursor is immediately positioned at the first occurrence of the character string "CIS 10". From there, you can step through other occurrences by pressing the appropriate key. You can also *search and replace*. For example, the professor can selectively replace "CIS 10" with "PSY 310". In Figure S-44, all occurrences of "CIS 10" are selectively replaced with "PSY 310". This could have been done instantly with a *global search and replace*. Besides copying the performance record report, the only other changes the professor had to make to the original memo were to delete the "s" in "nominees" and "students" and change "their" to "his". Only one student was recommended in PSY 310.

FIGURE S-44
Word Processing: Search and Replace
The text of the memo of Figure S-43 can be easily revised and used for PSY 310. With the search and replace command, the two occurrences of "CIS 10" are automatically located and replaced with "PSY 310".

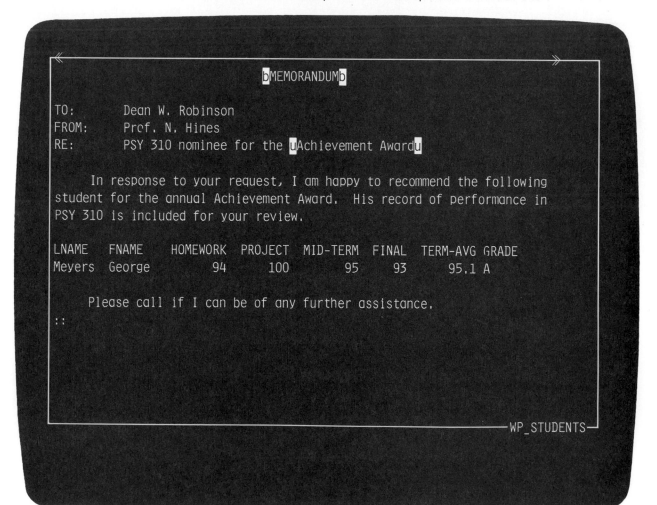

```
                              MEMORANDUM

  TO:        Dean W. Robinson
  FROM:      Prof. N. Hines
  RE:        CIS 10 nominees for the Achievement Award

       In response to your request, I am happy to recommend the following
  students for the annual Achievement Award.  Their record of performance
  in CIS 10 is included for your review.

  LNAME    FNAME     HOMEWORK   PROJECT   MID-TERM   FINAL   TERM-AVG  GRADE
  Jones    Sam            96        98         99      95      96.8 A
  Kane     Kathleen       98       100         95      97      97.3 A

       Please call if I can be of any further assistance.
```

FIGURE S-45
Word Processing: Printing Text
The memo of Figure S-43 is printed.

Other word processing features include automatic *centering* of titles. In Figure S-43, the center command was issued to cause the word "MEMORAN-DUM" to be centered. You can also center or *indent* blocks of text.

Word processing provides the facility to *boldface* and/or *underline* parts of the text for emphasis. In the memo of Figure S-43, the reverse video "b" before and after the word "MEMORANDUM" causes it to appear in boldface print on output (see Figure S-45). The reverse video "u" before and after the phrase "Achievement Award" (see Figure S-43) causes it to be underlined on output (see Figure S-45). Depending upon the type of software and printer you have, you may even be able to mix the size and style of type fonts in a single document. For example, you might wish to print the word "MEMORANDUM" in 48 point (about $\frac{1}{2}$ inch high) old English print.

Word processing software automatically prints *header* and *trailer labels*, if you so desire. The *pagination* feature automatically numbers the pages. On long reports, you might wish to repeat the report title at the top of each page and number each page at the bottom.

Advanced Features.   The features discussed in this section are available with the more sophisticated word processing packages. For example, some word processing software has sophisticated features for writers. A simple command creates a *table of contents*, with page numbers, from the first-level headers. An alphabetical *index of key words* can be created that lists the page numbers for each occurrence of designated words. One of the most tedious typing chores, *footnoting*, is done automatically. Footnote spacing is resolved electronically before anything is printed.

Have you ever been writing along and been unable to put your finger on the right word? Well, some word processing packages have a built-in *thesaurus*! Suppose you have just written: "The Grand Canyon certainly is beautiful." But "beautiful" is not quite the right word. Your electronic thesaurus is always ready with suggestions: pretty, elegant, exquisite, angelic, pulchritudinous, ravishing, ... Pulchritudinous? Oh, well.

If spelling is a problem, then word processing is the answer. Once you have entered the text and formatted the document the way you want it, you can call on the *spell* feature. The spell feature checks every word in the text against an electronic dictionary (usually from 75,000 to 150,000 words), then alerts you if a word is not in the dictionary. Upon finding an unidentified word, the spell function will normally give you several options.

1. You can correct the spelling.
2. You can ignore the word and continue scanning the text. Normally you do this when a word is spelled correctly but is not in the dictionary (e.g., a company name such as Diolab).
3. You can ask for possible spellings. The spell function then gives you a list of words of similar spelling from which to choose. For example, upon finding the nonword "persors," the spell function might suggest: person, persona, persons, personal, and personnel.
4. Or, you can add the word to the dictionary and continue scanning.

The *grammar* feature highlights grammatical concerns and deviations from conventions. For example, it highlights split infinitives, phrases with redundant words (e.g., "very highest"), misuse of caps (e.g., JOhn or MarY), sexist phrases, double words (e.g., and and), and sentences that are written in the passive voice (versus the active voice).

Use

You can create just about any kind of document with word processing. If your word processing software is part of an integrated microcomputer software package, you have the added advantage of being able to merge parts of the data base (see Figure S-45), and even graphics, with the text of the document. For example, a common application of word processing is to merge the names and addresses in a data base with the text of a letter to create "personalized" letters (see an example of this merge application in Chapter 12, "Information Systems in Business and Industry").

Some people use their word processing software to process ideas. They do this by organizing their thoughts hierarchically in an outline format that can be easily revised. In fact, several commercially available software packages are designed especially for "idea processing."

When working with word processing software, you are likely to enter long, continuous strings of text, as opposed to commands and data for the other components of integrated software. Therefore, if you expect to use word processing capabilities frequently, you might consider acquiring a solid foundation in keyboarding skills, if you have not already done so.

MEMORY BITS

WORD PROCESSING TEXT MANIPULATION

- Common features
    Replace and insert data
        entry modes
    Copy and move
    Search and replace
    Center
    Indent
    Boldface and underline
    Header and trailer labels
    Pagination
- Advanced features
    Table of contents
    Index of key words
    Footnoting
    Thesaurus
    Spell
    Grammar

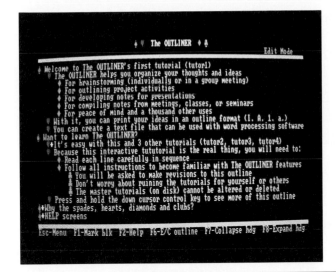

Idea processors are designed to help users organize their thoughts. Also called brainstorming software, idea processors have some word processing features. In the OUTLINER, each line represents a thought or an idea. Lines or blocks of lines can be manipulated until your thoughts are organized to your liking. The hard copy is produced in an outline format. (Long and Associates)

```
              The OUTLINER - Tutorial 1

  I.       Welcome to The OUTLINER's first tutorial (tutor1)
           A.   The OUTLINER helps you organize your thoughts and ideas
                1.   For brainstorming (individually or in a group meeting)
                2.   For outlining project activities
                3.   For developing notes for presentations
                4.   For compiling notes from meetings, classes, or seminars
                5.   For peace of mind and a thousand other uses
           B.   With it, you can print your ideas in an outline format (I. A. 1.
                a.)
           C.   You can create a text file that can be used with word processing
                software
 II.       Want to learn The OUTLINER?
           A.   It's easy with this and 3 other tutorials (tutor2, tutor3, tutor4)
           B.   Because this interactive tutorial is the real thing, you will
                need to:
                1.   Read each line carefully in sequence
                2.   Follow all instructions to become familiar with The OUTLINER
                     features
                     a.   You will be asked to make revisions to this outline
                     b.   Don't worry about ruining the tutorials for yourself or
                          others
                     c.   The master tutorials (on disk) cannot be altered or
                          deleted
           C.   Press and hold the down cursor control key to see more of this
                outline
 III.      Why the spades, hearts, diamonds and clubs?
 IV.       HELP screen
```

REVIEW EXERCISES (S-7)

1. What is the function of word processing software?

2. What must be specified when formatting a document?

3. What is meant when a document is formatted to be right and left justified?

4. Text is entered in either of what two modes? What mode would you select to change "the table" to "the long table"? What mode would you select to change "pick the choose" to "pick and choose"?

5. What causes text to wrap around?

6. Give an example of when you might issue a global search and replace command.

7. When running the "spell" function, what options does the system present to you upon encountering an unidentified word?

HANDS-ON EXERCISES

1. Enter the following text into your word processing system:

    Too Much Paper!

    Last year, the Public Relations Department's paper budget was overrun by $350. Therefore, Public Relations personnel are requested to learn word processing. It is apparent that Public Relations has not taken full advantage of the word processing capabilities of its microcomputers.

    Use the default layout line options (normally $8\frac{1}{2}$ by 11 inch document size, 1 inch right and left margins, 6 lines per inch, and so on). Justify on the right margin. Print the document.

    In the exercises that follow, make the changes cumulative; that is, revise whatever text is left after the previous revision. Each exercise builds on the results of the previous exercise.

2. In insert mode, insert the word "all" before "Public" in the second sentence. In replace mode, replace the lower-case letters in the title with capital letters. Print the document.

3. Center the title. Print the document.

4. At the end of the second sentence, add "by the end of the month". Observe how words at the end of the line wrap around to the next line. Print the document.

5. Use the move command to move the second sentence to the end of the document. Print the document.

6. Designate the word "all" to be underlined and the title to be in boldface when printed. Print the document.

7. Place the "page" (new page) marker at the end of the document and use the copy command to produce another copy of the entire document just below the original. Print the documents.

8. Use the search and replace command to replace all occurrences of "Public Relations" in the second document with "Research and Development". Revise $350 in the second document to be $525. Print the documents.

9. Run the spell function. Print the document. If you performed all of the hands-on exercises, then your printed output should appear as follows:

TOO MUCH PAPER!

Last year, the Public Relations Department's paper budget was overrun by $350. It is apparent that Public Relations has not taken full advantage of the word processing capabilities of its microcomputers. Therefore, all Public Relations personnel are requested to learn word processing by the end of the month.

TOO MUCH PAPER!

Last year, the Research and Development Department's paper budget was overrun by $525. It is apparent that Research and Development has not taken full advantage of the word processing capabilities of its microcomputers. Therefore, all Research and Development personnel are requested to learn word processing by the end of the month.

S-8   COMMUNICATIONS

Function

Communications software makes the microcomputer more than just a "dumb" terminal that just transmits and receives data to/from a remote computer. The microcomputer can process and store data as well. The communications software of integrated software automatically "dials up" a remote computer (another micro or a mainframe), then "logs-on" (establishes a link with a remote computer). Once on-line, you can communicate and share data with a remote computer.

After logging on, communications software allows you to **download** data; that is, you can request and receive data that are transmitted from a remote computer. Once the data have been downloaded to your micro, you can select any of the integrated software components to work with the data. Once processing is complete, you can use the communications software to **upload** the data to a remote computer. Uploading is the opposite of down-loading.

Concepts

You use the communications component to link your microcomputer via telephone lines to another computer system anywhere in the world. Your PC must be equipped with a *modem* before you can use the communications software. The modem links your PC with the telephone line that connects the two computers. On most microcomputers the modem is an optional plug-in board. You can purchase it with your micro or you can add it later as the need arises. A modem can also be purchased as a separate unit and connected to the micro with an electrical cable.

The communications software can be set up to automatically dial and log-on to frequently accessed computer systems. It will even redial if a busy signal is detected.

A micro with a modem and communications software can be on the receiving end as well. The microcomputer with these capabilities can automatically answer "calls" from other computers.

Use

Many *information services*, such as flight and hotel information, stock quotes, and even restaurant menus, are available to microcomputer owners with communications capabilities. A few information services are gratis, but most require a fee. The fee normally consists of a set monthly charge plus an amount based on usage.

Just about every city with a population of 25,000 or more has at least one *computer bulletin board*, often sponsored by a local computer club. Members "post" messages, announcements, for-sale notices, and so on, to the computer bulletin board by transmitting them to a central computer, usually another micro. To scan the bulletin board, members again use communications software to link up to the central computer. This software component also opens the door to sending and receiving *electronic mail*.

In the coming years, we'll probably see a shift to smaller briefcases. Why? With communications software and an ever-growing number of home computers, people won't need to lug their paperwork between home and office every day. For a great many white collar workers, at all levels, much of their work is on computers. Continuing their work at home is simply a matter of establishing a link between their home and office computers.

The combination of microcomputers and communications software has fueled the growth of *cottage industries*. The world has been made a little more compact with the computer revolution. Stock brokers, financial planners, writers, programmers, and people from a wide variety of professions may not need to "go to the office." They can live wherever they choose. Micros make it possible for these people to access needed information, communicate with their clients, and even deliver products of their work (e.g., programs, stories, recommendations).

To report end-of-term grades, the professor in our example (see Figure S-28) might wish to take advantage of the capabilities of communications software. Rather than duplicate the data entry effort and run the risk of a transcription error, the student names and their respective grades are simply transmitted directly to the college's computer center.

If you have a micro, communications software, a modem, and a telephone line, you can tap into a wide variety of information services, such as home banking.
(Copyright Viewdata Corporation of America 1984)

REVIEW EXERCISES (S-8)

1. What is the function of communications software?
2. Why would you download data? Upload data?
3. Why is a modem needed to upload data via telephone lines?

4. Some communications software has automatic dial and redial capabilities. Describe these capabilities.

5. One popular information service is home banking. Describe an interactive session with at least one transaction to both a checking and savings account. Begin from the time you turn on your microcomputer.

HANDS-ON EXERCISES

1. Upload the text created in the Section S-7 Hands-on Exercises to another computer. Download the data to your microcomputer.

2. Send a message via electronic mail to a friend.

3. Tap into and scan a local computer bulletin board.

S-9 ADVANCED FEATURES OF INTEGRATED SOFTWARE

So far, we have covered only the fundamental concepts and uses of integrated microcomputer software. As you familiarize yourself with a particular integrated software package, you will inevitably learn more sophisticated uses. For instance, you can actually do some tasks that would normally require a program. Advanced features even permit you to accomplish programming functions such as *loops* and *subroutines*.

Integrated micro software is *dynamic*; that is, it can actually "learn" the sequence of commands used in frequent requests. This capability vastly reduces the number of keystrokes required to work with a spreadsheet template or a data base screen. For example, a sales manager might wish to update sales and produce a bar chart each day. The menu selections and commands needed to do this can be stored and recalled from storage rather than entered each day.

As you progress in your knowledge of integrated microcomputer software, you will become more comfortable with using the wide range of functions that assists you in statistical and financial analysis.

S-10 BACKUP: BETTER SAFE THAN SORRY

The safeguarding of software and the data base may be more important than the safeguarding of hardware. If files and programs are destroyed, it may be impossible for them to be re-created within a reasonable period of time. If, on the other hand, the hardware is destroyed, it can be replaced fairly quickly. The impact of losing critical software or a data base makes **backup** a major concern.

When you create a document, a spreadsheet, or chart and you wish to recall it at a later time, you *store* the file on secondary storage (disk). You can, of course, store several files on a single disk. If the disk is in some way destroyed (e.g., scratched, demagnetized), then you have lost your files, unless you have a backup disk. To minimize the possibility of losing valuable files, you should periodically back up (make a copy of) your work disk.

(By permission of Michael Artell)

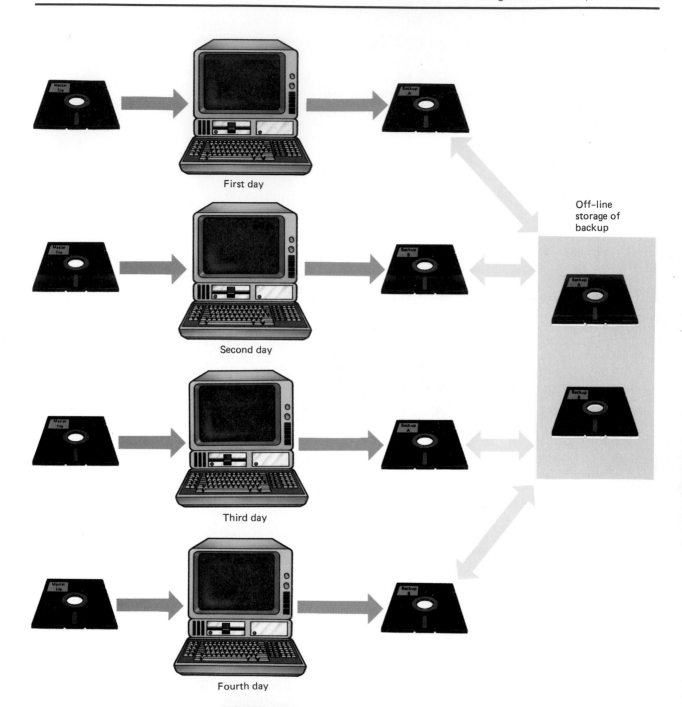

FIGURE S-46
Backup Procedure for a Diskette-Based Master File
The master file is backed up alternately to diskette A or B at the end of each day such that one backup file is always current within one day's processing.

The frequency with which a work disk is backed up depends on its *volatility*, or how often you use the files on the disk. If you spend time every day working with files on a work disk, then you should back it up each day. Others are backed up no more often than they are used. Since some updating will occur between backup runs, the re-creation of the files means that subsequent updates and changes must also be reaccomplished from the point of the last backup.

Figure S-46 illustrates the backup procedure for a work diskette that is used daily. Two *generations* of backup are maintained on backup diskettes A and B. After each day's processing, the contents of the work diskette are copied (or dumped) alternately to diskette A or B. In this manner, one backup is always current within a day's processing. If the work diskette and the most recent backup are accidentally destroyed, a third backup is current within two days' processing. Diskettes A and B are alternated as the most current backup.

At one time or another, just about every computer specialist has experienced the trauma of losing work for which there was no backup. It is no fun seeing several weeks of work go down the drain, but it does drive home the point that it is well worth the effort to make backup copies of your work.

S-11   SUMMARY

Integrated software lets you work the way you think, and think the way you work. Several projects are at the tips of your fingers, and you can switch easily between them. You can even use windows to display the output from one project while working on another.

Commercially available integrated software packages vary greatly in capabilities. Before buying, have an idea of how you plan to use the software, then check it out thoroughly to make sure it has the features you want. Ask the salesperson to demonstrate each of the components, especially those that you plan to use most. Software with essentially the same capabilities may be priced as much as several hundred dollars apart. Some graphics software creates displays of charts in seconds while others take minutes. Some integrated software packages are easy to learn and are accompanied by good documentation; others are not. Considering the amount of time that you might spend using micro software, any extra time you spend in evaluating the software will be time well spent.

In order to make the most effective use of the "integrated" aspects of integrated software, it is important to "think ahead" about what you wish to accomplish. A little prior planning goes a long way with integrated software.

Not all integrated software is as "user friendly" as vendors would have us believe. This is also true of the individual software components. Vendors are sometimes overzealous in their use of the phrase, "easy to learn." However, hundreds of thousands of computer novices and experts have mastered the use of these valuable productivity tools, and with a little study and practice, you will too.

During the learning stages, keep a list of error messages handy; you will probably need them. A word of warning: manuals and disk tutorials tell you *everything* you *can* do but say very little about what you *cannot* do. That may take a bit of "trial and error" to learn.

Perhaps the best way to learn integrated software is to use it. Anticipate some frustrations, but before you know it, you too will be a software wizard. What you do with the software, though, is 10% skills and 90% imagination.

REVIEW EXERCISES (S-9 through S-11)

1. What is it that integrated software can "learn"?
2. Why is it a good idea to maintain two generations of backup?
3. What do you look for when buying integrated software?

HANDS-ON EXERCISES

1. If you are using a diskette-based microcomputer, make a backup copy of your work diskette.
2. If you are in the market for integrated software, test out at least two packages at a computer store and write up a brief comparison, noting the strengths and weaknesses of each.

BASIC
PROGRAMMING

BASIC PROGRAMMING

Learning Module	BASIC Instructions						BASIC Functions
	Input/output	Data transfer and assignment	Computation	Control	Format	Other	
II*	INPUT PRINT LPRINT	LET	LET	GOTO GOSUB/RETURN END IF/THEN		REM	
III				FOR/NEXT WHILE/WEND			

IV	PRINT USING
	LPRINT USING
		READ/DATA
		RESTORE
					PRINT
					    USING
					LPRINT
					    USING
						DIM	TAB

V	CLS LINE INPUT			ON GOSUB ON GOTO			
VI							String Operations: CHR$, LEN, VAL, STR$, LEFT$, RIGHT$, MID$, INSTR Arithmetic operations: See Figure B–15 DEF FN
VII	OPEN CLOSE WRITE # INPUT # GET PUT	FIELD LSET RSET				KILL	File processing: LOC, LOF, EOF, MKS$, CVS
VIII	LINE PRINT PLAY SOUND					LOCATE SCREEN	
IX				DO/LOOP IF/THEN/ELSE (ELSEIF) SELECT CASE SUB SUB END CALL			

*Module II – System commands: NEW, LOAD, SAVE, KILL, LIST, LLIST, AUTO, EDIT, DELETE, RENUM, RUN

LEARNING MODULE 1

BASIC Basics

B-1 LEARNING TO WRITE PROGRAMS

PROGRAMMING
CONCEPTS

ANS Standards
Modules
Driver Module
Structured Programming
Program Logic
Variables/Constants
Reserved Words
Line Numbers
Free Form

Why Learn Programming. We communicate what we want the computer to do through the act of programming. This section of the book is about learning to program in the BASIC programming language. A knowledge of programming will always be a plus, even if you don't plan to write programs at home or at work. The following are just a few of the many benefits of learning to program in BASIC.

1. You will gain an appreciation for what the computer can and cannot do.
2. You will develop good logic skills.
3. You will be able to communicate more effectively with other programmers and systems analysts.
4. You will be able to write your own "custom" programs.

An enormous number of commercial software packages are available for everything from home accounting to computer-aided design (CAD). Even so, you may have unique information needs that are not met by any of these packages. In these cases, you will probably need *custom* software, or software developed especially to meet your information needs. Once you learn some BASIC programming, you should have the capability to develop your own custom software, and have fun doing it to boot!

Not only will programming experience be a valuable asset in attaining your career objectives, it can be fun, especially once you gain proficiency. If this is your first exposure to programming, expect a few frustrating moments. However, the excitement of completing your first program softens the frustration and beckons you to seek other programming challenges.

BASIC is the most widely-available programming language. BASIC programs can be run on any size computer system—from micros to mainframes.
Courtesy of Apple Computer, Inc.)
(Control Data Corporation)

Learning Modules.   This special section, "BASIC Programming," is divided into nine learning modules. Learning Module I provides some background information, an overview of BASIC, and a description of how the material is presented. Learning Modules II through IX introduce you to increasingly more sophisticated BASIC instructions, concepts, and features. Learning Modules I–III will give you an overview at the *beginning* level of BASIC. Learning Modules IV–VI take you up to the *intermediate* level. Learning Modules VII–IX present *advanced* topics in BASIC. Each learning module has Review Exercises to help you reinforce your understanding of the material. Learning Modules II through VIII also contain BASIC Programming Assignments for "hands on" experience.

If you have not already done so, you should read the "Programming Concepts" chapter. This chapter presents a general perspective on programming and its principles. It includes ideas on problem solving and program logic; techniques for designing programs; structured programming concepts; and the steps to program development.

This "BASIC Programming" section is constructed in learning modules. As figures and example programs are referenced in the text, carefully examine and study each before continuing. These important learning tools will help you get the most benefit from your study time.

MEMORY BITS

PROGRAM DEVELOPMENT STEPS

1. Describe the problem
2. Analyze the problem
3. Design the general logic of the program
4. Design the detailed logic of the program
5. Code the program
6. Test and debug the program
7. Document the program

B-2   BASIC: A PROGRAMMING LANGUAGE

The Beginning.   In the early 1960s, Dr. Thomas Kurtz and Dr. John Kemeny of Dartmouth College began developing a programming language that a beginner could learn and use quickly. Their work culminated, in 1964, with BASIC. Over the years, BASIC has gained widespread popularity and has evolved from a teaching language into a versatile and powerful language for both business and scientific applications. BASIC is supported on more computers than any other language. It is available on everything from microcomputers to the world's most powerful mainframe computers. Even with its expanded capabilities and universal acceptance, BASIC is still an excellent language for beginners.

With a little effort, you can learn enough BASIC to write substantial programs. With a little more effort, you can learn some of the many special features of BASIC that allow you to do sophisticated programming tasks.

This "BASIC Programming" section contains BASIC's fundamentals and many of its more advanced features. Depending on how much material you cover, you can achieve a beginning (Learning Modules I–III), intermediate (Learning Modules IV–VI), or advanced (Learning Modules VII–IX) level of competency.

ANS BASIC.   An American National Standard (ANS) for Minimal BASIC was established in 1978 and another more comprehensive standard, ANS BASIC, was introduced in 1985. However, even with a standard, hardware and software vendors tend to alter ANS BASIC to better accommodate the features of their products. As a result, a number of slightly different versions, or "dialects," exist for BASIC. The BASIC presented in Learning Modules I–VIII is a "BASIC-in-practice." That is, the instructions presented are applicable to most versions of BASIC. Any "nonstandard" features presented are widely accepted and are more the rule than the exception.

The BASIC presented in Learning Module IX—"The 'New' ANS BASIC"—adheres strictly to the standards set forth in the 1985 ANS BASIC. Dr. Kurtz, the co-developer of the original BASIC, served as chairman of the ANS committee charged with developing the new standard for BASIC. Relatively few existing versions of BASIC adhere to the new standard. Widespread implementation of a new programming standard will typically take three to five years.

B-3   METHOD OF PRESENTATION

A Single Application.   The focus of this "BASIC Programming" section is to present material so that you can understand BASIC programming. Application is the secondary focus: therefore, all example programs, except Example Program #14 (sound and music), are based on one familiar application—*grades*.

The "grade" example is presented in a series of programs, each of increasing challenge and complexity. The first example program illustrates a BASIC program to average three grades. Eventually, example programs illustrate on-line reporting and inquiry, disk file processing, and graphics. Each of the example programs introduces and demonstrates the use of additional BASIC programming instructions and techniques.

Structured Programming.   A *program description*, a *structure chart*, a *flowchart*, and an example *interactive session* accompany a *listing* of each of the 15 example programs. Figure B-1 highlights these items for Example Program #1. Example Program #1 is repeated and discussed in Learning Module II, "Getting Started in BASIC."

A structure chart breaks a programming problem into a hierarchy of tasks. A task can be broken down into subtasks, as long as a finer level of detail is desired. The most effective programs are designed so they can be designed and written in **modules**, or independent tasks. In structured programming, each program has a **driver module** (called "Main" in our examples) that causes other modules to be executed as they are needed. It is much easier to address a programming problem in small, more manageable

BASIC is a versatile language. Programs written in BASIC are used to keep track of everything from money to musical instruments.
(National Computer Systems)

EXAMPLE PROGRAM #1

This program accepts three quiz scores then computes and displays the average.

Program Description

Structure Chart ➡

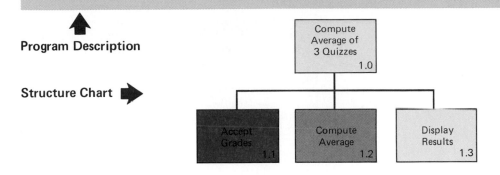

Flowchart ➡

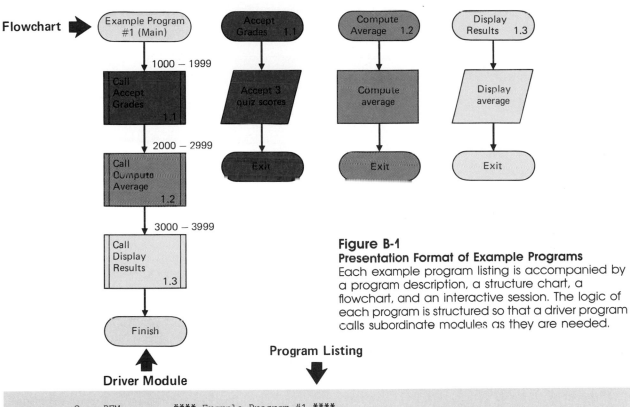

Figure B-1
Presentation Format of Example Programs
Each example program listing is accompanied by a program description, a structure chart, a flowchart, and an interactive session. The logic of each program is structured so that a driver program calls subordinate modules as they are needed.

Driver Module

Program Listing ⬇

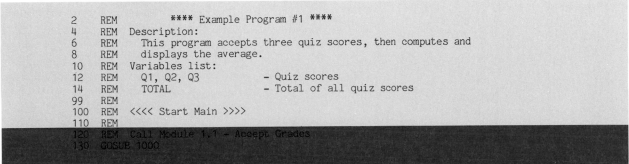

```
2     REM           **** Example Program #1 ****
4     REM    Description:
6     REM      This program accepts three quiz scores, then computes and
8     REM      displays the average.
10    REM    Variables list:
12    REM      Q1, Q2, Q3          - Quiz scores
14    REM      TOTAL               - Total of all quiz scores
99    REM
100   REM    <<<< Start Main >>>>
110   REM
120   REM    Call Module 1.1 - Accept Grades
130   GOSUB 1000
```

continued

Figure B-1 continued

```
140  REM  Call Module 1.2 - Compute Average
150  GOSUB 2000
160  REM  Call Module 1.3 - Display Results
170  GOSUB 3000
180  END
190  REM  <<<< End Main >>>>
999  REM
1000 REM  ==== Module 1.1 - Accept Grades
1010 INPUT Q1, Q2, Q3
1999 RETURN
2000 REM  ==== Module 1.2 - Compute Average
2010 LET TOTAL = Q1 + Q2 + Q3
2020 LET AVERAGE = TOTAL / 3
2999 RETURN
3000 REM  ==== Module 1.3 - Display Results
3010 PRINT AVERAGE
3999 RETURN
```

Interactive Session ▶

```
 run
? 73,91,85
 83
Ok
```

modules than as one big task. This is done using the principles of **structured programming**.

In structured programming, the logic of the program is addressed hierarchically in logical modules (see Figure B-1). In the end, the logic of each module is translated into a sequence of program instructions that are called and executed as a unit. By dividing the program into modules, you can use the structured approach to program development and thereby reduce the complexity of the programming task. Some programs are so complex that, if taken as a single task, they would be almost impossible to conceptualize, design, and code. The idea behind structured programming is to "divide and conquer." See the *Programming Concepts* chapter for a detailed explanation of structured programming.

Flowcharting, one of the most popular design techniques, permits you to illustrate data, information, and work flow through the interconnection of *specialized symbols* with *flow lines*. The combination of symbols and flow lines portrays the logic of the program. Each symbol indicates the *type of operation to be performed*, and the flowchart graphically illustrates the *sequence in which the operations are to be performed*. Flow lines depict the sequential flow of the program logic. The more commonly used flowchart symbols are: computer process ☐ , predefined process ▯ , generalized input/output ▱ , decision ◇ , connector ○ , and termination ⬭ . Flowcharting and other flowchart symbols are discussed in the "Programming Concepts" chapter.

The numbers just outside the upper right-hand corner of all predefined functions provide cross references to appropriate program *statement numbers* (see Figure B-1).

Input/Output.   The *interactive* nature of BASIC makes it necessary to distinguish between end-user input and computer output. To do this, example interactive sessions present *output* in yellow type and *input* in green type. In the text, output is shown in light type and input in **bold type.** For example,

Enter employee name and hours worked? **L. James, 38**

Presentation of Example Programs.   The 15 example programs are the basis for demonstrating the principles of programming in BASIC. Each example is presented with a *program description*, a *structure chart*, a *flowchart*, a *program listing*, and an example *interactive session*. These five items, which always appear together, are collectively referenced as Example Program #1, Example Program #2, and so on. To avoid confusion, only support graphics and special program segments will have figure numbers. Unless otherwise stated, any textual reference to an example program (e.g., Example Program #1) refers to all five of the above items.

B-4   VARIABLES AND CONSTANTS _____

Numeric and alphanumeric values, such as 14 and "DP101", are stored in primary storage locations within the computer and recalled by **identifiers**. Identifiers are used to name these storage locations, which are called **variables**. Identifiers are also used to name arrays (discussed in Learning Module IV), functions (Learning Module VI), and programs.

Numeric values are referenced by *numeric identifiers*. Alphanumeric values are referenced by *string identifiers*. These identifiers, or **variable names**, represent the actual values of the storage locations. In the input/output example above, the values of "L. James" and 38 are stored in locations referenced by the variable names EMPLOYEE$ and HOURS. "L. James" is a **string constant** (also called a **literal value**) and 38 is a **numeric constant**. When found in programming instructions, string constants like "DP101" and "L. James" are placed within quotation marks. This convention is followed in the discussion material as well.

The range of allowable numeric and string values depends on the version of BASIC used and available memory. The minimum and maximum values for numeric constants normally range from $1 * 10^{-99}$ to $1 * 10^{+99}$. The maximum length of string constants varies from 256 to 32,000 characters.

Most versions of BASIC in use today use the following naming conventions. The identifier:

1. Is normally no more than 40 characters in length.
2. Must begin with a letter.
3. Contains only letters and digits (no spaces).
4. Becomes a string variable name when a dollar sign ($) is appended to the end of the name.
5. Does not distinguish between upper- and lower-case letters (i.e., Part = PART).

We assign variable names so that we can recall and use data from primary storage. One of these memory chips contains the number of hours worked by a security guard. The payroll program, which is written in BASIC, references this value with the variable name HOURS. (Lisp Machine Inc.)

Example identifiers for numeric and string values are listed below.

Numeric Variable Names	String Variable Names
B	Z$
PartNumber	PARTNAME$
BIOLOGY318	U11a$

In some versions of BASIC, *only the first two characters are interpreted by the computer*. In the above examples, "Part Number" is interpreted as "PA" and "U11a$" is interpreted as "U1$". The remaining characters are purely for programmer convenience and documentation. For example, the numeric variable name AVERAGE in the program listing of Figure B-1 (Example Program #1) is more descriptive than simply AV.

In the program of Figure B-1 (Example Program #1), the variable names for quiz scores are Q1, Q2, and Q3. You might say, "Why not use QUIZ1, QUIZ2, and QUIZ3?" If your version of BASIC only recognizes the first two characters as being significant, then QUIZ1, QUIZ2, and QUIZ3 would all be interpreted as QU.

Another consideration in naming variables is that you must avoid using **reserved words**, such as READ, PRINT, and END. These words are reserved for the exclusive use of the BASIC interpreter and will be assumed to be a command, not a variable name.

B-5 STYLE AND SPACING

In BASIC, each program statement can be automatically assigned a **line number**. You, as the programmer, can select the beginning number and the increment. Programmers often begin each second-level module (i.e., those that are called from the driver module) with some multiple of a thousand, then increment by ten (see Figure B-1). This makes it easier to distinguish between modules and permits you to insert statements at a later date. The numbering scheme in the examples is designed to make it easier for you to cross-reference the program listing, the textual material, the structure chart, and the flowchart. For each example program (see Figure B-1), statements are numbered as follows:

Program description:	10–99	(increment 2)
Driver module (Main):	100–999	(increment 10)
Module 1.1:	1000–1999	(increment 10)
Module 1.2:	2000–2999	(increment 10)
Module 1.3:	3000–3999	(increment 10)
Module 1.4:	4000–4999	(increment 10)
Module 1.5:	5000–5999	(increment 10)
Module 1.6:	6000–6999	(increment 10)
Module 1.7:	7000–7999	(increment 10)

The increment is set to 5 when the number of statements in a module exceeds 99. Modules called by a second-level module (e.g., Module 1.1.2 or Module

1.3.1) are contained within the statement-number range of the calling module. That is, Module 1.1.2 might begin with statement number 1350, which is within the Module 1.1 range of 1000–1999.

BASIC is a **free form** language. This means you have a lot of flexibility in the way the statements are entered. There is only one requirement. There must be at least one space between each of the following: variable names, constants, and reserved words. You may place operators [+ − * / ^ = < >], symbols [' ( ) "], and delimiters [, ; :] next to each of these items, or you can insert spaces for better readability. The following statements are the same:

```
2010 LET TOTAL=Q1+Q2+Q3
2010 LET   TOTAL  =  Q1  +  Q2  +  Q3
```

To include more than one BASIC *instruction* on a single numbered *statement*, separate the instructions with a colon (:) [some systems use a backslash (\)]. For example:

```
2010 LET TOTAL = Q1 + Q2 + Q3: LET AVERAGE = TOTAL / 3
```

It's a good idea to adopt a personal style, then be consistent throughout your program. A well-formatted program is easier to debug and revise. Indenting certain parts of the program will improve readability of the source code and help you to spot program modules, remarks, loops, and so on, more quickly.

In the example programs, all variable names (e.g., AVERAGE) and BASIC commands (e.g., INPUT, PRINT, END) are in upper-case letters. All remarks are in upper/lower-case letters. The start and end of the "Main" driver program are indicated as follows:

```
REM <<<< Start Main >>>>
    :
REM <<<< End Main >>>>
```

The boundaries of each subordinate module are indicated as follows:

```
1000 REM ==== Module 1.1—Accept Grades
    :
1999 RETURN
```

Program sequences are often indented to improve readability.

Astronauts are conducting more and more scientific experiments while in space. They take microcomputers along so they can analyze the data from certain experiments while they are still in orbit. The language on these micros is BASIC.
(NASA)

REVIEW EXERCISES (LEARNING MODULE I)

1. Classify each of the following as a string or numeric constant.
   (a) 12.456   (c) "Rocky Mountains"   (e) 789
   (b) "12.456"   (d) "ROCKY"   (f) 987654.0
   Which of the above are literal values?

2. Identify legal and illegal variable names from the following list. Explain what rule or rules are violated for the illegal variable names. Which are numeric and which are string variable names?

(a)	A1111	(e)	5SALARY	(i)	DESCRIP$
(b)	B$	(f)	END	(j)	SUM
(c)	ALPHA1A	(g)	*SCORE	(k)	SUM1
(d)	NET PAY	(h)	LET		
		(l)	ECONOMICORDERQUANTITY		

3. In an inventory control program, variable A contains "parts on hand," variable B contains "parts used," and variable C contains "parts added." Rename the variables in the following statement so that they can be more easily understood.

   100 A=B−B+C

4. The following special characters are used to formulate BASIC instructions. Classify each as being an operator, a symbol, or a delimiter.

   (a) *   (d) :   (g) ^
   (b) ,   (e))   (h) +
   (c) /   (f) =   (i) "

5. What is the purpose of: (a) a driver module? (b) a line number?

6. For your computing environment, determine the following:
   (a) minimum and maximum values for numeric constants
   (b) maximum length of string constants
   (c) maximum length of variable names
   (d) number of significant characters in variable names

B-6 BASIC INSTRUCTION SET: LEARNING MODULE II GROUP

BASIC instructions are executed sequentially, unless the sequence of execution is altered by a *control* instruction. Like other languages, BASIC's instruction set has at least one instruction in each of the major instruction categories. The instructions that we will discuss fall into the following categories:

- Input/output instructions
- Data transfer and assignment instructions
- Computation instructions
- Control instructions
- Format instructions
- Other instructions

The "Programming Concepts" chapter contains a detailed explanation of all instruction categories. For ease of reference, a summary of BASIC instructions can be found at the end of the "BASIC Programming" section.

A chart on the page preceding the start of Learning Module I summarizes the BASIC instructions in each instruction category and by the Learning Module in which they are introduced. The Learning Module II instruction set, presented below in this section, contains several of the most commonly used BASIC instructions. The use of these instructions is illustrated in Example Programs #1 and #2. The same pattern of introduction and illustration is followed in subsequent learning modules. Some of the advanced features of the instructions are introduced in context with the discussions of the example programs.

The line numbers have been omitted in most of the examples that are given in the textual material to help you focus on the **syntax**, or the rules of formulating instructions. The general format and at least one example are presented for each new instruction.

INPUT/OUTPUT INSTRUCTIONS

INPUT. An INPUT instruction causes program execution to pause and an optional *prompt* to be displayed on the terminal. When a semicolon (;) follows the prompt, a *question mark* (?) is displayed to signal the user that the program is waiting for data to be entered. When a comma (,) follows the prompt, the *question mark* (?) does not appear.

> *Format*:   INPUT "prompt"; list of variables

PROGRAMMING CONCEPTS

Categories of Instructions
Instruction Syntax
Arithmetic Operators
Hierarchy of Operations
Subroutines
GOTO-less Programming
Relational Operators
System Commands
Input/Processing/Output
Internal/External
    Documentation
Editing Programs
Loops
Counters
Bugs (Logic and I/O)
Debugging

The keyboard is still our primary means of entering data into a computer system. But at one character at a time, keyboard data entry can be slow and cumbersome for some applications. Another input device, called the mouse (in right hand of person in photo), is rolled across the desktop to move the cursor quickly about the screen.
(Summagraphics Corporation)

Examples:
without prompt
   INPUT EMPLOYEE$, HOURS

with prompt
   INPUT "Enter employee name and hours worked"; EMPLOYEE$, HOURS

If you executed a program with the above INPUT instruction, a prompt and question mark would appear as shown below.

   Enter employee name and hours worked? **L. James, 38**

The variables take on the corresponding input data. In the example, EMPLOYEE$ takes on the value of "L. James", and HOURS takes on the value of 38. Good interactive programs have plenty of input prompts. If you did not have a prompt and saw only a question mark (or nothing), how would you know what to enter?

PRINT.   When BASIC was developed, most terminals were teleprinters with key input and printer output. Therefore, it was only logical that the primary output instruction be called PRINT. The PRINT instruction has stuck, even though most output is soft copy on video display terminals or microcomputer monitors. The PRINT instruction causes output to be displayed on a monitor or printed on a teleprinter terminal, depending on which one you are using.

Format: PRINT list of variables and/or expressions

The PRINT instruction displays (or prints) the values of variables, constants, and the results of any arithmetic expressions.

Example: PRINT "The pay of", EMPLOYEE$, "is", HOURS*8.50

Using the values from the above INPUT example (L. James, 38), the output would be as follows:

   The pay of   L. James   is   323

The *value* of EMPLOYEE$ and the two other string constants are displayed as is. The arithmetic expression (38*8.50 = 323) is resolved and displayed. In BASIC, the asterisk (*) is the symbol for the multiplication operation.
   A numeric constant is, itself, an arithmetic expression. See what happens when a single number is included in the PRINT list.

Example: PRINT "Hours worked is", 38

The output becomes

   Hours worked is   38

The *delimiters* (, ;) that separate the items in the print list determine *where* the values and constants are displayed on the line. The display line is divided into *zones* (see Figure B-2). The first item in the print list is displayed (or printed) in the first zone, the second item in the second zone, and so on. Some versions of BASIC have a preset zone width, usually from 14 to 18 character positions wide. On others, you can set the zone width to be whatever you want. For the purposes of illustration, we will assume a zone width of 14 characters in all examples.

The two print list delimiters, the *comma* (,) and the *semicolon* (;), serve a dual purpose. The delimiters separate the items in the print list and position the cursor of VDTs and micros, or the print head for teleprinter terminals.

- The *comma* positions the cursor/print head at the *beginning of the next complete zone.*
- The *semicolon* positions the cursor/print head at the next display/print position. When separated by a semicolon, items in the print list would be displayed next to one another.

Figure B-2 illustrates how the PRINT instruction can be used for a variety of display requirements. Figure B-2(a) is a repeat of the above example. Notice that the 323 in Figure B-2(a) begins in the second position of zone 4. All numbers are displayed with a leading space to permit a minus sign for negative numbers.

Figure B-2(b) shows what happens when semicolons are used as delimiters. Figure B-2(c) illustrates how a report title and column headings can be generated with a series of PRINT instructions. Notice that a PRINT instruction with no item list (statement 300) causes a blank line to be displayed. Figure B-2(d) illustrates how readability can be improved by using commas and semicolons in combination. Notice that the character strings "Gross pay

(a)
```
300 PRINT "The pay of", EMPLOYEE$, "is", HOURS*8.5
```

```
The pay of     L. James       is              323
zone 1--------zone 2---------zone 3--------zone 4--------zone 5--------
```

Figure B-2
Uses of the PRINT Instruction
These outputs are discussed in the text material.

(b)
```
300 PRINT "The pay of "; EMPLOYEE$; " is "; HOURS*8.5
```

```
The pay of L. James is   323
zone 1--------zone 2--------zone 3--------zone 4--------zone 5--------
```

(c)
```
300 PRINT "                PAYROLL REGISTER"
310 PRINT
320 PRINT "EMPLOYEE", "DEPARTMENT", "GROSS", "NET"
330 PRINT "NAME", , "PAY", "PAY"
340 PRINT "_____", "_____", "_____", "___"
```

```
                PAYROLL REGISTER

EMPLOYEE      DEPARTMENT    GROSS         NET
NAME                        PAY           PAY
_____      _____    _____         ___
zone 1--------zone 2--------zone 3--------zone 4--------zone 5--------
```

(d)
```
300 PRINT "Gross pay is "; GROSS, "Net pay is "; GROSS - DEDUCTIONS
```

```
Gross pay is  323           Net pay is  280
zone 1--------zone 2--------zone 3--------zone 4--------zone 5--------
```

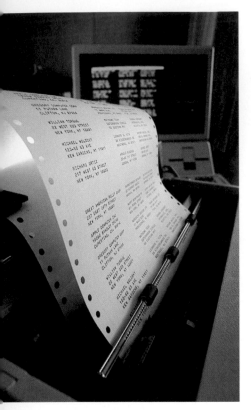

Use the LPRINT instruction to route an output line to a printer. Mailing labels are being printed on this printer. Printers vary in output speeds from 40 characters per second to 40,000 lines per minute.
(SCM Corporation)

is " and "Net pay is " both have a blank space at the end of the string. This provides a space between the string and the following number.

LPRINT. Use the LPRINT instruction when you are working on a VDT or micro, have a printer available, and want a hard copy output. LPRINT causes the output line to be routed to a printer.

Data Transfer and Assignment Instructions

LET. The LET expression can be used to assign values to variables and to perform computations. The LET computation capabilities are discussed later in the computation instruction category.

Format: LET variable = variable or constant value

Examples: LET SCORE = 95
LET GRADE$ = "A"
LET X = Y
LET EMPLOYEE$ = E$

In the above assignment examples, the constant values of 95 and "A" are assigned to storage locations referenced by the variable names SCORE and GRADE$, respectively. In the latter two examples, the values of the data referenced by the variables Y and E$ are transferred to the storage locations referenced by X and EMPLOYEE$, respectively. The values of Y and E$ are unchanged. The values previously in SCORE, GRADE$, X, and EMPLOYEE$ are replaced with the values of the constants and variables on the right-hand side.

In those versions of BASIC released prior to the new ANS BASIC standard, the addition of the reserved word LET is optional. However, in ANS BASIC, the LET is part of the command structure and is, therefore, required.

Any variable that is used in an instruction and has not been previously assigned a value is set equal to *zero* (0) for numeric variables and to the *null* ("") character for string variables. The null character is a string value that has no length.

Computation Instructions

LET. The LET instruction is also used for computation.

Format: LET variable = expression

Example: LET X = (A+B−C)^3

An *expression* consists of numeric variables and constants, and **arithmetic operators** ($+ - */ \char`\^$). Arithmetic expressions are more cumbersome in all programming languages because they must be entered on the same level

OPERATION	OPERATOR
Exponentiation	$\wedge$ or $\uparrow$ or **
Multiplication–Division	* /
Addition–Subtraction	+ –

Figure B-3
Hierarchy of Operations

(or one continuous line). In our handwritten calculations, we put the numerator physically over the denominator (e.g., $\frac{1}{2}$) and denote exponentiation with superscripts (e.g., A^2). In programming, however, we have to put the numerator, denominator, and superscripts on the same level.

When more than one operator is included in a single expression, the computer must determine which to perform first. Because of this, a standard **hierarchy of operations** was established to provide rules by which the computer evaluates arithmetic expressions. The hierarchy is illustrated in Figure B-3. Exponentiation ($\wedge$, $\uparrow$, or **) has the highest priority, followed by multiplication-division (*, /) and addition-subtraction (+, –). Notice that multiplication and division have the same priority, and addition and subtraction have the same priority. In the case of a tie, the expression is evaluated from *left to right*.

Parentheses override the priority rules for the hierarchy of operations. What would happen if we removed the parentheses from the above arithmetic expression: $X = (A+B-C)\wedge 3$? Without the parentheses, the first operation would be the exponentiation, C^3. The parentheses override the hierarchy priority and cause the expression within the parentheses to be resolved first. The result of $A+B-C$ is then raised to the third power. *When in doubt, use parentheses*. When you have a set of parentheses within a set of parentheses, the innermost expression is evaluated first. Always make sure that you have the same number of open and close parentheses in arithmetic expressions. Figure B-4 illustrates the order in which the expression for the future value of an annuity would be resolved by a computer.

Figure B-4
Evaluation of an Arithmetic Expression
The formula for the future worth of an annuity is shown algebraically and as a BASIC computation instruction. The expression is resolved by the computer in stages, according to the hierarchy of operations.

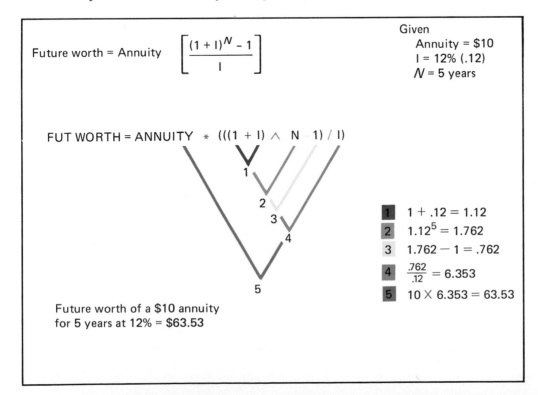

Future worth = Annuity $\left[\dfrac{(1 + I)^{N} - 1}{I} \right]$

Given
Annuity = $10
I = 12% (.12)
N = 5 years

FUT WORTH = ANNUITY * (((1 + I) $\wedge$ N - 1) / I)

1
2
3
4
5

1	$1 + .12 = 1.12$
2	$1.12^5 = 1.762$
3	$1.762 - 1 = .762$
4	$\frac{.762}{.12} = 6.353$
5	$10 \times 6.353 = 63.53$

Future worth of a $10 annuity
for 5 years at 12% = $63.53

B.17

Let me rephrase that. Lightning *probably* won't strike if you enter the wrong command.
(By permission of Anthony Cresci)

Control Instructions: Unconditional Transfer

GOTO.   The GOTO instruction causes an unconditional branch in the sequence of execution. The next statement to be executed is the statement at the line number specified in the GOTO instruction.

Format: GOTO line number

Example: GOTO 440

GOSUB/RETURN.   The driver program uses the GOSUB/RETURN combination of instructions to call and execute a module. The modules, also called **subroutines**, are a sequence of program instructions that are called and executed as needed.

Subroutines are used for the following reasons:

1. When a series of statements are to be executed several times throughout the program, or
2. To improve the logic of the program (i.e., structured programming).

The GOSUB/RETURN instruction pair gives us the capability to write structured programs.

Format: GOSUB line number

        subroutine statement
           ⋮
        subroutine statement
        RETURN [line number]

Example: 130   GOSUB 1000
            140   REM Call Module 1.2—Compute Average
            150   GOSUB 2000

                  ⋮

           1000 REM ==== Module 1.1—Accept Grades
           1010 INPUT Q1, Q2, Q3
           1999 RETURN

The GOSUB instruction is a control instruction that causes an unconditional branch to the statement at the designated line number (1000 in the above example). Statement 1000 is the first statement for the subroutine of Module 1.1 of Example Program #1. The subroutine statements are executed in sequence through the RETURN instruction (1999). The RETURN instruction causes a branch to the instruction following the original GOSUB. In the above example, the next instruction is at statement 140. When the RETURN is followed by a line number, the explicit line number overrides the default branch (instruction following GOSUB) and control of execution is passed to the statement at the line number. If your version of BASIC does not permit RETURNs to have a line number, *you will need to use alternative logic*, perhaps using GOTOs.

For now, the GOSUB/RETURN instruction pair is supported in the new ANS BASIC. However, GOSUB is designated for future removal from the standard as soon as the more sophisticated control structures (see Learning Module IX, "The New ANS BASIC") have been implemented in most versions of BASIC. In many versions of BASIC, the GOSUB/RETURN combination is still the primary instruction for creating structured programs, but the GOTO is seldom needed. In keeping with the trend to *GOTO-less programming* (see the "Programming Concepts" chapter), *we will use the GOTO instruction sparingly*. The GOTO is used only when its use is necessary to maintain structured logic.

END.   The purpose of the END instruction is to terminate program execution. Every program must have an END instruction. The END instruction can be placed anywhere in the program. Often the best place for it is at the end of the driver module. See Example Program #1, statement 180.

    Example: 999 END

Control Instructions: Conditional Transfer

IF/THEN.   An IF/THEN instruction is a conditional "branch" instruction. *If* a condition is evaluated to be true, *then* one of two things happens: (1) control of execution is transferred (a branch) to someplace else in the program, or (2) the instruction(s) following THEN is executed.

> *Format*:   IF   expression   relational operator   expression
>   THEN line number (or executable instruction(s))

The **relational operators** shown in Figure B-5 are used to compare numeric or string expressions.

COMPARISON	OPERATOR
Equal to	=
Less than	<
Greater than	>
Less than or equal to	< =
Greater than or equal to	> =
Not equal to	<>

Figure B-5
Relational Operators

Example: IF CODE$ = "S" THEN 440

IF AVERAGE >= 90 THEN PRINT "GRADE IS A"

COURSE$="DP101"
IF COURSE$ < "DP206" THEN 650

In the first example, if the value of CODE$ is equal to "S", then the statement at line number 440 is executed next. If the expressions are not equal, then the next sequential statement is executed. In the second example, "GRADE IS A" is displayed only if the value of AVERAGE is greater than or equal to 90. Any other values of AVERAGE would cause the next sequential statement to be executed.

Inequality comparisons can also be made between string variables. The comparison is strictly alphabetic (e.g., SMITH before or less than SMYTH) for *alpha* comparisons. For *alphanumeric* comparisons, a number character is considered "less than" an alpha character (in the ASCII code, see Figure B-6), and the comparison is made from left to right, one character at a time. For example, "1" is less than "A"; that is, the decimal ASCII code for "1" is numerically less than the decimal code for "A" (i.e., 48 < 65). In the third example above, no action is taken until the third characters are compared and found to be not equal.

Figure B-6
ASCII Encoding System
(Decimal)

ASCII code	Character	ASCII code	Character	ASCII code	Character	ASCII code	Character
000	Null	032	(space)	064	@	096	
001		033	!	065	A	097	a
002		034	"	066	B	098	b
003		035	#	067	C	099	c
004		036	$	068	D	100	d
005		037	%	069	E	101	e
006		038	&	070	F	102	f
007	beep or bell	039	'	071	G	103	g
008		040	(	072	H	104	h
009	tab	041	)	073	I	105	i
010	line feed	042	*	074	J	106	j
011		043	+	075	K	107	k
012		044	,	076	L	108	l
013	carriage return	045	–	077	M	109	m
014		046	.	078	N	110	n
015		047	/	079	O	111	o
016		048	0	080	P	112	p
017		049	1	081	Q	113	q
018		050	2	082	R	114	r
019		051	3	083	S	115	s
020		052	4	084	T	116	t
021		053	5	085	U	117	u
022		054	6	086	V	118	v
023		055	7	087	W	119	w
024		056	8	088	X	120	x
025		057	9	089	Y	121	y
026		058	:	090	Z	122	z
027		059	;	091	[	123	{
028	right ⎫ cursor	060	<	092	\	124	|
029	left ⎬ move-	061	=	093	]	125	}
030	up ⎭ ment	062	>	094	^	126	~
031	down	063	?	095	_	127	⌂

D = D = 68
P = P = 80
1 ≠ 2   (49, the ASCII code for 1, is less than
         50, the ASCII code for 2)

Because 1 < 2, the comparison ("DP101" < "DP206") is true and the statement at 650 is executed next.

Notice in Figure B-6 that the ASCII code values of upper- and lower-case letters are different. In comparing "SMYTH" to "Smith", the comparison "SMYTH" < "Smith" would be true because the ASCII value of an upper-case "M" is less than that of a lower-case "m" (77 < 109).

In the example programs, most lines contain only one instruction. However, there are circumstances that call for combining several instructions in a single statement, usually on one line. To do this, simply end one instruction with a *colon* (:) [a *backslash* (\) on some systems] and begin another instruction on the same line. In the example below, the line number 3030 refers to both an IF and a GOSUB instruction. If the expression in the following example is true, then both of the instructions that follow the THEN clause are executed.

3030 IF AVERAGE >= 90 THEN PRINT "GRADE IS A": GOSUB 2000

The IF/THEN/ELSE, a more versatile version of the IF/THEN instruction, is introduced in Learning Module IX.

Other Instructions

REM.   REM, or "remark," instructions are a programmer convenience. All comments prefaced by REM are ignored by the computer and can be placed anywhere in the program. Use REM instructions to document your programs (see any of the example programs).

A programmer discusses the format of a case load report with a social worker. The programmer is a computer specialist and the social worker is a computer user. Since the social worker took a course in BASIC, she has a better feel for what can and cannot be done and is better equipped to relate her information needs to a programmer.
(Cromemco, Inc.)

Format: REM remarks

Example: REM ==== Module 1.1—Accept Grades

Remarks can be added to the end of a statement by prefacing the remarks with a single quote (') or, in some BASIC dialects, an exclamation mark (!).

Example: LET COUNT = 1   'Initialize counter to 1

MEMORY BITS
PROGRAM INSTRUCTION CLASSIFICATIONS
■ Input/output
■ Data transfer and assignment
■ Computation
■ Control   Unconditional branch   Conditional branch
■ Format

B-7   SYSTEM COMMANDS

We use *system commands* to communicate to the computer what we want done with our BASIC program. For example, with system commands we can store, retrieve, and execute BASIC programs. System commands are not part of the program and are, therefore, not assigned line numbers.

These "command level" instructions are only partially standardized and vary considerably between computers. The following system commands are common to many computers.

RUN. The RUN command causes the program currently in primary storage to be executed.

NEW. The NEW command clears primary storage and readies the computer to accept a new BASIC program.

LOAD. The LOAD command causes the program identified by "program name" to be retrieved from secondary storage and loaded to primary storage.

Format: LOAD program name

Example: LOAD PROG1

Some versions of BASIC require system command references to a program name to be prefaced by or enclosed in quotes.

Example: LOAD "PROG1

LOAD "PROG1"

SAVE. With the SAVE command, the program currently in primary storage is saved on secondary storage, probably magnetic disk, for recall at a later time. The format is similar to the LOAD command.

KILL. The KILL command deletes a named file, program, or data, from disk. The format is similar to the LOAD command.

LIST. The LIST command causes all or part of the program currently in primary storage to be displayed on the workstation monitor.

Examples:
```
LIST            (display the entire program)
LIST 1000       (display statement 1000)
LIST 1000–1999  (display statements from 1000 through 1999)
LIST 2000–      (begin with 2000 and display the remainder
                of the program)
```

LLIST. The LLIST command causes all or part of the program currently in primary storage to be printed on a printer.

AUTO. The AUTO command causes line numbers to be generated automatically according to your specifications (e.g., start with 100 and increment by 10).

EDIT. The EDIT command puts you in *edit mode*. In edit mode you can modify or edit portions of an instruction without having to reenter it.

DELETE.   The DELETE command deletes those lines in the program that you designate (e.g., 1000 or 3000–3500).

RENUM.   The RENUM command causes all or part of the program lines to be renumbered according to your specifications (e.g., beginning at existing line 140, renumber starting at 100 and incrementing by 10).

The above command level instructions are only a subset of available system commands. Your instructor will point out any variations in the above list and explain other helpful commands for your computing environment.

B-8   EXAMPLE PROGRAM #1: INPUT, PROCESSING, OUTPUT

The example programs are designed to illustrate the use of BASIC programming instructions and the structure of BASIC programs. Each example program introduces different BASIC features and general programming techniques. Example Program #1 accepts three quiz scores (input), computes the average (processing), then displays the result (output).

This simple program is divided into three modules (see the structure chart): Module 1.1—Accept Grades, Module 1.2—Compute Average, and Module 1.3—Display Results. The first module is *input*, the second is *processing*, and the third is *output*. This is a common modular structure for straightforward programs. The driver module (Main: 100–999) calls each of these modules in sequence (see flowchart) to produce the interactive session or RUN (execution) of the program. In the interactive session, three scores are entered and the resulting average is displayed.

Statement 130 GOSUB 1000, the first *executable instruction*, causes the execution of Module 1.1—Accept Data (1000–1999). An executable instruction causes some type of processing activity (e.g., I/O, assignment, computation, and so on) to occur. Control is transferred to statement 1000, and, since REM is a *nonexecutable instruction,* control is passed on to statement 1010 INPUT Q1, Q2, Q3. Once the three grades have been entered, the RETURN at 1999 causes control to be passed back to the driver module at statement 140, the statement following the original GOSUB at 130. The other two modules are called and executed in a similar manner. The END at 180 is encountered and execution is terminated.

Inquiry and Response.   The interactive session of Example Program #1 is typical of the inquiry/response style of programming. In the interactive session, a question mark (?) is displayed to signal the user (inquiry) that the computer is ready to accept data (response). In Example Program #1 there are no prompts that tell the user what to enter, so the user must know that three grades are to be entered (the use of prompts is discussed in the next learning module). The user enters the three grades, separated by a comma (,) and the result is displayed on the next line. The program must be RUN again to compute the average of three more scores. Remember that input is shown in **bold type** so that you can distinguish between what is entered by the user and what is produced as a result of programming.

EXAMPLE PROGRAM #1

This program accepts three quiz scores then computes and displays the average.

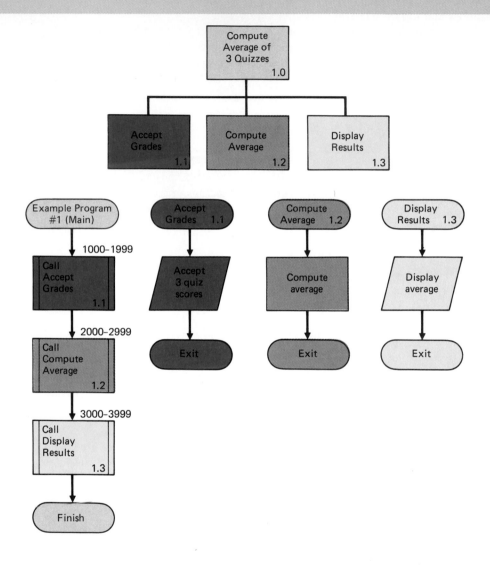

```
2    REM         **** Example Program #1 ****
4    REM  Description:
6    REM    This program accepts three quiz scores, then computes and
8    REM    displays the average.
10   REM  Variables list:
12   REM    Q1, Q2, Q3           - Quiz scores
14   REM    TOTAL                - Total of all quiz scores
99   REM
100  REM  <<<< Start Main >>>>
110  REM
120  REM  Call Module 1.1 - Accept Grades
130  GOSUB 1000
140  REM  Call Module 1.2 - Compute Average
150  GOSUB 2000
160  REM  Call Module 1.3 - Display Results
170  GOSUB 3000
180  END
190  REM  <<<< End Main >>>>
999  REM
1000 REM  ==== Module 1.1 - Accept Grades
1010 INPUT Q1, Q2, Q3
1999 RETURN
2000 REM  ==== Module 1.2 - Compute Average
2010 LET TOTAL = Q1 + Q2 + Q3
2020 LET AVERAGE = TOTAL / 3
2999 RETURN
3000 REM  ==== Module 1.3 - Display Results
3010 PRINT AVERAGE
3999 RETURN
```

```
run
? 73,91,85
 83
Ok
```

Developing Good Programming Habits.   The following BASIC statement produces exactly the same interactive session as Example Program #1.

```
10 INPUT A,B,C: PRINT (A+B+C)/3
```

So why do we need all the extraneous comments and instructions? The answer is simple: *to develop good programming habits from the very start*. The source code of Example Program #1 includes:

1. A program name (statement 2).
2. A program description (statements 4–8).
3. A list and description of all variable names (statements 10–14).
4. Internal comments (statements 120, 140, and others).
5. A structured design with a driver program (100–999) and subordinate modules (1000–3999)

All other example programs are organized in a similar manner. The above are considered to be the minimal *internal* documentation requirements for a program. The minimal *external* documentation requirements are the struc-

Most computer programs accept the input of data, do some processing, and generate some kind of output. In the textile business, pay is based on piecework. Employees affix labels with their employee number and part number to each item they complete. An optical character recognition (OCR) wand scanner reads these data as input, the data are processed based on the piece rate, and the printed payroll checks are the output.
(CAERE Corporation)

ture chart, a logic diagram (e.g., flowchart), and an interactive session. This amount of internal documentation may seem excessive for such a simple program, but it is important to practice good documentation and program design starting with your first program. You will not only learn to program more quickly, but you will be a better programmer, as well.

Entering and Editing Programs.   To write a BASIC program, you must first inform the computer that you wish to enter a program. Do this by entering the word BASIC (or some variation, e.g., BASICA, MBASIC5) after the *operating system prompt* (e.g., A>, >,], Ok) and pressing the carriage return. The BASIC software is loaded and an "Ok" prompt appears. This prompt means you are in *BASIC mode* and the system is ready to accept your program. Your instructor will provide the specifics for your hardware/software environment. The session might appears as follows:

```
A> BASIC
Ok
10 INPUT A, B, C
20 LET AVERAGE = (A+B+C) / 3
30 PRINT AVERAGE
99 END
RUN
? 73,91,85
  83
Ok
```

Programs are entered one statement at a time. You can elect to number the statements yourself or request that the system do it automatically (i.e., use the AUTO system command). Editing procedures (modifying statements) vary widely between versions of BASIC, but the following are standard:

1. Backspace to delete the last character entered.
2. To replace a statement with another, key in the number of the statement to be replaced and the new statement.
3. To insert a statement in the program, key in a number that is numerically between the statement numbers adjacent to the desired location (e.g., key 15 to insert a statement between statements 10 and 20), then key in the statement.
4. To delete a statement from the program, key in the number of the statement, then press the carriage return.

B-9   EXAMPLE PROGRAM #2: LOOP AND COUNTER _____

Example Programs #2, #3, and #4 are extensions of Example Program #1. Each of the three programs accomplishes the same task: *for any number of students*, three quiz scores are accepted, then the average is computed and displayed for *each student*. The logic of each program varies slightly because different BASIC features are introduced in each program. Example Programs #2 and #3 produce the same interactive session. Input and output prompts are added in Example Program #4.

EXAMPLE PROGRAM #2

This program accepts three quiz grades from each of any number of students. The average is computed and displayed for each student.

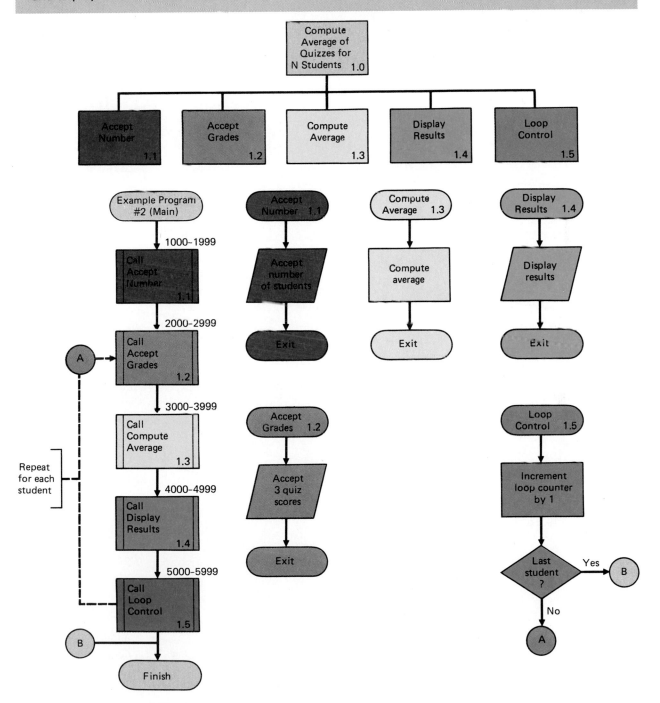

continued

Example Program 2 continued

```
2    REM          **** Example Program #2 ****
4    REM   Description:
6    REM     This program accepts three quiz grades from each of any number of
8    REM     students.  The average is computed and displayed for each student.
10   REM   Variables list:
12   REM     NUMBER            - Number of students
14   REM     Q1, Q2, Q3        - Quiz scores
16   REM     AVERAGE           - Average of quiz scores
18   REM     COUNT             - Loop counter
99   REM
100  REM   <<<< Start Main >>>>
110  REM
120  REM   Call Module 1.1 - Accept Number
130  GOSUB 1000
140  REM   Call Module 1.2 - Accept Grades
150  GOSUB 2000
160  REM   Call Module 1.3 - Compute Average
170  GOSUB 3000
180  REM   Call Module 1.4 - Display Results
190  GOSUB 4000
200  REM   Call Module 1.5 - Loop Control
210  GOSUB 5000
220  END
230  REM   <<<< End Main >>>>
999  REM
1000 REM   ==== Module 1.1 - Accept Number
1010 INPUT NUMBER
1999 RETURN
2000 REM   ==== Module 1.2 - Accept Grades
2010 INPUT Q1, Q2, Q3
2999 RETURN
3000 REM   ==== Module 1.3 - Compute Average
3010 AVERAGE = (Q1 + Q2 + Q3) / 3
3999 RETURN
4000 REM   ==== Module 1.4 - Display Results
4010 PRINT AVERAGE
4999 RETURN
5000 REM   ==== Module 1.5 - Loop Control
5010 REM   Increment loop counter & test if last student
5020 COUNT = COUNT + 1
5030 IF NUMBER = COUNT THEN RETURN 220
5999 RETURN 140
```

```
run
? 3
? 73,91,85
 83
? 86,88,99
 91
? 66,84,75
 75
Ok
```

In Example Program #2, the process of computing and displaying the
average for one student (2000–4999, essentially Example Program #1) is

included in a *loop* and repeated for each student. Module 1.1—Accept Number accepts the number of students to be processed. The loop is controlled by Module 1.5—Loop Control.

The Loop.   The loop is created by a *counter* (5020) and an IF instruction (5030). The loop (140–210) is repeated until the value of NUMBER (the number of students entered in Module 1.1) is equal to the value of COUNT (the counter). Since the test-on-condition is at the end of the loop, the loop is a DOUNTIL loop structure (see the *Programming Concepts* chapter). The DOWHILE loop structure is demonstrated in Example Program #4.

In BASIC, all numeric variables are set to zero at the start of program execution, so the value of COUNT is zero until the first execution of statement 5020. After the first time through the loop, the value of COUNT is 1. Thereafter, statement 5020 increments COUNT by 1 for each repetition of the loop (another student processed). The THEN clause of the IF instruction at 5030 is ignored until COUNT equals NUMBER. In these cases, the RETURN at 5040 returns control of execution to the driver program and the loop is repeated. When NUMBER equals COUNT, the THEN clause is taken and the END instruction is executed causing program execution to be terminated.

Variable Values During Execution.   The interactive session of Example Program #2 shows how the scores of three students are entered and the resulting averages are displayed. Figure B-7 illustrates the value of each variable during program execution. Variable values are not altered in the chart,

Line numbers in order executed	NUMBER	Q1	Q2	Q3	AVERAGE	COUNT
2–1000		0	0	0	0	0
1010	3	0	0	0	0	0
1999–2000	3	0	0	0	0	0
2010	3	73	91	85	0	0
2999–3000	3	73	91	85	0	0
3010	3	73	91	85	83	0
3999–5010	3	73	91	85	83	0
5020	3	73	91	85	83	1
5030–2000	3	73	91	85	83	1
2010	3	86	88	99	83	1
2999–3000	3	86	88	99	83	1
3010	3	86	88	99	91	1
3999–5010	3	86	88	99	91	1
5020	3	86	88	99	91	2
5030–2000	3	86	88	99	91	2
2010	3	66	84	75	91	2
2999–3000	3	66	84	75	91	2
3010	3	66	84	75	75	2
3999–5010	3	66	84	75	75	2
5020	3	66	84	75	75	3
5030	3	66	84	75	75	3
220	3	66	84	75	75	3

Figure B-7
Values of Variables During Interactive Session of Example Program #2
During the interactive session for Example Program #2, all variables except NUMBER change during program execution. For example, the values of Q1, Q2, and Q3 take on the values of new quiz scores after each execution of statement 2010 (INPUT Q1, Q2, Q3). The statement numbers on the left-hand side show the order in which the statements are executed. Figure B-8 contains a "trace" of Example Program #2 that shows all line numbers in the order in which they are executed.

or in primary storage, unless they change during execution. For example, the value of NUMBER is 3 after the execution of statement 1010 and is not changed thereafter. On the third time through the loop, the value of COUNT equals the value of NUMBER. When this happens, the loop is *not* repeated and the program is terminated.

To get a better idea of how the values in primary storage are affected during the execution of a program, spend a few minutes stepping through Figure B-7 while looking at the program listing and interactive session of Example Program #2.

B-10   GETTING THE BUGS OUT: DEBUGGING

Once you have entered a program into the system, you may need to do a little **debugging** before the program works properly. A **bug** is a name given to an error in program syntax or logic.

Syntax Errors.   Debugging a program is a repetitive process, whereby each successive attempt gets you one step closer to a working program. The first step is to eliminate *syntax errors*. You get a syntax error when you violate one of the rules for writing instructions (e.g., placement of parentheses, spelling of commands, and so on). For example, you will get an error message if you enter PRNT rather than PRINT in statement 4010 of Example Program #2.

Logic and I/O Errors.   Once all the syntax errors have been removed, the program can be executed, but that does not always mean that you have a working program. You now have to debug the *logic of the program* and the *input/output formats*. To do this, you need to create *test data* and, perhaps, a *test data base* so you know what to expect as output. In Example Program #2, you would expect the average to be 85 if the test data are 85, 95, and 75. If this is not the case, then there is a bug in the program logic. A program whose logic is sound might have input or output formats that need to be "cleaned up" (e.g., columns properly aligned, heading center, and so on). Do this after you have eliminated all the syntax and logic errors.

Debugging Aids.   Among the most helpful debugging aids, especially for finding logic errors, are the *trace* commands. These debugging aids permit a "trace" of the execution sequence of the program statements. When you ask for a trace, you get a sequential log of the order in which statements or sections of the program are executed. The trace also shows you which branches were taken during execution. By comparing the *actual* sequence of execution against the *expected* sequence of execution, you can usually isolate the error. The trace commands are:

        TRACE ON   (or TRON on some versions of BASIC)
        TRACE OFF   (or TROFF)

The TRACE ON command enables the display of each line number as the associated statement is executed. The TRACE OFF command disables the trace. Figure B-8 illustrates a trace of an execution of Example Program #2.

No more bugs! Every programmer has a sense of relief and accomplishment when the program finally runs. Some just lean back in their chair and grin—others explode with emotion.
(Photo supplied courtesy of Epson America)

```
TRON
Ok
RUN
[2][4][6][8][10][12][14][16][99][100][110][120][130][1000][1010]? 2
[1999][140][150][2000][2010]? 73,91,85
[2999][160][170][3000][3010][3999][180][190][4000][4010] 83
[4999][200][210][5000][5010][5020][5030][5999][140][150][2000][2010]? 86,88,99
[2999][160][170][3000][3010][3999][180][190][4000][4010] 91
[4999][200][210][5000][5010][5020][5030][220]
Ok
```

Programmers often add "extra" PRINT instructions to display the values of selected variables during the execution of a program. This technique helps you determine whether or not your program is doing what it is supposed to, when it is supposed to. Of course, once the program is working properly, the "extra" instructions are deleted.

The "Programming Concepts" chapter contains a detailed discussion of the program development process and debugging concepts.

Figure B-8
Interactive Session of Example Program #2 with the Trace "On"
The trace is an excellent debugging aid that enables you to monitor the logic of your program while it is being executed. The bracketed numbers list the sequence in which the statements are executed.

REVIEW EXERCISES (LEARNING MODULE II) _____

BASIC Instructions and Concepts

1. What is the general function of system commands? Describe the specific function of LIST, LLIST, SAVE, LOAD, RUN, and NEW.

2. Associate each of the following BASIC instructions with an instruction category.
   (a) PRINT
   (b) IF/THEN
   (c) LET (2 categories)
   (d) GOSUB/RETURN

3. "Trace" the execution of the following program by listing the line numbers in the order in which they are executed.

   ```
   100 GOSUB 400
   200 PRINT "The sum is ", X
   300 GOTO 700
   400 INPUT A, B
   500 X = A + B
   600 RETURN
   700 END
   ```

4. Identify the syntax error(s) in each of the following instructions.
   (a) 10 PRINT "   STATUS REPORT,
   (b) 10 INPUT "Enter starting month and day": MONTH, DAY
   (c) 10 LET X$=Y+Z
   (d) 10 GOSUB 400 THEN 500
   (e) 10 IF NAME = "Jones" THEN PRINT NAME

5. Use your hand calculator to determine what value of X would be printed.

```
100 A=1
200 B=3
300 C=−4
400 X=(A/B+C)*B
500 PRINT X
600 END
```

6. Refer to the above exercise. Use your hand calculator to determine what value of X would be printed if statement 400 were replaced with the following statement.

```
400 X=(−B+(B‿2−4*A*C)‿.5)/(2*A)
```

7. In which of the IF instructions below is the comparison true?

```
100 A$="LESS"
200 B=5
300 IF "MORE" > A$ THEN 950
400 IF "LESS" <= A$ THEN 960
500 IF B‿2 <= 28 THEN 970
600 IF C >= B THEN 980
700 DP$="DP101"
700 IF DP$ < "DP100" THEN 990
```

8. Which of the following statements will result in a program error? Describe the cause of each error.

```
100 REM PRINT "GRADE IS", A$
200 GOTO 10
300 A=4
351 C=0
500 X=(X*A)/2)
600 X$="(X*A)/2)"
700 PRINT "X=, X
800 Y=A/C
```

9. Write the print instructions that would produce the following output.
   (a)

```
ZONE 1--------    ZONE 2--------        ZONE 3--------    ZONE 4--------    ZONE 5-----
                               INVENTORY STATUS REPORT

PART NAME         PART NUMBER           ON HAND           USED-TO-DATE  ON ORDER
```

   (b)

```
ZONE 1--------    ZONE 2--------    ZONE 3

QUANTITY ON HAND IS                 S99999
QUANTITY ON HAND IS                 S99999
```

   where S = sign, 9 = number

Example Program #1

10. Follow the logic for the program, and manually perform the operations for quiz grades 95, 84, 91. For 86, 75, and 83.

11. How would you modify the program to average five grades?

12. How would you modify the program to route the output to the printer?

Example Program #2

13. What is the fundamental difference in the logic of Example Programs #1 and #2?

14. What is the value of COUNT before any values have been entered? Why?

15. Follow the logic for the program, and manually perform the operations for two students with grades of 95, 84, 91 and 86, 75, 83. Complete a table, as shown in Figure B-7, illustrating the values of the variables during execution.

16. Fill in the blanks below to achieve the same objectives as the original statements 5030 and 5999.

    5030 IF NUMBER > COUNT THEN RETURN____
    5999 RETURN____

17. What is the purpose of statement 5020, the "counter"?

18. What statements in the Main program are within the "loop"?

19. How would you modify the program to eliminate Module 1.5?

BASIC PROGRAMMING ASSIGNMENTS _____

1. Get acquainted with the computer and BASIC by entering and executing Example Program #1. Using the computer access procedures discussed in class, prepare to enter Example Program #1. Enter and execute this program and check your interactive session with that of the text.

2. Perform the following system level operations on Example Program #1: name and SAVE the program; return to SYSTEM mode; return to BASIC mode; LOAD the program; EDIT Q1, Q2, and Q3 to be E1, E2, and E3; RUN the program; LIST Module 1.3; KILL, or delete, the program file; and, finally, SAVE the file again using the same name.

3. Review Example Program #1 to be like Example Program #2. Execute, then save it for later recall. RENUMber the lines starting with 100 and incrementing by 10. Now, Renumber lines 200 and after in increments of 5.

4. Execute Example Program #2 with the trace command on. Compare your results with Figure B-8.

5. The number of widgets sold during each of the five days this last week is 71, 46, 92, 27, and 104. Write a program to enter the sales data and compute the total sales for the week, and to figure the average sold per day. The output (total sales and average) should appear as shown below:

340
68

6. Prepare a table converting centigrade temperatures from 0–31 degrees to Fahrenheit temperatures. The conversion formula is

F=(9/5)*C+32

The output should appear in columns in the first two print zones as shown below.

0	32
1	33.8
2	35.6
:	:
31	87.8

B-11 BASIC INSTRUCTION SET:
LEARNING MODULE III GROUP _____

In this learning module, two more control instructions are introduced. Both the FOR/NEXT and the WHILE/WEND instruction pairs make it easier to create loops. The three types of control instructions are *unconditional transfer* (e.g., GOSUB), *conditional transfer* (e.g., IF/THEN), and *loop* (e.g., FOR/NEXT and WHILE/WEND, both described below).

Control Instructions: Loop

FOR/NEXT. The FOR/NEXT combination of statements creates a loop in which the statements between a FOR instruction and a NEXT instruction are executed repeatedly. The FOR instruction specifies the number of times the sequence of statements is executed.

The FOR/NEXT combination is a programmer convenience for creating loops. We could do the same thing with an IF/THEN instruction and a counter (see Example Program #2), but the FOR/NEXT instruction just makes it easier to program and understand. The FOR/NEXT loop alternative is illustrated in Example Programs #3.

PROGRAMMING CONCEPTS
Conditional/Unconditional Transfers
Test-On-Condition
DOUNTIL and DOWHILE Loops
Infinite Loops
Nested Loops
Input Prompts
Output Descriptions

Format: FOR variable = initial value TO limit value [STEP increment value]

   statements

      ⋮

NEXT [index variable]

Examples:
1. FOR I=1 TO N
   statements
   ⋮
   NEXT I
2. FOR I=2 TO 10 STEP 3
   statements
   ⋮
   NEXT I
3. FOR I=2 TO −2 STEP −1
   statements
   ⋮
   NEXT I

In the above examples, the *variable* I first takes on the value of the *initial value*. I is then incremented by the *incremental value*, which is determined by the STEP clause, after each execution of the loop. When the STEP clause is omitted (as in example 1 above), the increment value is 1. Once the value of I passes the value of *limit value* (either positive or negative), the looping process is terminated and the statement following NEXT is executed. The initial value, limit value, and increment value can be either variables or constants.

For the above three examples, the values of I for each time through the loop are:

Example 1:   1, 2, 3, 4, 5, 6, 7 (for N=7)
Example 2:   2, 5, 8
Example 3:   2, 1, 0, −1, −2

The two variations of the loop structure are *DOUNTIL* and *DOWHILE* (see the "Programming Concepts" chapter for details). The net effect of a FOR/NEXT loop is a DOUNTIL loop. The loop designated by the FOR/NEXT instructions is repeated *until* the limit value is equal to or exceeded by the value of the variable. When this happens, the statement following the NEXT is executed. Each execution of the NEXT instruction causes the variable to be incremented by the value in the STEP clause.

The loop in Example Program #2 is also a DOUNTIL structure. Notice that in a DOUNTIL loop, the statements in the loop are executed at least once.

WHILE/WEND.   The WHILE/WEND instruction pair permits DOWHILE looping. That is, the statements in a loop are executed repeatedly *while* the

Because programmers may spend four or more hours each day at a workstation, vendors are paying more attention to the ergonomics (efficiency of the man-machine interface) of the programmer workstation. Features of these ergonomic workstations include a high resolution and non-glare display, tilt and swivel adjustments for the display, tilt adjustment for the keyboard, and noise level adjustments for prompting alarms.
(Sperry Corporation)

test-on-condition in the WHILE instruction is true. The use of the WHILE/
WEND instruction pair is illustrated in Example Program #4.

Format: WHILE   expression   relational operator   expression
            statements
                  ⋮
            WEND

Example: WHILE COUNT <= 50
             statements
                   ⋮
             WEND

In the above example, the statements between the WHILE and WEND
are executed repeatedly "WHILE" the condition (COUNT <= 50) is true.
The value of COUNT is in some way altered during processing so that eventually the condition is false (e.g., COUNT = 63). If a WHILE/WEND condition
can never become false, your program will enter an *infinite loop* when executed. That is, the loop is repeated until you either cause a "break" in the
program execution or turn off the computer. Later, we will learn that infinite
loops have their uses.

In a WHILE/WEND loop, the condition is examined just prior to each
pass (the execution of the instructions within the loop). If the condition is
true, the loop is repeated. If the condition is false, the loop is bypassed
and the statement following the WEND is executed. In the DOWHILE structure, if the condition is false when the WHILE is first encountered, the loop
statements are bypassed completely and not executed.

Both the WHILE and FOR instructions must always be accompanied
by their counterparts, WEND and NEXT—and vice versa. Of course, when
you forget a WEND or a NEXT, you will soon be reminded of the omission
when your program run is terminated prematurely and you get an error
message. If you branch into the middle of a WHILE/WEND or FOR/NEXT
loop and a WEND or a NEXT instruction is encountered without an accompanying WHILE or FOR, you will also get an error message.

Nested Loops: Loops Within Loops.   When a *complete* loop is entirely
within another loop, then the pair are referred to as **nested loops**. You
can create all kinds of nested loops. You can program loops within loops,
within loops, and so on. You can have several loops within a single loop.
You will probably not run into any trouble as long as you follow one simple
rule: *Do not overlap loops*. That is, don't nest the FOR or WHILE instructions
inside one loop and the corresponding NEXT or WEND inside another loop.

Figure B-9 shows how a FOR/NEXT loop can be nested within another
FOR/NEXT loop. Figure B-10 shows how two WHILE/WEND loops can
be nested within a FOR/NEXT loop.

Figure B-9
Nested Loops
The flowchart logic, the
corresponding BASIC code,
and the results are shown for
a FOR/NEXT loop that is nested
within another FOR/NEXT loop.

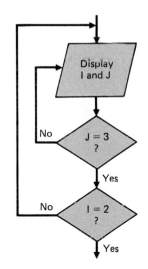

```
FOR I = 1 TO 2
   FOR J = 1 TO 3
      PRINT "I = "; I, "J = "; J
   NEXT J
NEXT I
```

Results:	
I = 1	J = 1
I = 1	J = 2
I = 1	J = 3
I = 2	J = 1
I = 2	J = 2
I = 2	J = 3

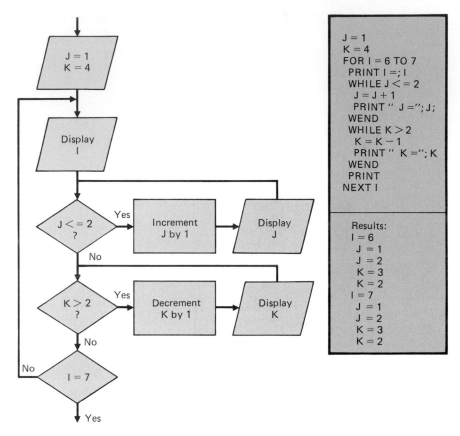

Figure B-10
Nested Loops
The flowchart logic, the corresponding BASIC code, and the results are shown when a couple of WHILE/WEND loops are nested within a FOR/NEXT loop.

B-12 EXAMPLE PROGRAM #3: AN EASIER WAY TO CREATE A LOOP

Example Program #3 performs exactly the same function as Example Program #2. The difference is that the FOR/NEXT instruction combination creates the loop rather than the IF-counter combination. The interactive session is also the same.

The counter is embedded in the FOR/NEXT combination. The variable COUNT is incremented by 1 each time the loop in the Main program module (150–220) is executed. Therefore, the loop is repeated until the value of COUNT becomes greater than the value of NUMBER. In our example, the loop is executed three times with the variable COUNT taking on values of 1, 2, and 3. After the third loop (COUNT=NUMBER=3), processing "drops through" to the END instruction and execution is terminated.

B-13 EXAMPLE PROGRAM #4: BEING "USER FRIENDLY"

Example Program #4 is another variation of Example Programs #2, except this time the WHILE/WEND instruction pair creates the loop and the program input/output is made more "user friendly."

EXAMPLE PROGRAM #3

This program accepts three quiz grades from each of any number of students. The average is computed and displayed for each student. It is the same as Example Program #2 with FOR/NEXT statements used to create the loop.

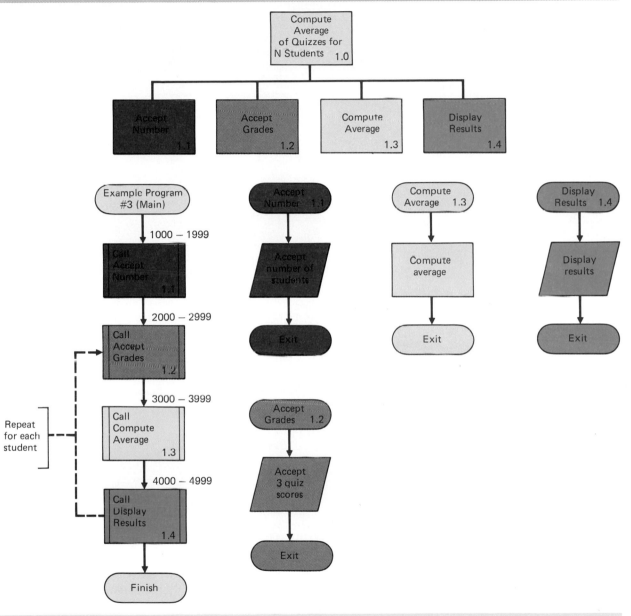

```
2    REM              **** Example Program #3 ****
4    REM   Description:
6    REM      This program accepts three quiz grades from each of any number of
8    REM      students.  The average is computed and displayed for each student.
10   REM      It is the same as Example Program #2 with FOR/NEXT statements
12   REM      used to create the loop.
14   REM   Variables list:
16   REM      NUMBER              - Number of students
18   REM      Q1, Q2, Q3          - Quiz scores
20   REM      AVERAGE             - Average of quiz scores
99   REM
```

continued

Example Program 3 continued

```
100  REM  <<<< Start Main >>>>
110  REM
120  REM  Call Module 1.1 - Accept Number
130  GOSUB 1000
140  REM  Begin loop to be executed 'NUMBER' times
150  FOR I=1 TO NUMBER
160     REM  Call Module 1.2 - Accept Grades
170     GOSUB 2000
180     REM  Call Module 1.3 - Compute Average
190     GOSUB 3000
200     REM  Call Module 1.4 - Display Results
210     GOSUB 4000
220  NEXT I
230  END
240  REM  <<<< End Main >>>>
999  REM
1000 REM  ==== Module 1.1 - Accept Number
1010 INPUT NUMBER
1999 RETURN
2000 REM  ==== Module 1.2 - Accept Grades
2010 INPUT Q1, Q2, Q3
2999 RETURN
3000 REM  ==== Module 1.3 - Compute Average
3010 AVERAGE = (Q1 + Q2 + Q3) / 3
3999 RETURN
4000 REM  ==== Module 1.4 - Display Results
4010 PRINT AVERAGE
4999 RETURN
```

```
run
? 3
? 73,91,85
 83
? 86,88,99
 91
? 66,84,75
 75
Ok
```

As long as the condition in the WHILE instruction is met (COUNT <= NUMBER), the loop is repeated and another student is processed. COUNT is initially set to 1 (150), then incremented by 1 (2040) after each student's grades are entered (Module 1.2). COUNT could just as well have been incremented in Modules 1.3 or 1.4. The condition is true during the first three passes through the loop, but after the third student's grades have been processed, the value of COUNT is 4. When COUNT = 4, the condition becomes false and the statement following WEND (240 END) is executed and program execution is terminated.

The input/output is made more user friendly by adding *input prompts* (1010, 2020) and *output descriptions* (4010). In the previous examples, the

EXAMPLE PROGRAM #4

This program accepts three quiz grades from each of any number of students. The average is computed and displayed for each student. It is the same as Example Programs #2 and #3 with input prompts and WHILE/WEND loop replacing the FOR/NEXT loop.

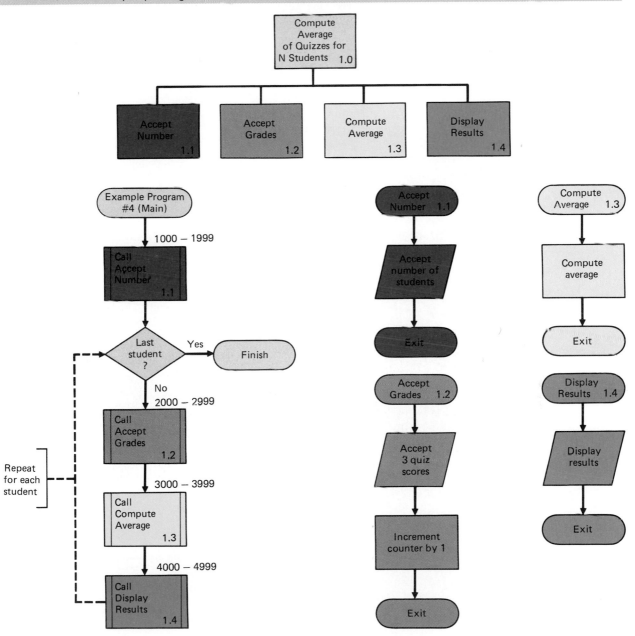

continued

Example Program 4 continued

```
2    REM           **** Example Program #4 ****
4    REM  Description:
6    REM    This program accepts three quiz grades from each of any number of
8    REM    students.  The average is computed and displayed for each student.
10   REM    It is the same as Example Program #2 and #3 with input prompts and
12   REM    WHILE/WEND loop replacing the FOR/NEXT loop.
14   REM  Variables list:
16   REM    NUMBER                 - Number of students
18   REM    Q1, Q2, Q3             - Quiz scores
20   REM    AVERAGE                - Average of quiz scores
99   REM
100  REM  <<<< Start Main >>>>
110  REM
120  REM  Call Module 1.1 - Accept Number
130  GOSUB 1000
140  REM  Begin loop to be executed 'NUMBER' times
150  COUNT = 1
160  WHILE COUNT <= NUMBER
170    REM  Call Module 1.2 - Accept Grades
180    GOSUB 2000
190    REM  Call Module 1.3 - Compute Average
200    GOSUB 3000
210    REM  Call Module 1.4 - Display Results
220    GOSUB 4000
230  WEND
240  END
250  REM  <<<< End Main >>>>
999  REM
1000 REM  ==== Module 1.1 - Accept Number
1010 PRINT "Enter total number of students";
1020 INPUT NUMBER
1030 PRINT
1999 RETURN
2000 REM  ==== Module 1.2 - Accept Grades
2010 REM   Input student grades and add one to loop counter 'COUNT'
2020 PRINT "Enter three quiz scores separated by commas";
2030 INPUT Q1, Q2, Q3
2040 REM   Increment loop counter
2050 COUNT = COUNT + 1
2999 RETURN
3000 REM  ==== Module 1.3 - Compute Average
3010 AVERAGE = (Q1 + Q2 + Q3) / 3
3999 RETURN
4000 REM  ==== Module 1.4 - Display Results
4010 PRINT "The average grade is "; AVERAGE
4020 PRINT
4999 RETURN
```

```
run
Enter total number of students? 3

Enter three quiz scores separated by commas? 73,91,85
The average grade is  83

Enter three quiz scores separated by commas? 86,88,99
The average grade is  91

Enter three quiz scores separated by commas? 66,84,75
The average grade is  75

Ok
```

only signal given the user to enter data is a question mark. Nothing is displayed to tell the user what to enter. The result is simply a number with no description. A user executing Example Program #3 would have to know what, and how many, data items to enter, as well as how to interpret the results. We make programs more user friendly by requesting input data through prompts and by describing the output.

Besides the input prompts and output description, blank lines (1030, 4020) are inserted in the interactive session to improve readability. Also, the semicolons (;) at the end of the PRINT instructions for the input prompts (e.g., 1010) cause the cursor to remain positioned at the ends of the prompts. This permits data to be entered on the same line and adjacent to the prompts. The semicolon in the PRINT for the output description causes the result to be displayed adjacent to the description (4010). In the interactive session, notice that the numerical output begins in the second space of the display zone. The extra space is always reserved for an implied plus sign or an actual minus sign.

Numerous input prompts and output descriptions were added to an office directory program to make it more "user friendly" and, therefore, easier to use.
(Computer Consoles Inc.)

REVIEW EXERCISES (LEARNING MODULE III)

BASIC Instructions and Concepts

1. Identify the syntax error(s) in each of the following instructions.
    (a)   10 FOR COUNT$ = 1 TO 10 STEP 3
    (b)   10 WEND NUMBER < > 10
    (c)   10 WHILE COUNT$ < = − 1
    (d)   10 FOR J = I UP TO J

2. Write instructions to produce the following interaction with the user.

    Enter quantity of part used today
    ? **4**
    Enter quantity of part received today
    ? **8**

3. What values of X and I are displayed?

    (a)   100 X=5
          200 FOR I=1 TO 8 STEP 3
          300 X=X + 1
          400 PRINT X,I
          500 NEXT I
          600 END
    (b)   100 X=2
          200 WHILE X <= 8
          300 X=X + 2
          400 PRINT X
          500 WEND
          600 END

4. Use a FOR/NEXT combination and write the sequence of instructions needed to produce the following output.

```
zone 1--------zone 2--------zone 3--------
X                 X SQUARED  X CUBED
 1                    1         1
 2                    4         8
 3                    9        27
 4                   16        64
```

5. Use a WHILE/WEND combination and write the sequence of instructions needed to produce the output described in exercise 3 above.

6. How many times is the PRINT instruction executed? What values of X, I, and J are displayed? Remember, all undefined variables are initially set to zero.

```
100 FOR I=1 TO 5
200   FOR J=2 TO 7
300     X=X + 1
400     PRINT X, I, J
500   NEXT
600   NEXT
700 END
```

Example Program #3

7. The FOR/NEXT combination effectively replaces statements 5020 and 5030 of Example Program #2. What are the advantages of this substitution?

8. What is the purpose of the index variable I? Could it just as well have been called COUNT?

Example Program #4

9. What makes Example Program #3 a DOUNTIL structure and Example Program #4 a DOWHILE structure?

10. What is the purpose of the PRINT instruction at 4020?

11. If the semicolon in 4010 were replaced with a comma, in what zones would the string constant and the value of AVERAGE be displayed?

12. If the value of COUNT were set to 100 rather than 1 in statement 150, how would you revise the WHILE instruction to keep the same logic?

BASIC PROGRAMMING ASSIGNMENTS _____

1. Load Example Program #2 to memory and revise it to be like Example Program #3, then execute and save the revised program. If you did not have Example Program #2 saved, enter Example Program #3 and save it. Revise Example Program #3 to be like Example Program #4, then execute and save it. Now load, list (on the monitor and printer), and execute these programs again.

2. Combine instructions in Example Program #4 when possible to eliminate two unnecessary instructions. Execute the program again and verify its accuracy. [*Hint*: Integrate input prompts in INPUT instructions.]

3. Write a centigrade-to-Fahrenheit conversion program to list the output in four columns as shown below. The conversion formula is: $F=(9/5)*C+32$.

CENTIGRADE	FAHRENHEIT	CENTIGRADE	FAHRENHEIT
0	32	16	60.8
1	33.8	17	62.6
2	35.6	18	64.4
:	:	:	:
15	59	31	87.8

4. Write a program to accept the course data shown below (no more than three different courses). No course has more than two sections, and the data for multiple-section courses are to be entered consecutively.

COURSE NUMBER	SECTION	# OF STUDENTS ENROLLED
CIS 11	1	30
CIS 11	2	21
CIS 41	1	72
CIS 88	1	25
CIS 88	2	23

Through comparisons and calculations, produce the following output.

COURSE NUMBER	NUMBER OF SECTIONS	TOTAL STUDENTS
CIS 11	2	51
CIS 41	1	72
CIS 88	2	48

5. Write a program to compute an electric utility bill that is based on time-of-day usage. The utility company charges $.03/kilowatt-hour from 8:00 P.M. until 6:00 A.M. The charge during the remainder of the day is $.07/kilowatt-hour. Use the following data:

Customer #	Prime time usage	Non-prime-time usage
44561	620	409
62178	780	165
55612	410	650

Produce the following interactive session and output for the first customer and similar I/O for the other two customers:

Enter number of customers to be processed? **3**

Enter customer #? **44561**
Enter prime time usage? **620**
Enter non-prime time usage? **409**

Charges for customer #44561 are $55.67

6. Prepare an interactive program to illustrate to the novice BASIC programmer the use of the separators (comma and semicolon) and zones in the PRINT instructions. The instructive interactive session should illustrate the PRINT instruction features presented in Figure B-2.

B-14 BASIC INSTRUCTION SET: LEARNING MODULE IV GROUP

Several more instructions are introduced in this learning module. The PRINT USING instruction, which is both an I/O and a format instruction, offers enhancements over the PRINT instruction. The READ/DATA/RESTORE is a data transfer and assignment instruction combination that provides an alternative to the LET assignment instruction. Also introduced is the DIM statement, which does not fall into any of the major instruction categories.

> **PROGRAMMING CONCEPTS**
>
> Formatting Output Fields
> Arrays/Subscripted Variables
> Initialization Routines
> Logical Operators
> Index Variables
> End-of-File Entry
> Report Formatting

Input/Output Instructions and Format Instructions

PRINT USING.   The PRINT USING instruction differs from the Print instruction in that it ignores the print zones and lets you display print list items in a specified format.

> *Format*:   PRINT USING   format string; list of variables and/or
>   expressions

> *Examples*:   PRINT USING "# # #. # #"; PAY, DEDUCT, NET
>   FORMAT$="\   \"
>   PRINT USING FORMAT$; NAME$
>
>   PRINT USING "**$# # #. # #"; PAY, NET
>
>   PRINT USING "# #-"; CREDIT, DEBIT
>
>   PRINT USING "# # # # #,. # # #"; 1367.5, 32850.789,
>   TOTAL

In the examples, notice that the format string can be either a string variable (e.g., FORMAT$) or a string constant (e.g., "**$###.##"). Some versions of BASIC permit only one format field per PRINT USING instruction (as shown in the examples), and all of the like print-list items (numeric or string) are displayed according to the specifications in the format string. Other versions of BASIC permit several format fields to be specified in a single format string (see Example Program #15 in Learning Module IX, "The 'New' ANS BASIC"). In the following discussion, we'll focus on PRINT USING instructions with a single format string.

The format string is made up of special *formatting characters*. Commonly used formatting characters are described and illustrated below: + − . , * $ and ˄ for numeric formats; and ! \ and & for string formats.

> BASIC is not only the most widely available language, it is also the most widely taught language. For the majority of students, their first programming language is BASIC.
> (The DeVry Institutes)

Numeric Format Fields

\#
The number sign represents a digit position. A number is right justified in the print field and preceded by spaces as applicable.

```
10   A=12: B=123: C=123.45
20   PRINT USING "#####"; A, B, C
RUN
     12  123    123
```

The decimal point defines the location of the decimal in the format field. Numbers are rounded when the number of decimal places in the format is fewer than in the value of the number to be displayed.

```
10   A=12: B=345.67: C=−.8
20   PRINT USING "####.#"; A, B, C
RUN
      12.0  345.7    −0.8
```

Zeroes are displayed to fill print positions for A and C. Only one zero is printed to the left of the decimal point. The value of B was rounded to one decimal point.

+ and −
A plus sign placed at the beginning or end of the format field causes the sign of the number (i.e.., + or −) to be displayed just before or after the number. A minus sign placed at the end of the format field causes negative numbers to be displayed with a trailing minus sign.

```
10 A=12.34: B=−123: C=−12.34: D=−.01
20 PRINT USING "+####.##"; A, B
30 PRINT USING "####.##−"; C, D
RUN
    +12.43 −123.00
    12.34−    0.01−
```

**
The double asterisk at the beginning of the format field causes leading spaces in the number to be filled with asterisks.

```
10 A=12: B=1234
20 PRINT USING "**#####"; A, B
RUN
```

*****12***1234

The asterisk fill is often used to make printed output more difficult to alter (e.g., net pay on a payroll check).

$$
A double dollar sign placed at the beginning of the format field causes a dollar sign to be displayed immediately to

the left of the leftmost digit in the displayed number. The $$ adds two more positions, one of which is the dollar sign, to the format field.

```
10 A=1.23: B=12.00: C=1234.56
20 PRINT USING "$$####.##"; A, B, C
RUN
        $1.23 $12.00 $1234.56
```

$ An asterisk/dollar sign combination ($) placed at the beginning of the format field causes a dollar sign to be displayed immediately to the left of the leftmost digit in the displayed number and any remaining leading spaces to be filled with asterisks. The **$ adds three more positions, one of which is the dollar sign, to the format field.

```
10 A=1.23: B=12.00: C=1234.56
20 PRINT USING "**$###.##"; A, B, C
RUN
****$1.23***$12.00*$1234.56
```

,   A comma to the left of the decimal point in the format field causes three-digit groups to the left of the decimal point to be separated by a comma.

```
10 A=1234.56: B=1234567.89
20 PRINT USING "#########,.##"; A, B
RUN
        1,234.56 1,234,567.89
```

On a few systems, the comma has to be inserted in the format field (i.e., "##,###,###.##").

~~~~   Four carets to the right of the digit positions in the format field cause the number to be displayed in exponential format. The four positions added to the field are needed to allow space for the exponential notation. The significant digits are left justified in the digit format and the exponent is adjusted accordingly.

```
10 A=-.12: B=12.345: C=123.45
20 PRINT USING "###.#~~~~"; A, B, C
RUN
-12.0E-02 12.3E+00 12.3E+01
```

If you wish to evenly align columns of numeric data, simply pad the format field with extra digit positions (#). For example, the following PRINT USING instruction creates columns that are 15 positions in width.

```
10 A=12.34: B=345.67: C= 7.89: D=56789.1
20 PRINT USING "############.##"; A, B, C, D
RUN
        12.34           345.67          7.89        56789.10
```

String Format Fields

! The exclamation point causes only the first character in the string to be displayed.

```
10 A$="Linda": B$="Bell"
20 PRINT USING "!"; A$, B$
RUN
LB
```

\n spaces\ The format beginning and ending with back slashes specifies that the string is to be left justified in a field that is $2 + n$ positions in length. The 2 backslashes in the format string represent 2 display positions. In the following examples, "Linda" and "Bell" are displayed in adjacent 5-position fields in statement 20 and in adjacent 6-position fields in statement 30.

```
10 A$="Linda":  B$="Bell"
20 PRINT USING "\     \"; A$, B$
30 PRINT USING "\      \"; A$, B$
RUN
LindaBell
Linda Bell
```

& An "and" sign in the format field causes the string to be displayed as it is defined.

```
10 A$="Linda": B$=" E. ": C$="Bell"
20 PRINT USING "&"; A$, B$, C$
RUN
Linda E. Bell
```

Figure B-11 illustrates example format fields and the resulting display for various numeric (N) and string (A$) constants.

LPRINT USING. The LPRINT USING works like the PRINT USING except the output line is routed to a printer instead of the monitor.

MEMORY BITS

SPECIAL CHARACTERS FOR PRINT USING FORMAT FIELDS

Numeric Format Characters

#	Digit position.
.	Decimal point alignment.
+ and −	Display + or − with number.
**	Asterisk fill.
$	Leading double dollar.
**$	Asterisk fill with leading dollar sign.
,	Insert comma.
^^^^	Exponential notation.

String Format Characters

!	Display first character.
\n spaces\	Display in field of $2 + n$ length.
&	Display as defined.

```
        PRINT USING FORMAT$; N                        PRINT USING FORMAT$; A$

FORMATS$=        N=          Displayed        FORMAT$=        A$=          Displayed
"#####"        12345            12345         "\  \"         "ONE"        ONE
"###.###"      23.45           23.450         "\  \"         "Two (2)"    Two
"**###.##"     23.45         ***23.45         "!"            "Three"      T
"$$###.##"     23.45           $23.45         "&"            " 4-Four"    4-Four
"**$##.##"     23.45         **$23.45         "\        \"   "FIVE SIX"   FIVE S
"##.###^^^^-"  -1234.56    12.346E+02-
"+##"          12                 +12
"###"          -12                -12
"##-"          -12                12-
```

Figure B-11
The PRINT USING Instruction
Example PRINT USING format fields and their resulting displays are shown for a variety of numeric (N) and string (A$) constants.

Data Transfer and Assignment Instructions

Read/Data/Restore.   The *values* in a DATA statement(s) are assigned to the corresponding *variables* in a READ statement(s). Numeric variables must be matched with numeric constants, and string variables must be matched with string constants. A mismatch of variables and constants will result in a program error. If there are more variables than data, you will also get an error.

Format: READ list of variables
            DATA constant values

Example: READ COURSE$, NUMBER
             DATA "Government", 101
             DATA "French III", 206
             DATA "Management", 320

The DATA statements have no effect on program execution and can appear any place in the program. The first time the above READ statement is executed, it has the same effect as:

COURSE$ = "Government"
NUMBER = 101

A "software" *pointer* monitors which data values have been assigned and is continually moved to "point" to the value to be assigned next. In the example, each time the READ statement is executed, two values in the DATA statements are assigned to COURSE$ and NUMBER. The first READ assigns the value of the string constant "Government" to the variable COURSE$ and the value of the numeric constant 101 to the variable NUM-

Although there are languages designed specifically for the development of educational software, many developers still prefer to use BASIC because of its versatility. Besides having a good time, these children are learning to read.
(Courtesy of Apple Computer, Inc.)

BER. With the assignment of the first two values, the pointer is moved and "points" to the next value to be assigned ("French III"). The next time the READ statement is executed, COURSE\$ and NUMBER are assigned new values ("French III" and 206) and the pointer is moved to the next value ("Management").

The RESTORE statement causes the pointer to be repositioned at the first value in the *first* DATA statement ("Government"). The values in the data statements can then be reread.

The six values in the three DATA statements in the example above could just as well have been included in one DATA statement or six DATA statements. The computer assumes the values in the DATA statements to be one continuous list of values. The following DATA statements are equivalent to the DATA statements in the example above.

```
DATA "Government", 101, "French III"
DATA 206, "Management", 320
```

The READ instruction in the above example alternately "reads" a string constant and a numeric constant. The values in the DATA statements must match variable types in the READ statement. If the first two values in the above DATA statement were "Government" and "French III", then you would get a type mismatch error (the second must be numeric), and program execution would be terminated.

Other Instructions

DIM.   The DIM or dimension statement permits you to specify and allocate storage for **array** variables. In one dimension (one subscript), an array is the same as a list of similar data elements (e.g., employee names). In two dimensions (two subscripts), an array is the same as a table (e.g., table of employee names and pay rates). *Subscripts* [(1), (2), and so on] provide each storage location in the array with a unique name.

Format: DIM list of array variables with subscript maximums

Examples: DIM EMPLOYEE\$(50), PAY(50)

DIM EMPLOYEE\$(50,2)

The first example DIM statement sets aside 50 primary storage locations for string constants and 50 primary storage locations for numeric values. The string constant locations are referenced by the variable names EMPLOYEE\$(1), EMPLOYEE\$(2), EMPLOYEE\$(3), . . . , EMPLOYEE\$(50), and the numeric locations are referenced by the variable names PAY(1), PAY(2), . . . , PAY(50). The DIM statement, which is usually included in an initialization subroutine, can define any number of array variables. The use of one-dimensional array variables is discussed and illustrated in Example Programs #6 and #7.

The second example DIM sets up a *two-dimensional* array, or a table. In this way the employee's first name and last name can be referenced separately. The first subscript designates a particular employee and the second subscript designates whether the array variable refers to the first or last name. For example, consider the following table:

	1	2
1	Joyce	Cass
2	Harry	Jones
3	Mike	Green
4	Sally	Ackers

EMPLOYEE$(1,1) refers to "Joyce" and EMPLOYEE$(1,2) refers to "Cass"; EMPLOYEE$(3,1) refers to "Mike" and EMPLOYEE$(3,2) refers to "Green"; and so on.

B-15 EXAMPLE PROGRAM #5: LOGICAL OPERATORS AND MULTIPLE CONDITIONAL STATEMENTS _____

Example Program #5 is a logical extension of the previous example programs. The program logic is shown in the structure chart and flowchart. The program not only computes the grades for any number of students (Example Programs #2 through #4), it accepts student identification data (name and ID) and assigns a letter grade of A, B, C, D, or F. The program also permits the instructor to assign a weighting factor to each of the three grades.

Initialization. Most programs require that certain variables be set, or *initialized*, to particular values prior to processing. In Example Program #5, the letter grades are assigned string variable names in Module 1.1—Assign Constants. In future example programs we will initialize the dimensions (DIM) for lists and tables. In this example the READ/DATA statements (1020–1030) are used to assign letter-grade values to string variables. These two statements are equivalent to:

```
1020 A$="A": B$="B": C$="C": D$="D": F$="F"
```

The Loop. The DOUNTIL loop (for each student) is created in a slightly different manner from previous example programs. The instructor does not have to know the number of students for which grades are to be computed. Instead, after each student is processed, the instructor is asked if there are more students to be processed (6020). If the instructor responds with Y or y (yes), then the loop (Modules 1.2 through 1.6) is repeated so that another student can be processed.

You can see from the flowchart that each student is completely processed (input, processing, output) before the next. Within the loop, letter grades are assigned in a series of conditional IF/THEN statements (4030–4070).

Embedded Input Prompts. In Example Program #4, the input prompts

EXAMPLE PROGRAM #5

This program computes the final numeric grade and assigns a letter grade for any number of students. The instructor assigns weighting factors to each of three test scores.

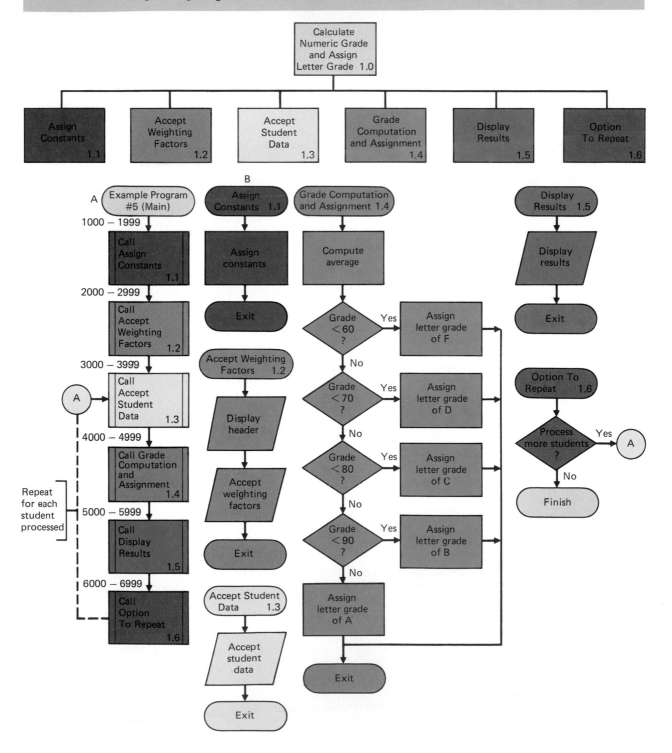

```basic
2     REM          **** Example Program #5 ****
4     REM   Description:
6     REM     This program computes the final numeric grade and assigns
8     REM     a letter grade for any number of students. The instructor
10    REM     assigns weighting factors to each of three test scores.
12    REM   Variables list:
14    REM     A$, B$, C$, D$, F$   - Letter grades
20    REM     STNAME$              - Student name
22    REM     ID                   - Student ID
24    REM     Q1, Q2, FINAL        - Test scores
26    REM     NUMGRADE             - Weighted final numeric grade
28    REM     GRADE$               - Letter grade earned
30    REM     ANSWER$              - Y or N response to inquiry
32    REM     F1$, F2$             - Strings for print using statements
99    REM
100   REM   <<<< Start Main >>>>
110   REM
120   REM   Call Module 1.1 - Assign Constants
130   GOSUB 1000
140   REM   Call Module 1.2 - Accept Weighting Factors
150   GOSUB 2000
160   REM   Call Module 1.3 - Accept Student Data
170   GOSUB 3000
180   REM   Call Module 1.4 - Grade Computation and Assignment
190   GOSUB 4000
200   REM   Call Module 1.5 - Display Results
210   GOSUB 5000
220   REM   Call Module 1.6 - Option to Repeat
230   GOSUB 6000
240   END
250   REM   <<<< End Main >>>>
999   REM
1000  REM   ==== Module 1.1 - Assign Constants
1010  REM   Assign letter grade constants to string variables
1020  READ A$, B$, C$, D$, F$
1030  DATA "A","B","C","D","F"
1999  RETURN
2000  REM   ==== Module 1.2 - Accept Weighting Factors
2010  PRINT "   --------- Grade Assignment Program ---------"
2020  PRINT "Separate multiple entries by commas."
2030  PRINT
2040  INPUT "Enter weighting factor for quiz1, quiz2, and final: ", W1, W2, WF
2999  RETURN
3000  REM   ==== Module 1.3 - Accept Student Data
3010  PRINT
3020  INPUT "Student name: ", STNAME$
3030  INPUT "Student ID: ", ID
3040  INPUT "Enter grades for quiz1, quiz2, and final: ", Q1, Q2, FINAL
3999  RETURN
4000  REM   ==== Module 1.4 - Grade Computation and Assignment
4010  REM       Compute numeric grade and assign letter grade
4020  NUMGRADE = W1*Q1 + W2*Q2 + WF*FINAL
4030  IF NUMGRADE < 60 THEN GRADE$ = F$ : RETURN
4040    IF NUMGRADE < 70 THEN GRADE$ = D$ : RETURN
4050      IF NUMGRADE < 80 THEN GRADE$ = C$ : RETURN
4060        IF NUMGRADE < 90 THEN GRADE$ = B$ : RETURN
4070          GRADE$ = A$
4999  RETURN
5000  REM   ==== Module 1.5 - Display Results
5010  F1$="#####          "
5020  F2$="###.##          "
5030  PRINT
5040  PRINT "Student Name","ID Number","Numeric Grade","Letter Grade"
5050  PRINT STNAME$,:PRINT USING F1$; ID,:PRINT USING F2$; NUMGRADE,:PRINT GRADE$
5060  PRINT
5999  RETURN
6000  REM   ==== Module 1.6 - Option to Repeat
6010  REM       Give the user the option to process another student
6020  INPUT "More students? (Y or N) ",ANSWER$
6030  IF ANSWER$ = "Y" OR ANSWER$ = "y" THEN RETURN 160
6999  RETURN 240
```

continued

Example Program 5 continued

```
run
     --------- Grade Assignment Program ---------
Separate multiple entries by commas.

Enter weighting factor for quiz1, quiz2, and final :.3,.3,.4

Student name :Charles Roth
Student ID :46912
Enter grades for quiz1, quiz2, and final :73,91,85

Student Name  ID Number      Numeric Grade Letter Grade
Charles Roth  46912             83.20          B

More students? (Y or N) y

Student name :Lucy Cook
Student ID :77878
Enter grades for quiz1, quiz2, and final :86,88,99

Student Name  ID Number      Numeric Grade Letter Grade
Lucy Cook     77878             91.80          A

More students? (Y or N) y
```

```
Student name :Wayne Evans
Student ID :66941
Enter grades for quiz1, quiz2, and final :66,84,75

Student Name  ID Number      Numeric Grade Letter Grade
Wayne Evans   66941             75.00          C

More students? (Y or N) n
Ok
```

are displayed with PRINT instructions. Using the PRINT/INPUT combination, an alternative to statement 3020 of Example Program #5 would have been:

```
3020 PRINT "Student name: ";
3025 INPUT STNAME$
```

In Example Program #5, a prompt is embedded in the INPUT instructions before the variables list (see statements 3020–3040). This consolidates the PRINT/INPUT combination illustrated in Example Program #4 into a single instruction.

When the descriptive prompt in an INPUT instruction is followed by a semicolon, a question mark prompt (?) is displayed immediately following and on the same line as the descriptive prompt. The following instruction:

INPUT "Student name: "; STNAME$

results in the following prompt being displayed:

Student Name: ?

A question mark is not needed here. To suppress the generic input prompt (?) in the INPUT instruction, follow the descriptive prompt ("Student name: ") by a *comma* rather than a semicolon. The following version of the above example eliminates the "?" when the descriptive prompt is displayed:

INPUT "Student name: ", STNAME$

The prompt is displayed as follows:

Student Name:

The INPUT instructions in Example Program #5 employ a comma to suppress the "?" (see the interactive session).

This portable computer fits neatly into a back pack (or briefcase). Nevertheless, it has the same kinds of BASIC programming instructions as mainframe computers.
(Photo supplied courtesy of Epson America)

Assigning Grades.   The numerical grade (NUMGRADE) is computed in statement 4020. Because the multiplication arithmetic operator has a higher priority than the addition arithmetic operator, the weighting factors (entered in Module 1.2) are first multiplied by the quiz scores and the products are then added. To avoid confusion, you might prefer to insert parentheses.

4020 NUMGRADE=(W1*Q1) + (W2*Q2) + (WF*FINAL)

In statements 4030–4070, a letter grade is assigned to each student based on the value of NUMGRADE (the weighted final numeric grade). IF the value of NUMGRADE meets the condition, THEN the appropriate letter grade constant is assigned to the variable GRADE$. If the first condition is not met, processing "drops through" to the next IF instruction, and so on, until the condition is met. When the condition is met, a letter grade is assigned and control is RETURNed to driver module.

Logical Operators.   We have already discussed arithmetic operators (Figure B-3) and relational operators (Figure B-5) in Learning Module II: Getting Started with BASIC. **Logical operators**, such as AND and OR (see Figure B-12), are placed between conditional expressions in an IF or WHILE instruction. In effect, logical operators enable us to combine conditional expressions. When the OR operator is used, the condition is considered true if *at least*

Figure B-12
Logical Operators

OPERATION	OPERATOR
For the condition to be true:	
Both subconditions must be true	AND
At least one subcondition must be true	OR

one subcondition is true. For example, at statement 6030, the THEN clause is taken and the loop is repeated IF the first OR the second expression is true. In this instance, the user can enter either "Y" or "y" to process another student.

Without the logical operator, statement 6030 would be written as two IF instructions:

```
6030 IF ANSWER$ = "Y" THEN RETURN 160
6035 IF ANSWER$ = "y" THEN RETURN 160
```

When the AND operator is used, *both* conditions must be true for the THEN clause to be executed. An alternative way to write statements 6030 and 6999 in Example Program #5 is:

```
6030 IF ANSWER$ <> "Y" AND ANSWER$ <> "y" THEN RETURN 240
6999 RETURN 160
```

In the above case, for the THEN clause to be taken, the character entered cannot be a "Y" AND it cannot be a "y". If both of these conditions are met, control is RETURNed to the driver module at the END instruction (240) and program execution is terminated.

The NOT operator reverses the logic of the expression it precedes. When the NOT operator is placed before a conditional expression, the condition must be false for the instruction following THEN to be executed. For example, the following instructions are equivalent to the above example:

```
6030 IF NOT ANSWER$ = "Y" AND NOT ANSWER$ = "y" THEN RETURN 240
6040 RETURN 160
```

Display of Results.   In statement 5050, the PRINT and PRINT USING instructions are combined in a single statement to create a better display of the results. The comma at the end of each instruction causes the cursor to remain on the same display line. In this way, the numeric values of ID and NUMGRADE can be displayed in formatted fields with PRINT USING instructions. For most versions of BASIC, two PRINT USING instructions would be necessary since two different formats are desired.

B-16   EXAMPLE PROGRAM #6: ARRAYS AND REPORT FORMATTING

The input, processing, and output of Example Program #6 are similar to that of Example Program #5 except *all student data are entered and processed prior to being displayed.* Once entered, the data are processed and displayed in the form of a "GRADE SUMMARY" report.

Arrays.   To present the results in a report format, the data for each student must be kept in memory. In Example Program #5, when the test scores of the second student are entered, a new value is computed for NUMGRADE, thereby erasing the numerical grade of the first student. We can use *arrays* (see DIM in the Learning Module IV instruction set) to retain data in primary storage so that they can be displayed together in a report format. To do this, a one-dimensional array, or list, is created for each student data element

EXAMPLE PROGRAM #6

This program computes the final numeric grade and assigns a letter grade for any number of students. The program uses arrays to compute and assign grades. The input and results are the same as that of Example Program #5, but the results are displayed in a report format.

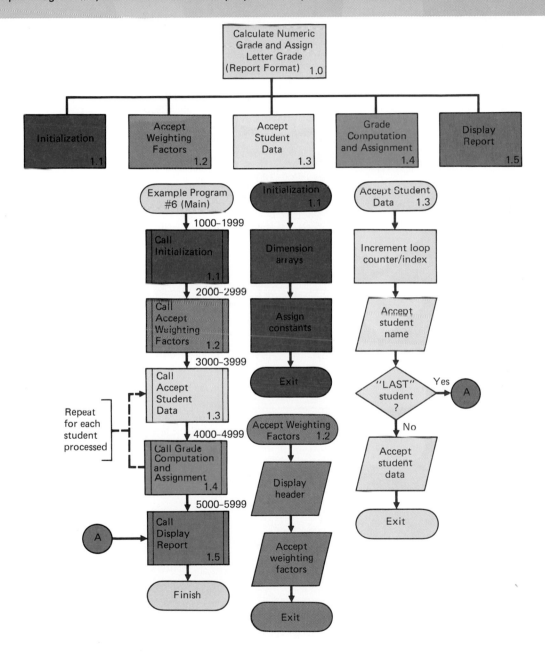

continued

Example Program 6 continued

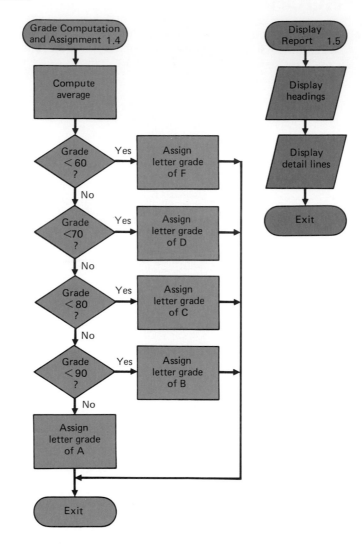

```
2    REM          **** Example Program #6 ****
4    REM   Description:
6    REM      This program computes the final numeric grade and assigns
8    REM      a letter grade for any number of students.  The program uses
10   REM      arrays to compute and assign grades.  The input and results are
12   REM      the same as that of Example Program #5, but the results are
14   REM      displayed in a report format.
16   REM   Variables list: () indicates array
18   REM      A$, B$, C$, D$, F$    -Letter grades
20   REM      W1, W2, WF            -Weighting factors
22   REM      COUNT                 -Counter for the number of students
24   REM      STNAME$()             -Student name
26   REM      ID()                  -Student ID
28   REM      Q1(), Q2(), FINAL()   -Test scores
30   REM      NUMGRADE()            -Weighted final grade
32   REM      GRADE$()              -Letter grade earned
34   REM      I                     -Index for display loop
36   REM      F1$, F2$              -Strings for PRINT USING statements
99   REM
100  REM   <<<< Start Main >>>>
110  REM
```

```
120  REM   Call Module 1.1 - Initialization
130  GOSUB 1000
140  REM   Call Module 1.2 - Accept Weighting Factors
150  GOSUB 2000
160  REM   Call Module 1.3 - Accept Student Data
170  GOSUB 3000
180  REM   Call Module 1.4 - Grade Computation and Assignment
190  GOSUB 4000
200  REM   Call Module 1.5 - Display Report
210  GOSUB 5000
220  END
230  REM   <<<< End Main >>>>
999  REM
1000 REM   ==== Module 1.1 - Initialization
1010 REM   Dimension arrays
1020 DIM STNAME$(50),ID(50),Q1(50),Q2(50),FINAL(50),NUMGRADE(50),GRADE$(50)
1030 REM   Assign letter grade constants to string variables
1040 READ A$, B$, C$, D$, F$
1050 DATA "A","B","C","D","F"
1999 RETURN
2000 REM   ==== Module 1.2 - Accept Weighting Factors
2010 PRINT "     -------- Grade Report Program --------"
2020 PRINT "Separate multiple entries by commas"
2030 PRINT
2040 INPUT "Enter weighting factors for quiz1, quiz2, and final"; W1, W2, WF
2999 RETURN
3000 REM   ==== Module 1.3 - Accept Student Data
3010 REM   Increment loop counter/index
3020 COUNT = COUNT + 1
3030 INPUT "Student name (Enter LAST when complete)";STNAME$(COUNT)
3040 IF STNAME$(COUNT) = "LAST" OR STNAME$(COUNT) = "last" THEN RETURN 200
3050 INPUT "Student ID";ID(COUNT)
3060 INPUT "Enter grades for quiz1, quiz2, and final"; Q1(COUNT), Q2(COUNT),
        FINAL(COUNT)
3999 RETURN
4000 REM   ==== Module 1.4 - Grade Computation and Assignment
4010 REM   Compute numeric grade and assign letter grade
4020 NUMGRADE(COUNT) = W1*Q1(COUNT) + W2*Q2(COUNT) + WF*FINAL(COUNT)
4030 IF NUMGRADE(COUNT) < 60 THEN GRADE$(COUNT) = F$ : RETURN 160
4040   IF NUMGRADE(COUNT) < 70 THEN GRADE$(COUNT) = D$ : RETURN 160
4050     IF NUMGRADE(COUNT) < 80 THEN GRADE$(COUNT) = C$ : RETURN 160
4060       IF NUMGRADE(COUNT) < 90 THEN GRADE$(COUNT) = B$ : RETURN 160
4070         GRADE$(COUNT) = A$
4999 RETURN 160
5000 REM   ==== Module 1.5 - Display Report
5010 REM   Display header
5020 F1$="#####             "
5030 F2$="###.##            "
5040 PRINT
5050 PRINT TAB(20);"Grade Summary"
5060 PRINT
5070 PRINT "Student Name","ID number","Numeric Grade","Letter Grade"
5080 PRINT "------------","---------","-------------","------------"
5090 PRINT
5100 REM   Generate report
5110 COUNT = COUNT - 1
5120 REM   Begin loop to display detail lines - execute 'COUNT' times
5130 FOR I=1 TO COUNT
5140   PRINT STNAME$(I),:PRINT USING F1$; ID(I);:PRINT USING F2$; NUMGRADE(I);
        :PRINT GRADE$(I)
5150 NEXT I
5999 RETURN
```

continued

Example Program 6 continued

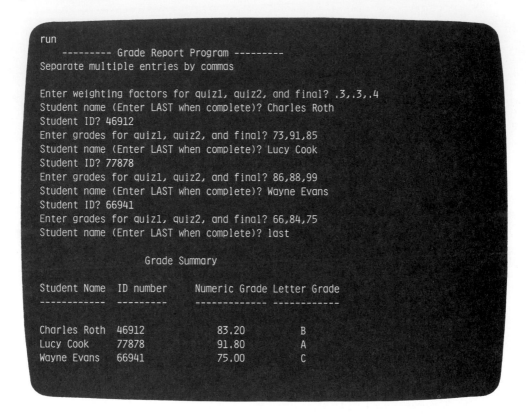

```
run
     --------- Grade Report Program ---------
Separate multiple entries by commas

Enter weighting factors for quiz1, quiz2, and final? .3,.3,.4
Student name (Enter LAST when complete)? Charles Roth
Student ID? 46912
Enter grades for quiz1, quiz2, and final? 73,91,85
Student name (Enter LAST when complete)? Lucy Cook
Student ID? 77878
Enter grades for quiz1, quiz2, and final? 86,88,99
Student name (Enter LAST when complete)? Wayne Evans
Student ID? 66941
Enter grades for quiz1, quiz2, and final? 66,84,75
Student name (Enter LAST when complete)? last

                  Grade Summary

Student Name  ID number     Numeric Grade Letter Grade
------------  ---------     ------------- ------------

Charles Roth  46912             83.20          B
Lucy Cook     77878             91.80          A
Wayne Evans   66941             75.00          C
```

(e.g., STNAME$, ID, Q1, Q2, FINAL, and so on). It is not necessary to dimension Q1, Q2, and FINAL to generate the report shown in the interactive session. These variables are dimensioned now so that the data are available if more sophisticated reporting is desired (see Example Program #7). This approach is common practice.

The DIM instruction in Module 1.1—Initialization (1020) sets aside, or "declares," 50 memory positions for each of seven array variables. The first five variables contain student data entered by the instructor. The last two array variables, NUMGRADE(50) and GRADE$(50), are determined and filled during processing.

In an array, values are stored and retrieved from a particular location by a *subscripted variable name*. All variables in a particular array have the same variable name (i.e., STNAME$), but each has a subscript to make it unique. The value of the subscript determines which of the 50 locations is referenced. For example, STNAME$(1) and ID(1) refer to the first items in the respective one-dimensional arrays. In the example programs, all subscripted variables with the subscript of (1) reference to the data for the first student. Those with the subscript of (2) reference the data for the second student, and so on.

In Example Program #6, COUNT is the **index variable**. An array index can be a *constant*, a *variable*, or even an *expression*. The value of COUNT is the subscript for the array variables and designates which data are for which student. The value of COUNT is incremented by 1 (3020) with each repetition of the loop (Modules 1.3–1.4). During the first time through the loop, COUNT is set to 1. Data that are entered, calculated, and processed are loaded to the first location in their respective arrays: STNAME$(1), ID(1), and so on. During the second pass through loop, or second *iteration*, the value of COUNT is equal to 2, and data are loaded to the second location in their respective arrays: STNAME$(2), ID(2), and so on. Because only 50 positions have been set aside in memory (1020), the maximum number of students that can be processed is 50.

The End-of-File Entry.   Example Program #6 illustrates how an *end-of-file* entry can be used to signal the program that data entry is complete. The INPUT instruction (3030) prompts the instructor to enter "LAST" instead of a student's name when all data entry is complete. "LAST" is the end-of-file entry. The IF instruction at 3040 checks each name entered to see if it equals "LAST" or "last". When "LAST" is entered, statement 3040 causes a RETURN to the driver module at Module 1.5—Display Report for the printing of the GRADE SUMMARY report.

The end-of-file entry gives the instructor greater flexibility in entering data than in the previous example programs. In Example Programs #2, #3, and #4, the instructor had to count and enter the number of students to be processed. This approach provides too much of an opportunity for human error. In Example Program #5, the instructor has to respond to a "More students?" inquiry for each student processed. This approach demands excessive user interaction.

Report Formatting.   Module 1.5—Display Report causes the report *header* to be displayed. A header normally consists of a report title (5050) and column headings (5070). Blank lines are inserted to make the report easier to read. Notice that TAB(20) is used in the PRINT instruction at 5050. The TAB(20) causes the report title to be displayed 20 spaces from the left margin. The **TAB** function is a handy tool for report generation.

The *detail lines* for each student are displayed in a FOR/NEXT loop (5130–5150). For the data of the example interactive session, the index variable I is incremented from 1 to 3 (the number of students processed) so that data for each student are displayed.

The column headings are displayed in *zones*, since commas are used to separate the display list (5070). The detail line is displayed using a combination of PRINT and PRINT USING instructions (see discussion of Example Program #5).

Obtaining a Hard Copy.   The PRINT and PRINT USING instructions in Module 1.5—Display Report generate output for the workstation display screen. If a hard copy of the GRADE SUMMARY report is preferred, simply change the PRINT and PRINT USING instructions in Module 1.5 to LPRINT and LPRINT USING. This modification would result in a hard copy report being produced on a printer.

The most common configuration for a microcomputer is a video monitor, a processor, at least one disk drive, and a printer. In this compact system, the monitor, processor, and disk drive are all in the same unit. The mouse, which is now standard on many micros, is also part of this system's configuration.
(Courtesy of Apple Computer, Inc.)

REVIEW EXERCISES (LEARNING MODULE IV) _____

BASIC Instructions and Concepts

1. Identify the syntax error(s) in each of the following instructions.

    (a) 10 DIMENSION DESCRIPTION$(100)
    (b) 10 LPRINT USING "*$$# #.# #", AMOUNT
    (c) 10 READ A: DATUM 345
    (d) 10 LET X(1,−1)=0

2. What PRINT USING format fields would produce the following numeric and string displays?

PRINT USING FORMAT$; 45.6789   PRINT USING FORMAT$; "Computers"
(a) 45.679   (e) C
(b) **45.7   (f) Compute
(c) 4.6E+01   (g) Computers
(d) $45.68   (h) Co

3. What are the problems in the following instruction sequence?

    100 READ A,A$,B,C
    200 DATA 8,4,"BOLT"

4. What values of A, B, and C are displayed?

    100 READ A
    200 RESTORE
    300 READ C, B
    400 READ A
    500 DATA 1, 2, 3, 4
    600 PRINT A, B, C
    700 END

5. Combine the following statements into two statements without the use of a colon:

    100 PRINT "Enter hours worked and rate"
    200 INPUT HRSWORK, RATE
    300 SALARY=HRSWORK*RATE
    400 PRINT "Salary is", SALARY

6. Modify the PRINT instruction in the above program segment to an LPRINT USING/LPRINT combination of instructions that produce the following hard copy output. [*Hint*: Put several instructions on the same line.]

    SALARY IS $350.00 FOR   40 HOURS AT $8.75 PER HOUR

7. Name and dimension arrays that will hold data for the following circumstances:
    (a) quarterly sales figures for 18 regional offices.
    (b) the location (city) for 18 regional offices.
    (c) the first name, middle initial, and last name of at least 300 customers.
    (d) the identification number for at least 300 customers.

8. Six letters are accepted and loaded to a 3-row by 2-column array, called LETTER$. The letters are entered in this order: A, E, I, O, U, and Y. Row is filled first, then rows 2 and 3. What is the value of:
   (a) LETTER$(2,1)   (c) LETTER$(1,2)
   (b) LETTER$(3,1)   (d) LETTER$(2,2)

9. Which of the following conditional expressions are true?

```
100 X=10
200 Y=20
300 IF X<>Y AND Y<21 THEN PRINT "True"
400 IF Y=X+10 OR X=Y+10 THEN PRINT "True"
500 IF X<>Y OR NOT Y=20 THEN PRINT "True"
```

Example Program #5

10. What do the PRINT USING instructions do in this program that cannot be done with PRINT instructions?

11. How would you modify the program to completely eliminate the need for Module 1.2—Assign Constants?

12. Describe in words what you would do to revise the program so that an instructor can enter and assign weighting factors for four grades.

13. How would the program logic change if the instructor were permitted to enter up to three grades and weighting factors?

14. What happens if you enter a "Z" rather than a "Y" or "N" in response to the "More students?" prompt in Module 1.6—Option to Repeat?

Example Program #6

15. Compare the logic of Example Programs #5 and #6. Could #5 have been modified to produce a report without the use of arrays? Why or why not?

16. How many primary storage locations are declared in the DIM statement at 1020 for numeric values and string values?

17. What must be done to modify the program to accommodate 60 students?

18. Compared to entering the number of students to be processed (Example Program #4) or asking the instructor after each entry if more students are to be processed (Example Program #5), what are the advantages to using an EOF entry (i.e., "LAST")?

BASIC PROGRAMMING ASSIGNMENTS _____

1. To optimize inventory, companies calculate the economic order quantity (EOQ) that would meet the company's demand for a particular item, yet minimize the cost of buying and holding the inventory.

This is a tradeoff between the number of times that a particular item must be ordered and the holding cost. Write a program to calculate the economic order quantity.

$$EOQ = (2*P*R/C)^{.5}$$

where P = preparation cost per order
         R = annual requirement for an inventory item
         C = storage cost per item per year

Make the program interactive so that any number of EOQs can be computed until the operator enters -999.

2. Write an interactive program (without arrays) to compute gross pay and net pay for salaried, hourly, and commissioned employees. Assume that deductions are 20% of gross pay. For salaried employees, gross pay is entered directly. For hourly employees, the gross pay is equal to the number of hours worked times the pay rate. For commissioned employees, gross pay is equal to the rate of commission times total sales.
    Present the following menu to the operator:

TYPE PAY
1 Salaried
2 Hourly
3 Commissioned
Select pay type?

Use the following prompts to enter pay data:

Enter salary:
Enter hours worked and pay rate:
Enter total sales and percent commission:

The output line for each employee should be:

EMPLOYEE NAME	PAY TYPE	GROSS PAY	NET PAY
T. Jones	Salaried	$3000.00	$2400.00

Note that the heading would be printed for each calculation.

3. Modify the above program to use arrays so that a payroll register can be produced that lists all the names and results consecutively rather than individually. The program should accommodate up to 20 employees.

PAYROLL REGISTER

EMPLOYEE NAME	PAY TYPE	GROSS PAY	NET PAY
T. Jones	Salaried	$3000.00	$2400.00
D. Mattis	Hourly	$2100.00	$1680.00
D. Guyer	Commission	$3800.00	$3040.00
	TOTAL	$8900.00	$7120.00

B-17 BASIC INSTRUCTION SET: LEARNING MODULE V GROUP

Four instructions are introduced in this group. One rather straightforward I/O instruction will give us the flexibility to substantially improve the appearance of the output displays. Two others are variations on the GOSUB and GOTO (see the Learning Module II instruction set). And the fourth is a variation on the INPUT instruction.

Input/Output Instructions

CLS. The "clear screen" instruction removes any output on the display screen and positions the cursor to the "home" position, normally the upper-left corner of the screen.

> *Format*: CLS

In Example Program #6, the CLS instruction could have been inserted at the start of Module 1.5—Display Report to clear the input data from the screen so that the GRADE REPORT could be positioned at the top of the screen.

On some systems, the clear screen command is CLEAR or HOME.

LINE INPUT. The LINE INPUT instruction accepts whatever is entered, including delimiters such as commas, into a single string variable.

> *Format*: LINE INPUT "prompt"; string variable

> *Example*: LINE INPUT "Enter comments"; COMMENTS$

In the above instruction, all characters (including spaces, commas, semicolons, etc.) entered prior to pressing the carriage return become a string constant and are assigned to the string variable COMMENT$.

Control Instructions: Conditional and Unconditional Transfer

ON GOSUB/RETURN. An optional form of the GOSUB instruction is used to direct processing to branch to a specified line number based on the value of a numeric expression. Processing is RETURNed to the statement following the ON GOSUB.

For the last several years, this product manager spent one hour each week tallying the regional sales figures. He finally spent five hours writing a BASIC program to help with this task. Now, his weekly sales reports take only 15 minutes and they are more accurate. In every office, there are many tasks for which a single BASIC program can be a real timesaver.
(Photo courtesy of Hewlett-Packard Company)

"A simple error message will do!"
(By permission of Brian Hansen)

> *Format*:   ON numeric expression GOSUB line number, line number, . . .

Example: 100 ON I GOSUB 2000, 3000, 4000

            2000 INPUT A, B
            2999 RETURN
            3000 INPUT A$
            3999 RETURN
            4000 INPUT C, D$
            4999 RETURN

In the example, control of execution is transferred to one of three line numbers depending on the value of I. If I=1, then control passes to the instruction at 2000, the first line number in the list; if I=2, then control passes to the instruction at 3000, the second line number; and so on. The value of the numeric expression is rounded to an integer, if needed. When the resultant value is negative, zero, or greater than the number of line numbers in the list, then control is passed to the statement following the ON GOSUB. A RETURN instruction must be associated with each line number so that control can be returned to the statement following the ON GOSUB instruction.

ON GOTO.   The ON GOTO counterpart of ON GOSUB causes an unconditional branch to a specified line number.

> *Format*:   ON numeric expression GOTO line number, line number, . . .

Example: 100 ON I GOTO 2000, 3000, 4000

The "Bread and Butter" BASIC Instructions

You now have an arsenal of programming tools at your disposal. With the few BASIC instructions presented and explained in the instruction set groups in Learning Modules II, III, IV, and V, you should be able to model almost any business or scientific procedure. These "bread and butter" instructions comprise about 20% of the total number of BASIC instructions, yet they account for about 80% of the instructions in a typical program. In the remaining learning modules you will learn instructions that permit more sophisticated programming activities, such as disk file manipulation, graphics, and music.

B-18   EXAMPLE PROGRAM #7: INTERACTIVE INQUIRY ___

Example Program #7 is Example Program #6 with an add-on *Inquiry* module (Module 1.6). We will focus our attention on this inquiry module. The inquiry module permits the instructor to make inquiries about the student data. For

EXAMPLE PROGRAM #7

This program computes the final numeric grade and assigns a letter grade for any number of students. The same report as in Example Program #6 is generated. An inquiry module allows the instructor to interactively make inquires with regard to: 1. Numeric averages for each quiz and overall; 2. Breakdown by letter grade; 3. High and low students.

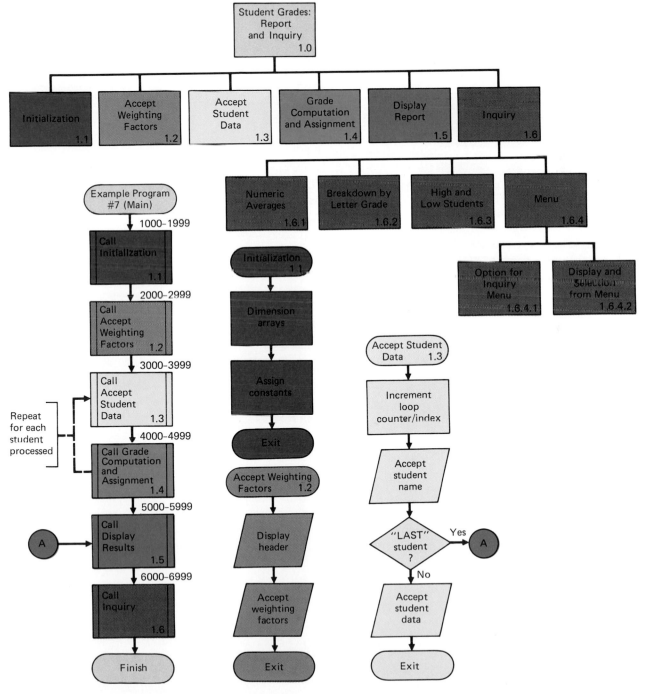

continued

Example Program 7 continued

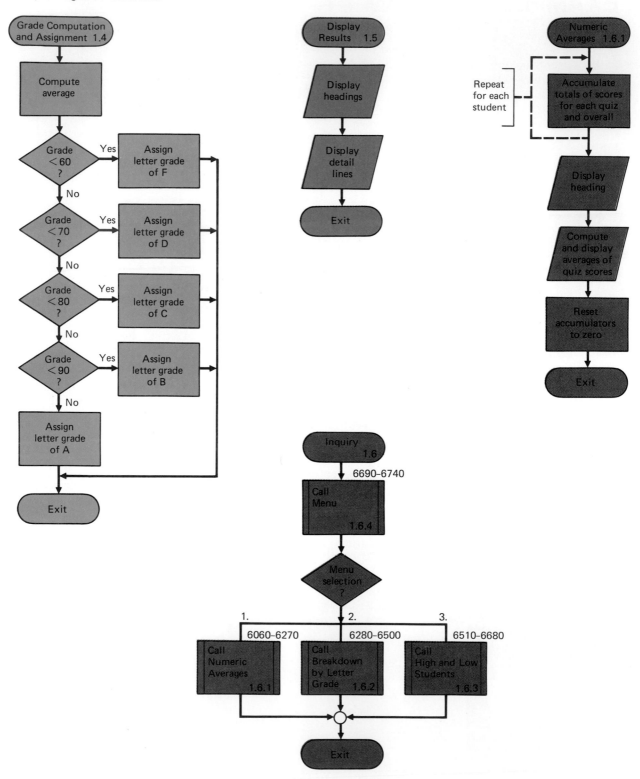

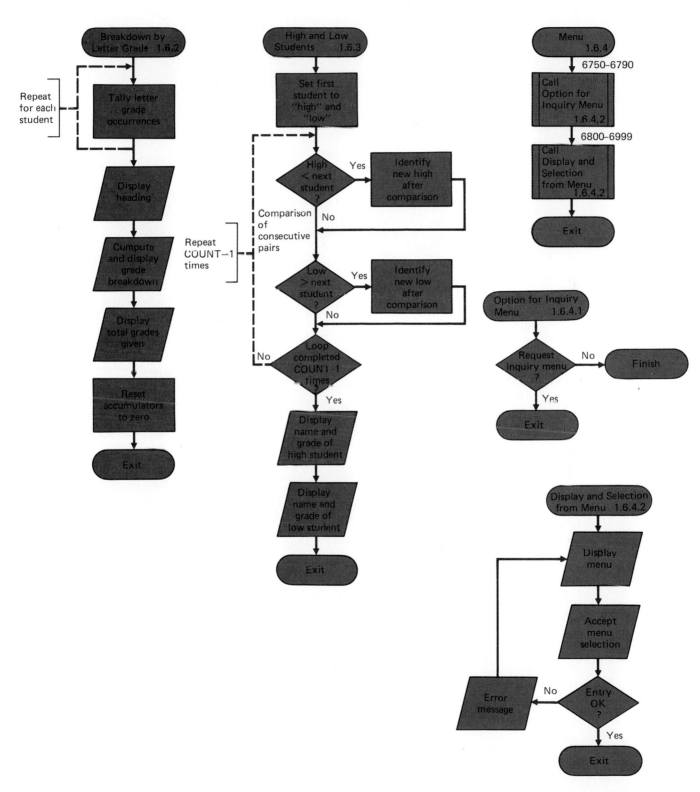

continued

```
2    REM          **** Example Program #7 ****
4    REM   Description:
6    REM      This program computes the final numeric grade and assigns a
8    REM      letter grade for any number of students. The same report as in
10   REM      Example Program #6 is generated. An inquiry module allows the
12   REM      instructor to interactively make inquiries with regard to:
14   REM              1. Numeric averages for each quiz and overall
16   REM              2. Breakdown by letter grade
18   REM              3. High and low students
20   REM   Variables list:
22   REM      A$, B$, C$, D$, F$   -Letter grades
24   REM      W1, W2, WF           -Weighting factors
26   REM      COUNT                -Counter for the number of students
28   REM      STNAME$()            -Student name
30   REM      ID()                 -Student ID
32   REM      Q1(), Q2(), FINAL()  -Test scores
34   REM      NUMGRADE()           -Weighted final grade
36   REM      GRADE$()             -Letter grade earned
38   REM      I                    -Index for display loop
40   REM      F1$, F2$, F3$        -Strings for PRINT USING statements
42   REM      MENU                 -Menu item selected
44   REM      T1, T2, T3, T4       -Accumulators to compute quiz averages
46   REM      HIGH, LOW            -Indices for high and low students
99   REM
100  REM   <<<< Start Main >>>>
110  REM
120  REM   Call Module 1.1 - Initialization
130  GOSUB 1000
140  REM   Call Module 1.2 - Accept Weighting Factors
150  GOSUB 2000
160  REM   Call Module 1.3 - Accept Student Data
170  GOSUB 3000
180  REM   Call Module 1.4 - Grade Computation and Assignment
190  GOSUB 4000
200  REM   Call Module 1.5 - Display Report
210  GOSUB 5000
220  REM   Call Module 1.6 - Inquiry
230  GOSUB 6000
240  REM
250  REM   <<<< End Main >>>>
999  REM
1000 REM   ==== Module 1.1 - Initialization
1010 REM   Dimension Arrays
1020 DIM STNAME$(50),ID(50),Q1(50),Q2(50),FINAL(50),NUMGRADE(50),GRADE$(50)
1030 REM   Assign letter grade constants to string variables
1040 READ A$, B$, C$, D$, F$
1050 DATA "A","B","C","D","F"
1999 RETURN
2000 REM   ==== Module 1.2 - Accept Weighting Factors
2010 PRINT "     -------- Grade Report Program --------"
2020 PRINT "Separate multiple entries by commas"
2030 PRINT
2040 INPUT "Enter weighting factors for quiz1, quiz2, and final: ", W1, W2, WF
2999 RETURN
3000 REM   ==== Module 1.3 - Accept Student Data
3010 REM   Increment loop counter/index
3020 COUNT = COUNT + 1
3030 INPUT "Student name (Enter LAST when complete): ",STNAME$(COUNT)
3040 IF STNAME$(COUNT) = "LAST" OR STNAME$(COUNT) = "last" THEN RETURN 200
3050 INPUT "Student ID: ",ID(COUNT)
3060 INPUT "Enter grades for quiz1, quiz2, and final: ", Q1(COUNT), Q2(COUNT),
        FINAL(COUNT)
3999 RETURN
4000 REM   ==== Module 1.4 - Grade Computation and Assignment
4010 REM   Compute grade and assign a letter grade
4020 NUMGRADE(COUNT) = W1*Q1(COUNT) + W2*Q2(COUNT) + WF*FINAL(COUNT)
4030 IF NUMGRADE(COUNT) < 60 THEN GRADE$(COUNT) = F$ : RETURN 160
4040   IF NUMGRADE(COUNT) < 70 THEN GRADE$(COUNT) = D$ : RETURN 160
4050     IF NUMGRADE(COUNT) < 80 THEN GRADE$(COUNT) = C$ : RETURN 160
4060       IF NUMGRADE(COUNT) < 90 THEN GRADE$(COUNT) = B$ : RETURN 160
4070         GRADE$(COUNT) = A$
4999 RETURN 160
```

```
5000 REM  ==== Module 1.5 - Display Report
5010 CLS
5020 REM  Display header
5030 PRINT
5040 PRINT TAB(20);"Grade Summary"
5050 PRINT
5060 PRINT "Student Name","ID Number","Numeric Grade","Letter Grade"
5070 PRINT "------------","---------","-------------","------------"
5080 PRINT
5090 F1$="#####           "
5100 F2$="###.##          "
5110 REM  Generate report
5120 COUNT = COUNT - 1
5130 REM  Begin loop to display detail lines - execute 'COUNT' times
5140 FOR I=1 TO COUNT
5150   PRINT STNAME$(I),:PRINT USING F1$; ID(I);:PRINT USING F2$; NUMGRADE(I);
          :PRINT GRADE$(I)
5160 NEXT
5999 RETURN
6000 REM  ==== Module 1.6 - Inquiry
6010 REM  Call Module 1.6.4 - Menu
6020 GOSUB 6690
6030 REM  Call appropriate inquiry module
6040 ON MENU GOSUB 6060, 6280, 6510
6050 GOTO 6010
6060 REM  ==== Module 1.6.1 - Numeric Averages
6070 REM  Compute numeric averages for each quiz and display them
6080 REM
6090 REM  Accumulate totals for each quiz
6100 FOR I=1 TO COUNT
6110   T1 = T1 + Q1(I)
6120   T2 = T2 + Q2(I)
6130   T3 = T3 + FINAL(I)
6140   T4 = T4 + NUMGRADE(I)
6150 NEXT I
6160 PRINT
6170 REM  Display quiz averages
6180 PRINT ,"Weighting","Average for"
6190 PRINT ,"Factor",COUNT;"Students"
6200 PRINT
6210 PRINT "Quiz 1", W1*100 ;"%", T1/COUNT
6220 PRINT "Quiz 2", W2*100 ;"%",T2/COUNT
6230 PRINT "Final", WF*100 ;"%",T3/COUNT
6240 PRINT "Overall",, T4/COUNT
6250 REM  Reset accumulators to zero
6260 T1 = 0 : T2 = 0 : T3 = 0 : T4 = 0
6270 RETURN
6280 REM  ==== Module 1.6.2 - Breakdown By Letter Grade
6290 REM  Tally letter grade occurrences
6300 FOR I=1 TO COUNT
6310   IF GRADE$(I) = A$ THEN AGRADE = AGRADE + 1
6320   IF GRADE$(I) = B$ THEN BGRADE = BGRADE + 1
6330   IF GRADE$(I) = C$ THEN CGRADE = CGRADE + 1
6340   IF GRADE$(I) = D$ THEN DGRADE = DGRADE + 1
6350   IF GRADE$(I) = F$ THEN FGRADE = FGRADE + 1
6360 NEXT I
6370 REM  Display letter grade breakdown
6380 PRINT "Grade","Number","Percent"
6390 F3$ = "###.##"
6400 PRINT
6410 PRINT A$, AGRADE,:PRINT USING F3$; (AGRADE/COUNT) * 100
6420 PRINT B$, BGRADE,:PRINT USING F3$; (BGRADE/COUNT) * 100
6430 PRINT C$, CGRADE,:PRINT USING F3$; (CGRADE/COUNT) * 100
6440 PRINT D$, DGRADE,:PRINT USING F3$; (DGRADE/COUNT) * 100
6450 PRINT F$, FGRADE,:PRINT USING F3$; (FGRADE/COUNT) * 100
6460 PRINT
6470 PRINT "Total number of grades given is"; COUNT
6480 REM  Reset grade counters to zero
6490 AGRADE = 0 : BGRADE = 0 : CGRADE = 0 : DGRADE = 0 : FGRADE = 0
6500 RETURN
```

continued

Example Program 7 continued

```
6510 REM  ==== Module 1.6.3 - High And Low Students
6520 REM  Find and display students with highest and lowest grades
6530 REM
6540 REM  Set both HIGH and LOW to first student
6550 HIGH = 1 : LOW = 1
6560 REM  Compare student pairs to identify
6570 REM  high and low students
6580 FOR I=2 TO COUNT
6590   IF NUMGRADE(HIGH) < NUMGRADE(I) THEN HIGH = I
6600   IF NUMGRADE(LOW) > NUMGRADE(I) THEN LOW = I
6610 NEXT I
6620 REM  Display high and low students
6630 PRINT "The high student is "; STNAME$(HIGH) ;" with an overall"
6640 PRINT "   grade of"; NUMGRADE(HIGH)
6650 PRINT
6660 PRINT "The low student is "; STNAME$(LOW) ;" with an overall"
6670 PRINT "   grade of"; NUMGRADE(LOW)
6680 RETURN
6690 REM  ==== Module 1.6.4 - Menu
6700 REM  Call Module 1.6.4.1 - Option for Inquiry Menu
6710 GOSUB 6750
6720 REM  Call Module 1.6.4.2 - Display and Selection from Menu
6730 GOSUB 6800
6740 RETURN
6750 REM  ==== Module 1.6.4.1 - Option for Inquiry Menu
6760 PRINT
6770 INPUT "Would you like to see the inquiry menu? (Enter Y or N) ",ANSWER$
6780 IF ANSWER$ = "N" OR ANSWER$ = "n" THEN RETURN 6999
6790 RETURN
6800 REM  ==== Module 1.6.4.2 - Display and Selection from Menu
6810 PRINT
6820 PRINT "   ---- INQUIRY MENU ----"
6830 PRINT "1. Numeric averages for each quiz and overall"
6840 PRINT "2. Breakdown by letter grade"
6850 PRINT "3. High and low students"
6860 PRINT
6870 REM  Accept menu selection
6880 INPUT "Make a selection from the menu: ", MENU
6890 CLS
6900 IF MENU > 0 AND MENU < 4 THEN RETURN
6910 REM  Error message
6920 PRINT "That was not a valid response, try again."
6930 GOTO 6800
6999 END
```

```
run
-------- Grade Report Program --------
Separate multiple entries by commas

Enter weighting factors for quiz1, quiz2, and final :.3,.3,.4
Student name (Enter LAST when complete) :Charles Roth
Student ID :46912
Enter grades for quiz1, quiz2, and final :73,91,85
Student name (Enter LAST when complete) :Lucy Cook
Student ID :77878
Enter grades for quiz1, quiz2, and final :86,88,99
Student name (Enter LAST when complete) :Wayne Evans
Student ID :66941
Enter grades for quiz1, quiz2, and final :66,84,75
Student name (Enter LAST when complete) :last
```

```
                    Weighting       Average for
                    Factor          3 Students

Quiz 1              30 %            75
Quiz 2              30 %            87.66666
Final               40 %            86.33334
Overall                             83.33334

Would you like to see the inquiry menu? (Enter Y or N) y

    ---- INQUIRY MENU ----
1. Numeric averages for each quiz and overall
2. Breakdown by letter grade
3. High and low students

Make a selection from the menu :2
```

```
                  Grade Summary

Student Name  ID Number     Numeric Grade Letter Grade
------------  ---------     ------------- ------------

Charles Roth  46912            83.20         B
Lucy Cook     77878            91.80         A
Wayne Evans   66941            75.00         C

Would you like to see the inquiry menu? (Enter Y or N) y

    ---- INQUIRY MENU ----
1. Numeric averages for each quiz and overall
2. Breakdown by letter grade
3. High and low students

Make a selection from the menu :1
```

```
Grade         Number        Percent

A             1             33.33
B             1             33.33
C             1             33.33
D             0             0.00
F             0             0.00

Total number of grades given is 3

Would you like to see the inquiry menu? (Enter Y or N) y

    ---- INQUIRY MENU ----
1. Numeric averages for each quiz and overall
2. Breakdown by letter grade
3. High and low students

Make a selection from the menu :3
```

```
The high student is Lucy Cook with an overall
   grade of 91.8

The low student is Wayne Evans with an overall
   grade of 75

Would you like to see the inquiry menu? (Enter Y or N) n
Ok
```

example, the instructor can ask for a breakdown by letter grade. These inquiries are possible because any student data entered and generated in Modules 1.1–1.5 (essentially Example Program #6) are still available in primary storage in the student data arrays (see 1020).

This is the first example program for which the logic of the program dictates a third level in the structure chart. At the third level are the three types of inquiries (Modules 1.6.1, 1.6.2, and 1.6.3) and the menu module (1.6.4), all of which are subordinate to Module 1.6—Inquiry. For illustrative purposes, Module 1.6.4 is subdivided into a fourth level (Module 1.6.4.1—Option for Inquiry Menu, and Module 1.6.4.2—Menu Display and Selection). In practice, a program of this level of complexity would not require a fourth-level breakdown. However, the level of detail in the program structure chart and flowchart is a matter of personal preference and logic complexity.

The Program. Don't let the 184 statements in Example Program #7 overwhelm you. Keep in mind that this program was compiled from several well-defined logical modules. When you consider that we have already discussed Modules 1.1 through 1.5 (Example Program #6) and the REM statements are nonexecutable, 68 statements are left. Now let's see how these statements are generated.

From the structure chart for Example Program #7 we know that Module 1.6–Inquiry is made up of the three inquiry options and the menu routine. A list of options presented to an operator is commonly referred to as a **menu**. The use of menus is an important facet of on-line interactive programs. The inquiry options, or menu items, are:

1. Numeric averages for each quiz and overall (Module 1.6.1),
2. Breakdown by letter grade (Module 1.6.2), and
3. High and low students (Module 1.6.3).

The interactive session of Example Program #7 demonstrates the outcome for inquiries to each menu item.

Module 1.6.4—Menu. The first processing activity of the Module 1.6—Inquiry is to call Module 1.6.4—Menu (6020). Module 1.6.4 is further subdivided into Module 1.6.4.1—Option for Inquiry Menu and Module 1.6.4.2—Menu Display and Selection. The purpose of Module 1.6.4.1 is to determine whether or not the user would like to see the inquiry menu (see interactive session).

Compare the IF instructions in Example Program #5 (6030) and Example Program #7 (6780). Both evaluate the user's request, but in different ways. In Example Program #5, the THEN clause is taken (process another student) if the character entered is "Y" or "y." In Example Program #7, the THEN clause is taken (end program) if the character is an "N" or "n." The menu is displayed when any character but an "N" or an "n" is entered.

Module 1.6.4.2 displays the menu on the screen and permits the user to make a selection from the list of items in the menu. As a programmer you must assume that if anything can go wrong, it will. You cannot assume that the user will always select one of the available menu items. If the user selects other than 1, 2, or 3, the error routine (6900–6930) displays an error message, then asks the user to try again.

Once the user has made a valid menu selection, control is RETURNed (6900) to Module 1.6—Inquiry, where the ON GOSUB instruction (6040) is used to direct processing to the appropriate module. At statement 6040, control is passed to a subroutine statement (6060, 6280, or 6510) *depending on* the value of MENU (menu item selected). If menu item 1 is selected (MENU=1), then Module 1.6.1—Numeric Averages is executed. If menu item 2 (MENU=2) is selected, then Module 1.6.2—Breakdown by Letter Grade is executed, and so on.

Module 1.6.1—Numeric Averages.   To compute the numeric averages for each quiz and overall, the scores of all quizes must be totaled. This is done in a FOR/NEXT loop containing four *accumulators* (6100–6150), one for each quiz (T1, T2, and T3) and the weighted final numeric grade (T4). An accumulator format has the assignment variable on both sides of the equation. In this way, the current value of the accumulator is added to other values on the right side to obtain a new accumulator value. The process is repeated, as illustrated below, until all scores (three in our example) are accumulated.

$$6110 \; T1 = T1 + Q1(I)$$

For: I=1	$73 =$	$0 + 73$
I=2	$159 =$	$73 + 86$
I=3	$225 = 159 + 66$	

The total of all quiz 1 scores, now in T1, is 225.

Arithmetic expressions are embedded in the PRINT statement item lists (6210–6240) to save programming time and simplify the program logic.

It is unlikely that the user will request menu item 1 again, but just in case, the accumulators must be reset to zero (6260). If this is not done, the accumulation of scores would begin, not with T1=0, but with T1=225.

Module 1.6.2—Breakdown by Letter Grade.   To achieve a breakdown by letter grade, the second inquiry option, a series of IF statements is embedded in a loop (6300–6360). In the loop, each student's letter grade is compared in successive IF statements to string constant values of "A", "B", "C", "D", or "F". Only one of the five conditions will be met for any given student. Each THEN clause contains a counter (AGRADE, BGRADE, etc,) which is incremented by one when a condition is met. In this way, letter grade occurrences are tallied. In the example interactive session of Example Program #7, Charles Roth earned a B (GRADE$(1)="B"). Since GRADE$(1)=B$, BGRADE is incremented from 0 to 1.

Again, in case the user selects menu item 2 a second time, the counters must be reset to zero (6490).

Module 1.6.3—High and Low Students.   Of the menu options, the logic of Module 1.6.3—High and Low Students is the most challenging. In this module the students with the highest and lowest numeric averages are displayed. The approach illustrated in the flowchart of Example Program #7 compares consecutive numerical grades in the array NUMGRADE. NUMGRADE(1) is compared to NUMGRADE(2); NUMGRADE(2) is compared to NUMGRADE(3), and so on through the array.

These programmers routinely use word processing software to prepare and maintain program documentation. This company's documentation policy calls for a detailed written description and a flowchart for each program. (AT&T Information Systems)

Figure B-13
**Index Values for Module
1.6.3—High and Low Students**
This figure shows how the index
values of HIGH and LOW
change as Module 1.6.3 of
Example Program #7 is
executed with the data from
the example interactive
session.

		Value		
		HIGH	LOW	COUNT
Initialize {	6550	1	1	
First pass of loop {	6590	2	1	2
	6600	2	1	2
Second pass of loop {	6590	2	1	3
	6600	2	3	3

The comparison is made in a loop which is repeated COUNT-1 (from 2 to COUNT) times, so that all pairs of grades can be compared. In our example, the loop is repeated twice (3−1=2, see Figure B-13). The first student (Charles Roth in the example) is arbitrarily identified as being both the high and the low student at the start of the pairs comparisons. That is, HIGH=LOW=1. On the first pass through the loop, the grade of the first student (83.2) is compared to the grade of the second student (91.8). Since the condition in statement 6590 is met (NUMGRADE(1) < NUMGRADE(2) or 83.2 < 91.8), the index HIGH takes on the current value of I, which in the first loop is 2. With HIGH equal to 2, the second student has the highest grade so far in the comparison.

The same procedure is followed for the determination of the low student. Since the condition in statement 6600 is not met (NUMGRADE(1) > NUMGRADE(2) or 83.2 > 91.8), the value of the index LOW is unchanged (LOW=1). The first student continues to have the lowest grade so far in the comparison.

Once the loop has been repeated the required number of times (twice in our example), the index of the high and low students is contained in the variables HIGH and LOW (see Figure B–13). These values then become the subscripts for the STNAME$ and NUMGRADE arrays when the high and low students are displayed (6630–6670).

B-19   EXAMPLE PROGRAM #8: TWO-DIMENSIONAL ARRAYS AND INPUT VALIDATION

Working with Tables: Two-dimensional Arrays.   In Example Program #7, the student grades and the resultant numeric average were stored in lists (one-dimensional arrays). Each of these lists required a unique name: Q1, Q2, and so on. In Example Program #8, these like data (student grades) are entered and processed in a single table, or two-dimensional array, called STUGRADES. STUGRADES is DIMensioned in statement 1020 to have up to 50 rows and 4 columns. The lists of Example Program #7 are equated to their Example Program #8 table equivalent next and in Figure B-14.

Example Program #7	Example Program #8
Q1(COUNT)	STUGRADES(COUNT,1)
Q2(COUNT)	STUGRADES(COUNT,2)
FINAL(COUNT)	STUGRADES(COUNT,3)
NUMGRADE(COUNT)	STUGRADES(COUNT,4)

In a two-dimensional array, the first subscript is conceptualized as the row number and the second as the column (see Figure B-14). In effect, the first subscript refers to a particular student and the second subscript depicts which grade is being referenced. For example, STUGRADES(3,2) references the third student's quiz 2 grade.

By using arrays, you don't have to worry about creating slightly different names for like data. For example, consider the accumulators in Module 1.6.1—Numeric Averages of Example Program #7 and #8. Compare the accumulators in Example Program #7 (6110–6140) to the accumulators in Example Program #8 (6100–6120). In Example Program #7, it was necessary to assign a unique variable name to each accumulator (e.g., T1, T2). In example Program #8, all grades are stored in the two-dimensional array STUGRADES. This permits the totals of the grades to be accumulated in nested loops and stored in the array TOTAL (e.g., TOTAL(1), TOTAL(2)). With only four grades, this approach is only marginally more efficient, but what if each student had 24 grades? In Example Program #7, you would need to identify 20 more accumulators and add 20 more accumulator instructions. With the nested loop logic of Example Program #8 (6090–6130), you would need only to change the limit value for the internal loop from 4 to 24, and redimension the student grades array from STUGRADES(50,2) to STUGRADES(50,24).

Input Validation and Control Techniques.   A good programmer assumes that the user will not always enter the correct data. In Example Program #7, the menu item selection was validated on input. The same routine is

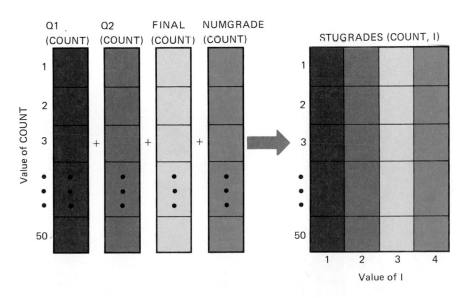

Figure B-14
Combining Related Lists into a Table
The one-dimensional lists of Example Program #7 are combined into a two-dimensional table in Example Program #8.

EXAMPLE PROGRAM #8

This program computes the final numeric grade and assigns a letter grade for any number of students. The same report as in Example Program #7 is generated. An inquiry module allows the instructor to interactively make inquires with regard to: 1. Numeric averages for each quiz and overall; 2. Breakdown by letter grade; 3. High and low students. It is the same as Example Program #7 except that two-dimensional arrays are used for student grades and some simple input validation routines are added.

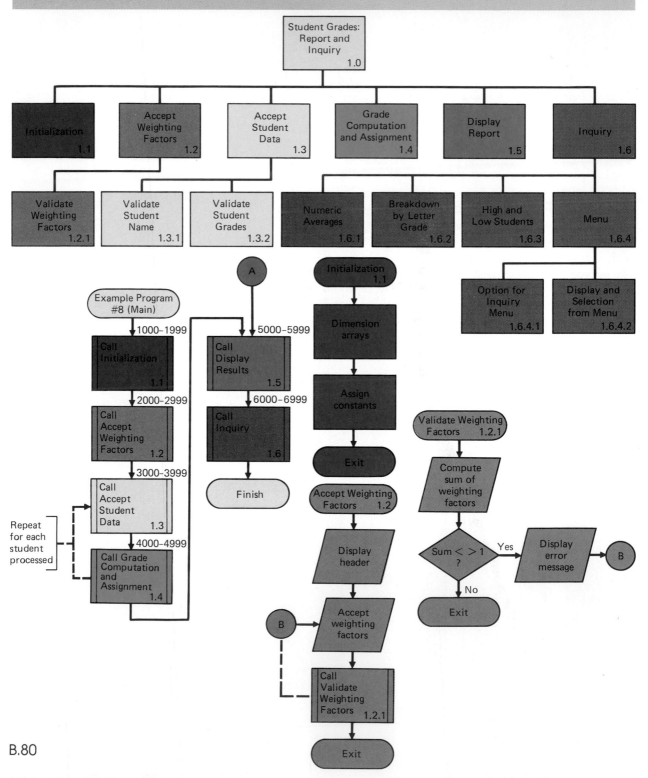

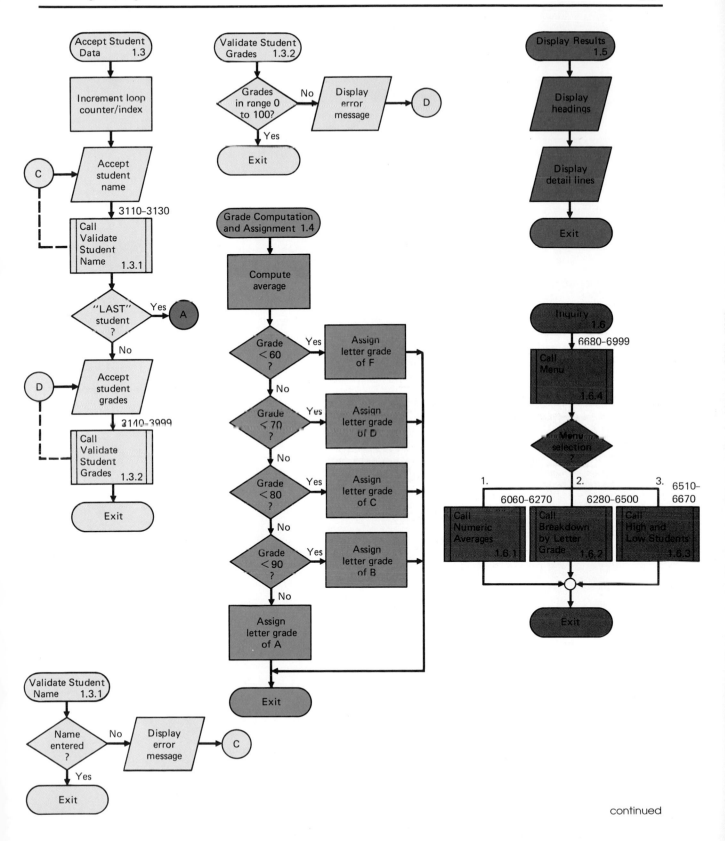

continued

Example Program 8 continued

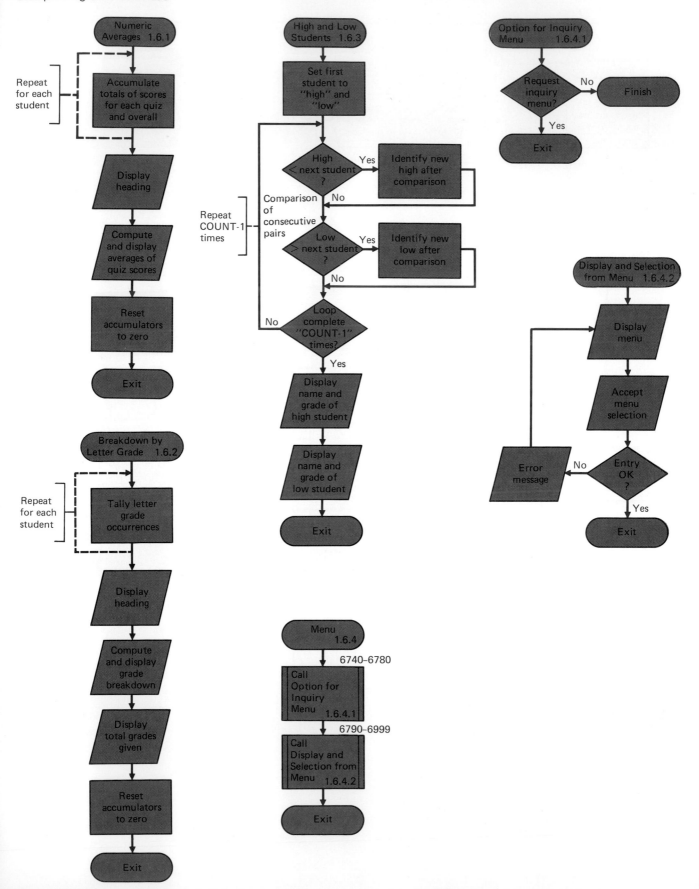

```
2    REM           **** Example Program #8 ****
4    REM   Description:
6    REM     This program computes the final numeric grade and assigns a
8    REM     letter grade for any number of students. The same report as in
10   REM     Example Program #7 is generated. An inquiry module allows the
12   REM     instructor to interactively make inquiries with regard to:
14   REM           1. Numeric averages for each quiz and overall
16   REM           2. Breakdown by letter grade
18   REM           3. High and low students
20   REM     It is the same as Example Program #7 except that two-dimensionl
22   REM     arrays are used for student grades and some simple input validation
24   REM     routines are added.
27   REM   Variables list:
28   REM     A$, B$, C$, D$, F$      -Letter grades
30   REM     W1, W2, WF             -Weighting factors
32   REM     COUNT                  -Counter for the number of students
34   REM     STNAME$()              -Student name
36   REM     ID()                   -Student ID
38   REM     STUGRADES( , )         -Test scores and weighted final grade
40   REM                             for each student
42   REM     GRADE$()               -Letter grade earned
44   REM     I                      -Index for display loop
46   REM     F1$, F2$, F3$          -Strings for PRINT USING statements
48   REM     MENU                   -Menu item selected
50   REM     TOTAL()                -Accumulator to compute quiz averages
52   REM     HIGH, LOW              -Indices for high and low students
54   REM     HIGH, LOW              -Indices for high and low students
99   REM
100  REM   <<<< Start Main >>>>
110  REM
120  REM   Call Module 1.1 - Initialization
130  GOSUB 1000
140  REM   Call Module 1.2 - Accept Weighting Factors
150  GOSUB 2000
160  REM   Call Module 1.3 - Accept Student Data
170  GOSUB 3000
180  REM   Call Module 1.4 - Grade Computation and Assignment
190  GOSUB 4000
200  REM   Call Module 1.5 - Display Report
210  GOSUB 5000
220  REM   Call Module 1.6 - Inquiry
230  GOSUB 6000
240  REM
250  REM   <<<< End Main >>>>
999  REM
1000 REM   ==== Module 1.1 - Initialization
1010 REM   Dimension Arrays
1020 DIM STNAME$(50),ID(50),STUGRADES(50,4),GRADE$(50)
1030 REM   Assign letter grade constants to string variables
1040 READ A$, B$, C$, D$, F$
1050 DATA "A","B","C","D","F"
1999 RETURN
2000 REM   ==== Module 1.2 - Accept Weighting Factors
2010 PRINT "     -------- Grade Report Program --------"
2020 PRINT "Separate multiple entries by commas"
2030 PRINT
2040 INPUT "Enter weighting factors for quiz1, quiz2, and final: ", W1, W2, WF
2050 REM   Call Module 1.2.1 - Validate Weighting Factors
2060 GOSUB 2080
2070 RETURN
2080 REM   ==== Module 1.2.1 - Validate Weighting Factors
2090 SUM = W1 + W2 + WF
2100 IF SUM <> 1 THEN PRINT "Weighting factors must sum to one (1)" : RETURN
        2030
2999 RETURN
3000 REM   ==== Module 1.3 - Accept Student Data
3010 COUNT = COUNT + 1
3020 INPUT "Student name (Enter LAST when complete): ", STNAME$(COUNT)
3030 REM   Call Module 1.3.1 - Validate Student Name
3040 GOSUB 3110
```

continued

```
3050 IF STNAME$(COUNT) = "LAST" OR STNAME$(COUNT) = "last" THEN RETURN 200
3060 INPUT "Student ID: ",ID(COUNT)
3070 INPUT "Enter grades for quiz1, quiz2, and final: ",STUGRADES(COUNT,1),
         STUGRADES(COUNT,2),STUGRADES(COUNT,3)
3080 REM  Call Module 1.3.2 - Validate Student Grades
3090 GOSUB 3140
3100 RETURN
3110 REM  ==== Module 1.3.1 - Validate Student Name
3120 IF STNAME$(COUNT) = "" THEN PRINT "Null student name not allowed":PRINT:
         RETURN 3020
3130 RETURN
3140 REM  ==== Module 1.3.2 - Validate Student Grades
3150 FOR I = 1 TO 3
3160  IF STUGRADES(COUNT,I) < 0 OR STUGRADES(COUNT,I) > 100 THEN PRINT
         "Grades must be in the range 0 to 100":PRINT:RETURN 3070
3170 NEXT I
3999 RETURN
4000 REM  ==== Module 1.4 - Grade Computation and Assignment
4010 REM  Compute numeric grade and assign letter grade
4020 REM
4030 STUGRADES(COUNT,4) = W1*STUGRADES(COUNT,1) + W2*STUGRADES(COUNT,2) +
         WF*STUGRADES(COUNT,3)
4040 IF STUGRADES(COUNT,4) < 60 THEN GRADE$(COUNT) = F$ : RETURN 160
4050  IF STUGRADES(COUNT,4) < 70 THEN GRADE$(COUNT) = D$ : RETURN 160
4060   IF STUGRADES(COUNT,4) < 80 THEN GRADE$(COUNT) = C$ : RETURN 160
4070    IF STUGRADES(COUNT,4) < 90 THEN GRADE$(COUNT) = B$ : RETURN 160
4080     GRADE$(COUNT) = A$
4999 RETURN 160
5000 REM  ==== Module 1.5 - Display Report
5001 CLS
5010 F1$="#####        "
5020 F2$="###.##       "
5030 PRINT
5040 PRINT TAB(20);"Grade Summary"
5050 PRINT
5060 PRINT "Student name","ID number","Numeric grade","Letter grade"
5070 PRINT "------------","---------","-------------","------------"
5080 PRINT
5090 REM  Generate Report
5100 COUNT = COUNT - 1
5110 REM  Begin loop to display detail lines - execute 'COUNT' times
5120 FOR I=1 TO COUNT
5130   PRINT STNAME$(I),:PRINT USING F1$; ID(I);:PRINT USING F2$;
         STUGRADES(I,4);:PRINT GRADE$(I)
5140 NEXT
5999 RETURN
6000 REM  ==== Module 1.6 - Inquiry
6010 REM  Call Module 1.6.4 - Menu
6020 GOSUB 6680
6030 REM  Call appropriate inquiry module
6040 ON MENU GOSUB 6060, 6280, 6510
6050 GOTO 6010
6060 REM  ==== Module 1.6.1 - Numeric Averages
6070 REM  Compute numeric averages for each quiz and display them
6080 REM  Accumulate totals for each quiz
6090 FOR I = 1 TO COUNT
6100  FOR J = 1 TO 4
6110   TOTAL(J) = TOTAL(J) + STUGRADES(I,J)
6120  NEXT J
6130 NEXT I
6140 PRINT
6150 REM  Display quiz averages
6160 PRINT ,"Weighting","Average for"
6170 PRINT ,"Factor",COUNT;"Students"
6180 PRINT
6190 PRINT "Quiz 1", W1*100 ;"%", TOTAL(1)/COUNT
6200 PRINT "Quiz 2", W2*100 ;"%", TOTAL(2)/COUNT
6210 PRINT "Final", WF*100 ;"%", TOTAL(3)/COUNT
6220 PRINT "Overall",, TOTAL(4)/COUNT
```

```
6230 REM   Reset accumulators to zero
6240 FOR J = 1 TO 4
6250    TOTAL(J) = 0
6260 NEXT J
6270 RETURN
6280 REM   ==== Module 1.6.2 - Breakdown By Letter Grade
6290 REM   Tally letter grade occurrences
6300 FOR I=1 TO COUNT
6310    IF GRADE$(I) = A$ THEN AGRADE = AGRADE + 1
6320    IF GRADE$(I) = B$ THEN BGRADE = BGRADE + 1
6330    IF GRADE$(I) = C$ THEN CGRADE = CGRADE + 1
6340    IF GRADE$(I) = D$ THEN DGRADE = DGRADE + 1
6350    IF GRADE$(I) = F$ THEN FGRADE = FGRADE + 1
6360 NEXT I
6370 REM  Display letter grade breakdown
6380 PRINT "Grade","Number","Percent"
6390 F3$ = "###.##"
6400 PRINT
6410 PRINT A$, AGRADE,:PRINT USING F3$; (AGRADE/COUNT) * 100
6420 PRINT B$, BGRADE,:PRINT USING F3$; (BGRADE/COUNT) * 100
6430 PRINT C$, CGRADE,:PRINT USING F3$; (CGRADE/COUNT) * 100
6440 PRINT D$, DGRADE,:PRINT USING F3$; (DGRADE/COUNT) * 100
6450 PRINT F$, FGRADE,:PRINT USING F3$; (FGRADE/COUNT) * 100
6460 PRINT
6470 PRINT "Total number of grades given is"; COUNT
6480 REM   Reset grade counters to zero
6490 AGRADE = 0 : BGRADE = 0 : CGRADE = 0 : DGRADE = 0 : FGRADE = 0
6500 RETURN
6510 REM   ==== Module 1.6.3 - High And Low Students
6520 REM  Find and display students with highest and lowest grades
6530 REM
6540 REM  Set both HIGH and LOW to first student
6550 HIGH = 1 : LOW = 1
6560 REM  Compare student pairs to identify
6570 REM  high and low students
6580 FOR I=2 TO COUNT
6590    IF STUGRADES(HIGH,4) < STUGRADES(I,4) THEN HIGH = I
6600    IF STUGRADES(LOW,4) > STUGRADES(I,4) THEN LOW = I
6610 NEXT I
6620 REM  Display high and low students
6630 PRINT "The high student is "; STNAME$(HIGH) ;" with an overall"
6640 PRINT "   grade of"; STUGRADES(HIGH,4)
6650 PRINT "The low student is "; STNAME$(LOW) ;" with an overall"
6660 PRINT "   grade of"; STUGRADES(LOW,4)
6670 RETURN
6680 REM   ==== Module 1.6.4 - Menu
6690 REM  Call Module 1.6.4.1 - Option for Inquiry Menu
6700 GOSUB 6740
6710 REM  Call Module 1.6.4.2 - Display and Selection from Menu
6720 GOSUB 6790
6730 RETURN
6740 REM   ==== Module 1.6.4.1 - Option for Inquiry Menu
6750 PRINT
6760 INPUT "Would you like to see the inquiry menu? (Enter Y or N) ",ANSWER$
6770 IF ANSWER$ = "N" OR ANSWER$ = "n" THEN RETURN 6999
6780 RETURN
6790 REM   ==== Module 1.6.4.2 - Display and Selection from Menu
6800 PRINT
6810 PRINT "   ---- INQUIRY MENU ----"
6820 PRINT "1. Numeric averages for each quiz and overall"
6830 PRINT "2. Breakdown by letter grade"
6840 PRINT "3. High and low students"
6850 PRINT
6860 REM  Accept menu selection
6870 INPUT "Make a selection from the menu: ",MENU
6880 CLS
6890 IF MENU > 0 AND MENU < 4 THEN RETURN
6900 REM  Error message
6910 PRINT "That was not a valid response. Try again."
6920 GOTO 6800
6999 END
```

continued

Example Program 8 continued

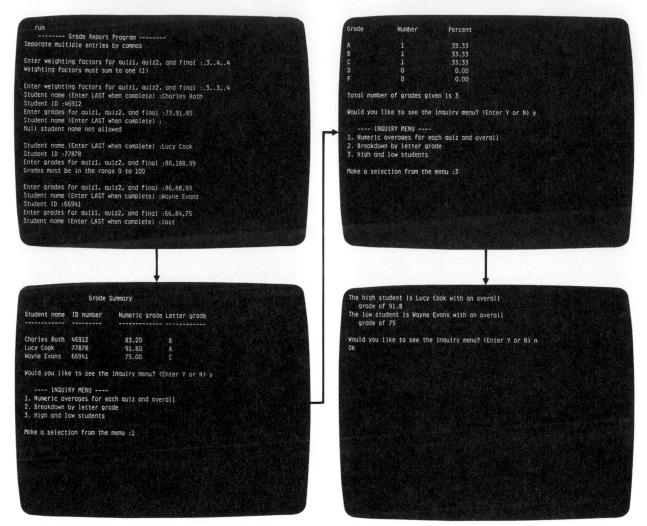

also included in Example Program #8 (6890–6920). Example Program #8 demonstrates several other ways in which we can use programming techniques to validate the accuracy of the input. We build validation procedures into a program to alert users that their input is inconsistent with that expected. Of course, there are limits to what types of errors can be detected using programming techniques. For example, a validation routine will not detect when a grade of 85 is incorrectly entered as 83.

Control Total.   An input control total is a value that is known to be the accumulated sum of several variables. In every case, the sum of the weighting factors for the quiz scores should be 1. In Module 1.2.1—Validate Weighting Factors (2080–2999), 1 is the control total. If the sum of the weighting factors entered is not equal to the control total (W1+W2+WF <> 1), then the user is alerted and asked to enter the weighting factors again. The use of this and the following validation procedures is demonstrated in the interactive session.

Check for No Entry.   In Example Program #8, the first piece of student data accepted is the student name (STNAME$(COUNT)). In Example Program #7, if the carriage return key is pressed before a name is entered, then a null is entered to a field in the STNAME$ array. A null ("") is a characterless string constant. To avoid this possibility, Module 1.3.1—Validate Student Name (3110–3130) was inserted in Example Program #8. When the user does not make any entry for student name, a warning appears on the screen, and the user is given another opportunity to enter a student's name.

Limits Check.   A limits check assesses whether the value of an entry is out of line with that expected. In our example, all grades must be in the range 0 to 100, inclusive. To ensure that negative values or grades in excess of 100 are not entered. Module 1.3.2—Validate Student Grades (3140–3999) alerts the user when a grade entered is not within the limits and requests that the grades be reentered. Since STUGRADES is an array, each grade can be examined separately by incrementing the second subscript in a FOR/NEXT loop.

Another example of a limits check is the input validation routine in Module 1.6.4.2—Menu Display and Selection (6790–6920). If the user does not select one of the available menu options, then an error message is displayed and the user is asked to "try again."

Other Input Control Techniques.   When writing a program that may be used often by a number of people, it is a good idea to check input data as thoroughly as you can during the course of the interactive session. In our example, besides checking the limits of the grades entered, you could also use a *reasonableness check*. For example, you could compare each score to the average of the other two. If they differ by more than some arbitrary amount, say 20 points, then a message is displayed and the user is requested to reenter that student's grades.

For the student name entry, you could also use a *character-type check*. The more advanced features of BASIC permit you to check each character of a name to ensure that it is a letter. The check would ensure that numbers are not accidentally keyed in the name field (e.g., Cha4les).

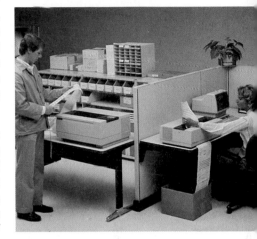

Input controls, such as limits and reasonableness checks, were designed into an order processing system to help this data entry operator verify the accuracy of her input. (Photo courtesy of Hewlett-Packard Company)

REVIEW EXERCISES (LEARNING MODULE V) _____

BASIC Instructions and Concepts

1. Identify the syntax error(s) in each of the following instructions.

    (a)   10 ON I>3 GOSUB 40
    (b)   10 CLS: "CLEAR THE SCREEN"
    (c)   10 ON COUNT GOTO 40; 50; 60
    (d)   10 LINT INPUT ALPHA

2. In what order are the animal names displayed in the following program?

```
100 ON COUNT GOSUB 400, 500, 600
200 PRINT "Cat"
300 COUNT = COUNT +1: GOTO 100
400 PRINT "Dog": RETURN
500 PRINT "Horse": RETURN
600 END
```

3. Explain the use of a menu in interactive inquiry programming.
4. Under what circumstances would you use the LINE INPUT instruction in lieu of the INPUT instruction?

Example Program #7

5. Why is it necessary to subtract 1 from COUNT at statement 5120?
6. List the beginning and ending statement numbers of all of the loops in Modules 1.6.1, 1.6.2, and 1.6.3.
7. What is the general name applied to statements like 6110–6140?
8. Why is it necessary to initialize certain variables to zero in statements 6260 and 6490?
9. How would you modify the program to include a menu item option 4 that permits the instructor to request a hard copy of the grade summary report?

Example Program #8

10. What are the advantages of storing student grade data in a single two-dimensional array (Example Program #8), as opposed to the several one-dimensional arrays in Example Program #7?
11. Write the code for a data entry reasonableness check that warns the professor if the average of the quiz 1 and quiz 2 grades differs by more than 20 points from the final exam grade.
12. Of the data entered for each student, which data element would be the best for a control total?

BASIC PROGRAMMING ASSIGNMENTS _____

1. Write a program to compile a sales report listing salespeople by sales (most sales first). Use the following input data.

Salesperson	Monthly Sales
Monro	28672
Wilson	14006
Plebani	22871
Kane	38222
Groover	76800

The output should appear as shown below:

```
            SALES REPORT
SALESPERSON         MONTHLY SALES
Groover                $76800
Kane                   $38222
Monro                  $28672
Plebani                $22871
Wilson                 $14006
```

Sort the sales data in arrays to prepare the sales report.

Once the program has been debugged and can be executed to produce the above output, modify it to accumulate and display total sales at the bottom of the report as shown below.

```
TOTAL SALES         $180571
```

2. Write a program that accepts an individual's birth date in the MM, DD, YY format, then translates the date to display the following:

The birth date of T. Jones is December 18, 1947

3. Companies "age" their accounts receivable records so that accounting can concentrate collection efforts on those companies that are most delinquent in their payments. Periodically, a report is prepared listing those accounts that are 30 days, 60 days, and 90 days overdue (to simplify the program, assume that each month has 30 days). Write a program to produce such a report. The program should accept the current date, then load customers in arrears to one of three arrays, depending upon whether they are 30, 60, or 90 days in arrears. Use the following input format.

```
Enter current date (MM, DD, YY):
Enter customer name:
Enter amount due:
Enter date due (MM, DD, YY):
```

Include appropriate heading for output.

4. Prepare a program that generates a bar chart showing the schedules for four projects: A, B, C, and D. The start and completion days (if before day 30) are entered for each project. Use the following input format.

```
Enter data for Project A
Start day (1–30): 3
Completion day (1–30): 15
```

An example bar chart appears below.

```
Project
   A    *     ////////////////////
   B    *          ////////////////////
   C    *             ////////////////////////
   D    *                         ///////////
        0 1 2 3 4 5 6 7 8 9 1 1 2 3 4 5 6 7 8 9 2 1 2 3 4 5 6 7 8 9 3
                           0                   0                   0
```

B-20 INTRINSIC FUNCTIONS: LET THE COMPUTER DO IT

PROGRAMMING CONCEPTS

Intrinsic Functions
User-Defined Concepts
Arguments
Parameters
String Processing
Concatenation

Certain **intrinsic functions** are provided with a BASIC interpreter. Intrinsic functions save us a lot of time by performing routine processing tasks that would otherwise need to be programmed (e.g., take a square root or count the number of characters in a string constant).

A function consists of the *function name* and *argument*. The function names are signals to the BASIC interpreter to "call" a system-supplied BASIC program segment. The argument may contain one or several elements, depending on the function. The argument elements may be the variable or expression that is to be acted upon or specification data for the function. A function with its argument can appear in any place in the program that a regular variable can appear. *The occurrence of a function and argument represents the result of a function acting upon the argument.* That is, when the function SQR(4), the square root of 4, appears in a program, it actually represents the resultant value or 2.

Intrinsic functions are discussed in two parts. Those that deal primarily with *string operations* are discussed first, then those that deal primarily with *arithmetic operations*. The material in section B-21 describes how you can define your own *user-defined functions*.

String Operations

String operations are performed by those BASIC functions that allow us to manipulate alphanumeric character strings. Word processing is a good example of string manipulation. For example, to center a heading on a line, it is necessary to know how many characters are in the heading string constant. Or, suppose you wanted to display only the first name of a student from a field (e.g., STNAME$) that contained both the first and last names. The following functions enable you to perform these and other types of string operations.

CHR$. The CHR$ (character string) function converts the decimal value of a specified ASCII code to its character equivalent (see Figure B-6).

Format: CHR$(decimal value of ASCII code)

Example: FOR N = 48 TO 57
    IF RESPONSE$ = CHR$(N) THEN PRINT CHR$(7)
    NEXT N

In the above example, if RESPONSE$ equals "0" (ASCII code of 48), "1"

(ASCII code of 49), and so on to "9", then a tone is sounded (ASCII code of 7) on the workstation's speaker.

LEN.   The LEN (length) function takes on the value of the number of characters in the string specified in the argument.

> *Format*:   LEN(string variable or constant)

>   *Example*:   LET FIRSTNAME$ = "Carl"
>   LET TOTAL = LEN(FIRSTNAME$) + LEN("Brooks")

The value of TOTAL is 10: 4 (number of characters in "Carl") plus 6 (number of characters in "Brooks").

VAL.   The VAL (value) function takes on the numerical value of the string specified in the argument.

> *Format*:   VAL(string variable or constant)

>   *Example*:   LET BALANCE$="$ 42.55 CR"
>   LET BALANCE = VAL(BALANCE$)

Any characters that are not numeric are stripped from the character string, and the value of BALANCE becomes 42.55. The VAL is handy for obtaining the numeric portion of an alphanumeric character string, such as a street address.

STR$.   The STR$ (string) function is the reverse of the VAL function. It takes on the string value of the number specified in the argument.

> *Format*:   STR$(numeric variable or constant)

>   *Example*:   LET BALANCE = 42.55
>   LET BALANCE$ = "$" + STR$(42.55) + " CR"

In this example, 42.55 is made a string constant so that it can be joined together with a $ and CR. The plus sign in the above example permits character strings to be "added" together, or *concatenated*. After the concatenation, BALANCE$="$ 42.55 CR". Notice that the STR$ function and its argument result in a string value that includes a space for the implied plus sign.

LEFT$. The LEFT$ function takes on the value of the *n* leftmost characters of the string specified in the argument.

> *Format*: LEFT$(string variable or constant, *n*)

> *Example*: LET FIRSTNAME$ = LEFT$("Barbara L. Shaw", 7)

The first seven characters of the argument string are selected, and the value of FIRSTNAME$ becomes "Barbara".

RIGHT$. The RIGHT$ function takes on the value of the *n* rightmost characters of the string specified in the argument.

> *Format*: RIGHT$(string variable or constant, *n*)

> *Example*: LET LASTNAME$ = RIGHT$("Barbara L. Shaw", 4)

The last four characters of the argument string are selected, and the value of LASTNAME$ becomes "Shaw".

MID$. Use the MID$ function to:

1. Extract a portion of a string, or
2. Replace a portion of a string with another string.

In the first instance, the MID$ function takes on the value of the *m* characters in the string specified in the argument, beginning at the *n*th character from the left. In the second instance, MID$ is used as an instruction. Remember, all characters, including spaces, are counted. The *m* value is optional. If omitted, all of the rightmost characters are extracted beginning at the *n*th character.

> *Format*: MID$(string variable or constant, *n*[,*m*])

> *Examples*: LET INITIAL$ = MID$("Barbara L. Shaw",9,2)
> LET STREET$ = MID$("317 High St.",5)

In the first example above, the value of INITIAL$ becomes "L." In the second example, STREET$ becomes "High St.".

In the following example, MID$ is used as an instruction.

> *Example*: LET NAME$ = "Barbara L. Shaw"
> LET MID$(NAME$,12,4) = "Harrison"

In the example, the four characters starting with the twelfth character in NAME$ ("Shaw") are replaced with "Harrison". The value of NAME$ is now "Barbara L. Harrison".

INSTR. The INSTR (in string) function permits you to search for the first occurrence of a particular character string in another character string. The value of the function becomes the starting character position of the first occurrence of the search string.

> *Format*:   INSTR(string variable 1, string variable 2)
>   Where, string variable 1 is the string to be searched
>   and string variable 2 is the search string.

    Example: LET NAME$ = "Barbara L. Shaw"
                LET PERIOD$ = "."
                LET POSITION = INSTR(NAME$,PERIOD$) − 1
                LET INITIAL$ = MID$(POSITION,1)

The above series of instructions assigns the value of INITIAL$ to be the middle initial of a name. The INSTR function first locates the period in NAME$ and returns a 10 as the character position of the ".". One is subtracted from the location of the "." to identify the location of the initial (POSITION = 9). The MID$ function is then used to extract the initial from the NAME$ character string so that it can be assigned the variable name INITIAL$. In the example above, INITIAL$ becomes "L".

Arithmetic Operations

Intrinsic functions are provided for many common arithmetic operations. As an example, recall from algebra that the roots of a second degree polynomial $(AX^2 + BX + C = 0)$ are determined by the quadratic formula:

$$X = \frac{-B \pm \sqrt{B^2 - 4AC}}{2A}$$

The BASIC expression for one root is:

    LET X = (−B + (B^2 − 4*A*C)^.5) / (2*A)

Instead of raising B^2−4*A*C to the .5 power, we can use the *square root function (SQR)*. The statement then becomes:

    LET X = (−B + SQR(B^2 − 4*A*C)) / (2*A)

The *integer function (INT)* returns the largest whole number that is not greater than the value of the argument. For example:

    LET X=INT(14.7)
    LET Y=INT(−14.7)

After execution of the above statements, X=14 and Y=−15.

ABS(X)	Absolute value
COS(X)	Cosine of X in radians
EXP(X)	e(2.71828) to power of X
FIX(X)	Integer part of X
INT(X)	Largest integer not greater than X
LOG(X)	Natural logarithm of X
RND(X)	Generates a random number between zero and one (use RANDOMIZE instruction to seed RND function)
SGN(X)	Value of 1, 0, or −1 if X is positive, zero or negative, respectively
SIN(X)	Sine of X in radians
SQR(X)	Square root of X
TAN(X)	Tangent of X in radians

Figure B-15
BASIC Intrinsic Arithmetic Functions

Other intrinsic arithmetic functions are listed and defined in Figure B-15.

B-21 USER-DEFINED FUNCTIONS

The intrinsic functions do not always cover the circumstances for which we want a function. For these cases, BASIC permits us to define our own *user-defined functions*.

Format: DEF FN function name (parameter list) = definition of function

The function name follows the same naming rules as variable identifiers (*see* Learning Module I, Section B-4). The parameter list contains those variable names used in the definition of the function. The variables in the calling function are replaced *one for one* in the parameter list.

A FN (function) statement could be DEFined, named (PER), and used in the following statements in Example Program #8.

Examples:

Without FN:

```
6410 PRINT A$, AGRADE,: PRINT USING F3$; (AGRADE/COUNT)*100
6420 PRINT B$, BGRADE,: PRINT USING F3$; (AGRADE/COUNT)*100
```

With FN:

```
6405 DEF FN PER(A,B)=(A/B)*100
6410 PRINT A$, AGRADE,: PRINT USING F3$; FN PER(AGRADE, COUNT)
6420 PRINT B$, BGRADE,: PRINT USING F3$; FN PER(BGRADE, COUNT)
```

The values of AGRADE and COUNT are substituted, respectively, for A and B in the definition of the function. The result is returned and printed in statements 6410 and 6420. A function must be defined before it can be called.

B-22 EXAMPLE PROGRAM #9: STRING PROCESSING ____

Example Program #9 illustrates the use of several functions in the manipulation of text data. The program permits the user to enter a person's name and address data. The data are then merged with a form letter to produce a "personalized" letter, such as the one shown in the interactive session. The program must be run again to produce another letter.

Module 1.1—Accept Data. The name and address data are entered in three lines: name, street address, and city-state-zip. The LINE INPUT instruction, introduced in Learning Module V, is often used when the program is designed to accept textual data. This is because it will accept whatever characters are entered, including commas. Notice in the interactive session that city, state, and zip are entered to a single character string (CITYSTATEZIP$) with a comma between city and state. In contrast, when the INPUT instruction is used, a comma serves as a delimiter between the data items entered and cannot be part of an input character string.

Module 1.2—Preparation. This module prepares appropriate character strings so that they can be merged with the text of the letter. The name and address data are inserted at several locations within the text of the letter: the inside address, the first name in the salutation and in the third sentence, the city in the second sentence, and the last name in the third sentence. The inside address is not a problem; the input strings are simply output to the printer. However, the first name, last name, and city must be extracted from the input strings. We do this with the string functions.

Several steps are needed to extract the person's first name. The INSTR function is used (2010) to determine the position of the first blank in the name string. Presumably the first name would precede the first blank. The LEFT$ function in statement 2020 extracts the characters to the left of the first blank, or the first name (FIRSTNAME$). The city is extracted from the CITYSTATEZIP$ field in a similar manner.

Extracting the last name is a little more tricky—but not much. We are assuming that each name is entered with a middle initial. In this case, we know that a blank separates the "." and the last name. The INSTR function is used to locate the period (2050). The starting character position of the last name is determined by subtracting the length of all of the characters that precede the last name (up to the "." plus 1) from the length of FULL-NAME$. The RIGHT$ function (2060) extracts the last name and stores it in LASTNAME$.

The salutation is a concatenation of three strings: "Dear", FIRSTNAME$, and ":". The plus signs (+) in statement 2070 cause the three strings to be concatenated. The resultant string is stored in SALUTATION$.

Module 1.3—Print Letter. The letter, with appropriate character strings inserted, is routed to a printer for output.

EXAMPLE PROGRAM #9

This program merges user-entered name and address data with the text of a form letter and prints the results.

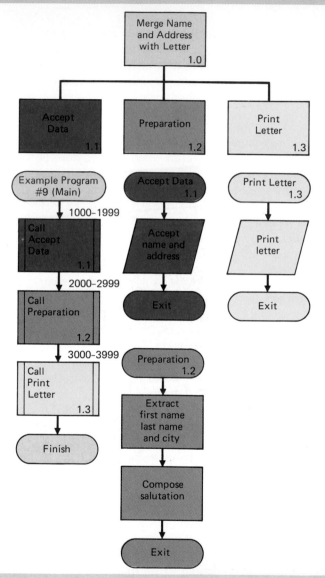

```
2    REM          **** Example Program #9 ****
4    REM  Description:
6    REM     This program merges user-entered name and address data with
8    REM      the text of a form letter and prints the results.
10   REM  Variables list:
12   REM     FULLNAME$              - Full name including middle initial
14   REM     STREET$                - Street address
16   REM     CITYSTATEZIP$          - City, state, and zip code
18   REM     FBLANK                 - Location of first blank in FULLNAME$ string
20   REM     FIRSTNAME$             - First name
22   REM     COMMAPOSITION          - Location of first comma in CITYSTATEZIP$
24   REM     CITY$                  - City
26   REM     LASTNAME$              - Last name
28   REM     SALUTATION$            - Salutation
99   REM
```

```
100  REM   <<<< Start Main >>>>
110  REM
120  REM   Call Module 1.1 - Accept Data
130  GOSUB 1000
140  REM   Call Module 1.2 - Preparation
150  GOSUB 2000
160  REM   Call Module 1.3 - Print Letter
170  GOSUB 3000
180  END
190  REM   <<<< End Main >>>>
999  REM
1000 REM   ==== Module 1.1 - Accept Data
1010 INPUT "Enter full name ( FIRST MI. LAST ): ",FULLNAME$
1020 LINE INPUT "Enter street address: ",STREET$
1030 LINE INPUT "Enter city, state, and zip code: ",CITYSTATEZIP$
1999 RETURN
2000 REM   ==== Module 1.2 - Preparation
2010 FBLANK = INSTR(FULLNAME$," ")
2020 FIRSTNAME$ = LEFT$(FULLNAME$,FBLANK-1)
2030 COMMAPOSITION = INSTR(CITYSTATEZIP$,",")
2040 CITY$=LEFT$(CITYSTATEZIP$,COMMAPOSITION-1)
2050 PERIOD = INSTR(FULLNAME$,".")
2060 LASTNAME$ = RIGHT$(FULLNAME$,LEN(FULLNAME$) - (PERIOD+1))
2070 SALUTATION$ = "Dear " + FIRSTNAME$ + ":"
2999 RETURN
3000 REM   ==== Module 1.3 - Print Letter
3010 CLS
3020 LPRINT
3030 LPRINT
3040 LPRINT FULLNAME$
3050 LPRINT STREET$
3060 LPRINT CITYSTATEZIP$
3070 LPRINT
3080 LPRINT SALUTATION$
3090 LPRINT
3100 LPRINT "     We are happy to announce a private showing of some of"
3110 LPRINT "the finest computer artists in the country.  This traveling"
3120 LPRINT "gallery will be coming to the ";CITY$;" area very soon (details"
3130 LPRINT "are enclosed).  ";FIRSTNAME$;
          ", we appreciate your patronage and hope"
3140 LPRINT "to see you and the ";LASTNAME$;" family at the showing."
3150 LPRINT
3160 LPRINT "                         Sincerely,"
3170 LPRINT : LPRINT
3180 LPRINT "                         Kim Hitchings,"
3190 LPRINT "                         Director"
3999 RETURN
```

```
run
Enter full name ( FIRST MI. LAST ): Marty E. Chambers
Enter street address: 115 Vista Drive
Enter city, state, and zip code: Walla Walla, WA 99362
Ok
```

continued

Example Program 9 continued

```
                    The Contemporary Art Gallery
                       1791 Brookhaven Avenue
                        Baltimore, MD 21233
                             CAG

Marty E. Chambers
115 Vista Drive
Walla Walla, WA 99362

Dear Marty:

     We are happy to announce a private showing of some of
the finest computer artists in the country.  This traveling
gallery will be coming to the Walla Walla area very soon (details
are enclosed).  Marty, we appreciate your patronage and hope
to see you and the Chambers family at the showing.

                             Sincerely,

                             Kim Hitchings

                             Kim Hitchings,
                             Director
```

Programmers with an interest and background in the sciences and mathematics may prefer scientific programming to business programming. This programmer writes programs relating to oil exploration and routinely takes advantage of the availability of arithmetic functions.
(Chevron Corporation)

B-23 EXAMPLE PROGRAM #10: ARITHMETIC AND USER-DEFINED FUNCTIONS

Example Program #10 illustrates the use of arithmetic and user-defined functions. Here is the problem. A professor would like to randomly seat students as they enter the classroom for the last personal enrichment opportunity (the final exame). The classroom has 8 rows, each with 10 seats across. The rows are numbered 1 to 8 from front to back and the seats are number 1 to 10 from left to right. Example Program #10 produces a listing (see interactive session) that the professor can use to seat students as they enter the classroom. The program is set up to randomly assign all seats numbered 1 (for all 8 rows), then all seats numbered 2, and so on.

Module 1.1—Initialization.   This short program has more to initialize than most of the programs that we have examined thus far. The array POSITION$ is dimensioned, and each location is loaded with the string constant "UNOCCUPIED" (1050–1070). This array represents the status of a given seat number for all 8 rows.

A user-defined function, called ROWEND, is defined in 1080. It is always a good idea to define user-defined functions in the initialization module. The use of ROWEND is explained in the Module 1.2 discussion.

The RANDOMIZE instruction is used in conjunction with the RND function (random number generator). On some systems, the random number generator must be "seeded" for each execution of the program; otherwise, the same "random" numbers are generated for each running of the program. The SEED is accepted in statement 1090.

EXAMPLE PROGRAM #10

This program produces a list from which students can be randomly seated in a classroom having rows, each with 10 seats across. All seat #1's are filled, then #2's, and so on.

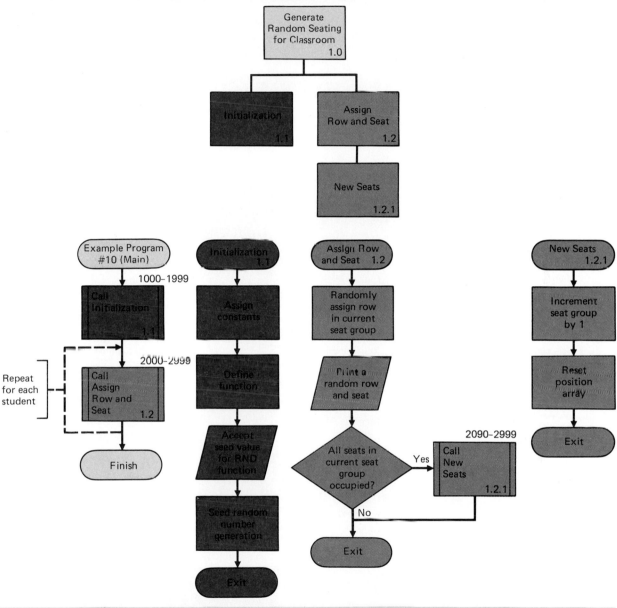

```
 2    REM              **** Example Program #10 ****
 4    REM     Description:
 6    REM        This program produces a list from which students can be randomly
 8    REM        seated in a classroom having rows, each with 10 seats across.
10    REM        All seat #1's are filled, then #2's, and so on.
12    REM     Variables list:
14    REM        SEED         - Seed for RND function
16    REM        STUDENT      - Student number (1-80)
18    REM        ROW          - Row number
20    REM        SEAT         - Seat number
22    REM        POSITION()   - Array which is randomly filled for each
24    REM                       seat position
```

continued

Example Program 10 continued

```
26   REM    LOCATION            - Function parameter
28   REM    I                   - Loop index
99   REM
100  REM  <<<< Start Main >>>>
105  REM
110  REM  Call Module 1.1 - Initialization
120  GOSUB 1000
130  FOR STUDENT = 1 TO 80
140    REM  Call Module 1.2 - Assign Row and Seat
150    GOSUB 2000
160  NEXT STUDENT
170  END
180  REM  <<<< End Main >>>>
999  REM
1000 REM   ==== Module 1.1 - Initialization
1010 REM
1020 DIM POSITION$(8)
1030 REM  Define function to determine if a multiple of 8 students have been
1040 REM  assigned seats
1050 DEF FN ROWEND(LOCATION) = (LOCATION / 8) - INT(LOCATION / 8)
1060 FOR COUNT = 1 TO 8
1070   POSITION$(COUNT) = "UNOCCUPIED"
1080 NEXT COUNT
1090 INPUT "Enter a seed for the random number generator (1 to 1000): ",SEED
1100 RANDOMIZE SEED
1110 SEAT = 1
1999 RETURN
2000 REM   ==== Module 1.2 - Assign Row and Seat
2010 REM  Randomly assign a row in the current group of seats
2020 ROW = INT(RND * 8) + 1
2030 IF POSITION$(ROW) = "OCCUPIED" THEN 2010
2040 POSITION$(ROW) = "OCCUPIED"
2050 PRINT "Student";STUDENT;TAB(16);"Row";ROW;", Seat";SEAT
2060 REM  All 8 seat positions in the current group of seats occupied?
2070 IF FN ROWEND(STUDENT) = 0 THEN GOSUB 3000 'Call Module 1.2.1 - New Seats
2999 RETURN
3000 REM   ==== Module 1.2.1 - New Seats
3010 REM  Increment current group of seats
3020 SEAT = SEAT + 1
3030 REM  Reset position array to "UNOCCUPIED"
3040 FOR COUNT = 1 TO 8
3050   POSITION$(COUNT) = "UNOCCUPIED"
3060 NEXT COUNT
3999 RETURN
```

```
run
Enter a seed for the random number generator (1 to 1000) :   765
Ok
```

```
Student  1        Row  1  ,  Seat  1
Student  2        Row  3  ,  Seat  1
Student  3        Row  5  ,  Seat  1
Student  4        Row  2  ,  Seat  1
Student  5        Row  8  ,  Seat  1
Student  6        Row  6  ,  Seat  1
Student  7        Row  4  ,  Seat  1
Student  8        Row  7  ,  Seat  1
Student  9        Row  7  ,  Seat  2
Student  10       Row  2  ,  Seat  2
Student  11       Row  8  ,  Seat  2
Student  12       Row  4  ,  Seat  2
Student  13       Row  6  ,  Seat  2
Student  14       Row  3  ,  Seat  2
Student  15       Row  1  ,  Seat  2
Student  16       Row  5  ,  Seat  2
Student  17       Row  2  ,  Seat  3
Student  18       Row  6  ,  Seat  3
Student  19       Row  7  ,  Seat  3
Student  20       Row  5  ,  Seat  3
         .                 .
         .                 .
         .                 .
Student  79       Row  8  ,  Seat  10
Student  80       Row  5  ,  Seat  10
```

Module 1.2—Assign Row and Seat.   Module 1.2 is called 80 times from Main, once for each of the 80 chairs in the classroom. A row is randomly assigned (2020–2040) within a particular seat group (e.g., seat number 1) for each pass through the loop in Main. The RND function in statement 2020 generates a random number between 0 and 1. The INT function in the same statement returns the greatest integer not larger than the value of the argument. In the example, this number will always be 0 to 7; therefore, 1 is added to randomly select 1 of 8 rows. Statements 2020–2030 are repeated until an "UNOCCUPIED" seat is found; then it becomes the ROW selected. The selected position is identified as "OCCUPIED", and a row and seat number are output to the printer.

The ROWEND function equals 0 once an even multiple of 8 students have been seated. This is a signal that all 8 fields in the POSITION$ array are "OCCUPIED". When this happens, the THEN clause is taken in statement 2070 and Module 1.2.1—New Seats is called. This module resets the POSITION$ array to "UNOCCUPIED" and bumps the seat number by 1.

REVIEW EXERCISES (LEARNING MODULE VI) _____

BASIC Instructions and Concepts

1. Identify the error(s) in each of the following instructions.
    (a)   10 PRINT CHR$(265)
    (b)   10 LET ANSWER = 4/LEN("")
    (c)   10 VALUE = VAL(ANSWER)
    (d)   10 INT = FIX(NUMBER)
    (e)   10 DEF FN ADDLIST (SUM) = A+B+C+D
    (f)   10 CHARPOS = CHARPOS + INSTR(DESCRIP$,HYPHEN)

2. Which of the following statements has the intrinsic function and which has the user-defined functon? Identify the function names of each.

```
300 SR=SQR(Y*Z)
400 X=FN DP(Y,Z)
```

3. Define a function for the following arithmetic expression and call it FUTVAL. The expression represent the future value of a uniform series of $1 investments for n periods at i interest.

$$\frac{(1+i)^n - 1}{i}$$

4. What values are displayed as a result of the following string operations?

```
100 ADDRESS$ = "135 New Street"
200 N$="N"
300 PRINT VAL(ADDRESS$)
400 PRINT INSTR(ADDRESS$,N$)
500 PRINT MID$(ADDRESS$,5,3)
600 PRINT RIGHT$(ADDRESS$,10)
700 PRINT STR$(VAL(ADDRESS$))
800 PRINT LEN(ADDRESS$)
```

Example Program #9

5. How would you modify the program to accept data and print the letter for any number of customers?

6. From a data entry operator's viewpoint, would it be easier to enter city, state, and zip together (as in the program) or separately? Explain.

7. How would you modify the program to eliminate the semicolons in statement 3140?

Example Program #10

8. How would the program change if the classroom had 16, rather than 8, rows?

9. The way the program is written, is it possible for two students who enter the classroom one after another to be assigned adjacent seats in the same row? Explain.

10. How many times is statement 2040 executed?

BASIC PROGRAMMING ASSIGNMENTS _____

1. The director of the Residence Operations at the college would like to send a personalized welcome memo to all students living on campus. One memo is to be sent to each room. All rooms are doubles. An example memo follows.

To: Harry Barnes and Jack Noble, Room 205

   I would like to take this opportunity, Harry and Jack, to welcome you back to campus and the pursuit of knowledge. Good luck! If I or my staff can be of service, please call.

                          Mike Phillips, Director

Write a program that accepts student name, last name first (e.g., Barnes, Harry), and room number (e.g., 205) for up to 100 students and in any order. The program should match roommates and produce a memo for each room. Notice the insertion of the students' first names in the text of the memo. [*Hint*: Consider sorting an array of room numbers by comparing consecutive values, then switching array positions as needed. Continue comparing and switching pairs until the room numbers are in an array in ascending order. Be sure to keep the names matched with the proper room numbers.]

2. Enhance the above progam so that the director has the option of producing an alphabetical listing of students (see below) and/or the memos. The report should have the following format.

STUDENT NAME	ROOM NUMBER
Barnes, Harry	205
Cole, Sally	106
Lupus, Janet	312
Noble, Jack	205

3. By using both intrinsic and user-defined functions, write a program to produce the following table:

X	X SQUARED	X CUBED	SQUARE ROOT OF X
1	1	1	1
2	4	8	1.414212
3	9	27	1.732051
⋮	⋮	⋮	⋮
20	400	8000	4.472136

4. Use the trigonometric functions of sine (SIN), cosine (COS), and tangent (TAN) to complete the following table. Remember that the argument must be expressed in radians. The 360 degrees of the circle have 2 pi (pi = 3.141592) radians. Each 45-degree increment is 1/8 (45/360) of 2 pi radians. [*Hint*: Use the STEP clause in the FOR/NEXT statement.]

                     TRIGONOMETRIC TABLE

DEGREES	SINE	COSINE	TANGENT
0			
45			
90			
135			
⋮			
315			
360			

B-24 DATA MANAGEMENT AND FILE PROCESSING _____

PROGRAMMING CONCEPTS

Program/Data Files
Hierarchy of Data Organization
Key Data Element
Sequential File Processing
Random File Processing
Internal Index File

This learning module presents the BASIC instructions and programming techniques for storing and retrieving data from disk storage. By now you will already have stored and retrieved many files from disk storage. These, however, were *program files*. You used the SAVE system command to store program files on disk storage for later recall with the LOAD command. Now we are ready to learn how to store and retrieve *data files*. When you store and retrieve a program file, it is relatively easy, because you store the entire file and retrieve the entire file. Manipulation of data files is more challenging than program files, because you may want to work with only a portion of the file.

The Hierarchy of Data Organization. We can use the *hierarchy of data organization* to illustrate how data are stored on disk. At the lowest level of the hierarchy is the *bit* (0 or 1). A series of *bits* are configured to represent a *character* or *byte*. For example, an ASCII byte 01000001 represents the character A inside the computer and on disk. At the next level of the hierarchy, characters are combined to represent the value of a *data element*, or *field*. In our example programs, student name (STNAME$) and the score of quiz 1 (Q1) are fields. Related data elements are grouped to form *records*. In the example programs, a student record would consist of student name, identification number, quiz 1 score, quiz 2 score, and the score of the final exam.

At the fourth level of the hierarchy, records with the same data elements are combined to form a *file*. Figure B-16 shows a student file with three records. This permanent source of student data is called a *master file*. In traditional file processing, files are sorted, merged, and processed by a *key data element*. In the example programs that follow, we'll use student identification number (ID) as the key data element. The key could just as well have been student name.

Sequential and Random Processing. In BASIC, data are manipulated and retrieved using *sequential processing* or *random processing*. In sequential processing, records are written to the disk in sequence and they are accessed in that same sequence. If a particular student's record is desired, each record, beginning with the first, is retrieved and loaded to memory one at a time until the value of that record's student ID (the key) matches that of the desired student.

Data are "written" to a spinning magnetic disk as "on" and "off" signals called bits. On input, several bits are combined to represent a character. On output, a bit string is interpreted by the computer system and translated to a character so that we can understand it. (Seagate Technology)

Figure B-16
Student File with Three Records

	STNAME$	ID	Q1	Q2	FINAL	
Record 1	Charles Roth	46912	73	91	85	Student file
Record 2	Lucy Cook	77878	86	88	99	
Record 3	Wayne Evans	66941	66	84	75	

A sequential file is processed from start to finish. Records can be added, or *appended*, to the end of the file, but if you wish to change an existing record, you would use the existing file to create a new file that includes the changed record. Sequential processing is demonstrated in Example Program #11.

A random file is a collection of records that can be processed randomly (in any order). This is called random processing. To do this in BASIC, however, you must know the *absolute location of the record within the file*. That is, you must know that a particular student is the third record on the file. Some languages (and the more advanced versions of BASIC) permit you to use the key data element to retrieve a record, but for most versions of BASIC, a record is randomly retrieved by its absolute location in the file. But, with a little programming ingenuity, we can create fairly sophisticated file access capabilities in BASIC. In Example Program #12, only the value of the record's key field (student ID) is needed for a record to be retrieved or changed.

B-25 BASIC INSTRUCTION SET: LEARNING MODULE VII GROUP

There are over 100 slightly different versions of BASIC. We are beginning to discuss the more advanced features of the BASIC language. As we do, there is a higher probability that there will be differences in the BASIC presented and that which you use. For example, the format of an instruction presented in the text may have a semicolon (;), but your BASIC may use a comma (,). You should be able to grasp the concepts and use of the instructions presented in this and subsequent learning modules, but check the *BASIC Reference Manual* for your system to get the exact syntax of these more advanced instructions.

Input/Output Instructions

OPEN.   A disk file must be OPENed before you can do anything with it, and it must be CLOSEd when you are finished with it. The OPEN instruction permits input/output to a disk file.

Format: OPEN filename$ [FOR mode] AS #filenumber
[LEN=record length]

Examples: OPEN "INVENTORY" FOR OUTPUT AS #1

SEQFILE$ = "INVENTORY"
OPEN SEQFILE$ FOR INPUT AS #1

OPEN "INVRANDOM" AS #2 LEN=50

The first two examples open a sequential file named "INVENTORY". Sequential files are opened FOR INPUT, OUTPUT, or APPEND. For the modes of INPUT and OUTPUT, processing is begun with the first record. The APPEND mode, a special case of the OUTPUT mode, causes processing to begin after the last record.

The omission of mode in the third example implies that a random file ("INVRANDOM") is opened. Once opened, a random file is both input and output. The record length (LEN) must be specified for random files. The record length of "INVRANDOM" is set at 50 bytes. The record length is important, because a file on a disk is simply a continuous string of characters. By setting the record length of INVRANDOM at 50 bytes, the system is instructed to find the first record in the first 50 bytes of the file, the second record in the second 50 bytes, and so on.

CLOSE.   The CLOSE instruction signals the completion of input/output to a file.

Format: CLOSE [#filenumber[, #filenumber . . .]]

Examples: CLOSE #1

            CLOSE

The first example closes the file that was OPENed as file number 1. The second example closes all files. To read a sequential file that has been opened as OUTPUT, the file must be closed and opened as INPUT, and vice versa.

WRITE #.   The WRITE instruction causes a record to be written to a sequential file.

Format: WRITE #filenumber, list of data elements

Example: WRITE #1, PARTNO, DESCRIP$, PRICE, QUANTITY

In the example, the values of the four data elements are written to the file opened as number 1. Some versions of BASIC employ a derivation on the PRINT statement (e.g., PRINT #1, PARTNO, DESCRIP$, PRICE, QUANTITY) to write to a disk file. Some versions have both. In these versions, the PRINT # instruction writes the image to disk as if it were to be displayed on a screen. This means there are no delimiters to distinguish between the fields unless you put them there.

The system software maintains a file *pointer* for WRITE # (and INPUT #) instructions. The pointer "points" to where the next record is to be written (or from where the next record is to be read). Each execution of a WRITE # instruction causes the pointer to be positioned to write the next sequential record on the file.

INPUT #. The INPUT # instruction reads a record from a sequential file and assigns the values in the data elements to variable names.

Format:　INPUT #filenumber, list of data elements

Example:　INPUT #1, PARTNO, DESCRIP$, PRICE, QUANTITY

The above instruction reads four data elements from the file opened as number 1. The file must have been opened as INPUT. The type of the data read, numeric or string, must match up with the types in the list of data elements or an error will result. In the example, the second data element read must be a string constant.

GET. The GET instruction causes the specified record to be retrieved from a random file.

Format:　GET #filenumber[, record number]

Example:　RECNO = 3
GET #1, RECNO
GET #1

In the example, the third record in a random file opened as file number 1 is retrieved, and the values in the data elements are assigned to the variable names specified in the FIELD instruction (see "Data Transfer and Assignment Instructions"). When no record number is specified, the next record after the last GET is retrieved. In the example, the fourth record is retrieved.

PUT. The PUT instruction causes a record to be written to a random file.

Format:　PUT #filenumber[, record number]

Example:　RECNO = 3
PUT #1, RECNO

In the example, a record containing the values of the data elements assigned to the variable names specified in the FIELD instruction (see "Data Transfer and Assignment Instructions") is written as record number 3 in a random file opened as file number 1.

Data Transfer and Assignment Instructions

FIELD.   The FIELD instruction defines the format of the intermediate storage area (in RAM) in which data are placed as a result of a GET (record) from a random file or a PUT (record) to random file.

> *Format*:   FIELD #filenumber, length AS string variable
> [, length AS string variable,]. . .

> *Example*:   FIELD # 1, 5 AS PARTNO$, 10 AS DESCRIP$

The above instruction sets aside 15 bytes (5 for PARTNO$ and 10 for DE-SCRIP$) for an intermediate storage area, called the *random file buffer*. Data are written from the file buffer to disk storage or read into the file buffer from disk storage. In either case, the data become the values of the variables in the FIELD instruction based on their relative location in the file buffer. The first 5 bytes are assigned to the variable PARTNO$ and the next 10 to DESCRIP$. Notice that all variables must be string variables. We'll discuss the reason for this later.

LSET and RSET.   The LSET and RSET instructions transfer data into a random file buffer (FIELD instruction) in preparation to be PUT, or written, to disk storage. LSET left-justifies the string in the field and RSET right-justifies it.

> *Format*:   LSET string variable from FIELD instruction
> = string variable
> RSET string variable from FIELD instruction
> = string variable

> *Example*:   FIELD # 1, 5 AS PARTNO$, 10 AS DESCRIP$
> LSET DESCRIP$ = PARTDESCRIP$

The value of PARTDESCRIP$ is loaded and left-justified in the DESCRIP$ field in the file buffer.

Other Instructions

KILL.   The appropriately named KILL instruction deletes the specified file from disk storage.

> *Format*:   KILL filename$

Example: KILL "INVENTORY"

The example deletes, or "erases," the file named "INVENTORY" from disk storage. KILL is also a system command on some versions of BASIC.

File Processing Functions

LOC.   The LOC (location) function takes on the value of the pointer's absolute location in the file.

> *Format*:   LOC(filenumber)

Example: WHILE LOC(1) < 20

In a sequential file, the value of LOC equals the number of records processed (read or written) since the file specified was opened. In random processing, the value of LOC is equal to the number of the last record read or written to the file.

LOF.   The LOF (length-of-file) function takes on the value of the number of bytes allocated to the file specified in the argument.

> *Format*:   LOF(filenumber)

Example: LENGTH = LOF(1)

LENGTH contains the number of bytes allocated to file number 1.

EOF.   The EOF (end-of-file) function is used to signal the end of a sequential file.

> *Format*:   EOF(filenumber)

Example: IF EOF(1) THEN END

The value of the EOF function becomes −1 when the end-of-file for file number 1 is reached. In the IF instruction example, the THEN clause is taken when the test on condition is false or the end-of-file is detected (value of the expression is −1).

MKS$.   The MKS$ function converts a numeric value to a string value.

> *Format*:   MKS$(numeric expression)

> *Example*:   LSET PARTNO$ = MKS$(PARTNO)

Before a numeric value can be stored in a random file it must be converted to a string value. And conversely, before you can perform arithmetic operations on a numeric "string" value that is read from a random file, it must be converted back to a numeric value. The MKS$ and CVS (see below) functions differ slightly from the STR$ and VAL functions (introduced in Learning Module VI) in that they do not change the bytes of the data. However, they do change the manner in which they are interpreted by BASIC. Therefore, MKS$ and CVS are used primarily in random file processing (see Section B-27).

In the above example, the numeric value of PARTNO is converted to a string value called PARTNO$. The LSET instruction loads and left-justifies the value of PARTNO$ to the random file buffer.

CVS.   The CVS function converts a string constant to a numeric constant.

> *Format*:   CVS(string)

> *Example*:   PARTNO = CVS(PARTNO$)

The string value of PARTNO$ is converted to a numeric value called PARTNO. Typically, PARTNO$ would have originally been a number that was prepared for storage on a random file with an LSET instruction and an MKS$ function.

B-26   EXAMPLE PROGRAM #11: SEQUENTIAL FILE PROCESSING

Example Program #11 illustrates how the student data used in previous example programs can be stored permanently in a sequential disk file. The program is a menu-driven program that permits a professor to *create the file*, *add student records*, *list student records*, and *delete the entire file*. In a sequential file, records are stored in the order in which they are written to disk and are retrieved in the same order. Sequential and random processing are discussed in Section B-24.

The Example Program #11 structure chart shows the hierarchical organization of the program. The three modules called from the driver module, and their subordinate modules, are discussed individually below.

Driver Module.   Subroutines are called from the driver module in a DO-WHILE loop. Loop processing continues while the value of MENU is not equal to 5 (entered in Module 1.1).

EXAMPLE PROGRAM #11

This program permits the creation or deletion of a sequential file and, also, the addition or listing of student records.

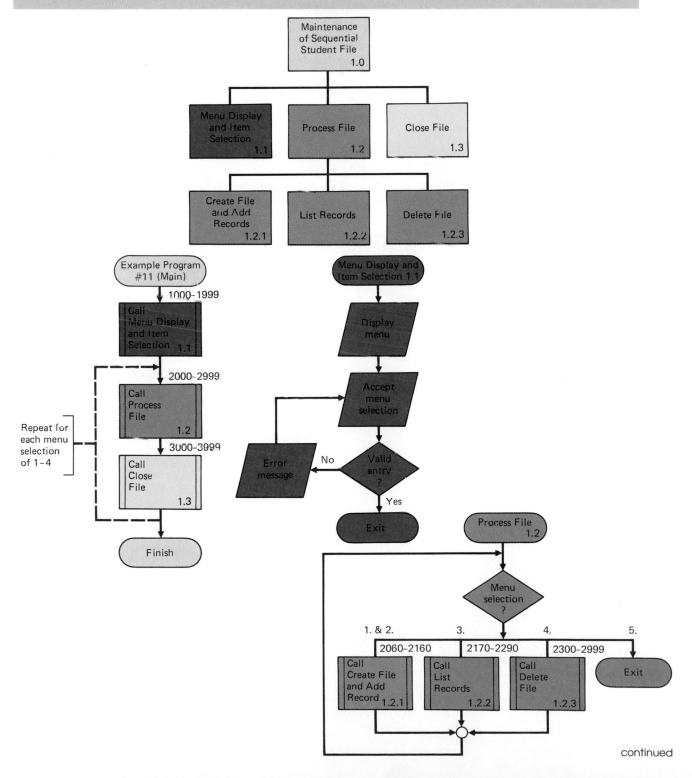

continued

Example Program 11 continued

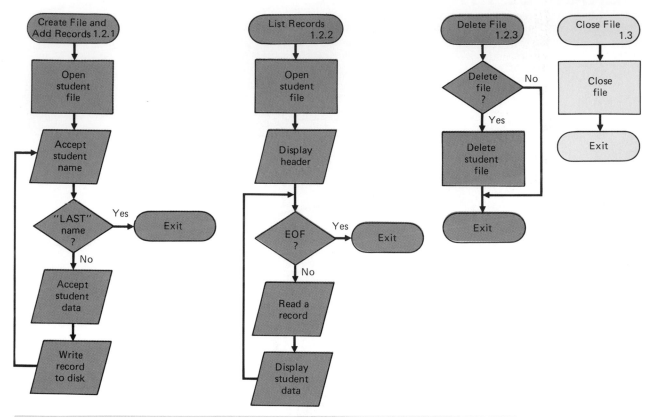

```
2     REM          **** Example Program #11 ****
4     REM   Description:
6     REM      This program permits the creation or deletion of a sequential
8     REM      file and, also, the addition or listing of student records.
10    REM   Variables list:
14    REM     STNAME$              - Student name
24    REM     Q1, Q2, FINAL        - Test scores
25    REM     ID                   - Student ID
30    REM     ANSWER$              - Y or N response to inquiry
32    REM     MENU                 - Menu item selected
99    REM
100   REM   <<<< Start Main >>>>
110   REM
120   WHILE MENU <> 5
130      REM  Call Module 1.1 - Menu Display and Item Selection
140      GOSUB 1000
150      CLS
160      REM  Call Module 1.2 - Process File
170      GOSUB 2000
180      REM  Call Module 1.3 - Close File
190      GOSUB 3000
200   WEND
210   END
220   REM   <<<< End Main >>>>
999   REM
```

```
1000 REM  ==== Module 1.1 - Menu Display and Item Selection
1010 REM  Display menu
1020 PRINT
1030 PRINT "        ****** Sequential Student File Program ******"
1040 PRINT
1050 PRINT "              1. Create student data file."
1060 PRINT "              2. Add student records."
1070 PRINT "              3. List student records."
1080 PRINT "              4. Delete student data file."
1090 PRINT "              5. Exit Program."
1100 PRINT
1110 REM  Accept menu selection
1120 INPUT "Make a selection from the menu: ",MENU
1130 PRINT
1140 IF MENU > 0 AND MENU < 6 THEN RETURN
1150 REM  Error message
1160 PRINT "That was not a valid response. Try again."
1170 PRINT
1999 GOTO 1120
2000 REM  ==== Module 1.2 - Process File
2010 IF MENU = 1 OR MENU = 2 THEN GOSUB 2060 'Call Module 1.2.1 - Create File
        and Add Records
2020    IF MENU = 3 THEN GOSUB 2170 'Call Module 1.2.2 - List Records
2030      IF MENU = 4 THEN GOSUB 2300 'Call Module 1.2.3 - Delete File
2040        IF MENU = 5 THEN RETURN
2050 RETURN
2060 REM  ==== Module 1.2.1 - Create File and Add Records
2070 REM
2080 REM  Open student data file for appending
2090 OPEN "STUDENTS" FOR APPEND AS #1
2100 PRINT
2110 INPUT "Student name (Enter LAST when complete): ",STNAME$
2120 IF STNAME$ = "LAST" OR STNAME$ = "last" THEN RETURN
2130 INPUT "Student ID: ",ID
2140 INPUT "Enter grades for quiz1, quiz2, and final: ",Q1, Q2, FINAL
2150 WRITE #1,STNAME$, ID, Q1, Q2, FINAL
2160 GOTO 2100
2170 REM  ==== Module 1.2.2 - List Records
2180 REM
2190 REM  Open student data file for input
2200 OPEN "STUDENTS" FOR INPUT AS #1
2210 PRINT
2220 PRINT "Student Name";TAB(22);"ID","Quiz 1","Quiz 2","Final"
2230 PRINT
2240 IF EOF(1) THEN 2280
2250 INPUT #1, STNAME$, ID, Q1, Q2, FINAL
2260 PRINT STNAME$;TAB(20);ID, Q1, Q2, FINAL
2270 GOTO 2240
2280 PRINT
2290 RETURN
2300 REM  ==== Module 1.2.3 - Delete File
2310 PRINT
2320 INPUT "Do you wish to delete the file? (Enter Y or N) ",ANSWER$
2330 IF ANSWER$ <> "Y" AND ANSWER$ <> "y" THEN 2999
2340 KILL "STUDENTS"
2999 RETURN
3000 REM  ==== Module 1.3 - Close File
3010 CLOSE #1
3999 RETURN
```

continued

Example Program 11 continued

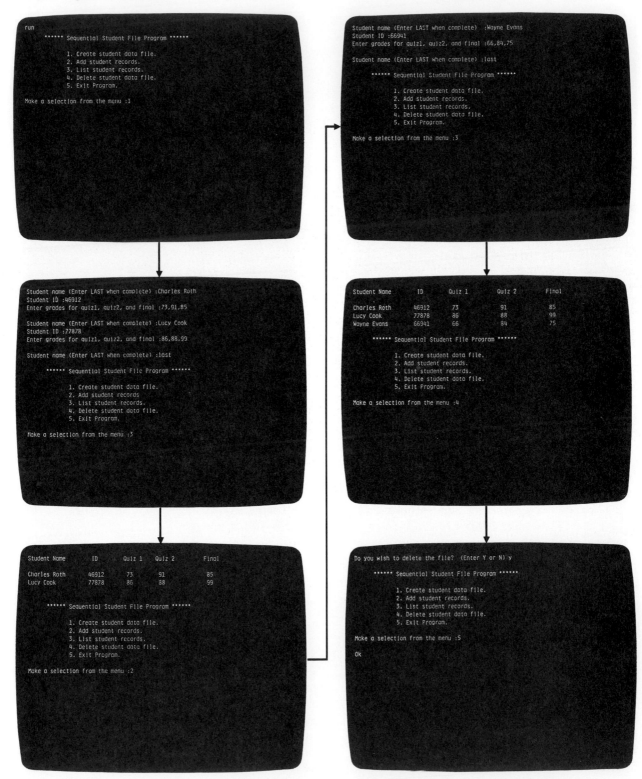

Module 1.1—Menu Display and Item Selection. In this module, the user is asked to make a selection from a menu of possible processing activities (see interactive session).

Module 1.2—Process File. The value of MENU obtained from Module 1.1 causes processing to be directed to one of several file activities. Each of these activities is handled in a subroutine that is subordinate to Module 1.2 (see the structure chart).

Module 1.2.1—Create File and Add Records. The same set of program instructions can be used to create the file and add records to the file. Notice that statement 2010 in Module 1.2 directs processing to Module 1.2.1 when MENU=1 (create file) or 2 (add records).

In statement 2090, the STUDENT file is opened for APPENDing records. The APPEND mode positions the pointer at the next available record position. When creating the file, the pointer is at the start of the file. When adding to an existing file, the pointer is at the end of the file.

Data are entered and written to the sequential file in a loop. Once the data have been entered for a single student, a WRITE # instruction (2150) writes a student record to disk. The loop is repeated until the professor enters "LAST" for student name. Control of processing is then passed to Module 1.1—Display Menu to permit further file processing.

Module 1.2.2—List Records. The instruction sequence in Module 1.2.2 causes all records on the STUDENT file (#1) to be read and listed (see interactive session). The file is OPENed for INPUT in statement 2200. A heading is displayed; then, for each pass of a loop, a record is read (INPUT # at statement 2250), then displayed until the end-of-file (EOF) is reached. When the EOF is detected (2240), control of execution is returned to Module 1.2, the calling module.

Module 1.2.3—Delete File. The execution of this module results in the STUDENT file being deleted from disk storage. The KILL instruction (2340) performs the delete operation. It is good programming practice to force a user to make two separate requests before deleting an entire file. In Example Program #11, the user must select menu item 4 *and* enter an affirmative answer to a followup request (see interactive session) before the file is deleted.

Module 1.3—Close File. The STUDENT file (#1) is CLOSEd in statement 3010. The file can now be reopened to service other user selections from the menu.

B-27 EXAMPLE PROGRAM #12: RANDOM FILE PROCESSING _____

From a programming standpoint, sequential files are more straightforward and require considerably less programming than random files, but random files can make life a lot easier for the people using the program. For example, if a professor desires to change a student's grade after creating the sequential file in Example Program #11, the entire file must be recreated. The use of a random file in Example Program #12 makes it possible for the professor to make changes to a student's record without affecting the other records

EXAMPLE PROGRAM #12

This program permits the addition, revision, deletion, and listing of the student records in a random file.

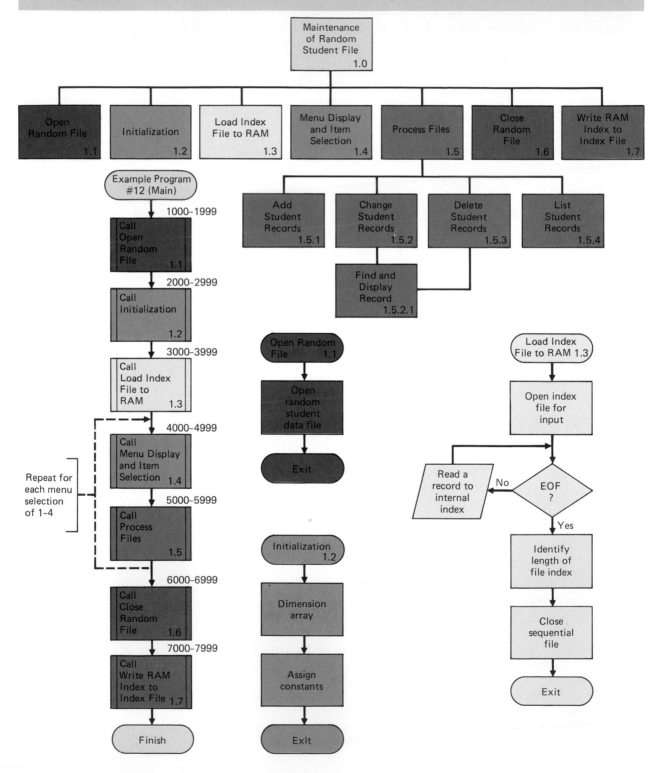

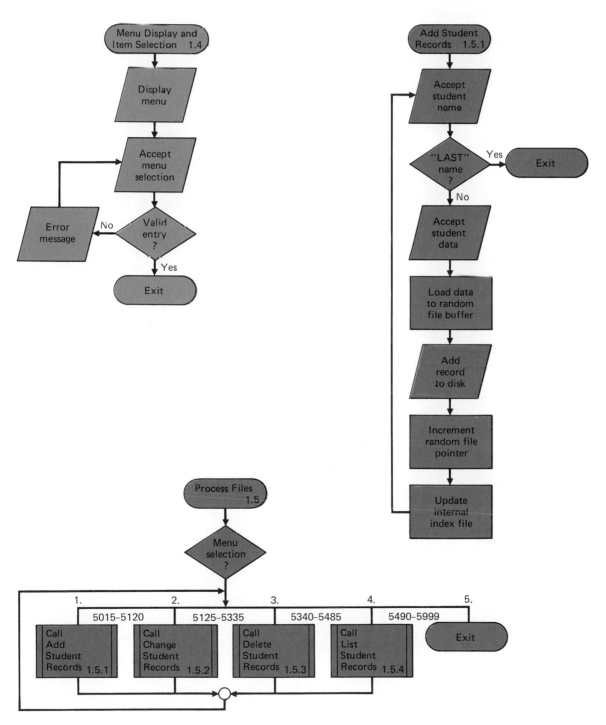

continued

Example Program 12 continued

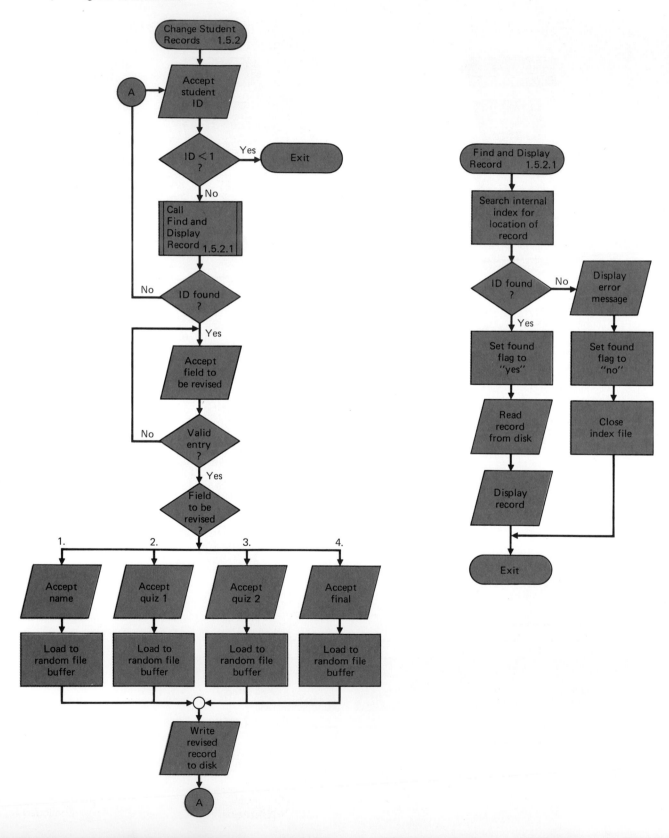

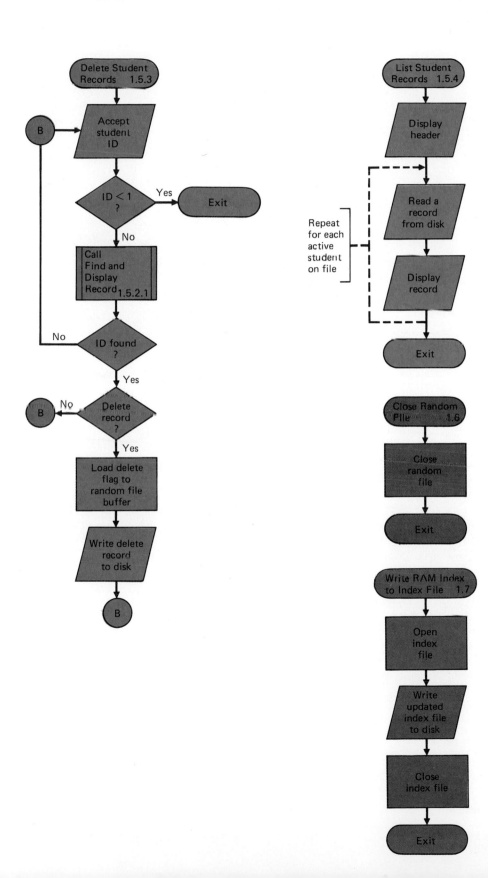

continued

Example Program 12 continued

```
2    REM           **** Example Program #12 ****
4    REM   Description:
6    REM     This program permits the addition revision, deletion, and
8    REM     listing of the student records in a random file.
10   REM   Variables list:
12   REM     STNAME$              - Student name
14   REM     Q1, Q2, FINAL        - Test scores
16   REM     ID                   - Student ID
18   REM     ANSWER$              - Y or N response to inquiry
20   REM     MENU                 - Menu item selected
22   REM     STUDENTNAME$         - Random buffer for variable STNAME$
24   REM     Q1$, Q2$, FINAL$     - Random buffer for variables Q1, Q2, FINAL
26   REM     DEL$                 - Delete flag
28   REM     RAMINDEX( , )        - Internal search index
30   REM     LENGTHRANDOM         - Length of random file (records)
32   REM     COUNT                - Index record subscript
34   REM     INDEXID              - Index variable for RAMINDEX array
36   REM     INDEXLEN             - Length of file index
38   REM     RECORDNUMBER         - Random file record number
40   REM     FOUND$               - Search status flag (YES/NO)
99   REM
100  REM   <<<< Start Main >>>>
110  REM
120  REM   Call Module 1.1 - Open Random File
130  GOSUB 1000
140  REM   Call Module 1.2 - Initialization
150  GOSUB 2000
160  REM   Call Module 1.3 - Load Index File to RAM
170  GOSUB 3000
180  REM   Return to activities menu as long as exit item is not selected
190  WHILE MENU <> 5
200     REM   Call Module 1.4 - Menu Display and Item Selection
210     GOSUB 4000
220     CLS
230     REM   Call Module 1.5 - Process Files
240     GOSUB 5000
250  WEND
260  REM   Call Module 1.6 - Close Random File
270  GOSUB 6000
280  REM   Call Module 1.7 - Write RAM Index to Index File
290  GOSUB 7000
300  END
310  REM   <<<< End Main >>>>
999  REM
1000 REM   ==== Module 1.1 - Open Random File
1010 OPEN "DATAFILE" AS #1 LEN=33
1020 FIELD #1, 20 AS STUDENTNAME$, 4 AS Q1$, 4 AS Q2$, 4 AS FINAL$, 1 AS DEL$
1999 RETURN
2000 REM   ==== Module 1.2 - Initialization
2010 DIM RAMINDEX(100,2)
2020 REM   Set LENGTHRANDOM equal to the number of records in the file
2030 LENGTHRANDOM = LOF(1)/33
2999 RETURN
3000 REM   ==== Module 1.3 - Load Index File to RAM
3010 REM
3020 OPEN "INDEX" FOR INPUT AS #2
3030 COUNT = 1
3040 REM   Test if end-of-file
3050 IF EOF(2) THEN 3110
3060 INPUT #2, INDEXID, RECORDNUMBER
3070 RAMINDEX(COUNT,1) = INDEXID
3080 RAMINDEX(COUNT,2) = RECORDNUMBER
3090 COUNT = COUNT + 1
3100 GOTO 3050
3110 INDEXLEN = COUNT - 1
3120 CLOSE #2
3999 RETURN
```

```
4000 REM  ==== Module 1.4 - Menu Display and Item Selection
4010 PRINT
4020 PRINT "       ****** Random Student File Program ******"
4030 PRINT
4040 PRINT "              1. Add student records."
4050 PRINT "              2. Change student records."
4060 PRINT "              3. Delete student records."
4070 PRINT "              4. List student records."
4080 PRINT "              5. Exit program."
4090 PRINT
4100 REM  Accept menu selection
4110 INPUT "Make a selection from the menu: ",MENU
4120 PRINT
4130 IF MENU > 0 AND MENU < 6 THEN RETURN
4140 REM  Error message
4150 PRINT "That was not a valid response. Try again."
4160 PRINT
4999 GOTO 4110
5000 REM  ==== Module 1.5 - Process Files
5005 ON MENU GOSUB 5015, 5125, 5375, 5440 'Call appropriate subroutine
5010 RETURN
5015 REM  ==== Module 1.5.1 - Add Student Records
5020 REM
5025 PRINT
5030 INPUT "Student name (Enter LAST when complete): ",STNAME$
5035 IF STNAME$ = "LAST" OR STNAME$ = "last" THEN 5120
5040 INPUT "Student ID: ",ID
5045 INPUT "Enter grades for quiz1, quiz2, and final: ", Q1, Q2, FINAL
5050 REM  Add student name and grades to random file
5055 LSET STUDENTNAME$ = STNAME$
5060 LSET Q1$ = MKS$(Q1)
5065 LSET Q2$ = MKS$(Q2)
5070 LSET FINAL$ = MKS$(FINAL)
5075 REM
5080 LSET DEL$=" "
5085 PUT #1, LENGTHRANDOM + 1
5090 LENGTHRANDOM = LENGTHRANDOM + 1
5095 REM  Add student ID and random record number to RAMINDEX
5100 INDEXLEN = INDEXLEN + 1
5105 RAMINDEX(INDEXLEN,1) = ID
5110 RAMINDEX(INDEXLEN,2) = LENGTHRANDOM
5115 GOTO 5025
5120 RETURN
5125 REM  ==== Module 1.5.2 - Change Student Records
5130 REM
5135 PRINT
5140 INPUT "Enter ID number of student record to change (Enter -1 when complete)
: ",ID
5145 IF ID < 1 THEN GOTO 5245
5150 GOSUB 5250  'Call Module 1.5.2.1 - Find and Display Record
5155 IF FOUND$ = "NO" THEN GOTO 5130
5160 INPUT "Enter the number of the field you wish to change (1-4): ",FLDNUM
5165 IF FLDNUM < 1 OR FLDNUM > 4 THEN
       PRINT "*** That was not a valid response ***" : GOTO 5160
5170 ON FLDNUM GOTO 5175, 5190, 5205, 5220
5175 INPUT "Enter correct student name: ",STNAME$
5180 LSET STUDENTNAME$ = STNAME$
5185 GOTO 5230
5190 INPUT "Enter correct quiz 1 score: ",Q1
5195 LSET Q1$ = MKS$(Q1)
5200 GOTO 5230
5205 INPUT "Enter correct quiz 2 score: ",Q2
5210 LSET Q2$ = MKS$(Q2)
5215 GOTO 5230
5220 INPUT "Enter correct final  score: ",FINAL
5225 LSET FINAL$=MKS$(FINAL)
5230 REM  Put revised record in random file
5235 PUT #1, RAMINDEX(COUNT,2)
5240 GOTO 5130
5245 RETURN
```

continued

Example Program 12 continued

```
5250 REM   ==== Module 1.5.2.1 - Find and Display Record
5255 REM
5260 REM   Search RAMINDEX for ID
5265 FOR COUNT = 1 TO INDEXLEN
5270   IF ID = RAMINDEX(COUNT,1) THEN 5310
5275 NEXT COUNT
5280 REM  Student ID not found in index file
5285 PRINT
5290 PRINT "Error: Student ID";ID;"was not found in index file."
5295 FOUND$ = "NO"
5300 CLOSE #2
5305 GOTO 5370
5310 REM  Student ID found in RAMINDEX
5315 FOUND$ = "YES"
5320 GET #1, RAMINDEX(COUNT,2)
5325 IF DEL$=CHR$(127) THEN 5275
5330 PRINT
5335 PRINT "Student ID:";ID
5340 PRINT
5345 PRINT "          1. Student name: ";STUDENTNAME$
5350 PRINT "          2. Quiz 1 score:";CVS(Q1$)
5355 PRINT "          3. Quiz 2 score:";CVS(Q2$)
5360 PRINT "          4. Final  score:";CVS(FINAL$)
5365 PRINT
5370 RETURN
5375 REM  ==== Module 1.5.3 - Delete Student Records
5380 REM
5385 PRINT
5390 INPUT "Enter ID number of student record to delete (Enter -1 when complete)
: ",ID
5395 IF ID < 1 THEN 5435
5400 GOSUB 5250   'Call Module 1.5.2.1 - Find and Display Record
5405 IF FOUND$="NO" THEN GOTO 5380
5410 INPUT "Do you wish to delete this record? (Y or N) ",ANSWER$
5415 IF ANSWER$ <> "Y" AND ANSWER$ <> "y" THEN 5430
5420 LSET DEL$ = CHR$(127) 'Set delete flag to ascii DEL
5425 PUT #1, RAMINDEX(COUNT,2)
5430 GOTO 5380
5435 RETURN
5440 REM  ==== Module 1.5.4 - List Student Records
5445 REM
5450 PRINT
5455 PRINT "Student Name";TAB(30);"ID";TAB(43);"Quiz 1";TAB(55);"Quiz 2";
     TAB(67);"Final"
5460 PRINT
5465 FOR COUNT = 1 TO INDEXLEN
5470   ID = RAMINDEX(COUNT,1)
5475   RECORDNUMBER = RAMINDEX(COUNT,2)
5480   GET #1,RECORDNUMBER
5485   IF DEL$ <> CHR$(127) THEN PRINT STUDENTNAME$; TAB(27); ID;TAB(36);
       :PRINT USING "      ###.##";CVS(Q1$), CVS(Q2$), CVS(FINAL$)
5490 NEXT COUNT
5999 RETURN
6000 REM   ==== Module 1.6 - Close Random File
6015 CLOSE #1
6990 RETURN
7000 REM   ==== Module 1.7 - Write RAM Index to Index File
7005 OPEN "INDEX" FOR OUTPUT AS #2
7010 FOR COUNT = 1 TO INDEXLEN
7015   WRITE #2, RAMINDEX(COUNT,1),RAMINDEX(COUNT,2)
7020 NEXT COUNT
7025 CLOSE #2
7999 RETURN
```

Screen 1 (top-left):

```
Enter ID number of student record to delete (Enter -1 when complete) :46912

Student ID : 46912

Student name : Charles Roth
Quiz 1 score : 73
Quiz 2 score : 91
Final  score : 85

Do you wish to delete this record? (Y or N) y

Enter ID number of student record to delete (Enter -1 when complete) :23670

Error: Student ID 23670 was not found in index file.

Enter ID number of student record to delete (Enter -1 when complete) :-1

        ****** Random Student File Program ******

          1. Add student records.
          2. Change student records.
          3. Delete student records.
          4. List student records.
          5. Exit program.

Make a selection from the menu :4
```

Screen 2 (top-right):

```
Enter ID number of student record to change (Enter -1 when complete) :77878

Student ID : 77878

          1. Student name : Lucy Cook
          2. Quiz 1 score : 86
          3. Quiz 2 score : 88
          4. Final score : 99

Enter the number of the field you wish to change (1-4) :3
Enter correct quiz 2 score :94

Enter ID number of student record to change (Enter -1 when complete) :-1

        ****** Random Student File Program ******

          1. Add student records.
          2. Change student records.
          3. Delete student records.
          4. List student records.
          5. Exit program.

Make a selection from the menu :3
```

Screen 3 (left, "run"):

```
run

        ****** Random Student File Program ******

          1. Add student records.
          2. Change student records.
          3. Delete student records.
          4. List student records.
          5. Exit program.

Make a selection from the menu :1
```

Screen 4 (right):

```
Student name (Enter LAST when complete) :Charles Roth
Student ID :46912
Enter grades for quiz1, quiz2, and final :73,91,85

Student name (Enter LAST when complete) :Lucy Cook
Student ID :77878
Enter grades for quiz1, quiz2, and final :86,88,99

Student name (Enter LAST when complete) :last

        ****** Random Student File Program ******

          1. Add student records.
          2. Change student records.
          3. Delete student records.
          4. List student records.
          5. Exit program.

Make a selection from the menu :4
```

Screen 5 (left):

Student Name	ID	Quiz 1	Quiz 2	Final
Charles Roth	46912	73.00	91.00	85.00
Lucy Cook	77878	86.00	88.00	99.00

```
        ****** Random Student File Program ******

          1. Add student records.
          2. Change student records.
          3. Delete student records.
          4. List student records.
          5. Exit program.

Make a selection from the menu :1
```

Screen 6 (right):

Student Name	ID	Quiz 1	Quiz 2	Final
Lucy Cook	77878	86.00	94.00	99.00
Wayne Evans	66941	66.00	84.00	75.00

```
        ****** Random Student File Program ******

          1. Add student records.
          2. Change student records.
          3. Delete student records.
          4. List student records.
          5. Exit program.

Make a selection from the menu :5

OK
```

Screen 7 (bottom-left):

```
Student name (Enter LAST when complete) :Wayne Evans
Student ID :66941
Enter grades for quiz1, quiz2, and final :66,84,75

Student name (Enter LAST when complete) :last

        ****** Random Student File Program ******

          1. Add student records.
          2. Change student records.
          3. Delete student records.
          4. List student records.
          5. Exit program.

Make a selection from the menu :2
```

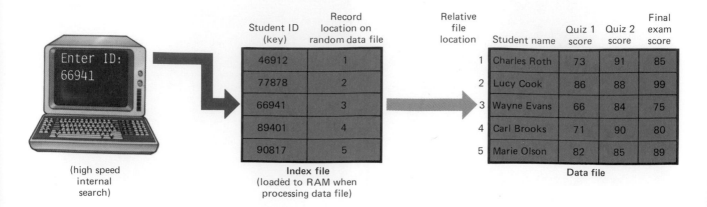

Figure B-17
Random Access in BASIC
Rapid random access is achieved in BASIC by maintaining an index file and a data file. The index file is loaded to primary storage prior to processing the data file. A high-speed search of the index file yields the physical location of the desired record. The record is then retrieved directly from the data file.

in the file. Random processing is also faster because a given record can be retrieved "directly," without the need for a time-consuming sequential search.

Records are stored and retrieved from a BASIC random file based on the record's absolute location in the file. This means that we must know what record is stored in location 1, 2, 3, and so on. Random processing is very convenient with BASIC random files when the key data element is equal to a record's storage location. For example, if a company manufactured 200 different parts and assigned them part numbers (the key) of 1 to 200, random processing is a breeze. But in practice the part numbers will look more like L3005AC and M4235AD than 1 and 2. The same is true of other key values. Even so, this minor hurdle can be overcome by using two files: a random *data file* and a sequential *index file*.

The *data file* contains the records (e.g., for each student, for each inventory item); the smaller *index file* has a record that contains the key and absolute location for each record on the data file. A request for a particular record is first directed to the index file, which, in turn, "points" to the physical location of the desired record in the data file. Figure B-17 graphically illustrates the relationship between the two files. The index file, which is usually much smaller than the data file, is loaded to primary storage (random-access memory or RAM) prior to processing. This permits an *internal search* of the index file. An internal search, which is done entirely in RAM, takes only a fraction of a second. A disk search for a particular record could take several seconds.

The following module-by-module discussion of Example Program #12 focuses on concepts and instructions that were not discussed for Example Program #11.

Driver Module. The driver module is set up similar to the driver module in Example Program #11. Processing is continued in a DOWHILE loop as long as the value of MENU is not equal to 6 (entered in Module 1.4).

Module 1.1—Open Random File. RAMINDEX is dimensioned as a two-dimensional array (100,2). RAMINDEX holds the key (ID) and pointer (to student record in "DATAFILE") for up to 100 students.

The student random file "DATAFILE" is OPENed and given a record length (LEN) of 33 bytes in statement 1010. The format of the file buffer is defined in the FIELD instruction (1020). All variables in the buffer are string variables. Since the key, ID, is stored in the index file ("INDEX"), there is no need to maintain ID in the "DATAFILE" (see Figure B-17). The DEL$ field is used to designate, or "flag," those records which are logically deleted.

Module 1.2—Initialization. Statement 2030 sets LENGTHRANDOM equal to the length of the random file in records. The length of the file in bytes (LOF function) is divided by the record length in bytes (33 from the FIELD instruction). If five records of 33 bytes are on the "DATAFILE" file, then the value of LENGTHRANDOM would be 5 (165/33).

Module 1.3—Load Index File to RAM. The sequential "INDEX" file is opened and its contents are loaded to the array RAMINDEX. This enables a high-speed sequential search for a particular student ID and the associated record's location (record number) in the random file, "DATAFILE". The contents of "INDEX" are loaded to RAMINDEX in a loop. At EOF, statement 3110 is executed to save the length of the file index (INDEXLEN) for future processing; then the file is closed.

Module 1.4– Menu Display and Item Selection. In this module, the user is asked to make a selection from a menu of possible processing activities (see interactive session).

Module 1.5—Process File. The ON GOSUB instruction (5005) causes processing to be directed to one of several file activities, depending on the value of MENU obtained from Module 1.4. Each of these activities is handled in a subroutine that is subordinate to Module 1.5 (see structure chart).

Module 1.5.1—Create File and Add Records. Just as in Example Program #11, the same set of program instructions can be used to create the files and to add records to the files. Remember from discussions of the BASIC instruction set in Section B-25 that all data elements in a record for a random file must be converted to string constants before they are loaded to the buffer. In statements 5060–5070, the three numeric test scores are converted to string values with the MKS$ function. In the same statements, the LSET instruction loads these values to the string variables specified in the FIELD instruction at statement 1020 (the random file buffer). Since STNAME$ is already a string variable, it is simply loaded as is to the buffer (5055).

The PUT instruction (5085) writes the contents of the random file buffer to the disk. The location in which the record is written is specified by the value of LENGTHRANDOM+1. When creating the file, the value of LENGTHRANDOM is 0, so the first record is written, or PUT, to location 1. When adding to an existing file, LENGTHRANDOM points to the last record in the file, so the next record is added at the end of the file. The student ID and location are added to the end of the RAMINDEX array in statements 5100–5110.

A bank teller enters your name or account number to call up your banking record from a direct access file. The teller can update the record to reflect a deposit or withdrawal, or the teller can request status information, such as an account balance.
(Courtesy of International Business Machines)

The loop is repeated until the professor enters "LAST" for student name. The INDEX file is then closed and control of processing is then passed to Module 1.4—Menu Display and Item Selection to permit further file processing.

Module 1.5.2—Change Records.   The processing activities in this module demonstrate the advantages of random processing over sequential processing. The interactive session of Example Program #12 illustrates how the professor has only to enter the ID number of the student record to be changed (statement 5140). Module 1.5.2.1—Find and Display Record is called (statement 5150) to retrieve and display the selected record.

As you can see from the interactive session, the user selects which data element is to be revised, then enters the revised data. The revised record is then written, or PUT, to the same location in the "DATAFILE" file from which it was read. A loop (5130–5240) is repeated until the professor enters a −1 for ID.

Module 1.5.2.1—Find and Display Record.   This module is called by both Module 1.5.2—Change Records and Module 1.5.3—Delete Records to retrieve and display the selected record. A rapid internal search of RAMINDEX yields the location of the record in the data file (RAMINDEX(COUNT,2)). The student's record is then retrieved with a GET instruction (5320). Depending on whether a record is found or not, a flag, FOUND$, is set to "YES" or "NO". The value of FOUND$ effects processing in Modules 1.5.2 and 1.5.3.

Module 1.5.3—Delete Records.   The logic for this module is similar to that of Module 1.5.2—Change Records. A record is not *physically* deleted; it is *logically* deleted. This is done by inserting an ASCII character, CHR$(127), in the DEL$ field. Any record flagged with a CHR$(127) in the DEL$ is ignored in future processing (see statement 5325) in Module 1.5.2.1—Find and Display Record. The record continues to exist physically, but logically it is no longer part of the file. The interactive session demonstrates the I/O for this module.

Module 1.5.4—List Records.   In this module, all records on the "DATA-FILE" file (#1) are read and listed (see interactive session).

Module 1.6—Close Random File.   The random file STUDENT (#1) is CLOSEd.

Module 1.7—Write RAM Index to Index File.   An updated "INDEX" file, the contents of the RAMINDEX array, is written to disk.

REVIEW EXERCISES (LEARNING MODULE VII) _____

BASIC Instructions and Concepts

1.   Identify the syntax error(s) in each of the following instructions.
     (a)   10 FIELD #2, 22 AS NAME$, 6 AS ID, 12 AS JOBTITLE$
     (b)   10 LET TOTAL = MKS$(SUM)
     (c)   10 OPEN #1, #2, #3

(d)   10 SIZE = EOF(#1)
(e)   10 INPUT #3 A,B,C

2. What are the differences in the way program files are retrieved from secondary storage and the way data files are retrieved?

3. Describe the relationship between the key data element and a master file.

4. In BASIC, data are manipulated and retrieved from disk storage using what two types of processing?

5. Start at the lowest level of the hierarchy of data organization and name each level.

6. Detail exactly what happens when a GET instruction is issued.

7. What is meant by a reference to the absolute location of a record within a file?

8. What is the difference between the LSET and RSET instructions?

Example Program #11

9. Module 1.2.1 is called when the file is to be created and when records are to be added to an existing file. Explain how the same instructions can accomplish two tasks.

10. Why would another file be needed to permit changes to the data for a particular record?

11. Why is it necessary to close a newly created file before listing the records?

12. Suppose you selected menu item 1 and created a file with three records, then selected menu item 5. Suppose you did exactly the same thing again. What would be the contents of the file?

Example Program #12

13. What is the significance of the 33 in the OPEN instruction at 1010?

14. What is the maximum number of student records that can be stored and processed by this program?

15. Why is the entire index file loaded to primary storage prior to processing?

16. Records are deleted logically, not physically. Explain.

17. What must be done to a record before it is loaded to the random file buffer for output to disk?

BASIC PROGRAMMING ASSIGNMENTS _____

1. The state highway patrol has asked you to write an interactive file processing program that would permit the creation of a sequential file of all licensed operators of vehicles. Each record would contain the following: an eight-digit operator ID (OPERATORID), the key;

the full name of the operator (FULLNAME$); the street address (STREET$); the city (CITY$); the state (STATE$); and the zip (ZIP).

Once the file has been created, permit the user to add records, list the records, or delete the entire file.

2. Modify the above program to add another user option. Permit the user of the program to select an option that would produce a report listing the operator ID and name of all licensed drivers in a particular city. The user would enter the name of the city (e.g., New Mayberry) and the following report would be produced.

Driver Summary—New Mayberry
======================

OPERATOR ID	NAME
56729789	Mary Metler
34978436	Mark Bass
⋮	⋮

3. The state highway patrol has asked you to write a program that would permit the creation and maintenance of a random vehicle file. Each record would contain the following: a six-letter license plate number (LICENSE$), the key; the make of the car (MAKE$); the model (MODEL$); the year (YEAR); and the eight-digit operator ID of the owner (OPID). Once the file has been created, permit the user to add records, change the operator ID of any record, list the records, or delete individual records.

Use the technique illustrated in Example Program #12; that is, use an index file and a data file.

4. Write a program that will permit a highway patrolperson to make inquiries that involve the licensed operator and vehicle files created in programming assignments 1 and 3 above. Often, patrolpersons need to know the name of the owner of a particular vehicle. Create the following interactive session for each inquiry.

Enter vehicle license number (enter LAST to quit): **ABC345**

VEHICLE DESCRIPTION
  Make: Mercedes-Benz
  Model: 380 SL
  Year: 1986

OWNER (Operator ID is 56729789):
  Mary Metler
  630 Pine Street
  Charlotte, NC 28205

B-28 BASIC INSTRUCTION SET: LEARNING MODULE VIII GROUP

The BASIC instructions presented in this group let you present numeric results graphically, create elementary pictorial images, and output sound and music. It is important to reemphasize that the syntax of these more advanced BASIC instructions may vary considerably between versions of BASIC. Check the *BASIC Reference Manual* for your system for the exact instruction syntax and for other related instructions.

Input/Output Instructions

LINE. The LINE instruction causes a *line* or a *box* of specified dimensions to be drawn on the screen.

> Format: LINE $[(x_1,y_1)]-(x_2,y_2)$ [,[color][,B[F]]]
> Where x_1, y_1, x_2, y_2 (the graphics coordinates)
> and "color" are numeric constants or expressions

Examples:
```
10  LINE (X1,Y1) — (X2,Y2)
20  LINE (20,20) — (280,20),1        'horizontal line of color 1
30  LINE (20,20) — (20,100),2        'vertical line of color 2
40  LINE (20,20) — (280,100),3       'diagonal line of color 3
50  LINE —(280,20),3                 'vertical line of color 3
60  LINE (10,10) — (290,110),2,B     'box of color 2
70  LINE (10,120) — (290,140),3,BF   'filled-in box of color 1
80  FOR X = 10 TO 250 STEP 40
90   LINE (X,150) — STEP(35,—35),2,B  'square boxes of color 2
100 NEXT X
```

Pixels and Resolution.   When doing programming in *graphics mode*, as opposed to *text mode*, you work with the screen as a *grid* of *picture elements*, or **pixels**. A pixel is a rectangular point on the screen to which light can be directed under program control. The number of pixels on the screen determines the **resolution** of the display. The resolution of a graphics display can vary from about 65,000 pixels for low-resolution screens to about 16 million pixels for very high-resolution screens.

Coordinates.   A particular pixel is identified by its coordinate location on the screen's grid. For our examples, we will assume a low-resolution screen with a 320 by 200 grid (see Figure B-18). That is, the grid is divided into 320 horizontal positions (across) and 200 vertical positions (up and down).
    A pixel coordinate is its horizontal and vertical position on the screen. The horizontal, or *x*, coordinate is first and the vertical, or *y*, coordinate is second. The coordinates of the *origin* of the grid, the upper left corner of

PROGRAMMING CONCEPTS

Graphics
Pixels
Resolution
Screen Coordinates
Relative Coordinates
Bar Charts
Nassi-Shneiderman Charts
Sound
Music

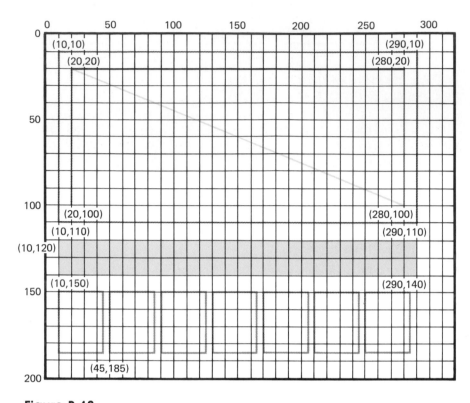

Figure B-18
Graphics-Mode Grid and Layout
The figure shows the output layout for the example LINE instructions in the text material.

You can use BASIC's graphics capabilities to produce graphic images for a wide variety of applications.
(Gerber Scientific, Inc.)

the screen, are 0,0. On some systems the origin is the lower left corner of the screen.

Creating Lines and Boxes. The coordinates in a LINE instruction specify the end points, or *range,* of a line or box. The range of a box is the coordinates of any two opposite corners. The lines and boxes resulting from example statements 20–70 above are illustrated in Figure B-18. Statements 20–40 cause horizontal, vertical, and diagonal lines to be drawn between the coordinates specified in the color specified: 1=red, 2=orange, and 3=yellow. Statement 50 causes a line to be drawn from the current position of the cursor (280,100) to the coordinates specified (280,20). Since the x coordinate is unchanged, the result is a vertical line.

The "B" option at the end of the LINE statement at 60 causes a box to be drawn in the range specified (see Figure B-18). The "BF" option at the end of the LINE statement at 70 causes a box filled with color 1 to be drawn in the range specified (see Figure B-18).

Relative Coordinates. The concept of relative coordinates is illustrated in example statements 80–100. When coordinates are prefaced by STEP, the position depicted is *relative* to the last coordinate position referenced. In statement 90 above, the second endpoint is relative to the first; that is, it is always 35 positions to the right and 35 positions down (a negative *y* coordinate signifies down) form the first endpoint. For the first execution of the loop, the range of the box is (10,150)–(45,185). Repeated execution of the loop causes seven equal-size boxes of color 2 to be created along the horizontal (see Figure B-18).

PRINT. We, of course, are very familiar with the PRINT instruction, but we have not used it to create graphic images. When in text mode, the PRINT instruction can be used in conjunction with the LOCATION instruction (see "Other Instructions" below) and the CHR$ function to produce any of a variety of special characters on the screen. The special characters associated with ASCII codes vary between computers. A few of the possible characters are illustrated in Figure B-19.

Figure B-19
Example Special Characters
Many special characters and symbols can be displayed by designating the decimal ASCII code in a PRINT CHR$( ) instruction.

Format: PRINT CHR$(ASCII code)

Example: FOR I = 10 TO 60
             LOCATE 20,I
             PRINT CHR$(219)
             NEXT I

The above loop causes the ASCII character of decimal value 219 (■) to be displayed across row 20. The result is a thick solid line starting at column 10 and ending after column 60 (see explanation of LOCATE instruction). With a little imagination, you can be very creative with these special characters.

SOUND. The SOUND statement generates a tone of a particular *frequency* and *duration*.

Format: SOUND frequency, duration

Example: LET FREQ = 440
             LET DURATION = 100
             SOUND FREQ, DURATION

A tone of 440 cycles per second (the A above middle C on a piano) is sounded for 100 time units. A time unit is a fraction of a second and could vary from one computer to the next.

PLAY. The PLAY instruction uses the sound output capability of computers to play music.

Format: PLAY string variable or constant

Example:
A$ = "DDAABBA2"
B$ = "GGF+F+EED2"
C$ = "AAGGF+F+E2"
PLAY "MN T120 O3 L4 XA$; XB$; XC$; XC$; MS T240 O4 XA$; GGF+F+P4ED2"

In the discussion that follows, we will assume some knowledge of music concepts and notation. The character string following the PLAY is simply BASIC's version of standard music notation. We still have quarter notes, rests, and sharps, but they are just written in a different manner.

The following characters have a special meaning when placed in the string in a PLAY instruction.

A–G, + −	Notes to be played. A plus or minus following the note indicates a sharp or a flat (e.g., F+ is F sharp).
On	Sets the octave. Octaves (the notes C up to B) are numbered (value of n) 0–6, with octave 3 beginning at middle C.
Ln	Sets length of notes. The notes following an Ln character combination take on a certain length (duration) unless otherwise specified on a note by note basis. The value of n ranges from 1 to 64. L8 specifies eighth notes, L4 specifies quarter notes, L2 specifies half notes, and so on. Override the L specification by placing the length after a particular note. For example, the string "L4ABCD" results in four quarter notes being played, and the string "L4ABC2D" results in two quarter notes, a half note C, and a quarter note being played.
Pn	A rest. The Pn character combination causes a pause of length n.
Tn	Sets the tempo. The value of n is the number of quarter notes per minute.
MN, ML, MS	Sets the way the notes are played. MN is for normal duration; ML is for legato; and MS is for staccato.
X	"Plays" the following character string. The contents of the string variable following an X are played.

In the example, a variation on "Twinkle Twinkle Little Star" is "played" in the key of D (two sharps at F and C). Contrast the BASIC notation to the

---

MEMORY BITS

STRING CONSTANT CHARACTERS FOR PLAY INSTRUCTION

A–G, + −	Notes to be played.
On	Sets octave.
Ln	Sets length of notes.
Pn	A rest.
Tn	Sets tempo.
MN, ML, MS	Sets the way notes are played.
X	"Plays" the following character string.

Figure B-20
A Variation on "Twinkle Twinkle Little Star" in Music Notation
This tune is translated into BASIC notation in the PLAY instruction example in the text material.

musical notation in Figure B-20. Blanks in the string are ignored and the semicolons are required when using an X followed by a string. In the song, two character strings are repeated several times. The last four measures are played twice as fast, in staccato, and an octave higher.

INKEY$.   INKEY$ is both an instruction and a variable. INKEY$ accepts a single character from the keyboard into the variable INKEY$.

Format: INKEY$

Example: 10 PRINT "Press any key to clear the graph and continue."
            20 IF INKEY$ = "" THEN 20

INKEY$ is automatically set to the null character ("") initially. Because IN-KEY$ = "", statement 20 above is itself a loop until a character is entered from the keyboard to give INKEY$ a value other than null. Upon encountering statement 20, the program enters an "infinite loop." This is a good way to pause processing or hold a graph on the screen until the user is ready to continue.

Other Instructions

LOCATE.   The LOCATE instruction positions the cursor on the text-mode screen at the display row and column specified.

Format: LOCATE row, column

Example: LOCATE 22,30

The LOCATE instruction deals with the rows and columns in which characters are displayed, not with pixels and coordinates, as in graphics mode. A typical screen has 24 or 25 rows and 80 columns. The LOCATE instruction positions the *text cursor*, as opposed to *graphics cursor,* at one of the 24 or 25 rows (its vertical position) and one of the 80 columns (its horizontal position). The example LOCATE instruction positions the cursor at row 22 (from the top) and column 30 (from the left). Notice that the vertical designator (row) is first in the LOCATE instruction. In the LINE instruction, the horizontal designator (*x* coordinate) is first.

The LOCATE instruction is handy for displaying titles and labels on graphs that are produced in graphics mode.

SCREEN.   A complete explanation of the SCREEN instruction is beyond the scope of this book. The SCREEN instruction statement sets a variety of screen attributes, including setting the computer to text or graphics mode. The fundamental use of the SCREEN instruction is illustrated in Example Program #13.

B-29   EXAMPLE PROGRAM #13: GRAPHICS

Graphics adds another dimension to the presentation of data and information. The graphic images that you produce on the screen are not only visually stimulating, but they can convey information very effectively. It is much easier to detect trends and proportions from a bar or pie graph than it is from data that are in tabular form (rows and columns).

Graphics, however, is the most *machine-dependent* processing activity. What you can and cannot do depends very much on what kind of hardware you have. For example, most mainframe computers support graphics, but if you do not have a graphics workstation, you are limited in what you can do. To get graphics capability on some microcomputers, you may need to purchase an optional circuit board. Options for monitors include color and high resolution. Because there are so many hardware variables, the syntax for BASIC graphics instructions has evolved to using the capabilities of a particular hardware environment. This means that the BASIC graphics instructions vary a lot; therefore, we'll confine our discussion to fundamental graphics operations.

In Example Program #13, a *bar graph* is produced that graphically illustrates the end-of-term class averages for each of three instructors. The term grade for any number of students can be entered for each class (see the interactive session). By now you are already familiar with the concepts illustrated in Modules 1.1—Initialization, 1.2—Accept Instructor Data, and 1.3—Accept Student Data, so we'll focus on Module 1.4—Draw Graph.

Module 1.4—Draw Graph.   This module calls six subroutines that process the data and draw the bar graph (see the interactive session).

Module 1.4.1—Initialize Graphics Screen.   The SCREEN instruction (4170) selects medium-resolution graphics as the processing mode. Other options are text mode and high-resolution graphics mode.

EXAMPLE PROGRAM #13

This program accepts student grade data for three instructors, then prepares and displays a bar graph showing class averages for the courses of each instructor.

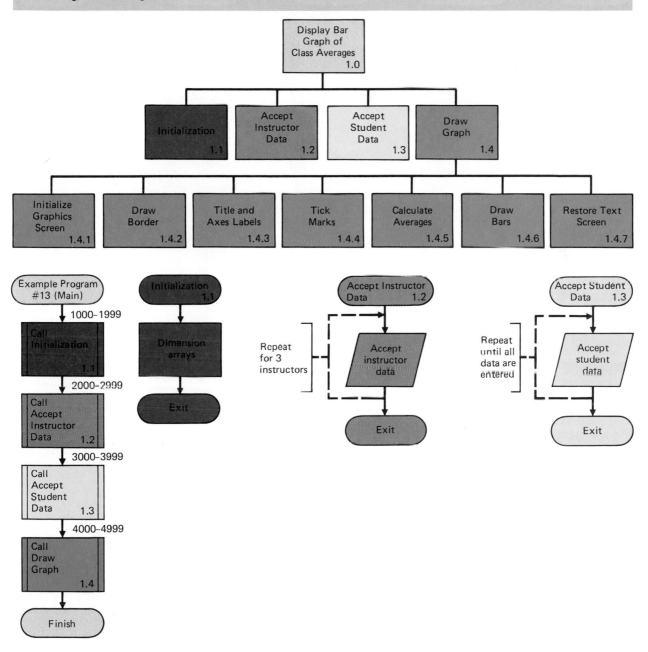

continued

Example Program 13 continued

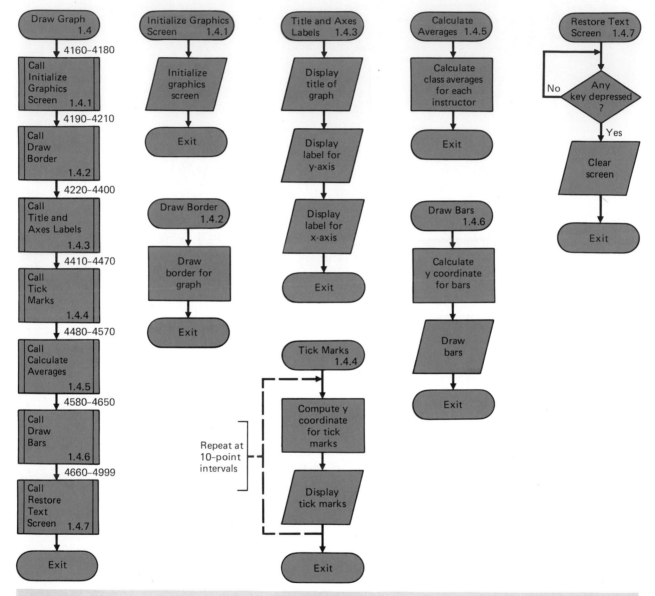

```
     2   REM            **** Example Program #13 ****
     4   REM   Description:
     6   REM      This program accepts student grade data for three instructors,
     8   REM      then prepares and displays a bar graph showing class averages
    10   REM      for the courses of each instructor.
    12   REM   Variables list:
    14   REM      GRADE( , )              - Grade array (instructor,student)
    16   REM      INAME$()                - Instructor name array
    18   REM      NUMSTUDENTS()           - Number of students in each class
    20   REM      AVERAGE()               - Array for class averages
    22   REM      COUNT                   - Index for loop control
    24   REM      STUDENT                 - Student index
    26   REM      INSTRUCTOR              - Instructor index
    28   REM      YPOINT                  - Y coordinate of tick marks
    30   REM      SCALE                   - Scaling factor
    32   REM      Y1, Y2, Y3              - Y coordinates of upper-left corner of bars
    99   REM
```

```
100   REM   <<<< Start Main >>>>
105   REM
110   REM   Call Module 1.1 - Initialization
120   GOSUB 1000
130   REM   Call Module 1.2 - Accept Instructor Data
140   GOSUB 2000
150   REM   Call Module 1.3 - Accept Student Data
160   GOSUB 3000
170   REM   Call Module 1.4 - Draw Graph
180   GOSUB 4000
190   END
200   REM   <<<< End Main >>>>
999   REM
1000  REM   ==== Module 1.1 - Initialization
1010  DIM GRADE(3,50), INAME$(3), NUMSTUDENTS(3), AVERAGE(3)
1999  RETURN
2000  REM   ==== Module 1.2 - Accept Instructor Data
2010  FOR COUNT = 1 TO 3
2020    PRINT "Enter last name of instructor #";COUNT;": ";
2030    INPUT "", INAME$(COUNT)
2040    INPUT "How many students does this instructor have";NUMSTUDENTS(COUNT)
2050    PRINT
2060  NEXT COUNT
2070  INPUT "Enter the course title (ie. CS105): ",COURSE$
2080  PRINT
2999  RETURN
3000  REM   ==== Module 1.3 - Accept Student Data
3010  FOR INSTRUCTOR = 1 TO 3
3020    PRINT
3030    PRINT "Enter grades for students of ";INAME$(INSTRUCTOR)
3040    FOR STUDENT = 1 TO NUMSTUDENTS(INSTRUCTOR)
3050      PRINT "Enter final grade for student #";STUDENT;": ";
3060      INPUT "", GRADE(INSTRUCTOR,STUDENT)
3070    NEXT STUDENT
3080  NEXT INSTRUCTOR
3999  RETURN
4000  REM   ==== Module 1.4 - Draw Graph
4010  REM   Call Module 1.4.1 - Initialize Graphics Screen
4020  GOSUB 4160
4030  REM   Call Module 1.4.2 - Draw Border
4040  GOSUB 4190
4050  REM   Call Module 1.4.3 - Title and Axes Labels
4060  GOSUB 4220
4070  REM   Call Module 1.4.4 - Tick Marks
4080  GOSUB 4410
4090  REM   Call Module 1.4.5 - Calculate Averages
4100  GOSUB 4480
4110  REM   Call Module 1.4.6 - Draw Bars
4120  GOSUB 4580
4130  REM   Call Module 1.4.7 - Restore Text Screen
4140  GOSUB 4660
4150  RETURN
4160  REM   ==== Module 1.4.1 - Initialize Graphics Screen
4170  SCREEN 1   ' Medium resolution
4180  RETURN
4190  REM   ==== Module 1.4.2 - Draw Border
4200  LINE (20,20) - (299,170),3,B
4210  RETURN
4220  REM   ==== Module 1.4.3 - Title and Axes Labels
4230  LOCATE 1,4
4240  PRINT COURSE$;" - Averages by Instructor"
4250  LOCATE 5,1:PRINT "A"
4260  LOCATE 6,1:PRINT "v"
4270  LOCATE 7,1:PRINT "e"
4280  LOCATE 8,1:PRINT "r"
4290  LOCATE 9,1:PRINT "a"
4300  LOCATE 10,1:PRINT "g"
4310  LOCATE 11,1:PRINT "e"
4320  LOCATE 13,1:PRINT "G"
4330  LOCATE 14,1:PRINT "r"
```

continued

```
4340 LOCATE 15,1:PRINT "a"
4350 LOCATE 16,1:PRINT "d"
4360 LOCATE 17,1:PRINT "e"
4370 LOCATE 23,7:PRINT INAME$(1);
4380 LOCATE 23,18:PRINT INAME$(2);
4390 LOCATE 23,29:PRINT INAME$(3);
4400 RETURN
4410 REM  ==== Module 1.4.4 - Tick Marks
4420 SCALE = 1.5
4430 FOR G = 0 TO 100 STEP 10
4440   YPOINT = 170 - SCALE * G
4450   LINE (15,YPOINT) - (20,YPOINT)
4460 NEXT G
4470 RETURN
4480 REM  ==== Module 1.4.5 - Calculate Averages
4490 REM
4500 FOR INSTRUCTOR = 1 TO 3
4510   INSTRUCTORSUM = 0
4520   FOR STUDENT = 1 TO NUMSTUDENTS(INSTRUCTOR)
4530     INSTRUCTORSUM = INSTRUCTORSUM + GRADE(INSTRUCTOR,STUDENT)
4540   NEXT STUDENT
4550   AVERAGE(INSTRUCTOR) = INSTRUCTORSUM / NUMSTUDENTS(INSTRUCTOR)
4560 NEXT INSTRUCTOR
4570 RETURN
4580 REM  ==== Module 1.4.6 - Draw Bars
4590 REM  Calculate Y coordinates for bars
4600 Y1 = 170 - SCALE * AVERAGE(1)
4610 Y2 = 170 - SCALE * AVERAGE(2)
4620 Y3 = 170 - SCALE * AVERAGE(3)
4630 LINE (43,Y1) - (89,170),1,BF
4640 LINE (133,Y2) - (179,170),2,BF
4650 LINE (223,Y3) - (269,170),3,BF
4660 RETURN
4670 REM  ==== Module 1.4.7 - Restore Text Screen
4680 REM  Wait until a key is pressed to clear graph
4690 IF INKEY$ = "" THEN 4690
4700 CLS
4999 RETURN
```

```
run
Enter last name of instructor # 1 : Finley
How many students does this instructor have? 3

Enter last name of instructor # 2 : Dow
How many students does this instructor have? 2

Enter last name of instructor # 3 : West
How many students does this instructor have? 2

Enter the course title (i.e. CS105) : HIST 309


Enter grades for students of Finley
Enter final grade for student # 1 : 83.2
Enter final grade for student # 2 : 91.8
Enter final grade for student # 3 : 75

Enter grades for students of Dow
Enter final grade for student # 1 : 71
Enter final grade for student # 2 : 83.7

Enter grades for students of West
Enter final grade for student # 1 : 75.4
Enter final grade for student # 2 : 86
```

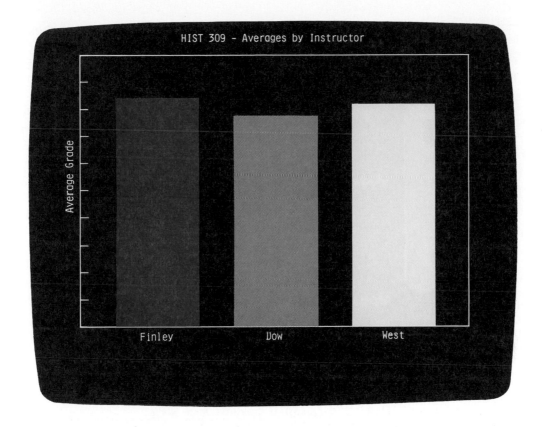

Module 1.4.2—Draw Border.   The LINE instruction at 4200 creates a box
which serves as the border for the bar graph. The x, y coordinates identify
the range, which is any two opposite corners of the box.

Module 1.4.3—Title and Axes Labels.   The LOCATE instructions position
the text cursor at a particular row and column. The title is printed beginning
at row 1, column 4 (statement 4230–4240). The LOCATE/PRINT combination is also used to display the labels for both axes.

Module 1.4.4—Tick Marks.   In this module, tick marks are added to the
y axis at 10-point increments. It is sometimes necessary to make an adjustment
to the value of the data to be graphed in order to make use of available
screen space. The maximum possible class average is 100, but the bar is to
be extended over 150 vertical coordinate positions (from 20 to 170, or 150
positions); therefore a scaling factor of 1.5 (150/100) is used (statement
4420).

Eleven tick marks, which are actually short horizontal lines, are drawn
on the y axis in a FOR/NEXT loop (4430–4460). On the first pass through
the loop, a line is drawn from coordinate positions 15,170 to 20,170 (bottom
tick mark). On the next pass, a line is drawn from 15,155 to 20,155, and
so on.

Module 1.4.5—Calculate Averages.   In this module, the end-of-term class
averages are calculated in nested FOR/NEXT loops. The outer loop (4500–
4560) is repeated for each instructor, or three times. The inner loop (4520–

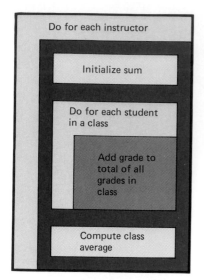

Figure B-21
Nassi-Shneiderman Chart
Nassi-Shneiderman charts are
handy for depicting the logic
of nested loop structures.

4540) is repeated a variable number of times, depending on the number of students (NUMSTUDENTS) in a particular class. In the inner loop, a summation instruction (4530) calculates the sum of all grades for a particular instructor. The class average is calculated in the outer loop and stored in the array AVERAGE (4550).

The **Nassi-Shneiderman chart** in Figure B-21 is provided to illustrate an alternative method for depicting the logic of the nested loop structures in Module 1.4.5. Compare the Nassi-Shneiderman chart of Figure B-21 with the flowchart for Module 1.4.5.

Module 1.4.6—Draw Bars.   Now for the fun part. All drawing and calculating thus far are done in preparation for the module. First, the *y* coordinates, which designate the height of the bars, are determined (4590–4610). These values define the upper left corner of the boxes that create the bars. The opposite corner is to the right and on the *x* axis. The LINE instructions (4620–4640) draw the boxes and fill them with three different colors (see the interactive session).

Module 1.4.7—Restore Text Screen.   The statement loop at 4680 causes the bar graph to stay on the screen until the user presses any key on the keyboard (see INKEY$ explanation in the instruction set for this module). The CLS at 4690 clears the screen in preparation for further text-mode processing.

B-30   EXAMPLE PROGRAM #14: SOUND AND MUSIC

Many workstations and microcomputers are being equipped with sound-producing speakers for sound and music output. We, as programmers, can piece together sounds of particular *frequencies* and *durations* to create interesting sounds, such as sirens, beeps, and warning signals, and we can even play music.

Example Program #14 demonstrates the use of sound and music instructions. Within the Main driver, three modules are called that produce a siren-type sound and give the user an opportunity to "play" a fanfare any number of times.

Module 1.1—Sound Siren.   A SOUND instruction is used in conjunction with several loop structures to create a siren-type sound. Within the main loop (1010–1080), the frequencies of the sounds produced are raised (1020–1040) then lowered (1050–1070). When the main loop is executed repeatedly, the frequencies oscillate and the result is a siren-type sound.

Module 1.2—Play Fanfare.   The PLAY instruction allows you to "play" the melodic line to an aria from Bizet's *Carmen*, a pop song, or your own composition. In Example Program #14, the character string following the PLAY instruction is the BASIC representation of the "trumpet" fanfare shown in musical notation in Figure B-22.

Figure B-22
Fanfare of Example Program #14 in Music Notation

EXAMPLE PROGRAM #14

This program sounds a siren, then plays a "trumpet" fanfare.

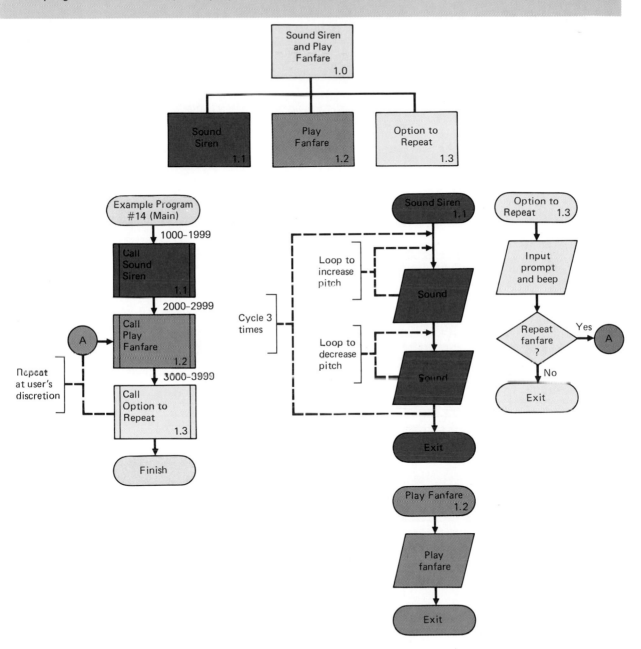

continued

Example Program 14 continued

```
2    REM          **** Example Program #14 ****
4    REM   Description:
6    REM      This program sounds a siren, then plays a "trumpet" fanfare.
8    REM   Variables list:
10   REM    COUNT                - Index for loop control
12   REM    PITCH                - Pitch of tone
14   REM    FANFARE$             - Music string for fanfare
99   REM
100  REM   <<<< Start Main >>>>
105  REM
110  REM   Call Module 1.1 - Sound Siren
120  GOSUB 1000
130  REM   Repeat fanfare while REPEAT$ is not equal to "NO"
140  WHILE REPEAT$ <> "NO"
150     REM   Call Module 1.2 - Play Fanfare
160     GOSUB 2000
170     REM   Call Module 1.3 - Option to Repeat
180     GOSUB 3000
190  WEND
200  END
210  REM   <<<< End Main >>>>
999  REM
1000 REM   ==== Module 1.1 - Sound Siren
1010 FOR COUNT = 1 TO 3
1020    FOR PITCH = 500 TO 1000 STEP 10
1030       SOUND PITCH,.4
1040    NEXT PITCH
1050    FOR PITCH = 1000 TO 500 STEP -10
1060       SOUND PITCH,.4
1070    NEXT PITCH
1080 NEXT COUNT
1999 RETURN
2000 REM   ==== Module 1.2 - Play Fanfare
2010 FANFARE$="MS T60 O3 L8 FF24F24F24FA O4 CC24C24C24C O3 AB- O4 D24C24 O3
ML B-24A O4 GF F4P8"
2030 PLAY FANFARE$
2999 RETURN
3000 REM   ==== Module 1.3 - Option to Repeat
3010 PRINT
3020 PRINT "Would you like to play the fanfare again (Y or N) ";
3030 REM   Sound beep
3040 SOUND 700,.5
3050 SOUND 32767,.25
3060 SOUND 800,.5
3070 INPUT ANSWER$
3080 IF ANSWER$ = "N" OR ANSWER$ = "n" THEN REPEAT$="NO"
3999 RETURN
```

The first portion of the string (2010), "MS T60 O3 L8," defines how the fanfare is to be played. The MS causes the notes to be played staccato. The tempo (T60) is set at 60 beats (quarter notes) per minute and play begins at the third octave (O3). Since most of the notes are eighth notes, the length of the note is set to L8. Triplets replacing the time span of an eighth note are given a length of 24 (3∗8). The ML causes the last three notes to be played legato. A pause of length 8 (P8) rounds out the last measure.

Module 1.3—Option to Repeat.   In this module, a two-tone "beep" is sounded to alert the user of an option to play the fanfare again. Such sounds are often used to alert users of a need for data entry and of erroneous data entry.

(By permission of Bob Glueckstein)

B-31   BUILDING ON A BASIC FOUNDATION _____

After studying and practicing BASIC, you should have acquired a solid foundation in BASIC and become a pretty good programmer. BASIC is a powerful and dynamic language, and we have covered only part of it.

There are half again as many instructions that we did not cover. Depending on the version of BASIC you are using, you may have: instructions that permit input from light pens, joysticks, and the mouse; a family of instructions, called MAT instructions, that permit manipulation of matrices; a family of graphics instructions that lets you create a variety of images (e.g., ellipses) on the screen; and much more. You can even build on the instructions you have learned by investigating their more sophisticated uses.

Many workstations and micros have function keys, or "soft"(ware) keys. BASIC permits you to write program instructions that are activated when a particular function key (e.g., F1) is pressed. This capability gives you considerable flexibility in designing the program to be "user friendly."

We were able to illustrate and discuss only a few example uses of each instruction. As a rule of thumb: if you can imagine it, you can write a program to do it.

If you wish to pursue BASIC in greater depth on your own, you now have the background necessary to go directly to the *BASIC Reference Manual*. Each version of BASIC has such a guide. Several reference copies are usually made available for student use in the computer center or computer laboratory. And, of course, if you have your own computer, chances are it comes with BASIC and a *BASIC Reference Manual*.

REVIEW EXERCISES (Learning Module VIII) _____

BASIC Instructions and Concepts

1.   Identify the syntax error(s) in each of the following instructions.
    (a)   10 LINE (20,40)—(40,60)—(60,80)
    (b)   10 FOR I=1 TO 50: PRINT CHR$(0101010);: NEXT I
    (c)   10 LOCATE(24,270)
    (d)   10 PLAY "MS—T40—L2—CDEFGFEDC"
    (e)   10 SOUND FREQ, 85
2.   Write the instructions that would draw a border around the screen that is 25 pixels wide and of color 2.
3.   What is the relationship between pixels and screen resolution?

4. The following instructions create the "board" for what game?

```
100 LINE (50,70)–(230,70)
200 LINE (50,130)–(230,130)
300 LINE (110,10)–(110,190)
400 LINE (170,10)–(170,190)
```

5. What characters are displayed by the following instructions?

```
100 FOR I=65 TO 90
200 PRINT CHR$(I);
300 NEXT I
```

6. What special characters in a PLAY instruction would result in the notes being played in the fifth octave, in stacatto, at a tempo of 200 beats per minute?

7. What single instruction would hold a graph on the screen until the user entered a "C"?

Example Program #13

8. Assume that the characters in the y-axis label (Average Grade) were individually defined in DATA statements in Module 1.1—Initialization.

```
1020 DATA "A", "V", "E", "R," "A", "G", "E", "   "
1030 DATA "G", "R", "A", "D", "E"
```

How would you modify the program to print the y-axis label with only one LOCATE instruction? Write the code that would replace statements 4250–4360.

9. What is the purpose of statement 4690?

10. What is accomplished in the inner loop in Module 1.4.5?

11. How would you modify the program to include numerical labels on the y-axis?

Example Program #14

12. How would the siren sound be affected if the duration of the sounds produced were revised from .4 to 1.2?

13. How would you modify the program such that the fanfare would play in half the time?

14. Musicians often add embellishments to the written music. One embellishment is the trill. In a trill, the note and the note above are alternated in rapid succession. How would you modify the program to trill the last note in the fanfare?

BASIC PROGRAMMING ASSIGNMENTS

1. Write a program that "plays" the melodic line of at least eight measures of one of your favorite tunes. Give the "musician" that executes the program an option to repeat the tune.

2. Write a program that permits the user to define the frequency and duration for each of three successive sounds. The user should select from these menu options: (a) listen to the sounds, (b) change the frequency and duration of the three sounds, and (c) exit the program. Give the sounds these initial frequencies and durations: 1800,2 ; 800,1 ; and 2500,3.

3. An arpeggio is the playing in sequence of the individual notes in a chord. Write a program to play arpeggios of a major chord (first, third, and fifth note) over three octaves (up, then down for each arpeggio), first in the key of C (i.e., CEGCEGCEGECGECGEC), then in G, then in F, then in C again.

4. Repeat programming assignment 4 of Learning Module V, except this time use graphics capabilities to produce a more sophisticated bar chart. The bar chart should be titled and have borders, labels for the axes, and solid horizontal bars to represent project schedules.

B-32   A COMPARISON

An American National Standard (ANS) for Minimal BASIC was established in 1978. In 1985 a "new" standard for ANS BASIC was introduced. The original standard describes what is now a relatively primitive form of BASIC. Without any standards for the advanced BASIC features, over a hundred slightly different versions, or dialects, of BASIC evolved. As a result, a BASIC program written for one computer may need to be revised before it can be run on another computer.

The 1985 standard describes a modern BASIC. The existence of an up-to-date standard will encourage developers of future BASICs to conform to ANS BASIC. In a few years, we won't be so concerned about the differences between BASIC dialects. If you write a program using a BASIC that conforms to the new standard, the program will be mostly machine independent; that is, a single BASIC program can be run on a variety of different computers.

ANS BASIC is more an extension of the BASIC presented in this book than a revision. Most of the BASIC that you have learned to date is the same as, or very similar to, the new standard. The following point summarize the major differences.

1. The new standard contains sophisticated instructions that facilitate the development of structured programs.

2. The new standard discourages the use of statement numbers in favor of named subroutines. This, of course, makes the GOTO and GOSUB series of statements obsolete.

3. The new standard permits subroutines to be internal or external. External subroutines are defined, called, and stored as separate program units. In most current versions of BASIC, the subroutines are internal; that is, they are included in the same program as the main calling module.

Dr. Thomas Kurtz (second from left) and Dr. John Kemeny (seated) created the BASIC programming language over 20 years ago. Kurtz, Kemeny, and other computer scientists in this photo recently joined forces to create a modern version of BASIC. They call this version, which is based on the new BASIC standard, True BASIC. Example Program #15 in this learning module is written in True BASIC.
(True BASIC Inc.)

The new standard also offers numerous enhancements to the individual instructions. New standards are defined for the precision of numeric constants and the maximum lengths of string constants. Graphics capabilities are substantially enhanced. There is greater flexibility in identifying variables, functions, subroutines, and so on. For example, all characters in an identifier are significant and the underscore(_) is a valid character (e.g., Quiz_Average).

B-33   BASIC INSTRUCTION SET: LEARNING MODULE IX GROUP

Those ANS BASIC instructions that help facilitate the writing of structured programs are presented below. These instructions are especially formulated for the efficient handling of loop and decision structures (see the chapter on "Programming Concepts") and subroutines.

Control Instructions

DO/LOOP.   The DO/LOOP permits both DO WHILE and DO UNTIL loop structures.

Format: DO WHILE expression   relational   operator   expression
                statements
                   :
            LOOP

            DO
                statements
                   :
            LOOP UNTIL expression   relational operator   expression

Examples: DO WHILE Count <= 50
                  statements
                     :
              LOOP

              DO
                  statements
                     :
              LOOP UNTIL Count > 50

The DO WHILE structure is similar to the WHILE/WEND instruction pair introduced in Learning Module III: Adding to Your Foundation. The LOOP UNTIL structure places the test-on-condition at the end of the loop.

IF/THEN/ELSE

Format: IF expression   relational operator   expression THEN
           statements
              ⋮
           ELSE
             statements
              ⋮
           END IF

Example: IF Count = 50 THEN
              LET Sum = Sum + 1
              PRINT "TOTAL IS"; Sum
            ELSE
              LET Sum1 = Sum1 + 1
              PRINT "SUBTOTAL IS "; Sum1
            END IF

With the IF/THEN/ELSE instructions you can specify that a block of instructions be executed if the test-on-condition is true and you can specify that another block of instructions be executed if the condition is false. In either instance, once the appropriate block is executed, the next instruction is the one following the END IF.

A more sophisticated variation of the IF/THEN/ELSE instruction has an ELSEIF clause that permits you to make a series of test-on-conditions. The use of this clause is illustrated in Example Program #15.

SELECT CASE.   Like the IF/THEN/ELSEIF instructions, the SELECT CASE permits you to define a series of instruction blocks that are to be executed based on a test-on-condition. The difference is that each "case" is evaluated against the expression defined to the right of SELECT CASE.

Format: SELECT CASE expression
              CASE case-item
                statements
                   ⋮
              CASE case-item
                statements
                   ⋮
              CASE ELSE
                statements
                   ⋮
            END SELECT

Example: SELECT CASE Type_Employee$
                CASE "H"
                  PRINT "Employee is hourly"
                CASE "C"
                  PRINT "Employee is on commission"
                CASE ELSE
                  PRINT "Employee is salaried"
             END SELECT

In the above example, the block (in this instance, only one instruction) following the first "case" is executed if Type_Employee$ = "H". A block is executed only if a case test is positive. After the tests, processing continues after the END SELECT.

SUB/END SUB and CALL.   The SUB/END SUB instruction pair defines an internal subroutine. The subroutine is called by a CALL instruction.

Format: SUB subroutine identifier
               statements
                  ⋮
            END SUB
            CALL subroutine identifier

Example: SUB Get_Message
                INPUT Message$
             END SUB
             SUB Display_Message
                PRINT "The message is: "; Message$
             END SUB
             REM === Main Program ===
             CALL Get_Message
             CALL Display_Message
             END

The above example is a program unit with two internal subroutines and a main calling module (at bottom). Processing skips over the subroutines and begins with the first CALL.

B-34   EXAMPLE PROGRAM #15: STRUCTURED PROGRAMMING WITHOUT GOSUBS AND LINE NUMBERS

Example Program #15 accomplishes the same processing activities as Example Program #5, except for one added twist. Both programs compute the final numeric grade and assign a letter grade for any number of students. Example Program #15 goes one step further and evaluates a student's progress over the term. The only difference in the fundamental *logic* of the two

EXAMPLE PROGRAM #15

This program computes the final numeric grade and assigns a letter grade for any number of students. The instructor assigns weighting factors to each of three test scores. Student progress during the term is evaluated. This program is written using True BASIC, an ANS BASIC.

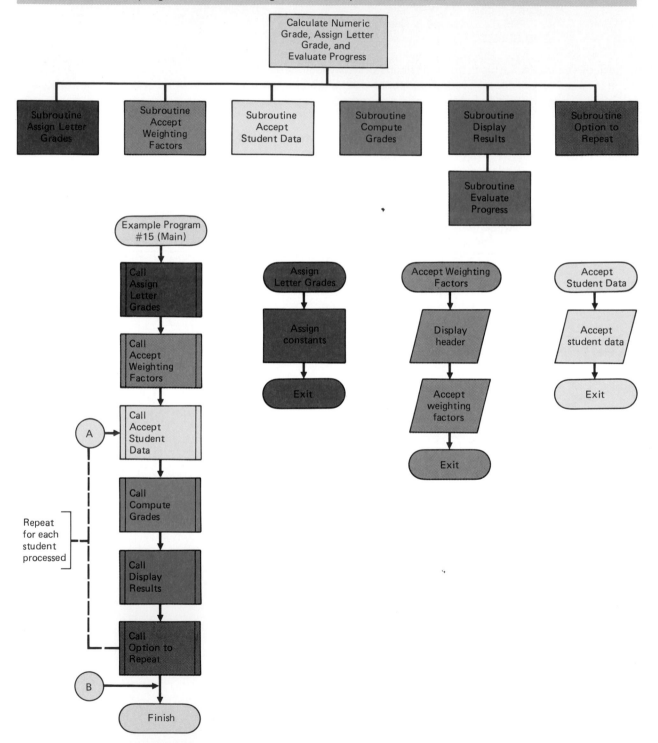

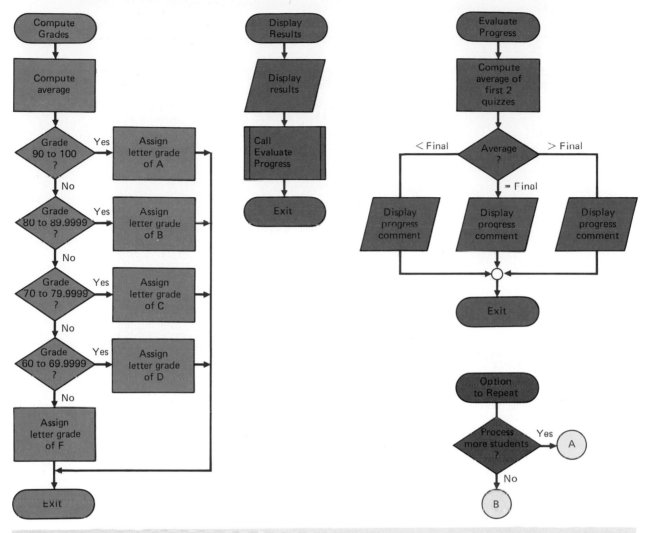

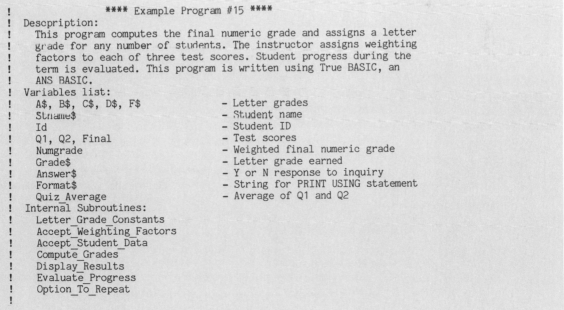

```
!                    **** Example Program #15 ****
! Descriprtion:
!   This program computes the final numeric grade and assigns a letter
!   grade for any number of students. The instructor assigns weighting
!   factors to each of three test scores. Student progress during the
!   term is evaluated. This program is written using True BASIC, an
!   ANS BASIC.
! Variables list:
!   A$, B$, C$, D$, F$              - Letter grades
!   Stname$                        - Student name
!   Id                             - Student ID
!   Q1, Q2, Final                  - Test scores
!   Numgrade                       - Weighted final numeric grade
!   Grade$                         - Letter grade earned
!   Answer$                        - Y or N response to inquiry
!   Format$                        - String for PRINT USING statement
!   Quiz_Average                   - Average of Q1 and Q2
! Internal Subroutines:
!   Letter_Grade_Constants
!   Accept_Weighting_Factors
!   Accept_Student_Data
!   Compute_Grades
!   Display_Results
!   Evaluate_Progress
!   Option_To_Repeat
!
```

continued

Example Program 15 continued

```
SUB Letter_Grade_Constants
!   Subroutine to assign letter grade constants to variables
READ A$,B$,C$,D$,F$
DATA "A","B","C","D","F"
END SUB

SUB Accept_Weighting_Factors
!   Subroutine for accepting weighting factors from keyboard
PRINT "   ---------- Grade Assignment Program ----------"
PRINT "Separate multiple entries by commas."
PRINT
INPUT PROMPT "Enter weighting factors for quiz1, quiz2, and final? ":W1,W2,Wf
END SUB

SUB Accept_Student_Data
!   Subroutine for accepting individual student data
PRINT
INPUT PROMPT "Student name? ":Stname$
INPUT PROMPT "Student ID? ":ID
INPUT PROMPT "Enter grades for quiz1, quiz2, and final? ":Q1,Q2,Final
END SUB

SUB Compute_Grades
!   Subroutine to compute numeric grade and assign a letter grade
!          for the student
LET Numgrade = W1*Q1 + W2*Q2 + Wf*Final
SELECT CASE Numgrade
    CASE 90 TO 100
        LET Grade$=A$
    CASE 80 TO 89.9999
        LET Grade$=B$
    CASE 70 TO 79.9999
        LET Grade$=C$
    CASE 60 TO 69.9999
        LET Grade$=D$
    CASE ELSE
        LET Grade$=F$
END SELECT
END SUB

SUB Display_Results
!   Subroutine to display grades (Both numeric and letter grades)
LET Format$="<##########     #####             ###.##             #"
PRINT
PRINT "Student Name","ID Number","Numeric Grade","Letter Grade"
PRINT USING Format$: Stname$,ID,Numgrade,Grade$
PRINT
CALL Evaluate_Progress
PRINT
END SUB

SUB Evaluate_Progress
!   Subroutine to evaluate student progress
PRINT ,"Comments:",
LET Quiz_Average=(Q1+Q1) / 2
IF Quiz_Average < Final THEN
    PRINT "Student shows progress"
    ELSEIF Quiz_Average > Final THEN
        PRINT "Student performance dropped"
        ELSE
            PRINT "Student is consistent"
END IF
END SUB

SUB Option_To_Repeat
!   Subroutine to ask if there are more students
INPUT PROMPT "More students? (Y or N) " : Answer$
END SUB
```

```
!  <<<< Start Main >>>>
CALL Letter_Grade_Constants
CALL Accept_Weighting_Factors
!  Do while there are more students to be processed
DO WHILE Answer$ <> "N" AND Answer$ <> "n"
   CALL Accept_Student_Data
   CALL Compute_Grades
   CALL Display_Results
   CALL Option_To_Repeat
LOOP
END
```

```
run
     --------- Grade Assignment Program ---------
Separate multiple entries by commas.

Enter weighting factor for quiz1, quiz2, and final? .3,.3,.4

Student name? Charles Roth
Student ID? 46912
Enter grades for quiz1, quiz2, and final? 73,91,85

Student Name      ID Number   Numeric Grade Letter Grade
Charles Roth      46912           83.20           B
                  Comments:   Student shows progress

More students? (Y or N) y

Student name? Tina Thomas
Student ID? 58843
Enter grades for quiz1, quiz2, and final? 86,85,78

Student Name      ID Number   Numeric Grade Letter Grade
Tina Thomas       58843           83.40           B
                  Comments:   Student performance dropped
```

```
More students? (Y or N) y

Student name? Wayne Evans
Student ID? 66941
Enter grades for quiz1, quiz2, and final? 66,84,75

Student Name      ID Number   Numeric Grade Letter Grade
Wayne Evans       66941           75.00           C
                  Comments:   Student is consistent

More students? (Y or N) n
Ok
```

programs is the add-on subroutine, Evaluate_Progress (compare structure charts), but the *implementation* of the logic is substantially different. Portions of the program that illustrate instructions presented in the previous section are discussed below.

Driver Program.   In ANS BASIC, subroutines must be defined before they are called; therefore, the Main program is placed at the end. Each student is processed in a DO WHILE loop. The loop is repeated while Answer$ (to an option-to-repeat inquiry) equals anything but "N" or "n".

SUB Compute_Grades.   The SELECT CASE instruction is a natural for assigning letter grades. Each of the four "cases" is compared to Numgrade. In the first case, if Numgrade is between 90 to 100, inclusive, then Grade$ is assigned A$, or "A." If the test is false, then the block of instructions (only the LET in our example) following the first case is bypassed. Each case is tested against Numgrade in a similar manner.

SUB Display_Results.   Notice the Format$ for the PRINT USING instruction. Four format fields, both numeric and string, are defined in a single format string. The "<" in the first format field causes the student name to be left-justified when it is displayed.

The subroutine, Evaluate_Progress, is called after each student's data are displayed.

SUB Evaluate_Progress.   This subroutine evaluates a student's progress during the term by comparing the final exam results to the average of the first two exams. This is done in an IF/THEN/ELSEIF series of statements. The block of statements following the THEN clause (only the PRINT in our example) is executed IF Quiz_Average < Final. If Quiz_Average > Final, the statements following the THEN are bypassed and the ELSEIF clause is taken. When Quiz_Average = Final, the ELSE clause is taken.

ANS BASIC Summary.   Several ANS versions of BASIC were available even before the 1985 standard became official! But historically, widespread implementation of a new programming standard will take from three to five years. If history repeats itself, ANS BASIC will be the norm toward the end of the decade.

The new ANS BASIC is one of many of the never-ending stream of changes in the computer industry. A good way to keep up with the recent innovations in hardware and software is to attend a computer exposition.
(Calma Company)

REVIEW EXERCISES (LEARNING MODULE IX) _____

BASIC Instructions and Concepts

1. Identify the syntax error(s) in each of the following.
   (a) DO UNTIL I=1 TO N
   (b) IF X<Y ELSE
       X=X + 1
       END IF
   (c) SELECT CASE Total
       CASE 0–1000
   (d) SUB Procedure Routine
2. What is the difference between an internal subroutine and an external subroutine?
3. What instructions permit you to define a series of instruction blocks that are to be executed based on a test-on-condition?

Example Program #15

4. Why do you suppose the program does not have any line numbers?
5. Compare Example Program #5 and this program. Besides the addition of the Evaluate_Progress module, point out major differences between the two programs.
6. Rewrite the Compute_Grades module and replace the usage of the SELECT CASE with IF/THEN/ELSEIF.

BASIC PROGRAMMING ASSIGNMENTS _____

1. Do programming assignment 2, Learning Module IV, in ANS BASIC.
2. Do programming assignment 2, Learning Module V, in ANS BASIC.
3. Do programming assignment 4, Learning Module V, in ANS BASIC.
4. Do programming assignment 3, Learning Module IV, in ANS BASIC.

GLOSSARY

Access arm The disk drive mechanism used to position the read/write heads over the appropriate track.

Access time The time interval between the instant a computer makes a request for a transfer of data from a secondary storage device and the instant this operation is completed.

Accumulator The computer register in which the result of an arithmetic or logic operation is formed.

Acoustical coupler A device in which a telephone handset is mounted for the purpose of transmitting data over telephone lines. Used with a modem.

Ada A multipurpose, procedure-oriented language.

Address (1) A name, numeral, or label that designates a particular location in primary or secondary storage. (2) A location identifier for terminals in a computer network.

Alpha A reference to the letters of the alphabet.

Alphanumeric Pertaining to a character set that contains letters, digits, punctuation, and special symbols (related to *alpha* and *numeric*).

APL [A Programming Language] An interactive symbolic programming language used primarily for mathematical applications.

Application A problem or task to which the computer can be applied.

Application generators Fifth generation of programming languages in which programmers specify, through an interactive dialog with the system, which processing tasks are to be performed.

Applications software Software that is designed and written for a specific personal, business, or processing task.

Arithmetic and logic unit That portion of the computer that performs arithmetic and logic operations (related to *accumulator*).

Artificial Intelligence [AI] The ability of the computer to reason, to learn, to strive for self-improvement, and to simulate human sensory capabilities.

Array A programming concept that permits access to a list or table of values by the use of a single variable name.

ASCII [American Standard Code for Information Interchange] An encoding system.

Assembler language A low-level symbolic language with an instruction set that is essentially one-to-one with machine language.

Asynchronous transmission Data transmission at irregular intervals that is synchronized with start/stop bits (contrast with *synchronous transmission*).

Automatic teller machine [ATM] An automated deposit/withdrawal device used in banking.

Auxiliary storage Same as *secondary storage*.

Back-end processor A host-subordinate processor that handles administrative tasks associated with retrieval and manipulation of data (same as *data base machine*).

Backup Pertaining to equipment, procedures, or data bases that can be used to restart the system in the event of system failure.

Backup file Duplicate of an existing production file.

Badge reader An input device that reads data on badges and cards (related to *magnetic stripe*).

Bar code A graphic encoding technique in which vertical bars of varying widths are used to represent data.

BASIC A multipurpose programming language that is popular on small computer systems.

Batch processing A technique in which transactions and/or jobs are collected into groups (batched) and processed together.

Binary notation Using the binary (base two) numbering system (0, 1) for internal representation of alphanumeric data.

Bit A *binary* digit (0 or 1).

Block A group of data that is either read from or written to an I/O device in one operation.

Blocking Combining two or more records into one block.

Boot The procedure for loading the operating system to primary storage and readying a computer system for use.

BPI [Bytes per inch] A measure of data-recording density on secondary storage.

Bug A logic or syntax error in a program, a logic error in the design of a computer system, or a hardware fault.

Byte A group of adjacent bits configured to represent a character.

C A transportable programming language that can be used to develop both systems and applications software.

CAD [Computer-aided design] Use of computer graphics capabilities to aid in the design, drafting, and documentation in product and manufacturing engineering.

CAI [Computer-assisted instruction] Use of the computer as an aid in the educational process.

CAM [Computer-aided manufacturing]   A term coined to highlight the use of computers in the manufacturing process.

Carrier, common [in data communications]   A company that furnishes data communications services to the general public.

Cathode ray tube   See *CRT*.

Cell   The intersection of a particular row and column in an electronic spreadsheet.

Cell address   The location, column and row, of a cell in an electronic spreadsheet.

Central processing unit [CPU]   Same as *processor*.

Channel   The facility by which data are transmitted between locations in a computer network (e.g., workstation to host, host to printer).

Character   A unit of alphanumeric datum.

COBOL [COmmon Business Oriented Language]   A programming language used primarily for administrative information systems.

Code   (1) The rules used to translate a bit configuration to alphanumeric characters. (2) The process of compiling computer instructions in the form of a computer program. (3) The actual computer program.

Collate   To combine two or more files for processing.

COM [Computer Output Microfilm/ Microfiche]   A device that produces a microform image of a computer output on microfilm or microfiche.

Common carrier (in data communications)   See *carrier, common*.

Communications   See *data communications*.

Compatibility   (1) Pertaining to the ability of one computer to execute programs of, access the data base of, and communicate with, another computer. (2) Pertaining to the ability of a particular hardware device to interface with a particular computer.

Compile   To translate a high-level programming language, such as COBOL, to machine language in preparation for execution (compare with *interpreter*).

Compiler   Systems software that performs the compilation process.

Computer   Same as *processor*.

Computer console   That unit of a

computer system that allows operator and computer to communicate.

Computer network   An integration of computer systems, workstations, and communications links.

Computer system   A collective reference to all interconnected computing hardware, including processors, storage devices, input/output devices, and communications equipment.

Computerese   A slang term that refers to the terms and phrases associated with computers and information processing.

Concentrator   Same as *down-line processor*.

Configuration   The computer and its peripheral devices.

Contention   A line control procedure in which each workstation "contends" with other workstations for service by sending requests for service to the host processor.

Contingency plan   A plan that details what to do in case an event drastically disrupts the operation of a computer center.

Control clerk   A person who accounts for all input to and output from a computer center.

Control field   Same as *key*.

Control total   An accumulated number that is checked against a known value for the purpose of output control.

Control unit   That portion of the processor that interprets program instructions.

Conversion   The transition process from one system (manual or computer-based) to a computer-based information system.

Counter   One or several programming instructions used to tally processing events.

CRT [Cathode Ray Tube]   The video monitor component of a workstation.

Cryptography   A communications crime-prevention technology that uses methods of data encryption and decryption to scramble codes sent over communications channels.

Cursor   A blinking character that indicates the location of the next input on the display screen.

Cyberphobia   The irrational fear of, and aversion to, computers.

Cylinder   A disk storage concept. A

cylinder is that portion of the disk that can be read in any given position of the access arm (contrast with *sector*).

Daisy-wheel printer   A letter-quality serial printer, whose interchangeable character set is located on a spoked print wheel.

DASD [Direct-Access Storage Device]   A random-access secondary storage device.

Data   A representation of fact. Raw material for information.

Data base   An organization's data resource for all computer-based information processing in which the data are integrated and related such that data redundancy is minimized.

Data base administrator [DBA]   The individual responsible for the physical and logical maintenance of the data base.

Data base machine   See *back-end processor*.

Data base management system [DBMS]   A systems software package for the creation, manipulation, and maintenance of the data base.

Data base record   Related data that are read from, or written to, the data base as a unit.

Data communications   The collection and/or distribution of data from and/or to a remote facility.

Data communications specialist   A person who designs and implements computer networks.

Data dictionary   A listing and description of all data elements in the data base.

Data element   The smallest logical unit of data. Examples are employee number, first name, and price (same as *field*; compare with *data item*).

Data entry   The transcription of source data into machine-readable format.

Data entry operator   A person who uses key entry devices to transcribe data into a machine-readable format.

Data flow diagram [DFD]   A design technique that permits documentation of a system or program at several levels of generality.

Data item   The value of a data element (compare with *data element*)

Data PBX   A computer that electronically connects computers and workstations for the purpose of data communication.

Data processing [DP] Using the computer to perform operations on data.

Debug To eliminate "bugs" in a program or system (related to *bug*).

Decimal The base-10 numbering system.

Decision support system [DSS] A sophisticated information system that uses available data, computer technology, models, and query languages to support the decision-making process.

Decision table A graphic technique used to illustrate possible occurrences and appropriate actions within a system.

Decode The reverse of the encoding process (contrast with *encode*).

Density The number of bytes per linear length of track of a recording media. Usually measured in bytes per inch (bpi) and applied to magnetic tapes and disks.

Desktop computer Any computer that can be placed conveniently on the top of a desk (e.g., *microcomputer*, *personal computer*).

Diagnostic The isolation and/or explanation of a program error.

Digitize To translate an image into a form that computers can interpret.

Direct access Same as *random access*.

Direct-access file Same as *random file*.

Direct-access processing Same as *random processing*.

Direct-access storage device See *DASD*.

Director of information services The person who has responsibility for computer and information systems activity in an organization.

Disk, magnetic A secondary storage medium for random-access data storage. Available as microdisk, diskette, disk cartridge, or disk pack.

Disk drive A magnetic storage device that records data on flat rotating disks (compare with *tape drive*).

Diskette A thin flexible disk for secondary random-access data storage (same as *floppy disk* and *flexible disk*).

Distributed processing Both a technological and an organizational concept based on the premise that information systems can be made more responsive to users by moving computer hardware and personnel physically closer to the people who use them.

Distributed processor The nucleus of a small computer system that is linked to the host computer and physically located in the functional area departments.

Documentation Permanent and continuously updated written and graphic descriptions of information systems and programs.

Down-line processor A computer that collects data from a number of low-speed devices, then transmits "concentrated" data over a single communications channel. Also called a multiplexor or concentrator.

Download The transmission of data from a mainframe computer to a workstation.

Downtime The time during which a computer system is not operational.

Driver module The program module that calls other subordinate program modules to be executed as they are needed.

Dump The duplication of the contents of a storage device to another storage device or to a printer.

EBCDIC [Extended Binary Coded Decimal Interchange Code] An encoding system.

Education coordinator The person who coordinates all computer-related educational activities within an organization.

EFT [Electronic Funds Transfer] A computer-based system allowing electronic transfer of money from one account to another.

Electronic funds transfer See *EFT*.

Electronic mail A computer application whereby messages are transmitted via data communications to "electronic mailboxes." Also called E-mail.

Electronic spreadsheet See *spreadsheet*.

Encode To apply the rules of a code (contrast with *decode*).

Encoding system A system that permits alphanumeric characters to be coded in terms of bits.

End user The individual providing input to the computer or using computer output. Same as *user*.

End-of-file [EOF] **marker** A marker placed at the end of a sequential file.

EPROM Erasable PROM [programmable read-only memory] (related to *PROM*).

Exception report A report that has been filtered to highlight critical information.

Expert system An interactive computer-based system that responds to questions, asks for clarification, makes recommendations, and generally aids in the decision-making process (related to *knowledge base*).

Feasibility study A study performed to determine the economic and procedural feasibility of a proposed information system.

Feedback loop In a process control environment, the output of the process being controlled is input to the system.

Field Same as *data element*.

File A collection of related records.

Firmware "Hard-wired" logic for performing certain computer functions; built into a particular computer, often in the form of ROM or PROM.

Flat files A traditional file structure in which records are related to no other files.

Flexible disk Same as *diskette*.

Floppy disk Same as *diskette*.

Flowchart A diagram that illustrates data, information, and work flow via specialized symbols which, when connected by flow lines, portray the logic of a system or program.

FORTRAN [FORmula TRANslator] A high-level programming language designed primarily for scientific applications.

Front-end processor A processor used to offload certain data communications tasks from the host processor.

Gateway Software that permits computers of different design architectures to communicate with one another.

General-purpose computer Those

computer systems that are designed with the flexibility to do a variety of tasks, such as CAI, payroll processing, climate control, and so on (contrast with *special-purpose computer*).

Gigabyte [G] Referring to one billion bytes of storage.

Grandfather-father-son method A secondary storage backup procedure that results in the master file having two generations of backup.

Hacker A computer enthusiast who uses the computer as a source of enjoyment.

Handshaking The process of establishing a communications link between the source and destination.

Hard copy A readable printed copy of computer output.

Hardware The physical devices that comprise a computer system (contrast with *software*).

Hashing A method of random access in which the address is arithmetically calculated from the key data element.

Hexadecimal A base-16 numbering system that is used in information processing as a programmer convenience to condense binary output and make it more easily readable.

High-level programming language A language with instructions that combine several machine-level instructions into one (compare with *machine language* or *low-level programming language*).

HIPO [Hierarchical Plus Input-Processing-Output] A design technique that encourages the top-down approach, dividing the system into easily manageable modules.

Host processor The processor responsible for the overall control of a computer system. The host processor is the focal point of a communications-based system.

Icons Pictographs that are used in place of words or phrases on screen displays.

Identifier A name used in computer programs to recall a value, an array, a program, or a function from storage.

I/O [Input/Output] Input or output, or both.

Index sequential-access method [ISAM] A direct-access data storage scheme that uses an index to locate and access data stored on magnetic disk.

Information Data that have been collected and processed into a meaningful form.

Information center A facility in which computing resources are made available to various user groups.

Information center specialist Someone who works with users in an information center.

Information system A computer-based system that provides both data processing capability and information for managerial decision making (same as *management information system* and *MIS*).

Information services department The organizational entity or entities that develop and maintain computer-based information systems.

Input Data to be processed by a computer system.

Inquiry An on-line request for information.

Instruction A programming language statement that specifies a particular computer operation to be performed.

Integrated software The integration of data management, electronic spreadsheet, graphics, word processing, and communications software.

Intelligent Computer aided.

Intelligent terminal A terminal with a build-in microprocessor.

Interactive Pertaining to on-line and immediate communication between the end user and computer (contrast with *batch*).

Interblock gap [IBG] A physical space between record blocks on magnetic tapes.

Interpreter Systems software that translates and executes each program instruction before translating and executing the next (compare with *compiler*).

ISAM See *indexed sequential access method*.

Job A unit of work for the computer system.

K (1) An abbreviation for "kilo,"

meaning 1,000. (2) A computerese abbreviation for 2 to the 10th power or 1,024.

Key data element The data element in a record that is used as an identifier for accessing, sorting, and collating records (same as *control field*).

Keyboard A device used for key data entry.

Knowledge base The foundation of a computer-based expert system (related to *expert system*).

Layout A detailed output and/or input specification that graphically illustrates exactly where information should be placed/entered on a VDT display screen or placed on a printed output.

Leased line A permanent or semi-permanent communications channel leased through a common carrier.

Lexicon The dictionary of words that can be interpreted by a particular natural language.

Librarian A person who functions to catalogue, monitor, and control the distribution of disks, tapes, system documentation, and computer-related literature.

Linkage editor An operating system program that assigns a primary storage address to each byte of an object program.

Load To transfer programs or data from secondary to primary storage.

Local area network [LAN or local net] A system of hardware, software, and communications channels that connects devices on the local premises.

Loop A sequence of program instructions that are executed repeatedly until a particular condition is met.

Low-level programming language A language comprised of the fundamental instruction set of a particular computer (compare with *high-level programming language*).

Machine cycle The time it takes to retrieve, interpret, and execute a program instruction.

Machine language The programming language in which a computer executes all programs, without regard to the language of the original code.

Magnetic disk See *disk*, *magnetic*.

Magnetic ink character recognition [MICR] A data entry technique used primarily in banking. Magnetic characters are imprinted on checks and deposits, then "scanned" to retrieve the data.

Magnetic stripes A magnetic storage medium for low-volume storage of data on badges and cards (related to *badge reader*).

Magnetic tape See *tape, magnetic*.

Main memory Same as *primary storage*.

Mainframe Same as *host processor*.

Maintenance The ongoing process by which information systems (and software) are updated and enhanced to keep up with changing requirements.

Management Information system [MIS] Same as *information system*.

Master file The permanent source of data for a particular computer application area.

Megabyte [M] Referring to one million bytes of primary or secondary storage capacity.

Memory Same as *primary storage*.

Menu A workstation display with a list of processing choices from which an end user may select.

Methodology A set of standardized procedures, including technical methods, management techniques, and documentation, that provides the framework to accomplish a particular function (e.g., system development methodology).

Message A series of bits sent from a workstation to a computer or vice versa.

Micro/mainframe link Linking microcomputers and mainframes for the purpose of data communication.

Microcomputer [or **micro**] A small computer.

Microcomputer specialist A specialist in the use and application of microcomputer hardware and software.

Microdisk A rigid $3\frac{1}{4}$- or $3\frac{1}{2}$-inch disk used for data storage.

Microprocessor A computer on a single chip. The processing component of a microcomputer.

Milestone A significant point in the development of a system or program.

Minicomputer [or **mini**] Computers with slightly more power and capacity than a microcomputer.

MIPS Millions of instructions per second.

MIS [Management Information System] Same as *information system*.

Mnemonics Symbols that represent instructions in assembler languages.

Modem [Modulator-Demodulator] A device used to convert computer-compatible signals to signals suitable for transmission facilities and vice versa.

Monitor A televisionlike display for soft copy output in a computer system.

Motherboard A microcomputer circuit board that contains the microprocessor, electronic circuitry for handling such tasks as input/output signals from peripheral devices, and "memory chips."

Multidrop The connection of more than one terminal to a single communications channel.

Multiplexor Same as *down-line processor*.

Multiprocessing Using two or more processors in the same computer system in the simultaneous execution of two or more programs.

Multiprogramming Pertaining to the concurrent execution of two or more programs by a single computer.

Natural language Sixth-generation language in which the programmer writes specifications without regard to instruction format or syntax.

Nested loop A programming situation where at least one loop is entirely within another loop.

Network, computer See *computer network*.

Node An endpoint in a computer network.

Numeric A reference to any of the digits 0–9 (compare with *alpha* and *alphanumeric*).

Object program A machine-level program that results from the compilation of a source program.

Octal A base-8 numbering system used in information processing as a programmer convenience to condense

binary output and make it easier to read.

Off-line Pertaining to data that are not accessible by, or hardware devices that are not connected to, a computer system (contrast with *on-line*).

Office automation [OA] Pertaining collectively to those computer-based applications associated with general office work.

Office automation specialist A person who specializes in the use and application of office automation hardware and software (see *office automation*).

On-line Pertaining to data and/or hardware devices that are accessible to and under the control of a computer system (contrast with *off-line*).

Operating system The software that controls the execution of all applications and systems software programs.

Operator The person who performs those hardware-based activities necessary to keep information systems operational.

Operator console The machine room operator's workstation.

Optical character recognition [OCR] A data entry technique that permits original-source data entry. Coded symbols or characters are "scanned" to retrieve the data.

Optical laser disk A read-only secondary storage medium that uses laser technology.

Output Data transferred from primary storage to an output device.

Packaged software Software that is generalized and "packaged" to be used, with little or no modification, in a variety of environments (compare with *proprietary software*).

Page A program segment that is loaded to primary storage only if it is needed for execution (related to *virtual storage*).

Parallel host processor A redundant host processor used for backup and supplemental processing.

Parity bit A bit appended to a bit configuration (byte) that is used to check the accuracy of data transmission from one hardware device to another (related to *parity checking* and *parity error*).

Parity checking   A built-in checking procedure in a computer system to help ensure that the transmission of data is complete and accurate (related to *parity bit* and *parity error*).

Parity error   Occurs when a bit is "dropped" in the transmission of data from one hardware device to another (related to *parity bit* and *parity checking*).

Pascal   A multipurpose procedure-oriented programming language.

Password   A word or phrase known only to the end user. When entered, it permits the end user to gain access to the system.

Patch   A modification to a program or information system.

Peripheral equipment   Any hardware device other than the processor.

Personal computer [PC]   Same as *microcomputer*.

Personal computing   A category of computer usage that includes individual uses of the computer for both domestic and business applications.

PL/I   A multipurpose procedure-oriented programming language.

Plotter   A device that produces hard copy graphic output.

Point-of-sale [POS] terminal   A cash-register-like terminal designed for key and/or scanner data entry.

Polling   A line control procedure in which each workstation is "polled" in rotation to determine whether a message is ready to be sent.

Port   An access point in a computer system that permits communication between the computer and a peripheral device.

Post-implementation evaluation   A critical examination of a computer-based system after it has been put into production.

Primary storage   The memory area in which all programs and data must reside before programs can be executed or data manipulated (same as *main memory*, *memory*, and *RAM*; compare with *secondary storage*).

Printer   A device used to prepare hard copy output.

Private line   A dedicated communications channel between any two points in a computer network.

Problem-oriented language   A high-level language whose instruction set is designed to address a specific problem (e.g., process control of machine tools, simulation).

Procedure-oriented language   A high-level language whose general-purpose instruction set can be used to model scientific and business procedures.

Process control   Using the computer to control an ongoing process in a continuous feedback loop.

Processor   The logical component of a computer system that interprets and executes program instructions (same as *computer*, *central processing unit*, *CPU*).

Program   (1) Computer instructions structured and ordered in a manner that, when executed, cause a computer to perform a particular function. (2) The act of producing computer software (related to *software*).

Programmer   One who writes computer programs.

Programmer/analyst   A position title of one who performs both the programming and systems analysis function.

Programming   The act of writing a computer program.

Programming language   A language in which programmers communicate instructions to a computer.

Project leader   The person in charge of organizing the efforts of a project team.

PROM   [Programmable Read-Only Memory]   ROM in which the user can load read-only programs and data.

Prompt   A program-generated message describing what should be entered by the end user operator at a workstation.

Proprietary software   Vendor-developed software that is marketed to the public. (related to *packaged software*).

Protocols   Rules established to govern the way that data are transmitted in a computer network.

Prototype system   A model of a full-scale system.

Pseudocode   Nonexecutable program code used as an aid to develop and document structured programs.

Query language   A fourth-generation programming language with English-like commands used primarily for inquiry and reporting.

RAM   [Random Access Memory]   Same as *primary storage*.

Random access   Direct access to records, regardless of their physical location on the storage medium (contrast with *sequential access*).

Random file   A collection of records that can be processed randomly.

Random processing   Processing of data and records randomly (same as *direct-access processing*; contrast with *sequential processing*).

Read   The process by which a record or a portion of a record is accessed from the magnetic storage medium (tape or disk) of a secondary storage device and transferred to primary storage for processing (contrast with *write*).

Read/write head   That component of a disk drive or tape drive that reads from and writes to its respective magnetic storage medium.

Record   A collection of related data elements (e.g., an employee record).

Register   A small, high-speed storage area in which data pertaining to the execution of a particular instruction are stored. Data stored in a specific register have a special meaning to the logic of the computer.

Reserved word   A word that has a special meaning to a compiler or interpreter.

Resolution   Referring to the number of addressable points on a monitor's screen. The greater the number of points, the higher the resolution.

Response time   The elapsed time between when a data communications message is sent and a response is received (compare with *turnaround time*).

Reusable code   Modules of programming code that can be called and used as needed.

Reverse video   Characters on a video display terminal presented as black on a light background; used for highlighting.

Robot   A computer-controlled manipulator capable of moving items through a variety of spacial motions.

Robotics   The integration of computers and industrial robots.

ROM [Read-Only Memory] RAM that can only be read, not written to.

RPG A programming language in which the programmer communicates instructions interactively by entering appropriate specifications in prompting formats.

Run The continuous execution of one or more logically related programs (e.g., print payroll checks).

Schema A graphical representation of the logical structure of a CODASYL data base.

Secondary storage Permanent data storage on magnetic disk and tape (same as *auxiliary storage*; compare with *primary storage*).

Sector A disk storage concept. A pie-shaped portion of a disk or diskette in which records are stored and subsequently retrieved (contrast with *cylinder*).

Sequential access Accessing records in the order in which they are stored (contrast with *random access*).

Sequential files Files that contain records that are ordered according to a key data element.

Sequential processing Processing of files that are ordered numerically or alphabetically by a key data element (contrast with *direct access* or *random processing*).

Set A CODASYL data base concept that serves to define the relationship between two records.

Smart card A card or badge with an embedded microprocessor.

Soft copy Temporary output that can be interpreted visually as on a workstation monitor (contrast with *hard copy*).

Software The programs used to direct the functions of a computer system (contrast with *hardware*).

Software package Same as *proprietary software*.

Sort The rearrangement of data elements or records in an ordered sequence by a key data element.

Source document The original hard copy from which data are entered.

Source program The code of the original program (compare with *object program*).

Special-purpose computer Computers that are designed for a specific application, such as CAD, video games, robots (contrast with *general-purpose computer*).

Spooling The process by which output (or input) is loaded temporarily to secondary storage. It is then output (or input) as appropriate devices become available.

Spreadsheet (electronic) Refers to software that permits users to work with rows and columns of data.

Statement Same as *instruction* (for a computer program).

Structured programming A design technique by which the logic of a program is addressed hierarchically in logical modules.

Structured walkthrough A peer evaluation procedure for programs and systems under development. It is used to minimize the possibility of something being overlooked or done incorrectly.

Subroutine A sequence of program instructions that are called and executed as needed.

Supervisor The operating system program that loads programs to primary storage as they are needed.

Switched line A telephone line used as a regular data communications channel. Also called dial-up line.

Synchronous transmission Terminals and/or computers transmit data at timed intervals (contrast with *asynchronous transmission*).

Syntax error An invalid format for a program instruction.

System development methodology Written standardized procedures that depict the activities in the systems development process and define individual and group responsibilities.

System life cycle A reference to the four stages of a computer-based information system—birth, development, production, and death.

Systems analysis The analysis, design, development, and implementation of computer-based information systems.

Systems analyst A person who does systems analysis.

Systems software Software that is independent of any specific applications area.

Tape, magnetic A secondary storage medium for sequential data storage. Available as a reel or a cassette.

Tape drive The secondary storage device that contains the read/write mechanism for magnetic tape.

Task The basic unit of work for a processor.

Technology transfer The application of existing technology to a current problem or situation.

Telecommunications Communication between remote devices.

Teleprocessing A term coined to represent the merging of telecommunications and data processing.

Template A model of a particular application of an electronic spreadsheet.

Terminal Any device capable of sending and/or receiving data over a communications channel.

Throughput A measure of computer system efficiency; the rate at which work can be performed by a computer system.

Timesharing Multiple end users sharing time on a single computer system in an on-line environment.

Top-down design An approach to system and program design that begins at the highest level of generalization; design strategies are then developed at successive levels of decreasing generalization, until the detailed specifications are achieved.

Trace A procedure used to debug programs whereby all processing events are recorded and related to the steps in the program. The objective of a trace is to isolate program logic errors.

Track, disk That portion of a magnetic disk face surface that can be accessed in any given setting of a single read/write head. Tracks are configured in concentric circles.

Track, tape That portion of a magnetic tape that can be accessed by any one of the nine read/write heads. A track runs the length of the tape.

Transaction A procedural event in a system that prompts manual or computer-based activity.

Transaction file A file containing records of data activity (transactions); used to update the master file.

Transcribe To convert source data to machine-readable format.

Transmission rate The number of characters per second that can be transmitted to/from primary storage from/to a peripheral device.

Transparent A reference to a procedure or activity that occurs automatically and does not have to be considered in the use or design of a program or an information system.

Turnaround document A computer-produced output that is ultimately returned to a computer system as a machine-readable input.

Turnaround time Elapsed time between the submission of a job and the distribution of the results.

Uninterruptible power source [UPS] A buffer between an external power source and a computer system that supplies clean and continuous power.

Universal product code [UPC] A 10-digit machine-readable bar code placed on consumer products.

Upload The transmission of data from a workstation to the mainframe computer.

User Same as *end user*.

User friendly Pertaining to an online system that permits a person with relatively little experience to interact successfully with the system.

User liaison A person who serves as the technical interface between the information services department and the user group.

Utility program An often-used service routine (e.g., a program to sort records).

Value added network [VAN] A specialized common carrier that "adds value" over and above the standard services of common carriers.

Variable A primary storage location that can assume different numeric or alphanumeric values.

Variable name An identifier in a program that represents the actual value of a storage location.

VDT [Video Display Terminal] A terminal on which printed and graphic information is displayed on a televisionlike monitor and data are entered on a typewriterlike keyboard.

Video display terminal See *VDT*.

Videodisk A secondary storage medium that permits storage and random access to "video" or pictorial information.

Videotext The merging of text and graphics in an interactive communications-based information network.

Virtual machine The processing capabilities of one computer system created through software (and sometimes hardware) in a different computer system.

Virtual memory The use of secondary storage devices and primary storage to effectively expand a computer system's primary storage.

Walkthrough, structured See *structured walkthrough*.

Window (1) A rectangular section of a display screen that is dedicated to a specific activity or application. (2) In integrated software, a "view" of a designated area of a worksheet, such as spreadsheet or word processing text.

Window panes Simultaneous display of subareas of a particular window (see *window*).

Word For a given computer, an established number of bits that are handled as a unit.

Word processing Using the computer to enter, store, manipulate, and print text.

Workstation The hardware that permits interaction with a computer system, be it a mainframe or a multiuser micro. A VDT and a microcomputer can be workstations.

Write To record data on the output medium of a particular I/O device (e.g., tape, hard copy, workstation display; contrast to *read*).

Zoom An integrated software command that expands a window to fill the entire screen.

INDEX

Note: When several page references are noted for a single entry, boldface denotes the page(s) on which the term is defined or discussed in some depth. Page references refer not only to the text material, but also to the photo captions, figure captions, and box items.

BASIC INSTRUCTIONS

FORMAT
DESCRIPTION

Input/Output Instructions

CLOSE [#filenumber[, #filenumber . . .]]
Signals the completion of input/output to a file.

CLS
Clears the display screen.

GET #filenumber[, record number]
Retrieves a record from a random file.

INKEY$
Accepts a single character from the keyboard into the variable INKEY$.

INPUT ["prompt";] list of variables
Accepts data from the keyboard.

INPUT #filenumber, list of data elements
Reads a record from a sequential file and assigns the data items to variable names.

LINE [(x_1,y_1)]—(x_2,y_2) [,[color][,B[F]]]
   where x_1, y_1, x_2, and y_2 are graphics coordinates
Displays a line or box of specified dimensions and color on the monitor.

LINE INPUT "prompt"; string variable
Accepts data into a single string variable.

LPRINT list of variables and/or expressions
Displays output line on a printer.

LPRINT USING format string; list of variables and/or expressions
Displays formatted output line on a printer.

OPEN filename$ [**FOR** mode] **AS** #filenumber [**LEN** = record length]
Permits input/output to a disk file.

PLAY string variable or constant
Plays musical notes as specified in a coded string value.

PRINT list of variables and/or expressions
Displays output line on the monitor.

PRINT USING format string; list of variables and/or expressions
Displays formatted output line on the monitor.

PUT #filenumber[, record number]
Writes a record to a random file.

SOUND frequency, duration
Generates a tone of a specified frequency and duration.

WRITE #filenumber, list of data elements
Writes a record to a sequential file.

Data Transfer and Assignment Instructions

FIELD #filenumber, length **AS** string variable [, length **AS** string variable,] . . .
Defines the format of the intermediate RAM storage area for GET and PUT operations.

LET variable = variable or constant value
Assigns a value to variable (see also *Computation Instructions*).

LSET string variable from **FIELD** instruction = string variable
Moves data into a random file buffer, right justified.

READ list of variables
DATA constant values
RESTORE
Assigns the values in DATA statements to corresponding variables in READ statements; repositions pointer to first value in first DATA statement.

RSET string variable from FIELD instruction = string variable
Moves data into a random file buffer, left justified.

Computation Instructions

LET variable = expression
Performs computations (^, *, /, +, −).

Control Instructions

END
Terminates program execution.

FOR variable = initial value **TO** limit value [**STEP** increment value]
   statements
NEXT [index variable]
Statements between FOR and NEXT are executed repeatedly a specified number of times.

GOSUB line number
   subroutine statement
Branches unconditionally to specified line number, then returns to the line following the GOSUB.

BASIC INSTRUCTIONS

FORMAT   **DESCRIPTION**

Control Instructions

RETURN [line number]

GOTO line number
Branches unconditionally to specified line.

IF expression relational operator expression **THEN** line number (or executable instruction(s))
If a condition is true, then a branch is taken to a specified line number or the instruction following THEN is executed.

ON numeric expression **GOSUB** line number, line number, . . .
Branches to a specified line number based on the value of a numeric expression. Processing is returned to the statement following the ON GOSUB.

ON numeric expression **GOTO** line number, line number, . . .
Branch unconditionally to a specified line number based on the value of a numeric expression.

WHILE expression relational operator expression
statements
WEND
Statements between the WHILE and WEND are executed while the test-on-condition is true.

Other Instructions

DIM list of array variables with subscript maximums
Specifies and allocates storage for array variables.

KILL filename$
Deletes a file from disk storage.

LOCATE row, column
Positions cursor on text-mode screen at specified row and column.

REM remarks
Remarks for internal documentation (ignored by computer).

User-defined Functions

DEF FN function name (parameter list) = definition of function
Defines a function.

ANS BASIC Instructions

DO
statements
LOOP UNTIL expression relational operator expression

DO WHILE expression relational operator expression
statements
LOOP
Permits both DOUNTIL and DOWHILE loop structures.

IF expression relational operator expression **THEN**
statements
ELSE
statements
END IF
Specifies that a block of instructions be executed if the test-on-condition is true and that another block of instructions be executed if the condition is false. The ELSEIF clause permits a series of test-on-conditions.

SELECT CASE expression
  CASE case-item
    statements
  CASE case-item
    statements
  CASE ELSE
END SELECT
Defines a series of instruction blocks to be executed based on a test-on-condition.

SUB subroutine identifier
statements
END SUB
The SUB/END SUB instruction pair defines an internal subroutine. The subroutine is called by a CALL instruction.

CALL subroutine identifier